TOKIMAKURE!

PART
3&4
LISTENING

解きまくれ！
リスニングドリル
TOEIC® L&R TEST PART 3&4

著：大里秀介

スリーエー
ネットワーク

Published by 3A Corporation
Trusty Kojimachi Bldg., 2F, 4, Kojimachi 3-Chome, Chiyoda-ku, Tokyo 102-0083, Japan

ISBN 978-4-88319-894-8 C0082

First published 2023
Printed in Japan

はじめに

　この度、解きまくれシリーズを執筆する機会をいただき、PART 3・4 が完成いたしました。この本でシリーズが完結となります。

　PART 3・4 といえば、まとまった会話やトークを聞いて設問を解く、という形式でリスニングセクション、ひいては PART 1 から 7 までの全体で見ても難易度は高いです。リーディングセクションとは異なり、時間が限られているため自由に気になる箇所に戻ることはできず、設問のセットごとの音声に沿ってリズムよく解かないと連鎖的に、解けない、聞き逃す、解くペースを乱してしまう、という負のスパイラルに陥ってしまう可能性のある PART です。そういう意味もあり、一連の PART でもとりわけ気力、体力が求められます。

　かくいう私も、PART 3・4 を攻略するのには時間を要しました。先読みスタイルを活用し、まとまった問題を集中して解き、一定数の会話やトークを暗唱して、苦手なナレーターの問題を集中的に音読して、少しずつ克服していきました。それでも、1 問正解の選択肢を選ぶのに時間がかかってしまうと、合計 23 セットある問題をリズムよく解くのは難しくなるため、どんなに練習していても今でも緊張感を持って臨む PART でもあります。

　本書は試験 8 回分の問題がありますので、例えば次のような使い方をするとよいでしょう。

1. 1 回分の TEST を音読用・設問先読み用にして徹底的に使い倒す
問題を通常どおり解くのではなく、音読をして苦手な音や音のつながりを押さえて、内容を理解しながらまとまった会話やトークを聞く態勢を整え、かつ設問で先読みする部分を集中して押さえることで、筋力アップに使用する。

2. 残りの 7 回分の TEST をとにかく解きまくる
毎日決まった時間に、1 回分の TEST、もしくは時間がない場合は、会話 1 セット、トーク 1 セットとドリルのように解いて、筋力アップした自分の実力を試す。これにより、さらに苦手な箇所をあぶりだす。

　上記はほんの一例ですので、みなさんに合った学習法であればそちらを優先してもかまいません。本書はボリュームがあるので、一度解いた問題でも次に出会ったときに忘れてしまう可能性もあります。とにかく聞きまくり解きまくることで、TOEIC リスニングセクションへの対応能力を上げて、ベストスコアを出すことを目指して進めていってください。私も 990 点を目指していた時に、旧作を使い倒して実力をつけました。問題の質も編集担当の方と相当推敲しましたので、自信を持ってオススメできます。たくさん解きまくって、これまで学習してきたあなたの実力を試験本番で全ての問題にぶつけてください。

　最後に、本書を使用してあなたの TOEIC 目標スコア取得と、取得後のさまざまな夢を達成されますことを心より祈念しております。

2023 年 3 月　大里　秀介

目次

はじめに …………………………………………… 3

「先読み」について ……………………………… 5

本書の構成と使い方 ……………………………… 8

音声について ……………………………………… 10

PART 3

TEST 1 ………………………………………… 13

TEST 2 ………………………………………… 69

TEST 3 ………………………………………… 125

TEST 4 ………………………………………… 181

TEST 5 ………………………………………… 237

TEST 6 ………………………………………… 293

TEST 7 ………………………………………… 349

TEST 8 ………………………………………… 405

PART 4

TEST 1 ………………………………………… 17

TEST 2 ………………………………………… 73

TEST 3 ………………………………………… 129

TEST 4 ………………………………………… 185

TEST 5 ………………………………………… 241

TEST 6 ………………………………………… 297

TEST 7 ………………………………………… 353

TEST 8 ………………………………………… 409

解答一覧 ………………………………………… 458

※ マークシート（解答用紙）は、一番最後のページに付いています。

「先読み」について

　PART 3・4 では「先読み」の解答方法でぐんと正答が捉えやすくなります。「先読み」は会話・トークの音声が流れる前に設問と選択肢に目を通して、場面や答えに関わる内容を予測し、音声が進むのと同時に解答を終え、設問が読み上げられるときには次の問題の設問・選択肢に目を通しているというサイクルで解答する方法です。

　設問パターンへの慣れや選択肢を読む力が必要になるため、無理は禁物です。自分の解答ペースとの相性や手ごたえを確かめながら、ばたつくことのない範囲で、以下のような方法を段階的に試してみることをお勧めします。

① **設問を読んで覚える**
② **選択肢を読む**
③ **①＋②の組み合わせを柔軟に行う**

詳細は以下の通りです。
① 設問を読んで覚える

設問を読んで内容をインプット（把握）しましょう。この際、質問はできるだけ省略して読むことがカギです。例えば、What is the topic? は What と topic を見ればよいです。

また、設問冒頭に According to the man, when did Mr. Kim order the printer? は和訳すると、「男性によると、Kim さんはいつプリンターを注文しましたか」ですが、少し長いですよね。この場合、According to the man を省略し、when Mr. Kim order the printer? すなわち、「いつ　Kim さん　買った　プリンター？」とするとよいでしょう。

そして、単に読むだけではなく覚えることも重要です。覚える際は英語や日本語で記憶してもかまいませんが、イラストを描くようなつもりで場面をイメージしてもよいでしょう。プリンター注文なら店頭もしくはオフィスでパソコンを使って発注するというイメージです。

② 選択肢を読む

余裕があったら選択肢を読みます。設問を読むので精いっぱいだったら、選択肢を読むのはそれができるようになってからでかまいません。選択肢もイメージで捉えると覚えやすいです。例えば、このような選択肢があったとします。

(A) A restaurant
(B) A park
(C) A school
(D) A dental clinic

訳すと、(A) レストラン　(B) 公園　(C) 学校　(D) 歯科医院　となりますが、4つの語を日本語に変換して、記憶保持しておくと少し負荷がかかりますよね。このような場合は、「行きつけのレストラン」「よく通る公園」「通った学校」「かかりつけの歯科医院」が選択肢を見たときにパッとイメージできるようにすると、会話やトークを聞いたときにふと「あ、これだ！」と思いつきます。選択肢が文の形になっていた場合は、①の**「設問を読んで覚える」**と同様に簡略化してイメージしましょう。

③ ①＋②の組み合わせを柔軟に行う。

実践では、これらの①・②の組み合わせを使います。PART 3・4の場合は限られた時間に読んで問題を解くことが求められますので、まずは以下を心がけながら取り組んでみてください。

・**最低限①「設問を読んで覚える」が3問ともできるようにする。**

・**余裕ができてくれば②「選択肢を読む」と組み合わせてイメージする。**

・**余裕が全くない場合は、1問でも先に読むことを心がけ、できるようになったら増やしていく。**

「先読み」の悩み

　そうは言っても先読みを安定させるのは難しいという声もよく聞きます。以下はよく聞かれる苦手なポイントとその克服方法の提案です。

悩み1　「先読みをすると聞き取りに集中できない」

問題パターンをまだつかめていないときに起こりやすいようです。設問と選択肢を完全に読み切ってから音声を流し始めて答えるというかたちで負荷を軽くして取り組んでみましょう。

どんなイメージを自分の中に描いて構えると解きやすいかが感覚的につかめてきます。その感覚を基本にしながら、

次のステップとして「**設問1問分だけ先読みして聞く**」

　　　　　　→「**設問2問分だけ先読みして聞く**」

と負荷を上げていくと無理なく段階的に慣れていくことができると思います。

悩み2　「次の設問を読もうとするときに流れている音声に耳がつられてしまう」

リスニングのトレーニングとしてシャドウイングに力を入れて取り組んでいる方にこの傾向があるようです。普段の練習のクセで耳が無意識のうちに音を追ってしまっているのではないでしょうか。耳が聞く態勢になっていること自体は悪いことではないですが、先読みができるように調整をしておきたいので、意識的に聞かないようにする練習をしてみましょう。別の問題の音声を流しながら目の前の設問文に集中し、ゆっくり丁寧に文字をなぞるように読んでいきます。あえて音読してもよいでしょう。これも慣れによる部分が大きいと思います。

悩み3　「先読みをしたのに正答に結びつかない」

先読みをするときに単語を意識するよりも場面のイメージを浮かべられているかがポイントになります。設問や選択肢にある言葉がそのまま音声に出てくることはまれで、言い換え表現を柔軟に考えられるかが勝敗を分けます。言葉を意識して待ち構えていると他の言葉が耳に入りにくくなりますが、場面や意味のイメージをつかんでいれば、表現をより大きなまとまりで処理できるようになるでしょう。これも**悩み1「先読みをすると聞き取りに集中できない」**と同様に段階的に取り組みながら、丁寧にイメージをつかんでいくとよいでしょう。

本書の構成と使い方

本書は、本試験と同様に問題ページでは PART 3 に続いて PART 4 があり、TEST ごとに PART 3 と PART 4 の解答・解説を収録しています。

【特長】

● 解答・解説ページの端に 3 回分のチェックボックスを設けています。間違えた問題にチェックを入れることで、復習の際に容易に探せるようになっています。

● 巻末にはマークシートが収録されています。

解答・解説ページには、リスニング音声のスクリプトと和訳、語注があります。

 ナレーターの発音と性別（W 女性／M 男性）

 3-1-32_34-01~02　音声のトラック番号（左は 2 つのファイルを表します。3-1-32_34-01「PART 3 の TEST 1 の問題 32 から 34 の会話の音声」と 3-1-32_34-02「PART 3 の TEST 1 の問題 32 から 34 の問題の音声」です。）

 訳

 語注

★★★☆☆　難易度

解説

解答

（問題ページ）

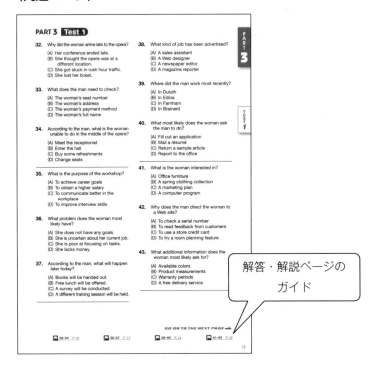

（解答・解説ページの ガイド）

「PART 3 の TEST 1 の問題 32 から 34 の会話の音声」が 3-1-32_34-01 に
「PART 3 の TEST 1 の問題 32 から 34 の問題の音声」が 3-1-32_34-02 に入っている
ことを示します。

（解答・解説ページ）

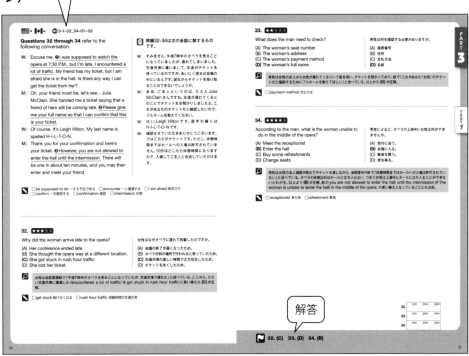

解答

音声について

リスニング問題で使用する音声は以下の方法で、すべて無料で聞くことができます。

パソコン・スマートフォンで聞く

インターネットにつながるパソコン・スマートフォンで、
「https://www.3anet.co.jp/np/resrcs/593320/」
または右のコードからアクセスしてください。

・ダウンロードする場合、音声ファイルは MP3 形式です。圧縮（zip 形式）されているので、
　パソコン上で解凍してください。
・MP3 プレイヤーへの取り込み方法などは各メーカーにお問い合わせください。
・ファイルダウンロード、ストリーミング再生には通信費が発生する場合があります。
・トラック名の番号は、PART・TEST・問題 XX から YY の会話の音声（-01）と問題の音声（-02）に対応
　しています。
　　　3-1-32_34-01.mp3 ⇒ PART 3・TEST 1・Q32〜34 の会話
・音声ファイルは各 TEST の冒頭に Directions があるものと、Directions がないものの 2 種類があります。
　本試験を意識した解答や復習などの用途に合わせてご利用ください。
　（紙面での Directions のスクリプトの表示はありません。）

アプリで聞く

■ AI 英語教材 abceed

株式会社 Globee が提供するマークシート連動型アプリ
アプリ内で「解きまくれ」で検索してください。

abceed
https://www.abceed.com/

　（アプリのダウンロード、その他アプリに関する不具合やご質問に関しましては、上記の配信元にお
問い合わせください。弊社ではお答えいたしかねますので、ご了承ください。）

TOKIMAKURE!

PART 3 & 4

Test

1

32. Why did the woman arrive late to the opera?

(A) Her conference ended late.
(B) She thought the opera was at a different location.
(C) She got stuck in rush hour traffic.
(D) She lost her ticket.

33. What does the man need to check?

(A) The woman's seat number
(B) The woman's address
(C) The woman's payment method
(D) The woman's full name

34. According to the man, what is the woman unable to do in the middle of the opera?

(A) Meet the receptionist
(B) Enter the hall
(C) Buy some refreshments
(D) Change seats

35. What is the purpose of the workshop?

(A) To achieve career goals
(B) To obtain a higher salary
(C) To communicate better in the workplace
(D) To improve interview skills

36. What problem does the woman most likely have?

(A) She does not have any goals.
(B) She is uncertain about her current job.
(C) She is poor at focusing on tasks.
(D) She lacks money.

37. According to the man, what will happen later today?

(A) Books will be handed out.
(B) Free lunch will be offered.
(C) A survey will be conducted.
(D) A different training session will be held.

38. What kind of job has been advertised?

(A) A sales assistant
(B) A Web designer
(C) A newspaper editor
(D) A magazine reporter

39. Where did the man work most recently?

(A) In Duluth
(B) In Edina
(C) In Farnham
(D) In Brainerd

40. What most likely does the woman ask the man to do?

(A) Fill out an application
(B) Mail a résumé
(C) Return a sample article
(D) Report to the office

41. What is the woman interested in?

(A) Office furniture
(B) A spring clothing collection
(C) A marketing plan
(D) A computer program

42. Why does the man direct the woman to a Web site?

(A) To check a serial number
(B) To read feedback from customers
(C) To use a store credit card
(D) To try a room planning feature

43. What additional information does the woman most likely ask for?

(A) Available colors
(B) Product measurements
(C) Warranty periods
(D) A free delivery service

GO ON TO THE NEXT PAGE ➔

🚩 32-34 *P. 20*   🚩 35-37 *P. 22*   🚩 38-40 *P. 24*   🚩 41-43 *P. 26*

44. What aspect of a charity event are the speakers discussing?

(A) Looking for volunteers
(B) Reserving a room
(C) Calling a caterer
(D) Providing entertainment

45. What concern does the woman have?

(A) An event space will be too crowded.
(B) Funding is limited.
(C) Invitations have not arrived.
(D) The weather forecast is not good.

46. What does the woman say she will do?

(A) Consult with a supervisor
(B) Update the Web site
(C) Speak to a decorator
(D) Perform at an event

47. What is the conversation mainly about?

(A) A competition
(B) A convention
(C) A report
(D) A banquet

48. What does the woman suggest doing?

(A) Booking a seat on a shuttle bus
(B) Taking a laptop computer
(C) Confirming some information online
(D) Arriving at the venue early

49. What does the man offer to do for the woman?

(A) Give her a ride
(B) Review her proposals
(C) Lend her his car
(D) E-mail a link to her

50. Where do the speakers most likely work?

(A) At a retail store
(B) At a movie theater
(C) At an art museum
(D) At a city hall

51. What have the men been working on?

(A) Taking inventory of new products
(B) Examining some orders
(C) Classifying returned products
(D) Correcting a marketing proposal

52. What does the woman suggest?

(A) Replacing the shipping company
(B) Working overtime
(C) Posting more visual aids
(D) Assigning more workers to the job

53. Where most likely are the speakers?

(A) At a restaurant
(B) At a warehouse
(C) At a music store
(D) At a concert hall

54. What problem does the man mention?

(A) A shipment has been delayed.
(B) An employee is absent.
(C) A store is closed.
(D) Some equipment is broken.

55. What does the man suggest the woman should do?

(A) Contact a manager
(B) Go to a different store
(C) Return to the store later that day
(D) Make an order online

56. What is the conversation mainly about?

(A) A monthly meeting
(B) A vacation period
(C) A sales target
(D) A project deadline

57. Why does the man say, "It'll be tough"?

(A) To ask for the women's assistance
(B) To express sympathy toward the women
(C) To show understanding of a task
(D) To give advice

58. What do the women imply about Albert?

(A) He is a valuable team member.
(B) He has received a promotion.
(C) He requires additional training.
(D) He received a sales award.

59. What are the speakers talking about?

(A) A knowledgeable coworker
(B) A professional training course
(C) A college class
(D) An investment opportunity

60. What does the woman mean when she says, "Hold on a moment"?

(A) She wants to finish writing an e-mail.
(B) She is waiting for an answer.
(C) She will check a document.
(D) She needs time to decide.

61. Who is Lena Pierce?

(A) An investor
(B) An entrepreneur
(C) An event planner
(D) A college professor

ITEM	PRICE
Internet Adapter	$30
Monthly service fee	$50
Two-year warranty	$60
Wi-fi router	$100
Total :	$240

62. Who most likely is the man?

(A) A television actor
(B) A sales clerk
(C) A telephone operator
(D) A repairperson

63. What does the woman ask about?

(A) A mobile application
(B) Cable television
(C) Online payments
(D) A subscription renewal

64. Look at the graphic. Which amount will be removed from the bill?

(A) $30
(B) $50
(C) $60
(D) $100

GO ON TO THE NEXT PAGE ➡

 56-58 *P. 36*   59-61 *P. 38*   62-64 *P. 40*

Agency	Hourly Wage /person	Workers	Total cost	Ending Time
Gracie	$9	60	$540	09:30 A.M.
Chad Place	$12	40	$480	12:00 P.M.
Madison High	$11	50	$550	11:00 A.M.
Romi Ocean	$10	50	$500	10:00 A.M.

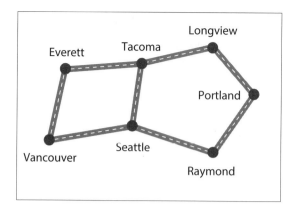

65. What will they do next Friday?

(A) They will select a good employment agency.
(B) They will hire more office workers.
(C) They will place an order for new computers.
(D) They will receive a shipment of new computers.

66. What does the man ask the woman to do?

(A) Help him select an agency
(B) Repair the old computers
(C) Contact job candidates
(D) Order some merchandise

67. Look at the graphic. Which agency will they choose?

(A) Gracie
(B) Chad Place
(C) Madison High
(D) Romi Ocean

68. What is taking place this weekend?

(A) A motor show
(B) A job fair
(C) A training seminar
(D) A sales promotion

69. What problem does the woman mention?

(A) She has another appointment this weekend.
(B) Her driver's license has expired.
(C) Her vehicle is being fixed.
(D) She does not know how to get there.

70. Look at the graphic. In which town does the man most likely want to stop for lunch?

(A) Seattle
(B) Tacoma
(C) Raymond
(D) Longview

🚩 65-67 *P. 42*   🚩 68-70 *P. 44*

71. What is being discussed?

(A) A change in convention dates
(B) A list of guest speakers
(C) A security policy
(D) An upcoming conference agenda

72. Why should listeners contact Johnny Alenko?

(A) To obtain a designated parking space
(B) To enroll in an event
(C) To receive extra information
(D) To add names to a list

73. What does the speaker say visitors will not be allowed to do?

(A) Take a photo
(B) Go to a different floor
(C) Copy documents
(D) Arrive late

74. What is the problem with the computer?

(A) The screen needs to be replaced.
(B) A button is malfunctioning.
(C) The battery is not charging.
(D) A program is not compatible with the device.

75. What does the speaker ask the listener to do?

(A) Pay a fee for the service
(B) Contact the repairperson
(C) Show the warranty certificate
(D) Purchase a new computer

76. What does the speaker offer?

(A) A discount
(B) A free carrying case
(C) An extended warranty
(D) A replacement device

77. Why is the speaker going to Kimberley?

(A) To look at its architecture
(B) To launch a real estate business
(C) To live with his relatives
(D) To teach at a school

78. What does the speaker mean when he says, "I'm really glad about that"?

(A) He can advertise a property.
(B) He can live with his family.
(C) He has found a suitable apartment.
(D) He does not have to move.

79. What additional information does the speaker want to know?

(A) Whether residents are permitted to have pets
(B) How much the security deposit is
(C) Where the nearest supermarket is
(D) Whether parking lots are available

80. Where does the talk most likely take place?

(A) At a coffee shop
(B) At a museum
(C) In a restaurant
(D) At a factory

81. What does the speaker show the listeners?

(A) Some chocolate
(B) A pamphlet
(C) Some coffee recipes
(D) Raw materials

82. What does the speaker ask the listeners to do?

(A) To stay within the marked boundaries
(B) To take photos without a flash
(C) To wear helmets
(D) To cover their shoes

GO ON TO THE NEXT PAGE ➡

 71-73 *P. 46*   74-76 *P. 48*   77-79 *P. 50*   80-82 *P. 52*

83. What kind of business does the speaker mainly focus on?

(A) Automobile wheels
(B) Ship building
(C) Bus renovations
(D) Traffic control systems

84. According to the speaker, what will the business do in October?

(A) Improve public awareness of the environment
(B) Open a new manufacturing plant
(C) Start an online advertising campaign
(D) Hold a press conference

85. What does the city official expect will take place in Austin?

(A) Employment opportunities will increase.
(B) More traffic regulations will be passed.
(C) Public transportation will improve.
(D) City taxes will be cut.

---

86. Who most likely is the speaker?

(A) An actor
(B) An event supporter
(C) A show coordinator
(D) A musician

87. What does the speaker say is special about the show?

(A) All the tickets have sold out.
(B) A complimentary souvenir will be given to all attendees.
(C) It was organized by a high school student.
(D) It has received many awards.

88. How will the profits of the show be used?

(A) To support programs in a local school
(B) To repair the concert hall
(C) To replace old musical instruments
(D) To build a community hall

---

89. Who most likely is the speaker?

(A) A museum director
(B) A seminar attendee
(C) A magazine editor
(D) A training instructor

90. What does the speaker mean when she says, "there have been many changes"?

(A) Previous experience is not so useful.
(B) The business has expanded into new areas.
(C) Some customers will be confused.
(D) It is necessary to raise prices.

91. What does the speaker ask listeners to do?

(A) Consult a manual
(B) Ask for help
(C) Update some software
(D) Practice at their office

---

92. What most likely will happen on Friday?

(A) A bicycle race
(B) A vote on a city development project
(C) Road closures
(D) An announcement of a plan

93. Where are the listeners recommended to make a detour?

(A) Central Avenue
(B) Tenth Avenue
(C) Mercury Street
(D) Delta Road

94. What is available on the Web site?

(A) Bicycle safety advice
(B) A visual guide to routes
(C) A construction schedule
(D) New bus times

🚩 83-85 *P. 54*   🚩 86-88 *P. 56*   🚩 89-91 *P. 58*   🚩 92-94 *P. 60*

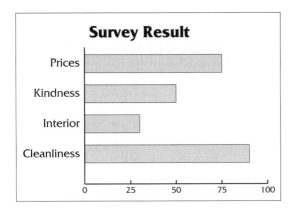

Survey Result

Prices	
Kindness	
Interior	
Cleanliness	

0   25   50   75   100

BOARDING PASS

Passenger Name: Mr.Volcan Danilov

Flight: HZ63   Seat: 17D

Date: March 10
     Departure Time: 2:45 P.M.(Gate E05)
     Boarding Starts: 2:15 P.M.
     Gate Closes: 2:35 P.M.

Anchorage to Saint Petersburg

95. Where does the speaker most likely work?

(A) At a restaurant
(B) At a consulting firm
(C) At a hotel
(D) At a theater

96. Look at the graphic. What does the speaker want to discuss?

(A) Prices
(B) Service
(C) Interior
(D) Cleanliness

97. What does the speaker ask the listeners to do?

(A) Receive a shipment
(B) Think of ways to improve customer satisfaction
(C) Make a report on the survey results
(D) Conduct another survey

98. What is the announcement mainly about?

(A) A flight delay
(B) A gate change
(C) An airport regulation
(D) A service cancellation

99. What does the speaker advise passengers to do?

(A) Get a new boarding pass
(B) Contact an airline official
(C) Show their passports
(D) Order a complimentary drink

100. Look at the graphic. When should Mr. Danilov be ready to board the airplane?

(A) At 1:55 P.M.
(B) At 2:15 P.M.
(C) At 2:25 P.M.
(D) At 2:35 P.M.

95-97   *P. 62*

98-100   *P. 64*

Questions 32 through 34 refer to the following conversation.

W: Excuse me. ❶I was supposed to watch the opera at 7:30 P.M., but I'm late. I encountered a lot of traffic. My friend has my ticket, but I am afraid she is in the hall. Is there any way I can get the ticket from her?

M: Oh, your friend must be, let's see... Julia McClain. She handed me a ticket saying that a friend of hers will be coming late. ❷Please give me your full name so that I can confirm that this is your ticket.

W: Of course. It's Leigh Hilton. My last name is spelled H-I-L-T-O-N.

M: Thank you for your confirmation and here's your ticket. ❸However, you are not allowed to enter the hall until the intermission. There will be one in about ten minutes, and you may then enter and meet your friend.

📝 問題32-34は次の会話に関するものです。

W: すみません、午後7時半のオペラを見ることになっていましたが、遅れてしまいました。交通渋滞に遭いまして。友達がチケットを持っているのですが、あいにく彼女は会場の中にいるんです。彼女からチケットを受け取ることはできないでしょうか。

M: ああ、ご友人というのは、ええとJulia McClainさんですね。友達が遅れてくるとのことでチケットをお預かりしましたよ。これがあなたのチケットだと確認したいので、フルネームを教えてください。

W: はい。Leigh Hiltonです。苗字の綴りはH-I-L-T-O-Nです。

M: 確認させていただきありがとうございます。ではこちらがチケットです。ただし、休憩時間まではホールへの入場は許可されていません。10分ほどしたら休憩時間になりますので、入場してご友人と合流していただけます。

✏️ □be supposed to *do* ～する予定である　□encounter ～に遭遇する　□I am afraid 残念だが
　□confirm ～を確認する　□confirmation 確認　□intermission 休憩

---

32. ★★★★☆

Why did the woman arrive late to the opera?

(A) Her conference ended late.
(B) She thought the opera was at a different location.
(C) She got stuck in rush hour traffic.
(D) She lost her ticket.

女性はなぜオペラに遅れて到着したのですか。

(A) 会議の終了が遅くなったため。
(B) オペラが別の場所で行われると思っていたため。
(C) 交通渋滞の激しい時間で立ち往生したため。
(D) チケットを失くしたため。

 女性は会話冒頭❶で「午後7時のオペラを見ることになっていたが、交通渋滞で遅れた」と述べている。ここから、ひどい交通渋滞に遭遇した (encountered a lot of traffic) を got stuck in rush hour traffic に言い換えた **(C)** が正解。

 □get stuck 動けなくなる　□rush hour traffic 混雑時間の交通渋滞

33. ★★☆☆☆

What does the man need to check?

(A) The woman's seat number
(B) The woman's address
(C) The woman's payment method
(D) The woman's full name

男性は何を確認する必要がありますか。

(A) 座席番号
(B) 住所
(C) 支払方法
(D) 名前

 男性は女性の友人から女性が遅れてくるという旨を伺い、チケットを預かっており、❷で「これがあなた(女性)のチケットだと確認するためにフルネームを教えてほしい」と述べている。以上から **(D)** が正解。

✎ □payment method 支払方法

---

34. ★★★★☆

According to the man, what is the woman unable to do in the middle of the opera?

(A) Meet the receptionist
(B) Enter the hall
(C) Buy some refreshments
(D) Change seats

男性によると、オペラの上演中に女性は何ができませんか。

(A) 受付に会う。
(B) 会場に入る。
(C) 軽食を買う。
(D) 席を移る。

 男性は女性の本人確認が取れてチケットを渡しながら、会話後半の❸で「休憩時間まではホールへの入場は許可されていない」と述べている。オペラの休憩以外はホールに立ち入れない、つまり女性は上演中にホールに立ち入ることができないとわかる。以上より **(B)** が正解。❸の you are not allowed to enter the hall until the intermission が The woman is unbale to (enter the hall) in the middle of the opera. の言い換えとなっていることにも注目。

✎ □receptionist 受付係　□refreshment 軽食

	1回目	2回目	3回目
32.			
33.			
34.			

🚩 **32. (C)　33. (D)　34. (B)**

Questions 35 through 37 refer to the following conversation.

M: Hello, ❶I'd like to thank all of you for attending this workshop on accomplishing your career goals. After you finish this workshop, you'll be able to focus much better on what you want to achieve in your career. First of all, does anyone have any questions?

W: Yes, actually. Will this workshop also help me identify the best career options for me? ❷At this point, I'm not entirely sure that I'm in the right career field.

M: I can see how that would be a useful topic, but that is not what we'll be working on in this workshop. ❸We do offer another workshop focusing on that topic, though, which is scheduled for later today. If you'd like, you can tell our organizer to move you to that workshop, then you can return to this workshop at a later date.

問題35-37は次の会話に関するものです。

M: こんにちは。キャリアの目標達成に関する本講習会にご参加くださりありがとうございます。本講習会を受講すればご自分のキャリアで達成したいことにもっと集中して向き合うことができるようになります。まず、何か質問のある方はいらっしゃいますか。

W: はい。この講習会は私にとっての最良の職業は何かを見極めるのにも役立ちますか。今、自分に合った業種にいるのか確信が持てていないんです。

M: それも有用なトピックになると思いますが、この講習の中で扱うものにはなっていません。ただ、そのトピックに焦点を当てた講習会が別にございます。本日、この後に開催する予定です。ご希望でしたら、そちらの講習会への変更希望の旨を主催者にお伝えください。こちらの講習会には後日またご参加いただくようにできます。

□workshop on ～に関する研修、講習会　□accomplish ～を達成する　□career goal キャリア目標
□focus on ～に集中する　□achieve ～を達成する　□first of all 最初に　□identify ～を特定する、見極める
□option 選択　□at this point 現時点で、この段階で　□entirely 全体的に　□right 適した　□career field 職業分野
□useful 役立つ　□topic 話題　□work on ～を行う、取り扱う　□organizer 主催者　□at a later date 後日

35. ★★★☆☆

What is the purpose of the workshop?

(A) To achieve career goals
(B) To obtain a higher salary
(C) To communicate better in the workplace
(D) To improve interview skills

この講習会の目的とは何ですか。

(A) キャリアの目標を達成すること。
(B) より高い給料を得ること。
(C) 職場でのコミュニケーションをより良くすること。
(D) 面接の技術を磨くこと。

会話の冒頭❶で男性が「キャリアの目標達成に関する本講習会」と述べているため、これを言い換えた **(A)** が正解。この問題では、accomplish と achieve の言い換えが問われている。研修・講習会の目的を問われたときは workshop on(about) 以下がどのような研修かという説明になることがあるため、注意して聞き取ろう。

□obtain ～を獲得する　□higher salary より高い給料　□communicate コミュニケーションを取る
□workplace 職場

36. ★★★★☆

What problem does the woman most likely have?

(A) She does not have any goals.
(B) She is uncertain about her current job.
(C) She is poor at focusing on tasks.
(D) She lacks money.

女性はどのような問題を抱えていると考えられますか。

(A) 目標が全くない。
(B) 現在の仕事について疑問がある。
(C) 職務に集中することが苦手である。
(D) お金がない。

🔍 女性は男性の講習会に関する説明の後で男性に質問し、❷で「今、自分に合った業種にいるのか確信が持てていない」と述べている。つまり、女性は今現在の仕事に疑問を抱えていることがわかるので、これを言い換えた **(B)** が正解。

✏️ □task 職務　□lack ～がない状態である

---

37. ★★★☆☆

According to the man, what will happen later today?

(A) Books will be handed out.
(B) Free lunch will be offered.
(C) A survey will be conducted.
(D) A different training session will be held.

男性によると、今日この後に何が起こりますか。

(A) 本が配られる。
(B) 無料の昼食が提供される。
(C) アンケート調査が実施される。
(D) 別の講習会が開催される。

🔍 男性は会話後半❸で「他のトピックに焦点を当てた講習会が別にあり、本日、この後に開催する」と述べている。「本日この後 (later today)」に開催される another workshop を a different training session に言い換えて、それが開催されるとした **(D)** が正解。

✏️ □hand out ～を手渡す　□offer ～を提供する　□survey 調査　□conduct ～を実行する

	1回目	2回目	3回目
35.			
36.			
37.			

🚩 **35. (A)　36. (B)　37. (D)**

Questions 38 through 40 refer to the following conversation.

M: Good morning, my name is Jonathan Feller. ❶I'm calling because I was reading the list of job openings on your newspaper's Web site and noticed that you intend to hire an assistant editor. Is that job still available?

W: Yes, it is. Do you have any relevant experience?

M: Yes. ❷I was working as an editor for a magazine called *The Dairy Industry* in Brainerd for the past five years, but I moved to Duluth a few weeks ago to be closer to my parents, who have a farm in Edina.

W: Oh, yes. I've heard of that magazine. ❸Why don't you send us your career history including educational background? We'll review it and contact you soon.

📝 問題38-40は次の会話に関するものです。

M: おはようございます。私は Jonathan Feller と申します。御社の新聞のウェブサイトにある求人欄で編集補佐を採用しようとしているのを見かけたのでお電話しました。その職はまだ空いていますでしょうか。

W: はい、空いています。何か関連するご経験はありますか。

M: はい、この5年間編集者として、Brainerd の Dairy Industry 誌で働いていましたが、Edina で牧場をやっている両親の近くで生活するために数週間前に Duluth に引っ越してきました。

W: まあ、そうですか。その雑誌でしたら聞いたことがあります。ぜひ、ご経歴と学歴を弊社にお送りいただけますか。拝見しましたら、じきにご連絡いたします。

✏️ □job opening 求人 □notice ～に気づく □intend to *do* ～するつもりである □editor 編集者 □available 可能である □relevant 関連した □hear of ～について聞く □Why don't you...? ～してはどうか □career history 職歴、経歴 □educational background 学歴 □review ～を確認する □contact ～に連絡する

38.

What kind of job has been advertised?

(A) A sales assistant
(B) A Web designer
(C) A newspaper editor
(D) A magazine reporter

どのような仕事が広報されていますか。

(A) 営業補佐
(B) ウェブデザイナー
(C) 新聞編集者
(D) 雑誌記者

🔍 男性は❶で「御社の新聞のウェブサイトにある求人欄で編集補佐を採用しようとしているのを見た」と言っている。ここから新聞会社の編集に関わる仕事だとわかる。以上から正解は **(C)**。Web という言葉から (B) を選ばないでほしい。Web site はあくまでも求人が掲載されていた情報先だ。

39. ★★☆☆☆

Where did the man work most recently?

(A) In Duluth
(B) In Edina
(C) In Farnham
(D) In Brainerd

男性は最近までどこで働いていましたか。

(A) Duluth
(B) Edina
(C) Farnham
(D) Brainerd

 男性は❷で「この5年間、Brainerd の Dairy Industry 誌で働いていた」と具体的な地名に言及している。以上から正解は **(D)**。(B) Edina は、男性の両親が農場を営んでいる地名なので不正解。

40. ★★★★☆

What most likely does the woman ask the man to do?

(A) Fill out an application
(B) Mail a résumé
(C) Return a sample article
(D) Report to the office

女性は男性に何をするように頼んでいると考えられますか。

(A) 申請書に記入すること。
(B) 履歴書を郵送すること。
(C) 記事のサンプルを返送すること。
(D) 事務所に行くこと。

 女性は❸で「経歴と学歴を弊社に送ってほしい」と述べている。ここから「経歴と学歴を記載したもの」＝「履歴書」ということがわかるので、それを résumé と言い換え、かつ送付することを mail と表現した **(B)** が正解。設問で ask を使って依頼内容や求めているものが問われる場合は、Why don't you...? で尋ねているところが狙われやすいので要注意。

□fill out 〜に記入する　□application 申込書　□mail 〜を送付する　□sample article 記事のサンプル
□report to 〜に行く

	1回目	2回目	3回目
38.			
39.			
40.			

38. (C)　39. (D)　40. (B)

Questions 41 through 43 refer to the following conversation.

W: ❶I'm calling to inquire about some new furniture for the conference room of my office. I've found a six-piece set from a copy of your spring catalog and I'm interested in buying it.

M: Thank you for calling. ❷Have you had an opportunity to visit our Web site yet? ❸We have an online tool that will enable you to upload a photo of your conference room to see what kind of furniture will go with your office.

W: Sure, I'll do that right away. ❹However, before I do, I'd like to make sure it'll fit in the room. ❺I don't see any measurements listed for the furniture in your catalog.

M: Please check page 17 in the back of the catalog. You can see the dimensions of all our items.

📝 問題41-43は次の会話に関するものです。

W: 当社の会議室のための新しいオフィス家具についてお尋ねしたいと思いお電話しました。御社の春のカタログで6点セットを見まして、それを購入しようか検討しています。

M: お電話ありがとうございます。弊社のウェブサイトをご覧になる機会はありましたでしょうか。会議室の写真をアップロードしていただければ、お客様のオフィスにどのような家具が合うかを見ていただけるオンラインツールがございます。

W: いいですね、すぐやってみます。ただ、その前に部屋に収まるかを確かめておきたいと思うのですが。カタログでは家具の大きさについての記載が見当たりません。

M: カタログ巻末の17ページをご確認ください。弊社の全商品の寸法をご覧いただけます。

✏️ □**inquire** 尋ねる、問い合わせる □**six-piece set** 6点のセット商品 □**opportunity** 機会
□**upload** 〜をアップロードする (ウェブサイトやクラウドにファイルを転送する) □**go with** 〜に合う
□**right away** すぐに □**fit in** 〜に収まる □**measurement** 測定 □**list** 〜を一覧にまとめる □**dimension** 寸法

---

41. ⭐☆☆☆☆

What is the woman interested in?

(A) Office furniture
(B) A spring clothing collection
(C) A marketing plan
(D) A computer program

女性は何に興味がありますか。

(A) オフィス用の家具
(B) 春の服のラインアップ
(C) マーケティング計画
(D) コンピュータープログラム

 会話の冒頭❶で女性は「会議室に置く新しいオフィス家具」について問い合わせている。ここから **(A)** が正解。興味があることについては inquire about 以降で話すことが多い。

 □**clothing** 服

42. ★★★★☆

Why does the man direct the woman to a Web site?

(A) To check a serial number
(B) To read feedback from customers
(C) To use a store credit card
(D) To try a room planning feature

男性はなぜ女性にウェブサイトを紹介していますか。

(A) シリアルナンバーを確認するため。
(B) 顧客の感想を読むため。
(C) 店のクレジットカードを使用するため。
(D) ルームプランニング機能を試すため。

男性は❷で自社ウェブサイトを見たことがあるか女性に尋ね、❸で女性の会議室写真をアップロードすると、どのような家具が合うか見ることのできるツールがあると述べている。ここから、部屋に何を設置すればよいかわかる機能を a room planning feature と表現した **(D)** が正解。a room planning feature は❸内の an online tool that ... your office までの表現を言い換えている。

□direct A to A に〜への行き方を教える　□serial number シリアルナンバー、製品の識別番号　□feedback 感想
□feature 機能

43. ★★★☆☆

What additional information does the woman most likely ask for?

(A) Available colors
(B) Product measurements
(C) Warranty periods
(D) A free delivery service

女性が追加情報として求めているものは何だと考えられますか。

(A) 取り扱っている色
(B) 製品の寸法
(C) 保証期間
(D) 無料配達サービス

女性は❹で「オンラインツール使用前に部屋に家具がそもそも収まるか確認したい」と切り出し、❺で「カタログ内に家具の大きさの記載がない」と言っている。つまり、家具のサイズに関する追加情報を求めていることが考えられ、この家具を product と表現した **(B)** が正解。

□available 入手可能な　□warranty period 保証期間

	1回目	2回目	3回目
41.			
42.			
43.			

🚩 **41. (A)　42. (D)　43. (B)**

Questions 44 through 46 refer to the following conversation.

M: Hello, Emily. ❶You're an organizer for the college's charity event this month, right? I'm sure you'll do a great job. I have a suggestion for the event. ❷A friend of mine is a member of a vocal group, and I think it would be great if they performed at the event.

W: Mick, that's a wonderful idea! ❸Regrettably, our budget isn't big enough to pay for performers.

M: No problem. ❹My friend told me they'd be happy to volunteer their services. The exposure would be good for them. And it might bring them future jobs.

W: ❺Right, I'll ask the director about it first and let you know.

📝 問題44-46は次の会話に関するものです。

M: こんにちは、Emily さん。今月は大学のチャリティーイベントの主催をするんですよね。きっと素敵な回になりますね。イベントについての提案があります。友達にボーカルグループのメンバーがいるのですが、彼らにイベントで公演してもらったら良いのではないかなと思うんです。

W: Mick さん、素晴らしいアイデアですね。ただ残念ながら私たちの予算は彼らに出演料を支払うには十分ではありません。

M: 大丈夫です。友達はぜひ無償で行いたいと言ってきています。公演ができることが彼らにとって良いことなんだと思います。将来の仕事につながるかもしれませんから。

W: わかりました。まずは委員長に尋ねてみてから、知らせます。

✎ □organizer 主催者　□charity event チャリティーイベント　□suggestion 提案
□it would be great if S *did* S が〜してくれるとよい　□regrettably 残念ながら　□pay for 〜に支払う
□volunteer 〜を無償で提供する　□director 委員長

---

44. ★★★☆☆

What aspect of a charity event are the speakers discussing?

(A) Looking for volunteers
(B) Reserving a room
(C) Calling a caterer
(D) Providing entertainment

話し手たちはチャリティーイベントのどんなことについて話し合っていますか。

(A) ボランティアを募ること。
(B) 部屋の予約をすること。
(C) ケータリング業者に電話をすること。
(D) 催しを用意すること。

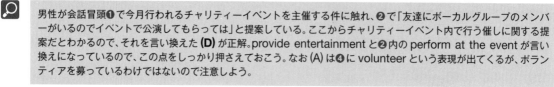

🔍 男性が会話冒頭❶で今月行われるチャリティーイベントを主催する件に触れ、❷で「友達にボーカルグループのメンバーがいるのでイベントで公演してもらっては」と提案している。ここからチャリティーイベント内で行う催しに関する提案だとわかるので、それを言い換えた **(D)** が正解。provide entertainment と❷内の perform at the event が言い換えになっているので、この点をしっかり押さえておこう。なお (A) は❹に volunteer という表現が出てくるが、ボランティアを募っているわけではないので注意しよう。

✎ □aspect 観点　□reserve 〜を予約する　□caterer ケータリング会社　□entertainment 催し

45. ★★★☆☆

What concern does the woman have?

(A) An event space will be too crowded.
(B) Funding is limited.
(C) Invitations have not arrived.
(D) The weather forecast is not good.

女性は何を心配していますか。

(A) 会場がひどく混雑すること。
(B) 資金が限られていること。
(C) 招待状が届いていないこと。
(D) 天気予報が良くないこと。

 女性は❸で「残念ながら、予算が男性の提案する催しの出演料を支払うには十分でない」と述べている。ここから予算自体が限定されていることがわかるので、この予算 (budget) を funding に言い換えた **(B)** が正解。心配・懸念は❸の regrettably に表れているので、この表現以降を狙い打つつもりで聞くことが重要。

✎ □crowded 混雑した　□funding 資金　□limited 制限された　□invitation 招待状　□weather forecast 天気予報

---

46. ★★★★☆

What does the woman say she will do?

(A) Consult with a supervisor
(B) Update the Web site
(C) Speak to a decorator
(D) Perform at an event

女性は何をすると言っていますか。

(A) 上司に相談する。
(B) ウェブサイトを更新する。
(C) 内装業者に話す。
(D) イベントで演奏する。

 女性は❺で「委員長に尋ねてみてから、男性に知らせる」と述べている。ここから、この部分の前半を言い換えた **(A)** が正解。director は何か事業をする場合の責任者を指し、このようなイベントでは「委員長」とされることが多い。ここでは、自分より立場が上の人＝supervisor と言い換えられている。(D) はイベントで演奏するのは、男性の友人であり、女性ではないため不正解。

✎ □consult with ～に相談する　□update ～を更新する　□decorator 内装業者

	1回目	2回目	3回目
44.			
45.			
46.			

 44. (D)　45. (B)　46. (A)

🔊 3-1-47_49-01~02

Questions 47 through 49 refer to the following conversation.

W: Paul, ❶I hear you'll be attending the Workplace Financial Management Conference next month. I think it's important for people in our line of work to network with others in the field.

M: Absolutely, Monica. I'm really excited. It's my first time to go to the conference, and I think it will be very helpful to have the chance to hear from those in the profession who are more experienced. It's an excellent way to enhance my skills.

W: I didn't know you hadn't been there before. ❷In that case, I recommend that you get to the conference center at least 30 minutes before it begins. ❸That way, you'll be able to get a seat near the front.

M: Thanks for the tip. ❹And I'm planning to drive there myself, so you're welcome to ride with me if you'd like.

問題47-49は次の会話に関するものです。

W: Paul さん、来月の職場の財務管理協議会に参加すると聞きました。私たちのような仕事に従事する者にとっては同業者同士の繋がりを持つことが重要だと思うのです。

M: そうですね。Monica さん。とても楽しみです。私は協議会に行くのは初めてですし、同じ職種での経験が長い方々の意見を聞く機会があれば大いにプラスになると思います。技術を向上させるのにとても良いです。

W: これまで行ったことがなかったとは知りませんでした。それなら、会場には遅くとも開始の30分前には到着しておいたほうがいいでしょう。そうすれば、前の方の席に座れますから。

M: アドバイスをありがとうございます。自分で車を運転して行こうと思っているんですが、よろしければ一緒に乗って行きませんか。

□Workplace Financial Management Conference 職場財務管理協議会　□network 情報交換する
□absolutely そのとおり　□helpful 役立つ　□those... ～の人々　□profession 職業　□experienced 経験のある
□excellent 素晴らしい　□enhance ～を強化する　□front 前方

---

47. ★★☆☆☆

What is the conversation mainly about?

(A) A competition
(B) A convention
(C) A report
(D) A banquet

会話の趣旨は何ですか。

(A) コンクール
(B) 代表者会議
(C) 報告
(D) 宴会

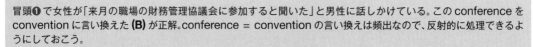

冒頭❶で女性が「来月の職場の財務管理協議会に参加すると聞いた」と男性に話しかけている。この conference を convention に言い換えた **(B)** が正解。conference = convention の言い換えは頻出なので、反射的に処理できるようにしておこう。

□competition 競技会、コンクール　□banquet 晩餐会、食事会

30

48. ★★★☆☆

What does the woman suggest doing?

(A) Booking a seat on a shuttle bus
(B) Taking a laptop computer
(C) Confirming some information online
(D) Arriving at the venue early

女性は何をすることを提案していますか。

(A) シャトルバスの席を予約すること。
(B) ノートパソコンを持っていくこと。
(C) インターネットで情報を確認すること。
(D) 会場に早めに到着すること。

❷で女性が「会場には遅くとも開始の30分前には到着しておいたほうがいい」と述べ、その後❸で「そうすれば、前方の席に座れる」と理由も添えている。ここから、会場を venue と言い換え、そこに早く着くという意味にした **(D)** が正解。❷にある I recommend that you ... は提案・助言の定型句で、この設問の正解を導くヒントになっている。

□book ～を予約する　□laptop ノートパソコン

---

49. ★★☆☆☆

What does the man offer to do for the woman?

(A) Give her a ride
(B) Review her proposals
(C) Lend her his car
(D) E-mail a link to her

男性は女性に何をすると申し出ていますか。

(A) 車で送ること。
(B) 計画を見直すこと。
(C) 車を貸すこと。
(D) リンクを E メールで送ること。

男性は❹で「自分で車を運転して行こうと思っているが、よければ一緒に乗って行かないか」と言っているため、車の同乗、つまり男性が運転する車に乗れば会場まで送ると申し出ていることがわかる。以上より、会話中の you're welcome to ride with me を言い換えた **(A)** が正解。

□give 人 a ride 人を車で送迎する　□review ～を確認する　□proposal 提案

	1回目	2回目	3回目
47.			
48.			
49.			

 47. (B)　48. (D)　49. (A)

Questions 50 through 52 refer to the following conversation with three speakers.

W: ❶Eddie and James. I know both of you are taking inventory of returned items and sorting them. Can I have an update on it?

M1: ❷James and I completed categorizing the returned products by the names of the goods. We are going to figure out why they were returned and check the state they are in.

M2: Yes, ❸we need to screen out the ones that customers returned because they simply changed their mind or purchased the wrong product. If the package is in its original state, we can just restock it for sale.

M1: If the package has been opened and it seems that the product has been used, we have to send it to the refurbishing center. However, it's taking more time than we thought.

W: Right. I think this should be done by this month so that we can reorganize our store for the summer holiday season. ❹I think this work requires more employees to be done quickly.

M2: That would be great.

📝 問題50-52は3人の話し手による次の会話に関するものです。

W: Eddie さんに James さん。返品商品の在庫の棚卸しと仕分けはお二人が行っていますよね。状況はどうですか。

M1: James さんと私とで返品商品を品名で分類する作業は終えました。これから返品された理由を調べ、状態を確認します。

M2: はい。単に気が変わったか、あるいは、間違った製品を購入したという理由でお客様から返品されたものを分けておきます。パッケージが元の状態であれば、そのまま販売用の在庫に戻すことができるので。

M1: パッケージが開封され、製品に使用の形跡がある場合は、改装センターに送らなければなりません。ただ、思った以上に時間がかかります。

W: そうですね。夏休みのシーズンに向けて店内を模様替えできるように、今月中に終わらせておきたいところです。この仕事を迅速に終えるためにはもっと従業員が必要ですね。

M2: そうだと助かります。

🖊 □take inventory 在庫棚卸を行う　□returned item 返品商品　□sort ～を整頓する、仕分けする　□update 最新版
□complete *doing* ～を完了する　□categorize ～を分類する　□figure out ～を調査する
□screen out ～を明らかにしておく　□change one's mind 決心する　□wrong 間違った
□original state 元の状態　□restock ～を在庫として戻す　□for sale 販売用 (に)
□refurbishing center 改装センター　□reorganize ～を模様替えする

---

50. ⭐⭐⭐⭐☆

Where do the speakers most likely work?

(A) At a retail store
(B) At a movie theater
(C) At an art museum
(D) At a city hall

話し手たちはどこで働いていると考えられますか。

(A) 小売店
(B) 映画館
(C) 美術館
(D) 市役所

🔍 女性は会話の冒頭❶で男性2人に「返品商品の在庫の棚卸しと仕分け」について尋ねている。ここから、商品の返品・在庫の仕分けを行う仕事と考えると選択肢の中では **(A)** の小売店舗と考えられるため、これが正解。most likely を使って勤務場所が問われたら、このように業務内容から推測して解くようにしよう。

 □retail store 小売店舗　□city hall 市役所

51. ★★★★☆

What have the men been working on?

(A) Taking inventory of new products
(B) Examining some orders
(C) Classifying returned products
(D) Correcting a marketing proposal

男性たちは何に取り組んでいますか。

(A) 新製品在庫の棚卸しをしている。
(B) 注文を調査している。
(C) 返品を分類している。
(D) マーケティング案を修正している。

🔍 1人目の男性が❷で「2人で返品商品を品名で分類する作業は終えた」と言い、2人目の男性が❸で「理由別にお客様から返品されたものを分ける」と述べている。ここから2人とも返品作業の仕分けをしていることがわかるので、この作業をclassify（〜を分類する）を使って言い換えた **(C)** が正解。この classify は categorize、screen out とそれぞれ言い換えられている。これらを聞いて選択肢と照合して解く必要があるため、しっかり押さえよう。

✏️ □work on 〜に取り組む　□examine 〜を調査する　□classify 〜を分類する　□correct 〜を修正する
□marketing proposal マーケティングに関する提案

52. ★★★★☆

What does the woman suggest?

(A) Replacing the shipping company
(B) Working overtime
(C) Posting more visual aids
(D) Assigning more workers to the job

女性は何を提案していますか。

(A) 運送会社を変更すること。
(B) 残業すること。
(C) 視覚資料をもっと掲示すること。
(D) もっと多くの作業員を配置すること。

🔍 女性は男性たちが取り組んでいる仕事に対して、❹で「この仕事を迅速に終えるためにはもっと従業員が必要だ」と述べている。ここから、より多くの従業員にこの仕事を割り当てることが考えられる。これを動詞 assign を使って言い換えた **(D)** が正解。(D) は会話中にある this work requires more employees to be done quickly と対応していることに着目しておこう。

✏️ □shipping company 運送会社　□work overtime 残業する　□post 〜を掲載する　□visual aid 視覚資料
□assign A to 〜に A を割り当てる

	1回目	2回目	3回目
50.			
51.			
52.			

🚩 **50. (A)　51. (C)　52. (D)**

Questions 53 through 55 refer to the following conversation.

W: Excuse me. ❶I'm searching for the latest album by the pop group, the Happy Guys. I've looked in the pop section, and also the sections for rock music. But I can't find it anywhere. Do you have any in your stock room?

M: ❷Unfortunately, we don't. I'm afraid we sold out of that particular album very quickly after we received it. ❸We expected to have more delivered this morning, but the delivery is late. We may receive them tomorrow morning. Could you come back again tomorrow afternoon?

W: That's a shame. I really wanted to buy it today for my brother's birthday. He turns 18 years old today, and that's one of his favorite bands. That's the only album I know he doesn't have yet.

M: ❹Well, how about trying one of our other stores in town? We have branches on York Avenue and Edinburgh Way. Those locations are much larger, so they usually have a lot more stock than we do here.

📝 問題53-55は次の会話に関するものです。

W: すみません。the Happy Guys というポップグループの最新アルバムを探しています。ポップスの棚とロックの棚は確認したのですが、どこにも見当たりません。在庫保管室にはありませんか。

M: 申し訳ありませんが、ございません。あいにく、そのアルバムは入荷してからすぐに売り切れてしまいました。今朝追加で届く予定でしたが、その配送が遅れています。明日の朝には入荷する見込みです。明日の午後にまたお立ち寄りいただけますか。

W: それは残念です。弟の誕生日なので、どうしても今日買いたかったのですが。今日18歳になって、それがお気に入りのバンドなので。私が知る限り、彼がまだ持っていないアルバムはこれだけなのです。

M: では、街にある他の店舗をあたってみてはいかがでしょうか。当社は York 大通りと Edinborough 街道にも店舗があります。そちらの店舗の方がはるかに大きいですし、大抵、ここよりもはるかに多くの在庫を置いています。

✏️ □search for ～を探す　□latest 最新の　□pop section ポップ音楽のコーナー　□stock room 在庫保管室
□I'm afraid (that) 残念ながら～だ　□particular 特定の　□That's a shame. それは残念だ。
□turn 18 years old 18歳になる　□favorite お気に入りの　□branch 支店、分店

53.

Where most likely are the speakers?

(A) At a restaurant
(B) At a warehouse
(C) At a music store
(D) At a concert hall

話し手たちはどこにいると考えられますか。

(A) レストラン
(B) 倉庫
(C) 音楽店
(D) コンサート会場

🔍 女性は❶で、あるバンドのアルバムを探していると言い、それに対して男性が❷で「残念ながらない」と伝えている。つまり音楽関係のアルバムを売買しているところでの会話だと考えることができる。以上より正解は **(C)**。音楽を想定すると (D) も考えられるが、会話全体がアルバムに関する在庫有無等の流れになり、コンサート会場に関連する話題はないため、ここでは不正解。

✏️ □warehouse 倉庫

54. ★★★☆☆

What problem does the man mention?	男性はどのような問題について話していますか。
(A) A shipment has been delayed.	**(A)** 配送が遅れている。
(B) An employee is absent.	(B) 従業員が不在である。
(C) A store is closed.	(C) 店が閉まっている。
(D) Some equipment is broken.	(D) 機材が壊れている。

🔍 男性は特定の商品の在庫がないことに触れた後、❸で「今朝追加で届く予定だったが、配送が遅れている」と述べている。ここから、商品の配送が遅れていることがわかるため、正解は **(A)**。(A) は❸の the delivery is late の言い換えになっている。

✏️ □absent 不在である　□equipment 装置

---

55. ★★☆☆☆

What does the man suggest the woman should do?	男性は女性に何をすることを提案していますか。
(A) Contact a manager	(A) 店長に問い合わせる。
(B) Go to a different store	**(B)** 別の店舗に行く。
(C) Return to the store later that day	(C) その日に時間をあらためて来店する。
(D) Make an order online	(D) インターネットで注文する。

🔍 男性は❹で「街にある他の店舗をあたってみてはどうか」と違う店舗でアルバムを探すことを提案している。以上から正解は **(B)**。

✏️ □contact 〜に連絡する

	1回目	2回目	3回目
53.			
54.			
55.			

 53. (C)　54. (A)　55. (B)

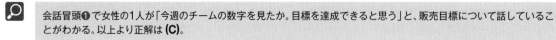

🇺🇸 W1　🇬🇧 M　🇦🇺 W2　🔊 3-1-56_58-01~02

Questions 56 through 58 refer to the following conversation with three speakers.

W1: ❶Have you seen our team's figures for this week? I think we can reach our target!

M: Let's hope so! If we do, it will be the first time in around six months.

W2: Well, ❷we only need to make thirty more sales, and we still have a week left.

M: ❸It'll be tough, ❹but we have a good chance.

W1: Albert gets back from his vacation tomorrow. That will help our figures.

M: For sure. He can probably get thirty sales by himself!

W2: ❺I'm so glad that he was moved over to our sales team.

W1: ❻Me, too. We would really struggle without him.

問題56-58は3人の話し手による次の会話に関するものです。

W1: 今週のチームの数字を見ましたか。目標を達成できると思います。

M: 幸運を祈りましょう。もし達成できたら、この6か月間で初めてのことです。

W2: あと30売り上げればいいだけですし、まだ1週間あります。

M: 大変ですが、チャンスは十分にあります。

W1: Albert が明日、休暇から戻ります。数字に貢献してくれるでしょう。

M: 確かに。彼一人でも30売り上げるかもしれません。

W2: 我々の営業チームに異動してきてくれて本当によかったです。

W1: 私もです。彼なしでは本当に苦労するところでした。

✎ □figure 数字　□reach one's target 目標に到達する　□tough 厳しい、大変な　□for sure 確かに
□move over to ～に異動する　□struggle 奮闘する、もがく

---

56. ⭐☆☆☆☆

What is the conversation mainly about?

(A) A monthly meeting
(B) A vacation period
(C) A sales target
(D) A project deadline

会話の趣旨は何ですか。

(A) 月例会議
(B) 休暇期間
(C) 販売目標
(D) プロジェクトの期限

🔍 会話冒頭❶で女性の1人が「今週のチームの数字を見たか。目標を達成できると思う」と、販売目標について話していることがわかる。以上より正解は **(C)**。

✎ □period 期間　□deadline 期限

36

57. ★★★★★

Why does the man say, "It'll be tough"?

(A) To ask for the women's assistance
(B) To express sympathy toward the women
(C) To show understanding of a task
(D) To give advice

男性はなぜ "It'll be tough" と言っていますか。

(A) 女性たちに協力を求めるため。
(B) 女性たちへの共感を表すため。
(C) 課題に対する見解を示すため。
(D) 助言を与えるため。

意図問題で問われている箇所は❸の「大変だろう」という意味である。この前後を見ていくと、❷あと30を1週間以内に売り上げる必要がある➡❸大変だろう➡❹でもチャンスは十分あるという流れになっており、厳しいが手が届かないわけではないということを意図しているとわかる。以上より、この課題に対する認識・見解を示すための表現だと考えられるので、それを言い換えた (C) が正解。(B) も思いつくかもしれないが、この場合は❸以前に、共感できるような tough に近い状況の言及がないと文脈に合わず、ここでは不正解。

□assistance 協力　□sympathy 共感　□understanding 見解　□task 課題

58. ★★★★★

What do the women imply about Albert?

(A) He is a valuable team member.
(B) He has received a promotion.
(C) He requires additional training.
(D) He received a sales award.

Albert さんについて女性たちは何を示唆していますか。

(A) 貴重なチームメンバーである。
(B) 昇進した。
(C) 追加の研修が必要である。
(D) 販売成績の賞を受け取った。

2人の女性は Albert さんについて、❺・❻でそれぞれ「我々のチームに異動して本当によかった」「彼なしでは苦労するところだった」と、彼がチームにとって重要な存在であることを述べている。以上から (A) が正解。(B) 昇進、(D) 受賞の事実はなく、いずれも不正解。

□valuable 貴重な　□promotion 昇進　□sales award 販売賞

	1回目	2回目	3回目
56.			
57.			
58.			

56. (C)　57. (C)　58. (A)

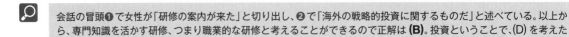

🇦🇺 W 🇨🇦 M 🔊 3-1-59_61-01~02

Questions 59 through 61 refer to the following conversation.

W: ❶I just received some information on the interactive training next week. I can't attend, but maybe you're available.

M: What's it about? I might want to go if it's about investments.

W: I'm sorry. I should have told you that. Yes, ❷it's about "Making strategic investments in overseas markets."

M: ❸Does it say who the speakers will be?

W: ❹Hold on a moment. ❺I have the letter right here. ❻The keynote speaker is Lena Pierce. I don't know who that is.

M: ❼She's a professor at Woodhole University. I took one of her classes a few years ago. She's very knowledgeable, so I think I might go.

📝 問題59-61は次の会話に関するものです。

W: 来週のインタラクティブトレーニングのお知らせが届きました。私は出席できませんが、ご都合はいかがでしょうか。

M: テーマは何ですか。投資についてでしたら行ってもいいかもしれません。

W: すみません。それをお伝えするべきでしたね。そうです。「海外市場への戦略的投資」に関するものです。

M: 講演者が誰だか書いてありますか。

W: 少々お待ちください。案内はここにありますので。基調講演者は Lena Pierce さんです。どんな方なのかはわかりません。

M: Woodhole 大学の教授です。私は数年前にその方の講義を受けました。とても知識が豊富な方ですから、行ってもいいかもしれませんね。

✏️ □interactive 相互の、お互いに行う □investment 投資 □strategic 戦略的な □overseas market 海外市場 □hold on a moment 少々待つ □keynote speaker 基調講演者 □professor 教授 □knowledgeable 知識が豊富である

59. ★★★★☆

What are the speakers talking about?

(A) A knowledgeable coworker
(B) A professional training course
(C) A college class
(D) An investment opportunity

話し手たちは何について話していますか。

(A) 知識が豊富な同僚
(B) 職業訓練コース
(C) 大学の授業
(D) 投資機会

🔍 会話の冒頭❶で女性が「研修の案内が来た」と切り出し、❷で「海外の戦略的投資に関するものだ」と述べている。以上から、専門知識を活かす研修、つまり職業的な研修と考えることができるので正解は (B)。投資ということで、(D) を考えた方もいるかもしれないが、❶で研修と言っているため、実際の投資機会ではないことに注意しよう。

✏️ □opportunity 機会

60. ★★★★☆

What does the woman mean when she says, "Hold on a moment"?

(A) She wants to finish writing an e-mail.
(B) She is waiting for an answer.
(C) She will check a document.
(D) She needs time to decide.

女性が "Hold on a moment" と言う際、何を意味していますか。

(A) E メールを打ってしまいたい。
(B) 回答を待っている。
(C) 書類を確認する。
(D) 決めるのに時間が要る。

 意図を問われている箇所は、❹で「少し待つように」と言っている。そこで前後を見ていくと、❸講演者は誰か➡❹少々お待ちを➡❺ここに案内がある➡❻講演者は Lena Pierce さんだと、手元の手紙から基調講演者を調べていることがわかる。よって、ある文書を確認するために時間が欲しいと伝える文脈だとわかるため、正解は **(C)**。

---

61. ★★☆☆☆

Who is Lena Pierce?

(A) An investor
(B) An entrepreneur
(C) An event planner
(D) A college professor

Lena Pierce とは誰ですか。

(A) 投資家
(B) 起業家
(C) イベントプランナー
(D) 大学教授

 ❻で女性が講演者は Lena Pierce だと述べ、❼で男性が「(彼女は) Woodhole 大学の教授だ」と言っているので、正解は **(D)**。

□investor 投資家　□entrepreneur 起業家

	1回目	2回目	3回目
59.			
60.			
61.			

 59. (B)　60. (C)　61. (D)

M: ▶M ▲W 🔊 3-1-62_64-01~02

Questions 62 through 64 refer to the following conversation and invoice.

M: ❶Is there anything else that I can help you with this morning, or is this all you are getting today, an Internet adapter?

W: In fact, I would like to ask one more thing before I buy the router. ❷Can I pay the monthly bill online? I go out of town often for my job, so I wouldn't be able to come here every month to pay on time.

M: You can access your account online through your computer. It means that you can pay your bill anytime, as long as you have a connection. You can also download our mobile application, so you can get a message when your bill is issued and see the status of your account anywhere.

W: Yes, I see. ❸However, I really don't think I'll need the extra 24-month warranty. Could you just take that off my bill?

M: Sure. Here's your bill for today.

ITEM	PRICE
Internet Adapter	$30
Monthly service fee	$50
❹Two-year warranty	❺$60
Wi-fi router	$100
Total:	$240

問題62-64は次の会話と請求書に関するものです。

M: 今朝は他に何かご入用のものはありませんか。本日のご購入はこちらのインターネットアダプターでよろしいですか。

W: 実は、もう一つ質問したいことがあって、その後でルーターを購入しようと思っているんです。月々の料金をインターネットで支払えますか。仕事でよく町を離れることがあるので、期限内に料金を支払いに来るのは難しいのです。

M: コンピューターからインターネットのアカウントにアクセスすることができます。なので、インターネットにつながっていれば、料金の支払いはいつでも好きなときにできます。携帯電話のアプリをダウンロードすれば、請求書が発行されたときにメッセージを受け取れますし、アカウントの状況がどこにいても確認できます。

W: はい、わかりました。ただ、24か月の追加保証は必要ないと思います。勘定から引いていただけますか。

M: わかりました。こちらが本日のお買い上げです。

商品	価格
インターネットアダプター	30ドル
月額使用料	50ドル
2年間保証	60ドル
Wi-fi ルーター	100ドル
合計	240ドル

□adapter アダプター □router ルーター □go out of town 町を離れる □access ～に接続する □bill 請求
□connection 接続 □download ～をダウンロードする (提供元から別のコンピューター等にデータを移す)
□mobile application 携帯電話のアプリケーション □issue ～を発行する □status 状態 □take off ～を取り除く

62.

Who most likely is the man?

(A) A television actor
(B) A sales clerk
(C) A telephone operator
(D) A repairperson

男性は誰であると考えられますか。

(A) テレビ俳優
(B) 販売員
(C) 電話のオペレーター
(D) 修理工

 会話冒頭❶で男性は女性に「今朝は他に何か入用のものはないか」と尋ね、特定の商品のみでよいか確認していることから、男性はある商品を販売している人だということがわかる。以上から正解は **(B)**。

✎ □actor 俳優　□sales clerk 販売員

63.

What does the woman ask about?

(A) A mobile application
(B) Cable television
(C) Online payments
(D) A subscription renewal

女性は何について尋ねていますか。

(A) 携帯電話のアプリ
(B) ケーブルテレビ
(C) インターネットでの支払い
(D) 購読契約の更新

 女性は、男性にルーターを購入したい旨を伝え、❷で「月々の料金をインターネットで支払えるか」と尋ねている。以上より正解は **(C)**。月々の支払ということで、(D) を考えた人もいるかもしれないが、これは renewal（更新）となっており、既に契約をしている人が更新をすることであるため、ここでは不正解。

✎ □subscription 定期購読　□renewal 更新

64.

Look at the graphic. Which amount will be removed from the bill?

(A) $30
(B) $50
(C) $60
(D) $100

図を見てください。請求書から引かれる金額はどれですか。

(A) 30ドル
(B) 50ドル
(C) 60ドル
(D) 100ドル

🔍 女性は❸で「24か月の追加保証は必要ないので勘定から引いてほしい」と述べている。ここから24か月＝2年の保証に該当する請求書の❹・❺を見ると、60ドルであることがわかる。以上から正解は **(C)**。年を月単位に置き換えて表現することはよくあるので、このような年月の変換はすぐにできるようにしておこう。

	1回目	2回目	3回目
62.			
63.			
64.			

 62. (B)　63. (C)　64. (C)

Questions 65 through 67 refer to the following conversation and list.

M: ❶Jasmine, we ordered 50 desktop computers last month and we will receive the shipment next Friday.

W: Really? Should we replace our current computers with the new ones by ourselves?

M: No, we don't need to. Because our budget permits it, we can hire temporary workers by the hour. ❷Can you help me choose the right employment agency?

W: Of course, what do we need?

M: ❸Our budget is $500 maximum. And we should finish the replacement of the old computers by 11 A.M. What agency should we call?

W: According to the information I received, it seems this one would be the perfect choice.

Agency	Hourly Wage /person	Workers	Total cost	Ending Time
Gracie	$9	60	$540	09:30 A.M.
Chad Place	$12	40	$480	12:00 P.M.
Madison High	$11	50	$550	11:00 A.M.
Romi Ocean	$10	50	❹$500	❺10:00 A.M.

問題65-67は次の会話とリストに関するものです。

M: Jasmine さん、先月デスクトップパソコンを50台注文したので、来週の金曜日に配送される予定です。

W: 本当ですか。今のコンピューターは自分たちで新しいコンピューターに取り替えなければならないのでしょうか。

M: いいえ、その必要はありません。予算があるので、時間単位で派遣社員を雇うことができます。適切な派遣会社を選ぶのを手伝ってもらえますか。

W: もちろん、どうしたらいいですか。

M: 予算は最大500ドルです。そして古いコンピューターの交換は11時までに終わらせる必要があります。どの派遣会社に頼むのがよいでしょうか。

W: いただいた条件で見ると、ここがちょうど良さそうです。

派遣会社	料金／人	作業員	費用合計	終了時刻
Gracie	9ドル	60人	540ドル	午前9時30分
Chad Place	12ドル	40人	480ドル	午後12時
Madison High	11ドル	50人	550ドル	午前11時
Romi Ocean	10ドル	50人	500ドル	午前10時

✏️ □desktop computer 卓上に置く比較的大型のパソコン　□shipment 送付物　□replace ～を更新する　□permit ～を許容する　□temporary 臨時の　□right 適切な　□employment agency 人材派遣会社　□replacement 交換　□choice 選択

65. ★★★★★

What will they do next Friday?

(A) They will select a good employment agency.
(B) They will hire more office workers.
(C) They will place an order for new computers.
(D) They will receive a shipment of new computers.

来週の金曜日に何がありますか。

(A) 良い派遣会社を選ぶ。
(B) より多くの事務員を雇う。
(C) 新しいコンピューターを注文する。
(D) 新しいコンピューターが届く。

 会話冒頭❶で男性が「先月デスクトップパソコンを50台注文したので、来週の金曜日に配送される予定だ」と述べている。以上から正解は **(D)**。

 □place an order 発注する

---

66. ★★★★★

What does the man ask the woman to do?

(A) Help him select an agency
(B) Repair the old computers
(C) Contact job candidates
(D) Order some merchandise

男性は女性に何をするように頼んでいますか。

(A) 派遣会社を選ぶのを手伝うこと。
(B) 古いコンピューターを修理すること。
(C) 求職者に連絡をすること。
(D) 商品を注文すること。

 男性は❷で「適切な派遣会社を選ぶのを手伝ってもらえないか」と尋ねている。以上から正解は **(A)**。

□job candidate 求職者　□merchandise 商品

---

67. ★★★★★

Look at the graphic. Which agency will they choose?

(A) Gracie
(B) Chad Place
(C) Madison High
(D) Romi Ocean

図を見てください。彼らはどの派遣会社を選びますか。

(A) Gracie
(B) Chad Place
(C) Madison High
(D) Romi Ocean

 男性は❸で派遣会社選定の条件を述べており、「予算は最大500ドル」「コンピューターの交換は午前11時までに終わらせる」と2つの条件を満たす必要があることがわかる。次に、表を見ていくと、2つの条件を満たすのは❹・❺から **(D)** だとわかる。よって、これが正解。今回は2つの条件を両方満たす項目を探す必要があるところが難しいポイント。価格・時間の一方のみに着目していると解答が複数出てきてしまうので、問われている条件を当てはめながら正解を選ぼう。

	1回目	2回目	3回目
65.			
66.			
67.			

 65. (D)　66. (A)　67. (D)

Questions 68 through 70 refer to the following conversation and map.

W: Hello, Scott. ❶Are you excited about the auto show in Portland on Sunday? I'm happy our president chose us to represent our firm.

M: Yes, it should be fun! However, how are we going to get there?

W: I'm sorry to say ❷my car is still in the auto shop. The mechanic is trying to repair the engine.

M: I don't mind driving. What's the best way to get from Vancouver to Portland?

W: We should take the highway to Seattle first. From there we can reach Portland. We need to avoid the heavy traffic around Raymond, though.

M: Sounds great. ❸And there's a nice little town between Seattle and Longview. Let's stop off at the bakery there for some lunch.

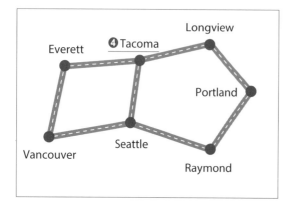

📝 問題68-70は次の会話と地図に関するものです。

W: こんにちは、Scott さん。日曜日の Portland の自動車展示会が楽しみですか。社長に会社の代表として選ばれてとてもうれしいです。

M: ええ、きっと楽しいと思いますよ。でも、現地まではどうやって行ったらいいのですか。

W: あいにく私の車はまだ自動車工場にあります。整備士にエンジンを修理してもらっているところなのです。

M: 私が車を出してもいいですよ。Vancouver から Portland までどうやって行くのが一番いいでしょうか。

W: まずは幹線道路で Seattle まで行きます。そこから Portland まで行けます。Raymond 周辺の交通渋滞は避けなければなりません。

M: いいですね。Seattle と Longview の間に小さな素敵な町があるんですよ。昼食はそこのパン屋に立ち寄りましょう。

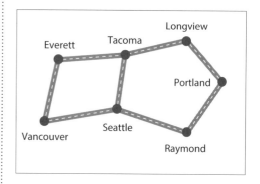

✏️ □auto show 自動車展示会　□represent ～を代表する　□firm 会社　□fun 楽しい　□auto shop 自動車修理工場　□mechanic 技術者、整備士　□I don't mind *doing* ～するのは構わない　□highway 幹線道路　□avoid ～を避ける　□heavy traffic 交通渋滞　□stop off 立ち寄る　□bakery パン屋、ベーカリー

68. ★★★★★

What is taking place this weekend?	今週末何がありますか。
(A) A motor show	**(A)** モーターショー
(B) A job fair	(B) 就職説明会
(C) A training seminar	(C) 研修セミナー
(D) A sales promotion	(D) 販売促進の活動

 会話冒頭❶で女性が「日曜日の Portland の自動車展示会が楽しみか」と尋ねていることから、週末に自動車の展示会があることがわかる。以上から正解は **(A)**。auto、motor ともに自動車を意味する。

✎ □motor show 自動車展示会、モーターショー　□job fair 就職説明会　□sales promotion 販売促進のキャンペーン

---

69. ★★★★★

What problem does the woman mention?	女性はどんな問題について話していますか。
(A) She has another appointment this weekend.	(A) 週末に別の用事がある。
(B) Her driver's license has expired.	(B) 彼女の運転免許証の有効期限が切れている。
(C) Her vehicle is being fixed.	**(C)** 彼女の車が修理中である。
(D) She does not know how to get there.	(D) そこに行く方法を知らない。

 女性は、週末の自動車展示会のイベントについて言及した後、❷で「あいにく私の車はまだ自動車工場にあり、修理中だ」と述べている。これを言い換えた **(C)** が正解。(C) は受け身の進行形でトーク内の、現在車が修理中だ、という表現の言い換え (Her vehicle is being fixed by the mechanic = The mechanic is fixing her vehicle.) になっていることを押さえておこう。

✎ □appointment 約束、用事　□driver's license 運転免許　□expire 期限が切れる　□fix ～を修理する

---

70. ★★★★★

Look at the graphic. In which town does the man most likely want to stop for lunch?	図を見てください。男性が昼食に立ち寄りたいのはどの町だと考えられますか。
(A) Seattle	(A) Seattle
(B) Tacoma	**(B)** Tacoma
(C) Raymond	(C) Raymond
(D) Longview	(D) Longview

 男性は❸で「Seattle と Longview の間でパン屋に立ち寄ろう」と提案している。そこで地図を見ると、Seattle と Longview の間は❹の Tacoma であることがわかる。よって正解は **(B)**。

	1回目	2回目	3回目
68.			
69.			
70.			

🚩 **68. (A)　69. (C)　70. (B)**

Questions 71 through 73 refer to the following excerpt from a meeting.

M: ❶Let's move on to the next item on the agenda. ❷We need to build up our in-house security. As our business is expanding, we get more visitors than ever. ❸From the beginning of October, our security desk at the lobby will screen all visitors to the company. ❹This means that before we allow visitors to enter our building, we will confirm their name, affiliation, purpose of visit, and who they are meeting from the visitors' list. ❺So please send the visitors' information to Johnny Alenko, our security manager, at least one day before their intended visit. If you have an unexpected guest, you'll be asked to come down to the desk, complete the form, and escort him or her in person. ❻Moreover, any recording devices are not allowed in our facility. We will cover and seal the camera lens of the visitors' mobile phones.

M: 議題の次の項目に移りましょう。当社は社内の警備を強化します。事業が拡大するにつれて、当社にはこれまで以上に多くの人が訪れています。10月の初めから、ロビーの警備デスクでは全ての来訪者を確認します。つまり来訪者がビルに入る前に、名前、所属、訪問の目的、誰を訪ねて来たのかを訪問者リストで確認します。そのため、来訪者情報を遅くとも訪問予定日の前日までに警備主任のJohnny Alenkoさんに伝えてください。予定外の来訪者に応対する場合は、デスクのところまで降りてきて、用紙に記入した上で直接ご案内していただきます。また、当施設では録画撮影の機器等の持ち込みは禁止されています。来訪者の携帯電話のカメラのレンズは覆って封をすることになります。

✏️ □next item on the agenda 次の議題の項目　□build up ～を強化する　□in-house 社内の　□security 警備
□expand 拡張する　□visitor 来訪者　□than ever 今まで以上に　□screen ～を検査する　□confirm ～を確認する
□affiliation 所属（関係）　□unexpected 予期しない　□escort ～を案内する　□in person 直接
□moreover さらに　□recording device 録音装置　□facility 施設　□cover ～を覆う　□seal ～に封をする

---

71. ★★★☆☆

What is being discussed?

(A) A change in convention dates
(B) A list of guest speakers
(C) A security policy
(D) An upcoming conference agenda

何の話をしていますか。

(A) 総会の日程の変更
(B) 招待講演者の一覧
(C) 警備の方針
(D) 今度の会議の議題

🔍 話し手は❶で「次に」と話題を切り替えて、❷で「社内警備を強化する」と述べている。これを言い換えた **(C)** が正解。❶のような話の切り出し方は、新たな話題提起だと思ってしっかり集中して正解を探していこう。

✏️ □convention 会議、総会　□security policy 警備方針　□upcoming 来たるべき

72. ★★★★☆

Why should listeners contact Johnny Alenko?

(A) To obtain a designated parking space
(B) To enroll in an event
(C) To receive extra information
(D) To add names to a list

聞き手はなぜ Johnny Alenko さんに連絡する
必要がありますか。

(A) 駐車場を割り当ててもらうため。
(B) イベントに参加登録するため。
(C) さらに情報を受け取るため。
(D) 名前をリストに追加するため。

 話し手は❷以降、会社の警備を強化する内容に触れ、❸で会社が来訪者を審査すること、❹で細かい情報をリストで確認することを述べ、❺でこれらを受けて「来訪者情報を Alenko さんに伝えておくように」と言っている。つまり、来訪者の名前等の情報を Alenko さんに伝える必要があることがわかる。正解はそれを言い換えた **(D)**。

✎ □designated 指定された、割り当てられた　□enroll in 〜に登録する

73. ★★★☆☆

What does the speaker say visitors will not be
allowed to do?

(A) Take a photo
(B) Go to a different floor
(C) Copy documents
(D) Arrive late

話し手は、来訪者は何をすることが許可されてい
ないと言っていますか。

(A) 写真を撮ること。
(B) 別の階に行くこと。
(C) 文書を複製すること。
(D) 遅れて到着すること。

 話し手は❻で「当施設では録画の機器等の持ち込みは禁止で、(携帯電話の) カメラレンズも覆って封をする」と言っている。ここから、撮影禁止であることがわかるので、これに関わる行為を指した **(A)** が正解となる。cover and seal the camera lens of the visitors' mobile phones から take a photo が禁じられることを導き出すという点で、言い換えレベルがやや高い。しっかり復習で押さえておこう。

	1回目	2回目	3回目
71.			
72.			
73.			

71. (C)　72. (D)　73. (A)

W 4-1-74_76-01~02

Questions 74 through 76 refer to the following telephone message.

W: Hello. ❶This is a message for Nathan Turner about the computer you brought to Nixon Technology for repair. ❷Our store's repairperson has found that the home button of the computer is not working properly and will need to be replaced. ❸Unfortunately, the warranty on your computer has expired, so you'll be charged for the new part and repair fee. ❹But, because you shop here regularly, we'd like to give you a 30 percent discount on the repair fee. If you need more information, call us at 888-2190. We're open from 9 to 5, Monday through Friday.

問題74-76は次の電話のメッセージに関するものです。

W: こんにちは。Nixon Technology社に修理のために持ち込まれたコンピューターについてNathan Turnerさんにご連絡します。当店の修理担当者によると、コンピューターのホームボタンが正常に機能しておらず、交換が必要とのことです。恐れ入りますが、コンピューターの保証期間が過ぎてしまっているため、交換部品と修理の代金が必要になります。ただ、お客様は当店をいつもご利用いただいているので、修理代から30パーセントをお値引きいたします。詳しい情報が必要でしたら、888-2190までお電話ください。月曜日から金曜日の9時から5時まで営業しております。

□bring A to A を～に持ち込む　□repairperson 修理担当者　□work properly 正常に作動する
□replace ～を交換する　□warranty 保証　□expire 期限が切れる　□regularly 定期的に

74. ★★★★★

What is the problem with the computer?

(A) The screen needs to be replaced.
(B) A button is malfunctioning.
(C) The battery is not charging.
(D) A program is not compatible with the device.

コンピューターの問題は何ですか。

(A) 画面の交換が必要である。
(B) ボタンが正常に動かない。
(C) バッテリーが充電されない。
(D) プログラムが機器に合わない。

話し手は❶で修理に持ち込まれたコンピューターについて言及し、❷でボタンが正しく動作していないと述べている。ここから、ボタンの動作に言及した **(B)** が正解。malfunctioning = not working properly と言い換えが可能なので、慣れておこう。

□malfunction 故障している　□battery バッテリー、電池　□compatible 互換性のある

75. ★★★☆☆

What does the speaker ask the listener to do?

(A) Pay a fee for the service
(B) Contact the repairperson
(C) Show the warranty certificate
(D) Purchase a new computer

話し手は聞き手に何をするように頼んでいますか。

(A) 作業料を支払う。
(B) 修理担当者に連絡する。
(C) 保証書を提示する。
(D) 新しいコンピューターを購入する。

話し手は❸で「保証期限が過ぎているので有償対応となる」と述べている。つまり、修理するには作業料金を払う必要があると述べているので、これを言い換えた **(A)** が正解。

□contact 〜に連絡する　□warranty certificate 保証書

---

76. ★★☆☆☆

What does the speaker offer?

(A) A discount
(B) A free carrying case
(C) An extended warranty
(D) A replacement device

話し手は何を提供しますか。

(A) 値引き
(B) 無料の持ち運び用ケース
(C) 保証期間の延長
(D) 交換品

話し手は❸で有償対応だと伝えながらも、❹で「(聞き手は) お得意様のため、値引きする」と述べている。以上から、話し手が申し出ているのは **(A)** だとわかる。

□carrying case 持ち運びケース　□extended 延長した　□replacement 交換

PART
4

TEST
1

	1回目	2回目	3回目
74.			
75.			
76.			

 74. (B)　75. (A)　76. (A)

Questions 77 through 79 refer to the following telephone message.

📄 問題77-79は次の電話のメッセージに関するものです。

M: I'm calling to ask about your advertisement for an apartment with a short-term lease in the downtown area of Kimberley. ❶I'm moving to Kimberley, because I was offered a teaching job at a local high school. And I'd be interested in renting your apartment starting August 15. ❷The ad mentioned that the lease is only for four months. ❸I'm really glad about that. ❹Since I'd like to get familiar with the area for a few months before committing to a longer lease, I think the apartment is a perfect match for me. ❺However, I'm wondering whether your building is pet-friendly or not. Please let me know.

M: Kimberley の中心地にある短期賃貸アパートの広告について伺いたくて、お電話しました。地元の高校で教員をすることになったので、Kimberley に引っ越しをします。8月15日からそちらのアパートをお借りしたいと考えています。広告には賃貸は4か月のみと記載されていました。それが本当に気に入っています。もっと長い期間の賃貸契約を結ぶ前に、数か月間でその地域のことをよく知りたいと思っているので、そのアパートはぴったりだと思います。ただ、建物でペットを飼えるかが気になっています。教えてください。

✏️ ☐short-term 短期間の　☐lease 賃貸　☐downtown area 中心部　☐be interested in ～に興味がある　☐ad 広告　☐mention ～に言及する　☐get familiar with ～に慣れる　☐commit to a lease 賃貸契約に同意する　☐perfect match for ～にぴったりである　☐pet-friendly ペット飼育可である

77. ⭐☆☆☆☆

Why is the speaker going to Kimberley?

(A) To look at its architecture
(B) To launch a real estate business
(C) To live with his relatives
(D) To teach at a school

話し手はなぜ Kimberley に行きますか。

(A) 建築物を見るため。
(B) 不動産事業を立ち上げるため。
(C) 彼の家族と暮らすため。
(D) 学校で教えるため。

🔍 話し手は❶で「地元の高校で教師をすることになったので、Kimberley に引っ越す」と述べている。以上から正解は **(D)**。

✏️ ☐architecture 建築物　☐launch ～を立ち上げる　☐real estate 不動産　☐relatives 親戚、家族 (の者)

78. ★★★★☆

What does the speaker mean when he says, "I'm really glad about that"?

(A) He can advertise a property.
(B) He can live with his family.
(C) He has found a suitable apartment.
(D) He does not have to move.

話し手が "I'm really glad about that" と言う際、何を意味していますか。

(A) 不動産を宣伝できる。
(B) 家族と一緒に暮らせる。
(C) 適当な場所が見つかった。
(D) 引っ越す必要はない。

 意図を問われている表現❸は「それについてうれしい」と言っている。この前後の流れを見ていくと、❷アパート賃貸は4か月のみ➡❸それがうれしい➡❹数か月間でその地域を知りたいのでぴったりだとなっている。ここから、話し手の要望に合う物件が見つかったことがわかるので、それを suitable apartment と言い換えた **(C)** が正解。

□property 不動産　□suitable 適した

---

79. ★★☆☆☆

What additional information does the speaker want to know?

(A) Whether residents are permitted to have pets
(B) How much the security deposit is
(C) Where the nearest supermarket is
(D) Whether parking lots are available

話し手はどんな追加情報が知りたいのですか。

(A) 居住者がペットを飼うことが許可されているか
(B) 敷金の金額がいくらか
(C) 最寄りのスーパーマーケットはどこか
(D) 駐車場が利用できるか

 話し手は❺で「建物でペットが飼えるのか気になっている」と述べている。これを言い換えた **(A)** が正解。

□security deposit 敷金　□nearest 最寄りの

	1回目	2回目	3回目
77.			
78.			
79.			

77. (D)　78. (C)　79. (A)

Questions 80 through 82 refer to the following announcement.

M: Welcome and thank you for joining us. ❶ This will be an exciting two-hour tour of complete indulgence. We'll begin with a short history of the product, then you'll see exactly how chocolate is made from the bean to the finished bar. ❷ Look, has anyone ever seen this? It's a cacao pod. And inside? These are beans. Along the way you'll try some wonderful cacao pulp, see the fermentation process, learn about the health benefits of chocolate, and of course taste the product at the end of the tour. Before we start, I ask that everyone put on these hairnets. This is to adhere to our sanitary guidelines. During the tour, ❸ please make sure you don't go beyond the red lines on both sides. I'll be happy to answer any questions about our chocolate factory along the way. If you have any allergies, please tell me now. OK, here we go.

問題80-82は次のお知らせに関するものです。

M: ご来場の皆さま、ご参加くださりありがとうございます。このツアーは心ゆくまでお楽しみいただける2時間のツアーです。まずは弊社製品の歴史をご覧いただき、次にチョコレートが豆から出来上がりの棒状になるまでを実際に見てまいりましょう。はい、これを見たことがある方はいらっしゃいますか。カカオの実です。そして中にあるのが、豆です。進んでいく中で、すりつぶしたおいしいカカオを試食して、醗酵の過程を見て、チョコレートの健康面への効能を学び、そして、もちろんツアーの最後には製品をご賞味いただけます。始める前に皆さまにこのヘアネットを常につけておいていただくようお願いします。これは当社の衛生規定に沿うためのものです。ツアー中は常に左右の赤い線を越えないようにご注意ください。チョコレート工場についてご質問がありましたら、途中でも喜んでお答えしてまいります。何かアレルギーのある方がいらっしゃいましたらお知らせください。では、まいりましょう。

☐ complete すっかりと　☐ indulgence 思いや楽しみにふけること、耽溺　☐ finished 最終製品の
☐ cacao pod カカオの実　☐ pulp すりつぶしたもの　☐ fermentation process 発酵工程
☐ health benefits 健康に関する効能　☐ taste ～を試食する　☐ hairnet ヘアネット　☐ adhere to ～を遵守する
☐ sanitary guideline 衛生規定　☐ along the way 途中で

---

80. ★★☆☆☆

Where does the talk most likely take place?

(A) At a coffee shop
(B) At a museum
(C) In a restaurant
(D) At a factory

この話はどこで行われていると考えられますか。

(A) コーヒーショップ
(B) 博物館
(C) レストラン
(D) 工場

🔍 話し手は❶で「これは2時間のツアーです」と紹介をしており、その後チョコレートの原材料や製品に言及していることから、この話は工場で行われていることがわかる。以上より正解は **(D)**。

81. ★★★☆☆

What does the speaker show the listeners?	話し手は聞き手に何を見せていますか。
(A) Some chocolate	(A) チョコレート
(B) A pamphlet	(B) パンフレット
(C) Some coffee recipes	(C) コーヒーの作り方
(D) Raw materials	**(D) 原材料**

 話し手は❷でカカオの実と豆を見せている。つまりチョコレートの原材料を見せていることがわかるため、正解は **(D)** となる。

 □raw material 原材料

---

82. ★★★★★

What does the speaker ask the listeners to do?	話し手は聞き手に何をするように頼んでいますか。
(A) To stay within the marked boundaries	**(A) 境界線の内側にいること。**
(B) To take photos without a flash	(B) フラッシュなしで写真を撮ること。
(C) To wear helmets	(C) ヘルメットをかぶること。
(D) To cover their shoes	(D) 靴を覆うこと。

話し手は❸でツアー中の注意事項について言及し、「ツアー中は常に左右の赤い線を越えないように」と述べている。ここから、境界線の中に滞まるようにお願いしていることがわかる。この越えてはいけない赤い線を marked boundaries と言い換えた **(A)** が正解となる。

□marked 印のついた　□boundary 境界線

	1回目	2回目	3回目
80.			
81.			
82.			

 80. (D)　81. (D)　82. (A)

Questions 83 through 85 refer to the following broadcast.

W: ❶ In business news, one of the world's biggest producers of vehicle wheels, Edward Wheels, has been contracted to supply passenger vehicle wheels for the new EZ-5 car. ❷ In order to be able to manufacture the large number of wheels required by the contract, Edward Wheels is scheduled to open another manufacturing plant at the beginning of October. The new plant will be located in the city of Austin. ❸ In a press conference earlier this morning, Kate Nelson, the mayor of Austin, expressed her delight at the opening of the facility, saying that it will likely bring up to 700 additional jobs to the community.

📝 問題83-85は次の放送に関するものです。

W: ビジネスのニュースです。世界最大の車輪メーカーの一つである Edward Wheels 社が新型車 EZ-5 のための乗用車用ホイールを供給する契約を結びました。契約で定められた大量のホイールを製造できるように Edward Wheels 社は10月初めに新たな製造工場を始動する予定です。新工場は Austin 市に置かれます。今朝行われた記者会見で、Austin 市長の Kate Nelson は開設への期待を示し、地域に700人規模に及ぶ雇用機会がもたらされると述べました。

✎ □contract ～と契約する　□vehicle wheel 車輪　□in order to *do* ～するため　□manufacture ～を製造する
□large number of 大多数の　□require ～を要求する　□manufacturing plant 製造工場
□press conference 記者会見　□delight 期待　□facility 施設　□likely おそらく　□bring ～をもたらす
□up to ～まで

---

83. ★★☆☆☆

What kind of business does the speaker mainly focus on?

(A) Automobile wheels
(B) Ship building
(C) Bus renovations
(D) Traffic control systems

話し手は主にどんな事業に焦点を当てていますか。

(A) 自動車用の車輪
(B) 造船
(C) バスの修理
(D) 交通管制システム

🔍 話し手は冒頭❶で「世界最大の車輪メーカーの一つである」と切り出している。ここから、車輪に関わる事業であることがわかる。以上から正解は **(A)**。

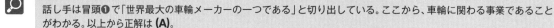

✎ □ship building 造船　□renovation 修理、改装　□traffic control 交通管制

84. ★★★★★

According to the speaker, what will the business do in October?

(A) Improve public awareness of the environment
(B) Open a new manufacturing plant
(C) Start an online advertising campaign
(D) Hold a press conference

話し手によると企業は10月に何をしますか。

(A) 環境に対する一般市民の意識を向上させる。
(B) 新しい製造工場を開設する。
(C) インターネットで広告キャンペーンを始める。
(D) 記者会見を開く。

話し手は❷で「Edward Wheels 社は10月初めに新たな製造工場を始動する予定だ」と述べているので、ここから **(B)** が正解となる。

□awareness 気づき、意識　□environment 環境

---

85. ★★★★★

What does the city official expect will take place in Austin?

(A) Employment opportunities will increase.
(B) More traffic regulations will be passed.
(C) Public transportation will improve.
(D) City taxes will be cut.

市の職員は Austin で何が起こることを望んでいますか。

(A) 雇用機会が増える。
(B) より多くの交通規制が可決される。
(C) 公共交通機関が改善される。
(D) 市の税額が下がる。

話し手は❸で「記者会見で、Austin 市長は地域に700人規模に及ぶ雇用機会がもたらされると述べた」と伝えている。つまり、市の職員の1人である市長が雇用の機会が増えることを望んでいるとわかるため、これを言い換えた **(A)** が正解となる。

□employment 雇用　□opportunity 機会　□regulation 規制　□pass ～を通過する、可決する
□public transportation 公共交通機関　□tax 税

	1回目	2回目	3回目
83.			
84.			
85.			

 83. (A)　84. (B)　85. (A)

PART 4 TEST 1

55

Questions 86 through 88 refer to the following announcement.

📝 問題86-88は次のお知らせに関するものです。

M: Hello, everyone! ❶ Welcome to this afternoon's show of Sugar Man. I'm Tammy Sinclair, the coordinator of this art and theater group. ❷ I am very excited to tell you that all the tickets for our show have sold out once again, which means we've sold every ticket to every show since opening day of this year. During a short intermission, please feel free to buy refreshments out in the hallway or visit our theater souvenir shop on the first floor. ❸ All proceeds from this afternoon's ticket sales will financially support the local arts program at our community high school, so thank you all for coming. Now, please enjoy the Sugar Man's concert.

M: 皆さん、こんにちは。午後の Sugar Man ショーへようこそ。この芸術と演劇グループの取りまとめ役の Tammy Sinclair です。当グループのショーのチケットが再度完売したことを大変喜ばしく思います。これはすなわち今年の初日からの全てのショーでチケットが完売したということです。短い休憩時間には玄関ホールでお気軽に軽食をお求めいただくか、または1階の劇場土産店にお立ち寄りください。本日の午後のチケット販売での収益は全て地域の高校の芸術プログラムの財政支援に充てられますので、お越しいただけたことを大変ありがたく思います。では、Sugar Man のコンサートをお楽しみください。

✏️ ☐coordinator 主催者　☐short intermission 小休止　☐feel free to *do* 自由に～する　☐refreshment 軽食
☐hallway ホール　☐souvenir お土産　☐proceeds 収益金　☐financially support ～を財政的に支援する

---

86. ★★☆☆☆

Who most likely is the speaker?

(A) An actor
(B) An event supporter
(C) A show coordinator
(D) A musician

話し手は誰であると考えられますか。

(A) 俳優
(B) イベントの後援者
(C) ショーのコーディネーター
(D) 音楽家

🔍 話し手は❶で「ショーへようこそ」と切り出し、「私はこの芸術と演劇団体の取りまとめ役だ」と述べていることから、正解は **(C)** とわかる。

✏️ ☐actor 俳優、演者　☐supporter 後援者、支援者

87. ★★★★★

What does the speaker say is special about the show?

(A) All the tickets have sold out.
(B) A complimentary souvenir will be given to all attendees.
(C) It was organized by a high school student.
(D) It has received many awards.

このショーについて話し手は何が特別であると言っていますか。

(A) チケットが完売した。
(B) 全ての参加者に無料の記念品が贈られる。
(C) 高校生によって準備された。
(D) 多くの賞を受賞した。

 話し手は❷で「チケットがまたも完売、つまり今年の初日からの全てのショーでチケットが完売したことになる」と述べている。ここから、チケットが立て続けに完売した、ということをがわかるので、これを言い換えた **(A)** が正解。

 □complimentary 無料の　□attendee 参加者　□award 賞

----

88. ★★★★★

How will the profits of the show be used?

(A) To support programs in a local school
(B) To repair the concert hall
(C) To replace old musical instruments
(D) To build a community hall

このショーの収益はどのように使われますか。

(A) 地元の学校のプログラムを支援するため。
(B) コンサートホールを改修するため。
(C) 古い楽器を交換するため。
(D) コミュニティホールを建造するため。

 話し手は❸で「収益金は地域の高校生のプログラムサポートに充てられる」と伝えているので、これを言い換えた **(A)** が正解となる。設問の profits = proceeds との言い換えは、リスニングだけではなく Part 7の長文問題にも登場するので押さえておこう。

 □musical instrument 楽器

	1回目	2回目	3回目
86.			
87.			
88.			

 86. (C)　87. (A)　88. (A)

Questions 89 through 91 refer to the following instructions.

W: Good morning, everyone! ❶I'm here to teach you how to use the Amee Editing software. Your art production director wants this two-day training session to improve office productivity and creativity. This software is a powerful graphic design tool that will help you create a better quality product with more variety in design. ❷I'm aware some of you have experience using a previous version, but ❸there have been many changes. ❹That's why we'll be starting from the basics then moving on to the many extra features. ❺If at any time you become lost or don't know what to do, please raise your hand. ❻I'll be pleased to assist you.

W: 皆さま、おはようございます。今日は Amee 編集ソフトウェアの使い方をお教えします。御社の芸術製作主任はこの二日間の研修をとおして、皆さまのお仕事での生産性と創造性を向上させることを期待していらっしゃいます。このソフトウェアはよりデザイン性に富んだ、より高品質の製品を制作するのに役立つ強力なグラフィックデザインツールです。皆さまの中には既に旧バージョンをご利用になられた方もあるようですが、多くの変更がなされています。そのため、基本事項から始めて数々の特徴を扱っていくことになっています。ついていけなくなったり、やり方がわからなくなったりした際には、いつでも手を挙げてください。すぐにお手伝いにまいります。

✏️ ☐director 監督、主任　☐productivity 生産性　☐creativity 創造性　☐quality 品質の良い　☐variety 多様性
☐previous 過去の　☐extra 他の　☐feature 特徴　☐at any time いつでも　☐raise one's hand 手を挙げる

---

89. ★★★☆☆

Who most likely is the speaker?

(A) A museum director
(B) A seminar attendee
(C) A magazine editor
(D) A training instructor

話し手は誰であると考えられますか。

(A) 美術館長
(B) セミナー参加者
(C) 雑誌編集者
(D) 研修会の講師

 話し手が❶で「今日は編集ソフトウェアの使い方を教えるために来た」と述べていることから、研修講師であることがわかるため、これを言い換えた **(D)** が正解。(B) は受講者のことを指すので不正解。

 ☐instructor 講師

90. ★★★★☆

What does the speaker mean when she says, "there have been many changes"?

(A) Previous experience is not so useful.
(B) The business has expanded into new areas.
(C) Some customers will be confused.
(D) It is necessary to raise prices.

"there have been many changes" と言う際、話し手は何を意味していますか。

(A) これまでの経験はあまり通用しない。
(B) 会社は新規分野に乗り出している。
(C) 顧客の混乱が予想される。
(D) 値上げが必要である。

意図を問われている表現は❸「多くの変更があった」である。この前後を見ていくと、❷参加者の何人かは経験者➡❸たくさん変更があった➡❹そのため基礎から始めるという流れになっている。つまり、最近たくさんの変更があったため、経験者が持っている知識も役に立たないことを意図しているとわかる。以上から、これを言い換えた **(A)** が正解。

□expand into ～に参入する　□confuse ～を混乱させる　□raise prices 値上げする

91. ★★★☆☆

What does the speaker ask listeners to do?

(A) Consult a manual
(B) Ask for help
(C) Update some software
(D) Practice at their office

話し手は聞き手に何をするよう求めていますか。

(A) 説明書を見る。
(B) 助けを求める。
(C) ソフトをアップデートする。
(D) 会社で練習する。

話し手は❺・❻で「不明な点があれば挙手してもらえればすぐに手伝う」と話しているため、わからなかった場合には助けを求めてほしいと言っていることがわかる。この助けを求めることを Ask for help と言い換えた **(B)** が正解。

□consult ～を調べる　□update ～を更新する

	1回目	2回目	3回目
89.			
90.			
91.			

89. (D)　90. (A)　91. (B)

Questions 92 through 94 refer to the following announcement.

W: With more and more bike commuters, the city transportation department voted to install bike lanes. After months of planning, throughout the city, bike lanes will now become a reality. ❶Beginning on Friday, July 16, the city will start roadworks on the southern side of Central Avenue as it intersects from Seventh Avenue to Tenth Avenue. ❷Therefore, Central Avenue and Mercury Street will not be accessible for six weeks. ❸Traffic will be diverted to Delta Road, and regular routes are expected to reopen on August 30. ❹To help see the situation clearly, a map showing alternate routes is on the city's Web site.

問題92-94は次のお知らせに関するものです。

W: 自転車通勤者が増えていることを受けて、市の交通局は自転車専用車線の設置を可決しました。数か月の準備期間を経て、市の全域での自転車専用車線がついに実現します。Central通りの南側が7番街から10番街までと交差しているため、7月16日の金曜日に市はそこから工事を開始します。従って、Central通りとMercury街は6週間以上通行できなくなります。通行の際はDelta道へ迂回することになり、通常経路の再開は8月30日になる見込みです。交通状況を詳しくご覧になる場合は、市のウェブサイトに迂回路を示す地図があります。

□commuter 通勤者　□transportation department 交通局　□vote ～を票決する　□reality 現実　□intersect ～と交差する　□accessible 到達できる、利用する　□divert ～を迂回させる　□regular route 通常経路　□reopen 再開する　□alternate 別の、もう1つの

92. ★★★★☆

What most likely will happen on Friday?

(A) A bicycle race
(B) A vote on a city development project
(C) Road closures
(D) An announcement of a plan

金曜日には何があると考えられますか。

(A) 自転車レース
(B) 都市開発プロジェクトに関する投票
(C) 道路の封鎖
(D) 計画の発表

話し手は❶・❷で「金曜日から始まる工事でしばらく通行できない道路がある」と述べている。つまり、道路が封鎖されることを伝えているため、正解は(C)となる。

□closure 閉鎖

93. ★★★★★

Where are the listeners recommended to make a detour?

聞き手はどこで迂回することを勧められていますか。

(A) Central Avenue
(B) Tenth Avenue
(C) Mercury Street
(D) Delta Road

(A) Central 通り
(B) 10番通り
(C) Mercury 街
(D) Delta 道

 話し手は❸で通行は Delta 道へ向けて迂回するように、と伝えている。以上から、正解は **(D)**。この問題は、be diverted to（～へ迂回する）という表現が設問で make a detour と言い換えられていることと、複数の通りの名前が出てくる中で、それらが通行できなかったり、迂回の対象ではないことを理解して解く必要がある。ここに出てくる言い換えは頻出なので、見抜けるようにしておこう。

---

94. ★★★★☆

What is available on the Web site?

ウェブサイトでは何が利用できますか。

(A) Bicycle safety advice
(B) A visual guide to routes
(C) A construction schedule
(D) New bus times

(A) 自転車安全利用案内
(B) 道路案内図
(C) 工事の予定表
(D) 新しいバスの時刻表

 話し手は❹で「市のウェブサイトに迂回路を示す地図（a map showing alternate routes）がある」と述べている。これを言い換えた **(B)** が正解。

✎ □visual guide 図解ガイド　□bus time バスの時刻表

	1回目	2回目	3回目
92.			
93.			
94.			

 92. (C)　93. (D)　94. (B)

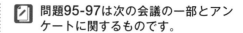
Questions 95 through 97 refer to the following excerpt from a meeting and survey.

M: ❶Please take a look at the next thing on our agenda, the results of the guest survey. ❷The survey was taken by all guests who dined here in the month of December. Astonishingly, the parts we were worried about seem to be fine, but ❸there is definitely an area we need to work on. I will be back here in about twenty minutes because I need to receive a shipment. Meanwhile, ❹please scan the comments the guests have made and think about how we can improve on the area we received the lowest rating on. I will then put together the best ideas and apply them here to provide our guests with better dining experiences.

📝 問題95-97は次の会議の一部とアンケートに関するものです。

M: 議題の次の項目を見てください。お客様へのアンケート調査の結果です。調査は12月にうちで食事をした全てのお客様に対して行いました。意外なことに懸念していた部分については問題がなさそうでしたが、確実に取り組みが必要となる面があります。私は配送物を受け取らなければなりませんが、20分ほどで戻ってきます。その間に、お客様が記入したコメントに目を通して、どうしたら最も評価の低かった点を改善できるか考えてください。そこから私が最適なアイデアをまとめて、それを当店で実行し、お客様により良い食事を体験していただけるようにします。

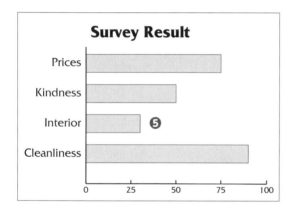

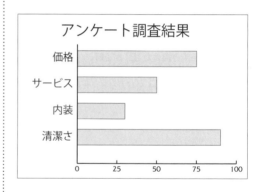

☐take a look at ～を見る   ☐dine 食事をする   ☐astonishingly 意外なことに   ☐be worried about ～を心配する
☐definitely 確実に   ☐meanwhile その間   ☐scan ～に目を通す   ☐put together ～をまとめる
☐apply ～を適用する   ☐cleanliness 清潔さ

95.

Where does the speaker most likely work?

(A) At a restaurant
(B) At a consulting firm
(C) At a hotel
(D) At a theater

話し手はどこで働いていると考えられますか。

(A) レストラン
(B) コンサルティング会社
(C) ホテル
(D) 劇場

 話し手は❶でアンケート調査結果について触れ、❷で「うちで食事をしたお客様に対して行ったアンケート」と述べている。ここから、食事を提供する場所であることがわかるので **(A)** が正解。

96.

Look at the graphic. What does the speaker want to discuss?

(A) Prices
(B) Service
(C) Interior
(D) Cleanliness

図を見てください。話し手は何について話し合いたいと思っていますか。

(A) 価格
(B) サービス
(C) 内装
(D) 清潔さ

 話し手はアンケート結果から、❸で「ある分野は改善の余地がある」ことに触れ、❹で「一番低評価のところについて改善案を考えてほしい」と述べている。グラフを見ると、一番評価が低く改善を考えたいものは❺の内装だとわかる。よって正解は **(C)**。

97.

What does the speaker ask the listeners to do?

(A) Receive a shipment
(B) Think of ways to improve customer satisfaction
(C) Make a report on the survey results
(D) Conduct another survey

話し手は聞き手に何をするように頼んでいますか。

(A) 配送物を受け取る。
(B) 顧客満足度の改善方法を考える。
(C) 調査結果の報告をする。
(D) 別のアンケート調査を実施する。

話し手は❹で、アンケートのコメントを確認するように求めている。そして、このアンケートはお客様からの回答であるため、この改善がお客様の満足度の向上につながることがわかる。以上から、このお客様の満足を customer satisfaction と言い換えた **(B)** が正解となる。

□customer satisfaction 顧客満足度　□conduct a survey 調査を行う

	1回目	2回目	3回目
95.			
96.			
97.			

95. (A)　96. (C)　97. (B)

Questions 98 through 100 refer to the following announcement and boarding pass.

M: This is an important announcement for all those at Gate E05 waiting to board Flight HZ63 to Saint Petersburg. ❶Because of the bad weather, this flight will leave a little later than scheduled. It is not at risk of being canceled, as we expect the snowstorm to end fairly soon. ❷In light of this inconvenience, you are entitled to request a free beverage from the coffee shop or bar next to Gate E05. Simply present your boarding pass at either of these places and you will not be charged for your order. ❸The departure time and boarding time printed on your boarding pass have both been pushed back by twenty minutes. Please be ready at the gate when boarding starts so that everything moves along smoothly. Thank you for your understanding.

📝 問題98-100は次のお知らせと搭乗券に関するものです。

M: 搭乗口E05にて、Saint Petersburg行きHZ63便にご搭乗をお待ちの全てのお客様に重要なお知らせをいたします。悪天候により、当便は予定されていたよりも少々遅れての出発となります。吹雪は間もなく収まるものと予想されており、欠航の可能性はありません。ご不便をおかけしておりますため、搭乗口E05の隣の喫茶店またはバーにて無料で飲み物をご利用いただけるよう手配しております。いずれかの店頭におきましても搭乗券をご提示いただけましたら、ご注文に対する料金はかかりません。搭乗券に記載の出発時刻と搭乗時刻は共に20分遅れとなっております。全ての手続きが円滑に進みますよう、搭乗開始時刻には搭乗口でお待ちください。ご了承のほど、お願い申し上げます。

BOARDING PASS

Passenger Name: Mr.Volcan Danilov

Flight: HZ63   Seat: 17D

Date: March 10
       Departure Time: 2:45 P.M. (Gate E05)
❹ Boarding Starts: 2:15 P.M.
       Gate Closes: 2:35 P.M.

Anchorage to Saint Petersburg

搭乗券

乗客名：Volcan Danilov 様

便名：HZ63   座席：17D

日付：3月10日
       出発時刻：午後2時45分(搭乗口E05)
       搭乗開始時刻：午後2時15分
       搭乗締切時刻：午後2時35分
Anchorage 発 Saint Petersburg 行

🖊 □at risk 危険、リスクがある　□snowstorm 吹雪　□fairly soon もうまなもく　□in light of ～を考慮し
□inconvenience 不便　□be entitled to *do* ～する資格がある　□simply 単に　□boarding pass 搭乗券
□charge (金額等)を課す　□push back ～を遅らせる　□move along smoothly 円滑に進む
□Thank you for your understanding. よろしくお願いします。

98.

What is the announcement mainly about?	アナウンスの趣旨は何ですか。
(A) A flight delay	**(A)** 飛行機の遅延
(B) A gate change	(B) 搭乗口の変更
(C) An airport regulation	(C) 空港の規定
(D) A service cancellation	(D) サービスの停止

 話し手は❶で「悪天候より飛行機の出発便が予定よりも遅れる」ということを述べている。以上から正解は **(A)**。

✎ □regulation 規定、ルール

99.

What does the speaker advise passengers to do?	話し手は乗客に何をするように勧めていますか。
(A) Get a new boarding pass	(A) 新しい搭乗券を受け取る。
(B) Contact an airline official	(B) 航空会社の職員に連絡する。
(C) Show their passports	(C) パスポートを見せる。
(D) Order a complimentary drink	**(D)** 無料の飲み物を注文する。

 話し手は❷で「搭乗口隣の喫茶店またはバーにて無料で飲み物をご利用いただけるよう手配した」と述べている。ここから、無料ドリンクを勧めていることがわかるので、正解は **(D)**。(C) は示すように言われているのがパスポートではなく搭乗券のため不正解。

✎ □airline official 空港職員　□complimentary 無料の

100.

Look at the graphic. When should Mr. Danilov be ready to board the airplane?	図を見てください。Danilov さんはいつ飛行機搭乗の準備ができていなければなりませんか。
(A) At 1:55 P.M.	(A) 午後1時55分
(B) At 2:15 P.M.	(B) 午後2時15分
(C) At 2:25 P.M.	(C) 午後2時25分
(D) At 2:35 P.M.	**(D)** 午後2時35分

 話し手は❸で「搭乗券に記載の出発時刻と搭乗時刻は共に20分遅れとなっている」と述べ、その直後に「搭乗開始時刻には搭乗口で待つように」とお願いしている。次に搭乗券を見ると、搭乗時間が❹より午後2時15分となっている。ここから、この搭乗時間から20分後の午後2時35分が現在の搭乗時間であり、この時間に搭乗口にいなくてはいけないことがわかる。以上から正解は **(D)**。

	1回目	2回目	3回目
98.			
99.			
100.			

🚩 **98. (A)　99. (D)　100. (D)**

GO ON TO THE NEXT TEST!

PART **3**&**4**

Test

2

32. What is the man working on?

    (A) A quarterly report
    (B) A budget plan
    (C) A meeting agenda
    (D) An office newsletter

33. What did the man just find out?

    (A) A conference has been rescheduled.
    (B) A sales report is lost.
    (C) A meeting room is already reserved.
    (D) A mistake has been discovered.

34. What does the woman agree to do in the afternoon?

    (A) E-mail a co-worker
    (B) Cancel an appointment
    (C) Take a look at a document
    (D) Postpone a meeting

35. What problem does the man talk about?

    (A) There is a lack of employees.
    (B) The business has fewer guests.
    (C) A bill has not been paid.
    (D) There is no record of a reservation.

36. What most likely does the woman recommend?

    (A) Discounting prices
    (B) Extending the hours of operation
    (C) Moving to larger facilities
    (D) Holding group parties

37. What does the man ask the woman to do?

    (A) Plan a renovation project
    (B) Host a staff meeting
    (C) Hire extra workers
    (D) List new service options

38. What most likely is the man's job?

    (A) A bank teller
    (B) A sales manager
    (C) A journalist
    (D) A store cashier

39. What change was recently made to the woman's workplace?

    (A) The security was increased.
    (B) Her offices were remodeled.
    (C) New employees were hired.
    (D) Operation hours were changed.

40. What does the woman say about her employees?

    (A) They are working more effectively.
    (B) They are pleased with the renovated interiors.
    (C) They are unhappy about a change.
    (D) They are keen to advance their careers.

41. What is the main topic of the conversation?

    (A) Budget deficits
    (B) Collaboration with another company
    (C) Merger and acquisition
    (D) Personnel changes

42. What has the speakers' company recently done?

    (A) Installed more energy-efficient equipment
    (B) Appointed a new president
    (C) Moved to a larger office
    (D) Received funds from the government

43. Why was Hollingsworth Steel chosen to be contacted?

    (A) It is skilled at production.
    (B) It is environment-friendly.
    (C) It is located nearby.
    (D) It has the lowest prices.

GO ON TO THE NEXT PAGE ➡

 32-34 *P. 76*　　📑 35-37 *P. 78*　　📑 38-40 *P. 80*　　📑 41-43 *P. 82*

44. Where does the woman most likely work?

(A) At a watch repair store
(B) At an electronic store
(C) At a technical school
(D) At a clothing shop

45. What does the woman show the man?

(A) A product catalog
(B) A shopping list
(C) A list of courses
(D) A range of components

46. What does the woman offer the man?

(A) A repairperson's contact details
(B) A training session
(C) A discounted price
(D) Another appointment time

47. What is mentioned about the tables?

(A) They are now on sale.
(B) They require some adjustments.
(C) They are made locally.
(D) They can be assembled easily.

48. What does the woman imply when she says, "I don't live alone"?

(A) She shouldn't choose the style by herself.
(B) She saves money on living expenses.
(C) She tries not to stay out too late.
(D) She doesn't have space for new furniture.

49. Why will the woman not take a picture?

(A) She ran out of power on her mobile phone.
(B) She can find the part in a catalog.
(C) She thinks it is prohibited in the store.
(D) She plans to visit the store again.

50. What does the company sell?

(A) Business clothing
(B) Display cases
(C) Eyewear
(D) Photographic equipment

51. What is the man surprised about?

(A) The price of a raw material
(B) The speed of a production process
(C) The popularity of a product
(D) The range of available sizes

52. What will the woman do?

(A) Compare a competitor's prices
(B) Order additional stock
(C) Update a Web site
(D) Organize promotional photos

53. What are the speakers talking about?

(A) A discounted accommodation rate
(B) A lodging's location
(C) An incomplete booking
(D) An overcharged purchase

54. According to the woman, what does the man need to send?

(A) A personal review
(B) His credit card number
(C) A photograph ID
(D) His e-mail address

55. What does the man ask the woman to do?

(A) Confirm receipt of a message
(B) Submit a picture of the room
(C) Provide a credit card number
(D) Reduce the price of his next stay

44-46 *P. 84*   47-49 *P. 86*   50-52 *P. 88*   53-55 *P. 90*

56. What is the main topic of the conversation?

(A) The winner of a game
(B) The technique of an artist
(C) The format of a contest
(D) The price of a piece of art

57. What did Ms. Townsend recently do?

(A) Moved a sculpture
(B) Appeared on television
(C) Resigned from her job
(D) Negotiated a new contract

58. What does the man mean when he says, "I think I'll pass"?

(A) He will not buy an item.
(B) He is on his way through an area.
(C) He expects to be allowed to enter.
(D) He is prepared for an important test.

59. Why did the man visit the gallery?

(A) To promote a product
(B) To deliver a package
(C) To see an exhibit
(D) To fill in a signature card

60. What does the woman say about Ms. Coleman?

(A) She does not allow visitors.
(B) She starts work at 12.
(C) She is not working today.
(D) She will be available shortly.

61. What does the man say he will do next?

(A) Return the following day
(B) Wait in the lobby
(C) Finish another task first
(D) Call Ms. Coleman later

The Butterfield Cinema is proud to host
The 10th Dayton Ocean Independent Movie Festival

"The Book of Eli"

Time: 8:00 P.M.   **Screen:** 5
Seat: A03   **Price:** $25

62. What will the woman receive for free?

(A) Some event souvenirs
(B) A movie program
(C) Some refreshments
(D) A book about film making

63. Who most likely is the man?

(A) A box office agent
(B) A movie critic
(C) A festival planner
(D) A film director

64. Look at the graphic. What type of seat did the woman select?

(A) A standard Seat
(B) A comfort Seat
(C) A deluxe Seat
(D) A VIP Seat

GO ON TO THE NEXT PAGE ➡

56-58 *P. 92*   59-61 *P. 94*   62-64 *P. 96*

Daily Train Schedule (Dallas-Austin)	
Train	**Departure**
ANT201	09:30 A.M.
ANT303	11:00 A.M.
ANT405	1:30 P.M.
ANT507	4:00 P.M.

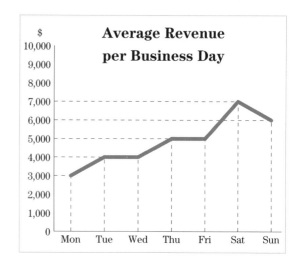

65. What is the main topic of the conversation?

(A) A tourist attraction
(B) An annual event
(C) A work schedule
(D) A new train service

66. What will the speakers do on Wednesday afternoon?

(A) Attend a conference
(B) Visit their company headquarters
(C) Interview a new branch manager
(D) Submit a travel expenses report

67. Look at the graphic. What train will the speakers most likely take on Wednesday?

(A) ANT201
(B) ANT303
(C) ANT405
(D) ANT507

68. What is the main topic of the conversation?

(A) Maximizing profits
(B) Changing suppliers
(C) Decreasing prices
(D) Attracting customers

69. When will the coffee shop begin holding live music?

(A) Next week
(B) Next month
(C) Next quarter
(D) Next year

70. Look at the graphic. On which day will business hours most likely be reduced?

(A) On Mondays
(B) On Tuesdays
(C) On Wednesdays
(D) On Thursdays

65-67 *P. 98*

68-70 *P. 100*

71. What is the purpose of the speech?

(A) To remind staff of a next step
(B) To acknowledge employees' efforts
(C) To accept a proposal
(D) To discuss a new regulation

72. Where does the speaker most likely work?

(A) At a manufacturing company
(B) At a travel agency
(C) At a construction company
(D) At a state government

73. What does the speaker say about the government plan?

(A) It will cause state taxes to rise.
(B) It will encourage tourism.
(C) It will expand the company's market area.
(D) It will increase the company's sales.

74. What is the speech mainly about?

(A) Hiring more employees
(B) Increasing efficiency
(C) Relocating the company
(D) Spreading workload

75. Who most likely are the listeners?

(A) Company managers
(B) Small vendors
(C) Researchers and developers
(D) Potential recruits

76. Why does the speaker say, "You know your staff better than anyone"?

(A) To understand a common complaint
(B) To clarify a procedure
(C) To praise strong team spirit
(D) To ask for proposals

77. According to the speaker, when will the snowboard lesson start?

(A) At 2:00 P.M.
(B) At 2:30 P.M.
(C) At 3:00 P.M.
(D) At 3:30 P.M.

78. What problem does the speaker mention?

(A) An instructor has been delayed.
(B) Some attendees have canceled their registration.
(C) A snowboard slope has been closed.
(D) Some equipment is unusable.

79. What does the speaker mean when he says, "Don't wander off"?

(A) He wants the listeners to stay near a meeting point.
(B) He advises the listeners to remain indoors.
(C) He forbids the listeners to stand close to equipment.
(D) He instructs the listeners to go to a rental office.

80. What change has been made?

(A) Working hours have been decreased.
(B) A warehouse has been moved.
(C) Corporate headquarters has been expanded.
(D) A new service provider has been hired.

81. According to the speaker, what has the staff been worried about?

(A) The speed of Internet services
(B) A small work space
(C) Levels of noise
(D) Lack of environmental policies

82. What does the speaker remind the listeners to do?

(A) Check a notice
(B) Attend a staff meeting
(C) Log into a homepage
(D) Read their e-mail

GO ON TO THE NEXT PAGE ➡

 71-73 *P. 102*   **74-76** *P. 104*   **77-79** *P. 106* **80-82** *P. 108*

83. What is the problem with the desk?

(A) It has been discontinued.
(B) It has been out of stock.
(C) It is damaged.
(D) It is too big.

84. According to the speaker, what will the listener have to do?

(A) Visit the company headquarters
(B) Contact a sales representative
(C) Show proof of purchase
(D) Input a voucher number

85. What will the speaker send?

(A) A refund
(B) An extended warranty
(C) A replacement
(D) A voucher

86. What does the speaker imply when he says, "Make sure you check your schedule"?

(A) The day of the radio show will change.
(B) Ticket sales may end earlier than expected.
(C) An event will start soon.
(D) A construction process will cause delays.

87. What will happen on Sunday?

(A) A musical event
(B) A community party
(C) A culinary festival
(D) A sports game

88. Who most likely is Ms. Della?

(A) A celebrated musician
(B) The festival coordinator
(C) A local politician
(D) A renowned chef

89. Why is the business closed today?

(A) All the employees are taking a vacation.
(B) The shop is being cleaned.
(C) It's a public holiday.
(D) New appliances are being installed.

90. Why does the speaker mention Billy's Market?

(A) It is also closed today.
(B) The owner is an excellent baker.
(C) They have a business relationship.
(D) It is conveniently located.

91. What does the business plan for September involve?

(A) Offering a delivery service
(B) Opening another store
(C) Hiring more workers
(D) Starting a new promotion

92. Where most likely are the listeners?

(A) On a bus
(B) On an airplane
(C) On a ship
(D) On a train

93. What has caused the problem?

(A) A gate number has not been assigned.
(B) An equipment malfunction has been found.
(C) A trip has been overbooked.
(D) Inclement weather has caused a delay.

94. What is the new departure time?

(A) 6:00 P.M.
(B) 7:00 P.M.
(C) 8:00 P.M.
(D) 9:00 P.M.

83-85 *P. 110*   86-88 *P. 112*   89-91 *P. 114*   92-94 *P. 116*

Roles	Zone
Janitor: Tables and Floors	1
Janitor: Bathrooms	
Grill Cook	2
Line Cook	
Drive-Through Cashier	3
Main Restaurant Cashier	
Delivery Driver	4

95. Where most likely does the speaker work?

(A) In a hotel
(B) In a restaurant
(C) In a recruitment agency
(D) In a food wholesaler

96. What are the listeners asked to do?

(A) Prepare a meal
(B) Check a schedule
(C) Review a shift
(D) Choose a job duty

97. Look at the graphic. What zone is a delivery driver in?

(A) Zone 1
(B) Zone 2
(C) Zone 3
(D) Zone 4

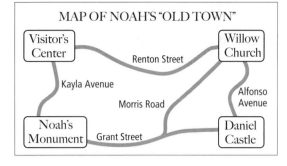

MAP OF NOAH'S "OLD TOWN"

98. Who most likely are the listeners?

(A) Passengers
(B) Tourists
(C) Trainees
(D) Guides

99. Look at the graphic. Which place can listeners see as a bonus?

(A) Willow Church
(B) Daniel Castle
(C) Noah's Monument
(D) Renton Street

100. What does the speaker remind the listeners to do?

(A) Gather at a hotel for a meal
(B) Return to the bus on time
(C) Take part in the event
(D) Put their belongings on the bus

95-97 *P. 118*

98-100 *P. 120*

Questions 32 through 34 refer to the following conversation.

M: Hello, Lisa. ❶I am now preparing the budget plan for the next quarter, which we will be discussing at Monday's meeting.

W: I don't think you know yet. ❷Mr. Cameron just told me that the meeting has been postponed until next Wednesday.

M: ❸That's a relief. But still, ❹I was hoping that you could give me some feedback on it.

W: ❺I'm very sorry, but I'm quite busy at the moment since I have a sales report that I have to send by noon. ❻However, I would be able to review it around 4 P.M. ❼So, why don't you submit the draft to me by e-mail?

📝 問題32-34は次の会話に関するものです。

M: こんにちは、Lisa さん。今、月曜日の会議で話し合う次の四半期の予算計画を準備しているんです。

W: まだご存じじゃないかもしれませんね。私も Cameron さんから聞いたばかりなのですが、会議は来週の水曜日に延期されたそうです。

M: それはよかった。でも、これについて意見をお聞きできたらと思うのですが。

W: 大変申し訳ないのですが、正午までに送らなければいけない売上報告があって、今はとても忙しいのです。ただ、午後4時ごろでしたら確認できそうなので、草案を E メールで送ってもらえますか。

✏️ □prepare ～を準備する □quarter 四半期 □That's a relief. それはよかった。 □feedback 感想、意見
□at the moment 今現在 □review ～を確認する □Why don't you...? ～してはどうか □draft (文書等の) 草案

---

32. ⭐☆☆☆☆

What is the man working on?

(A) A quarterly report
(B) A budget plan
(C) A meeting agenda
(D) An office newsletter

男性は何に取り組んでいますか。

(A) 四半期報告書
(B) 予算計画
(C) 会議の議題
(D) 社内報

 男性は会話冒頭❶で「次の四半期の予算計画を準備している」と述べている。そこから、取り組んでいるものは予算計画だとわかるので、正解は **(B)**。

 □office newsletter 社内報

33. ★★★☆☆

What did the man just find out?

(A) A conference has been rescheduled.
(B) A sales report is lost.
(C) A meeting room is already reserved.
(D) A mistake has been discovered.

男性は何を知りましたか。

(A) 会議の日程が変更されたこと。
(B) 売上報告書が紛失したこと。
(C) 会議室が既に予約されたこと。
(D) 間違いが発見されたこと。

 男性の冒頭の発言の後、女性が❷で「（男性は知らないかもしれないが）会議は来週の水曜日に延期された」と述べている。その後、男性が❸で「それはよかった」と述べていることから、この情報が男性にとって初耳だとわかる。以上より、正解は **(A)**。(A) は❷の the meeting has been postponed の言い換えになっていることに注目。

 □discover ～を発見する

---

34. ★★★★☆

What does the woman agree to do in the afternoon?

(A) E-mail a co-worker
(B) Cancel an appointment
(C) Take a look at a document
(D) Postpone a meeting

女性は午後何をすることを承諾していますか。

(A) 同僚に E メールを送ること。
(B) 約束を取り消すこと。
(C) 書類に目を通すこと。
(D) 打ち合わせを遅らせること。

 男性が❹で作成した予算案について意見を求めているのに対し、女性は❺で「今は忙しい」と断りながらも、❻で「午後4時ごろなら確認できそうだから、メールで送ってほしい」と言っている。つまり、男性の予算案を確認してほしいという依頼を承諾したことになる。これを言い換えた **(C)** が正解。❺ の review を take a look at、❼ の draft を a document と言い換えていることに注意。この問題の難しいところは、❹の代名詞 it = a budget plan であること、また女性は一度依頼を断るが、❺で However... と逆接の接続詞に続く部分で承諾したというストーリーをつかむ点にある。しっかり復習しておこう。

 □take a look at ～に目を通す

	1回目	2回目	3回目
32.			
33.			
34.			

 32. (B)　33. (A)　34. (C)

Questions 35 through 37 refer to the following conversation.

M: Hi, Wendy. Here's the situation. ❶For the past few months, we haven't had as many clients as we had last year at this time. ❷We need to do something to attract more people to the spa. If you have experienced a similar situation before, I'd like to hear how you dealt with it.

W: ❸In the past under our previous manager, we held a 'Winter Spa Month' during which we offered new spa packages at reduced prices.

M: ❹That sounds like a wonderful plan. ❺Can you go ahead and make a list of spa packages? However, I'd like to look it over before we start advertising them.

問題35-37は次の会話に関するものです。

M: こんにちは、Wendy さん。状況をお知らせします。直近の数か月間の顧客数は昨年の同期ほどではありませんでした。スパへの来場者を増やすために何か手を打つ必要があります。以前にも似たような状況があったのでしたら、どう対処されたのかお聞きしたいのですが。

W: 前任の部長のときには、新しいスパのパッケージを割引で提供する「冬のスパ月間」を開催しました。

M: それはいい案ですね。スパパッケージのリストの作成に着手してもらえますか。ただ、確認をしてから宣伝に移りたいと思います。

✎ □situation 状況　□past 直近の、過去の　□as many A as ～と同じくらいの A　□attract ～を引き付ける
□spa 温泉　□deal with ～に対処する　□under 人 人のもとで　□at reduced prices 割引価格で
□go ahead 進む

35.

What problem does the man talk about?

(A) There is a lack of employees.
(B) The business has fewer guests.
(C) A bill has not been paid.
(D) There is no record of a reservation.

男性はどのような問題について話していますか。

(A) 従業員が不足している。
(B) 顧客が減っている。
(C) 請求金額が支払われていない。
(D) 予約の記録がない。

🔍 男性は❶・❷で「直近数か月間の顧客数が昨年比を下回ったため、スパの来場者数を増やすために何かをする必要がある」と述べている。ここから、最近お客様の入りが減っていることが問題だとわかる。それを fewer guests と言い換えた **(B)** が正解となる。

✎ □a lack of ～の不足　□bill 請求書、請求額

36. ★★★☆☆

What most likely does the woman recommend?

(A) Discounting prices
(B) Extending the hours of operation
(C) Moving to larger facilities
(D) Holding group parties

女性は何を勧めていると考えられますか。

(A) 値下げ価格
(B) 営業時間の延長
(C) より大きな施設への移転
(D) グループパーティーの開催

> 女性は男性が問題について言及した後、❸で「前任の部長のもとで、パッケージ割引プランを行った」と過去の経験を話し、それに対して男性は❹で「よい計画のようだ」と述べている。ここから、女性がこの発言内容を勧めていることがわかるため、割引プランを意味する **(A)** が正解。(A) の discounting を会話❸では reduced と言っていることも押さえておこう。

🖊 □extend 〜を延長する　□facility 施設　□hold a party パーティーを開催する

37. ★★★★☆

What does the man ask the woman to do?

(A) Plan a renovation project
(B) Host a staff meeting
(C) Hire extra workers
(D) List new service options

男性は女性に何をするように頼んでいますか。

(A) 改修プロジェクトを組むこと。
(B) スタッフ会議を主催すること。
(C) さらに多くのスタッフを雇うこと。
(D) 新しいサービス項目を一覧にすること。

> 男性は会話後半❺で女性に「スパパッケージのリストの作成に着手してほしい」と依頼している。ここから、スパパッケージ＝新しいサービスと考えると、選択肢の中で言い換えとなっている **(D)** が正解だとわかる。

🖊 □renovation 改修　□list 〜を一覧化する

	1回目	2回目	3回目
35.			
36.			
37.			

🚩 **35. (B)　36. (A)　37. (D)**

Questions 38 through 40 refer to the following conversation.

M: Good morning, ❶I'm Keith Jackson from Riverbank Daily Tribune. ❷I heard that you recently introduced a revolutionary change in your working environment. ❸It's really surprising that your firm decided to reduce the total working time by two hours per day. ❹Would you tell me how this recent change has affected your company?

W: ❺Thus far, the new policy has been very successful. Our workers appear to be satisfied and the working atmosphere is very positive.

M: You sound quite satisfied with the result. But has it increased the productivity of your workers?

W: Yes, it has. ❻Our employees are now working with more energy. ❼We've seen output go up by 10 percent since introducing this change.

📝 問題38-40は次の会話に関するものです。

M: おはようございます。Riverbank Daily Tribune 紙の Keith Jackson と言います。先日、御社で職場環境における革新的な変更を行ったとお聞きしました。御社が総労働時間を1日あたり2時間短縮すると決定したということにとても驚いています。この改革が会社に与えた影響がどのようなものだったかお聞かせいただけますか。

W: これまでのところ、新方針は大変成功しています。従業員は満足している様子で、職場の雰囲気はとても前向きです。

M: 結果には非常に満足なさっているようですね。ただ、従業員の生産性は向上したのでしょうか。

W: ええ、向上しています。当社の従業員はより精力的に仕事に取り組んでいます。変更を導入してから、生産高は10パーセント増えています。

✏️ □introduce ~を導入する　□working environment 職場環境　□surprising 驚くべきこと
□working time 勤務時間　□affect ~に影響する　□thus far これまでのところ　□policy 方針
□working atmosphere 職場の雰囲気　□positive 前向き　□productivity 生産性　□with energy 精力的に
□output 生産高　□go up by (数値)ほど上昇する

---

38. ⭐⭐⭐⭐⭐

What most likely is the man's job?

(A) A bank teller
(B) A sales manager
(C) A journalist
(D) A store cashier

男性の仕事は何であると考えられますか。

(A) 銀行員
(B) 営業部長
(C) 記者
(D) レジ係

🔍 男性はまず❶で「Riverbank Daily Tribune」と所属先を伝え、❷で聞いた出来事に触れ、❹でその感想を求めている。ここで、あるニュースについての情報を聞き出す、という仕事をしていることから、選択肢の中で一番関連がある **(C)** の記者だとわかる。なお、Daily Tribune というのは日刊紙＝新聞を指す場合が多いので、この名前から「記者では？」と勘を働かせても構わない。

 □bank teller 銀行員　□cashier レジ係

39. ★★★★☆

What change was recently made to the woman's workplace?

(A) The security was increased.
(B) Her offices were remodeled.
(C) New employees were hired.
(D) Operation hours were changed.

女性の職場で最近変わったこととは何ですか。

(A) 警備が厚くなった。
(B) 彼女の仕事場が改築された。
(C) 新入社員が採用された。
(D) 業務時間が変更になった。

会話冒頭で男性が問いかけた際に、❸で「（女性の）会社が総労働時間を1日あたり2時間短縮すると決定した」と述べ、❺で女性が「これまでのところはうまくいっている」とその内容を認めているため、業務時間が変更になった、と言い換えている **(D)** が正解。(D) が❸内の your firm decided to reduce the total working time by two hours per day から言い換えられていることをチェックしておこう。

□security 警備　□remodel ～を改装する　□operation hours 営業時間

40. ★★★☆☆

What does the woman say about her employees?

(A) They are working more effectively.
(B) They are pleased with the renovated interiors.
(C) They are unhappy about a change.
(D) They are keen to advance their careers.

女性は従業員について何と言っていますか。

(A) 前より効率的に働いている。
(B) 屋内の改装に満足している。
(C) 変化について不満がある。
(D) 昇進に熱意を抱いている。

女性は❻・❼で「当社の従業員はより精力的に仕事に取り組むようになり、生産高は10パーセント増加した」と述べていることから、この会社の生産性が上がったことがわかる。この状況を working more effectively と言い換えた **(A)** が正解。

□effectively 効果的に　□renovated 改装された　□be unhappy about ～に対して不満である
□be keen to *do* ～することに熱心である　□advance one's career 昇進する

	1回目	2回目	3回目
38.			
39.			
40.			

38. (C)　39. (D)　40. (A)

81

Questions 41 through 43 refer to the following conversation with three speakers.

M1: ❶Are the meetings with Hollingsworth Steel about the joint venture going well?

M2: Not really. We spent a lot of time discussing details of the project, but nothing was decided.

W: We got stuck on the issue of who will oversee the project. If they accept Rainbow Plastics from our firm, everything will progress much better than now.

M2: I think you're right. I don't like to see so much time and energy wasted.

M1: I couldn't agree with you more. ❷Now that our company has received a lot of funding from the government, we just want to work with a business that is good at production. ❸That's why we contacted them.

W: I agree. We need to reach an agreement about who will provide the supervisors as soon as possible. Otherwise, we may need to look for another partner.

📝 問題41-43は次の3人の話し手による会話に関するものです。

M1: Hollingsworth Steel 社との提携の話し合いはうまく行っていますか。

M2: そうでもありません。プロジェクトの詳細についての話し合いに時間を多く費やしましたが、何も決まりませんでした。

W: どちらがプロジェクトの監督をするかという問題で行き詰まったんです。先方が当社の Rainbow Plastics を受け入れるならば、全てが今よりも大幅に進展するのでしょうけど。

M2: そのとおりですね。多くの時間や労力が無駄になるのを見たくはありません。

M1: 全くです。当社は政府からたくさんの資金をもらっているので、生産力がある企業と一緒に仕事がしたいだけなのに。そのためにあちらに声をかけたわけですから。

W: そうですね。どちらが監督者を出すかは早急に合意を取りつけたいところです。それができないのであれば、他の提携先を探すことになるでしょう。

✎ □joint venture 共同事業　□go well うまくいく　□detail 詳細　□get stuck on ～で行き詰まる
□oversee ～を監督する　□firm 会社　□waste ～を浪費する
□I couldn't agree with you more そのとおりである (直訳：これよりも同意できないだろう)　□funding 資金
□be good at ～に強みを持つ　□otherwise さもなければ

---

41. ★★★☆☆

What is the main topic of the conversation?

(A) Budget deficits
(B) Collaboration with another company
(C) Merger and acquisition
(D) Personnel changes

会話の話題は何ですか。

(A) 予算不足
(B) 他社との協力
(C) 吸収合併
(D) 人事異動

🔍 会話冒頭❶で男性が企業間の共同事業について話していることから、それを言い換えた **(B)** が正解。joint venture は難しい言い回しだが、TOEIC にはよく登場するのでしっかり押さえておこう。

✎ □deficit 不足　□merger 合併　□acquisition 買収　□personnel change 人事異動

42. ★★☆☆☆

What has the speakers' company recently done?

(A) Installed more energy-efficient equipment
(B) Appointed a new president
(C) Moved to a larger office
(D) Received funds from the government

話し手たちの会社が先日行ったこととは何ですか。

(A) さらにエネルギー効率がいい設備を設置した。
(B) 新しい社長を任命した。
(C) さらに広いオフィスに移転した。
(D) 政府から資金を受け取った。

🔍 ❷で男性の1人が「最近政府から金銭的支援を受けた」と言っていることから、それを言い換えた **(D)** が正解。

✏️ □install 〜を設置する　□energy-efficient エネルギー効率の良い、省エネの　□appoint 〜を任命する

---

43. ★★★★☆

Why was Hollingsworth Steel chosen to be contacted?

(A) It is skilled at production.
(B) It is environment-friendly.
(C) It is located nearby.
(D) It has the lowest prices.

Hollingsworth Steel 社に声がかけられたのはなぜですか。

(A) 生産に長けているため。
(B) 環境に配慮しているため。
(C) 近くにあるため。
(D) 最低価格のため。

🔍 1人目の男性が❷で「政府から資金提供を受けているので、生産力があるところと手を組みたい」と話し、❸で「だから彼らに声をかけた」と述べている。この彼らこそ、手を組む＝共同で事業を行おうとしている会社であり、冒頭❶で登場してきた Hollingsworth Steel 社だとわかる。以上より正解は **(A)**。❷の good at が (A) で skilled at に言い換えられているところもチェックしておこう。

✏️ □be skilled at 〜に長けている　□environment-friendly 環境に配慮した

	1回目	2回目	3回目
41.			
42.			
43.			

 41. (B)　42. (D)　43. (A)

Questions 44 through 46 refer to the following conversation.

M: Good morning, ❶I've never been here before, but your watch repair shop was strongly recommended. ❷Can you mend this watch? The hour hand is broken and I'd like to have it replaced with a new one.

W: ❸We have a large selection of parts for watches. Regrettably, I don't think I have the exact one you need. However, if you want, I can replace both the hour and minute hand so they match. ❹Here, take a look in the display case.

M: I really like the black ones up there. I will go with those ones. Are they very expensive?

W: It's one of our most expensive styles, but because I couldn't fulfill your original request, ❺I'll give you 30% off the price.

📝 問題44-46は次の会話に関するものです。

M: おはようございます。初めてなのですが、こちらの時計修理店がとてもいいと聞きました。この時計を修理してもらえませんか。時針が壊れているので新しいのに交換してほしいんです。

W: 当店では時計の部品を豊富に取り揃えておりますが、あいにく、お客様のご希望どおりのものは用意がございません。ただ、もしよろしければ、時針と分針の両方を交換して、2つが合うようにできます。こちらの陳列ケースをご覧ください。

M: 上の方にある黒いのはいいですね。あれにしようと思います。お値段は結構かかりますか。

W: 当店では最も高額なモデルの一つですが、お客様の最初のご希望に添えなかったこともありますし、価格は30パーセントお引きします。

✏️ □repair shop 修理店　□strongly とても　□mend ～を修理する　□hour hand (時計の) 時針
□replace with ～に交換する　□a large selection of 豊富な品揃えの　□regrettably 残念ながら
□exact ちょうど合う　□minute hand (時計の) 分針　□match 調和する　□take a look 見る
□display case 陳列ケース　□up there 上の方にある　□go with ～の商品にする、～を選択する　□style (品物の) 型
□fulfill ～を満たす

---

44. ★★☆☆☆

Where does the woman most likely work?

(A) At a watch repair store
(B) At an electronic store
(C) At a technical school
(D) At a clothing shop

女性はどこで働いていると考えられますか。

(A) 時計修理店
(B) 電子機器店
(C) 専門学校
(D) 衣料品店

🔍 会話冒頭❶・❷で男性が「女性の店を強く薦められたので自分の時計を修理してくれないか」と女性に頼んでいる。ここから、女性は時計修理店で働いていることがわかる。以上より正解は **(A)**。

✏️ □technical school 専門学校

45. ★★★★☆

What does the woman show the man?

(A) A product catalog
(B) A shopping list
(C) A list of courses
(D) A range of components

女性は男性に何を見せていますか。

(A) 製品カタログ
(B) 買い物リスト
(C) コースの一覧
(D) 部品の品揃え

❸で女性は男性に「幅広い種類の時計の部品を持っている」と述べ、❹でディスプレイケースを見るように促している。ここから、女性は男性にいろいろな種類の時計パーツを見せていることがわかる。以上より、時計パーツをcomponents と言い換えて表現した **(D)** が正解。「品揃えがある」という表現は❸の a selection of 以外に、(D) の a range of、そのほかに a variety of、an array of があるが、TOEIC ではいずれも頻出の表現なので、しっかり覚えておこう。

□a list of 〜の一覧　□a range of 豊富な　□component 構成部品

46. ★★★★☆

What does the woman offer the man?

(A) A repairperson's contact details
(B) A training session
(C) A discounted price
(D) Another appointment time

女性は男性に何を申し出ていますか。

(A) 修理工の連絡先
(B) 研修会
(C) 値引き価格
(D) 別の予約時間

女性は会話の最後に❺で「お客様の最初のご希望に添えなかったため、価格は30パーセント値引きする」と言っている。つまり、値下げを申し出ていることがわかるため、正解は **(C)**。

□contact detail 連絡先詳細　□training session 研修　□appointment time 予約時間

	1回目	2回目	3回目
44.			
45.			
46.			

 44. (A)　45. (D)　46. (C)

Questions 47 through 49 refer to the following conversation.

M: Hey, Sara! ❶Check out these tables.

W: Yes, ❷the unique design caught my eye from across the store. ❸And it says on the sign that they're made right here in Bayville City.

M: Don't you need a new table for your dining room? This one would be ideal.

W: ❹I like the bright colors, but ❺I don't live alone. ❻I share an apartment with my sister.

M: ❼Maybe you could take a picture and send it to her.

W: ❽That won't be necessary. ❾We're going shopping in this mall on Sunday, so I'll bring her here to see it for herself. I'm sure they won't be sold out by then.

問題47-49は次の会話に関するものです。

M: やあ、Sara さん。このテーブルを見てください。

W: ええ、店の反対側からも独創的なデザインが目に入りました。それに案内にはここ Bayville 市で作られたと書いてありますね。

M: お宅のダイニング用に新しいテーブルが必要なのではないですか。これならぴったりですよ。

W: その明るい色は気に入りましたが、私は一人暮らしではないのです。同じアパートで妹と一緒に暮らしているので。

M: 写真に撮って送ったりしてはどうですか。

W: それは必要ありません。日曜日にこのモールに二人で買い物に来るので、ここに連れてきて直接見てもらいます。それまでに売り切れてしまうことはないと思います。

□check out ～を確認する　□unique 独創的な　□catch one's eye 目を引く　□ideal 理想的な　□bright 明るい
□Maybe you could ～してみてはどうか　□necessary 必要である　□sold out 売り切れ

---

47. ★★★☆☆

What is mentioned about the tables?

(A) They are now on sale.
(B) They require some adjustments.
(C) They are made locally.
(D) They can be assembled easily.

テーブルについて何と言っていますか。

(A) 現在販売中である。
(B) 調整が必要である。
(C) 地元で作られている。
(D) 組み立てが簡単である。

まず会話冒頭❶で、男性がテーブルについて触れ、女性が❷でそれが独創的なデザインであることと、❸でこの地域で製作したサインがあることを述べている。ここから、❸の内容にあたる **(C)** が正解。

□on sale 発売中である　□require ～を要求する　□adjustment 調整　□locally 地元で
□assemble ～を組み立てる

48. ★★★★☆

What does the woman imply when she says, "I don't live alone"?

(A) She shouldn't choose the style by herself.
(B) She saves money on living expenses.
(C) She tries not to stay out too late.
(D) She doesn't have space for new furniture.

女性が "I don't live alone" と言う際、何を意図していますか。

(A) 自分一人で形を選ぶわけにはいかない。
(B) 生活費を節約している。
(C) 遅くまで出かけていないようにしている。
(D) 新しい家具を置くスペースがない。

意図を問われている対象の❺は「私は1人暮らしではない」と述べている。この前後を見ると、❹女性は明るい色が気に入った➡❺女性は1人暮らしではない➡❻妹とアパートをシェアしていると話している。ここから、自分一人で住んでいるわけではないので自分一人の好みで決定するわけにはいかない、という意図であることがわかる。以上より、正解は **(A)**。ここで (A) の style は色のことを抽象的に表現していると捉えれば正答にたどり着けるはずだ。

□style 型、様式　□living expense 生活費　□stay out 外に出たままである

---

49. ★★★☆☆

Why will the woman not take a picture?

(A) She ran out of power on her mobile phone.
(B) She can find the part in a catalog.
(C) She thinks it is prohibited in the store.
(D) She plans to visit the store again.

女性はなぜ写真を撮らないのですか。

(A) 携帯電話の電池が切れた。
(B) 部品はカタログで見つけられる。
(C) 店内では禁止されていると思っている。
(D) また店を訪れる予定である。

❼「テーブルの写真を撮影して妹に送っては」という男性からの提案に対して、女性は❽で必要ないと断り、❾で「週末の買い物で妹に直接見てもらう」と述べている。つまり、女性は日を改めて店舗を再訪するとわかるので、これを言い換えた **(D)** が正解。他の選択肢はいずれも該当する発言がないため、不正解。

□run out of ～を使い切る　□prohibit ～を禁じる

	1回目	2回目	3回目
47.			
48.			
49.			

47. (C)　48. (A)　49. (D)

Questions 50 through 52 refer to the following conversation.

W: ❶The first boxes of new frames for our summer collection of sunglasses have just arrived. Take a look, they are exactly as we designed them.

M: They certainly are. ❷And so soon! The manufacturer has done an amazing job in such a short time. These are bound to sell well on our Web site.

W: ❸First we need to get a range of images of models wearing the new styles. ❹I'll contact the studio to arrange a fashion shoot. Can you start thinking about Web page design?

M: I'll get on it right away. We should be aiming to start sales by the end of May.

📖 問題50-52は次の会話に関するものです。

W: 夏のサングラスコレクション用の新フレームの初めの配送分が届きましたよ。ほら、ちゃんとデザインしたとおりになっています。

M: 確かにそうですね。それに本当に早かったです。メーカーはこの短期間で見事に仕上げてくれましたね。ウェブサイトでよく売れるに違いありません。

W: まずはモデルが新デザインを着用している画像を揃えましょう。スタジオに連絡をしてファッション写真の手はずを整えておきます。ウェブページのデザインを考えておいてもらえますか。

M: すぐに取りかかります。5月末までには売り出せるようにしたいですね。

✏️ □frame フレーム、枠　□collection コレクション、シリーズ商品　□take a look 見る
□exactly as ちょうど〜のとおりの　□certainly 確かに　□manufacturer 製造者　□amazing 素晴らしい
□in such a short time そんな短い時間で　□be bound to *do* 〜するだろう　□sell well よく売れる
□a range of さまざまな　□image 画像　□style 型、デザイン　□contact 〜に連絡する　□arrange 〜を設定する
□fashion shoot ファッション写真の撮影

50.

What does the company sell?

(A) Business clothing
(B) Display cases
(C) Eyewear
(D) Photographic equipment

会社は何を販売していますか。

(A) ビジネス用衣類
(B) 陳列ケース
(C) 眼鏡類
(D) 撮影用機器

🔍 会話冒頭❶で女性が「フレーム」「サングラス」に関連する納品が来たことを伝えているので、この会社は眼鏡類を扱っていることがわかる。以上より正解は **(C)**。

✏️ □eyewear 眼鏡類　□photographic equipment 撮影機器

51. ★☆☆☆☆

What is the man surprised about?

(A) The price of a raw material
(B) The speed of a production process
(C) The popularity of a product
(D) The range of available sizes

男性は何に驚いていますか。

(A) 原料の価格
(B) 製造工程の速さ
(C) 商品の人気
(D) 対応可能なサイズの幅

 男性は❷で「すぐに来た！」と驚き、「こんなにも短い期間で素晴らしい仕事をした」と話している。以上から、製造工程のスピードの速さに驚いていることがわかるため、正解は **(B)**。

□raw material 原料　□production process 製造工程　□popularity 人気　□range 幅、範囲

---

52. ★☆☆☆☆

What will the woman do?

(A) Compare a competitor's prices
(B) Order additional stock
(C) Update a Web site
(D) Organize promotional photos

女性はこれから何をしますか。

(A) 競合他社の価格を比べる。
(B) 在庫品を追加注文する。
(C) ウェブサイトを更新する。
(D) 広告写真をまとめる。

女性は❸・❹で「モデルが着用している画像を揃える」「スタジオ会社に連絡して撮影の手配をする」と述べているので、商品の販売促進に取りかかろうとしていることがわかる。正解はそれを言い換えた **(D)**。商品を売るための活動全般が promotional という表現で選択肢によく登場するので慣れておこう。

□compare ～を比較する　□competitor 競合　□stock 在庫　□organize ～を整理する
□promotional 販売促進の、広告の

	1回目	2回目	3回目
50.			
51.			
52.			

🚩 **50. (C)　51. (B)　52. (D)**

Questions 53 through 55 refer to the following conversation.

W: Hello, Mr. Lewis. ❶This is Vicky calling from the Eddie Hotel about the reservation that you recently made. ❷The room you requested is available on the date you want, but we need a credit card number to finish the reservation.

M: I've made reservations at the Eddie Hotel before and I never needed to provide a credit card number beforehand.

W: You're right, Mr. Lewis, but management recently had to change our policy to comply with the Ministry of Commerce. ❸Because of security concerns, I can't take your credit card number over the phone, but if you e-mail it to the address listed on our Web site, your reservation will be finished.

M: I see. I'll take care of it as soon as I can. ❹After the number has been received, I'd appreciate it if you could send an e-mail to me to confirm that the reservation has been accepted.

問題53-55は次の会話に関するものです。

W: こんにちは、Lewis さん。Eddie Hotel の Vicky と申しますが、先日予約された件についてお電話いたしました。ご指定のお日にちでご希望のお部屋のご利用が可能ですが、予約を完了するためにクレジットカードの番号をいただく必要がございます。

M: 以前に Eddie Hotel で予約をしたことがありますが、クレジットカード番号を事前にお伝えする必要はありませんでしたよ。

W: おっしゃるとおりです、Lewis さん。しかし弊社は最近、商務省の規約に従うために方針を変えなければなりませんでした。防犯上、電話でクレジットカード番号をお尋ねすることはできませんが、当館のウェブサイトに載っているアドレスまで E メールを送っていただけましたら、予約を完了できます。

M: わかりました。できるだけ早くやります。番号が届いたら、予約ができたことを確認するために E メールでお知らせいただければ幸いです。

🖊 □beforehand 以前は　□management 経営陣　□policy 会社　□comply with ～を遵守する
□the Ministry of Commerce 商務省　□security concerns 安全上の懸念、防犯の観点　□over the phone 電話で
□list ～を掲載する　□take care of ～を処理する　□I'd appreciate it if you could ～していただけるとありがたい
□confirm ～を確認する

---

53. ★★★★☆

What are the speakers talking about?

(A) A discounted accommodation rate
(B) A lodging's location
(C) An incomplete booking
(D) An overcharged purchase

話し手たちは何について話していますか。

(A) 割引宿泊料金
(B) 宿泊施設の所在地
(C) 未完了の予約
(D) 過大請求された購入

🔍 会話冒頭❶で女性が男性の行った予約について触れ、❷で「部屋は確保できるものの、予約を終えるためにクレジットカードナンバーが必要」と述べている。つまり、予約がまだできていないことが示されているので、それを言い換えた **(C)** が正解。(C) は❷の後半の to finish the reservation が対応している。

🖊 □discounted 割り引きした　□accommodation rate 宿泊費　□lodging 宿泊施設
□overcharged 過大に請求された

54. ★★★☆☆

According to the woman, what does the man need to send?

(A) A personal review
(B) His credit card number
(C) A photograph ID
(D) His e-mail address

女性によると、男性は何を送る必要がありますか。

(A) 個人の批評
(B) クレジットカード番号
(C) 写真付き身分証明書
(D) Eメールアドレス

 女性は❸で「電話でクレジットカード番号を尋ねることができないので、Eメールで送ってほしい」と依頼している。つまり、Eメールでクレジットカード情報を送る必要があるとわかる。以上より正解は **(B)**。

✎ □review 感想、批評

55. ★★★★☆

What does the man ask the woman to do?

(A) Confirm receipt of a message
(B) Submit a picture of the room
(C) Provide a credit card number
(D) Reduce the price of his next stay

男性は女性に何をするように頼んでいますか。

(A) メッセージの受領を確認する。
(B) 部屋の写真を提出する。
(C) クレジットカード番号を教える。
(D) 次回の宿泊料を下げる。

🔍 男性は会話終盤の❹で「番号が届いたら、予約ができたことを確認するためにEメールで知らせてほしい」と言っている。つまり、男性が送るメッセージの受領を確認してほしいと述べているので、**(A)** が正解。(C) はクレジットカード番号を教えるのが男性の側なので不正解。

✎ □receipt 受領　□provide ～を提供する　□stay 滞在、宿泊

	1回目	2回目	3回目
53.			
54.			
55.			

🚩 **53. (C)　54. (B)　55. (A)**

Questions 56 through 58 refer to the following conversation.

M: Hi. ❶I'm interested in one of the sculptures in the garden. ❷Can you tell me its price?

W: Of course. Which one?

M: That one next to the entrance. ❸The artist's name is Melissa Townsend.

W: Ah, yes. Some people have been asking about that. ❹She was featured on a television show recently and has become quite famous. ❺I'm afraid that piece is very expensive. It's 25,000 dollars.

M: What!? ❻I think I'll pass. ❼Unfortunately, I can't afford it.

W: I see. Would you like to ask Ms. Townsend if she would be willing to reduce the price?

M: I don't think she'll negotiate it down to the price I'm able to pay. I'll take a look at some of the other pieces.

📝 問題56-58は次の会話に関するものです。

M: あの、お庭にある彫刻の一つに興味があるんですが。お値段を教えてもらえますか。

W: はい。どちらでしょうか。

M: 入口の横のです。作者の名前はMelissa Townsendです。

W: わかりました。あちらについては数件問い合わせをいただいています。彼女は先日テレビ番組で取り上げられて、非常に有名になりました。ただ、かなりお値段はかかります。2万5千ドルです。

M: なんですって。それはもう諦めます。残念ながら手が出ません。

W: そうですか。Townsendさんにもっと安くできないかお聞きになりますか。

M: 私が払える金額に下がるまで応じてもらえるとは思えません。他の作品を見てみます。

✏️ □interested in ～に興味がある □sculpture 彫刻像 □entrance 入口 □feature ～を特集する
□pass やめておく □afford ～に対する (金銭的) 余裕がある □willing to *do* ～する気がある
□negotiate ～を交渉する □take a look at ～を見る

---

56. ★★☆☆☆

What is the main topic of the conversation?

(A) The winner of a game
(B) The technique of an artist
(C) The format of a contest
(D) The price of a piece of art

会話の話題は何ですか。

(A) 試合の勝者
(B) 芸術家の技巧
(C) コンテストの方式
(D) 芸術作品の価格

🔍 会話冒頭❶・❷で男性がある彫刻に興味を持ち、その価格について質問していることがわかるため、正解は **(D)**。

✏️ □format 方式

57.

What did Ms. Townsend recently do?

(A) Moved a sculpture
(B) Appeared on television
(C) Resigned from her job
(D) Negotiated a new contract

最近 Townsend さんは何をしましたか。

(A) 彫刻を移動した。
(B) テレビに出演した。
(C) 仕事を辞めた。
(D) 新規契約を結んだ。

 ❸から Townsend さんは話題にしている彫刻を制作したアーティストだとわかる。そして❹で「最近テレビショーに出演した」と述べていることから、正解は **(B)**。

□negotiate a contract 契約を締結する

58.

What does the man mean when he says, "I think I'll pass"?

(A) He will not buy an item.
(B) He is on his way through an area.
(C) He expects to be allowed to enter.
(D) He is prepared for an important test.

男性が "I think I'll pass" という際、何を意図していますか。

(A) 商品を購入しない。
(B) 区域を通り抜けて行こうとしている。
(C) 入場を許可されると思っている。
(D) 重要なテストの準備ができている。

TEST 2

 意図を問われている発言❻は「やめておこうと思う」という意味である。この前後を見てみると、❺彫刻の価格は高額で25,000ドル➡❻やめておく➡❼購入する余裕がない、という流れになっているため、欲しかった彫刻品が高額のため購入することをやめるという意図であることがわかる。以上から、彫刻品を an item と言い換えて表現した **(A)** が正解。

□on one's way ある目的地に向かう途中にいる

	1回目	2回目	3回目
56.			
57.			
58.			

🚩 **56. (D)   57. (B)   58. (A)**

Questions 59 through 61 refer to the following conversation.

M: Hello. ❶This is the Milford Gallery, isn't it? ❷I have a package to deliver to Tanisha Coleman. Do you happen to know where I can find her? I have to get a signature from her before I can drop it off.

W: ❸She is currently in a meeting. It was supposed to wrap up at 12 o'clock. ❹It's already quarter after 12, so she should be done any minute now. ❺Would you like to wait for her here in the lobby?

M: ❻Actually, I have another delivery to make across the street, so I will be back in 30 minutes.

W: Sure. I'll let her know that you will be returning soon. That way, she can make sure she's here when you get back.

📝 問題59-61は次の会話に関するものです。

M: こんにちは。こちらは Milford Gallery でお間違いないでしょうか。Tanisha Coleman さんにお届け物です。どちらにいらっしゃるかおわかりになりますか。お渡しの際に署名をいただく必要があるんですが。

W: 現在会議中です。12時ちょうどに終わる予定でしたが、既に12時を15分過ぎていますので、じきに終わると思います。こちらのロビーでお待ちになりますか。

M: 実は通りの反対側にも配達があるので、30分後にこちらに戻ってきます。

W: わかりました。すぐにお戻りになるとお伝えしておきます。そうすれば、戻られた際に必ず Coleman がここにおりますので。

✏️ □signature 署名　□drop off ～を届ける、渡す　□be supposed to *do* ～する予定である　□wrap up 終了する
□quarter after ～時15分過ぎ　□any minute now 今すぐにでも

---

59. ★★★☆☆

Why did the man visit the gallery?

(A) To promote a product
(B) To deliver a package
(C) To see an exhibit
(D) To fill in a signature card

男性はなぜ画廊を訪れましたか。

(A) 製品を宣伝するため。
(B) 小包を配達するため。
(C) 展示を見るため。
(D) 署名欄に記入するため。

🔍 会話冒頭❶・❷で男性は今いる場所が画廊かを尋ね、Coleman さん宛ての荷物を持ってきたことを伝えている。以上から正解は **(B)**。(D) は Coleman さんの署名が必要であって、男性が書き入れるわけではないため、不正解。

✏️ □promote ～を販売促進する、広告宣伝する　□exhibit 展示物　□fill in ～に書き入れる

60. ★☆☆☆

What does the woman say about Ms. Coleman?

(A) She does not allow visitors.
(B) She starts work at 12.
(C) She is not working today.
(D) She will be available shortly.

女性は Coleman さんについて何と言っていますか。

(A) 訪問者の入場を許可していない。
(B) 12時に仕事を始める。
(C) 今日は働いていない。
(D) 間もなく手が空く。

 まず❷から Coleman さんは荷物を受け取る人物だと把握できる。次に、女性は❸で今現在打ち合わせ中だと述べ、❹で「もうまもなく打ち合わせが終わるはずだ」と言っている。つまり、まもなく手が空くということがわかるので、正解はそれを表した **(D)**。関わっている用事がまもなく終わる➡ available shortly という表現での言い換えは使われることが多いので慣れておこう。

✎ □allow a visitor 訪問者入場を許可する　□available 手が空いている　□shortly まもなく

---

61. ★★★☆☆

What does the man say he will do next?

(A) Return the following day
(B) Wait in the lobby
(C) Finish another task first
(D) Call Ms. Coleman later

男性は次に何をすると言っていますか。

(A) 翌日に戻ってくる。
(B) ロビーで待つ。
(C) 先に別の用件を済ます。
(D) Coleman さんに後で電話をする。

 ❺で男性は女性にロビーで待つか尋ねられ、❻で別の配送を先に済ませてくると答えている。ここから、他の業務を先に行うことがわかるので、another delivery を another task と言い換えた **(C)** が正解。(B) は明確に否定していないが、男性の❻の発言以降、女性が "Sure." と了解し、男性が戻るまでに行う対応を伝えていることから、この後ロビーで待つことは考えにくいため、不正解。

✎ □the following day 翌日　□task 業務

	1回目	2回目	3回目
59.			
60.			
61.			

 59. (B)　60. (D)　61. (C)

Questions 62 through 64 refer to the following conversation and ticket.

M: ❶Welcome to the Dayton Ocean Movie Festival! We have several movies showing this evening, and many of the directors are here in person.

W: Right, and I heard that the famous film critic Amy Davidson is here too. ❷I'd like a ticket for The Book of Eli at 8 P.M., please.

M: Sure. ❸Also, the festival organizers have arranged for all guests to receive complimentary popcorn and a drink.

W: Great! Yes, I read about the special offers in this month's Film Bee Magazine.

M: ❹Which would you prefer? Standard seats are 15 dollars, and comfort seats are 20. ❺And there are deluxe seats for 25 and VIP seats for 30.

W: ❻I enjoyed seat A03 the last time I was here, so I'd like the same seat this time.

問題62-64は次の会話とチケットに関するものです。

M: Dayton Ocean 映画祭にようこそ。今晩はいくつかの映画を上映しますが、監督の皆さんもこの会場にいらっしゃっていますよ。

W: そうなんですね。有名な映画評論家の Amy Davidson さんも来ていると聞きました。8時の The Book of Eli のチケットをください。

M: 承知しました。また、主催者の提供で、ご来場者の方全員に無料のポップコーンと飲み物を差し上げております。

W: うれしいです。そうそう、この特別サービスのことは今月の Film Bee Magazine で読みました。

M: お席はどちらがよろしいですか。普通席は15ドル、ゆったり席は20ドルです。25ドルの特別席と30ドルの VIP 席もあります。

W: 前回ここに来たときは A03席がよかったので、今回も同じ席がいいです。

The Butterfield Cinema is proud to host
The 10ᵗʰ Dayton Ocean Independent Movie Festival

"The Book of Eli"

Time: 8:00 P.M.　　**Screen:** 5
❼**Seat:** A03　　❽**Price:** $25

The Butterfield Cinema が満を持してお送りする
第 10 回 Dayton Ocean 自主製作映画祭

The Book of Eli

時間：午後 8 時　　スクリーン：5
座席：A03　　　　価格：25 ドル

✎ □in person 直接　□film critic 映画評論家　□organizer 主催者　□complimentary 無料の　□prefer ～を好む
□deluxe 特別の　□VIP 重要人物 (Very Important Person の略)　□be proud to *do* ～することを誇りに思う
□host ～を主催する　□independent movie 自主製作映画

62. ★★★☆☆

What will the woman receive for free?

(A) Some event souvenirs
(B) A movie program
(C) Some refreshments
(D) A book about film making

女性は無料で何を受け取りますか。

(A) イベントの記念品
(B) 映画のプログラム
(C) 軽食
(D) 映画作りに関する書籍

 ❶・❷から男性が映画祭の受付、女性が映画祭に来た客だとわかる。次に❸で映画祭の客全員にポップコーンとドリンクが無料で提供されることがわかる。この飲食物を refreshments と言い換えた **(C)** が正解。設問中にある free が❸の complimentary から言い換えられていることにも注目。

 □souvenir お土産　□refreshment 軽食　□film making 映画作り

---

63. ★★★☆☆

Who most likely is the man?

(A) A box office agent
(B) A movie critic
(C) A festival planner
(D) A film director

男性は誰であると考えられますか。

(A) チケットの販売員
(B) 映画評論家
(C) 祭りの企画者
(D) 映画監督

 女性が❷でチケットが欲しいと言ったのに応じて、男性が❹・❺で座席別の料金を提示していることから、ここでチケットを販売していることがわかる。以上より、男性はチケット販売員とわかるため、正解は **(A)**。

□box office agent チケット販売員　□film director 映画監督

---

64. ★★★★★

Look at the graphic. What type of seat did the woman select?

(A) A standard Seat
(B) A comfort Seat
(C) A deluxe Seat
(D) A VIP Seat

図を見てください。女性が選んだのはどの種類の座席であると考えられますか。

(A) 普通席
(B) ゆったり席
(C) 特別席
(D) VIP 席

 まず❹・❺の男性の情報から4種類の価格帯があることがわかる。次に女性の❻の発言から前回同様 A03席を望んでいることがわかる。その情報をもとにチケットを見ると、❼でこの座席が A03 となっていることから、このチケットは女性が望んでいるものであり、かつ価格が❽で25ドルになっていることがわかる。❺の発言にあった情報と結びつけると、正解は **(C)** となる。

□comfort 心地よさ、快適

	1回目	2回目	3回目
62.			
63.			
64.			

 62. (C)　63. (A)　64. (C)

Questions 65 through 67 refer to the following conversation and schedule.

W: ❶It's been a long day! Are there any other business meetings we should attend this week?

M: ❷The last one is on Wednesday at 2:00 P.M. ❸It's a brief meeting, so it'll probably be over by 3 P.M. Afterwards, we will visit one of our branches in Austin.

W: Oh, I see. ❹What railway are we using?

M: Alamo North Texas Railways. ❺It takes about an hour and 50 minutes to get there by train.

W: ❻The branch manager told me that someone will pick us up at Austin Train Station at 6:00 P.M. We should arrive before then.

M: Good! I'll book two tickets right away online.

📝 問題65-67は次の会話と予定表に関するものです。

W: 長い一日でした。今週は他に私たちが参加する商談がありますか。

M: 水曜日の午後2時からのが最後です。簡単な打ち合わせなので、午後3時までには終わるでしょう。その後で、Austin にある当社の支部の1つを訪問します。

W: わかりました。どの鉄道を使いますか。

M: Alamo North Texas 鉄道です。あそこまで電車で約1時間50分かかります。

W: 支部長は午後6時に Austin 鉄道駅に誰かが迎えに来ると言っていましたから、その前には到着する必要があります。

M: わかりました。すぐにインターネットでチケットを2枚予約します。

Daily Train Schedule (Dallas-Austin)	
Train	**Departure**
ANT201	09:30 A.M.
ANT303	11:00 A.M.
ANT405	1:30 P.M.
❼ANT507	❽4:00 P.M.

列車時刻表 (Dallas - Austin)	
列車	**出発時刻**
ANT201	午前9時30分
ANT303	午前11時00分
ANT405	午後1時30分
ANT507	午後4時00分

✏️ □business meeting 商談 □be over 終了する □afterwards その後 □branch 支店, 支社 □railway 鉄道 □pick up 〜を車で迎えに行く □book 〜を予約する □right away すぐに

65.

What is the main topic of the conversation?

(A) A tourist attraction
(B) An annual event
(C) A work schedule
(D) A new train service

会話の話題は何ですか。

(A) 観光名所
(B) 毎年の恒例行事
(C) 仕事の予定
(D) 列車の新サービス

 会話冒頭❶で女性が商談の有無について質問していることから、この会話の話題は仕事の予定についてであることがわかる。以上より、正解は **(C)**。

✏ □tourist attraction 観光名所

66.

What will the speakers do on Wednesday afternoon?

(A) Attend a conference
(B) Visit their company headquarters
(C) Interview a new branch manager
(D) Submit a travel expenses report

話し手たちは水曜日の午後に何をしますか。

(A) 会議に参加する。
(B) 本社を訪問する。
(C) 新しい支部長と面談する。
(D) 旅費の報告を提出する。

 ❶で女性が仕事の予定について尋ね、それに対して男性が❷・❸で「水曜日の午後2時からの打ち合わせが最後で、午後3時までには終わる」と述べている。ここから、この2人は会議に参加することがわかる。business meeting を conference に言い換えた **(A)** が正解。

✏ □travel expense 旅費

67.

Look at the graphic. What train will the speakers most likely take on Wednesday?

(A) ANT201
(B) ANT303
(C) ANT405
(D) ANT507

図を見てください。話し手たちは水曜日にどの電車に乗ると考えられますか。

(A) ANT201
(B) ANT303
(C) ANT405
(D) ANT507

 女性が❹で「どの電車に乗るか」尋ねている。男性が❺で「電車で1時間50分かかる」と述べ、女性が❻で「午後6時に駅に迎えが来るので、その前に到着を」と述べている。そこで、打ち合わせが終わる午後3時以降で午後6時前に到着する一番タイミングのよい電車は、スケジュール表❼・❽から午後4時発の ANT507 だとわかる。以上から正解は **(D)**。

	1回目	2回目	3回目
65.			
66.			
67.			

 65. (C) 66. (A) 67. (D)

Questions 68 through 70 refer to the following conversation and graph.

M: Hello, Samantha. ❶ I've been trying to find ways to improve the overall earnings of our coffee shop.

W: Good. I think that's so important. Have you found a new supplier who charges lower prices?

M: Not yet. But right now we're spending too much money on labor on our quietest days. ❷ So, I'd like to close the shop three hours earlier on our quietest day.

W: ❸ Good idea. Remember that we'll be beginning the evening concert series from next Wednesday. And obviously we can't shut early on Saturday or Sunday.

M: Sure. ❹ So, except for Wednesdays and weekends, we should close early on our least busy day.

W: You know, your plan might work. Let's take a look at our average revenue throughout the week.

📝 問題68-70は次の会話とグラフに関するものです。

M: こんにちは、Samantha さん。うちの喫茶店の全体的な収益を増やすにはどうすればいいか考えているんです。

W: そうですね。本当に重要だと思います。今より安い価格で取り引きをしてくれる新しい仕入れ先は見つかりましたか。

M: まだです。ただ、現状では特に閑散とした日の人件費が余計にかかっています。ですので、特に閑散とする日は、3時間早く店を閉めたいと思います。

W: いいアイディアですね。今度の水曜日から夜のコンサートシリーズが始まることは忘れないでください。そして、もちろん土曜日と日曜日は閉店を早められません。

M: わかりました。水曜日と週末を除いた上で特に閑散としている日は早めに閉店するようにしましょう。

W: ええ、その方針はきっとうまくいきます。週を通した平均収益を見てみましょう。

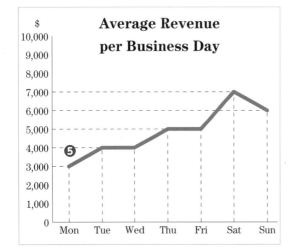

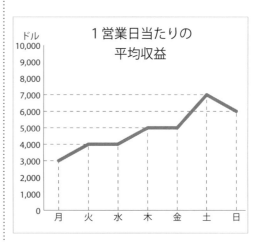

✏️ □improve 〜を改善する □overall 全体の □earning 収益 □supplier 供給業者 □charge (費用等) を請求する □right now 今現在 □spend on labor 人件費に支出する □on our quietest days 閑散期に □obviously 明らかに、もちろん □shut 閉店にする □except for 〜を除き □work うまくいく □take a look at 〜を見る □revenue 収益 □business day 営業日

68.

What is the main topic of the conversation?

(A) Maximizing profits
(B) Changing suppliers
(C) Decreasing prices
(D) Attracting customers

会話の話題は何ですか。

(A) 収益を最大化すること。
(B) 仕入れ先を変更すること。
(C) 値下げすること。
(D) 客を引き付けること。

🔍 会話冒頭❶で男性が「うちの喫茶店の全体的な収益を増やすにはどうすればいいか考えている」と述べているので、収益最大化について話していると言える。以上から、正解は **(A)**。(A) は❶の find ways to improve the overall earnings の言い換えになっていることを押さえておこう。なお、(B)・(C)・(D) は、収益を上げるための手段だが、会話には具体的な内容は出てこないため、いずれも不正解。

✏️ □maximize ～を最大化する　□profit 収益　□decrease ～を減少させる　□attract ～を引き付ける

69.

When will the coffee shop begin holding live music?

(A) Next week
(B) Next month
(C) Next quarter
(D) Next year

喫茶店はいつ生演奏を始めますか。

(A) 来週
(B) 来月
(C) 来期
(D) 来年

🔍 男性が❷で店舗を早く閉めることに触れた際に、女性が❸で「来週の水曜日から夜の演奏会があることを忘れずに」と述べているので正解は **(A)**。ポイントは、いつ早く閉店するかについてと、コンサート開催という情報が設問で holding live music と言い換えられていることをスムーズに処理できるかどうかにある。しっかり復習しておこう。

✏️ □hold ～を開催する

70.

Look at the graphic. On which day will business hours most likely be reduced?

(A) On Mondays
(B) On Tuesdays
(C) On Wednesdays
(D) On Thursdays

図を見てください。どの日の営業時間が短縮されると考えられますか。

(A) 月曜日
(B) 火曜日
(C) 水曜日
(D) 木曜日

🔍 男性が❹で「水曜日と週末を除いた上で特に閑散としている日は早めに閉店しよう」と提案している。次に、グラフを見ると、❺の月曜日が一番閑散としているので、営業時間を短縮するのは月曜日だとわかる。以上より正解は **(A)**。

✏️ □business hours 営業時間

	1回目	2回目	3回目
68.			
69.			
70.			

 68. (A)　69. (A)　70. (A)

Questions 71 through 73 refer to the following speech.

📝 問題71-73は次のスピーチに関するものです。

M: Hello, everyone! Welcome to the year-end party of All-star Technology. ❶We are here to recognize the continuous efforts put in by each of you. ❷As a result of your excellent contribution, we've managed to remain one of the top five bathtub manufacturers in the country. Due to the increasing amount of new construction, our sales revenues are rising. ❸As you already know, the governor's decision to modernize state housing will benefit us, since the plan involves the installation of countless bathtub fixtures and we are the main supplier for the project. So, let's congratulate ourselves on the great job we're doing!

M: 皆さん、こんにちは。All-star Technology 社の忘年会にようこそ。一人ひとりのたゆみない努力を労いましょう。皆さんの素晴らしい貢献のおかげで、当社は浴槽メーカーの上位5社に入り続けています。新築の数が増えているため、当社の売上高は増加しています。ご存じのとおり、州の住宅を現代的にするという知事の決定は、その計画に膨大な数の浴槽の設置が必要であり、当社がプロジェクトの主要な供給業者であることから、当社に利益をもたらすことになります。ですので、我々の仕事をともにたたえましょう。

✏️ □year-end party 忘年会　□recognize ～を認める　□continuous effort 継続的な努力
□as a result of ～の結果として　□contribution 貢献　□manage to do 何とかして～する　□bathtub バスタブ
□manufacturer 製造会社　□due to ～により　□amount 量　□revenue 収入　□modernize ～を現代的にする
□state housing 州の住宅　□benefit ～に利益をもたらす　□involve ～を含む　□installation 組み込み、設置
□countless 多くの　□fixture 設置　□supplier 供給会社　□congratulate A on ～について A を祝う

---

71. ★★★☆☆

What is the purpose of the speech?

(A) To remind staff of a next step
(B) To acknowledge employees' efforts
(C) To accept a proposal
(D) To discuss a new regulation

スピーチの目的は何ですか。

(A) 社員に次の段階を意識させること。
(B) 従業員の努力に謝意を示すこと。
(C) 提案を受け入れること。
(D) 新しい規制について話し合うこと。

🔍 話し手はスピーチの冒頭で All-star Technology 社の忘年会への歓迎の言葉を述べた後、❶で「ここで一人ひとりのたゆみない努力を労いましょう」と述べているので、これを言い換えて表した **(B)** が正解。❶の recognize には、人を認め、称えるという意味があり、(B) の acknowledge と同義語になっている。

✏️ □remind A of A に～を思い出させる　□acknowledge ～を認める、～に感謝する　□proposal 提案

72. ★★★☆☆

Where does the speaker most likely work?

(A) At a manufacturing company
(B) At a travel agency
(C) At a construction company
(D) At a state government

話し手はどこで働いていると考えられますか。

(A) 製造会社
(B) 旅行代理店
(C) 建設会社
(D) 州政府

 話し手は❷で「皆さんの努力のおかげで、浴槽メーカーの上位5位に入っている」と述べている。ここから、この話し手の会社は浴槽を製造しているメーカーだとわかる。それを manufacturing company と言い換えた **(A)** が正解。❷を聞き逃しても、❸の後半に supplier という表現があるため、バスタブの供給会社、というところからもヒントは得られる。

✎ □construction company 建設会社　□state government 州政府

73. ★★★☆☆

What does the speaker say about the government plan?

(A) It will cause state taxes to rise.
(B) It will encourage tourism.
(C) It will expand the company's market area.
(D) It will increase the company's sales.

話し手は政府の計画について何と言っていますか。

(A) 州税の引き上げにつながる。
(B) 観光業を振興する。
(C) 会社の市場地域を拡大する。
(D) 会社の売り上げを伸ばす。

 ❸で州政府が公営住宅を現代的にする動きがあって、浴槽設置をすることで利益がもたらされると述べている。ここから、この州政府の計画は話し手の会社の売り上げアップにつながることがわかるため、これを言い換えた **(D)** が正解。(C) は、トークでは浴槽の設置数には触れられているが、設置エリアには触れられていないので、不正解。

✎ □cause A to *do* A が〜することを引き起こす　□encourage 〜を振興する、奨励する　□tourism 観光業
□expand 〜を拡張する

	1回目	2回目	3回目
71.			
72.			
73.			

 71. (B)　72. (A)　73. (D)

Questions 74 through 76 refer to the following speech.

📝 問題74-76は次のスピーチに関するものです。

W: ❶Please take a look at the next item on the agenda. ❷In order to expand our profits, we need to reduce costs and improve productivity. We should consider the various ways that can make our team more productive. ❸I've already asked the personnel department to look into some further benefits we could offer as a way to raise company morale, and now I'd like to talk with you, the leaders, on how we can motivate our teams. ❹I'm open to talk about things that don't require much on our part, like longer lunches or shorter Friday work hours and even more vacation days to reward productivity. ❺You know your staff better than anyone. ❻I'm totally flexible, so the floor is yours.

W: 議題の次の項目を見てください。利益を拡大するためには、費用を削減し、生産性を向上させることが必要です。チームの生産性を高めるさまざまな方法を検討するべきです。会社の士気を高める方法として、より充実した提供可能な福利厚生を検討するように人事部に依頼してあります。そして、今はリーダーの皆さまにどうすればチームのやる気を引き出せるかについて話したいと思います。会社側へ求めることがあまり大きくないもので、例えば昼休みの延長、金曜日の就業時間の短縮、あるいは生産性への報奨として休暇日数を追加するようなことについてお話を受けたいと思います。皆さまの方がよりスタッフの方のことをわかっていると思います。柔軟に対応しますので、どうぞお考えをお聞かせください。

✏️ □take a look at 〜を見る　□next item on the agenda 次の議題　□in order to *do* 〜するために
□expand 〜を拡大する、発展させる　□profit 利益　□reduce cost コストを削減する
□improve productivity 生産性を改善する　□various さまざまな　□productive 生産的な
□personnel department 人事部　□look into 〜を検討する　□further さらなる　□benefit 福利厚生
□as a way to *do* 〜する方法として　□raise 〜を高める　□company morale 社内のモラール (やる気)
□motivate 〜の意欲を向上させる　□be open to *do* 進んで〜するよう受け入れる　□require 〜を要求する
□reward 〜に報酬を与える　□flexible 柔軟に対応できる　□The floor is yours. どうぞお話しください。

---

74. ⭐⭐⭐⭐☆

What is the speech mainly about?

何についてのスピーチですか。

(A) Hiring more employees
(B) Increasing efficiency
(C) Relocating the company
(D) Spreading workload

(A) 従業員をさらに雇うこと。
(B) 効率を上げること。
(C) 会社を移転すること。
(D) 仕事量を分散させること。

🔍 話し手はトーク冒頭❶で「次の議題」と切り出し、❷で「利益拡大のためには経費節減と生産性向上が必要だ」と述べている。ここから、より業務を効率的に行うことについて話すとわかる。それを抽象度をやや高くして言い換えた **(B)** が正解となる。

✏️ □efficiency 効率　□spread workload 作業量を分散させる

75. ★★★★☆

Who most likely are the listeners?	聞き手は誰であると考えられますか。
(A) Company managers	**(A)** 会社の管理職
(B) Small vendors	(B) 小規模な販売業者
(C) Researchers and developers	(C) 研究者と開発者
(D) Potential recruits	(D) 内定者

 話し手は❸で人事部に福利厚生について問い合わせをしていることに触れ、その後で、「今はリーダーの皆さまにどうすればチームのやる気を引き出せるかについて話したい」と述べている。つまり、聞き手は会社の中でメンバーを率いているリーダーであり、マネジャーとしての役割を担う人たちだとわかるため、正解は **(A)** となる。

✎ □vendor 販売業者

---

76. ★★★★☆

Why does the speaker say, "You know your staff better than anyone"?	話し手はなぜ "You know your staff better than anyone" と言っていますか。
(A) To understand a common complaint	(A) よくある不満を理解するため。
(B) To clarify a procedure	(B) 手順を明確にするため。
(C) To praise strong team spirit	(C) 力強いチーム精神を称えるため。
(D) To ask for proposals	**(D)** 提案を求めるため。

 意図を問われている箇所❺は「誰よりも皆さまがスタッフのことをわかっている」という意味である。この前後を見ていくと、❸会社の士気を高め、チームを活気づけるために話したい➡❹改善案について話を聞きたい➡❺聞き手がスタッフのことをよくわかっている➡❻柔軟に対応するので話してほしい、という流れになっている。つまり、現場のメンバーをよく知っていることを踏まえて意見・要望を伝えてほしいという意図であるとわかる。この意見・要望を proposal と言い換えた **(D)** が正解。(C) は強いチーム精神をつくっていくのは今後のことであり、まだ褒める段階ではないため、不正解。

✎ □common complaint よくある不満、クレーム □clarify ～を明確にする □procedure 手順 □praise ～を褒める
□team spirit チーム精神 □proposal 提案

	1回目	2回目	3回目
74.			
75.			
76.			

🚩 **74. (B) 75. (A) 76. (D)**

Questions 77 through 79 refer to the following announcement.

📝 問題77-79は次のアナウンスに関するものです。

M: ❶This is an announcement for all of you who are waiting for the snowboarding lesson with Julia Palmore. ❷The lesson was scheduled to begin at 2:30 this afternoon, but we're afraid it has been postponed by thirty minutes. We apologize for this, but ❸Ms. Palmore will take longer than usual to get here since one of the mountain roads has been closed for repaving. She assures us she'll try to get here as quickly as possible. In the meantime, ❹please make sure that you have rented any snowboard equipment that you require, and then make your way over to the bottom of the west slope where your lesson will take place. ❺Don't wander off. ❻Some of the areas nearby can be very steep and dangerous.

M: Julia Palmore のスノーボードレッスンをお待ちの皆さまにお知らせです。レッスンは午後2時半に開始を予定していましたが、恐れ入りますが30分の延期となりました。申し訳ありません。山道の一つが再舗装により閉鎖されているため、Palmore がここに到着するまでに通常よりも時間がかかります。なるべく早くこちらに着けるようにすると言っております。その間に、必要なスノーボード用品をレンタルしてあることを確認し、レッスンを行う西斜面のふもとまでお越しください。道からは離れないでください。付近は非常に急で危険な所もあります。

✏️ ☐be scheduled to *do* ～する予定である ☐take longer than usual 通常より時間がかかる
☐get here ここに到着する ☐repaving （道路等の）再舗装 ☐assure A that A に～であることを保証する
☐as quickly as possible できるだけ早く ☐in the meantime その間 ☐rent ～を借りる ☐equipment 器具、用具
☐require ～を必要とする ☐make one's way over to ～のところまで寄る ☐slope 斜面 ☐take place 開催する
☐wander off 道からそれる ☐nearby 近くの ☐steep 険しい、急な

---

77. ★★★☆☆

According to the speaker, when will the snowboard lesson start?

(A) At 2:00 P.M.
(B) At 2:30 P.M.
(C) At 3:00 P.M.
(D) At 3:30 P.M.

話し手によるとスノーボードのレッスンはいつ開始しますか。

(A) 午後2時
(B) 午後2時半
(C) 午後3時
(D) 午後3時半

🔍 話し手は❶で「Palmore 講師のスノーボード講習」についての案内を切り出し、❷で「スノーボードレッスンは当初午後2時30分からだったが、30分延期になった」と述べている。以上より正解は **(C)**。

78. ★★★★☆

What problem does the speaker mention?

(A) An instructor has been delayed.
(B) Some attendees have canceled their registration.
(C) A snowboard slope has been closed.
(D) Some equipment is unusable.

話し手はどんな問題について言及していますか。

(A) 講師が遅れている。
(B) 参加者が登録を取り消した。
(C) スノーボード場が閉鎖されている。
(D) 使えない器具がある。

 ❶で触れた講師の Palmore さんが❸で「到着に時間がかかっている」と伝えているため、講師の到着が遅れていることがわかる。以上より正解は (A)。この問題は❶の段階で、Palmore さんがレッスン講師だとわからないと正解にたどり着けなくなってしまうので注意しよう。

□instructor 講師　□attendee 参加者　□registration 登録　□unusable 使用できない

---

79. ★★★★☆

What does the speaker mean when he says, "Don't wander off"?

(A) He wants the listeners to stay near a meeting point.
(B) He advises the listeners to remain indoors.
(C) He forbids the listeners to stand close to equipment.
(D) He instructs the listeners to go to a rental office.

話し手が "Don't wander off" と言う際、何を意図していますか。

(A) 聞き手に集合場所の近くで待っていてほしい。
(B) 聞き手に屋内に留まるよう忠告している。
(C) 聞き手が設備の近くに立つことを禁止している。
(D) 聞き手にレンタル事務所に行くよう指示をしている。

意図を問われている発言❺は「離れないで」という意味である。この前後を見ていくと、❹「レッスン場所の斜面ふもとまで来てほしい」➡❺「離れないで」➡❻「付近は非常に危険である」という流れになっている。つまり、道からそれると非常に危ないため、集合場所にいてほしいという意図であると考えられる。それを言い換えた (A) が正解となる。なお、❹でレンタル部品の確認については言及しているが、レンタル事務所に行くことまでは指示していないため、ここでは不正解。

□stay near 近くに留まる　□advise A to do A に〜するように忠告する　□remain 留まる　□indoors 屋内に
□forbid A to do A が〜するのを禁止する　□instruct A to do A に〜するように指示する

	1回目	2回目	3回目
77.			
78.			
79.			

77. (C)　78. (A)　79. (A)

Questions 80 through 82 refer to the following excerpt from a meeting.

M: The first topic on this staff meeting agenda is the new waste disposal program. ❶We've changed the company that provides our waste removal services, since with the former company we had to use five separate bins. ❷Many of you complained that they were taking up too much room in the office, and you know it's already not big enough. However, with the new service everything can be thrown away in one container, which should free up some much-needed space. ❸As usual, when you throw something away, please remember to check the notice near the bin for our waste disposal policies.

📝 問題80-82は次の会議の一部に関するものです。

M: 職員会議の最初の議題は新しいごみ処理事業です。以前の会社では別々のごみ箱を5つ使う必要があったため、ごみ処理を請け負う会社を変更しました。多くの方から、事務所の空間を占めすぎているという不満が出ていましたし、またご存じのとおり大きさも十分ではありません。ですが、新しいサービスでは、全部一つの容器に捨てることができ、大いに必要とされていたスペースが使えるようになります。いつものように、何かを捨てる際には、ごみ箱の近くにあるごみ処理の方法の掲示を忘れずに確認してください。

✏️ □topic 題材　□waste disposal 廃棄物処理　□waste removal service 廃棄物処理会社　□former 以前の
□separate 別々の　□bin ゴミ箱　□complain ～という不満を言う　□take up too much room 場所を取りすぎる
□throw away ～を捨てる　□container 容器　□free up ～の制限を解く、～を自由に使えるようにする
□as usual いつもどおりに　□notice 知らせ　□waste disposal policy ごみ処理方法

---

80. ★★★☆☆

What change has been made?

(A) Working hours have been decreased.
(B) A warehouse has been moved.
(C) Corporate headquarters has been expanded.
(D) A new service provider has been hired.

どんな変更がありましたか。

(A) 就業時間が減った。
(B) 倉庫が移転した。
(C) 本社が拡張された。
(D) 新しいサービス提供者が採用された。

🔍 話し手は❶でごみ処理会社の変更について触れている。これを言い換えた **(D)** が正解。

✏️ □working hours 就業時間　□decrease ～を減少させる　□warehouse 倉庫　□corporate headquarters 本社
□expand ～を拡張する　□provider 供給業者

81. ★★★☆☆

According to the speaker, what has the staff been worried about?

(A) The speed of Internet services
(B) A small work space
(C) Levels of noise
(D) Lack of environmental policies

話し手によると、職員は何を心配していますか。

(A) インターネットサービスの速さ
(B) 職場の狭さ
(C) 騒音の大きさ
(D) 環境方針の欠如

 話し手は❷で職員の苦情に触れ、「従来のごみ処理方法では職場のスペースをかなり占有していた」と話している。これを言い換えた **(B)** が正解となる。ごみ処理に関連して、(C) 騒音、(D) 環境方針に関わることも想定されるが、トーク内では言及がないため、いずれも不正解。

 □noise 騒音　□environmental policy 環境方針

---

82. ★★☆☆☆

What does the speaker remind the listeners to do?

(A) Check a notice
(B) Attend a staff meeting
(C) Log into a homepage
(D) Read their e-mail

話し手は聞き手に何をするように呼びかけていますか。

(A) 通達を確認すること。
(B) 職員会議に出席すること。
(C) ホームページにログインすること。
(D) E メールを読むこと。

 話し手は❸で「ゴミ捨て時に掲示内容を確認してほしい」と述べている。以上より正解は **(A)**。(A) と同様の表現が❸にあるため、素早く正解を見つけられるようにしよう。

 □notice 通知、通達

	1回目	2回目	3回目
80.			
81.			
82.			

🚩 **80. (D)　81. (B)　82. (A)**

Questions 83 through 85 refer to the following recorded message.

📝 問題83-85は次の録音メッセージに関するものです。

W: Hello. This is Bonnie from All-Star Office Furniture calling for Tommy Nelson. ❶We've taken a careful look at your newly purchased desk and confirmed that it has some scratches. ❷We consider them to be manufacturing defects. Because this is not your fault, you will not have to pay for the repair. ❸You will only need to present the receipt of your purchase at the customer service desk in any of our locations. ❹We will then send your product back to you promptly. ❺We will also include a coupon worth $300 with the item. We are very sorry for the inconvenience caused to you due to our error.

W: こんにちは。All-Star Office Furniture の Bonnie ですが、Tommy Nelson さんにおかけしています。新しくご購入いただいた机を綿密に確認したところ、いくつか擦り傷が見つかりました。これらは製造上の欠陥です。これはお客様の過失によるものではありませんので、修繕代をお支払いになる必要はございません。ご購入時の領収書を弊社のいずれかの支店のお客様サービスコーナーでご提示いただくだけで十分です。その後、製品をすぐにご返送いたします。また、製品と一緒に300ドル分のクーポンをお付けします。当社の不手際によりご不便をおかけし、誠に申し訳ありません。

✏️ □take a careful look at ～を注意深く確認する　□confirm ～を確認する　□scratch ひっかき傷
□manufacturing defect 製造上の不具合　□one's fault ～の非　□repair 修理　□present ～を提示する
□receipt of one's purchase ～の購入領収書　□promptly 直ちに　□include ～を含める
□sorry for the inconvenience caused to you 不便をかけ申し訳ない　□due to ～が原因で　□error 誤り

---

83. ★★☆☆☆

What is the problem with the desk?

(A) It has been discontinued.
(B) It has been out of stock.
(C) It is damaged.
(D) It is too big.

机にはどんな問題がありますか。

(A) 生産中止になっている。
(B) 在庫切れになっている。
(C) 破損している。
(D) 大きすぎる。

🔍 話し手は❶でお客様の購入した机を確認したところ見つかったという傷に言及している。以上より、机が損傷していることがわかる。これを言い換えた **(C)** が正解。

✏️ □discontinued 製造が中止された　□out of stock 在庫切れである

84. ★★★☆☆

According to the speaker, what will the listener have to do?

(A) Visit the company headquarters
(B) Contact a sales representative
(C) Show proof of purchase
(D) Input a voucher number

話し手によると、聞き手は何をしなければなりませんか。

(A) 本社を訪問する。
(B) 営業担当者に連絡する。
(C) 購入証明を提示する。
(D) バウチャーの番号を入力する。

🔍 話し手は❸で「購入した領収書を提示してほしい」と伝えている。それを proof of purchase と言い換えた **(C)** が正解。

✎ □contact ～に連絡する　□proof of purchase 購入証明　□input ～を入力する　□voucher 金券、クーポン

---

85. ★★★☆☆

What will the speaker send?

(A) A refund
(B) An extended warranty
(C) A replacement
(D) A voucher

話し手は何を送りますか。

(A) 返金
(B) 延長保証
(C) 交換品
(D) バウチャー

🔍 話し手は❹で製品の返送について触れた後、❺で一定金額のクーポンを付けることについても言及している。これを言い換えた **(D)** が正解。coupon = voucher は言い換えとしてお馴染みなので、しっかり押さえておこう。

✎ □refund 払い戻し　□extended 延長した　□warranty 保証書　□replacement 交換品　□voucher 金券、クーポン

	1回目	2回目	3回目
83.			
84.			
85.			

🚩 **83. (C)　84. (C)　85. (D)**

Questions 86 through 88 refer to the following broadcast.

問題86-88は次の放送に関するものです。

M: To all our loyal listeners, thank you for tuning in to 95.7 JAK radio. ❶As you may already know, the ninth Annual Miami Beach Festival is just around the corner! ❷Make sure you check your schedule. ❸The festival will take place in Margaret Pace Park from Friday to Sunday. As thousands of people are expected to gather there, there might be heavy traffic on Biscayne Bay Street this weekend. The festival will be packed with various exciting events, including the Baby Blue Eyes' show on the opening night, and ❹the Surfside Dance Music Concert on the closing night, in which a number of nationally famous musicians will perform. ❺We will be back after a commercial break with one of the guests at the event on the Sunday, Daria Della.

M: リスナーの皆さま、95.7 JAK ラジオをお聞きいただきありがとうございます。きっとご存じのことと思いますが、毎年恒例 Miami Beach Festival の第9回が間近に迫ってきています。スケジュールを確かめてください。祭典は Margaret Pace Park で金曜日から日曜日まで開催されます。数千人が集まることが予想され、今週末 Biscayne Bay 通りでは渋滞が発生する可能性があります。祭典には、開会の日の夜の Baby Blue Eyes のショーや、閉会の日の夜の、全国的に有名なミュージシャンが複数出演する Surfside ダンスミュージックコンサートなど、さまざまな楽しいイベントが盛りだくさんです。コマーシャルの後は、日曜日のイベントに出演するゲストの Daria Della さんをお迎えします。

✎ □tune in to ～（の番組）にチャンネルを合わせる　□just around the corner 間近に迫っている　□take place 開催する
□be expected to *do* ～することが予想される　□gather 集まる　□heavy traffic 交通渋滞
□be packed with ～でいっぱいである　□various さまざまな　□including ～を含めて、～など
□commercial break コマーシャル休憩

---

86. ★★★☆☆

What does the speaker imply when he says, "Make sure you check your schedule"?

"Make sure you check your schedule" と言う際、話し手は何を意図していますか。

(A) The day of the radio show will change.
(B) Ticket sales may end earlier than expected.
(C) An event will start soon.
(D) A construction process will cause delays.

(A) ラジオ番組の曜日が変わる。
(B) チケットが予想より早く売り切れそうである。
(C) まもなくイベントが始まる。
(D) 工事の過程により遅れが生じる。

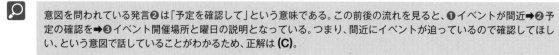

🔍 意図を問われている発言❷は「予定を確認して」という意味である。この前後の流れを見ると、❶イベントが間近➡❷予定の確認を➡❸イベント開催場所と曜日の説明となっている。つまり、間近にイベントが迫っているので確認してほしい、という意図で話していることがわかるため、正解は **(C)**。

✎ □construction process 工事の工程　□cause ～の原因となる　□delay 遅延

87. ★★★★★

What will happen on Sunday?

(A) A musical event
(B) A community party
(C) A culinary festival
(D) A sports game

日曜日に何がありますか。

(A) 音楽イベント
(B) 地域のパーティー
(C) 料理の祭典
(D) スポーツの試合

 ❸の from Friday to Sunday から日曜日はイベント最終日だとわかる。そして❹で、最終日の夜 (the closing night) にはコンサートがある、と話していることから、音楽イベントが日曜日にあるとわかるため、正解は **(A)**。この問題は、日曜日＝イベント最終日だと気づかないと正解を選ぶことができないので、しっかりヒントの部分を聞き取るようにしよう。

 □culinary 料理の

---

88. ★★★★☆

Who most likely is Ms. Della?

(A) A celebrated musician
(B) The festival coordinator
(C) A local politician
(D) A renowned chef

Della さんは誰であると考えられますか。

(A) 名高い音楽家
(B) 祭典のコーディネーター
(C) イベントの主催者
(D) 有名な料理人

 ❺から Della さんは日曜日のイベントのゲストだとわかる。Q.87で触れたとおり、音楽イベントがあることを関連づけて考えると、正解は **(A)** だとわかる。この問題のように、前の問題で関連したヒントを活用して解く問題もあるので気を付けよう。

 □celebrated 高名な　□renowned 著名な

	1回目	2回目	3回目
86.			
87.			
88.			

86. (C)　87. (A)　88. (A)

Questions 89 through 91 refer to the following recorded message.

W: Hello, thank you for calling Clifton Bakery. ❶We are closed all day today, as we are installing new ovens. All the installation work will be completed today, and we will be open at 7:00 A.M. tomorrow as usual. ❷However, don't forget you can still buy a wide range of our delicious baked goods at Billy's Market on 85 Midway Avenue. ❸Moreover, starting September, you can get our custom-made cakes delivered to your home for special events. For more information, you can call our store or you are welcome to come by and ask our staff.

📝 問題89-91は次の録音メッセージに関するものです。

W: こんにちは、Clifton Bakery にお電話いただきありがとうございます。新しいオーブンを設置するため、本日は終日閉店しております。設置作業は本日全て完了する予定ですので、明日は通常どおり午前7時に開店いたします。ですが、当店の美味しい焼き菓子等の商品の幅広いラインアップは85 Midway 大通りの Billy's Market で変わらずにご購入いただけます。また、9月から特別なイベント用の特注ケーキの宅配をご利用いただけます。詳しくは当店へのお電話、またはご来店の際にスタッフまでお問い合わせください。

✏️ □all day 一日中　□install ～を設置する　□oven オーブン　□as usual いつもどおり　□a wide range of 豊富な～
□baked goods 焼き菓子　□moreover さらに　□custom-made 特注の

89.

Why is the business closed today?

(A) All the employees are taking a vacation.
(B) The shop is being cleaned.
(C) It's a public holiday.
(D) New appliances are being installed.

なぜ今日は店が閉まっていますか。

(A) 全従業員が休暇を取っている。
(B) 店は清掃中である。
(C) 祝祭日である。
(D) 新しい設備を取り付けているところである。

🔍 話し手は❶で本日の閉店はオーブン設置のため、と述べている。これを oven = appliance と言い換えて表した **(D)** が正解。

✏️ □public holiday 公休日、祝祭日　□appliance 設備、器具

90. ★★★☆☆

Why does the speaker mention Billy's Market?

(A) It is also closed today.
(B) The owner is an excellent baker.
(C) They have a business relationship.
(D) It is conveniently located.

話し手はなぜ Billy's Market に言及していますか。

(A) 同様に閉店している。
(B) 店主がパン焼きの名人である。
(C) 業務の関係がある。
(D) 便利な場所にある。

 話し手は❷で閉店の間は Billy's Market で自分たちの焼き菓子を購入してほしい旨を伝えている。ここから、話し手のお店は Billy's Market に商品を卸している、つまり共にビジネスをする関係にあることがわかる。以上から正解は **(C)**。

 □baker パン焼き職人　□relationship 関係　□conveniently located 便利な場所に位置している

91. ★★★★☆

What does the business plan for September involve?

(A) Offering a delivery service
(B) Opening another store
(C) Hiring more workers
(D) Starting a new promotion

9月の事業計画には何が含まれますか。

(A) 配送サービスを提供すること。
(B) 新しい店を開くこと。
(C) さらに労働者を雇うこと。
(D) 新しい販促活動を始めること。

話し手は❸で9月の事業計画について触れ、特注ケーキの宅配サービスを行うと伝えている。以上より正解は **(A)**。

□promotion 販促活動

	1回目	2回目	3回目
89.			
90.			
91.			

89. (D)　90. (C)　91. (A)

Questions 92 through 94 refer to the following announcement.

W: ❶Attention, Eval Air passengers. ❷We would like to inform you of unforeseen bad weather in the form of high winds. Therefore, we will have to make a short stop at Philadelphia. It's 7 P.M. local time. Happily, ❸the winds are expected to pass in approximately two hours, which means we expect to take off again at 9 P.M. We apologize for the inconvenience that this may cause you. ❹On landing, all passengers are asked to stay near the gate so that updated information may be heard. Thank you for flying with us, and we'll try to keep further disruptions to a minimum.

📝 問題92-94は次のお知らせに関するものです。

W: Eval 航空でご旅行中の皆さまにお知らせです。強風による急な悪天候についてお知らせします。このため、少しの間 Philadelphia に寄航をする必要があります。ただいまの現地時刻は午後7時です。幸い、風はおよそ2時間のうちに通過する見込みですので、午後9時には再び離陸することになります。これによってご不便をおかけしてしまい申し訳ありません。着陸しましたら、最新情報をお聞きいただけるよう、乗客の皆さまは搭乗口の近くでお待ちください。当社をご利用いただきありがとうございます。その他の混乱が最小限におさまるよう努めてまいります。

✏️ □attention 注目　□inform you of ～について知らせる　□unforeseen 不測の　□in the form of ～の形、状態の
□make a short stop ちょっと立ち寄る、寄航する　□local time 現地時間　□happily 幸いにして
□be expected to *do* ～する見込みである　□pass 通過する　□approximately およそ　□take off 離陸する
□inconvenience 不便　□cause 人 A 人に A を引き起こす　□on landing 着陸時に、着陸したらすぐに
□updated information 最新情報　□disruption 混乱　□minimum 最低限

92.

Where most likely are the listeners?

(A) On a bus
(B) On an airplane
(C) On a ship
(D) On a train

聞き手はどこにいると考えられますか。

(A) バス
(B) 飛行機
(C) 船
(D) 電車

🔍 話し手は❶で乗客に話しかけている。そして❸で離陸の見込み時間、❹で着陸や搭乗ゲートに関する案内をしている。ここから、聞き手は飛行機の中にいることがわかる。以上から正解は **(B)**。

93. ★★★☆☆

What has caused the problem?

(A) A gate number has not been assigned.
(B) An equipment malfunction has been found.
(C) A trip has been overbooked.
(D) Inclement weather has caused a delay.

問題の原因は何ですか。

(A) 搭乗口の番号が決まっていない。
(B) 設備の故障が見つかった。
(C) ツアーのオーバーブッキングがあった。
(D) 悪天候が遅れを生じさせた。

 話し手は❷で不測の悪天候に触れ、その後一時的にフィラデルフィアに立ち寄る等で飛行機が遅れることを伝えている。以上から悪天候を inclement weather と言い換えた **(D)** が正解。

✏ □assign ～を割り当てる　□malfunction 故障　□overbook ～の予約が重複する　□inclement weather 悪天候

---

94. ★★☆☆☆

What is the new departure time?

(A) 6:00 P.M.
(B) 7:00 P.M.
(C) 8:00 P.M.
(D) 9:00 P.M.

新たな出発時刻は何時ですか。

(A) 午後6時
(B) 午後7時
(C) 午後8時
(D) 午後9時

 話し手は❸で「午後9時には離陸する予定だ」と述べている。以上から正解は **(D)**。

PART 4

TEST 2

	1回目	2回目	3回目
92.			
93.			
94.			

 92. (B)　93. (D)　94. (D)

Questions 95 through 97 refer to the following excerpt from a meeting and list.

W: ❶Good morning, South Street Burger's newest employees! Welcome to the training program. We try to make our training both fun and memorable. The first item on our agenda is role assignments. As you know, each one of you may be scheduled to fill many different kinds of shifts in a week. However, we want to take advantage of your best skills. ❷If you're good at math, you should be on the cash register. If you move very quickly, we'd like you to be on the grill. The roles are divided into several zones. ❸Take a look at our available roles, and decide which zone you think you would be best suited for. ❹I'm afraid that there was a printing error and the roles in Zone 1 and Zone 4 have been mixed up. Please keep that in mind when reading.

📝 問題95-97は次の会議の一部と一覧表に関するものです。

W: South Street Burger に新しく入った皆さん、おはようございます。研修プログラムにようこそ。私たちは研修を楽しく、かつ記憶に残りやすいものにしたいと思っています。話し合いの最初のテーマは職務の割り当てです。ご存じのとおり、一週間の中のさまざまな種類のシフトを埋めるように皆さんは予定が組まれます。しかし、当店では皆さんの最も得意な技術を生かしたいと思っています。計算が得意なら、レジを担当するのがよいでしょう。動作が早い人は、グリルを担当してほしいと思います。職務はいくつかの領域に分けられています。入ることが可能な当店での役割を見て、自分に最も合っていると思う領域を決めてください。申し訳ありませんが、印刷のミスがありまして、領域1と領域4の職務が逆になっています。読む際は、その点に注意してください。

Roles	Zone
Janitor: Tables and Floors	❺1
Janitor: Bathrooms	
Grill Cook	2
Line Cook	
Drive-Through Cashier	3
Main Restaurant Cashier	
❻Delivery Driver	4

役割	領域
管理：テーブルとフロア	1
管理：トイレ	
グリル調理	2
ライン調理	
ドライブスルーのレジ	3
メインのレストランのレジ	
配達運転手	4

✏️ ☐training program 研修 ☐memorable 記憶に残る、思い出となる ☐the first item on the agenda 最初の議題
☐role assignment 職務の割り当て ☐be scheduled to *do* ～する予定である ☐shift 交替勤務、シフト
☐take advantage of ～を活用する ☐math 計算、数学 ☐cash register レジ ☐grill (調理場の) グリル
☐be divided into ～に分かれる ☐zone 領域 ☐be suited for ～に合う ☐I'm afraid すまないが
☐printing error 印刷上のミス ☐mix up ～を混乱させる ☐keep that in mind その点に注意する ☐janitor 管理人
☐line cook 一連の調理過程 (材料準備から盛り付けまで) に関わる調理師

95.

Where most likely does the speaker work?

(A) In a hotel
(B) In a restaurant
(C) In a recruitment agency
(D) In a food wholesaler

話し手はどこで働いていると考えられますか。

(A) ホテル
(B) レストラン
(C) 人材派遣会社
(D) 食品卸

 話し手は冒頭❶で、ハンバーガーショップと思われる場所の新規従業員に向けて朝の挨拶をしており、その後❷で調理や注文に関する話をしていることから、このトークは食事を受注し提供する場所で行われていることが考えられる。以上より、これを言い換えた **(B)** が正解。

✎ □recruitment agency 人材派遣会社

96.

What are the listeners asked to do?

(A) Prepare a meal
(B) Check a schedule
(C) Review a shift
(D) Choose a job duty

聞き手は何をするよう求められていますか。

(A) 食事を用意する。
(B) 予定表を確認する。
(C) シフトを見直す。
(D) 職務を選択する。

 話し手は❸で「入ることが可能な当店での役割を見て、自分に最も合っていると思う領域を決めてほしい」と述べている。ここから、どの仕事にするか決めることが求められているとわかるため、正解は **(D)**。他の選択肢にある項目も業務上必要そうだが、トーク内では特に求められておらず、不正解。

✎ □review 〜を見直す　□shift 交替勤務、シフト　□job duty 職務

97.

Look at the graphic. What zone is a delivery driver in?

(A) Zone 1
(B) Zone 2
(C) Zone 3
(D) Zone 4

図を見てください。配達担当の運転手はどの領域に入りますか。

(A) 領域 1
(B) 領域 2
(C) 領域 3
(D) 領域 4

 表を見ると、配送担当者は Zone 4 となっているが、話し手は❹でミスプリントがあると述べ、Zone 1 と Zone 4 に記載されている役割が入れ替わっていることを伝えている。これより、❻の Zone 4 にある役割が本当は❺の Zone 1 に属することがわかる。以上より正解は **(A)**。グラフィック問題は、リスニングか表のどちらか一方の情報で解くことは絶対にできないように作られているため、表だけ一見して解ける！と思うような問題はトーク内で訂正や説明が入ると思って聞いていこう。

	1回目	2回目	3回目
95.			
96.			
97.			

95. (B)　96. (D)　97. (A)

Questions 98 through 100 refer to the following talk and map.

📝 問題98-100は次の話と地図に関するものです。

W: Hello, everyone. ❶My name is Nicole Green and I'll be your tour guide during your walk around Noah's historical Old Town. ❷After we leave Noah's monument, our destination is Willow Church. ❸If you refer to this map, we usually walk there by taking a short cut, but Morris Road is closed for repairs today. ❹We will need to go the long way round. Happily, this means we can view an extra sight. After the church, you can take your time and view all the structures and alleyways on your way back along Renton street. ❺Make sure you get back by 5:00 P.M., though, as the bus will be leaving promptly to return to the hotel.

W: 皆さま、こんにちは。私の名前は Nicole Green です。Noah の歴史的旧市街を巡る間のツアーガイドを務めます。Noah の記念碑を出発しましたら、私たちの行き先は Willow 教会です。地図を見ると、通常は近道をすることになっていますが、今日は補修工事のために Morris 通りが閉鎖されています。私たちは回り道をすることになります。幸い、これによって1つ多く名所を観光することができます。教会の後は、Renton 街を通って戻ってくるまで、自由に時間を過ごして、建物や路地などをご覧いただけます。ただ、ホテルに戻るバスはすぐに出発しますので、午後5時までには必ず戻ってくるようにしてください。

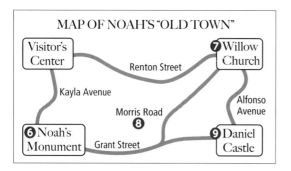

MAP OF NOAH'S "OLD TOWN"

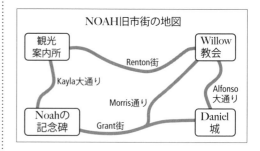

NOAH旧市街の地図

✏️ ☐tour guide ツアーガイド ☐historical 歴史的な ☐monument 記念碑 ☐destination 目的地
☐refer to ～を参照する ☐short cut 近道 ☐be closed for ～で閉鎖している ☐repair 補修
☐go the long way round 回り道をする ☐view ～を見る ☐an extra sight もう1つの名所 ☐structure 建造物
☐alleyway 路地 ☐on one's way back 戻る際に ☐promptly 直ちに

98.

Who most likely are the listeners?

(A) Passengers
(B) Tourists
(C) Trainees
(D) Guides

聞き手は誰であると考えられますか。

(A) 乗客
(B) 観光客
(C) 研修生
(D) ガイド

 話し手は❶でツアーガイドだと名乗り、これから始めるウォーキングツアーについて伝えている。つまり、聞き手はガイド付きツアーの参加者だとわかるため、正解は **(B)**。

□trainee 訓練生

99.

Look at the graphic. Which place can listeners see as a bonus?

(A) Willow Church
(B) Daniel Castle
(C) Noah's Monument
(D) Renton Street

図を見てください。聞き手が特典として見られるのはどの場所ですか。

(A) Willow 教会
(B) Daniel 城
(C) Noah の記念碑
(D) Renton 街

話し手は❷で「Noah's monument（❻）を出て Willow Church（❼）を目的地としている」と述べている。次に❸・❹で通常であれば近道をするところが Morris Road（❽）が閉鎖されているので回り道をしなくてはいけないが、このおかげでもう1つ見学地が増えたと言っている。つまり、この「もう1つの見学地」が設問の bonus だとわかる。この情報をもとに地図を見ると、Daniel Castle（❾）を経由して❼に向かう必要があるため、正解は **(B)** となる。この問題は、情報を聞きながら地図の位置関係を整理して正解を求める必要があるため、しっかり情報処理をして解いていこう。

□bonus 特典

100.

What does the speaker remind the listeners to do?

(A) Gather at a hotel for a meal
(B) Return to the bus on time
(C) Take part in the event
(D) Put their belongings on the bus

話し手は聞き手に何を忘れずにするように伝えていますか。

(A) 食事のためにホテルに集合すること。
(B) 時間どおりにバスに戻ること。
(C) イベントに参加すること。
(D) 持ち物をバスの中に置くこと。

話し手は❺で、「ホテルに戻るバスはすぐに出発するので、午後5時までには必ず戻ってくるように」と聞き手にお願いしている。つまり、時間どおりに戻りのバスに乗ることを忘れないよう伝えていることがわかる。以上から正解は **(B)**。

□gather 集まる　□on time 時間どおりに　□take part in ～に参加する　□belonging 所有物

	1回目	2回目	3回目
98.			
99.			
100.			

 98. (B)　99. (B)　100. (B)

Test

3

TOKIMAKUREI!

PART **3** & **4**

32. What is the woman working on?

(A) A shop window display
(B) A slide presentation
(C) An advertising campaign
(D) A fashion show

33. What does the man say is impressive?

(A) Some workers' experience
(B) A model's career
(C) A new retail catalog
(D) Some sales reports

34. What will the speakers do tomorrow?

(A) Prepare a media conference
(B) Create some new sales strategies
(C) Select some final pictures
(D) Hold a runway show

35. Why is the man going to California?

(A) To visit his relatives
(B) To report on an event
(C) To compete in a contest
(D) To enjoy his vacation

36. What does the man say he wants to do before his travels?

(A) Buy a guidebook
(B) Contact local businesspeople
(C) Reserve a hotel
(D) Collect information

37. What does the woman offer to do?

(A) Prepare a trip schedule
(B) Confirm a flight
(C) Pass on some contact details
(D) Send an e-mail to an artist

38. What is the conversation mainly about?

(A) An advertising presentation
(B) A free workshop
(C) An European visitor
(D) A possible company expansion

39. What will the woman do on Wednesday?

(A) Go to another city
(B) Meet her family
(C) Get a promotion
(D) Train her colleagues

40. What does the man mean when he says, "It comes as no surprise"?

(A) He expected a high number of attendees.
(B) He believes the woman deserves a promotion.
(C) A weather forecast is usually correct.
(D) Many companies have experienced sales decreases.

41. How did the woman get to know about the restaurant?

(A) Through a newspaper
(B) Through a flyer
(C) Through a magazine
(D) Through her friend

42. What does the man say about the restaurant?

(A) It has a large menu.
(B) It has quick service.
(C) It serves local produce.
(D) It employs a well-known cook.

43. What do the speakers agree to do?

(A) Order the same dessert
(B) Split the bill
(C) Take their food home
(D) Divide some food between them

GO ON TO THE NEXT PAGE ➡

🔖 **32-34** *P. 132*   🔖 **35-37** *P. 134*   🔖 **38-40** *P. 136*   🔖 **41-43** *P. 138*

44. What are the speakers talking about?

(A) Stopping mail delivery
(B) Finding a lost item
(C) Reserving a conference place
(D) Moving an office

45. Why does the man decline the woman's suggestion?

(A) The quality of service is low.
(B) The room is cramped.
(C) He has already received information.
(D) He will be out of the country.

46. What will the man most likely tell the woman next?

(A) The date of his return
(B) His office expansion plan
(C) His temporary address
(D) The topic of his speech

47. Where is the conversation taking place?

(A) In a restaurant
(B) In a bakery
(C) In a hotel
(D) In a department store

48. What does the woman mean when she says, "That'll do"?

(A) She accepts the man's recommendation.
(B) She doesn't want to order anything else.
(C) She wants the man to stop working.
(D) She already has what she needs.

49. What will most likely happen next?

(A) The speakers will go for a drive.
(B) The speakers will confirm a booking.
(C) A dinner reservation will be canceled.
(D) An order will be relayed to the kitchen.

50. Why is the woman calling?

(A) To register for an event
(B) To order some software
(C) To hold a workshop
(D) To pay an invoice

51. According to the man, what does the woman have to do?

(A) Call him back later
(B) Submit an expense form
(C) Rearrange an appointment
(D) Make a booking online

52. What does the man ask for?

(A) Presentation material
(B) Details of a bill
(C) Proof of employment
(D) Some contact information

53. What is the topic of the conversation?

(A) Organizing a sales event
(B) Renovating a store
(C) Looking for a property
(D) Buying a bookstore

54. What does the woman ask the man about?

(A) The dimensions of a shop
(B) A company's target market
(C) The location of a business
(D) Items he would like to order

55. What does the woman say she will do next?

(A) Send a list of furnishings
(B) Buy some supplies
(C) Come to the man's store
(D) Contact a designer

44-46 *P. 140*   47-49 *P. 142*   50-52 *P. 144*   53-55 *P. 146*

56. Who most likely is the woman?

(A) A nurse
(B) A doctor
(C) A patient
(D) A receptionist

57. Why is Dr. Gibson unavailable?

(A) She is performing an operation.
(B) She is attending a meeting.
(C) She is having a patient consultation.
(D) She is talking on the phone.

58. What problem does the woman say she has?

(A) A pharmacy doesn't carry the drug she needs.
(B) Her prescribed medication does not work well.
(C) She is worried about the cost of a drug.
(D) The hospital made a mistake with her prescription.

59. What kind of event is mainly discussed?

(A) A closing speech
(B) An employee's promotion
(C) A hiring process
(D) A company's anniversary

60. What does Bianca imply about the company?

(A) It offers competitive salaries.
(B) All of its items are expensive.
(C) New employees will be hired.
(D) It supports local charities.

61. According to the man, what is the company offering?

(A) Merchandise price cuts
(B) Complimentary beverages
(C) Free furniture
(D) Membership rewards

Conference Room Reservations: June 15	
09:30 A.M.	General conference
10:00 A.M.	Leadership workshop
10:30 A.M.	Intern interviews
11:00 A.M.	Headquarters meeting

62. Where do the speakers most likely work?

(A) At an accounting firm
(B) At a magazine publisher
(C) At a manufacturing facility
(D) At a fashion studio

63. Look at the graphic. Which event was Mr. Lopez planning to attend?

(A) General conference
(B) Leadership workshop
(C) Intern interviews
(D) Headquarters meeting

64. What does the woman plan to do?

(A) Send an e-mail to Wayne Fashion
(B) Discuss her career
(C) Visit her client's office
(D) Ask a colleague to reschedule an event

GO ON TO THE NEXT PAGE ➡

🚩 56-58 *P. 148*   🚩 59-61 *P. 150*   🚩 62-64 *P. 152*

Contents

History / 5

Our Products

Tablet Computers / 14

Laptop Computers / 15

Desktop Computers / 16

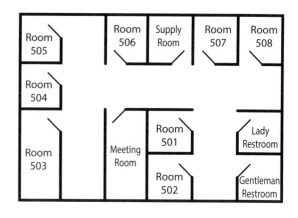

65. Why is the man calling?

(A) To pay a bill
(B) To place an order
(C) To arrange an appointment
(D) To talk about a problem

66. What does the woman offer?

(A) Complimentary express shipping
(B) A gift certificate
(C) A discounted product
(D) A free accessory

67. Look at the graphic. Which page should the man refer to?

(A) P.5
(B) P.14
(C) P.15
(D) P.16

68. What most likely is the woman's job?

(A) An interior designer
(B) A financial advisor
(C) A bank clerk
(D) An event planner

69. What is the man planning to do tomorrow?

(A) Train some workers
(B) Interview job applicants
(C) Go to the woman's office
(D) Attend a meeting

70. Look at the graphic. Where is the woman's office located?

(A) Room 501
(B) Room 504
(C) Room 506
(D) Room 507

65-67 *P. 154*   68-70 *P. 156*

71. Where does the speaker most likely work?

(A) At a bookstore
(B) At an advertising agency
(C) At a print shop
(D) At a publishing company

72. What will happen at the start of next month?

(A) Opening hours will be lengthened.
(B) The product will be distributed.
(C) An advertising campaign will launch.
(D) An anniversary will be celebrated.

73. What does the speaker ask for help with?

(A) Planning an author lecture
(B) Promoting a new store location
(C) Preparing for an event
(D) Setting up new equipment

74. Who most likely is the speaker?

(A) A tenant
(B) A carpenter
(C) A repairperson
(D) A home owner

75. What is the purpose of the call?

(A) To make an appointment
(B) To settle a bill
(C) To ask for advice
(D) To report a problem

76. What does the caller request?

(A) A product manual
(B) A return call
(C) A full refund
(D) A replacement

77. What type of business is being advertised?

(A) A cleaning service
(B) A car repair shop
(C) A hardware shop
(D) An auto dealership

78. According to the advertisement, what has the company recently done?

(A) Introduced a new service
(B) Changed its hours of operation
(C) Opened a new office
(D) Remodeled its branch

79. What does the speaker mean when she says, "How can you pass up this opportunity"?

(A) She does not understand why a decision was made.
(B) She wants the listeners to change a schedule.
(C) She predicts a rival company will steal market share.
(D) She believes the offer is a great deal for customers.

80. Why did the speaker meet with Mr. Eisenhower?

(A) To discuss an agreement
(B) To promote a new product
(C) To prepare for a presentation
(D) To organize a special promotion

81. What does the speaker offer Mr. Eisenhower?

(A) A dinner invitation
(B) A free product sample
(C) A promotional discount
(D) A job opportunity

82. According to the speaker, what must Mr. Eisenhower do before Friday?

(A) Cancel a subscription
(B) Pay a deposit
(C) Renew a contract
(D) Make a decision

GO ON TO THE NEXT PAGE ➡

 71-73 *P. 158*   **74-76** *P. 160*   **77-79** *P. 162*   📑 **80-82** *P. 164*

83. What is being advertised?

(A) Custom-made suits
(B) Handmade leather goods
(C) Wedding attire rental
(D) Shoes for special purposes

84. What is highlighted about the service?

(A) All goods are unique.
(B) The first fitting is complimentary.
(C) Fabrics and leather are from organic sources.
(D) Cotton and wool are hand dyed.

85. What is mentioned about the fabrics?

(A) Some of them are not waterproof.
(B) Some of them are imported.
(C) They are colorful.
(D) They can be ordered online.

86. What is the purpose of the announcement?

(A) To update a policy
(B) To announce a new plan
(C) To introduce a new colleague
(D) To set up a new team

87. What does the speaker mention about Alegra Wallace?

(A) She has already shown her competence.
(B) She is an experienced software designer.
(C) She has started many businesses.
(D) She is a retired engineer.

88. What will the speaker do for each listener?

(A) Edit a report
(B) Arrange a meeting
(C) Make a phone call
(D) Give a job evaluation

89. What business does the speaker most likely work in?

(A) Cosmetics manufacturing
(B) Importing and exporting
(C) Corporate accounting
(D) Offline marketing

90. What does the speaker mean when she says, "As a result of your efforts"?

(A) Sufficient employees have been hired for a project.
(B) A business partnership has been agreed.
(C) A persistent problem has been fixed.
(D) Salaries will be raised.

91. What does the speaker ask the listeners to do?

(A) Prepare for online advertisements
(B) Examine the buyers' feedback
(C) Decide on the price of the product
(D) Consider how to survey consumers

92. Where does the speaker most likely work?

(A) At a pharmaceutical company
(B) At a hotel
(C) At a drug store
(D) At a hospital

93. Why does the speaker say, "she will be more than that"?

(A) To explain a salary increase
(B) To warn against making too many requests
(C) To clarify an employee's schedule
(D) To emphasize a set of skills

94. What event will take place tomorrow?

(A) A welcoming reception
(B) A retirement celebration
(C) A grand opening party
(D) An awards ceremony

83-85 *P. 166*   86-88 *P. 168*   89-91 *P. 170*   92-94 *P. 172*

City	Date
Portland	May 6
Los Angeles	May 10
San Jose	May 16
San Diego	May 19

95. What is the main purpose of the announcement?

(A) To highlight benefits of a membership
(B) To help a local charity
(C) To update a performance schedule
(D) To announce a venue grand opening

96. What does the speaker say about the original tickets?

(A) They could not be bought online.
(B) They must be returned.
(C) Their prices were cheaper.
(D) They are sold out.

97. Look at the graphic. On what date will the band most likely perform in San Francisco?

(A) May 8
(B) May 12
(C) May 16
(D) May 19

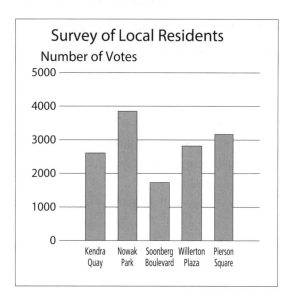

Survey of Local Residents
Number of Votes

98. Who most likely are the listeners?

(A) Residents' association members
(B) City officials
(C) Survey respondents
(D) Market research specialists

99. What is indicated about the city?

(A) It has undergone much urban development.
(B) It has experienced a decline in tourism.
(C) It had to cancel several construction projects.
(D) It has seen a decrease in residents' satisfaction.

100. Look at the graphic. Which location will most likely be chosen?

(A) Kendra Quay
(B) Nowak Park
(C) Willerton Plaza
(D) Pierson Square

95-97 *P. 174*

98-100 *P. 176*

Questions 32 through 34 refer to the following conversation.

W: Peter, ❶I'm making a slide show for my presentation to Michael's clothing shop. The store is interested in selling our jeans, and they want to learn more about our sales at other retail locations.

M: ❷I'm sure they'll be very impressed by our sales totals of the last few seasons. Our jeans have been selling very well at the other stores that carry them. Have you chosen any photographs from our fashion show to include in the presentation?

W: We have some really great photos from that runway show. However, I'm having a hard time deciding which one looks the best. ❸Will you come by my office tomorrow to help me make a final decision on what photos to include?

問題32-34は次の会話に関するものです。

W: Peter さん、私は今 Michael 洋品店に行うプレゼンテーション用のスライドを作っているのですが。このお店は当社のジーンズの販売に興味を示していて、他の小売店での売上についてもっと知りたいそうです。

M: 過去数シーズンの当社の総売上を知れば間違いなく驚くことでしょう。他の取扱店で当社のジーンズは非常によく売れています。プレゼンテーションに入れる当社のファッションショーの写真は選びましたか。

W: あのショーでの写真はとてもいいのがあります。でも、どれが一番見栄えがいいか決めあぐねています。明日私のオフィスに来て、どの写真を入れるか最終的に決定するのを手伝っていただけませんか。

✏️ □slide show （プレゼン等の）投影用スライド資料　□be interested in ～に興味がある　□jeans （衣類の）ジーンズ　□retail 小売店舗　□be impressed by ～に感銘を受ける　□the last few seasons 過去数シーズン　□sell well 売れ行きが良い　□carry ～を取り扱う　□runway （ファッションショーなどの）ランウェイ

---

32. ★★☆☆☆

What is the woman working on?

(A) A shop window display
(B) A slide presentation
(C) An advertising campaign
(D) A fashion show

女性は何に取り組んでいますか。

(A) 店のショーウインドウの展示
(B) プレゼンテーションのスライド
(C) 広告キャンペーン
(D) ファッションショー

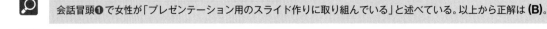

🔍 会話冒頭❶で女性が「プレゼンテーション用のスライド作りに取り組んでいる」と述べている。以上から正解は **(B)**。

✏️ □advertising campaign 広告キャンペーン

33. ★★★★★

What does the man say is impressive?

(A) Some workers' experience
(B) A model's career
(C) A new retail catalog
(D) Some sales reports

男性は何が強い印象を与えると言っていますか。

(A) 従業員の経験
(B) モデルの経歴
(C) 新しい商品カタログ
(D) 売上報告

 男性は❷で「過去数シーズンの当社の総売上を知れば間違いなく驚く」と述べている。以上より、会話中の our sales total を言い換えた **(D)** が正解となる。

 □impressive 印象的な　□career 経歴

34. ★★★★★

What will the speakers do tomorrow?

(A) Prepare a media conference
(B) Create some new sales strategies
(C) Select some final pictures
(D) Hold a runway show

話し手たちは明日何をしますか。

(A) 記者会見の準備をする。
(B) 新しい販売戦略を立てる。
(C) 最終的な写真を選ぶ。
(D) ファッションショーを開催する。

 会話の最後❸で女性が「明日オフィスに来て、どの写真を入れるか決めるのを手伝ってほしい」と言っている。以上より正解は **(C)**。(C) は会話中の make a final decision on what photos to include の言い換えになっていることにも注目しておこう。

 □media conference 記者会見　□sales strategy 販売戦略

	1回目	2回目	3回目
32.			
33.			
34.			

 32. (B)　33. (D)　34. (C)

Questions 35 through 37 refer to the following conversation.

M: Hello, Lauren. ❶I am leaving for California next month to attend an art exhibition at Todd Modern Gallery. ❷I am going to be covering the event and writing an article for the August issue. You've been there before, right?

W: I have. And that reminds me, a friend of mine is an artist who will exhibit some of her artwork there next month. If you want, I can give you her number.

M: That would certainly help me. You know, ❸I wanted to get as much information as possible about the artists before attending the event.

W: ❹I'm glad to help you out. ❺I have her business card at home, so I will e-mail you her number after work.

□art exhibition 美術展　□cover 〜を報道する　□that reminds me それで思い出したが　□artwork 芸術作品
□certainly 確かに　□as much A as possible できるだけ多くの A　□help out 〜を手伝う、〜の役に立つ
□business card 名刺

問題35-37は次の会話に関するものです。

M: こんにちは、Lauren さん。私は Todd 近代美術ギャラリーの美術展を見るために来月カリフォルニアに行きます。8月号のためにイベントを取材して記事を書くためです。あちらには以前行ったことがありますよね。

W: はい。そういえば、友達に芸術家がいるのですが、来月そこで作品を展示するんです。もしよければ、彼女の電話番号をお伝えできますが。

M: それは本当に助かります。イベントに参加する前に芸術家の情報を出来るだけ多く得ておきたいと思っていましたので。

W: お役に立てたら幸いです。彼女の名刺が家にありますので、仕事の後に電話番号を E メールで送ります。

---

35. ★★☆☆☆

Why is the man going to California?

(A) To visit his relatives
(B) To report on an event
(C) To compete in a contest
(D) To enjoy his vacation

男性はなぜカリフォルニアに行きますか。

(A) 親族を訪ねるため。
(B) イベントについて報道するため。
(C) コンテストに出場するため。
(D) 休暇を楽しむため。

男性は会話の冒頭❶で「美術展を見るために来月カリフォルニアに行く」と述べ、その後❷で「イベントを取材して記事を書くため」と話している。以上より、正解は **(B)**。❷の cover は多義語だが、今回は report と同義語になっている。

□relatives 親族　□compete in a contest コンテストに出場する

36. ★★★★☆

What does the man say he wants to do before his travels?

(A) Buy a guidebook
(B) Contact local businesspeople
(C) Reserve a hotel
(D) Collect information

男性は旅行の前に何がしたいと言っていますか。

(A) ガイドブックを買う。
(B) 地元の事業家と連絡を取る。
(C) ホテルの予約をする。
(D) 情報を収集する。

 男性は❸で「イベントに参加する前に芸術家の情報をできるだけ多く得ておきたい」と言っている。以上より、正解は **(D)**。get と collect が言い換えになっている。(B) は連絡を取るのは地元の芸術家であって、事業家ではない。(A) や (C) も通常は旅行前にする行動かもしれないが、会話中では触れられていないので、ここでは不正解。

□guidebook (旅行案内等の) ガイドブック　□contact 〜と連絡を取る

---

37. ★★★★☆

What does the woman offer to do?

(A) Prepare a trip schedule
(B) Confirm a flight
(C) Pass on some contact details
(D) Send an e-mail to an artist

女性は何をすると申し出ていますか。

(A) 旅行日程の準備をすること。
(B) 飛行機の便の確認をすること。
(C) 連絡先を伝えること。
(D) 芸術家に E メールを送ること。

 女性は男性が❸で「できるだけ情報を集めたい」と話していることを受け、❹で「お役に立てたらうれしい」と述べつつ、❺で知人の連絡先をメールで送る、と言っている。ここから、連絡先を伝えることがわかるので、正解は **(C)**。述語の pass on が e-mail の言い換えとなっていることにも注目。(D) は彼女自身が美術家にメールを添付するとは言っていないので、ここでは不正解。

□trip schedule 旅程　□confirm 〜を確認する　□pass on 〜を伝える、渡す　□contact detail 詳細な連絡先

	1回目	2回目	3回目
35.			
36.			
37.			

 35. (B)　36. (D)　37. (C)

Questions 38 through 40 refer to the following conversation.

M: Did you sign up to participate in the training session next month?

W: No. Didn't you hear the news?

M: What news?

W: ❶I was chosen to represent our company at the negotiations with a potential buyer located in Paris. ❷If it goes well, we might end up expanding into France!

M: Fantastic, congratulations! ❸So, when are you leaving?

W: ❹Maybe on Wednesday. ❺I might be promoted and be put in charge of the new Paris branch.

M: ❻It comes as no surprise. ❼I know you've been putting in lots of additional work to get that position. In addition, if we open a Paris branch, we'll be in 20 different countries!

問題38-40は次の会話に関するものです。

M: 来月の研修会への参加申し込みをしましたか。

W: いいえ、お知らせを聞かなかったのですか。

M: どんなお知らせですか。

W: 私が社を代表してバイヤーになる見込みのあるパリの業者との交渉に行くことになったのです。うまくいけば、フランスに展開することになるかもしれません。

M: 素晴らしいですね。おめでとうございます。それで、いつ出発するのですか。

W: おそらく水曜日です。昇進してパリの新支店の責任者になるかもしれません。

M: そうなるのも当然だと思いますよ。その役職に就くために人一倍の努力をしてきたんですから。それで、パリ支店を開設したら、20か国で展開することになります。

□sign up to *do* ～することを申し込む　□participate in ～に参加する　□training session 研修
□represent ～を代表する　□negotiation 交渉　□potential buyer 将来見込みのあるバイヤー (仕入れ調達担当者)
□go well うまくいく　□end up *doing* 最終的に～する　□expand into ～に参入する　□be promoted 昇進する
□put A in charge of A を～の責任者にする　□come as no surprise 驚くことではない　□lots of たくさんの
□additional 追加の

---

38. ★★★★★

What is the conversation mainly about?

(A) An advertising presentation
(B) A free workshop
(C) An European visitor
(D) A possible company expansion

会話の趣旨は何ですか。

(A) 広告のプレゼンテーション
(B) 無料の研修
(C) ヨーロッパからの訪問者
(D) 事業拡大の可能性

❶・❷で女性が「自分が会社を代表してパリの業者との交渉に行くことになった」ことと「うまくいけば、フランスに事業展開できるかも」と述べている。ここから、今後の有望な事業展開についての話題だとわかる。以上より、正解は **(D)** となる。会話冒頭では研修の話題となっていたが、それを女性が変えて❶・❷の会話の流れになっているところがポイント。

□visitor 訪問者　□possible 可能性のある　□expansion 拡大

39.

What will the woman do on Wednesday?

(A) Go to another city
(B) Meet her family
(C) Get a promotion
(D) Train her colleagues

水曜日に女性は何をしますか。

(A) 別の都市に行く。
(B) 家族に会う。
(C) 昇進する。
(D) 同僚に向けて研修を行う。

男性が❸で「いつ（パリに）出発するのか」と尋ね、その後❹で女性が「おそらく水曜日」と言っている。以上から、水曜日にパリに行くことがわかるため、パリを another city と言い換えて表した **(A)** が正解。

40. ★★★★★

What does the man mean when he says, "It comes as no surprise"?

(A) He expected a high number of attendees.
(B) He believes the woman deserves a promotion.
(C) A weather forecast is usually correct.
(D) Many companies have experienced sales decreases.

男性が "It comes as no surprise" という際に意図していることとは何ですか。

(A) 大勢の参加があることを予測していた。
(B) 女性が昇進に値すると思っている。
(C) 天気予報はたいてい当たる。
(D) 多くの会社が売り上げの減少に見舞われている。

意図を問われている表現❺「驚くことではない」の前後を見ていくと、❺「（女性が）新しいパリ支店の責任者になるかもしれない」➡❻「それは驚くべきことではない」➡❼「女性がそのような役職に就くため努力していることは知っている」という流れになっている。つまり、女性は昇進するのが当然だと思えるくらい努力しているという意図で話していることがわかる。それを deserve a promotion（昇進に値する）と言い換えた **(B)** が正解。

□a high number of 大多数の　□attendee 参加者　□deserve 〜に値する　□promotion 昇進
□weather forecast 天気予報　□correct 的確である　□experience 〜を経験する　□decrease 減少、落ち込み

	1回目	2回目	3回目
38.			
39.			
40.			

38. (D)　39. (A)　40. (B)

Questions 41 through 43 refer to the following conversation.

W: ❶George, thanks for bringing me to this restaurant. ❷I've been wanting to try the food here ever since I read the feature about it in the newspaper.

M: I've heard great reviews from some of my friends, too. And I can see why. ❸They have very efficient service. ❹We were shown to our table so fast, and the waiter has already brought us our drinks.

W: It's quite impressive. I also like the wide menu selection. However, I can't decide what to order. The barbecue chicken looks delicious, but this place is famous for its steaks. ❺How about we order both of these entrées and share them?

M: ❻That would be fine with me.

問題41-43は次の会話に関するものです。

W: George さん、このレストランに連れてきてくださってありがとうございます。新聞の特集記事を読んでから、ここで食事をしてみたいとずっと思っていたんです。

M: 友達からも良かったという感想を聞きました。それも当然だと思います。サービスの効率がとてもいいですよね。すぐにテーブルに案内してもらえましたし、ウエイターはもう飲み物を用意してくれています。

W: 本当に印象的ですね。メニューが幅広いのも気に入りました。でも、何を注文したらいいか迷ってしまいますね。バーベキューチキンはおいしそうですが、ここはステーキが有名なんです。メインディッシュを両方注文して分け合うのはどうでしょうか。

M: それがいいですね。

□bring 人 to 人を~に連れてくる　□feature 特集 (記事)　□review 感想　□efficient 効率的な
□impressive 印象的な、感銘を受ける　□wide 豊富な　□what to order 何を注文するか
□famous for ~で有名である　□entrée メインディッシュ　□fine with ~にとってよい

---

41. ★★☆☆☆

How did the woman get to know about the restaurant?

(A) Through a newspaper
(B) Through a flyer
(C) Through a magazine
(D) Through her friend

女性はどうやってレストランのことを知りましたか。

(A) 新聞で
(B) チラシで
(C) 雑誌で
(D) 友達の話で

女性は会話冒頭❶で今いるレストランに連れてきてもらったことの礼を述べ、❷で「新聞の特集記事を読んでから、ここで食事をしてみたいとずっと思っていた」と述べている。以上から、新聞を通じて知ったことがわかるので正解は **(A)**。

□flyer チラシ

42.

What does the man say about the restaurant?

(A) It has a large menu.
(B) It has quick service.
(C) It serves local produce.
(D) It employs a well-known cook.

男性はレストランについて何と述べていますか。

(A) メニューが豊富である。
(B) サービスが迅速である。
(C) 地元の農産物で提供している。
(D) 有名な料理人を雇用している。

 男性はこのレストランについて❸で、サービスの効率が良いと述べ、例として❹で「テーブルに案内するのも飲み物を用意するのも早い」と述べている。ここから、サービスが早いことがわかる。それを言い換えた **(B)** が正解となる。

 □produce 農産物　□employ ～を雇う　□well-known 有名な

43.

What do the speakers agree to do?

(A) Order the same dessert
(B) Split the bill
(C) Take their food home
(D) Divide some food between them

話し手たちは何をすることに同意していますか。

(A) 同じデザートを注文すること。
(B) 会計を折半すること。
(C) 料理を家に持ち帰ること。
(D) 料理を分け合うこと。

 女性が❺で、メインディッシュを複数注文して分け合おうと提案し、男性が❻でそれに応じている。以上から、正解は **(D)**。この設問のように「同意している」場合は、どちらかが提案し、相手がそれに応じている会話を狙って聞き取る必要がある。

 □split the bill 割り勘にする　□divide 分ける

	1回目	2回目	3回目
41.			

	1回目	2回目	3回目
42.			

	1回目	2回目	3回目
43.			

 41. (A)　42. (B)　43. (D)

Questions 44 through 46 refer to the following conversation.

M: ❶I'm going to be away on vacation beginning Thursday, April 15, and I'd like you to put a hold on my mail.

W: Of course. We can keep your mail here at the post office until you get back, sir. ❷Did you know that you can have your mail delivered to another address instead?

M: ❸Yes, I'm aware of that. However, I'm actually going to be traveling overseas. Therefore, I don't think I could use that service. I'd like you to keep everything at the post office while I am out of town.

W: ❹When do you want the delivery to restart?

📝 問題44-46は次の会話に関するものです。

M: 4月15日木曜日から休暇で出かけるので、郵便物を保管しておいてもらえますか。

W: 承知しました。戻られるまで、こちらの局でお預かりします。Jackson さん、保管の代わりに郵便物を別の住所に配達できることはご存じですか。

M: はい、知っています。でも、実は外国を旅行するんです。だから、そのサービスは使えないと思っています。町を出ている間は全て郵便局で保管していただきたいのですが。

W: いつから配達を再開すればよろしいですか。

✏️ □be away on ～で不在にする　□put a hold on ～を保留する　□mail 郵送物　□get back 戻る
□instead 代わりに　□be aware of ～のことを知っている　□out of town 町を出て　□restart ～を再開する

44.

What are the speakers talking about?

(A) Stopping mail delivery
(B) Finding a lost item
(C) Reserving a conference place
(D) Moving an office

話し手たちは何について話していますか。

(A) 郵便物の配送を停止すること。
(B) 遺失物を見つけること。
(C) 会議場を予約すること。
(D) 事務所を移転すること。

🔍 会話冒頭❶で男性が「木曜日から出かけるので、郵便物を保管しておいてほしい」とお願いしている。ここから、郵送物の配送を止めてほしい、という話をしていることがわかるので、正解は **(A)**。

✏️ □lost item 遺失物

45. ★★★☆☆

Why does the man decline the woman's suggestion?

(A) The quality of service is low.
(B) The room is cramped.
(C) He has already received information
(D) He will be out of the country.

男性はなぜ女性の提案を断っていますか。

(A) サービスの質が低いため。
(B) 部屋が狭いため。
(C) 情報を既に受け取っているため。
(D) 国外にいる予定のため。

 女性が❷で不在時に別住所に配達できるサービスを提案しているが、男性は❸でそのサービスを知っているものの、海外に行くので利用が難しい旨を伝えている。以上から、正解は海外に行くことを別の表現に言い換えた **(D)** となる。

 □cramped 窮屈な、狭苦しい

46. ★★★★☆

What will the man most likely tell the woman next?

(A) The date of his return
(B) His office expansion plan
(C) His temporary address
(D) The topic of his speech

男性は女性に次に何を伝えると考えられますか。

(A) 戻ってくる日にち
(B) 事務所の拡張計画
(C) 暫定の住所
(D) スピーチのトピック

 会話の最後❹で女性が「いつから配達を再開するか」と、配達が可能になる日、つまり男性が戻ってくる日を尋ねていることがわかる。以上から、正解は **(A)**。

 □expansion plan 拡張計画　□temporary 仮の、一時的な

	1回目	2回目	3回目
44.			
45.			
46.			

44. (A)　45. (D)　46. (A)

141

M1 W M2 🔊 **3-3-47_49-01~02**

Questions 47 through 49 refer to the following conversation with three speakers.

M1: ❶Welcome to Ashton Steak House! Would you like some more time to look at the menu, or have you decided what you would like?

W: I think we're ready. I'll have the Philly cheesesteak with a glass of white wine. Can I get that steak medium?

M1: Of course you may. And for you?

M2: Um, what are your specials tonight?

M1: Tonight's special is barbecued ribs with buffalo wings.

M2: Alright, I'll go with that. And I'm driving, so I'll just have a glass of soda to go with my dinner.

M1: Great. ❷Will that be all or would you like any appetizers?

W: ❸That'll do. Thanks.

M1: ❹OK. ❺I'll place your order now and be right back with your drinks.

📝 問題47-49は次の3人の話し手による会話に関するものです。

M1: Ashton ステーキハウス店にようこそ。もうしばらくメニューをご覧になりますか、それともご注文はお決まりでしょうか。

W: 決まったと思います。フィリーチーズステーキと白ワインをグラスで。ステーキの焼き加減はミディアムでお願いできますか。

M1: はい、承知しました。お客様は？

M2: ええと、今夜のスペシャルメニューは何ですか。

M1: 今夜のスペシャルメニューはバーベキューリブとバッファローウイングです。

M2: わかりました、それにします。それから私は運転しますので、ソーダをください。

M1: かしこまりました、以上でよろしいですか。前菜などいかがでしょうか。

W: それで結構です。ありがとうございます。

M1: 承知しました。注文を通してから、すぐにお飲み物をお持ちします。

✏️ □a glass of グラス1杯の □medium (ステーキの焼き方の) ミディアムレア □rib リブ (あばら骨周辺の部位の肉)
□buffalo wing バッファローウイング (鶏の手羽フライ) □go with ～にする □appetizer 前菜
□be right back すぐに戻る

47.

Where is the conversation taking place?

(A) In a restaurant
(B) In a bakery
(C) In a hotel
(D) In a department store

会話はどこで行われていますか。

(A) レストラン
(B) パン屋
(C) ホテル
(D) デパート

🔍 会話冒頭❶で男性の1人が「ステーキハウス店にようこそ」と言っているので、食事をする場所での会話だとわかる。以上から正解は **(A)**。

✏️ □bakery パン屋、ベーカリー

48. ★★★☆☆

What does the woman mean when she says, "That'll do"?

(A) She accepts the man's recommendation.
(B) She doesn't want to order anything else.
(C) She wants the man to stop working.
(D) She already has what she needs.

女性が "That'll do" と言う際、意味していることは何ですか。

(A) 男性の勧めを受ける。
(B) 他に注文するつもりはない。
(C) 男性に作業を停止してもらいたい。
(D) 必要なものは既に持っている。

🔍 意図を問われている箇所は❸で「もう十分」と言っている。この会話の流れを見ていくと、❷で男性の1人が「他に注文はないか」と尋ね➡❸女性「十分だ」➡男性の1人「了解」という流れになっている。ここから、女性はこれ以上注文しない、という意図で発言したことがわかるので、正解は **(B)**。That'll do.「それで十分だ」は Part 2の会話問題でも正解の応答として出てくることがあるため、押さえておこう。

✏️ □anything else 他に何か

---

49. ★★★★☆

What will most likely happen next?

(A) The speakers will go for a drive.
(B) The speakers will confirm a booking.
(C) A dinner reservation will be canceled.
(D) An order will be relayed to the kitchen.

次に何が起こると考えられますか。

(A) 話し手たちがドライブをしに行く。
(B) 話し手たちが予約を確認する。
(C) 夕食の予約が取り消される。
(D) 注文が厨房に伝えられる。

🔍 男性の1人が会話の最後❺で「注文をとおしてから、すぐに飲み物を持ってくる」と述べている。ここから、注文を厨房にいる人に伝えに行き、飲み物を用意して戻ってくる行動が考えられる。それを言い換えた **(D)** が正解。relay はリレー競走のバトンを渡すように、ある行為を中継することを意味する。それが、このレストランの場面では、お客様の注文を受け、厨房に注文を通す流れを表現していることにも注目。

✏️ □go for a drive ドライブに行く　□confirm ～を確認する　□booking 予約　□relay ～を中継で伝える

	1回目	2回目	3回目
47.			
48.			
49.			

🚩 **47. (A)　48. (B)　49. (D)**

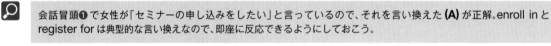

Questions 50 through 52 refer to the following conversation.

W: Hello. ❶I'm calling as I'm interested in enrolling in the economics seminar. I have a group of 30 people who would like to attend it.

M: Regrettably, ❷we don't process group registrations over the phone. ❸You should complete a form online.

W: You know, I just tried completing that form many times. However, whenever I pressed the send button, I received an error message. Is there any other way to enroll?

M: I'm so sorry to hear that. ❹Could you please give me your name, e-mail address and phone number? I'll have our technical support team contact you right away.

問題50-52は次の会話に関するものです。

W: こんにちは。経済学セミナーの申し込みについて伺いたくてお電話しました。30人のグループでの参加なんですが。

M: 申し訳ございませんが、グループでのお申し込みは電話では承っておりません。インターネットでフォームに入力してください。

W: 実はそのフォームへの入力は何度もやってみたのですが。でも、送信ボタンを押したところでいつもエラーメッセージが出るんです。他に申し込む方法はありませんか。

M: 申し訳ありませんでした。お名前とEメールアドレス、電話番号を教えていただけますか。すぐにテクニカルサポートチームからご連絡を差し上げます。

□be interested in ～に興味がある　□enroll in ～に登録する　□regrettably 残念ながら
□process ～を扱う、処理する　□group registration 団体登録　□over the phone 電話ごしに
□complete a form 書式に記入する　□send button 送信ボタン　□error エラー、誤り　□contact ～に連絡する
□right away すぐに

---

50. ★★★☆☆

Why is the woman calling?

(A) To register for an event
(B) To order some software
(C) To hold a workshop
(D) To pay an invoice

女性はなぜ電話をしていますか。

(A) イベントの参加登録をするため。
(B) ソフトウェアを注文するため。
(C) セミナーを行うため。
(D) 請求書の支払いをするため。

🔍 会話冒頭❶で女性が「セミナーの申し込みをしたい」と言っているので、それを言い換えた **(A)** が正解。enroll in と register for は典型的な言い換えなので、即座に反応できるようにしておこう。

□register for ～に登録する　□invoice 請求書

51. ★★★☆☆

According to the man, what does the woman have to do?

(A) Call him back later
(B) Submit an expense form
(C) Rearrange an appointment
(D) Make a booking online

男性によると、女性は何をしなければなりませんか。

(A) 彼に電話をかけ直す。
(B) 支出に関する書式を提出する。
(C) アポイントメントを再設定する。
(D) インターネットで予約する。

🔍 男性は❷・❸で女性に「グループ申し込みは電話で受け付けられないので、オンラインで行ってほしい」と述べている。以上から **(D)** が正解。registration = booking と言い換えられている。

✏️ □expense form 支出に関する書式　□rearrange 再調整する

52. ★★★★☆

What does the man ask for?

(A) Presentation material
(B) Details of a bill
(C) Proof of employment
(D) Some contact information

男性は何を求めていますか。

(A) プレゼンテーションの素材
(B) 請求明細
(C) 雇用証明
(D) 連絡先の情報

🔍 男性は会話後半❹で「名前とEメールアドレス、電話番号を教えてほしい」と述べている。ここから、女性の連絡先を尋ねていることがわかるので、正解は **(D)**。

✏️ □presentation material プレゼン素材　□detail 詳細、明細　□bill 請求　□proof of employment 雇用証明
□contact information 連絡先

	1回目	2回目	3回目
50.			
51.			
52.			

 50. (A)　51. (D)　52. (D)

Questions 53 through 55 refer to the following conversation.

M: ❶Hello, I'm trying to reach Langston Interiors. ❷I manage a bookstore and I'd like to remodel my sales floor. I'd like to get an estimate for installing new floors, as well as for new furnishings.

W: We can certainly help with that. I will need some more information first. ❸Do you know what kind of floor and furnishings you would like us to install in your shop?

M: For the floor, I am thinking that I'd like a polished granite floor so that it would be easy to clean. I mostly need bookshelves and tables for the furnishings, but I'm uncertain about the style that I will go with.

W: I understand. Prices on those kinds of furnishings can vary widely because we offer many different styles. ❹If you'd like, I can mail you a catalog with all of the furnishings that we offer after I hang up and you can call me back after you've decided.

📝 問題53-55は次の会話に関するものです。

M: こんにちは、Langston Interiors 店さんですか。私は書店を経営しておりまして、売り場の改装をしたいのですが。床を新しくして、オフィス家具も新調する場合の見積もりをお願いします。

W: ご希望のとおりにご用意いたします。まずは詳しい情報をいただきたいのですが、店内に設置する床や家具の種類についてご希望はありますか。

M: 床は清掃しやすいように研磨した御影石がいいです。家具で主に必要なのは本棚とテーブルなんですが、どんな様式にするかは明確に考えていません。

W: わかりました。弊社は多くのスタイルをご提供していますので、そういった家具は値段にかなり幅があります。よろしければ、いったん電話を切って弊社が取り扱っている全ての家具を掲載したカタログをお送りしますので、お決まりになりましたときにまたお電話ください。

✏️ □reach 〜と連絡を取る　□manage 〜を経営する　□remodel 〜を改装する　□estimate 見積もり
□install 〜を設置する　□furnishing オフィス家具　□polish 〜を磨く　□granite 御影石
□uncertain よくわからない　□go with 〜を選ぶ　□vary 変わる　□widely 幅広く　□hang up 電話を切る

---

53. ★★☆☆☆

What is the topic of the conversation?

(A) Organizing a sales event
(B) Renovating a store
(C) Looking for a property
(D) Buying a bookstore

会話の話題は何ですか。

(A) 販売イベントを開催すること。
(B) 店舗を改装すること。
(C) 物件を探すこと。
(D) 書店を購入すること。

🔍 男性は会話冒頭❶・❷である内装業者に連絡し、「経営している書店の売り場の改装をしたい」と述べている。ここから、店舗改装をしたいことがわかるので、正解は **(B)**。

✏️ □organize 〜を開催する　□renovate 〜を改装する　□property 物件

54. ★★★☆☆

What does the woman ask the man about?

(A) The dimensions of a shop
(B) A company's target market
(C) The location of a business
(D) Items he would like to order

女性は男性に何について尋ねていますか。

(A) 店の規模
(B) 企業がターゲットとする市場
(C) 店の所在地
(D) 注文したい商品

女性は❸で「店内に設置する床やオフィス家具の種類について希望があるか」と尋ねている。つまり、男性の注文したい商品について尋ねていることがわかるので、正解は **(D)**。

□dimension 規模、面積　□target market ターゲットとする市場

55. ★★★★☆

What does the woman say she will do next?

(A) Send a list of furnishings
(B) Buy some supplies
(C) Come to the man's store
(D) Contact a designer

女性は次に何をするつもりであると言っていますか。

(A) オフィス家具の一覧を送る。
(B) 物資を購入する。
(C) 男性の店に行く。
(D) デザイナーに連絡する。

女性は会話後半❹で「弊社が取り扱っている全ての家具を掲載したカタログを送る」と言っている。それを言い換えた **(A)** が正解となる。a list と catalog が言い換えとなっている。

□supply 備品、物資

	1回目	2回目	3回目
53.			
54.			
55.			

53. (B)　54. (D)　55. (A)

■✦■ M　🇺🇸 W　🔊 3-3-56_58-01～02

Questions 56 through 58 refer to the following conversation.

M: Hello. Thank you for calling Karston Skin Clinic. May I help you?

W: ❶Yes, this is Dorothy Canter calling. Is Dr. Gibson available? ❷I made an appointment with her yesterday, and I just have a quick question for her about my prescription.

M: ❸I'm afraid she's not here at the moment. ❹She was just called into an urgent meeting at the hospital. Would you like to speak to another doctor on duty?

W: No, I don't think that's necessary. Maybe you can answer my question. ❺Dr. Gibson wrote me a prescription, but the pharmacy doesn't have the prescribed medication. Do you think I should ask for a different prescription?

📄 問題56-58は次の会話に関するものです。

M: こんにちは。Karston皮膚科医院にお電話くださりありがとうございます。どうされましたか。

W: ええ、Dorothy Canterと申しますが、Gibson先生はいらっしゃいますか。昨日、診察を受けたのですが、処方箋についてちょっと質問があるのです。

M: 恐れ入りますが、今、席を外しております。ちょうど病院の緊急会議に呼ばれたところなんです。勤務中の別の医師とお話しされますか。

W: いいえ、それは必要ないと思います。おそらく、あなたにもお答えいただけるかもしれません。Gibson先生に処方箋を書いていただきましたが、薬局には処方された薬がないのです。別の処方箋をお願いしたほうがよいでしょうか。

✏️ □available 空いている　□quick question ちょっとした質問　□prescription 処方箋
□I'm afraid すまないが、あいにく　□at the moment 今現在　□call ～を招集する　□urgent 緊急の
□on duty 勤務中　□pharmacy 薬局　□prescribed medication 処方薬

56.

Who most likely is the woman?

(A) A nurse
(B) A doctor
(C) A patient
(D) A receptionist

女性は誰であると考えられますか。

(A) 看護師
(B) 医者
(C) 患者
(D) 受付係

🔍 女性は❶・❷で医者に診察を受け、自分の処方箋について質問があると伝えていることから、患者であることがわかる。以上から正解は **(C)**。(B) は電話で話したい相手なので、ここでは不正解。

✏️ □patient 患者　□receptionist 受付

57. ★★★★★

Why is Dr. Gibson unavailable?

(A) She is performing an operation.
(B) She is attending a meeting.
(C) She is having a patient consultation.
(D) She is talking on the phone.

なぜGibson 医師は手が空いていないのですか。

(A) 手術を執り行っているから。
(B) 会議に出席しているから。
(C) 患者の診察を行っているから。
(D) 電話で話しているから。

🔍 男性は❸・❹で緊急の打ち合わせが入ったため、Gibson 医師は電話に出られないと伝えている。正解はそれを言い換えた **(B)**。

✎ □perform an operation 手術を行う　□patient consultation 診察

58. ★★★★★

What problem does the woman say she has?

(A) A pharmacy doesn't carry the drug she needs.
(B) Her prescribed medication does not work well.
(C) She is worried about the cost of a drug.
(D) The hospital made a mistake with her prescription.

女性はどんな問題があると言っていますか。

(A) 薬局が薬を扱っていない。
(B) 処方された薬があまり効かない。
(C) 薬の費用が気にかかっている。
(D) 病院が処方を間違えた。

🔍 女性は❺で「Gibson 先生に処方箋を書いてもらったが、薬局には処方された薬がない」と述べている。ここから、訪ねた薬局では処方薬を扱っていないことがわかるので、処方薬を drug と言い換えて、その状況を表現した **(A)** が正解。

✎ □carry 〜を取り扱う　□drug 薬　□work well うまく効力を発する　□be worried about 〜について心配する

	1回目	2回目	3回目
56.			
57.			
58.			

🚩 **56. (C)　57. (B)　58. (A)**

Questions 59 through 61 refer to the following conversation with three speakers.

W1: ❶That fireworks show was just the best way to end the ceremony.

M: I agree!

W2: ❷I can't believe the company's been in business for 20 years already. I've worked here since it opened its first store, and it seems like yesterday!

M: That's amazing, Ronda. ❸Haven't you been here for a long time too, Bianca?

W1: I have, yes. ❹It's such a supportive atmosphere, and the company is the best in the industry in terms of pay and benefits.

M: ❺By the way, I heard the company is offering big discounts on furniture in celebration of its anniversary.

W2: I heard that, too. It's a great way not only to celebrate, but also to increase sales.

📝 問題59-61は次の3人の話し手による会話に関するものです。

W1: あの花火ショーは式典の締めくくりに最高でしたね。

M: 私もそう思います。

W2: 会社がもう20年も営業しているなんてびっくりしました。私は最初の店が開店してから、ここで働いていますが、まるで昨日のことのようです。

M: すごいですよ、Rondaさん。Biancaさんも長い間ここにいるのではないですか。

W1: そうです。とても協力的な環境ですし、うちは給与と福利厚生においては業界で一番ですから。

M: ところで、会社は記念日のお祝いに家具の大幅値引きを行うそうです。

W2: 私も聞きました。お祝いをするだけでなくて、売り上げを増やすのにもいい手ですよね。

✏️ □fireworks show 花火大会　□ceremony 式典　□be in business 事業をしている　□amazing 素晴らしい
□supportive atmosphere 協力的な環境　□industry 業界　□in terms of ～の観点で
□pay and benefits 給与と福利厚生　□by the way ところで

---

59. ★★★☆☆

What kind of event is mainly discussed?

(A) A closing speech
(B) An employee's promotion
(C) A hiring process
(D) A company's anniversary

どんな出来事について主に話し合っていますか。

(A) 閉会の挨拶
(B) 従業員の昇進
(C) 採用手順
(D) 会社の創立記念

🔍 会話冒頭❶で女性の1人が式典に関わる花火のショーについて言及し、その後もう1人の女性が❷「会社が20年営業している」と伝えている。ここから、会社の20周年記念のイベントが行われたことについて話しているとわかるので、それを言い換えた **(D)** が正解。

✏️ □closing 閉会　□promotion 昇進　□hiring process 採用手順

60. ★★★★★

What does Bianca imply about the company?

(A) It offers competitive salaries.
(B) All of its items are expensive.
(C) New employees will be hired.
(D) It supports local charities.

Bianca さんは会社について何を示唆していますか。

(A) 水準以上の給料が支払われている。
(B) 全ての商品が高額である。
(C) 新しく雇用される人がいる。
(D) 地域の慈善事業を支援している。

 Bianca さんは男性からの❸「この会社に長い間いるのではないか」という問いかけに対して、❹で「とても協力的な環境で、給与と福利厚生においては業界で一番だ」と答えている。この中の、給与が業界一番という点を competitive salaries と言い換えて表している **(A)** が正解だとわかる。この問題は Bianca さんが誰なのかというところと、その後の会話の内容を聞いて、言い換えを探すところが難しい。しっかり復習しておこう。

□competitive 競争力のある、魅力的な　□charity 慈善事業

---

61. ★★★★★

According to the man, what is the company offering?

(A) Merchandise price cuts
(B) Complimentary beverages
(C) Free furniture
(D) Membership rewards

男性によると会社は何を提供しますか。

(A) 商品価格の割引
(B) 無料の飲み物
(C) 無料の家具
(D) 会員への見返り

男性は❺で「会社が記念の祝いとして、家具を大幅割引する」と言っている。この商品の値引きを merchandise price cuts と言い換えた **(A)** が正解。(A) cut という表現を使っているため、コスト削減や商品の流通停止、あるいは簡略化のようなニュアンスにも感じられるが、ここでは「値引き」を指す。

□merchandise price cuts 商品価格の割引　□complimentary 無料の　□reward 見返り

	1回目	2回目	3回目
59.			
60.			
61.			

59. (D)　60. (A)　61. (A)

Questions 62 through 64 refer to the following conversation and schedule.

W: Great news! ❶The owner of Wayne Fashion recommended us to one of his contacts, an apparel maker, and it's interested in using our accounting services. The director of the company wants to meet here on June 15th.

M: Great! We've been making a real effort to expand our client base, and signing with a major client like this is exactly what we need.

W: The only problem is with the conference room. Check out the schedule. ❷The client wants to meet at 10, but the room's already been reserved by Mr. Lopez.

M: Not to worry. I'm sure he could move his event to the afternoon. This is more important.

W: All right. ❸I'll e-mail him to explain the situation and ask him to do that.

Conference Room Reservations: June 15	
09:30 A.M.	General conference
❹10:00 A.M.	❺Leadership workshop
10:30 A.M.	Intern interviews
11:00 A.M.	Headquarters meeting

📝 問題62-64は次の会話と予定表に関するものです。

W: 朗報です。Wayne Fashion 社のオーナーが付き合いのあるアパレルメーカーに当社を推薦してくださいました。そこは当社の会計サービスの導入に興味を持っていただけているそうです。取締役の方が6月15日に当社での面談を希望されているそうです。

M: いいじゃないですか。当社は顧客基盤を広げるために大変な努力をしてきているわけで、このような大手の顧客との契約は正に当社が求めているものです。

W: 唯一の問題は会議室です。予定表を見てください。お客様は10時に面談を希望していらっしゃいますが、部屋は Lopez さんがもう予約しています。

M: 心配ありません。その予定は午後にずらせると思います。こちらの方が重要ですから。

W: わかりました。E メールで状況を説明して、そうしてもらえるように頼みます。

会議室の予約：6月15日	
午前9時半	総会
午前10時	リーダーシップ研修会
午前10時半	インターン面接
午前11時	本社会議

✏️ ☐contact 知り合い　☐apparel maker 衣類製造業者　☐be interested in ～に興味がある、関心を寄せている
☐accounting 会計 (の)　☐director (事業、会社等の) 部長、取締役　☐make an effort to *do* ～する努力をする
☐client base 顧客基盤　☐expand ～を拡大する　☐general conference 総会　☐headquarters 本社

62. ★★★☆☆

Where do the speakers most likely work?

(A) At an accounting firm
(B) At a magazine publisher
(C) At a manufacturing facility
(D) At a fashion studio

話し手たちはどこで働いていると考えられますか。

(A) 会計事務所
(B) 雑誌の出版社
(C) 製造施設
(D) ファッションスタジオ

会話冒頭❶で女性が「ある会社のオーナーが当社を他の会社に紹介してくれて、そこが当社の会計サービス導入に興味を持っている」と述べている。ここから、この女性たちの会社が会計サービスを提供する会社、つまり会計に関する会社だとわかる。以上から正解は **(A)**。

 □accounting firm 会計事務所　□facility 施設

---

63. ★★★★☆

Look at the graphic. Which event was Mr. Lopez planning to attend?

(A) General conference
(B) Leadership workshop
(C) Intern interviews
(D) Headquarters meeting

図を見てください。Lopez さんが参加しようとしていたのはどのイベントですか。

(A) 総会
(B) リーダーシップ研修会
(C) インターン面接
(D) 本社会議

女性は❷で「10時に使用したいと思っている部屋は Lopez さんが確保している」と述べている。次に会議室予約の表❹・❺を見ると、10時のところには研修名が書いてある。よって Lopez さんが参加しようとしているイベントは **(B)**。Lopez さんは会話を聞かないと、どこで登場するか不明なので、しっかり聞き取って解こう。

---

64. ★★★★☆

What does the woman plan to do?

(A) Send an e-mail to Wayne Fashion
(B) Discuss her career
(C) Visit her client's office
(D) Ask a colleague to reschedule an event

女性は何をするつもりですか。

(A) Wayne Fashion 社に E メールを送る。
(B) キャリアについて話し合う。
(C) 事務所を訪ねる。
(D) イベントの予定変更を同僚にお願いする。

女性は❸で、メールでお願いする、と言っている。このお願いは直前の男性の発言にある「予定を午後に移してもらう」ことを意味している。つまり、イベント開催時間の変更をお願いするつもりであることがわかるので、正解は **(D)**。(A) はメールの送り先が異なるので、ここでは不正解。

 □career 経歴

	1回目	2回目	3回目
62.			
63.			
64.			

 62. (A)　63. (B)　64. (D)

Questions 65 through 67 refer to the following conversation and contents page.

M: Good afternoon, this is Gary from Timbercrest Construction. ❶I'm calling to confirm that I received our order today, but I have a question about the invoice.

W: Thanks for letting me know that. What is your question?

M: ❷I remember you said all shipping fees would be waived for any purchase over $3,000, but I found $20 was charged.

W: Oh, there must have been an error. I will submit a revised invoice as soon as possible. ❸As an apology, I will send a $10 voucher which can be used at our shops.

M: Wait, one more thing! ❹I want to buy accessory kits for the Palmtop Computers, but I couldn't find any information on the tablet computers page.

W: Sorry for the inconvenience. You must have an old version of our brochure. ❺They are listed at the bottom of the laptop computers page.

Contents

History	/ 5
Our Products	
Tablet Computers	/ 14
❻Laptop Computers	/ 15
Desktop Computers	/ 16

問題65-67は次の会話と目次に関するものです。

M: こんにちは、Timbercrest Construction社のGaryと申します。本日は注文品を受け取ったことをお知らせするためにお電話しましたが、請求書について質問があります。

W: ご連絡くださりありがとうございます。ご質問は何でしょうか。

M: 3000ドル以上の購入をした場合は送料がかからなくなると聞いた記憶があるのですが、20ドルが請求されています。

W: ああ、それは手違いがあったのだと思います。訂正した請求書を出来るだけ早くお送りします。お詫びとして、当店で使える10ドル分のクーポンをお送りします。

M: 待ってください。もう一点あるのですが。Palmtopパソコン用のアクセサリーを購入したいと思っていますが、タブレットパソコンのページで何も見つけられないんです。

W: ご不便をおかけして、申し訳ありません。弊社の古い版のパンフレットをお持ちのようです。そちらはノートパソコンのページの下の方に掲載されております。

目次

会社の歴史	/ 5
当社の製品	
タブレットパソコン	/ 14
ノートパソコン	/ 15
デスクトップパソコン	/ 16

✏️ □confirm ～を確認する □invoice 請求書 □shipping fee 送料 □waive ～を適用除外とする
□charge ～を請求する □revised 改定した □as soon as possible できるだけ早く
□as an apology お詫びとして □voucher 金券、クーポン □accessory kit アクセサリー部品
□tablet computer タブレット型のコンピューター □inconvenience 不便、不都合 □brochure パンフレット

65. ★★★☆☆

Why is the man calling?	男性はなぜ電話をしていますか。
(A) To pay a bill	(A) 請求書の支払いをするため。
(B) To place an order	(B) 注文をするため。
(C) To arrange an appointment	(C) アポイントメントを取るため。
(D) To talk about a problem	**(D)** 問題について話すため。

男性は❶で「本日受け取った注文品の受領と請求書について質問がある」と述べ、❷で「かからないはずの送料が請求されている」と述べている。ここから、請求書に関して問題が発生していることがわかるので、正解は **(D)**。

☐bill 請求書　☐place an order 発注する

---

66. ★★★☆☆

What does the woman offer?	女性は何を申し出ていますか。
(A) Complimentary express shipping	(A) 無料の速達
(B) A gift certificate	**(B)** 商品券
(C) A discounted product	(C) 割引された製品
(D) A free accessory	(D) 無料のアクセサリー

女性は男性の言及している問題を受けて❸で「お詫びとしてクーポンを送付する」と述べている。このクーポンを言い換えた **(B)** が正解。

☐complimentary 無料の　☐express shipping 速達配送　☐gift certificate 商品券

---

67. ★★★★★

Look at the graphic. Which page should the man refer to?	図を見てください。男性はどのページを参照しますか。
(A) P.5	(A) 5ページ
(B) P.14	(B) 14ページ
(C) P.15	**(C)** 15ページ
(D) P.16	(D) 16ページ

男性は❹で「アクセサリーの情報が載っているページが見つからない」と追加で質問をしている。それに対して女性が❺「ノートパソコンのページの下の方に載っている」と答えていることから、男性の欲しい情報はノートパソコンのページにあることがわかる。表を参照すると、❻からノートパソコンは15ページにあるため、正解は **(C)**。表のノートパソコンの下にある (D) ではなく、あくまでノートパソコンが当てはまるページ内の下の方だということを正しく認識して解くようにしよう。

	1回目	2回目	3回目
65.			
66.			
67.			

 65. (D)　66. (B)　67. (C)

Questions 68 through 70 refer to the following conversation and floor plan.

M: Hello, Sierra. ❶I'd like to arrange an appointment with you to discuss my investments and short-term financial plans.

W: I'd be happy to discuss those things with you, Jimmy. ❷How about stopping by my office at 10 A.M. tomorrow?

M: ❸I'm afraid I'll be leading a staff training seminar at my company all day. So, how about Friday?

W: That works for me. I'm sure you remember where my company building is located. My office is still on the fifth floor.

M: Yes, I know. Your office is next to the supply room, just opposite the conference room, right?

W: No, I recently moved. ❹Now it's around the corner, right across from the women's bathroom.

M: OK. I'll see you at 10 on Friday.

📝 問題68-70は次の会話と見取り図に関するものです。

M: こんにちは、Sierraさん。投資と短期の資金計画についてお話し合いをするためにお時間をいただければと思います。

W: Jimmyさん、その件について是非お話しできればと思います。明日の午前10時に私の事務所にお立ち寄りいただくのはいかがですか。

M: 申し訳ありませんが、会社で終日、職員研修会を担当しておりまして。金曜日はいかがですか。

W: それでも大丈夫です。私の会社の所在地は覚えていらっしゃると思います。事務所は前と変わらず5階です。

M: ええ、わかりますよ。備品室の隣で、会議室の向かいですよね。

W: いえ、先日移動したんです。今は角を曲がったところで、女性用トイレの向かいです。

M: わかりました。金曜日の10時にお伺いします。

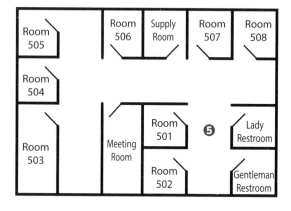

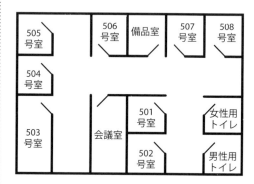

□arrange an appointment 約束を取り付ける　□investment 投資　□short-term 短期の
□financial plan 資金計画　□I'd be happy to do 喜んで〜する　□I'm afraid すまないが
□staff training seminar 従業員教育研修　□work for 〜に都合が良い　□supply room 備品室
□opposite 〜の向かい側　□bathroom トイレ、洗面所　□restroom トイレ

68. ★★★★☆

What most likely is the woman's job?

(A) An interior designer
(B) A financial advisor
(C) A bank clerk
(D) An event planner

女性の仕事は何であると考えられますか。

(A) 内装デザイナー
(B) 財務顧問
(C) 銀行員
(D) イベントプランナー

🔍 会話冒頭❶で男性が女性に「投資と短期の資金計画について話し合いをするために時間が欲しい」と述べている。ここから、女性は財務関連の仕事をしていることが考えられるため、**(B)** が正解となる。

 □interior 内装　□financial advisor 財務顧問

---

69. ★★★☆☆

What is the man planning to do tomorrow?

(A) Train some workers
(B) Interview job applicants
(C) Go to the woman's office
(D) Attend a meeting

男性は明日何をするつもりですか。

(A) 従業員の研修をする。
(B) 求職者の面接をする。
(C) 女性の事務所に行く。
(D) 会議に出席する。

🔍 女性が❷で「明日私のオフィスに立ち寄るのはどうか」と尋ねているのに対し、男性が❸で「その日は1日中スタッフ研修講師を行う」と述べている。つまり、男性が社員教育を行うことがわかるので、正解はこれを言い換えた **(A)** となる。この問題は女性の発言にある tomorrow が、男性が言及していない日取りを示しているので、その点に注意して解くようにしよう。

 □train ～を教育する　□job applicant 求職者

---

70. ★★★★☆

Look at the graphic. Where is the woman's office located?

(A) Room 501
(B) Room 504
(C) Room 506
(D) Room 507

図を見てください。女性の働く部屋はどこに位置していますか。

(A) 501号室
(B) 504号室
(C) 506号室
(D) 507号室

🔍 女性は❹で「今現在は角を曲がったところで、女性用のトイレの近く」と述べている。次に地図でこの女性の言及している箇所❺を見ると、Room 501 が該当することがわかる。以上から、正解は **(A)**。bathroom は、オフィスや公共施設などの場合は、トイレ（＝restroom）を指すことが多いので、気を付けておこう。

	1回目	2回目	3回目
68.			
69.			
70.			

 68. (B)　69. (A)　70. (A)

Questions 71 through 73 refer to the following talk.

W: Thank you for coming. ❶ This is our final promotional meeting before we publish the new East Slope adventure book in a month. We've been advertising this novel a great deal over the last six months, and book sellers across the country have already ordered a huge number of copies from us. ❷ Our shipping department will start delivering orders at the beginning of next month. Then on the night before the novel's official debut, we will be holding a special celebration at the Schneider Memorial Center. ❸ I need some assistance preparing for the celebration, so if you're not too busy and have time to help, please contact me as soon as possible. Thank you.

📝 問題71-73は次の話に関するものです。

W: ご出席いただきありがとうございます。これは新刊の East Slope 冒険物語を1か月後に発行する前の最後の販促会議です。この6か月間、この小説の宣伝に大いに取り組んできたこともあり、国内各地の書店から膨大な数の注文が来ています。出荷部は来月初めから注文の配送を始めます。そして小説の公式発売日の前夜、Schneider Memorial Center にて特別祝賀会を開催します。祝賀会の準備に人手が必要なので、もしあまりお忙しくなくてお手伝いいただける時間がありましたら、なるべく早くご連絡ください。よろしくお願いいたします。

✏️ □promotional meeting 販売促進会議　□adventure 冒険　□book seller 書店　□across the country 国中の
□a huge number of 大多数の　□copy（本などの）部　□shipping department 配送部門　□debut 初登場
□contact A as soon as possible 早急に A に連絡する

---

71. ★★☆☆☆

Where does the speaker most likely work?

(A) At a bookstore
(B) At an advertising agency
(C) At a print shop
(D) At a publishing company

話し手はどこで働いていると考えられますか。

(A) 書店
(B) 広告代理店
(C) 印刷所
(D) 出版社

 話し手は❶で「新刊を発行する前の販促会議」と述べており、この話し手の会社が本を発行する会社、つまり出版社だとわかる。以上より正解は **(D)**。

 □print shop 印刷店（所）

72. ★★★☆☆

What will happen at the start of next month?

(A) Opening hours will be lengthened.
(B) The product will be distributed.
(C) An advertising campaign will launch.
(D) An anniversary will be celebrated.

来月の初めに何がありますか。

(A) 開店時間が長くなる。
(B) 商品が配送される。
(C) 宣伝活動が始まる。
(D) 記念日が祝われる。

 話し手は❷で「出荷部が来月初めから注文の配送を始める」と述べている。以上から、来月から話し手の会社の製品である本の出荷が始まることがわかる。この出荷を be distributed と言い換えた **(B)** が正解。distribute には、商品が配給されて市場に流通する、というニュアンスが含まれている。

✎ □lengthen ～を長くする　□distribute ～を配送する、流通させる　□launch 始まる

---

73. ★★★★★

What does the speaker ask for help with?

(A) Planning an author lecture
(B) Promoting a new store location
(C) Preparing for an event
(D) Setting up new equipment

話し手は何を手伝ってほしいと言っていますか。

(A) 著者の講演を計画すること。
(B) 新店舗を宣伝すること。
(C) イベントの準備をすること。
(D) 新しい設備を調整すること。

 話し手は❸で「祝賀会準備の手伝いが必要なので、忙しくなければ連絡してほしい」と伝えている。以上より、❸の celebration を event と言い換えた **(C)** が正解。

✎ □set up ～を設定する、調整する

PART 4

TEST 3

	1回目	2回目	3回目
71.			
72.			
73.			

 71. (D)　72. (B)　73. (C)

Questions 74 through 76 refer to the following telephone message.

📝 問題74-76は次の電話のメッセージに関するものです。

M: Hello, this is Bert Ferrall, and I am calling at 10 o'clock on Tuesday morning. ❶I rent apartment 4G in the Belmont Park complex. ❷Due to the heavy rain we had last night, a lot of water came in around the living room window. ❸As you know, this is just the beginning of the rainy season, so it needs to be fixed urgently. I believe this kind of maintenance is covered under the rental agreement. ❹Please get back to me as soon as possible and let me know when you can come. Thanks very much.

M: こんにちは、Bert Ferrall です。火曜日の朝10時にお電話しています。私は Belmont Park 棟のアパート4G を借りています。昨晩の大雨のせいでリビングの窓の周辺から水がたくさん入ってきてしまいました。ご存じのとおり、雨季は始まったばかりですので、すぐに直していただく必要があります。この手の管理は賃貸借契約の中で補償されると思います。できるだけ早く折り返しいただいて、いつ来られるか教えてください。よろしくお願いいたします。

✏️ □complex（アパート、マンションなどの）集合住宅　□due to ～が原因で　□fix ～を修理する　□urgently 早急に
□this kind of この手の～　□cover ～を補償する　□under ～のもとで　□rental agreement 賃貸借契約
□get back to ～に返事する　□as soon as possible できるだけ早く

---

74. ★★★☆☆

Who most likely is the speaker?

(A) A tenant
(B) A carpenter
(C) A repairperson
(D) A home owner

話し手は誰であると考えられますか。

(A) 貸借人
(B) 大工
(C) 修理工
(D) 家主

🔍 話し手は❶で「アパートを借りている」ことに言及しているので、アパートの賃借人であることがわかる。これを意味する **(A)** が正解。tenant は住居の他に、商業用施設を借りている場合にも使うので押さえておこう。

✏️ □tenant 賃借人　□carpenter 大工　□repairperson 修理技術者　□home owner 家主、大家

75. ★★★★★

What is the purpose of the call?	電話の目的は何ですか。
(A) To make an appointment	(A) 予約をすること。
(B) To settle a bill	(B) 支払いをすること。
(C) To ask for advice	(C) 助言を求めること。
(D) To report a problem	**(D)** 問題を報告すること。

 話し手は❷で「大雨でリビングに水が入ってきた」と話し、❸で「すぐに修理してほしい」と話しているため、この電話で問題について伝えていることがわかる。以上より、正解は **(D)**。

 □settle a bill 支払いをする　□ask for ～を求める

---

76. ★★★★★

What does the caller request?	電話の発信者は何を求めていますか。
(A) A product manual	(A) 製品の取扱説明書
(B) A return call	**(B)** 折り返しの電話
(C) A full refund	(C) 全額返金
(D) A replacement	(D) 交換品

まず電話の発信者とは、このトークを話している話し手自身が、留守番電話に向かって "Hello" と切り出していることから、話し手＝発信者の関係だとわかる。次に、話し手は❹で「早めに折り返し電話してほしい」と伝えている。以上より、正解は **(B)**。

□refund 払い戻し　□replacement 交換品

	1回目	2回目	3回目
74.			
75.			
76.			

74. (A)　75. (D)　76. (B)

Questions 77 through 79 refer to the following advertisement.

W: ❶I'm Julia Adachi, owner of Adachi Ace Cars. ❷We have been Wellington's number one choice in auto sales for the last decade. Come by any one of our five Wellington locations to see the state's largest selection of new and used cars and trucks. ❸Moreover, we're proud to announce the introduction of our new tire care service. To launch our new service, we're offering a special promotional offer for this month only. ❹Purchase four new tires for your vehicle, and we'll fit them for free. ❺How can you pass up this opportunity?

📝 問題77-79は次の広告に関するものです。

W: Adachi Ace 自動車のオーナーの Julia Adachi です。当社は Wellington でこの10年間、自動車販売の一番手です。Wellington にある5つの店舗のいずれかにご来店いただき、州で最大の新車、中古車、トラックの取り揃えをご覧ください。そして、タイヤのお手入れの新サービスの開始を胸を張ってご案内いたします。新サービスの開始にあたり、今月に限り特別販売価格でご提供しております。新品のタイヤを4本ご購入いただきますと、無料で取り付けをいたします。この機会をお見逃しなく。

✏️ □number one choice 一番人気　□for the last decade この10年で　□the largest selection of 最大の品揃えの　□used car 中古車　□moreover さらに　□be proud to *do* 自信を持って〜する　□introduction 導入　□care 手入れ　□launch 〜を開始する　□promotional offer 販売促進のための価格　□pass up 〜を見逃す　□opportunity 機会

---

77. ★★☆☆☆

What type of business is being advertised?

(A) A cleaning service
(B) A car repair shop
(C) A hardware shop
(D) An auto dealership

どのような種類の事業が宣伝されていますか。

(A) 清掃サービス
(B) 自動車修理店
(C) 金物屋
(D) 自動車販売店

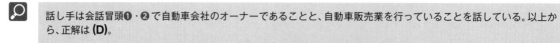

🔍 話し手は会話冒頭❶・❷で自動車会社のオーナーであることと、自動車販売業を行っていることを話している。以上から、正解は **(D)**。

✏️ □hardware shop 金物屋　□auto dealership 自動車販売店

78. ★★☆☆☆

According to the advertisement, what has the company recently done?

(A) Introduced a new service
(B) Changed its hours of operation
(C) Opened a new office
(D) Remodeled its branch

広告によると、会社は最近何をしましたか。

(A) 新しいサービスを開始した。
(B) 営業時間を変更した。
(C) 新しい営業所を開設した。
(D) 支店を改装した。

🔍 話し手は❸で「新たなタイヤのお手入れサービスをご案内」と述べている。これをシンプルに表現した **(A)** が正解。

✎ □hours of operation 営業時間　□remodel ～を改装する　□branch 支店

---

79. ★★★☆☆

What does the speaker mean when she says, "How can you pass up this opportunity"?

(A) She does not understand why a decision was made.
(B) She wants the listeners to change a schedule.
(C) She predicts a rival company will steal market share.
(D) She believes the offer is a great deal for customers.

"How can you pass up this opportunity" と言う際、話し手は何を意味していますか。

(A) なぜ決定が下されたか理解できない。
(B) 聞き手に予定を変更してもらいたい。
(C) 競合他社が市場のシェアを奪うと予想している。
(D) 提供は顧客にとってお得な取引きだと思っている。

🔍 意図を問われている表現❺はトークの最後にあり、「この機会をお見逃しなく」という意味である。この直前の❹を見ると「新品タイヤを4本購入すると取り付けが無料」と伝えている。つまり、❺はお客様にとって見逃せないようなおトクなサービスであることを意図した発言だとわかる。これを言い換えた **(D)** が正解。

✎ □predict ～と予想する　□rival company 競合他社　□market share 市場占有率、市場シェア
□great deal お得な取引

	1回目	2回目	3回目
77.			
78.			
79.			

🚩 **77. (D)　78. (A)　79. (D)**

163

Questions 80 through 82 refer to the following telephone message.

W: ❶Hello, Mr. Eisenhower. This is Sylvia Campbell. ❷Yesterday I was very happy to meet you to talk about a contract with your company. ❸Our accounts department will meet your request, and the rate for ground shipping within the state will be lowered. You mentioned that your company has a plan to expand into other states and countries in North America. ❹I talked with our international department and they said that our company is currently offering special rates on international shipping. ❺If you're interested in this promotion, please give me a call sometime this week, as the discount expires on Friday.

📝 問題80-82は次の電話のメッセージに関するものです。

W: こんにちは、Eisenhower さん。こちらは Sylvia Campbell です。昨日は御社との契約についてお会いしてお話しすることができ、大変うれしく思っております。弊社の会計部門が御社のご要望にお応えしまして、州内の地上配送価格の引き下げをいたします。御社は他の州や北米の他の国に事業を広げる計画があるとお話しされていました。弊社の国際部門と話したところ、弊社が現在、国際配送を特別価格で提供していることが確認できました。このキャンペーンにご関心をお寄せいただけましたら、割引は金曜日までしていますので、今週中のどこかでお電話ください。

✏️ □be happy to *do* ～することをうれしく思う　□contract with ～との契約　□accounts department 会計部門
□rate 料金　□ground shipping 地上配送　□lower (価格など) を下げる　□mention ～と言う
□expand into ～に拡大する、発展する　□be interested in ～に興味がある　□promotion (販売促進の) キャンペーン
□expire (期限が) 切れる

---

80. ★★★☆☆

Why did the speaker meet with Mr. Eisenhower?

(A) To discuss an agreement
(B) To promote a new product
(C) To prepare for a presentation
(D) To organize a special promotion

話し手はなぜ Eisenhower さんと会いましたか。

(A) 合意について話し合うため。
(B) 新製品を宣伝するため。
(C) 説明の準備をするため。
(D) 特別キャンペーンを企画するため。

🔍 話し手は❶で Eisenhower さんに話しかけ、❷で「昨日は契約について話せてよかった」と述べている。そして❸で Eisenhower さんの要望に応じるという発言もしていることから、話し手は昨日 Eisenhower さんとある合意について話をしたと考えられる。以上より、正解は **(A)**。

✏️ □agreement 合意　□promote ～を宣伝する　□organize ～を運営する、企画する

81. ★★★★★

What does the speaker offer Mr. Eisenhower?

(A) A dinner invitation
(B) A free product sample
(C) A promotional discount
(D) A job opportunity

話し手は Eisenhower さんに何を提供しますか。

(A) 夕食への招待
(B) 無料の製品見本
(C) キャンペーン割引
(D) 仕事の機会

 話し手は❹で「現在国際配送について特別価格で提供している」と話している。ここから、特別価格＝通常より安い価格だということがわかる。これを promotional discount と言い換えた **(C)** が正解。

 □promotional キャンペーンの

---

82. ★★★★★

According to the speaker, what must Mr. Eisenhower do before Friday?

(A) Cancel a subscription
(B) Pay a deposit
(C) Renew a contract
(D) Make a decision

話し手によると Eisenhower さんは金曜日までに何をしなければなりませんか。

(A) 購読を解約する。
(B) 保証金を支払う。
(C) 契約を更新する。
(D) 決定を下す。

 話し手は❺で「キャンペーンに興味があれば、割引が金曜日までなので、今週中に連絡してほしい」と伝えている。つまり、Eisenhower さんは今週金曜日までにキャンペーンに申し込むか決断して連絡する必要があることがわかる。以上より正解は **(D)**。このトーク内では契約に関する話題が出てきているが、契約を更新することには触れられていないので (C) は不正解。

 □subscription 定期購読　□deposit 保証料金　□renew 〜を更新する

PART 4

TEST 3

	1回目	2回目	3回目
80.			
81.			
82.			

 80. (A)　81. (C)　82. (D)

Questions 83 through 85 refer to the following advertisement.

📝 問題83-85は次の広告に関するものです。

M: In today's world, you have to stand out. ❶Whether you have an important interview or business deal, or you simply just enjoy looking smart, Kirkton Ford Tailors has what you're looking for. ❷Everything we offer is made to order, so you can be sure no one else will have the same style as you. Make an appointment with us, and we'll find the look that's right for you. ❸Select from classic or modern styles with more than 50 fabrics covering all seasons. ❹And if you are looking for an extra special fabric, we can order directly from our trusted producers around the world. For an individual consultation with our experienced staff, please call us at 777-9965 or go online at kirktontailors.org.

M: このご時世においては存在感を放っていなければなりません。重要な面接や商談があるときでも、ただおしゃれを楽しむときでも、Kirkton Ford 洋服店なら、お探しの物が見つかります。当店が販売するものは全てオーダーメイドのため、誰もお客様と同じスタイルになることはないと思って間違いありません。まずはご予約ください。お客様にぴったりの装いをご用意いたします。クラシックからモダンなスタイルまで、どの季節にも合う50以上の生地と合わせてお選びください。もしさらに特別な生地をお探しでしたら、私たちの信頼する世界中の生産者から、直接お取り寄せいたします。当店の経験豊かなスタッフとの個別相談は、777-9965までお電話いただくか、オンラインの kirktontailors.org にアクセスください。

✏️ □stand out 目立つ　□business deal 業務上の取引　□simply 単に　□look smart おしゃれをする
□made to order オーダーメイドの、受注生産品の　□no one else 他の誰も〜ない　□the same A as 〜と同じ A
□look ファッションスタイル　□right for 〜に適した　□fabric 生地　□cover 〜を対象とする
□trusted 信頼している　□individual consultation 個別相談　□experienced 経験豊富な

83.

What is being advertised?

(A) Custom-made suits
(B) Handmade leather goods
(C) Wedding attire rental
(D) Shoes for special purposes

何を宣伝していますか。

(A) カスタムメイドのスーツ
(B) 手作りの革製品
(C) ウェディング用貸衣装
(D) 特別な用途の靴

🔍 話し手は❶で「面接や商談があるときやおしゃれを楽しむときには当店を」と幅広い用途に言及し、その後❷で「オーダーメイドである」、❸で「どの季節にも合う生地から選ぶ」と言っているので、服装に関わるものであることがわかる。以上より、正解は **(A)**。(C) はウェディングもシーンとして考えられないことはないが、貸衣装ではなく、オーダーメイドで製作するものと言っているので、ここでは不正解。

✏️ □custom-made 顧客特注品の　□handmade 手作りの　□attire 衣装　□for special purpose 特別用途の

84. ★★★★☆

What is highlighted about the service?

(A) All goods are unique.
(B) The first fitting is complimentary.
(C) Fabrics and leather are from organic sources.
(D) Cotton and wool are hand dyed.

サービスでは何が強調されていますか。

(A) 商品は全て一点ものである。
(B) 初めの仮縫いは無料である。
(C) 生地と革はオーガニック由来のものである。
(D) 綿と毛糸は手染めである。

 話し手は❷で「オーダーメイドなので他の人と同じスタイルにはならない」と述べている。ここから、商品が全て一点ものであると強調していることがわかる。これを unique と言い換えた **(A)** が正解。設問で強調されているものが問われる場合、everything、whatever、all、no one や exact、very、never、ever のほかに疑問の形を用いた反語表現 (Who will recognize such a tiny difference? など) がヒントになることがある。

✎ □fitting 仮縫い　□complimentary 無料の　□organic source オーガニック原料　□cotton 綿　□wool 毛、ウール
□hand dyed 手染めの

---

85. ★★★★☆

What is mentioned about the fabrics?

(A) Some of them are not waterproof.
(B) Some of them are imported.
(C) They are colorful.
(D) They can be ordered online.

生地について何が言及されていますか。

(A) 防水ではないものがある。
(B) 輸入されているものがある。
(C) 色彩に富んでいる。
(D) オンラインで注文ができる。

 話し手は❹で「世界中から生地を取り寄せることができる」と話している。ここから、輸入品も扱っていると考えられる。これを言い換えた **(B)** が正解。(A)、(C) も多様な生地であれば可能性はあるかもしれないが、トーク内では言及がないため、いずれも不正解。

✎ □waterproof 防水の　□import 〜を輸入する

	1回目	2回目	3回目
83.			
84.			
85.			

🚩 **83. (A)　84. (A)　85. (B)**

Questions 86 through 88 refer to the following announcement.

M: As we get further along in planning, we've realized that we need help in supervising this project in every way. ❶So, we've been searching for a new manager of product development. ❷Alegra Wallace worked as a project director for a number of years before becoming head of production at Russel Industries and later at Ascot Software. ❸Her leadership got both companies through a rough time, and now they have a great reputation in the high technology industry. She'll be with us until the end of this project. ❹From next week, she'll be having face-to-face meetings with team members to analyze our project. ❺So please call me in order to schedule yours.

📝 問題86-88は次のお知らせに関するものです。

M: 計画を進めるにつれ、このプロジェクトをあらゆる点で監督するのに助けが必要であると感じました。そのため、当社は製品開発の新しい主任を探してきました。Alegra Wallace さんは数年間プロジェクトの指揮を務め、Russel Industries 社と、それに次いで Ascot Software 社で生産部長になりました。そのリーダーシップによって両社とも困難な時期を乗り越え、現在ではハイテク業界で高い評価を得ています。彼女はこのプロジェクトの終了まで我々のところにいる予定です。プロジェクトを分析するため、来週からチームのメンバーと対面の打ち合わせをします。それぞれの日時を決めるので、私までお電話をください。

✏️ □get along 先に進む　□realize ～であると理解する　□supervise ～を監督する　□search for ～を探す
□work as ～として務める　□a number of 複数の、いくつかの　□head of ～部門の上長
□a rough time 困難な時期　□reputation 評判、うわさ　□industry 業界
□face-to-face meeting 対面式の打ち合わせ　□analyze ～を分析する　□in order to *do* ～するため

---

86. ★★★☆☆

What is the purpose of the announcement?

(A) To update a policy
(B) To announce a new plan
(C) To introduce a new colleague
(D) To set up a new team

お知らせの目的は何ですか。

(A) 方針を改定すること。
(B) 新しい計画を発表すること。
(C) 新しい同僚を紹介すること。
(D) 新しいチームを作ること。

🔍 話し手は❶で、人材を探してきたと切り出し、❷・❸で Alegra Wallace さんの紹介と彼女の経歴に触れている。ここから、新たに加わった人員を同僚に紹介していることがわかる。以上より正解は **(C)**。

✏️ □update ～を更新する　□set up ～を作る

87. ★★★★☆

What does the speaker mention about Alegra Wallace?

(A) She has already shown her competence.
(B) She is an experienced software designer.
(C) She has started many businesses.
(D) She is a retired engineer.

話し手は Alegra Wallace さんについて何と言っていますか。

(A) 既に適性を証明している。
(B) 経験の豊かなソフトウェアデザイナーである。
(C) 多くの事業を立ち上げた。
(D) 引退したエンジニアである。

話し手が❸で、Alegra Wallace さんの以前の職場でのパフォーマンスについて「そのリーダーシップによって両社とも困難な時期を乗り越え、現在ではハイテク業界で高い評価を得ている」と話していることから、既に仕事の適性があることがわかる。以上から、これを competence（適性・能力）という語を用いて表した **(A)** が正解。(B) は経験はあるものの、ソフトウェアデザイナーとしての経験に関する言及はないため不正解。

□competence 適性、能力　□experienced 経験のある　□retired 引退した

---

88. ★★★★☆

What will the speaker do for each listener?

(A) Edit a report
(B) Arrange a meeting
(C) Make a phone call
(D) Give a job evaluation

話し手は聞き手に何をしますか。

(A) 報告書を編集する。
(B) 会議を設定する。
(C) 電話をする。
(D) 仕事の評価を行う。

話し手は❹・❺で、「Alegra Wallace さんとの対面ミーティングのスケジュール調整をするので電話してほしい」と言っている、ここから、ミーティングのスケジュール調整＝会議の設定、とわかるので、これを言い換えた **(B)** が正解。(C) は電話をかけるのが話し手ではなく聞き手の方なので不正解。

□edit 〜を編集する　□arrange 〜を設定する　□job evaluation 職務評価

	1回目	2回目	3回目
86.			
87.			
88.			

86. (C)　87. (A)　88. (B)

Questions 89 through 91 refer to the following excerpt from a meeting.

📝 問題89-91は次の会議の一部に関するものです。

W: Thank you for coming to this staff meeting, even though I called it so abruptly. ❶The prolonged negotiations in which we proposed the development of a new product for the Gelda Cosmetics brand have finally been concluded. ❷As a result of your efforts, ❸we need to start putting our plans into action. The first thing we need to do is to seek the perspectives of outsiders on our product idea. ❹Please think of ways to effectively gather prospective consumers' responses. For instance, we can ask them on social networking services if they would buy our product.

W: あまりに急な招集をしたのにもかかわらず、このスタッフ会議にお集まりくださってありがとうございます。Gelda Cosmetics ブランド向けの新製品開発の提案をした長期に渡る交渉がようやく落ち着きました。皆さんの努力の結果として、計画を実行に移し始める必要があります。まずするべきことは、当社の製品アイディアについての外部の人の視点を調べることです。どうすれば将来のお客様の反応を効果的に集めることができるか考えてください。例えば、当社の製品を購入するかどうか SNS で尋ねることもできるでしょう。

✏️ □abruptly 急に　□prolonged 長期化した　□negotiation 交渉　□propose ～を提案する　□conclude ～を終える
□as a result of ～の結果として　□put a plan into action 計画を実行に移す　□seek ～を探す　□perspective 視点
□outsider 外部の人　□effectively 効果的に　□gather ～を集める　□prospective 将来有望な
□for instance 例えば
□social networking service SNS (ソーシャルネットワークサービス：インターネット上の交流サイト)

---

89. ★★★★☆

What business does the speaker most likely work in?

(A) Cosmetics manufacturing
(B) Importing and exporting
(C) Corporate accounting
(D) Offline marketing

話し手はどの事業に従事していると考えられますか。

(A) 化粧品の製造
(B) 輸出入
(C) 企業会計
(D) オフラインマーケティング

🔍 話し手は❶である化粧品ブランドの新商品開発に関わる交渉について言及していることから、化粧品に関わる業務であることがわかる。以上から正解は **(A)**。この問題は「化粧品ブランドの新商品について交渉」という内容から、この業界に関わる事業と推測する視点が重要。

✏️ □corporate accounting 企業会計
□offline marketing オフラインマーケティング (インターネットを使わない直接対話式のマーケティング)

90. ★★★★☆

What does the speaker mean when she says, "As a result of your efforts"?

(A) Sufficient employees have been hired for a project.
(B) A business partnership has been agreed.
(C) A persistent problem has been fixed.
(D) Salaries will be raised.

話し手が "As a result of your efforts" と言う際、何を意味していますか。

(A) プロジェクトのために十分な数の従業員が雇われた。
(B) 事業提携が認められた。
(C) 続いていた問題が解決した。
(D) 給与が上げられる。

 意図を問われている箇所❷は「皆さんの努力の結果として」という意味である。この前後を見ると、❶新商品開発に関する交渉を行う➡❷皆さんの努力の結果➡❸計画を実行に移すという流れになっている。計画を実行できる＝提案が受け入れられ、交渉が締結した、と考えることができる。以上から、交渉相手との関係構築が合意に至ったことを言い換えて表した **(B)** が正解。

 □sufficient 十分な　□persistent 継続していた　□fix 〜を修復する　□raise salaries 給料を上げる

---

91. ★★★★★

What does the speaker ask the listeners to do?

(A) Prepare for online advertisements
(B) Examine the buyers' feedback
(C) Decide on the price of the product
(D) Consider how to survey consumers

話し手は聞き手に何をするように求めていますか。

(A) インターネット広告の準備をする。
(B) 購入者の感想を精査する。
(C) 製品の価格を決定する。
(D) 消費者の調査方法を考える。

 話し手は聞き手に❹で「どうすれば将来のお客様の反応を効果的に集めることができるか考えてほしい」と伝えている。つまり、お客様の反応を集める＝消費者を調査する方法を考えてほしい、と言えるので、その言い換えを表した **(D)** が正解。この (D) Consider how to survey consumers と❹think of ways to effectively gather prospective consumers' responses の言い換えは、文字でも、リスニングでもしっかり認識できるようにしておこう。

 □examine 〜を確認する　□decide on 〜について決定する

	1回目	2回目	3回目
89.			
90.			
91.			

 89. (A)　90. (B)　91. (D)

Questions 92 through 94 refer to the following excerpt from a meeting.

M: ❶I'd like to start today's meeting by welcoming a new accountant, Estrella Jimenez to our medical facility. ❷Ms. Jimenez has more than 15 years' experience as an accountant. ❸But she will be more than that. ❹With the ability to speak Spanish, her first official duty here at Cribbon Health Clinic will be to help negotiate a medicine contract with one of our Spain-based providers. ❺Tomorrow, there will be a welcoming party for Ms. Jimenez, beginning at 6 P.M. in the conference room on the sixth floor. I hope you will all join us for that.

問題92-94は次の会議の一部に関するものです。

M: 今日の会議は当診療所の新しい会計士 Estrella Jimenez さんを歓迎することから始めたいと思います。Jimenez さんは会計士として15年以上の経験をお持ちです。でも、それだけではありません。スペイン語を話す能力で、この Cribbon 診療所での最初の任務はスペインを拠点とする供給者の一つとの医薬品に関する契約交渉のサポートをすることです。明日 Jimenez さんの歓迎会を6階の会議室で午後6時から行います。皆さん全員にご参加いただけるとうれしいです。

✎ ☐accountant 会計士　☐with the ability to *do* 〜する能力をもって　☐official duty 任務
☐negotiate a contract 契約について取り決める　☐Spain-based スペインを拠点とする　☐provider 供給業者
☐welcoming party 歓迎会

---

92. ★★★☆☆

Where does the speaker most likely work?

(A) At a pharmaceutical company
(B) At a hotel
(C) At a drug store
(D) At a hospital

話し手はどこで働いていると考えられますか。

(A) 製薬会社
(B) ホテル
(C) ドラッグストア
(D) 病院

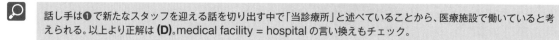

話し手は❶で新たなスタッフを迎える話を切り出す中で「当診療所」と述べていることから、医療施設で働いていると考えられる。以上より正解は **(D)**。medical facility = hospital の言い換えもチェック。

✎ ☐pharmaceutical company 製薬会社

93. ★★★★☆

Why does the speaker say, "she will be more than that"?

(A) To explain a salary increase
(B) To warn against making too many requests
(C) To clarify an employee's schedule
(D) To emphasize a set of skills

なぜ話し手は "she will be more than that" と言っていますか。

(A) 昇給について説明するため。
(B) 過多な要望を寄せることに対して警告するため。
(C) 従業員の予定を明らかにするため。
(D) 一連の技能を強調するため。

意図を問われている箇所❸は「でも彼女はそれだけではない」という意味になっている。その前後を見ると、❷Jimenez さんは会計士として15年以上の経験がある➡❸それだけではない➡❹堪能なスペイン語で現地サプライヤーとの契約関連の仕事をしてもらう、とある。ここから、会計士以外にも語学力、交渉力等さまざまなスキルを持っていることを強調しているとわかる。その彼女のひとそろいのスキルを a set of skills と表現した **(D)** が正解。

□warn against 〜に対して警告する　□clarify 〜を明確にする　□emphasize 〜を強調する
□a set of 一連の、ひとそろいの

94. ★★☆☆☆

What event will take place tomorrow?

(A) A welcoming reception
(B) A retirement celebration
(C) A grand opening party
(D) An awards ceremony

明日、どんな行事が開催されますか。

(A) 歓迎会
(B) 退職祝い
(C) 新規開店パーティ
(D) 授賞式

話し手は❺で「明日歓迎会を開く」と言っているので、正解は **(A)**。party = reception と捉えても OK。

□retirement celebration 退職のお祝い　□grand opening 新規開店　□award 賞

	1回目	2回目	3回目
92.			
93.			
94.			

 92. (D)　93. (D)　94. (A)

Questions 95 through 97 refer to the following announcement and schedule.

W: ❶For those who are fans of the Canadian rock group Son of Gregor, we have good news! ❷They have officially announced that they will add an extra concert to their Rock the West Coast Tour! The tour was originally scheduled to start in Seattle and go from Portland to San Diego with stops in Los Angeles and San Jose. ❸Because all of the original tickets have already sold out but so many fans online have been demanding more concerts, they have added a stop in San Francisco! ❹The band plans to stop there for a concert instead of going straight to San Jose from Los Angeles as was originally planned. Get your tickets now, since they're sure to sell out quick!

City	Date
Portland	May 6
❺Los Angeles	May 10
❻San Jose	May 16
San Diego	May 19

問題95-97は次のお知らせと予定表に関するものです。

W: カナダのロックグループ Son of Gregor のファンの皆さまに良いお知らせがあります。彼らの Rock the West Coast Tour で追加公演を行うことが公式に発表されました。当初の予定ではツアーは Seattle で始まり、Portland から Los Angeles と San Jose に寄って、San Diego で終わることになっていました。初めのチケットは既に完売しましたが、インターネットで多くのファンが追加の公演を求めたため、San Francisco に寄ることが追加されました。バンドは当初予定していた Los Angeles から San Jose へ直行することをやめ、そこに立ち寄ります。チケットは間違いなくすぐに売り切れるので、今すぐに手に入れましょう。

都市	日程
Portland	5月6日
Los Angeles	5月10日
San Jose	5月16日
San Diego	5月19日

□those who ～する人　□fan of ～のファン　□rock group ロック音楽のグループ　□extra 追加の
□be originally scheduled to do もともと～する予定だ　□demand ～を要求する　□stop 立ち寄り
□instead of ～の代わりに　□go straight to ～へ直行する　□as (it) was originally planned 当初予定していたとおり

95. ★★★☆☆

What is the main purpose of the announcement?

(A) To highlight benefits of a membership
(B) To help a local charity
(C) To update a performance schedule
(D) To announce a venue grand opening

お知らせの主な目的は何ですか。

(A) 会員の特典を強調すること。
(B) 地元の慈善活動を手伝うこと。
(C) 公演日程を更新すること。
(D) 新規会場の開始を発表すること。

🔍 話し手は❶でロックバンド Son of Gregor のファンに向けて、「良いお知らせがある」と切り出し、❷で追加公演の発表があったことを伝えている。以上から、最新スケジュールを案内しているとわかるので、これを言い換えた **(C)** が正解。(C) の update a performance schedule が❷の add an extra concert を指していると捉えよう。

✎ □highlight 〜を強調する　□benefit 特典、利益　□charity チャリティー、慈善事業　□update 〜を更新する　□venue 会場　□grand opening 新規開始、新規開店

---

96. ★★★☆☆

What does the speaker say about the original tickets?

(A) They could not be bought online.
(B) They must be returned.
(C) Their prices were cheaper.
(D) They are sold out.

話し手は最初のチケットについて何と言っていますか。

(A) オンラインで購入できなかった。
(B) 返品しなければならない。
(C) 価格はもっと安かった。
(D) 売り切れた。

🔍 話し手は❸で「最初のチケットは全て売り切れた」と言っているので、正解は **(D)**。この問題はトークの途中でサラッと言って通り過ぎているので、聞き逃さないようにしよう。

---

97. ★★★★★

Look at the graphic. On what date will the band most likely perform in San Francisco?

(A) May 8
(B) May 12
(C) May 16
(D) May 19

図を見てください。バンドが San Francisco で公演するのはどの日であると考えられますか。

(A) 5月8日
(B) 5月12日
(C) 5月16日
(D) 5月19日

🔍 話し手は❸で San Francisco での公演に触れ、❹で「Los Angeles 公演後に San Jose に直行せずに立ち寄って公演を行う」と言っていることから、Los Angeles と San Jose の公演の間に San Francisco 公演を行うことがわかる。次に表を見ると、❺・❻から Los Angeles 公演が5月10日、San Jose 公演が5月16日のため、この間の日程が公演日となることがわかる。以上より、正解は **(B)**。

	1回目	2回目	3回目
95.			
96.			
97.			

 95. (C)　96. (D)　97. (B)

Questions 98 through 100 refer to the following talk and graph.

📝 問題98-100は次の話とグラフに関するものです。

M: Hello, everyone. ❶I'd like to begin by discussing the results of the survey we conducted of ten thousand residents in our city. ❷In the survey, residents were informed that we, the city council, plan to build a monument to try to boost the falling number of domestic and foreign tourists who visit our city each year. Our construction and design specialists proposed five potential locations for the monument, and survey participants were asked to vote for their favorite site. ❸But we have since learned that the proposed site at Nowak Park will be used for a fountain, and that the spot in Pierson Square is too small for our plans. With that in mind, we'll have no choice but to choose the most popular of the remaining options. Let's take a look at the survey results.

M: こんにちは、皆さん。市内在住の1万人を対象に行った調査の結果について話し合うことから始めたいと思います。この調査では、我々、市議会が記念碑を建て、それにより年々減少している国内外からの観光客を増やす計画を立てていることを住民に伝えました。当市の建設とデザインの専門家から記念碑の候補地に5か所の提案がありましたので、調査の参加者に好きな場所を投票していただきました。しかし、その後でNowak公園の提案された場所は噴水に使われることと、Pierson広場は我々の計画には狭すぎることがわかりました。そのことを踏まえた上で、残りの選択肢の中で最も人気のあるものを選ぶことになります。調査結果を見てみましょう。

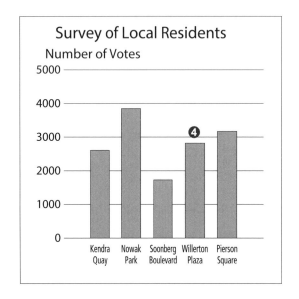

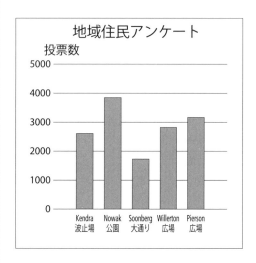

✏️ ☐conduct ～を実行する　☐be informed that ～だと知らされる　☐city council 市議会　☐monument 記念碑
☐boost ～を増やす　☐the falling number of ～の落ち込みつつある数　☐domestic and foreign 国内外の
☐potential 可能性のある　☐participant 参加者　☐favorite 好きな　☐fountain 噴水
☐with that in mind それを考慮して　☐have no choice but to *do* ～せざるを得ない　☐remaining 残っている
☐take a look at ～を見る　☐survey result 調査結果　☐number of votes 投票数

98. ★★★☆☆

Who most likely are the listeners?	聞き手は誰であると考えられますか。
(A) Residents' association members	(A) 地域自治会の会員
(B) City officials	**(B) 市の役人**
(C) Survey respondents	(C) 調査の回答者
(D) Market research specialists	(D) 市場調査の専門家

話し手は❶で「市内在住の1万人を対象に行った調査の結果について話し合うことから始めたい」と述べている。また❷で「我々、市議会は……」と言っていることから、話し手が市議会議員であることもわかる。ここから、聞き手も話し手と同様に市のアンケート結果を管理、共有できて、市議会に出席できる人物だと考えられる。以上より、正解は **(B)**。

□city official 市の役人、市職員　□respondent 回答者

---

99. ★★★★☆

What is indicated about the city?	市についてどんなことが示されていますか。
(A) It has undergone much urban development.	(A) 多くの都市開発が行われてきた。
(B) It has experienced a decline in tourism.	**(B) 観光業の衰退を経験している。**
(C) It had to cancel several construction projects.	(C) いくつかの建設計画を中止しなければならなかった。
(D) It has seen a decrease in residents' satisfaction.	(D) 住民の満足度が下がっていることがわかった。

話し手は❷で「我々、市議会が記念碑を建てることにより、年々減少している国内外からの観光客を増やす計画を立てている」と述べていることから、この市の観光業は衰退していることがわかる。これを言い換えた **(B)** が正解。❷の the falling number of ... tourists と (B) の a decline in tourism の言い換えを押さえておこう。

□undergo ～を経る、経験する　□urban development 都市開発　□decrease 減少

---

100. ★★★★★

Look at the graphic. Which location will most likely be chosen?	図を見てください。どの場所が選ばれると考えられますか。
(A) Kendra Quay	(A) Kendra 波止場
(B) Nowak Park	(B) Nowak 公園
(C) Willerton Plaza	**(C) Willerton 広場**
(D) Pierson Square	(D) Pierson 広場

❸で投票結果を受けて、「投票上位の Nowak 公園と Pierson 広場は他の建設予定やスペースの関係で難しいので、その次に人気のある場所を選ぶ」とある。ここから、グラフで3番目に人気のあるところ❹を見ると、**(C)** が正解だとわかる。❸から「3番目の投票獲得数」という情報を聞き出すことがカギ。

□quay 埠頭、波止場

	1回目	2回目	3回目
98.			
99.			
100.			

🏁 **98. (B)　99. (B)　100. (C)**

PART 4

TEST 3

GO ON TO THE NEXT TEST!

PART **3**&**4**

Test

4

PART 3 Test 4

32. What event is most likely being planned?

(A) A company party
(B) A training workshop
(C) An advertisement screening
(D) A marketing campaign

33. What has the hotel recently done?

(A) Waived a fee
(B) Installed new interior walls
(C) Changed the menu
(D) Renovated its facilities

34. According to the woman, how can the fee be reduced?

(A) By asking more people to attend
(B) By decreasing the length of an event
(C) By changing a food serving method
(D) By changing the date

35. What most likely is the man's job?

(A) A landscape designer
(B) An architect
(C) A gardener
(D) A programmer

36. What does the woman suggest adding to the plan?

(A) A light
(B) More plants
(C) A sculpture
(D) A path

37. What will the man do after receiving the woman's information?

(A) Sign an agreement
(B) Make an image
(C) Purchase materials
(D) Calculate the fee of a service

38. Where most likely are the speakers?

(A) At a stationery store
(B) At an electronics store
(C) At an antique store
(D) At a furniture store

39. What does the woman dislike about the product?

(A) The size
(B) The design
(C) The material
(D) The color

40. What will the man most likely do next?

(A) Show the woman other items
(B) Submit product samples to the woman
(C) Fetch another member of staff
(D) Give the woman delivery information

41. Why does the woman want to sell her vehicle?

(A) She plans to take public transportation.
(B) She has experienced breakdowns a few times.
(C) She will be transferred to a foreign branch.
(D) She needs a larger car.

42. According to the man, why will buyers like the vehicle?

(A) The exterior is in good condition.
(B) The model is currently very popular.
(C) It has brand new leather seats.
(D) It is fuel-efficient.

43. What will the man probably do next?

(A) Measure some fabric
(B) Clean the front seat
(C) Look for contact information
(D) Confirm a price online

GO ON TO THE NEXT PAGE ➡

 32-34 *P. 188*   35-37 *P. 190*   38-40 *P. 192*   41-43 *P. 194*

44. Where is the conversation most likely taking place?

(A) At a fruit shop
(B) At a farm
(C) At a bakery
(D) At a flower shop

45. Why does the man apologize?

(A) A bill was miscalculated.
(B) An order was sent to the wrong address.
(C) A reservation was canceled.
(D) A product has sold out.

46. What does the man suggest?

(A) Ordering in advance
(B) Canceling a party
(C) Calling another shop
(D) Asking a family member for help

47. What do the speakers want to do?

(A) Hire new workers
(B) Invite more guests
(C) Buy some furniture
(D) Prepare an event room

48. What does the man mean when he says, "I'm a bit worried"?

(A) Finding an interpreter is not easy.
(B) Attending two conferences at the same time is impossible.
(C) Using the planned space could cause a problem.
(D) He may not be able to attend the meeting.

49. What does Monica offer to do?

(A) Make the final arrangements
(B) Reschedule the demonstration
(C) Call a technician
(D) Buy some supplies

50. Who is Tanya Reed?

(A) An announcer at an event
(B) A manager of a company
(C) A designer of a Web site
(D) A computer programmer

51. What is unique about the product?

(A) It does not need an external power source.
(B) It can keep more data than any other computer.
(C) It is waterproof.
(D) It is eco-friendly.

52. According to the woman, what will happen in three months?

(A) A device will be on the market.
(B) A distribution center will be opened.
(C) An engineering problem will be solved.
(D) A software developer will be promoted.

53. Why is the woman calling the man?

(A) To get information on a job
(B) To make a proposal
(C) To ask for a discount
(D) To launch a new business

54. What will the company do next month?

(A) Host an orientation
(B) Offer discount coupons
(C) Prepare a presentation
(D) Conduct interviews

55. According to the man, what can the woman find on the company's Web site?

(A) New educational materials
(B) Information on employee benefits
(C) A sales commission calculator
(D) A list of lecturers

44-46 *P. 196*   47-49 *P. 198*   50-52 *P. 200*   53-55 *P. 202*

56. What is the topic of the conversation?

(A) A company picnic
(B) Plans for lunch
(C) Visiting old colleagues
(D) An annual celebration

57. What does the man mean when he says, "That depends"?

(A) He needs to know the start time.
(B) He is not sure of his plans.
(C) He is worried about the weather.
(D) He has a spending limit.

58. What will the woman most likely do next?

(A) Submit invitation cards
(B) Make some phone calls
(C) Book a restaurant
(D) Go to a grocery store

59. What does the man want to do?

(A) Take a cruise
(B) Register for college
(C) Begin his own company
(D) Remodel his store

60. What does the woman suggest?

(A) Getting a second job
(B) Employing an online resource
(C) Applying for a bank loan
(D) Consulting a financial planner

61. What is the man worried about?

(A) High interest rates
(B) Busy work schedules
(C) The price of a service
(D) The security of a homepage

Location	Max Occupancy
Rushden Center	300
Thornton College Gymnasium	700
Grant Athletic Center	800
Shaw Fitness	500

62. Who most likely is the man?

(A) An event planner
(B) A sports team coach
(C) A city official
(D) A maintenance worker

63. What problem does the woman report?

(A) A court was wet.
(B) A venue was double-booked.
(C) A structure was damaged.
(D) An event was canceled.

64. Look at the graphic. Where will the tournament most likely be held?

(A) Rushden Center
(B) Thornton College Gymnasium
(C) Grant Athletic Center
(D) Shaw Fitness

PART 3

TEST 4

GO ON TO THE NEXT PAGE ➡

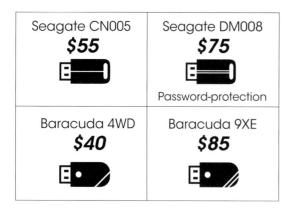

Seagate CN005 **$55** 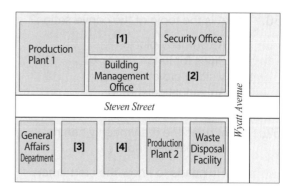	Seagate DM008 **$75** Password-protection
Baracuda 4WD **$40**	Baracuda 9XE **$85**

65. Where is the conversation most likely taking place?

(A) At a delivery company
(B) At a storage company
(C) At an electronics shop
(D) At a computer repair shop

66. What does the woman most likely give the man?

(A) A store flyer
(B) A membership card
(C) A discount voucher
(D) A delivery code

67. Look at the graphic. Which model will the man most likely select?

(A) Seagate CN005
(B) Seagate DM008
(C) Baracuda 4WD
(D) Baracuda 9XE

68. What are the speakers mainly talking about?

(A) A monthly work schedule
(B) An orientation agenda
(C) A job fair
(D) A site inspection

69. According to the woman, what will take place in the afternoon?

(A) A tour of the manufacturing plants
(B) A presentation on new products
(C) A visit to the building management office
(D) A discussion about waste disposal methods

70. Look at the graphic. In which location is the cafeteria most likely located?

(A) [1]
(B) [2]
(C) [3]
(D) [4]

🚩 **65-67** *P. 210*

🚩 **68-70** *P. 212*

71. What type of product is being discussed?

(A) Camping tools
(B) Office heaters
(C) Sports equipment
(D) Clothing

72. According to the speaker, what will the listeners receive?

(A) Completed questionnaires
(B) Sales targets
(C) A product sample
(D) Details of a marketing campaign

73. What are listeners asked to think about?

(A) Arranging items attractively
(B) Ways to cut costs
(C) Suggestions for attracting customers
(D) Possible locations for a shop

74. According to the speaker, why is Goldberg's Clinic currently closed?

(A) Dr. Goldberg is away on vacation.
(B) Doctors have to renew their licenses.
(C) It is moving to a new location.
(D) Its equipment is under repair.

75. What does the speaker say happens on Wednesdays?

(A) A nutrition expert is available.
(B) The office closes early.
(C) Another doctor substitutes for Dr. Goldberg.
(D) Waiting times are longer.

76. Why are first-time patients asked to visit a Web site?

(A) To make a medical appointment
(B) To confirm the new address
(C) To upload questions
(D) To download a required form

77. Where is this announcement taking place?

(A) At a train station
(B) At a bus terminal
(C) On an airplane
(D) At an airport

78. What does the speaker mean when she says, "our attendants have no access to further information"?

(A) She wants to apologize for a power outage.
(B) People should check updates by themselves.
(C) The company's staff have forgotten a password.
(D) Attendants need more technology training.

79. Who should go to Terminal E?

(A) Travelers taking a shuttle bus
(B) Passengers traveling without luggage
(C) Visitors who wish to upgrade their seats
(D) Those heading to foreign destinations

80. What does the speaker mention about Antonio Media?

(A) It has tried to expand abroad.
(B) It sells products made by Gillian World News Agency.
(C) Its new offering will be launched soon.
(D) It has experienced problems with leadership.

81. What does the speaker mean when she says, "Unfortunately it won't happen"?

(A) She will cancel her business trip.
(B) She thinks a product will be unavailable.
(C) She doesn't agree with a project.
(D) She is reporting on a plan's failure.

82. What is indicated about Gillian World News Agency?

(A) Its president left the company.
(B) It received investment funds.
(C) It changed its news sources.
(D) It acquired a company.

GO ON TO THE NEXT PAGE ➡

 71-73 *P. 214*   **74-76** *P. 216*   **77-79** *P. 218*   📗 **80-82** *P. 220*

83. What is the purpose of the talk?

(A) To thank staff members
(B) To look for volunteers
(C) To plan a ceremony
(D) To introduce a new executive

84. Where does the speaker most likely work?

(A) At a hotel
(B) At an apparel company
(C) At a catering firm
(D) At an advertising agency

85. According to the speaker, why was the project beneficial?

(A) It improved morale.
(B) It resulted in an award nomination.
(C) It attracted new customers.
(D) It helped a charitable organization.

86. What are listeners asked to provide?

(A) A work log
(B) A form of identification
(C) A signed employment contract
(D) A vacation schedule

87. What special feature is mentioned about the new digital key?

(A) It can confirm who enters a building.
(B) It can work in numerous branches.
(C) It can be set up by each employee.
(D) It can be used only on new doors.

88. What does the speaker mean when he says, "make sure to pick it up"?

(A) Staff members should review some information.
(B) Staff members should purchase some cards.
(C) Staff members should keep their offices clean.
(D) Staff members should collect their passes soon.

89. Why is the speaker calling?

(A) To report a problem with an order
(B) To give details of a health warning
(C) To apologize for an early billing
(D) To arrange a new delivery date

90. According to the speaker, what caused the issue?

(A) A misprint on an invoice
(B) A relocation of the business
(C) A database error
(D) A mechanical failure

91. What does the speaker say will happen next?

(A) The company will replace some produce.
(B) The business will forward another invoice.
(C) The customer will receive store credit.
(D) The membership number will be changed.

92. What is the main purpose of the broadcast?

(A) To announce a contest
(B) To advertise a local event
(C) To inform listeners of traffic conditions
(D) To provide a weather advisory

93. What will happen on Friday?

(A) Temperatures will go up.
(B) The area will experience light winds.
(C) It will rain.
(D) A cold front will bring snow.

94. Why would listeners send an e-mail?

(A) To share photographs of their area
(B) To see their names on the screen
(C) To contribute data to a report
(D) To register for a contest

Monthly Sales — September

Legend:
- ■ Entropixer 700
- ☐ Onda Cosmica

Salesperson	Entropixer 700	Onda Cosmica
Frank Lee	40	27
Gregory Matson	32	39
Liz Siegel	35	43
Karen Telford	30	30

95. What is the main purpose of the talk?

(A) To suggest ways to improve customer satisfaction
(B) To express gratitude to staff members
(C) To explain the reason for a price decrease
(D) To promote a member of staff

96. According to the speaker, what happened at the beginning of September?

(A) Employees attended a seminar.
(B) Customers received a discount.
(C) Meyer Electronics opened a new store.
(D) Several new products were launched.

97. Look at the graphic. Who will receive the monthly bonus?

(A) Frank Lee
(B) Gregory Matson
(C) Liz Siegel
(D) Karen Telford

BIG SALE

Monday	Team Sports Equipment
Tuesday	Fitness Sports Equipment
Wednesday	Footwear
Thursday	Return to Regular Prices

98. What is limited about this sale?

(A) How long the shop is open
(B) Which brands are available
(C) Which branches will run the promotion
(D) How many items receive the discount

99. What is the discount?

(A) Half off the regular price
(B) Two items for the price of one
(C) Five dollars off every item
(D) Ten dollars for all items

100. Look at the graphic. What product will be on sale on Thursday?

(A) All goods
(B) Team Sports Equipment
(C) Fitness Sports Equipment
(D) Footwear

95-97 *P. 230*

98-100 *P. 232*

Questions 32 through 34 refer to the following conversation.

M: Good afternoon, this is Brian Lee calling from Nancy Wireless. ❶We are having an end-of-year banquet this December and are currently searching for a location for two hundred people. I remember that your hotel held one of our last events and had a marvelous interior. I am wondering whether you have a ballroom to accommodate such a number of guests.

W: We certainly can. ❷A few months ago we remodeled our facility and some of our banquet halls are capable of seating up to three hundred people. Now, let's see on which dates the room is available. At present, it seems that the room can be reserved on any day from the 21st to the 24th. Our standard course menu per person is seventy dollars.

M: That might exceed our budget. By any chance, ❸could you reduce the price?

W: ❹Yes, if you don't mind buffet-style dining, it would be cheaper by more than thirty percent. However, as for the other service charges, I am afraid I can't do much.

M: こんにちは、Nancy Wireless 社の Brian Lee と申します。12月に忘年会がありまして、今200人が入れる場所を探しています。そちらのホテルには当社の直近のイベントを開催していただきましたが、内装が素晴らしかったのを覚えています。この人数を収容できる宴会場はありますか。

W: ご用意がございます。当館は数か月前に施設を改修しまして、300名様までのお席をご利用いただける宴会場もございます。ただいま、会場をいつご利用いただけるかお調べします。現時点ですと、21日から24日でしたら、いつでもご予約いただけそうです。当館の標準的なコースメニューは1名様当たり70ドルです。

M: それだと予算を超えてしまいそうです。どうにか価格を抑えられないでしょうか。

W: そうですね。ビュッフェスタイルのお食事でよろしければ、30パーセント以上はお安くなります。しかし、その他のサービス料については、恐れ入りますが、お応えができかねます。

□end-of-year 年末の　□banquet 夕食会　□search for 〜を探す　□marvelous 素晴らしい　□interior 内装　□ballroom 宴会場、ダンス場　□accommodate 〜を収容する　□a number of たくさんの、複数の　□remodel 〜を改装する　□facility 施設　□capable of 〜する能力がある、〜できる　□seat 〜を着席させる　□up to 上限〜まで　□at present 現在　□course コース料理　□exceed 〜を超過する　□by any chance もしかして　□buffet-style dining ビュッフェ形式の食事　□as for 〜に関して　□service charge サービス料金　□I am afraid すまないが　□do much 大いに尽力する

32. ★★☆☆☆

What event is most likely being planned?

(A) A company party
(B) A training workshop
(C) An advertisement screening
(D) A marketing campaign

どのようなイベントが予定されていると考えられますか。

(A) 会社のパーティー
(B) 研修会
(C) 広告審査
(D) マーケティングキャンペーン

🔍 会話の冒頭❶で男性が「12月に忘年会を行う」と述べている。ここから、パーティーのようなイベントだと考えられる。以上から正解は **(A)**。

✎ □training workshop 研修　□screening 審査

---

33. ★★☆☆☆

What has the hotel recently done?

(A) Waived a fee
(B) Installed new interior walls
(C) Changed the menu
(D) Renovated its facilities

ホテルは最近何をしましたか。

(A) 手数料を免除した。
(B) 新しい内壁を取り付けた。
(C) メニューを変更した。
(D) 施設を改装した。

🔍 女性は❷でホテルが最近施設を改修したと述べ、その後で詳細について話している。以上から、この中の remodel を renovate と言い換えた **(D)** が正解。

✎ □waive 〜を免除する　□install 〜を設置する　□renovate 〜を改装する

---

34. ★★★★☆

According to the woman, how can the fee be reduced?

(A) By asking more people to attend
(B) By decreasing the length of an event
(C) By changing a food serving method
(D) By changing the date

女性によると、どうすれば料金を下げることができますか。

(A) より多くの人に参加をお願いする。
(B) イベントの時間を短くする。
(C) 食事の提供方法を変更する。
(D) 日程を変更する。

🔍 男性が❸で「価格を下げられないか」と尋ねたのに対し、女性が❹で「ビュッフェにすると価格が安くなる」と述べている。ここから、食事をセルフ式の提供方法に変更することで価格が安くなることがわかる。以上から正解は **(C)**。❹の buffet が正解の選択肢では食事の提供方法（food serving method）という表現に言い換えられていることを押さえておこう。

✎ □decrease 〜を減らす　□length 長さ　□serving method 提供方法

	1回目	2回目	3回目
32.			
33.			
34.			

 32. (A)　33. (D)　34. (C)

Questions 35 through 37 refer to the following conversation.

M: Hello, Susan. ❶Sorry I couldn't take your call earlier, but I know that you wanted to discuss the front yard design of your house. Was there something wrong?

W: No. ❷It's just that I came up with an idea to make the area look better. ❸How about adding a stone walkway all the way to the entrance door? I think it might go well with the surrounding shrubbery which you suggested last time.

M: I couldn't agree with you more. ❹If you give me more information regarding the details by Friday, I can include it in the 3-D image. Let's see what we can do afterwards.

📝 問題35-37は次の会話に関するものです。

M: こんにちは、Susan さん。先ほどのお電話に出ることができず、申し訳ありませんでした。ただ、お宅の表の庭のデザインについてお話があるということだったと思います。何か問題がありましたか。

W: いいえ。ただ、もっと見栄えを良くするためのアイデアを思いついただけなんです。石の通路を玄関まで作ってみるなんてどうでしょうか。前回提案していただいた、周りを囲む低木とも合うと思います。

M: 私もそう思います。金曜日までにもっと情報を詳しく知らせていただければ、3D 画像に組み込めます。それから何ができるか考えましょうか。

✏️ □take one's call ～の電話に出る　□front yard 表の庭　□come up with ～を思いつく　□walkway 通路　□all the way to ～までずっと続く　□go well with ～に合う　□surrounding 取り囲む　□shrubbery 低木　□last time 前回　□regarding ～に関する　□detail 詳細　□include ～を含める　□3-D image 立体画像　□afterwards その後

---

35. ⭐⭐⭐☆☆

What most likely is the man's job?

(A) A landscape designer
(B) An architect
(C) A gardener
(D) A programmer

男性の仕事は何であると考えられますか。

(A) 造園デザイナー
(B) 建築家
(C) 庭師
(D) プログラマー

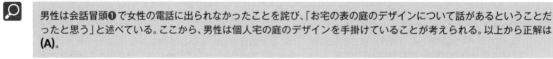

🔍 男性は会話冒頭❶で女性の電話に出られなかったことを詫び、「お宅の表の庭のデザインについて話があるということだったと思う」と述べている。ここから、男性は個人宅の庭のデザインを手掛けていることが考えられる。以上から正解は **(A)**。

✏️ □landscape 造園　□architect 建築家

36. ★★★☆☆

What does the woman suggest adding to the plan?

(A) A light
(B) More plants
(C) A sculpture
(D) A path

女性は計画に何を追加することを提案していますか。

(A) 明かり
(B) より多くの植物
(C) 彫刻
(D) 通り道

🔍 女性は❶で男性から「庭のデザインについて問題があるか」と尋ねられたのに対し、❷で「良くするためのアイデアを思い付いた」と言い、❸で「玄関まで石の通路を加えてみるのはどうだろうか」と提案している。つまり、玄関までの通路に関する提案だとわかる。以上から正解は **(D)**。❸の walkway が正解の選択肢の path に言い換えられている。path は Part 1でも登場する表現なので、しっかり押さえておこう。

✏️ □sculpture 彫刻　□path 通り道、小道

---

37. ★★★★☆

What will the man do after receiving the woman's information?

(A) Sign an agreement
(B) Make an image
(C) Purchase materials
(D) Calculate the fee of a service

男性は女性から情報を受けた後何をしますか。

(A) 同意書に署名する。
(B) 画像を作る。
(C) 材料を購入する。
(D) サービス料を計算する。

🔍 男性は❹で「金曜日までにもっと情報を詳しく知らせてくれれば、3D 画像に組み込める」と言っている。つまり、情報に基づいて画像を作成することがわかる。以上から正解は **(B)**。image は、日本語では概念的な印象や形を意味することが多いが、英語では画像を意味することもある。

✏️ □agreement 合意書　□image 画像　□material 材料、素材　□calculate 〜を計算する　□fee 料金

PART 3

TEST 4

	1回目	2回目	3回目
35.			
36.			
37.			

🚩 **35. (A)　36. (D)　37. (B)**

Questions 38 through 40 refer to the following conversation.

W: Excuse me, ❶I'm searching for a chair just like the one on your left, but I don't think that would fit in my office. ❷Do you have a smaller one in the same color and design?

M: ❸I'm afraid we don't have any smaller chairs in stock now. They are expected to arrive next week. Would you like me to set one aside for you when it comes?

W: I see. ❹I would rather find another design. I need it as soon as possible.

M: ❺Then allow me to recommend another design from our stock. We have a large selection in the other room.

📝 問題38-40は次の会話に関するものです。

W: すみません、その左側の椅子のようなものを探しているのですが、私の事務所には収まらないと思うんです。小さいサイズで色とデザインが同じものはありますか。

M: 申し訳ありませんが、今はこれより小さい椅子の在庫がございません。来週、入荷する予定になっております。到着時にお取り置きしておきましょうか。

W: そうですか。それよりは違うデザインを探したいと思います。出来るだけ早く揃えたいので。

M: それでしたら、在庫の中から別のデザインのものをご紹介させてください。別の部屋に豊富に取り揃えてございますので。

✏️ □search for ～を探す　□fit in ～に収まる　□I'm afraid すまないが　□have A in stock 在庫として A がある
□be expected to *do* ～する予定になっている　□set aside ～を取り置く　□would rather むしろ～したい
□as soon as possible できるだけ早く　□allow A to *do* A に～させる　□a large selection 豊富な品揃え

38.

Where most likely are the speakers?

(A) At a stationery store
(B) At an electronics store
(C) At an antique store
(D) At a furniture store

話し手たちはどこにいると考えられますか。

(A) 文房具店
(B) 電子機器店
(C) 骨董品店
(D) 家具店

🔍 会話冒頭❶・❷で女性が「椅子を探している」「小さいサイズはないか」と家具を探していることがわかる。ここから、この会話は家具店で行われていると考えられる。以上から正解は **(D)**。

✏️ □stationery store 文房具店　□antique 骨董品

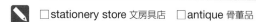

39. ★★★★★

What does the woman dislike about the product?

(A) The size
(B) The design
(C) The material
(D) The color

女性は製品の何が気に入っていませんか。

(A) 大きさ
(B) デザイン
(C) 素材
(D) 色

 女性は❷で「同じデザインで小さいものはないか」と尋ねている。ここから、女性は陳列されている椅子の大きさが気に入らないと考えられる。以上から正解は **(A)**。❷の Do you have a smaller one が聞こえた時点で、「あ、サイズの言及だな」と素早く反応できるようにしよう。

✎ □material 材料、素材

40. ★★★★★

What will the man most likely do next?

(A) Show the woman other items
(B) Submit product samples to the woman
(C) Fetch another member of staff
(D) Give the woman delivery information

男性は次に何をすると考えられますか。

(A) 女性に別の商品を見せる。
(B) 女性に製品サンプルを差し出す。
(C) 他の従業員を連れてくる。
(D) 女性に配送の情報を伝える。

 男性は❷女性の求める同じデザインでサイズが異なる椅子について、❸で現在は在庫がないと述べ、女性は❹で他の物を探す意向を述べている。そして男性は❺で「他の物を薦めたい」と述べている。つまり、男性がそれまで話していた商品とは別のものをこれから女性に見せることが考えられる。以上から正解は **(A)**。

✎ □fetch ～を連れてくる

	1回目	2回目	3回目
38.			
39.			
40.			

 38. (D) 39. (A) 40. (A)

Questions 41 through 43 refer to the following conversation.

W: Hello, Rick. Thanks for taking a look at my car to see whether it needs repair work. ❶I'd like to list it for sale by the end of this season since I need to buy a bigger vehicle.

M: ❷I think buyers will like it because the outside of the vehicle has been well maintained. But I can see small flaws on the leather of the driver's seat, so I strongly recommend having that repaired.

W: Right. Do you know how much it will cost to have new leather put on the seat?

M: I have a friend who does that kind of work, and the prices are fairly reasonable. ❸I'll find her business card so you can reach her anytime for an estimate.

📝 問題41-43は次の会話に関するものです。

W: こんにちは、Rick さん。車の修理が必要かどうか見てくださってありがとうございます。これより大きい車を買う必要があるので、今季が終わるまでにこの車を売りに出したいのです。

M: 車の外側の手入れが行き届いているので、買う人は気に入ると思います。でも、運転席の革に小さな傷が見られます。ですので、修繕することを強くお勧めします。

W: わかりました。座席に新しい革を張ってもらうのにいくらかかるかわかりますか。

M: その手の仕事をしている友人がいるのですが、価格はまずまず手頃です。彼女の名刺を捜してきますので、いつでも見積もりを依頼していただけます。

✏️ □take a look at ～を見る □see whether ～かどうか考える □repair work 修理作業
□list A for sale A を売りに出す □buyer 買い手 □well maintained 手入れが行き届いている □flaw 傷
□that kind of work その種の仕事 □fairly reasonable （価格が）かなりお手頃である □reach ～に連絡する

---

41. ★★★☆☆

Why does the woman want to sell her vehicle?

(A) She plans to take public transportation.
(B) She has experienced breakdowns a few times.
(C) She will be transferred to a foreign branch.
(D) She needs a larger car.

女性はなぜ車を売りたいと思っていますか。

(A) 公共交通機関を利用する予定であるため。
(B) 数回、故障に見舞われた経験があるため。
(C) 海外の支店に転勤になるため。
(D) 今より大きな車が必要であるため。

🔍 女性は❶で「大きい車を買う必要があるので、この車を売りに出したい」と述べている。ここから、女性が今所有しているものより大きい車を購入しようとしていることが理由であるとわかる。以上から正解は **(D)**。❶の since が理由を導く接続詞になっていることにも注目。

✏️ □public transportation 公共交通機関 □breakdown 故障 □be transferred to ～に異動する
□foreign branch 海外支店

42. ★★★☆☆

According to the man, why will buyers like the vehicle?

(A) The exterior is in good condition.
(B) The model is currently very popular.
(C) It has brand new leather seats.
(D) It is fuel-efficient.

男性によると、なぜ買い手は車を気に入るのですか。

(A) 外装の状態が良いから。
(B) この型は現在非常に人気があるから。
(C) 新品の革張りの座席が付いているため。
(D) 燃費が良いため。

 男性は❷で「車の外側の手入れが行き届いているので、買い手は気に入るだろう」と述べている。ここから、自動車の外装の状態が良いことが購入の動機につながると考えていることがわかる。以上から正解は **(A)**。(A) は❷の理由を導く接続詞 because 以降の the outside of the vehicle has been well maintained の言い換えになっている。

□exterior 外装　□good condition 良好な状態　□fuel-efficient 燃費の良い

43. ★☆☆☆☆

What will the man probably do next?

(A) Measure some fabric
(B) Clean the front seat
(C) Look for contact information
(D) Confirm a price online

男性はおそらく、次に何をしますか。

(A) 生地の寸法を取る。
(B) 前部座席を掃除する。
(C) 連絡先情報を探す。
(D) インターネットで価格を確認する。

男性は❸で「女性が修理の見積もりを取る連絡ができるように、友人の名刺を探す」と述べている。ここから、名刺を探す＝記載されている連絡先の情報を探す、という言い換えになっていると考えることができる。以上から正解は **(C)**。名刺も連絡先の手段として言い換えられると覚えておこう。

□measure ～を測定する　□fabric 生地　□contact information 連絡先　□confirm ～を確認する

	1回目	2回目	3回目
41.			
42.			
43.			

41. (D)　42. (A)　43. (C)

Questions 44 through 46 refer to the following conversation.

W: ❶I was wondering whether you have any strawberry cakes available. I can't see any in the display case.

M: ❷I'm very sorry. ❸All the strawberry cakes we made today have sold out. However, we still have a nice choice of other cakes.

W: Actually, ❹it's for my father's birthday party tomorrow and he really likes strawberries.

M: ❺If you don't need the cakes until tomorrow, I can take an order for them right now. You can specify exactly what you'd like and we can have them ready for you first thing tomorrow morning.

📖 問題44-46は次の会話に関するものです。

W: イチゴのケーキがあるか伺えますか。陳列ケースでは見当たらないので。

M: 大変申し訳ありません。今日作ったイチゴケーキは全て売り切れてしまいました。しかし、他のケーキでしたら良いものがございます。

W: 実は明日の父の誕生日パーティー用で、父はイチゴが大好きなのです。

M: 明日まででもよろしければ、今ここで注文を承ることができます。ご希望を詳しくお聞かせいただけましたら、明日の朝一番にご用意しておきます。

✏️ □display case 陳列ケース　□take an order for ～の注文を受ける　□right now 今すぐ
□specify ～を具体的に話す　□first thing tomorrow morning 明日の朝一番で

---

44. ⭐⭐☆☆☆

Where is the conversation most likely taking place?

(A) At a fruit shop
(B) At a farm
(C) At a bakery
(D) At a flower shop

会話はどこで行われていると考えられますか。

(A) 果物屋
(B) 農場
(C) ベーカリー
(D) 花屋

🔍 会話冒頭❶で女性が「ケーキがあるか」と尋ねている。ここから、この会話はケーキを販売しているお店で行われていると考えられる。以上から正解は **(C)**。

✏️ □bakery ベーカリー (パン・菓子類を販売している店)

45. ★★★★★

Why does the man apologize?

(A) A bill was miscalculated.
(B) An order was sent to the wrong address.
(C) A reservation was canceled.
(D) A product has sold out.

なぜ男性は謝罪していますか。

(A) 請求書の計算が間違っていたため。
(B) 注文品が違う住所に送られたため。
(C) 予約が取り消しになったため。
(D) 商品が完売したため。

 男性は❷で謝罪し、❸で「尋ねられたケーキは全て売り切れた」と述べている。ここから、ケーキ＝ある商品と言い換えられているとわかる。以上から正解は **(D)**。

 □bill 請求書　□miscalculate 〜を誤って計算する　□wrong 間違った

---

46. ★★★★★

What does the man suggest?

(A) Ordering in advance
(B) Canceling a party
(C) Calling another shop
(D) Asking a family member for help

男性は何を勧めていますか。

(A) 事前に注文をすること。
(B) パーティーを中止すること。
(C) 別の店に電話すること。
(D) 家族に手伝いをお願いすること。

 ❸で尋ねたケーキが売り切れたことを知った女性は、❹で「明日の父の誕生日パーティー用だ」と述べている。これに対して、男性が❺で「明日でよければ今注文をすることができる」と、今日注文すれば明日の朝一番で用意する、と提案している。ここから、事前注文を勧めていることがわかるため、正解は **(A)**。

 □in advance 前もって

	1回目	2回目	3回目
44.			
45.			
46.			

 44. (C)　45. (D)　46. (A)

197

Questions 47 through 49 refer to the following conversation with three speakers.

W1: ❶Let's set up Conference Room A for the demonstration tomorrow. We're expecting many visitors.

W2: For the new air conditioner project? They are coming from the European division, right? Do we need an interpreter?

W1: No, but we need a podium with a microphone and as many as fifty seats.

M: Why don't we use the convention room on the third floor? It has plenty of seating.

W1: ❷Riley will use that space tomorrow morning.

M: I see. In that case, ❸I'm a bit worried. ❹I used Room A previously with fifty people and it was uncomfortable. ❺It might be better if we tried to find a hall in a different building.

W2: I see. ❻Monica, how about we rent one of the halls in the municipal center next to the city hall? It's only one block from here.

W1: I'm happy to change plans based on what Bryan said. ❼I'll go and reserve one now.

問題47-49は3人の話し手による次の会話に関するものです。

W1: 明日の実演のために会議室Aの準備をしましょう。多くの来場者を見込んでいます。

W2: 新しいエアコンのプロジェクトのためですか。ヨーロッパ支社から来るんですよね。通訳者が必要でしょうか。

W1: いいえ、しかしマイクを設置した演壇と50ほどの座席が必要です。

M: 3階の会議室を使うのはどうですか。たくさんの座席があります。

W1: 明日の朝は Riley さんが使用するのです。

M: そうですか。そうなると、ちょっと心配です。私は以前、会議室Aを50人で使用したのですが落ち着かなかったです。別の建物で開催場所を探すほうがいいかもしれません。

W2: なるほど。Monica さん、市役所の隣の市民会館内のホールを一つ借りるのはどうでしょうか。ここからほんの1区画先にあります。

W1: Bryan さんが言ったとおりの案で予定を変えたいと思います。今から予約しに行きます。

✏️ □set up ～を設定する　□visitor 来訪者　□interpreter 通訳者　□podium 演壇
□as many as ～と同じくらいの多さの　□convention room 会議室　□plenty of 大量の　□seating 座席
□in that case その場合　□uncomfortable 心地の悪い　□it might be better if ～したほうがよいかもしれない
□municipal 公営の　□next to ～の隣にある　□based on ～に基づいて

---

47. ⭐⭐☆☆☆

What do the speakers want to do?

(A) Hire new workers
(B) Invite more guests
(C) Buy some furniture
(D) Prepare an event room

話し手たちは何をしたいと思っていますか。

(A) 新しい従業員を雇う。
(B) より多くの客を招待する。
(C) 家具を買う。
(D) 行事用の部屋を準備する。

🔍 会話冒頭❶で1人目の女性が「明日の実演のために会議室の準備をしよう」と述べていることから、会議室で明日のイベント準備を行おうとしていることがわかる。以上から正解は **(D)**。

48. ★★★★★

What does the man mean when he says, "I'm a bit worried"?

(A) Finding an interpreter is not easy.
(B) Attending two conferences at the same time is impossible.
(C) Using the planned space could cause a problem.
(D) He may not be able to attend the meeting.

男性が "I'm a bit worried" と言った際、何を意味していますか。

(A) 通訳を見つけるのは簡単なことではない。
(B) 2つの会議に同時に参加するのは不可能である。
(C) 予定していた場所を使うと問題が生じるかもしれない。
(D) 会議に参加できないかもしれない。

 意図を問われている表現❸「少し心配だ」の前後を見ていくと、❷「Riley さんが明日の朝そのスペース（たくさん座席のある会議室）を使う」→❸「それは少し心配だ」→❹・❺「会議室 A を50人前後で使用したら居心地が悪かったので、他を借りたほうがよいのでは」という流れになっている。今予約している会議室 A のまま続行すると、問題が発生する恐れがあるという意図で発言したことがわかる。以上から正解は **(C)**。問われている前後の文脈をしっかり意識して解くようにしよう。

✎ □planned 予定した　□cause a problem 問題を引き起こす

---

49. ★★★★☆

What does Monica offer to do?

(A) Make the final arrangements
(B) Reschedule the demonstration
(C) Call a technician
(D) Buy some supplies

Monica さんは何をすることを申し出ていますか。

(A) 最終的な手配をすること。
(B) 実演の日程を変更すること。
(C) 技術者に連絡をすること。
(D) 物資を購入すること。

 2人目の女性が❻で Monica さんに話しかけ、「市民会館内のホールを借りるのはどうか」と提案しているのに対して、Monica さんは❼で「今から予約しに行く」と言っている。ここから、Monica さんはこの後これまで話題にしていた準備の最終的な調整として会議室の変更手続きをしに行くことがわかる。以上から正解は **(A)**。Monica さんが会話中の誰なのかを理解して解く必要があるので、注意して登場人物を把握するようにしよう。

✎ □arrangement 手配　□demonstration 実演　□supply 備品

	1回目	2回目	3回目
47.			
48.			
49.			

🚩 **47. (D)　48. (C)　49. (A)**

Questions 50 through 52 refer to the following conversation.

M: We are back now to new technology. ❶Speaking with us live today is Tanya Reed, executive in charge of research and development at Tony Computer Technologies, who is here to discuss her company's new computer. Tanya, what do you have to say about your special new product?

W: ❷Our new computer, the Tony AY7788, will be the first commercial tablet computer that can operate completely under water. That is to say, this new product is the first commercially available device that can be used to play audio or browse Web sites at the beach or in a swimming pool.

M: I can't believe what I'm hearing! Exactly how long will it be until the production process is completed? And when will the computer be ready for sale?

W: The final review stage of development will be finished before the end of the year. ❸You can be sure that in just three short months, the Tony AY7788 will be available in stores and online.

📝 問題50-52は次の会話に関するものです。

M: 今度は新しい科学技術のコーナーです。今日、生出演でお話しいただくのは、Tony Computer Technologies 社の研究開発の取締役である Tanya Reed さんで、同社の新しいコンピューターについてお話しいただきます。Tanya さん、御社の特別な新製品について何をお聞かせいただけるのでしょうか。

W: 当社の新しいコンピューター、Tony AY7788は完全に水中に入ってしまっても稼働する初の商用タブレットとなります。つまり、この新製品はビーチやプールでラジオを聞いたりウェブサイトを閲覧したりできる初の市販機器というわけです。

M: お聞きしたことが信じられませんね。実際のところ、製造工程の完了まであとどのくらいかかる見込みですか。そして、発売はいつごろでしょうか。

W: 開発の最終確認段階は年末までには終了する予定です。わずか3か月後には Tony AY7788が店頭やインターネットでお求めになれるようになるとご期待いただければと思います。

✏️ ☐speaking with us live today is 本日生出演で我々と話すのは～です　☐executive in charge of ～の担当役員
☐research and development 研究開発　☐be here to *do* ～するために来ている　☐commercial 商業用の
☐tablet computer タブレット型コンピューター　☐operate 動作、稼働する　☐under water 水中で
☐that is to say つまり　☐device 装置　☐browse ～を閲覧する

---

50. ★★☆☆☆

Who is Tanya Reed?

(A) An announcer at an event
(B) A manager of a company
(C) A designer of a Web site
(D) A computer programmer

Tanya Reed さんとは誰ですか。

(A) イベントでのアナウンサー
(B) 会社の取締役
(C) ウェブサイトのデザイナー
(D) コンピュータープログラマー

🔍 男性が❶で Tanya Reed さんについて「Tony Computer Technologies 社の研究開発の取締役である」と述べていることから、ある会社の取締役であるとわかる。以上から正解は **(B)**。

51. ★★★☆☆

What is unique about the product?

(A) It does not need an external power source.
(B) It can keep more data than any other computer.
(C) It is waterproof.
(D) It is eco-friendly.

製品の特長とは何ですか。

(A) 外部電源が必要でない。
(B) 他のどのコンピューターよりも多くのデータを保存できる。
(C) 防水である。
(D) 環境に配慮している。

女性は❷で「完全に水中に入ってしまっても稼働する初の商用タブレット」と述べている。ここから、この製品の特長が防水仕様であることがわかる。以上から正解は、これを1語で言い換えた **(C)**。

□unique 独特である、特徴がある　□external power source 外部電源　□waterproof 防水の
□eco-friendly 環境に配慮した

52. ★★★★☆

According to the woman, what will happen in three months?

(A) A device will be on the market.
(B) A distribution center will be opened.
(C) An engineering problem will be solved.
(D) A software developer will be promoted.

女性によると3か月後には何が起こりますか。

(A) 製品が市場に出回る。
(B) 配送センターが開業する。
(C) 技術上の問題が解決する。
(D) ソフトの開発者が昇進する。

女性は❸で「紹介した商品が3か月後に店頭やインターネットで入手できると期待していていてほしい」と述べている。ここから、ある商品が3か月後に市場に出回ることがわかる。以上から、正解は the Tony AY7788という具体的な商品名を device と言い換えた **(A)**。

□on the market 市場に　□distribution center 配送センター　□solve 〜を解決する
□software developer ソフト開発者　□be promoted 昇進する

	1回目	2回目	3回目
50.			
51.			
52.			

50. (B)　51. (C)　52. (A)

Questions 53 through 55 refer to the following conversation.

W: Hi, my name is Estrella Hernandez. ❶I'm calling about the ad I saw online for the vacancy in your marketing department. ❷Has the position been filled?

M: No, it hasn't yet. ❸We are still accepting applications online and we plan to begin interviewing candidates here at our office next month. This position requires a bachelor's degree, but not necessarily in business. We also require at least three years of sales experience and a list of professional and personal references, of course.

W: Yes, I see. May I ask, is the salary based only on commission, or is there also a base salary?

M: There is a base salary. Moreover, commissions are paid monthly. ❹You can get more details of other benefits on our Web site, including our medical insurance plan and vacation policies.

問題53-55は次の会話に関するものです。

W: こんにちは、Estrella Hernandez と言います。御社のマーケティング部門の求人広告をインターネットで拝見して、お電話しました。もう募集枠は埋まってしまいましたか。

M: いいえ、まだです。インターネットでの応募はまだ受け付けていますし、候補者の面接は来月から弊社の事務所で始める予定です。この職には学士号が必要ですが、ビジネスの分野である必要はありません。それに最低3年間の営業経験と、もちろん職務経歴と身元保証人のリストが必要です。

W: はい、わかりました。給与は完全歩合制ですか、それとも基本給も支給されるか伺えますか。

M: 基本給はあります。それに加えるかたちで月ごとに歩合給を支払います。医療保険の種類や休暇制度などの福利厚生の詳細については当社のウェブサイトでご確認いただけます。

✎ □vacancy 求人、仕事の空き　□fill position 仕事の募集を埋める　□accept an application 応募を受け付ける
□interview a candidate 候補者と面接する　□require ～を必要とする　□bachelor's degree 大学の学士号
□not necessarily 必ずしも必要ではない　□in business ビジネスの分野で　□personal reference 身元保証人
□salary 給料　□based on commission (給料が) 業務に基づく、歩合制で　□base salary 基本給
□moreover さらに　□detail 詳細　□benefit 福利厚生　□including ～を含めて、～など
□medical insurance 医療保険　□vacation policy 休暇制度

---

53. ★★☆☆☆

Why is the woman calling the man?

(A) To get information on a job
(B) To make a proposal
(C) To ask for a discount
(D) To launch a new business

女性はなぜ男性に電話をしていますか。

(A) 仕事についての情報を得るため。
(B) 提案をするため。
(C) 割引を求めるため。
(D) 新事業を立ち上げるため。

🔍 会話冒頭❶で女性が求人広告を見て電話したと切り出し、❷で「募集枠は埋まってしまったか」と尋ねている。ここから、求人に関しての問い合わせで電話したことがわかる。以上から正解は **(A)**。

✎ □proposal 提案　□ask for ～を求める　□launch ～を立ち上げる

54. ★★★★★

What will the company do next month?

(A) Host an orientation
(B) Offer discount coupons
(C) Prepare a presentation
(D) Conduct interviews

来月会社は何をしますか。

(A) オリエンテーションを実施する。
(B) 割引クーポンを提供する。
(C) プレゼンテーションの準備をする。
(D) 面接を実施する。

男性は❸で「来月、候補者の面接を始める予定だ」と述べている。つまり、来月は求人応募者に対する面接が行われることがわかる。以上から正解は **(D)**。conduct は何かを実行することを意味する動詞で、目的語に interview を取ることができる。

□orientation オリエンテーション、新人研修　□conduct interview 面接を実施する

55. ★★★★★

According to the man, what can the woman find on the company's Web site?

(A) New educational materials
(B) Information on employee benefits
(C) A sales commission calculator
(D) A list of lecturers

男性によると女性は会社のウェブサイトで何を見ることができますか。

(A) 新しい教材
(B) 従業員の福利厚生に関する情報
(C) 売上歩合の計算表
(D) 講師一覧

男性は❹でウェブサイトの内容について言及しており、「医療保険の種類や休暇制度などの福利厚生の詳細について見ることができる」と述べている。ここから、会社の福利厚生に関する情報だとわかる。以上から正解は **(B)**。

□educational material 教材　□employee benefit 従業員の福利厚生　□commission calculator 歩合計算 (表)
□lecturer 講師

	1回目	2回目	3回目
53.			
54.			
55.			

53. (A)　54. (D)　55. (B)

Questions 56 through 58 refer to the following conversation.

W: Hello, Douglas! ❶I'm throwing a birthday party for my daughter next weekend. ❷Would you like to bring your daughter to it?

M: ❸That depends. ❹When will the party be held?

W: I was thinking of having it early Saturday evening. Then I'll have plenty of time during the day to get everything ready.

M: Ah, that wouldn't work so well for me. Some old friends are coming into town on Saturday at six, and I've already made plans with them.

W: That's too bad. I know our children really like playing together.

M: What if you change the party to begin at 1 o'clock? I could come over early and help you prepare for it.

W: Actually, that might be better! ❺I'll get in touch with the people I already informed to let them know about the change in plans.

📝 問題56-58は次の会話に関するものです。

W: こんにちは、Douglasさん。今度の週末に娘のために誕生日パーティーを開きます。お嬢さんを連れていらっしゃいませんか。

M: どうでしょう。パーティーを開くのはいつですか。

W: 土曜日の夜の早い時間を考えていました。そうすれば日中にいろいろと準備をする時間がたっぷり取れますから。

M: そうですか。それだと、ちょっと都合が合いません。土曜日の6時に親友が町にやってくるので、もう彼らとの予定があります。

W: 残念です。私たちの子どもたちは一緒に遊ぶのが大好きですから。

M: パーティーを午後1時に始めるようにするなんてどうですか。早めに来て準備をお手伝いできますが。

W: 実はその方がいいです。既にお知らせした人たちに連絡して予定の変更について伝えます。

✏️ □throw a party パーティーを行う　□that depends それは場合による　□plenty of たくさんの〜
□That's too bad. それは残念です。　□What if...? 〜してはどうか　□get in touch with 〜と連絡を取る
□inform 〜に知らせる　□change in plan 予定変更

---

56. ★★★☆☆

What is the topic of the conversation?

(A) A company picnic
(B) Plans for lunch
(C) Visiting old colleagues
(D) An annual celebration

会話の趣旨は何ですか。

(A) 会社のピクニック
(B) 昼食の計画
(C) 昔の同僚を訪ねること
(D) 毎年のお祝い

🔍 会話冒頭❶で女性が「週末に娘の誕生日パーティーを開く」と述べている。ここから、誕生日パーティ＝年に1回のお祝いだとわかる。以上から正解は **(D)**。

✏️ □annual 毎年の、年次の

57. ★★★☆☆

What does the man mean when he says, "That depends"?	男性が "That depends" と言う際、何を意味していますか。
(A) He needs to know the start time.	(A) 開始時間を知る必要がある。
(B) He is not sure of his plans.	(B) 自分の予定がわからない。
(C) He is worried about the weather.	(C) 天気を心配している。
(D) He has a spending limit.	(D) 使用限度額がある。

 意図を問われている表現❸「場合による」の前後を見ていくと、❷「男性の娘をパーティーに連れていきたいか」➡❸「場合による」➡❹「いつ開催するのか」という流れになっている。つまり、男性の娘が参加できるかは、いつ開催するかによるという意図で発言しているとわかる。以上から正解は **(A)**。

□start time 開始時間　□be worried about ～について心配している　□spending limit 使用限度額

58. ★★★★☆

What will the woman most likely do next?	女性は次に何をすると考えられますか。
(A) Submit invitation cards	(A) 招待状を送る。
(B) Make some phone calls	**(B)** 電話をかける。
(C) Book a restaurant	(C) レストランを予約する。
(D) Go to a grocery store	(D) 食料品店に行く。

 女性は会話の最後に❺「既にお知らせした人たちに連絡して予定の変更について伝える」と述べている。ここから、女性は複数の人に連絡を取ると考えられる。つまり、選択肢の中で変更の連絡をする手段になるものが正解の候補になる。以上から正解は **(B)**。

□invitation card 招待状　□grocery store 食料品店

	1回目	2回目	3回目
56.			
57.			
58.			

56. (D)　57. (A)　58. (B)

Questions 59 through 61 refer to the following conversation.

W: Hello, Jim. It's nice to see you.

M: Great to meet you, too. I've been meaning to talk to you. ❶I want to renovate my shop. I heard you recently remodeled yours.

W: Yes. I am really satisfied with my store.

M: ❷I think it will cost a lot more than I have in my budget. ❸How did you make it happen?

W: You know, these kinds of big projects usually require a lot of money. ❹However, I found a great comparison Web site, savemany.net. ❺It helped me a lot.

M: How does it work?

W: You just type in some information by following the simple steps. It will recommend the cheapest options for materials and professional services.

M: ❻Well, how much does it cost? I don't know whether it is a good idea to spend money in order to save money.

W: It charges you only if you use one of their recommendations.

📝 問題59-61は次の会話に関するものです。

W: こんにちは、Jim さん。お会いできてうれしいです。

M: こちらこそうれしいです。お話しできることを楽しみにしていました。店を改修したいと思っているんです。先日そちらのお店を改装されたとお聞きしましたが。

W: はい、とても満足しています。

M: 私の方は予算よりもはるかに費用がかかりそうなのです。どのようになさったのですか。

W: たいていの場合、この手の大プロジェクトには多額の費用がかかりますよね。でも、今回は savemany.net という比較用のウェブサイトを見つけたんです。これが大変に役立ちました。

M: それはどういうものですか。

W: 単純な手順に従って情報を入力するだけです。一番安い素材と専門サービスを勧めてくれます。

M: それで、それにはどのくらい費用がかかりますか。お金を節約するためにお金を使うのがいいことなのか判断できないですが。

W: 勧められたものを利用することにした場合だけ課金されます。

✏️ □mean to *do* ～するつもりである □renovate ～を改修する □remodel ～を改装する □be satisfied with ～に満足する □budget 予算 □make it happen 実現させる □require ～を必要とする □comparison 比較 □type in ～を入力する □step 手順 □material 材料、素材 □in order to *do* ～するために □save money お金を節約する □charge ～に課金する

---

59. ★★★★☆

What does the man want to do?

(A) Take a cruise
(B) Register for college
(C) Begin his own company
(D) Remodel his store

男性は何をしたいと思っていますか。

(A) 船旅に参加する。
(B) 大学の履修登録をする。
(C) 自分の会社を始める。
(D) 店を改修する。

🔍 男性は❶で「自分の店を改修したい」と述べている。以上から正解は **(D)**。remodel = renovate、store = shop が言い換えになっていることをしっかりチェックしておこう。

✏️ □cruise クルーズ、船旅 □register for ～に参加登録する

60. ★★★☆☆

What does the woman suggest?	女性は何を勧めていますか。
(A) Getting a second job	(A) 副業を見つける。
(B) Employing an online resource	**(B) オンラインの情報源を利用する。**
(C) Applying for a bank loan	(C) 銀行のローンを利用する。
(D) Consulting a financial planner	(D) ファイナンシャルプランナーに相談する。

 男性は自分の店の改修について❷で「予算超過するのでは」と懸念を示し、❸でどうすれば実現できるかを女性に尋ねている。それに対して女性は❹で比較できるウェブサイトに言及し、❺で「とても役立った」と述べている。つまり、女性はオンラインの情報の活用を勧めていることがわかる。以上から正解は **(B)**。ここでの employ は「雇用する」ではなく、何かの手段を「利用、活用する」という意味になっていることに注意しよう。

 □employ 〜を利用する　□apply for 〜に申し込む　□consult 〜に相談する

---

61. ★★★☆☆

What is the man worried about?	男性は何を心配していますか。
(A) High interest rates	(A) 高金利
(B) Busy work schedules	(B) 忙しい作業日程
(C) The price of a service	**(C) サービスの価格**
(D) The security of a homepage	(D) ホームページの安全性

 男性は女性に❹で薦められた比較用のウェブサイトについて、❻で「そのサービスの費用はどれくらいかかるのか」と尋ね、お金を使う判断ができないとサービスについて懸念を示していることがわかる。以上から正解は **(C)**。

 □interest rate 金利

	1回目	2回目	3回目
59.			
60.			
61.			

 59. (D)　60. (B)　61. (C)

Questions 62 through 64 refer to the following conversation and table.

W: ❶Hello, Coach Marley. Something came up with the location for the next basketball tournament.

M: What's the matter?

W: ❷I just found out this morning that all the snow piled up on top of the Thornton College Gymnasium caused part of the roof to collapse. We'll have to find another place for the games.

M: That's terrible! I hope no one was hurt.

W: No, luckily the building was vacant when it happened. However, as I said, we have to find another location to host the tournament. Where do you think would be best?

M: ❸We need somewhere that can seat at least seven hundred spectators. Could you find a location that would be appropriate?

Location	Max Occupancy
Rushden Center	300
Thornton College Gymnasium	700
❹Grant Athletic Center	800
Shaw Fitness	500

📝 問題62-64は次の会話と表に関するものです。

W: すみません、Marley コーチ。次のバスケットボールトーナメントの場所についてお伝えすることがあります。

M: どうしたのですか。

W: 今朝、Thornton College Gymnasium の上に積もった大量の雪で屋根の一部が壊れたことがわかりました。試合のために別の場所を探さなければなりません。

M: それは惨事ですね。誰もけがをしていないと良いのですが。

W: はい、そのときは幸い、建物には誰もいませんでした。ただ、今申し上げたように、トーナメントを行うために別の場所を探す必要があります。どこが最適だと思いますか。

M: 最低でも700人の観客を収容できる場所が必要です。適当な場所を見つけてもらえますか。

場所	最大収容人数
Rushden Center	300
Thornton College Gymnasium	700
Grant Athletic Center	800
Shaw Fitness	500

🖊 □something comes up with ～について何かが発生する　□tournament トーナメント
□What's the matter? 何かあったのですか。　□pile up 積み上がる　□cause ～を引き起こす　□collapse 破損する
□terrible ひどい　□be hurt 負傷する　□luckily 幸運にも　□vacant 空室の、誰もいない　□as I said 言ったとおり
□host ～を開催する　□spectator 観客　□appropriate 適切な

62. ★★★★☆

Who most likely is the man?	男性は誰であると考えられますか。
(A) An event planner	(A) イベントプランナー
(B) A sports team coach	**(B)** スポーツチームのコーチ
(C) A city official	(C) 市職員
(D) A maintenance worker	(D) 保守員

🔍 会話冒頭❶で女性が男性に「コーチ」と呼びかけ、「次のバスケットボールトーナメントの場所について伝えることがある」とスポーツに関する連絡をしている。ここから、男性がスポーツのコーチをしていると考えられる。以上から正解は **(B)**。

✏️ □city official 市職員

63. ★★★★★

What problem does the woman report?	女性はどのような問題を報告していますか。
(A) A court was wet.	(A) コートが濡れた。
(B) A venue was double-booked	(B) 会場が二重に予約された。
(C) A structure was damaged.	**(C)** 建物が損壊した。
(D) An event was canceled.	(D) イベントが中止された。

🔍 女性は❷で「今朝、Thornton College Gymnasium の上に積もった大量の雪で屋根の一部が壊れた」と述べている。ここから、ある建築物の屋根が破損したことがわかる。以上から正解は、建築物の屋根を a structure と抽象度を上げて表現した **(C)**。

✏️ □venue 開催場所　□double-book 〜を重複して予約する　□structure 建物

64. ★☆☆☆☆

Look at the graphic. Where will the tournament most likely be held?	図を見てください。どの場所でトーナメントが開催されると考えられますか。
(A) Rushden Center	(A) Rushden Center
(B) Thornton College Gymnasium	(B) Thornton College Gymnasium
(C) Grant Athletic Center	**(C)** Grant Athletic Center
(D) Shaw Fitness	(D) Shaw Fitness

🔍 男性は会話の後半❸で「最低でも700人の観客を収容できる場所が必要」と述べている。つまり、会場は700人を超える収容が可能である必要があることがわかる。次に表を見ると、❹からこの条件を満たすのは Grant Athletic Center だとわかる。以上から正解は **(C)**。❷で述べているため候補から外せるが、❸の「最低でも700」と述べている中の数字で (B) だと惑わされないようにしよう。

	1回目	2回目	3回目
62.			
63.			
64.			

 62. (B)　63. (C)　64. (C)

Questions 65 through 67 refer to the following conversation and table.

M: ❶May I ask you something? ❷I'm searching for an external memory device. ❸Could you tell me the difference between these?

W: Of course, sir. The Seagate models can read and write data faster, but the Baracuda models can store more data.

M: I think I would prefer the faster ones. How much are they?

W: ❹Here's our monthly special deals.

M: Let me see. ❺This one looks almost the same as the Seagate CN005.

W: ❻It is a newer model of the Seagate. ❼You can protect your data by password, so you don't have to be concerned about your data even if you lose the device.

M: That's fascinating. ❽I'll go for the cheaper one, though.

❾Seagate CN005 **$55**	❿Seagate DM008 **$75** Password-protection
Baracuda 4WD **$40**	Baracuda 9XE **$85**

📝 問題65-67は次の会話と表に関するものです。

M: 伺ってもよろしいですか。外付けの記憶媒体を探しているのですが。これらの違いを教えてもらえますか。

W: もちろんです。Seagate モデルの方がデータの読み書きは速いですが、Baracuda モデルの方がたくさんデータを保存できます。

M: 速い方にしようと思います。いくらですか。

W: こちらが当店の今月だけの特別料金です。

M: ええと、こちらは Seagate CN005とほとんど見た目が同じですが。

W: それは、Seagate の新しいモデルです。パスワードでデータを保護することができるので、紛失してもデータの心配をする必要はありません。

M: それは魅力的ですね。ただ、やはり安い方にします。

Seagate CN005 **55** ドル	Seagate DM008 **75** ドル パスワード保護
Baracuda 4WD **40** ドル	Baracuda 9XE **85** ドル

✏️ □search for ～を探す　□external memory device (PC 等に接続する) 外付けの記憶媒体　□store ～を保存する
□prefer ～を好む　□special deal 特別価格、お買い得品　□almost the same as ～とほぼ同じである
□protect ～を保護する　□be concerned about ～を気にかける、心配する　□even if たとえ～でも
□lose ～を紛失する　□fascinating 魅力的な　□go for ～の方を選ぶ、～にする

65. ★★★☆☆

Where is the conversation most likely taking place?

(A) At a delivery company
(B) At a storage company
(C) At an electronics shop
(D) At a computer repair shop

会話はどこで行われていると考えられますか。

(A) 配送会社
(B) 倉庫会社
(C) 電子機器店
(D) コンピューター修理店

🔍 会話冒頭❶で男性が女性に話しかけ、❷で「外部メモリー部品」に言及し、❸で複数の商品の違いについて聞いている。ここから、この場所は家電製品を取り扱っているところだとわかる。以上から正解は **(C)**。

✏️ □storage company 倉庫会社　□repair shop 修理会社、修理工場

66. ★★★★☆

What does the woman most likely give the man?

(A) A store flyer
(B) A membership card
(C) A discount voucher
(D) A delivery code

女性は男性に何を渡していると考えられますか。

(A) 店のチラシ
(B) 会員カード
(C) 割引券
(D) 配送番号

🔍 女性は男性に❹で「こちらが今月のお買い得品です」と、お店の商品情報を差し出している。つまり、チラシを男性に渡していると考えることができる。以上から正解は **(A)**。

✏️ □flyer チラシ　□voucher 金券、割引券

67. ★★★★★

Look at the graphic. Which model will the man most likely select?

(A) Seagate CN005
(B) Seagate DM008
(C) Baracuda 4WD
(D) Baracuda 9XE

図を見てください。男性はどのモデルを選ぶと考えられますか。

(A) Seagate CN005
(B) Seagate DM008
(C) Baracuda 4WD
(D) Baracuda 9XE

🔍 男性がチラシを手に取り、❺で Seagate CN005と同じに見える製品について女性に尋ねている。女性は❻・❼で「こちらは Seagate 製品の最新版でパスワード保護機能がある」と説明しており、表の❿よりこの説明が Seagate DM008についてだとわかる。ただ男性は最終的に❽で the cheaper one、つまり、Seagate シリーズの安い方にすると述べている。この情報をもとに表を見ると、Seagate シリーズで安いのは❾と❿の比較より Seagate CN005だとわかる。以上から正解は **(A)**。この問題は、最後に「やっぱりシリーズの安い方にする」と言う部分を理解することがミソ。一番安い (C) を選ばないように気を付けよう。

	1回目	2回目	3回目
65.			
66.			
67.			

 65. (C)　66. (A)　67. (A)

Questions 68 through 70 refer to the following conversation and map.

M: Excuse me. ❶I was recently hired and I'm here for my first day of work. ❷Can you tell me about today's schedules?

W: Of course. All new employees should report to the building management office by 10 A.M. for a welcome speech. Then you'll go to the security office around 10:30.

M: I see. Will we get a tour of the general affairs department today?

W: Yes, at around 11:30. They'll talk to you about all of the new projects that they're working on. ❸Then you'll have lunch from 12 to 1 in the employee cafeteria before looking around the production plants.

M: Sounds like we have an interesting day ahead. ❹In which building is the cafeteria?

W: ❺It's the building directly across the street from the waste disposal facility, not far from the security office.

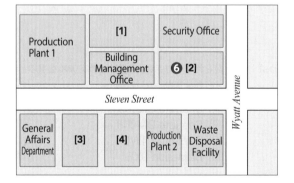

📝 問題68-70は次の会話と地図に関するものです。

M: すみません。こちらの会社で最近採用されたばかりで、勤務初日なのですが。今日の予定について教えてもらえますか。

W: もちろんです。新入社員は全員、歓迎のスピーチのために午前10時までに建物管理事務所に顔を出してください。その後、10時半ごろに警備室に向かいます。

M: わかりました。今日は総務部の見学がありますか。

W: はい、11時半ごろです。進行中の新プロジェクト全てについての話があります。その後、12時から1時は社員食堂で昼食を取っていただいてから、製造工場を見学します。

M: 興味深い一日になりそうですね。食堂はどの建物にありますか。

W: 廃棄物処理施設から道を挟んで真向かいの建物です。警備室からは遠くありません。

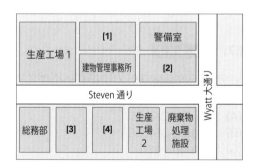

📝 □report to ～に出向く □management office 管理事務所 □welcome speech 歓迎の挨拶
□security office 警備室 □general affairs department 総務部 □work on ～に取りかかる
□employee cafeteria 社員食堂 □production plant 製造工場 □ahead これから
□waste disposal facility 廃棄物処理施設 □avenue 大通り

68. ★★★★☆

What are the speakers mainly talking about?	話し手たちは主に何について話していますか。
(A) A monthly work schedule	(A) 月の作業日程
(B) An orientation agenda	**(B) 説明会の議事**
(C) A job fair	(C) 就職説明会
(D) A site inspection	(D) 現場調査

🔍 会話冒頭❶・❷で男性が「勤務初日なのだが、今日の予定について教えてほしい」と女性に尋ね、女性がそれに答えている。ここから、男性は勤務初日で会社について説明を受けることがわかる。これを「会社説明のスケジュール（議事進行内容）」と言い換えた **(B)** が正解。

✎ □orientation 説明会　□agenda 議事　□job fair 就職説明会　□site inspection 現地調査

---

69. ★★★☆☆

According to the woman, what will take place in the afternoon?	女性によると午後何が行われますか。
(A) A tour of the manufacturing plants	**(A) 生産工場の見学**
(B) A presentation on new products	(B) 新製品の紹介
(C) A visit to the building management office	(C) 建物管理事務所の訪問
(D) A discussion about waste disposal methods	(D) 廃棄物処理方法についての討論

🔍 女性は❸で「12時から午後1時まで昼食を取って、その後工場見学に行く」と述べている。この工場見学を言い換えた **(A)** が正解。日本語の直訳だと、「工場見学前の12時から1時に昼食」となっているが、それはつまり「12時から1時に昼食で、その後工場見学」という意味になる。聞き取った内容はできるだけ戻り読みで訳さず、頭からイメージできるようにしておこう。

✎ □manufacturing plant 生産工場　□method 方法

---

70. ★★★★☆

Look at the graphic. In which location is the cafeteria most likely located?	図を見てください。食堂はどこに位置していると考えられますか。
(A) [1]	(A) [1]
(B) [2]	**(B) [2]**
(C) [3]	(C) [3]
(D) [4]	(D) [4]

🔍 男性が❹で食堂の位置について尋ね、女性が❺で「廃棄物処理施設から道を挟んで真向かいの建物で、警備室から遠くない」と述べている。この情報をもとに地図を見ると、この条件に当てはまるのは❻の [2] だとわかる。以上から正解は **(B)**。

	1回目	2回目	3回目
68.			
69.			
70.			

 68. (B)　69. (A)　70. (B)

Questions 71 through 73 refer to the following excerpt from a meeting.

W: I'd like to update you on recent developments. ❶As you know, our winter line of women's coats, jeans, and shirts hasn't been selling as well as we expected. We have unsold inventory at all of our store locations. ❷So in an attempt to make future sales promotions more successful, we handed out questionnaires to our shoppers asking them which types of garments or accessories they are most likely to buy and when. ❸I'm going to pass out some of the completed ones now for you to review. ❹For the remainder of the meeting, let's use this feedback to generate some new ways to attract potential customers, especially young women between the ages of 18 and 25.

📝 問題71-73は次の会議の一部に関するものです。

W: 最近の展開についてご報告をしたいと思います。ご存じのとおり、当社の冬物の女性用コート、ジーンズ、シャツは予想していたほどの売り上げが出ていません。全店舗が売れ残りの在庫を抱えています。そこで、今後の販促をより成功させるため、どの種類の衣服や小物をいつ買いたいか尋ねるアンケートをお客様に配布しました。記入されたものをご覧いただくために今からいくつか配ります。会議の残りの時間では、これらの意見をもとに、特に18歳から25歳の若い女性の潜在顧客を引き付ける新たな方法を考えたいと思います。

✏️ □update ～に近況を報告する　□development 進展　□winter line 冬物　□unsold inventory 売れ残りの在庫
□in an attempt to *do* ～するために、～する試みとして　□sales promotion 販売促進　□hand out ～を配布する
□questionnaire アンケート　□shopper 買い物客　□garment 衣類　□be likely to *do* ～しそうな
□pass out ～を配る　□completed 記入済の　□review ～を確認する　□remainder 残り　□feedback 感想、意見
□generate ～を生み出す　□attract ～を引き付ける　□potential customer 潜在顧客

---

71. ★★☆☆☆

What type of product is being discussed?

(A) Camping tools
(B) Office heaters
(C) Sports equipment
(D) Clothing

どんな種類の製品について話し合っていますか。

(A) キャンプ用品
(B) オフィス用ヒーター
(C) スポーツ器具
(D) 衣服

 話し手は❶で「当社の冬物の女性用コート、ジーンズ、シャツ」と言っているので、衣類関係の製品について話していることがわかる。以上から正解は **(D)**。

 □sports equipment スポーツ用品、スポーツ器具

72. ★★★☆☆

According to the speaker, what will the listeners receive?

(A) Completed questionnaires
(B) Sales targets
(C) A product sample
(D) Details of a marketing campaign

話し手によると、聞き手は何を受け取りますか。

(A) 記入済みのアンケート
(B) 売上目標
(C) 製品のサンプル
(D) マーケティングキャンペーンの詳細

🔍 話し手は❷で「お客様に製品アンケートを配布した」と述べ、❸で「記入されたものをこれから配る」と述べている。ここから、聞き手がこれからお客様の記入済アンケートを受け取るとわかるので、正解は **(A)**。❸the completed ones の one が❷の questionnaire であることを押さえておこう。

✏️ □sales target 売り上げ目標　□detail 詳細

73. ★★★★☆

What are listeners asked to think about?

(A) Arranging items attractively
(B) Ways to cut costs
(C) Suggestions for attracting customers
(D) Possible locations for a shop

聞き手は何について考えるよう求められていますか。

(A) 商品を魅力的に陳列すること
(B) コストを減らす方法
(C) 集客のための提案
(D) 新店舗の候補地

🔍 話し手は❹でアンケートの意見をもとに、特定層の潜在顧客を引き付ける新たな方法を考えたい、と言っている。ここから、聞き手は集客する方法の提案を求められているとわかるため、❹の new ways を suggestions と言い換えた **(C)** が正解となる。

✏️ □attractively 魅力的に　□cut cost コストを削減する　□suggestion 提案　□possible location 候補地

	1回目	2回目	3回目
71.			
72.			
73.			

🚩 **71. (D)　72. (A)　73. (C)**

Questions 74 through 76 refer to the following recorded message.

M: ❶Thank you for calling Goldberg's Clinic. ❷We are very sorry, but the office is closed for the entire week as we will be relocating to Brady Street. ❸We will resume business at the new location on Monday, April 10. Our business hours will remain the same, from 9 to 6, apart from Wednesdays when we close at 2 P.M. ❹For those wishing to make an appointment with us for the first time, please visit www. goldberghos.net and download the patient admission questionnaire, which you will need to submit upon your first visit. For further information, please press 1 to leave your message. One of our representatives will call you back the next business day.

📝 問題74-76は次の録音メッセージに関するものです。

M: Goldberg 診療所にお電話いただきありがとうございます。大変申し訳ございませんが、Brady 通りに移転するため、一週間全日休業いたします。移転先での診療再開は4月10日、月曜日からです。診療時間はこれまでと同じ、9時から6時です。水曜日は別で、午後2時に診療終了となります。初診の予約をご希望の方は www.goldberghos.net にアクセスし、問診票をダウンロードしてください。初回の診療時にご提出いただきます。さらに詳しい情報をお求めの方は1を押してメッセージを残してください。代表の者が次の営業日に折り返しお電話いたします。

✏️ □entire week 1週間丸々 　□relocate to 〜に移転する 　□resume 〜を再開する
□remain the same 同じままである 　□apart from 〜を除き 　□for those *doing* 〜する人に
□patient admission questionnaire 問診票 　□representative 代表者 　□next business day 翌営業日

---

74. ★★☆☆☆

According to the speaker, why is Goldberg's Clinic currently closed?

(A) Dr. Goldberg is away on vacation.
(B) Doctors have to renew their licenses.
(C) It is moving to a new location.
(D) Its equipment is under repair.

話し手によると、なぜ Goldberg 診療所は現在休診していますか。

(A) Goldberg 医師が休暇のため不在である。
(B) 医師が免許を更新する必要がある。
(C) 新しい場所に移転する。
(D) 設備が修理中である。

🔍 話し手は❶で Goldberg 診療所に電話をかけた人に対する挨拶をし、❷で「移転するため、一週間全日休業する」と述べている。以上から正解は **(C)**。

✏️ □away on vacation 休暇で不在である 　□renew 〜を更新する 　□under repair 修理中の

75. ★★★☆☆

What does the speaker say happens on Wednesdays?

(A) A nutrition expert is available
(B) The office closes early.
(C) Another doctor substitutes for Dr. Goldberg.
(D) Waiting times are longer.

話し手は水曜日に何がおこると言っていますか。

(A) 栄養の専門家が応じてくれる。
(B) 事務所が早く閉まる。
(C) 別の医師が Goldberg 医師の代わりをする。
(D) 待ち時間が長くなる。

🔍 話し手は❸で診療再開の情報を伝えており、「通常は9時から6時の営業だが、水曜日は午後2時に閉まる」と水曜日のみ他と比べ早く閉まると伝えている。これを言い換えた **(B)** が正解。

✏️ □nutrition expert 栄養士　□substitute for ～の代わりをする　□waiting time 待ち時間

76. ★★★★☆

Why are first-time patients asked to visit a Web site?

(A) To make a medical appointment
(B) To confirm the new address
(C) To upload questions
(D) To download a required form

なぜ初診患者はウェブサイトへのアクセスを求められていますか。

(A) 診療の予約を取るため。
(B) 新しい所在地を確認するため。
(C) 質問をアップロードするため。
(D) 必要な用紙をダウンロードするため。

🔍 話し手は❹で「初診予約希望の人は専用ウェブサイトにアクセスし、問診票をダウンロードするように」と述べていることから、問診票をダウンロードするためにアクセスを求めていることがわかる。この問診票を「必要な用紙 (a required form)」と言い換えた **(D)** が正解。

✏️ □medical appointment 診察予約　□confirm ～を確認する　□upload ～をアップロードする (ウェブ上に移す)
□download ～をダウンロードする (提供元から別のコンピューター等にデータを移す)　□required 必要な

	1回目	2回目	3回目
74.			
75.			
76.			

🚩 **74.** (C)　**75.** (B)　**76.** (D)

Questions 77 through 79 refer to the following announcement.

W: ❶Good morning. Thank you for flying on Allegiant Air Flight 225 to Detroit. We would like to update you on departure times for connecting flights. Flight SE490 to Houston has been delayed because of bad weather conditions at its destination. It has been rescheduled to depart one hour later than the original departure time. ❷Passengers who wish to board this flight should keep checking the departure information on display boards, as the flight schedule may change. ❸Display boards will be updated every five minutes. ❹Please note, our attendants have no access to further information. ❺All other flights to domestic destinations will depart on time. ❻If you are transferring to an international flight, please take the monorail to Terminal E. Have a nice trip.

W: おはようございます。Allegiant 航空225便 Detroit 行きにご搭乗いただきありがとうございます。乗り継ぎ便の出発時刻についての最新情報をお知らせいたします。SE490便 Houston 行きは目的地の悪天候により現在、出発に遅れが生じております。当初の出発予定時刻より1時間遅れての出発に変更となっております。この便にご搭乗されるお客様は掲示板の出発情報をこまめにご確認ください。フライトスケジュールは変更されることがございます。掲示板の内容は5分ごとに更新されます。私たち乗務員はこれ以上の情報を知り得ないことをご了承ください。その他の国内行きの全ての便は定刻どおりに出発する予定です。国際線にお乗り継ぎの場合は、モノレールでターミナルEまでお越しください。どうぞよいご旅行を。

✏️ □update 〜に最新情報を報告する　□connecting flight 乗継便　□destination 目的地
□be rescheduled to *do* 〜する予定を再度設定される　□depart 出発する　□display board 掲示板
□attendant 乗務員、添乗員　□have no access to further information これ以上の情報を入手できない
□domestic 国内の　□transfer to 〜に乗り継ぐ　□monorail モノレール

77.

Where is this announcement taking place?

(A) At a train station
(B) At a bus terminal
(C) On an airplane
(D) At an airport

このアナウンスはどこで流れていますか。

(A) 駅
(B) バスターミナル
(C) 飛行機の中
(D) 空港

🔍 話し手は❶で「Allegiant 航空225便 Detroit 行きにご搭乗いただき……」と飛行機の乗客に向けたアナウンスをしていることから、正解は **(C)**。飛行機のアナウンスを聞いてすぐに空港だと判断しないように注意しよう。途中❹で客室乗務員にも言及しており、飛行機内であることを裏付けるヒントが出ていることもチェックしておこう。

78. ★★★★☆

What does the speaker mean when she says, "our attendants have no access to further information"?

(A) She wants to apologize for a power outage.
(B) People should check updates by themselves.
(C) The company's staff have forgotten a password.
(D) Attendants need more technology training.

話し手が "our attendants have no access to further information" と言う際、何を意味していますか。

(A) 停電について謝罪したい。
(B) 乗客は最新情報を自ら確認しなければならない。
(C) 会社のスタッフがパスワードを忘れた。
(D) 添乗員はテクノロジー訓練をさらに行う必要がある。

 意図を問われている箇所❹は「乗務員はこれ以上の情報を持ち合わせていない」という意味で、前後を見ると、❷・❸「(SE490便の) フライトスケジュールは変更の可能性があり、掲示板に最新情報がある」➡❹添乗員はこれ以上の情報を持っていない➡❺他の飛行機は今のところ定刻、という流れになっている。それまでの SE490便に関する案内をここで終えていることから、❹は現段階での最新情報は伝えたが以降は各自で確認してほしいという意図の発言であることがわかる。以上から正解は **(B)**。

□power outage 停電　□update 最新情報

79. ★★☆☆☆

Who should go to Terminal E?

(A) Travelers taking a shuttle bus
(B) Passengers traveling without luggage
(C) Visitors who wish to upgrade their seats
(D) Those heading to foreign destinations

誰がターミナル E に行くべきですか。

(A) シャトルバスに乗る旅行者
(B) 荷物を持たずに旅行している乗客
(C) 座席のグレードアップを希望している訪問者
(D) 外国の目的地に向かう人々

話し手は❻「国際線へ乗り継ぐ場合はターミナル E まで」と言っているので、国際線の利用客、つまり海外に行く人だとわかる。以上より正解は **(D)**。(D) の Those は人々 (The people) を意味しており、(who are) heading 以降が後置修飾していることも理解しておこう。

□upgrade ～の級を上げる　□those 人々　□head to ～に向かう　□foreign destination 外国の目的地

	1回目	2回目	3回目
77.			
78.			
79.			

77. (C)　78. (B)　79. (D)

Questions 80 through 82 refer to the following news.

W: And now for today's business news. ❶Antonio Media has grown over the last seven years. ❷As a result, it has been trying to expand its reach overseas. ❸To do so, it attempted to merge with news provider Gillian World News Agency. ❹This would have helped sales, especially in Asia. ❺But Maria Hill, a spokesperson for Antonio Media gave an update on the status of the firm's business talks with the provider. ❻Unfortunately it won't happen. ❼Instead of pursuing the merger, Gillian accepted an investment offer from another company. Antonio Media is starting over, looking for other solutions to be competitive.

📝 問題80-82は次のニュースに関するものです。

W: では、今日のビジネスニュースをお伝えします。Antonio Media 社はこの7年間で成長をとげました。その結果、勢力範囲を海外に拡大しようとしています。そのために報道機関の Gillian World News Agency 社との合併を試みました。これは特にアジアでの売り上げを伸ばすことになっていたでしょう。しかし、Antonio Media 社の広報担当 Maria Hill 氏がその提供者との商談の状況を報告しました。残念ながら、その見通しはなくなりました。Gillian 社は、合併を求めるのをやめ、他社からの投資の申し出を受け入れました。Antonio Media 社はふりだしに戻り、競争力をつける他の方法を模索しています。

✏️ □now for（ニュース番組で）それでは〜をお伝えします　□as a result 結果として
□expand one's reach 力の範囲を拡大する　□attempt to *do* 〜しようと試みる　□merge with 〜と合併する
□news provider ニュース配信会社　□spokesperson 広報担当者　□status 状況　□business talk 商談
□instead of 〜の代わりに　□pursue 〜を追求する　□investment offer 投資の申し出　□start over やり直す
□solution 解決策　□competitive 競争力がある

---

80. ★★★☆☆

What does the speaker mention about Antonio Media?

(A) It has tried to expand abroad.
(B) It sells products made by Gillian World News Agency.
(C) Its new offering will be launched soon.
(D) It has experienced problems with leadership.

話し手は Antonio Media 社について何と言っていますか。

(A) 海外展開を試みた。
(B) Gillian World News Agency 社が作った製品を売っている。
(C) もうすぐ新しい提供品が売り出される。
(D) 指導力に関わる問題に苦しんだ。

 話し手は❶で Antonio Media 社がここ7年で成長を遂げ、❷で「結果として海外にその事業範囲を拡大しようとしている」と述べている。正解はこれを言い換えた **(A)**。

 □launch 〜を発売する、開始する

81. ★★★★★

What does the speaker mean when she says, "Unfortunately it won't happen"?

(A) She will cancel her business trip.
(B) She thinks a product will be unavailable.
(C) She doesn't agree with a project.
(D) She is reporting on a plan's failure.

話し手が "Unfortunately it won't happen" と言う際、何を意味していますか。

(A) 出張を取りやめるつもりだ。
(B) 製品が利用できなくなると考えている。
(C) プロジェクトに賛同しない。
(D) 計画の失敗を報告している。

 意図を問われている箇所❺は「残念ながらそれは起こらない」という意味である。トーク全体を踏まえた上でこの前後の流れを見てみると、❶～❹で Antonio Media 社が海外進出を図り、企業合併を画策しているという前段から、❺ Antonio Media 社の広報担当が商談状況を報告➡❻残念だがそれ（合併）は起こらない➡❼合併する予定の会社が代わりに他の会社から資本を受けることになった、となっている。もともと交渉していた合併が不発となり、他の道を探すことになったことを受けた意図として、合併計画が失敗になったことに対する「残念だが」という表現になっていることがわかる。以上より、合併の失敗を a plan's failure と表現した **(D)** が正解。

 □unavailable 入手できない

---

82. ★★★☆☆

What is indicated about Gillian World News Agency?

(A) Its president left the company.
(B) It received investment funds.
(C) It changed its news sources.
(D) It acquired a company.

Gillian World News Agency 社について何が示されていますか。

(A) 社長が会社を去った。
(B) 投資資金を受け取った。
(C) 情報源を変更した。
(D) ある会社を買収した。

 話し手は❼で「他社からの投資の申し出を受け入れた」と述べているので、正解は **(B)**。企業の合併や買収は中止になったことから (D) は不正解。

 □fund 資金　□source もと、源　□acquire ～を獲得する、買収する

	1回目	2回目	3回目
80.			
81.			
82.			

80. (A)　81. (D)　82. (B)

Questions 83 through 85 refer to the following talk.

M: Attention, employees. ❶Allow me to welcome you all to the Cameron company banquet. ❷We hold this yearly dinner party to show our appreciation for all your efforts over the past year. ❸Cameron continues to be a leader in the advertising industry because of your hard work and commitment. ❹I'd like to specifically thank all employees who worked on the Moreland Jeans promotion, creating the billboards and television commercials for the company's new line of jeans. ❺As you know, it was a very profitable account. ❻And it was also important to us since the work helped us get nominated for the Jackson Advertising Award.

📝 問題83-85は次の話に関するものです。

M: 従業員の皆さま。Cameron 社の宴会にご参加いただきありがとうございます。皆さまの1年間のご尽力に感謝するため、毎年このパーティーを開催しています。Cameron 社が広告業界のリーダーであり続けているのは、皆さまの熱心な仕事と献身のおかげです。特に Moreland Jeans の販促に携わり、そのジーンズの新作ラインアップのために看板広告やテレビコマーシャルを制作した従業員の皆さまに感謝を申し上げます。ご存じのとおり、莫大な利益になりました。またキャンペーンは、Jackson 広告賞にノミネートされることにつながった点で重要なものでもありました。

✏️ □allow me to *do* 私に〜させてください　□yearly 年次の　□appreciation 感謝　□effort 努力
□commitment 献身　□promotion 販売促進　□billboard 看板広告　□profitable 利益となる
□get nominated for 〜にノミネートされる

83.

What is the purpose of the talk?

(A) To thank staff members
(B) To look for volunteers
(C) To plan a ceremony
(D) To introduce a new executive

話の目的は何ですか。

(A) 従業員に感謝すること。
(B) ボランティアを探すこと。
(C) 式典を計画すること。
(D) 新しい取締役を紹介すること。

🔍 話し手は❶で Cameron 社の宴会に参加してくれた御礼を述べ、❷で「従業員に感謝するための会」と述べている。以上から正解は **(A)**。

✏️ □ceremony 式典

84. ★★★★★

Where does the speaker most likely work?

(A) At a hotel
(B) At an apparel company
(C) At a catering firm
(D) At an advertising agency

話し手はどこで働いていると考えられますか。

(A) ホテル
(B) 衣料品の会社
(C) ケータリング会社
(D) 広告代理店

 話し手が❸で「Cameron 社が広告業界のリーダーであり続けている」と述べていることから、話し手は広告関係の仕事をしていると考えられる。以上より正解は **(D)**。

□apparel 衣料 (品)

---

85. ★★★★★

According to the speaker, why was the project beneficial?

(A) It improved morale.
(B) It resulted in an award nomination.
(C) It attracted new customers.
(D) It helped a charitable organization.

話し手によると、なぜプロジェクトは有益でしたか。

(A) 労働意欲を高めた。
(B) 受賞候補につながった。
(C) 新規顧客を引きつけた。
(D) 慈善団体を支援した。

話し手は❹で、Moreland Jeans の販促について触れ、❺で莫大な利益になったと述べ、そして❻で「このキャンペーンが賞にノミネートされた点でも重要だった」と述べていることから、Moreland Jeans の販促＝project が利益と受賞候補の2つに繋がったことがわかる。この後者を指した **(B)** が正解。トーク中に project という直接的な言及はないが、このように設問文で特定の仕事を指す表現としても出てくることを押さえておこう。

□beneficial 有益である　□morale 労働意欲、モラール　□result in ～という結果になる
□charitable organization 慈善団体

	1回目	2回目	3回目
83.			
84.			
85.			

83. (A)　84. (D)　85. (B)

PART 4

TEST 4

223

Questions 86 through 88 refer to the following announcement.

M: Good evening, staff members. ❶Beginning next month, we are installing new digital locks on all doors into the building. ❷All employees will need to get a new digital key for entering the building. ❸You're asked to bring your ID card to the security office, where the guard will have a new key ready for you. ❹The new keys will be linked only to your ID. ❺Therefore, we will be able to monitor who enters and leaves the building 24 hours a day. ❻There's more information available about the upcoming security changes in the company magazine, so ❼make sure to pick it up. ❽After reading it carefully, if you have any questions, don't hesitate to contact your supervisor. Thank you.

📝 問題86-88は次のお知らせに関するものです。

M: こんばんは、従業員の皆さま。来月よりビルに入るための全てのドアに電子ロックを取り付けます。全従業員はビルに入る際に新しい電子キーが必要になります。警備員が新しい鍵を準備しますので、警備室にIDカードを持っていってください。新しい鍵は各自のIDにのみ対応しています。これにより、1日24時間、ビルに出入りする人を全て監視できるようになります。この警備関連の変更に関する詳細情報は社内報で確認できますので、忘れずにお持ちください。これをよく読んで、もし質問がある場合は遠慮なく上司に聞いてください。よろしくお願いいたします。

✎ □digital lock 電子ロック □digital key 電子キー □security office 警備室 □guard 警備員
□monitor ～を監視する □upcoming 来たるべき □don't hesitate to contact 遠慮なく～に連絡する
□supervisor 管理者、上司

---

86. ★★☆☆☆

What are listeners asked to provide?

(A) A work log
(B) A form of identification
(C) A signed employment contract
(D) A vacation schedule

聞き手は何を提供するように求められていますか。

(A) 業務記録
(B) 身分証明書
(C) 署名付き雇用契約書
(D) 休暇の予定

🔍 話し手は❶・❷でビル入館時のルール変更について言及し、❸で身分証明書を警備室に持っていくように伝えている。ここから、聞き手が提供するように求められているのは身分証明書だとわかるので、正解は **(B)**。

✎ □work log 業務記録 □form of identification 身分証明書 □signed 署名入りの
□employment contract 雇用契約

87. ★★☆☆☆

What special feature is mentioned about the new digital key?

(A) It can confirm who enters a building.
(B) It can work in numerous branches.
(C) It can be set up by each employee.
(D) It can be used only on new doors.

新しい電子キーのどんな特別な機能について述べられていますか。

(A) 誰がビルに入ってきたか確認できる。
(B) 数多くの支店で動作する。
(C) 各従業員が設定できる。
(D) 新しいドアにのみ使うことができる。

 話し手は❹・❺で「新しい鍵は各自の ID に対応しているので、ビルに出入りする人を全て監視できる」と述べている。これを言い換えた **(A)** が正解。(A) の confirm は❺の monitor の言い換えとなっている。

🖊 □numerous 数多くの

88. ★★★★☆

What does the speaker mean when he says, "make sure to pick it up"?

(A) Staff members should review some information.
(B) Staff members should purchase some cards.
(C) Staff members should keep their offices clean.
(D) Staff members should collect their passes soon.

話し手が "make sure to pick it up" と言う際、何を意味していますか。

(A) 従業員は情報を確認する必要がある。
(B) 従業員はカードを購入する必要がある。
(C) 従業員はオフィスを綺麗な状態に保っておく必要がある。
(D) 従業員は近々入場許可証を受け取る必要がある。

 意図を問われている箇所❼は「忘れずに持っていくように」という意味になっている。前後を見ていくと、❻「警備関連の変更に関する詳細情報は社内報で確認できる」➡❼「忘れずにそれ（社内報）を持っていくように」➡❽「読んで質問がある場合は上司に確認を」という流れになっている。ここから、it（社内報）を持っていくのは、情報を確認しておいてほしいという意図であるとわかる。以上から正解は **(A)**。電子キーの話をしているが、配付方法については言及していないため、(D) は不正解。

🖊 □review 〜を確認する　□collect 〜を受け取る　□pass 許可証

	1回目	2回目	3回目
86.			
87.			
88.			

 86. (B)　87. (A)　88. (A)

225

Questions 89 through 91 refer to the following telephone message.

M: Hello, Ms. Nakazawa. ❶This is James Kronenberg from Wilson Mart. ❷Unfortunately, your order was returned to our distribution center, as it appears the address we have for you in our records is wrong. ❸This is likely because we lost some updated information when we upgraded our customer database last week. Could you please call me at 888-6549 to let me know your current address? You will need your membership number when you call so that we can verify your identity. ❹Please be assured that the pork chops in your order will be replaced with fresh ones after we sort out the address problem. We apologize for the inconvenience.

問題89-91は次の電話のメッセージに関するものです。

M: こんにちは、Nakazawa さん。Wilson Mart 社の James Kronenberg です。あいにく、当店で伺っている住所が間違っていたようで、ご注文が配送センターに戻ってきました。これは、先週顧客データベースをバージョンアップした際に最新の情報が消えてしまったためだと思われます。888-6549までお電話いただき、現在のご住所をお知らせいただけますか。ご本人であると確認できるように、お電話をおかけいただく際は会員番号が必要です。当店が住所の問題を解決しましたら、ご注文いただいたポークチョップは新鮮なものに交換してお送りいたしますことをご承知おきください。ご迷惑をおかけし申し訳ありません。

□distribution center 配送センター □it appears どうやら〜である
□this is likely because これはおそらく〜が原因である □upgrade 〜をバージョンアップする □verify 〜を検証する
□identity 身元 □be assured that 〜を承知する □pork chop ポークチョップ (豚肉の切り身)
□be replaced with 〜に交換する □sort out 〜を解決する、整理する

89. ★★☆☆☆

Why is the speaker calling?

(A) To report a problem with an order
(B) To give details of a health warning
(C) To apologize for an early billing
(D) To arrange a new delivery date

話し手はなぜ電話をしていますか。

(A) 注文の問題について報告するため。
(B) 健康被害警告の詳細を知らせるため。
(C) 早期請求を謝罪するため。
(D) 新たな配送日を決めるため。

話し手は❶で社名と名前を名乗り、❷で「当店で伺っている住所が間違っており、注文が配送センターに戻ってきた」と述べている。以上より、ある注文に問題があって電話したことがわかるので、これを言い換えた **(A)** が正解。

□detail 詳細 □health warning 健康に関する警告 □early billing 早期請求

90. ★★★☆☆

According to the speaker, what caused the issue?

(A) A misprint on an invoice
(B) A relocation of the business
(C) A database error
(D) A mechanical failure

話し手によると問題の原因は何ですか。

(A) 明細書の誤植
(B) 事業所の移転
(C) データベースの不具合
(D) 機械の故障

話し手は❸で問題が起きた原因を「先週顧客データベースをバージョンアップした際に最新の情報が消えてしまったためだ」と推測している。これはデータベース上の問題であると言えるため、正解は **(C)**。❸の This is likely because は原因や理由を述べる際の表現なので、ここをキャッチして、その後を注意深く聞き取るようにしよう。

□misprint 誤植　□relocation 移転　□mechanical failure 機械の故障

---

91. ★★★☆☆

What does the speaker say will happen next?

(A) The company will replace some produce.
(B) The business will forward another invoice.
(C) The customer will receive store credit.
(D) The membership number will be changed.

話し手は何が起こると言っていますか。

(A) 農産物を取り替える。
(B) 企業は別の請求書を送る。
(C) 顧客は返品交換物を受け取る。
(D) 会員番号が変更される。

話し手はトークの後半❹で「注文を受けたポークチョップは新鮮なものに交換して送る」と述べている。ここから、送付予定のある食品については新しいものに交換することがわかる。以上の pork chops = produce（農産物）と言い換えた **(A)** が正解。

□produce 農産物　□forward 〜を送る
□store credit ストアクレジット（返品した品物と同じ金額分の買い物ができる権利）

	1回目	2回目	3回目
89.			
90.			
91.			

89. (A)　90. (C)　91. (A)

Questions 92 through 94 refer to the following broadcast.

W: ❶And now, the latest news on the weather. ❷It's been a pretty gray weekend across the country with rain in the south. Current temperatures this afternoon are still above average at 17 degrees in Montreal. Beginning tomorrow morning we'll experience very windy weather across the entire region, with a strong wind warning in the south. ❸Later in the week, beginning Friday we'll see more rainy conditions as the weather front heads south, lowering temperatures a few degrees. ❹Special thanks to Kirsty Russel of Ottawa for sending this beautiful photo of a deer playing in a snow-covered field near her house. ❺If you'd like to send in an image, please e-mail it to us at the address shown at the bottom of your screen.

📝 問題92-94は次の放送に関するものです。

W: では、最新の気象情報をお伝えします。全国的に曇り空の週末で、南部は雨となっています。現在の午後の気温は、Montreal では17度で、まだ平均を上回っています。明日の朝から地域全体で強風が発生し、南部では強風警報が出ています。週の後半は、金曜日から前線が南に向かうことで雨が増え、気温も数度下がるでしょう。家の近くの雪で覆われた野原で遊ぶ鹿の美しい写真を送っていただいた Ottawa の Kirsty Russel さんに感謝を申し上げます。画像を送ってくださる方は、画面の下に表示されているアドレスにEメールをお送りください。

✏️ □latest 最新の　□gray 曇った　□above average 平均を上回る　□degree 度　□windy 風が強い
□across the entire region その地域全体にわたって　□weather front 前線　□head ～に向かう
□lower ～を下げる　□snow-covered 雪で覆われている　□bottom of one's screen ～の画面下

92.

What is the main purpose of the broadcast?

(A) To announce a contest
(B) To advertise a local event
(C) To inform listeners of traffic conditions
(D) To provide a weather advisory

放送の主な目的は何ですか。

(A) コンテストのお知らせをすること。
(B) 地元のイベントを宣伝すること。
(C) 道路状況を伝えること。
(D) 気象関連の注意を提供すること。

🔍 話し手は❶で最新の天気情報を伝えると述べ、❷で「強風警報が出ている」と話している。以上から天気に関する注意を伝えていることがわかるので、正解は **(D)**。weather advisory とは天気の注意報のこと。

✏️ □inform A of A に～のことを伝える

93. ★★☆☆☆

What will happen on Friday?	金曜日に何が起こりますか。
(A) Temperatures will go up.	(A) 気温が上昇する。
(B) The area will experience light winds.	(B) 地域に弱い風が吹く。
(C) It will rain.	**(C)** 雨が降る。
(D) A cold front will bring snow.	(D) 寒冷前線が雪をもたらす。

話し手は❸で「金曜日から前線が南に向かうことで雨が増え、気温も数度下がる」と述べている。この前半部分に相当する **(C)** が正解。(A) は❸の内容と真逆なので不正解。

□go up 上昇する　□light wind 弱い風　□cold front 寒冷前線

---

94. ★★★☆☆

Why would listeners send an e-mail?	聞き手はなぜ E メールを送りますか。
(A) To share photographs of their area	**(A)** 地域の写真を送るため。
(B) To see their names on the screen	(B) 名前を画面上に映すため。
(C) To contribute data to a report	(C) データで報道に寄与するため。
(D) To register for a contest	(D) コンテストに参加登録するため。

話し手は❹である地域の写真を送付してくれた人に感謝をした後で、❺で「画像を送りたい人は、E メールを送ってほしい」と述べている。ここから、同様にある地域の写真を共有したい場合にメールを送るとわかる。以上から正解は **(A)**。❺にある image は、ここでは picture、photo (photograph) と同じ意味で使われている。

□contribute 〜を提供する　□register for 〜に参加登録する

	1回目	2回目	3回目
92.			
93.			
94.			

 92. (D)　93. (C)　94. (A)

Questions 95 through 97 refer to the following talk and chart.

📝 問題95-97は次の話と図表に関するものです。

M: As sales representatives of Meyer Electronics, your performance has a direct impact on the success or failure of our company. ❶So I'm very happy to tell you that our overall sales were up during September, and each of you successfully met your individual targets. ❷I really appreciate your efforts. ❸As you no doubt remember, September 1st saw the release of many new desktop models in our store, and we held a competition to see who could sell the most of the two most popular models. ❹In order to win a monthly bonus of $200, you had to sell at least thirty Entropixer 700s, and at least forty Onda Cosmicas. Only one of you managed to achieve this, in spite of your generally high sales. Let's take a look at the number of units sold and find out who won the bonus.

M: Meyer Electronics 社の営業担当者であるため、皆さんの成果は会社が成功するか失敗するかに直接的な影響を持ちます。ですから、9月の会社全体の売り上げが増え、各自が自身の目標を達成できたことを非常にうれしく思います。皆さんの尽力に大変感謝しています。皆さんが間違いなく記憶されているとおり、当店では9月1日に多くの新作デスクトップパソコンが発売となり、人気のモデル2機種を誰が一番多く売れるか競いました。200ドルの月のボーナスを獲得するには、Entropixer 700を最低30台と Onda Cosmica を最低40台売る必要がありました。皆さんの全体の売り上げは高いものでしたが、これを達成できたのは1人だけでした。では、販売台数を見て、誰がボーナスを勝ち取ったのか見てみましょう。

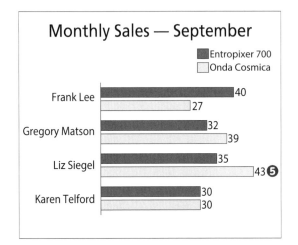

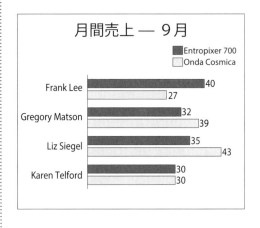

✏️ ☐sales representative 営業担当者 ☐direct impact on ～への直接的な影響 ☐failure 失敗 ☐overall 全体の
☐individual target 個別目標 ☐no doubt 間違いなく ☐release 発売 ☐hold a competition 競争をする
☐in order to *do* ～するために ☐manage to *do* 何とかして～する ☐achieve ～を達成する
☐in spite of ～にかかわらず ☐generally 一般的に ☐take a look at ～を見る ☐unit ユニット、個

95. ★★☆☆☆

What is the main purpose of the talk?

(A) To suggest ways to improve customer satisfaction
(B) To express gratitude to staff members
(C) To explain the reason for a price decrease
(D) To promote a member of staff

話の主な目的は何ですか。

(A) 顧客満足度を上げるための方法を提案すること。
(B) スタッフに感謝の意を表すること。
(C) 値下がりした理由を説明すること。
(D) スタッフの一人を昇進させること。

 話し手は❶で「9月の会社全体の売り上げが増え、各自が自身の目標を達成できたことが非常にうれしい」と述べ、❷で「皆さんの尽力に大変感謝している」と伝えている。ここから、スタッフに感謝を述べていることがわかるので、正解は**(B)**。

 □customer satisfaction 顧客満足　□express gratitude 感謝を伝える　□price decrease 値下がり

96. ★★★☆☆

According to the speaker, what happened at the beginning of September?

(A) Employees attended a seminar.
(B) Customers received a discount.
(C) Meyer Electronics opened a new store.
(D) Several new products were launched.

話し手によると9月の初めに何がありましたか。

(A) 従業員が講習に参加した。
(B) 顧客が割引を受けた。
(C) Meyer Electronics 社が新店舗を開いた。
(D) 新製品が数点発売された。

 話し手は❸で「当店では9月1日に多くの新作デスクトップパソコンが発売となり」と述べている。ここから、新製品が複数発売されたことがわかる。以上より、正解はこれを言い換えた**(D)**。(D)は❸の saw the release of many new desktop models の言い換えとなっている。

 □launch 〜を発売する

97. ★★★★☆

Look at the graphic. Who will receive the monthly bonus?

(A) Frank Lee
(B) Gregory Matson
(C) Liz Siegel
(D) Karen Telford

図を見てください。月のボーナスを受け取るのは誰ですか。

(A) Frank Lee
(B) Gregory Matson
(C) Liz Siegel
(D) Karen Telford

 話し手は❹で「Entropixer 700を最低30台と Onda Cosmica を最低40台売った人がボーナスを得る」と述べている。次にグラフを見ると、両方達成したのは❺から Liz Siegel さんだとわかる。以上より正解は**(C)**。

	1回目	2回目	3回目
95.			
96.			
97.			

 95. (B)　96. (D)　97. (C)

Questions 98 through 100 refer to the following announcement and flyer.

W: Hello, ❶Hamson's Sporting Goods shoppers! We are having a huge end-of-summer sale this week. ❷We'll be marking down 300 pieces of merchandise every day by 50 percent. The sale starts on Monday and ends on Thursday. On Monday, it's team sports equipment. On Tuesday, it's fitness equipment. And we apologize for the change on the schedule printed on the flyer. ❸It says prices will go back to normal on Thursday, but we've decided to extend the Wednesday sale into Thursday. Come on each day to enjoy great deals. ❹The special savings apply to a maximum of two items per customer and end when 300 items are sold on that day.

📝 問題98-100は次のアナウンスとチラシに関するものです。

W: こんにちは、Hamson スポーツ用品店でお買い物中の皆さま。今週当店では大規模な夏の終わりセールを行います。毎日300点の商品を50パーセント値下げいたします。セールは月曜日に始まり、木曜日に終了します。月曜日はチームスポーツ用品です。火曜日はフィットネス用品。そして、申し訳ありませんが、チラシに印刷されている予定に変更があります。木曜日に通常価格に戻ると書いていますが、水曜日のセールを木曜日まで延長することにいたしました。どの曜日もセールをお楽しみにお越しください。特別価格の品はお一人様最大2点までで、各日とも先着300点で終了となります。

BIG SALE

Monday	**Team Sports Equipment**
Tuesday	**Fitness Sports Equipment**
❺**Wednesday**	**Footwear**
Thursday	Return to Regular Prices

大セール

月曜日	チームスポーツ用品
火曜日	フィットネス用品
水曜日	靴
木曜日	通常価格に戻ります

✏️ □shopper 買い物客　□end-of-summer 夏の終わりの　□mark down 〜を値下げする　□merchandise 商品
□sports equipment スポーツ用品　□fitness equipment フィットネス用品　□flyer チラシ
□go back to normal 元に戻る　□extend A into A を〜まで延長する　□great deals お買い得セール
□saving 値引き　□apply to 〜に適用する　□return to 〜に戻る

98.

What is limited about this sale?

(A) How long the shop is open
(B) Which brands are available
(C) Which branches will run the promotion
(D) How many items receive the discount

セールでは何が制限されていますか。

(A) どのぐらい店が開いているか
(B) どのブランドが対象になるか
(C) どの支店で販促が行われるか
(D) いくつの商品で割引を受けられるか

 話し手は❶で買い物客に呼びかけて、今週のセールについて伝え、❷で「毎日300点の品物で半額セールを実施する」と述べている。ここから、割引の対象になる商品の数が限定されていることがわかる。以上から正解は **(D)**。ブランドについては言及していないため (B) は不正解。

✎ □run ～を行う、運営する

99.

What is the discount?

(A) Half off the regular price
(B) Two items for the price of one
(C) Five dollars off every item
(D) Ten dollars for all items

割引はどのぐらいですか。

(A) 通常価格の半分
(B) 商品2点で1点分の価格
(C) 各商品が5ドル引き
(D) 全商品10ドル引き

 ❷から割引額は50%、つまり半額だとわかるため、正解は **(A)**。(B) も実質半額だが、❹は「ひとり2点まで」と商品の購入個数の限度について述べているだけで、2点買ったら半額になるということではないため、ここでは不正解。

✎ □half off ～の半額である

100.

Look at the graphic. What product will be on sale on Thursday?

(A) All goods
(B) Team Sports Equipment
(C) Fitness Sports Equipment
(D) Footwear

表を見てください。木曜日にどの製品がセールになりますか。

(A) 全商品
(B) チームスポーツ用品
(C) フィットネス用品
(D) 靴

 話し手は❸で「チラシには木曜日に通常価格に戻ると書いているが、水曜日のセールを木曜日まで延長する」と述べている。つまり、水曜日のアイテムが木曜日もセール対象となることがわかる。表を見ると、❺から水曜日のセール品は靴であることがわかるため、正解は **(D)**。

✎ □footwear 靴

	1回目	2回目	3回目
98.			
99.			
100.			

 98. (D)　99. (A)　100. (D)

TOKIMAKURE!

PART **3**&**4**

Test

5

NOTE

LET'S GET STARTED!

32. What is the topic of the conversation?

(A) Harvesting some produce
(B) Hiring farm workers
(C) Buying farm equipment
(D) Preparing for the rainy season

33. What does the man mention about last year?

(A) A watering system was installed.
(B) Different fields were used.
(C) Some fruits were ruined.
(D) A different crop was planted.

34. What does the woman suggest they do now?

(A) Check a warehouse
(B) Send an invoice
(C) E-mail customers
(D) Meet with the visitors

35. What problem are the speakers talking about?

(A) A promotion has been unsuccessful.
(B) There are too many rivals.
(C) Customers are expecting various menus.
(D) There is a need to change the business hours.

36. Who most likely is Mr. Taylor?

(A) A manager
(B) A waiter
(C) A receptionist
(D) A customer

37. What does the man say he will do?

(A) Inform people of a change
(B) Give complimentary dinner coupons
(C) Speak to Mr. Taylor
(D) Send a memo to staff

38. Where does the woman most likely work?

(A) At a magazine publisher
(B) At a retail store
(C) At an auto dealership
(D) At a delivery company

39. Why is the woman calling?

(A) To give an update on an order
(B) To ask for an alternative address
(C) To inform someone of a product warranty
(D) To request a time for pickup

40. Why is Mr. Brooks unavailable?

(A) He is visiting a doctor.
(B) He is working at a different branch.
(C) He is handling a private matter.
(D) He is meeting a client.

41. What does the man say he must do by the end of today?

(A) Check a report
(B) Hand in some material
(C) Train some staff
(D) Complete the draft of a speech

42. What problem does the woman mention?

(A) The wrong program was used.
(B) A due date has passed.
(C) Some errors were found.
(D) An appointment has been missed.

43. What solution does the man propose?

(A) Distributing the work to other colleagues
(B) Providing an extension
(C) Looking for a different location
(D) Meeting at a later time

GO ON TO THE NEXT PAGE

 32-34 *P. 244*   35-37 *P. 246*   38-40 *P. 248*   41-43 *P. 250*

44. Where most likely are the speakers?

(A) At a newspaper company
(B) At a print shop
(C) At a library
(D) At a publishing company

45. What problem does the man mention?

(A) A facility is under construction.
(B) A printer is out of order.
(C) A newspaper is out of stock.
(D) A book delivery is late.

46. What does the man suggest the woman do?

(A) Return at a later time
(B) Go to another branch
(C) Renew a subscription
(D) Contact technical support

47. Where most likely do the speakers work?

(A) At a financial institution
(B) At an advertising agency
(C) At a construction company
(D) At an accounting firm

48. What does the woman mean when she says, "I haven't seen it"?

(A) She is unfamiliar with a policy.
(B) She is searching for a lost item.
(C) She cannot comment on a product.
(D) She cannot confirm her attendance.

49. What does the man offer to do?

(A) Accompany a colleague to a meeting
(B) Recommend the woman for an event
(C) Ask the supervisor for a raise
(D) Review some of the woman's work

50. Where do the speakers most likely work?

(A) At a museum
(B) At a graphic design studio
(C) At a book distributor
(D) At a newspaper company

51. Why will the man visit a client?

(A) To deliver some material
(B) To take an order
(C) To promote a new service
(D) To pick up an item

52. What does the woman suggest the man do?

(A) Take a company vehicle
(B) Use more photographs
(C) Invite a colleague to join him
(D) Check his work for errors

53. What is the topic of the conversation?

(A) A corporate banquet
(B) An advertising method
(C) A local festival
(D) A marketing event

54. According to the man, what is the marketing department busy doing?

(A) Providing special offers
(B) Looking for new contacts
(C) Composing a monthly plan
(D) Creating a marketing tool

55. What does the woman say she will do?

(A) Prepare for the event
(B) Respond to an e-mail
(C) Write an e-mail to her director
(D) Contact the receptionist

44-46 *P. 252*   47-49 *P. 254*   50-52 *P. 256*   53-55 *P. 258*

56. Where do the speakers most likely work?

(A) At a property rental office
(B) At a law firm
(C) At a photo studio
(D) At a record shop

57. What does Allegra recommend?

(A) Confirming a bank statement
(B) Speaking to an assistant
(C) Trying to access information on the Internet
(D) Scheduling a conference

58. Why is the man concerned?

(A) His computer is out of order.
(B) Some supplies have not been shipped.
(C) Some paperwork was signed incorrectly.
(D) He cannot locate a document.

59. What does the man say he did in college?

(A) He taught students to play the guitar.
(B) He gained work experience.
(C) He made a Web page.
(D) He played in a musical group.

60. What is available on the Web site?

(A) A list of local radio broadcasts
(B) Free downloadable music
(C) Educational videos
(D) Feedback from instructors

61. What does the man imply when he says, "That would be helpful"?

(A) He will join a mailing list.
(B) An e-mail address is unnecessary.
(C) A lesson seems competitively priced.
(D) He appreciates a schedule change.

HAWK'S VISIBILITY EYE CLINIC

Discount Coupon - - - - - - - - - - -

Eyeglasses ($50 or under) ---------------------- $5 off

Eyeglasses (Over $50) --------------------- $10 off

Contact Lenses ($50 - $100) ------------------ $20 off

Contact Lenses (Over $100) ------------------- $30 off

Expires 11/30

62. What did the woman do last Wednesday?

(A) She called an eye clinic.
(B) She purchased contact lenses.
(C) She had her eyes checked.
(D) She was given a coupon.

63. What does the man suggest the woman do?

(A) Pick up her order tomorrow afternoon
(B) Finalize some paperwork
(C) Contact him in November
(D) Come to his hospital today

64. Look at the graphic. What discount will the woman probably receive?

(A) $5
(B) $10
(C) $20
(D) $30

GO ON TO THE NEXT PAGE ➡

🚩 56-58 *P. 260*   🚩 59-61 *P. 262*   🚩 62-64 *P. 264*

Date	Available Time
March 19 (Monday)	10:00 A.M. - 11:00 A.M.
March 20 (Tuesday)	2:00 P.M. - 5:00 P.M.
March 21 (Wednesday)	2:00 P.M. - 4:00 P.M.
March 22 (Thursday)	1:30 P.M. - 3:00 P.M.

65. What does the man ask the woman to do?

(A) Call some applicants
(B) Arrange a customer's visit
(C) Prepare for job interviews
(D) Design a Web site

66. What problem does the woman talk about?

(A) A Web site is currently out of order.
(B) A call to an important customer was too late.
(C) A staff meeting has been delayed.
(D) There is a scheduling conflict.

67. Look at the graphic. What day will the woman reserve the meeting room for?

(A) Monday
(B) Tuesday
(C) Wednesday
(D) Thursday

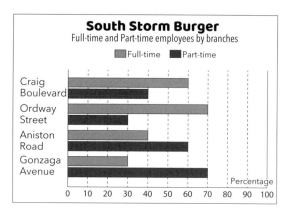

South Storm Burger
Full-time and Part-time employees by branches

68. What is the topic of the conversation?

(A) The changing of a menu
(B) The new location of a business
(C) The need to hire full-time staff
(D) The opening of a store

69. What problem does the man talk about?

(A) A location is understaffed.
(B) A manager is unavailable.
(C) A renovation is incomplete.
(D) A budget has been exceeded.

70. Look at the graphic. Which branch will the woman most likely contact?

(A) Craig Boulevard
(B) Ordway Street
(C) Aniston Road
(D) Gonzaga Avenue

🚩 **65-67** *P. 266*   🚩 **68-70** *P. 268*

71. What kind of business is being advertised?

(A) A travel agency
(B) A resort
(C) A hotel
(D) A restaurant

72. What added benefit does the speaker mention?

(A) Faster Internet booking
(B) Free meals
(C) Reduced prices
(D) Exclusive access

73. What are listeners invited to do on Wednesday?

(A) Tour Kelvin Convention Center
(B) Attend a presentation
(C) Collect discount vouchers
(D) Go to a dinner

74. What is the main purpose of the talk?

(A) To introduce a new employee
(B) To describe team performance
(C) To announce a change in policy
(D) To discuss company strategy

75. What is mentioned about the level of customer satisfaction?

(A) It is higher than the company's average.
(B) The firm has the best rate in the industry.
(C) It has been continuously increasing.
(D) It will soon be calculated differently.

76. What will happen next month?

(A) The firm will open a new office overseas.
(B) The president will be on vacation.
(C) A customer survey will be sent out.
(D) There will be training for new staff members.

77. What topic is the TV show discussing?

(A) The opening of a local restaurant
(B) Traffic conditions
(C) Saturday night entertainment
(D) The history of a community

78. Who is Mina Johnson?

(A) An author
(B) A television presenter
(C) A tour guide
(D) A chef

79. How can viewers win a prize?

(A) By accessing a homepage
(B) By participating in a quiz
(C) By attending a special meeting
(D) By making a donation

80. Where most likely are the listeners?

(A) At a government office
(B) At a construction site
(C) At an airport
(D) At a weather center

81. What is mentioned about the use of some equipment?

(A) It must be operated under supervision.
(B) It requires additional training.
(C) It is only allowed at certain times.
(D) It has caused complaints about noise.

82. What does the speaker mean when he says, "please do not rush"?

(A) There is enough time for everyone to receive food.
(B) There are new speed limits in place.
(C) A deadline has been extended.
(D) Safety steps must not be skipped.

GO ON TO THE NEXT PAGE ➡

 71-73 *P. 270*   74-76 *P. 272*   77-79 *P. 274*   80-82 *P. 276*

241

83. What is the purpose of the event?

(A) To announce a manager's retirement
(B) To collect funds for charity
(C) To honor new graduates
(D) To attract participants to a program

84. What will the video feature?

(A) The city's landmarks
(B) A training session
(C) A new teacher
(D) The company's history

85. What will take place after the meal?

(A) A speech by the president
(B) Small group discussions
(C) Individual interviews
(D) A dance party

86. What is the topic of the broadcast?

(A) A live performance
(B) Local traffic conditions
(C) A book launch
(D) An area festival

87. What does the speaker mean when she says, "Get yours quick"?

(A) The concert will finish soon.
(B) Parking spaces will be limited.
(C) Seats are expected to be taken quickly.
(D) The price of an item is due to increase.

88. What do the producers expect?

(A) More copies will be needed.
(B) Album sales will increase.
(C) Visitors will enjoy a redesign.
(D) A new composer will join.

89. Where is the speaker calling?

(A) An eye clinic
(B) A dental office
(C) A vehicle license center
(D) A hospital

90. What does the speaker imply when he says, "I know this is not the first time"?

(A) He is sorry for causing Ms. Holmes inconvenience again.
(B) He does not need to do the same training.
(C) He is unhappy at a repeated mistake.
(D) He expects Ms. Holmes to do a task easily.

91. What is the listener asked to do?

(A) Confirm Mr. Foreman's bill
(B) Participate in an event
(C) Return a call
(D) Reserve a hotel room

92. According to the speaker, what makes the Soar Wings Tower unique?

(A) Its unusual color
(B) Its intriguing histor
(C) Its construction style
(D) Its family ownership

93. What does the speaker suggest passengers do after the tour?

(A) Go to a souvenir shop
(B) Eat with the other passengers
(C) Take a photo of the Soar Wings Tower
(D) Reserve tickets for the next tour

94. What does the speaker remind the listeners to do?

(A) Climb the Soar Wings Tower
(B) Keep to a schedule
(C) Gather their belongings
(D) Offer a tip to the bus driver

83-85 P. 278   86-88 P. 280   89-91 P. 282   92-94 P. 284

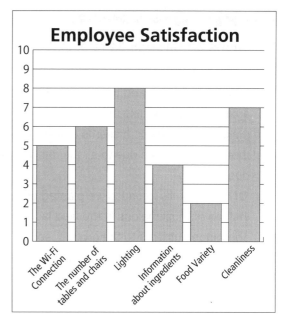

Madame Butterfly

At Hicks Opera House

Performance Starts: 7:00 P.M.

Ticket Price: $80

Seat: J15

Name: Mr. James Davenport

95. Why is the speaker calling?

(A) To explain a performance schedule
(B) To express gratitude to a sponsor
(C) To offer information about prices
(D) To give directions to an opera house

96. Look at the graphic. When did Mr. Davenport most likely attend an opera?

(A) On December 10
(B) On December 17
(C) On December 24
(D) On December 31

97. According to the speaker, how can Mr. Davenport buy a ticket?

(A) By using a Web site
(B) By going to the opera house
(C) By submitting an e-mail
(D) By making a phone call

98. What type of project is the speaker discussing?

(A) Opening a new dining area
(B) Improving employees' health
(C) Making improvements to a cafeteria
(D) Switching to a different Internet service provider

99. According to the speaker, what is the problem with the current Internet connection?

(A) The security is vulnerable.
(B) The signal frequently cuts off.
(C) It has restrictions on downloads.
(D) Its speed is too slow.

100. Look at the graphic. What does the speaker ask the listeners to discuss?

(A) Food variety
(B) The Wi-Fi connection
(C) Information about ingredients
(D) The number of tables and chairs

PART 4

TEST 5

95-97 *P. 286*

98-100 *P. 288*

Questions 32 through 34 refer to the following conversation.

W: Leo, ❶I have checked the muskmelon fields again, and it looks like they will be ready for picking in one week. It seems quicker than we thought. Maybe it's due to all the rain we've been getting.

M: ❷No, I think it's because we planted corn instead of muskmelons in the field last year. The corn adds nutrients to the ground, so the muskmelons should be growing faster this year.

W: You're right. It was a good idea to begin rotating between the two. ❸Why don't we forward our e-mail to customers right now to let them know the muskmelons will be ready for purchase sooner than we anticipated?

W: Leo さん、マスクメロンの畑をまた見て来たのですが、あと1週間で収穫できそうでした。思っていたよりも早そうですね。おそらくこのところの雨によるものでしょう。

M: いいえ、昨年マスクメロンの代わりにトウモロコシを畑に植えたからだと思います。トウモロコシが土壌に栄養を与えるので、必然的にマスクメロンが今年速く成長しているのです。

W: そのためですね。その2種類を順に作り始めたのは良いアイデアでした。すぐにお客様にEメールを送って、マスクメロンが予定していたよりも早く購入できるようになることを知らせましょう。

□muskmelon マスクメロン　□field 畑　□due to ～による　□plant ～を植える　□instead of ～の代わりに　□nutrient 栄養　□rotate between the two 2つを順に作る　□forward ～を送付する、転送する　□anticipate ～を予期する

32. ★★★☆☆

What is the topic of the conversation?

(A) Harvesting some produce
(B) Hiring farm workers
(C) Buying farm equipment
(D) Preparing for the rainy season

会話の話題は何ですか。

(A) 農産物を収穫すること。
(B) 農場作業員を補充すること。
(C) 農機具を購入すること。
(D) 雨季に備えること。

会話冒頭❶で女性が「マスクメロンの畑をまた見て来たが、もうすぐ収穫できそうだった」と述べている。ここから、農作物の収穫について話していることがわかる。以上から正解は **(A)**。会話中で picking = harvesting、muskmelon = produce と言い換えられていることも要チェック。

□harvest ～を収穫する　□produce 農作物　□farm equipment 農機具　□rainy season 雨期

33. ★★★☆☆

What does the man mention about last year?

(A) A watering system was installed.
(B) Different fields were used.
(C) Some fruits were ruined.
(D) A different crop was planted.

男性は昨年について何と言っていますか。

(A) 給水システムが設置された。
(B) さまざまな畑が使用された。
(C) 果物が台無しになった。
(D) 別の作物が植えられた。

 男性は❷で「昨年マスクメロンの代わりにトウモロコシを畑に植えた」と述べている。ここから、昨年はマスクメロン以外の作物を植えていたとわかるため、正解は **(D)**。

 □watering system 給水システム　□ruin 〜をだめにする　□crop 作物

---

34. ★★★☆☆

What does the woman suggest they do now?

(A) Check a warehouse
(B) Send an invoice
(C) E-mail customers
(D) Meet with the visitors

女性は今から何をすることを提案していますか。

(A) 倉庫を確認すること。
(B) 請求書を送ること。
(C) 顧客に E メールを送ること。
(D) 訪問者と会うこと。

 女性は❸で「お客様に E メールを送って、マスクメロンが予定よりも早く購入できることを知らせよう」と提案している。ここから、女性がお客様に E メールを送ることを提案しているとわかる。以上から正解は **(C)**。

 □invoice 請求書

	1回目	2回目	3回目
32.			
33.			
34.			

 32. (A)　33. (D)　34. (C)

Questions 35 through 37 refer to the following conversation.

W: Ever since our restaurant was shown on a TV program last week, our sales revenue has increased by 20 percent. But ❶many customers are complaining about the limited hours that our restaurant is operational. ❷We could increase our profit by adjusting the operational hours.

M: I agree. ❸But it will mean extending the working hours. ❹We need to contact Mr. Taylor about this change first.

W: In fact, he already approved my proposal for the increase this morning. Here are the proposed new times.

M: I see. ❺I'll make an announcement to all the workers about the amended working hours tonight.

📝 問題35-37は次の会話に関するものです。

W: 先週テレビ番組で当レストランが紹介されてから、売上高が20パーセント増加しました。しかしお客様の多くはレストランの営業時間がとても短いと不満を言っています。営業時間を調整することで利益を増やせそうです。

M: 私もそう思います。ただ、そうすると勤務時間が延びることになります。まず、レストランの責任者のTaylorさんに変更することを伝える必要がありますね。

W: 実は今朝、営業時間を延長する提案を承認してくださっています。新しい時間の案です。

M: わかりました。今夜、変更後の営業時間について全従業員に知らせます。

✏️ □ever since ～後ずっと □sales revenue 売上高 □increase by (数値)ほど増える
□complain about ～に対して苦情を言う □operational 稼働している □profit 利益 □adjust ～を調整する
□operational hours 営業時間 □extend ～を延長する □working hours 営業時間 □contact ～に連絡する
□proposed 提案された □amended 変更された

---

35. ★★★☆☆

What problem are the speakers talking about?

(A) A promotion has been unsuccessful.
(B) There are too many rivals.
(C) Customers are expecting various menus.
(D) There is a need to change the business hours.

話し手たちはどんな問題について話していますか。

(A) 販売促進キャンペーンは失敗だった。
(B) ライバルが多すぎる。
(C) 客は多様なメニューを期待している。
(D) 営業時間の変更が必要である。

🔍 女性は❶・❷で「お客様の多くがレストランの営業時間の短さに不満があり、営業時間を調整することで対応できそうだ」と述べている。ここから、営業時間変更の必要性について話していることがわかる。正解は営業時間をbusiness hoursと言い換えた**(D)**。

✏️ □promotion 販売促進 □unsuccessful 失敗である □rival ライバル、競合 □various さまざまな
□business hours 営業時間

36. ★★★★☆

Who most likely is Mr. Taylor?	Taylor さんは誰だと考えられますか。
(A) A manager	**(A)** 店長
(B) A waiter	(B) ウエイター
(C) A receptionist	(C) 受付係
(D) A customer	(D) 客

 女性が❶・❷で「営業時間を調整しては」と提案したのに対し、男性が❸・❹で「営業時間の調整は勤務時間を延長することになるので、最初に Taylor さんに話す必要がある」と述べている。ここから、Taylor さんは、勤務時間延長の権限がある管理者であると考えられる。以上から正解は **(A)**。❸の it = adjusting the operational hours ということも押さえておこう。

 □receptionist 受付

---

37. ★★★★★

What does the man say he will do?	男性は何をすると言っていますか。
(A) Inform people of a change	**(A)** 変更について人々に知らせる。
(B) Give complimentary dinner coupons	(B) 無料の夕食券を渡す。
(C) Speak to Mr. Taylor	(C) Taylor さんと話す。
(D) Send a memo to staff	(D) 書類を送信する。

 男性は❺で「今夜、変更後の営業時間について全従業員に知らせる」と述べている。以上から正解は **(A)**。

 □inform A of A に〜を知らせる　□complimentary 無料の

	1回目	2回目	3回目
35.			
36.			
37.			

 35. (D)　36. (A)　37. (A)

🇺🇸 W 🇨🇦 M 🔊 3-5-38_40-01~02

Questions 38 through 40 refer to the following conversation.

W: ❶Hello, this is Katherine calling from Francois Printers. ❷I would like to talk to Mr. Brooks about his personal order of a laser printer.

M: Sorry, but he is currently out of the office. What should I tell him when he comes back?

W: ❸Could you tell him that we got the printer today? ❹I initially told him that it would arrive at our store next month, but actually we received the shipment today, so it's in our inventory.

M: I see. ❺Mr. Brooks is at a business lunch with a customer right now, so, I will text him and tell him that he can pick it up from your store this afternoon.

問題38-40は次の会話に関するものです。

W: こんにちは、Francois Printers 社の Katherine です。Brooks さんが個人で注文されたレーザープリンターについてお話ししたいのですが。

M: すみませんが、彼はただいま外出しております。戻りましたら何とお伝えしたらよろしいですか。

W: では、本日プリンターが入荷したとお伝えいただけますか。初めは当店に届くのは来月だとお伝えしていましたが、実は本日配送がありまして、今、当店の在庫にあります。

M: わかりました。Brooks は現在、お客様と商談を兼ねた昼食会に行っておりますので、今日の午後にそちらのお店で引き取れることをテキストメッセージで伝えておきます。

□personal order 個人注文 □laser printer レーザープリンター □out of the office 外出している
□shipment 発送、送付 □inventory 在庫 □right now 今ちょうど □text ～にテキストメッセージを送る
□pick up ～を引き取る

---

38. ★★★★☆

Where does the woman most likely work?

(A) At a magazine publisher
(B) At a retail store
(C) At an auto dealership
(D) At a delivery company

女性はどこで働いていると考えられますか。

(A) 雑誌出版社
(B) 小売店
(C) 自動車の会社
(D) 宅配業者

 会話冒頭❶・❷で女性が「Francois Printers 社の者である」「注文されたレーザープリンターについて話したい」と述べている。以上から、女性はレーザープリンターを商品として取り扱っている会社で、顧客に販売している場所、つまり小売店舗で働いているとわかる。以上から正解は **(B)**。

 □magazine publisher 雑誌出版社 □retail store 小売店舗

39.

Why is the woman calling?

(A) To give an update on an order
(B) To ask for an alternative address
(C) To inform someone of a product warranty
(D) To request a time for pickup

女性はなぜ電話をしていますか。

(A) 注文に関する最新情報を伝えるため。
(B) 住所変更をお願いするため。
(C) 製品の保証について誰かに知らせるため。
(D) 受取時間の希望を伝えるため。

女性は❸・❹で「本日プリンターが入荷した」「来月届く予定だったが、今日店舗に届いた」と、お客様の注文に関する最新情報を伝えていることがわかる。以上から正解は **(A)**。

□update 最新情報、更新　□alternative 変更の　□inform A of A に～を知らせる
□product warranty 製品の保証　□pickup 受け取り

40.

Why is Mr. Brooks unavailable?

(A) He is visiting a doctor.
(B) He is working at a different branch.
(C) He is handling a private matter.
(D) He is meeting a client.

Brooks さんはなぜ不在なのですか。

(A) 医者の所に行っているため。
(B) 別の支店で働いているため。
(C) 私用があるため。
(D) 客に会っているため。

男性は❺で Brooks さんについて「現在、お客様と商談を兼ねた昼食会に行っている」と述べている。ここから、Brooks さんは現在顧客と会っていることがわかる。以上から正解は **(D)**。

□handle ～に対処する　□private matter 私用

	1回目	2回目	3回目
38.			
39.			
40.			

🚩 **38. (B)　39. (A)　40. (D)**

Questions 41 through 43 refer to the following conversation.

M: Hello, Rachel. Did you go over my draft of the company's new staff manual? ❶My supervisor wants me to finish the manual by the end of today. ❷He needs me to submit the final version before he leaves this evening around 6 P.M.

W: I ended reviewing it this morning, and ❸I found a misspelling on the third page. ❹Could we go over the error during our brief conference at 3 P.M.?

M: In fact, ❺I can't make it to the conference. I have a prior appointment with a customer. ❻Can we meet later instead, around 5 P.M.? Is that fine with you?

W: No problem at all. See you then.

問題41-43は次の会話に関するものです。

M: こんにちは、Rachel さん。新しい社員用マニュアルの草案は読んでもらえましたか。上司に今日中にマニュアルを完成させてほしいと言われたのです。今日の午後6時ごろ退社される前に最終版を提出しなければならないのです。

W: 今朝確認が終わりまして、3ページ目に誤字を見つけました。午後3時の話し合いのときに間違いについてお伝えしてもいいですか。

M: 実はその話し合いには参加できないのです。お客様と先に約束をしています。代わりにその後、午後5時くらいにお話ししてもいいですか。どうでしょうか。

W: まったく問題ありません。ではまた後で。

✏️ □go over 〜を確認する、検討する　□draft 草案　□supervisor 上司、監督者　□by the end of today 今日までに
□final version 最終版　□review 〜を確認する　□misspell つづりを誤る　□brief conference 小会議
□make it to 〜に行く、参加する　□prior 事前の　□Is that fine with you? それでよいですか。

---

41. ★★★☆☆

What does the man say he must do by the end of today?

(A) Check a report
(B) Hand in some material
(C) Train some staff
(D) Complete the draft of a speech

男性は今日中に何をしなければならないと言っていますか。

(A) 報告書を確認する。
(B) 資料を提出する。
(C) スタッフの訓練をする。
(D) スピーチの文案を完成させる。

🔍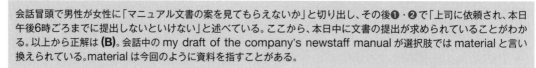
会話冒頭で男性が女性に「マニュアル文書の案を見てもらえないか」と切り出し、その後❶・❷で「上司に依頼され、本日午後6時ごろまでに提出しないといけない」と述べている。ここから、本日中に文書の提出が求められていることがわかる。以上から正解は **(B)**。会話中の my draft of the company's newstaff manual が選択肢では material と言い換えられている。material は今回のように資料を指すことがある。

✏️ □hand in 〜を提出する　□train 〜を訓練する

42. ★★☆☆☆

What problem does the woman mention?

(A) The wrong program was used.
(B) A due date has passed.
(C) Some errors were found.
(D) An appointment has been missed.

女性は男性にどんな問題を伝えていますか。

(A) 間違ったプログラムが使用された。
(B) 期日が過ぎている。
(C) 誤植が見つかった。
(D) 面会の約束が果たされていない。

❸で女性は男性に3ページ目にスペルミスがあったと伝えている。以上から正解は **(C)**。

□wrong 間違った　□due date 支払い締め切り日　□miss an appointment 約束をすっぽかす

43. ★★★★☆

What solution does the man propose?

(A) Distributing the work to other colleagues
(B) Providing an extension
(C) Looking for a different location
(D) Meeting at a later time

男性はどんな解決方法を提示しますか。

(A) 仕事を別の同僚に振り分ける。
(B) 期間を延長する。
(C) 別の場所を探す。
(D) 後で会う。

まず女性がマニュアルの誤字について❹で午後3時に打ち合わせを申し入れたが、男性は❺で用事があるので参加できないと言い、❻で代わりに午後5時ではどうかと尋ねている。以上から、女性の申し入れに対して、その後の別の時間に会うことを提案していることがわかるため、正解は **(D)**。

□distribute A to A を〜に渡す　□provide an extension 延長する　□at a later time 後に

	1回目	2回目	3回目
41.			
42.			
43.			

 41. (B)　42. (C)　43. (D)

Questions 44 through 46 refer to the following conversation.

📝 問題44-46は次の会話に関するものです。

W: ❶I'm here to look for an article that was written in the local newspaper about two years ago. ❷Is there a copy in the library? I don't know how far back you retain newspapers.

M: We only keep issues of the local paper for the last six months. However, articles from the last three years are kept on our Web site. Therefore, I can help you find an electronic copy of the article.

W: Great! How much will it cost to print?

M: It's 10 cents a page. ❸However, regrettably our printer is not working right now. ❹A technician is coming, and it should be fixed by noon. ❺It may be better to come back this afternoon.

W: 約2年前に地元の新聞に載った記事を探しに来たのですが、図書館で保管していますか。どのくらい前までの新聞が保存されているのかわからないのですが。

M: 地元の新聞は過去6か月の間に発行された号のみを保管しています。でも、記事でしたら過去3年分が当館のウェブサイトに保存されています。ですので、記事の電子版の検索であればお手伝いできます。

W: よかったです。プリントアウトにはいくらかかりますか。

M: 1ページにつき10セントです。ただあいにく、当館のプリンターは現在故障中なのです。技術者が来ますので、正午までには直るはずです。ですので、今日の午後、ご都合の良い時間にまたいらしてください。

✏️ □how far back どのくらいさかのぼって　□retain ~を保有する　□issue (雑誌等の) 号
□electronic copy 電子コピー　□regrettably 残念ながら　□work 作動する　□right now ただ今
□fix ~を修理する

44.

Where most likely are the speakers?

(A) At a newspaper company
(B) At a print shop
(C) At a library
(D) At a publishing company

話し手たちはどこにいると考えられますか。

(A) 新聞社
(B) 印刷屋
(C) 図書館
(D) 出版社

🔍 女性は❶で「約2年前に地元の新聞に載った記事を探しに来た」と切り出し、❷で「図書館内にその記事はあるか」と尋ねている。ここから、過去の新聞を保管している場所、つまり図書館が今いる場所だと考えることができる。以上から正解は **(C)**。後半にプリンターの話題が出てくるが、(B) と混同しないようにしよう。

✏️ □print shop 印刷屋

45. ★★☆☆☆

What problem does the man mention?

(A) A facility is under construction.
(B) A printer is out of order.
(C) A newspaper is out of stock.
(D) A book delivery is late.

男性はどんな問題に言及していますか。

(A) 施設が建設中である。
(B) プリンターが故障している。
(C) 新聞は在庫切れである。
(D) 本の宅配が遅れている。

🔍 男性は❸で「プリンターは現在作動していない」と述べている。以上から、正解は会話中の not working を out of order に言い換えた **(B)**。

✎ □facility 施設　□under construction 建設中である　□out of order 故障中である　□out of stock 在庫切れである

----

46. ★★★☆☆

What does the man suggest the woman do?

(A) Return at a later time
(B) Go to another branch
(C) Renew a subscription
(D) Contact technical support

男性は女性に何をすることを勧めていますか。

(A) 後で戻ってくる。
(B) 別の支店に行く。
(C) 購読契約を更新する。
(D) テクニカルサポートに連絡する。

🔍 男性は❸で図書館のプリンターが故障していることに触れ、❹・❺で「正午には復旧するので午後以降に再度来てほしい」と述べている。以上から、少し時間をおいて後で戻ってくるように勧めていることがわかるため、正解は **(A)**。❺の It may be better to *do* は「～したほうがよい」という提案表現になっていることを押さえておこう。

✎ □at a later time 後で　□renew ～を更新する　□subscription 定期購読　□contact ～に連絡する

	1回目	2回目	3回目
44.			
45.			
46.			

 44. (C)　45. (B)　46. (A)

Questions 47 through 49 refer to the following conversation.

M: Hi, Mary. I just got off the phone with the owner of Lucent Construction. ❶She was extremely satisfied with the service you gave her while helping to process her business loan.

W: That's good news.

M: I know that the loan account involved a lot of complex analysis, and you handled it well. I think you'd be a great representative for our company at the next industry meeting. Are you going?

W: ❷Mr. Gomez is choosing ten workers to go. ❸I've heard that he's already made his list, but ❹I haven't seen it.

M: ❺How about I talk to him and encourage him to add you, if he hasn't finalized it yet?

W: I'd really appreciate that.

📝 問題47-49は次の会話に関するものです。

M: こんにちは、Mary さん。ちょうど Lucent 建設社のオーナーと電話で話していたところです。彼女は企業融資の手続きをあなたが手伝った際の応対に非常に満足していらっしゃいましたよ。

W: それはよかったです。

M: 借入金勘定には複雑な分析をたくさんしなければなりませんでしたが、しっかりと対処されましたね。次回の業界会議では当社の代表を立派に務められると思います。出席されますか。

W: 出席する10人の社員は Gomez さんが決めます。既にリストはできたと聞きましたが、見てはいません。

M: もしまだ決まっていなければ、私から話してあなたを追加するように勧めてみましょうか。

W: それは大変ありがたいです。

✏️ ☐get off the phone 電話を切る ☐be extremely satisfied with ～にとても満足する ☐process ～の手続きをする ☐business loan 事業融資 ☐loan account 借入金勘定 ☐involve ～を含む、～に関与する ☐complex 複雑な ☐handle ～を処理する ☐representative 代表者 ☐encourage A to do A に～するように勧める ☐finalize ～を完成させる ☐appreciate ～に感謝する

---

47. ★★★★☆

Where most likely do the speakers work?

(A) At a financial institution
(B) At an advertising agency
(C) At a construction company
(D) At an accounting firm

話し手たちはどこで働いていると考えられますか。

(A) 金融機関
(B) 広告代理店
(C) 建設会社
(D) 会計事務所

🔍 まず男性が❶で「顧客が企業融資の手続き応対に非常に満足していた」と女性に伝えている。ここから、この二人は企業融資に関する仕事、つまり金融機関で働いていることが考えられる。以上から正解は **(A)**。

✏️ ☐financial institution 金融機関 ☐accounting firm 会計事務所

48. ★★★★☆

What does the woman mean when she says, "I haven't seen it"?

(A) She is unfamiliar with a policy.
(B) She is searching for a lost item.
(C) She cannot comment on a product.
(D) She cannot confirm her attendance.

女性が "I haven't seen it" と言う際、意味していることは何ですか。

(A) 方針をよく知らない。
(B) 遺失物を探している。
(C) 製品について意見を述べることができない。
(D) 出席できるか確認できない。

意図を問われている表現❹「それを見ていない」の前後を見ていくと、❷・❸「Gomez さんが出席する10人の社員を決め、リストはできていると聞いた」➡❹「でもまだ見ていない」➡❺「（男性が）女性を追加するように進言しようか」という流れになっている。つまり、女性は話題にしている会議のリストに入っているかわからず、参加の可否を伝えられないと言っていると考えられる。よって正解は **(D)**。

☐ be unfamiliar with ～をよく知らない　☐ lost item 遺失物　☐ confirm ～を確認する、承認する　☐ attendance 出席

---

49. ★★★★★

What does the man offer to do?

(A) Accompany a colleague to a meeting
(B) Recommend the woman for an event
(C) Ask the supervisor for a raise
(D) Review some of the woman's work

男性は何をすることを申し出ていますか。

(A) 同僚と会議に出ること。
(B) 女性をイベントに推薦すること。
(C) 上司に昇給をお願いすること。
(D) 女性の仕事を確認すること。

男性は❺で「私から彼（Gomez さん）に話して（女性を会議招集メンバーに）追加するように勧めようか」と申し出ている。ここから、女性がある会議に参加できるよう推薦しようという申し出だとわかる。正解はこの会議を an event と言い換えた **(B)**。男性自身が会議に出るわけではないので **(A)** は不正解。

☐ accompany A to A を～に同席させる　☐ raise 昇給　☐ review ～を確認する

	1回目	2回目	3回目
47.			
48.			
49.			

47. (A)　48. (D)　49. (B)

Questions 50 through 52 refer to the following conversation.

W: Hi, Jason. ❶Did the brochures you designed for the museum in Delaware come back from the printers?

M: Yes. The shipment arrived this morning, and they look really impressive. The graphic elements in particular turned out well. ❷Since this is for a new client, I was thinking I should deliver the first order in person.

W: I think they would appreciate that. We're hoping to receive repeat orders from this customer, so it's vital to build a strong relationship with them. Oh, and ❸you might want to take Owen along. ❹He took the photographs for the brochure.

M: OK. I'll go see if he's ready.

📝 問題50-52は次の会話に関するものです。

W: こんにちは、Jason さん。Delaware の美術館用にデザインしたパンフレットは印刷所から戻ってきましたか。

M: はい。荷物は今朝届いて、とても印象的な出来栄えです。写真の要素が特にうまく行きました。新しい顧客に向けたものなので、この最初の注文は直接届けようかと思っています。

W: 彼らもきっと喜ぶと思います。この顧客からはまた注文を受けられるといいと思いますので、強い信頼関係を築くことが大切です。ああ、Owen さんも一緒に行ってはどうでしょうか。彼がパンフレットの写真を撮りました。

M: そうですね。すぐ行けるか見に行きます。

✏️ □brochure パンフレット □shipment 送付物 □impressive 感銘を受ける □graphic elements 図や写真の要素 □in particular 特に □turn out well うまくいく □in person 直接 □appreciate ～に感謝する □repeat order リピート注文 □vital 必須の、不可欠な □build a strong relationship 強固な関係を築く □(you) might want to *do* ～してはいかがと思う □take A along A を同行させる

---

50. ★★★☆☆

Where do the speakers most likely work?

(A) At a museum
(B) At a graphic design studio
(C) At a book distributor
(D) At a newspaper company

話し手たちはどこで働いていると考えられますか。

(A) 美術館
(B) グラフィックデザイン事務所
(C) 書籍取次会社
(D) 新聞社

🔍 会話冒頭❶で女性が男性に「美術館用にあなたがデザインしたパンフレットは印刷所から戻ってきたか」と尋ねている。ここから、この話し手たちはパンフレットをデザインしている会社に勤めていると考えられる。以上から正解は **(B)**。美術館は依頼する側なので、ここでは不正解。

✏️ □book distributor 書籍取次業者

51. ★★★☆☆

Why will the man visit a client?

(A) To deliver some material
(B) To take an order
(C) To promote a new service
(D) To pick up an item

なぜ男性は顧客を訪ねますか。

(A) 材料を届けるため。
(B) 注文を受けるため。
(C) 新しいサービスを売り込むため。
(D) 物を取りに行くため。

 男性は❷で「新しい顧客に向けたものなので、この最初の注文は直接届けようかと思っている」と話している。つまり、男性が作成して印刷所から上がってきたパンフレットを顧客に直接届けるつもりだということがわかる。以上から、正解はこのパンフレット (brochure) を material と言い換えた **(A)**。

 □material 素材、材料　□promote 〜の販売を促進する、〜を売り込む　□pick up 〜を取りに行く

---

52. ★★★★☆

What does the woman suggest the man do?

(A) Take a company vehicle
(B) Use more photographs
(C) Invite a colleague to join him
(D) Check his work for errors

女性は男性に何をするよう提案していますか。

(A) 社用車を使うこと。
(B) もっと写真を使うこと。
(C) 参加するよう同僚を招くこと。
(D) 誤りを確認すること。

女性は❸で Owen さんを顧客への納品に同行させてはどうかと提案している。そして❹で Owen さんはパンフレットの写真を撮った同僚だとわかる。以上から正解は **(C)**。

□company vehicle 社用車

	1回目	2回目	3回目
50.			
51.			
52.			

 50. (B)　51. (A)　52. (C)

Questions 53 through 55 refer to the following conversation.

W: Hello, Kevin. ❶Did you get an invitation to the company dinner party? I haven't heard anything yet. I was wondering whether it was just me or not.

M: I didn't get one, either. ❷I heard the entire marketing department is busy making a promotional video for the new product scheduled to be launched next season. Maybe that's why they haven't sent out the invitation letters yet.

W: I don't think so. They are always busy, but this has never happened before. They have always kept us up-to-date. Now the dinner party is just around the corner, and nobody knows what's going on. ❸I think I'll send an e-mail to my director and ask about it.

M: I think that's a good idea. Let me know when you get a reply.

問題53-55は次の会話に関するものです。

W: こんにちは、Kevin さん。会社の夕食会への招待状は来ましたか。私はまだ何も聞いていないのですよ。自分だけなのかどうか知りたいと思いまして。

M: 私ももらっていません。マーケティング部の皆さんは来季に発売する新製品のための宣伝動画の制作で忙しいと聞いています。おそらく、そのせいでまだ招待状を送付していないのでしょう。

W: そうではないと思います。彼らはいつも忙しいけど、今までにこんなことはありませんでした。最新情報をいつも提供してくれています。会社の夕食会はもうすぐなのに、どうなっているのか誰も知らないんですよ。私が部長に E メールを送って尋ねてみます。

M: それがいいですね。返信があったら教えてください。

□invitation 招待状　□entire 全体の　□promotional video 宣伝動画
□be scheduled to *do* ～することを予定している　□send out ～を送付する
□keep A up-to-date A を最新の状態に保つ　□reply 返信

---

53. ★★☆☆☆

What is the topic of the conversation?

(A) A corporate banquet
(B) An advertising method
(C) A local festival
(D) A marketing event

会話の話題は何ですか。

(A) 企業の宴会
(B) 宣伝方法
(C) 地元のお祭り
(D) マーケティングイベント

🔍 会話冒頭❶で女性が「会社の夕食会の招待状が来たか」と尋ねている。ここから、会社の夕食会の話題であるとわかる。以上から、正解は company と corporate、dinner を banquet と言い換えた **(A)**。

□corporate banquet 会社の夕食会　□method 方法

54. ★★★☆☆

According to the man, what is the marketing
  department busy doing?

(A) Providing special offers
(B) Looking for new contacts
(C) Composing a monthly plan
(D) Creating a marketing tool

男性によると、マーケティング部は何をするのに
忙しいですか。

(A) 特価品を提供すること。
(B) 新たな人脈をつくること。
(C) 月次計画を作成すること。
(D) マーケティングツールを作成すること。

 男性は❷で「マーケティング部は来季の新製品宣伝動画の制作で忙しいと聞いている」と述べている。ここから、現在マーケティング部は宣伝動画、つまりマーケティングツールの作成で忙しいとわかる。以上から正解は **(D)**。

 □compose ～を作成する

---

55. ★★★★☆

What does the woman say she will do?

(A) Prepare for the event
(B) Respond to an e-mail
(C) Write an e-mail to her director
(D) Contact the receptionist

女性は何をすると言っていますか。

(A) イベントの準備をする。
(B) Eメールに返信をする。
(C) 部長にEメールを書く。
(D) 受付係に連絡をする。

女性は❸で「部長にEメールを送って尋ねてみる」と述べている。以上から正解は **(C)**。メールに返信するわけではないので (B) は不正解。

□respond to ～に返答する　　□receptionist 受付

	1回目	2回目	3回目
53.			
54.			
55.			

53. (A)　54. (D)　55. (C)

Questions 56 through 58 refer to the following conversation with three speakers.

M: ❶Hi, Allegra. ❷Do you have the contract ready for Charles Kross, the tenant at 43 Cobb Street? ❸He's coming by when he gets off work to update his rental agreement with our office.

W1: ❹The new secretary reorganized the contracts for the rental properties three days ago. ❺Ask her. ❻She might be able to help you.

M: Thanks a lot. I really hope she knows where it is. Mr. Kross will be here in the next hour, and ❼I'm afraid his contract won't be ready for him to sign if I don't find it soon. Oh, here she comes now. Excuse me. Hello!

W2: Hello, Mr. Gilmore. Do you need help?

M: Yes. Where did you leave the reorganized contracts?

W2: I put them on my manager's desk. Is there a problem?

問題56-58は次の3人の話し手による会話に関するものです。

M: こんにちは、Allegra さん。Cobb 通り43番地を借りている Charles Kross さんの契約書の準備はできていますか。うちとの賃貸契約の更新をするために、仕事の後に立ち寄っていただく予定なのです。

W1: 今度の補佐が3日前に賃貸物件の契約書を整理してくれましたから。彼女に聞いてください。彼女がお応えできるんじゃないかと思います。

M: ありがとうございます。どこにあるかわかるといいのですが。Kross さんは1時間しないうちにいらっしゃるのに、すぐに見つからなかったら契約書に署名してもらう準備ができませんから心配です。彼女が来ましたね。すみません。こんにちは。

W2: こんにちは、Gilmore さん。どうかされましたか。

M: ええ、整理してくれた契約書はどこにしまいましたか。

W2: 部長の机におきましたが。何か問題がありますか。

✎ □get off work 仕事を終える　□update rental agreement 賃貸借契約を更新する　□secretary 秘書、補佐役
□reorganize ～を再編成する　□contract 契約書　□rental property 賃貸物件　□I'm afraid すまないが

---

56. ★★★☆☆

Where do the speakers most likely work?

(A) At a property rental office
(B) At a law firm
(C) At a photo studio
(D) At a record shop

話し手たちはどこで働いていると考えられますか。

(A) 不動産事務所
(B) 法律事務所
(C) 写真館
(D) レコード店

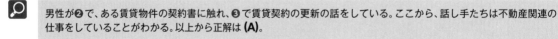

🔍 男性が❷で、ある賃貸物件の契約書に触れ、❸で賃貸契約の更新の話をしている。ここから、話し手たちは不動産関連の仕事をしていることがわかる。以上から正解は **(A)**。

✎ □property rental office 不動産事務所　□law firm 法律事務所

57. ★★★★★

What does Allegra recommend?

(A) Confirming a bank statement
(B) Speaking to an assistant
(C) Trying to access information on the Internet
(D) Scheduling a conference

Allegra さんは何を勧めていますか。

(A) 銀行の取引明細書を確認すること。
(B) 秘書に連絡すること。
(C) インターネット上の情報へのアクセスを試みること。
(D) 会議の予定を決めること。

まず、会話冒頭❶で男性が Allegra さんに話しかけているので、Allegra さんは男性に応えて次に話す女性だとわかる。そして Allegra さんは❹・❺・❻で新しい補佐役に聞いてみるとよい、と勧めている。よって、会話中の secretary を assistant と言い換えた **(B)** が正解。3人での会話は問われている人物がどこで話すかに注目する必要がある。

□confirm ～を確認する　□bank statement 銀行取引明細書　□access ～に接続する
□schedule ～の予定を決める

58. ★★★★☆

Why is the man concerned?

(A) His computer is out of order.
(B) Some supplies have not been shipped.
(C) Some paperwork was signed incorrectly.
(D) He cannot locate a document.

男性はなぜ心配していますか。

(A) コンピューターが故障したため。
(B) 消耗品が出荷されていないため。
(C) 事務処理が正しく行われなかったため。
(D) 書類を見つけることができないため。

男性は❼で「すぐに（契約書が）見つからなかったら契約書に署名してもらえないかもしれないので心配だ」と述べている。以上から、契約書類が見つかるかどうかを心配していることがわかる。よって正解は **(D)**。言い換えとなっている locate には「～を見つける」という意味もある。

□out of order 故障中　□supply 備品、消耗品　□ship ～を発送する　□incorrectly 間違って
□locate ～を見つける

	1回目	2回目	3回目
56.			
57.			
58.			

56. (A)　57. (B)　58. (D)

Questions 59 through 61 refer to the following conversation.

M: Hello. I heard on a local radio commercial that your shop offers guitar lessons, and I'd like to sign up.

W: Sure. Do you have any previous experience playing the guitar?

M: ❶Yes, I played a little in my college band.

W: I think you'll probably fit into our intermediate class, then. Those classes begin next month.

M: Fantastic!

W: ❷And there are instructional videos on our Web site. You can see them if you register for our monthly e-mails. ❸Would you like to join?

M: ❹That would be helpful. ❺My e-mail address is stodden36@semail.net.

W: OK, you're registered, and the first lesson will be next Friday at 7 P.M. See you then!

問題59-61は次の会話に関するものです。

M: こんにちは、地元ラジオ局のコマーシャルでそちらのお店がギターのレッスンを提供していると聞いて、申し込みをしたいのですが。

W: 承ります。ギターを弾いた経験はありますか。

M: はい、大学のバンドで少し演奏をしました。

W: でしたら、おそらく中級クラスがちょうどいいと思います。クラスは来月から始まります。

M: よかったです。

W: 当店のウェブサイトに講習ビデオがあります。毎月配信しているEメールに登録すればご覧いただけます。登録されますか。

M: それは助かりますね。私のEメールアドレスは stodden36@gmail.net です。

W: はい、登録いたしました。初回のレッスンは今度の金曜日の午後7時からです。そのときにまたお目にかかります。

✎ □sign up 参加登録する　□previous 過去の　□intermediate class 中級のクラス
□instructional video 教育ビデオ　□register for ～に登録する

---

59. ★★★☆☆

What does the man say he did in college?

(A) He taught students to play the guitar.
(B) He gained work experience.
(C) He made a Web page.
(D) He played in a musical group.

男性は大学で何をしたと言っていますか。

(A) ギターの弾き方を学生に教えた。
(B) 職務経験を積んだ。
(C) ウェブページを作った。
(D) 音楽グループで演奏した。

🔍 男性は❶で「大学時代少しバンドをしていた」と述べている。このバンドを a musical group と言い換えた **(D)** が正解。

✎ □gain experience 経験を積む

60. ★★★☆☆

What is available on the Web site?

(A) A list of local radio broadcasts
(B) Free downloadable music
(C) Educational videos
(D) Feedback from instructors

ウェブサイトには何がありますか。

(A) 地元のラジオ局の番組一覧
(B) 無料でダウンロードできる音楽
(C) 教育ビデオ
(D) 講師からのコメント

 女性は❷で「ウェブサイトに講習ビデオがある」と述べている。これを言い換えた **(C)** が正解。❷の instructional が educational に言い換えられている。

✎ □educational video 教育ビデオ　□feedback コメント　□instructor 講師

---

61. ★★★★☆

What does the man imply when he says, "That would be helpful"?

(A) He will join a mailing list.
(B) An e-mail address is unnecessary.
(C) A lesson seems competitively priced.
(D) He appreciates a schedule change.

男性が "That would be helpful" という際、何を意図していますか。

(A) メーリングリストに登録する。
(B) E メールアドレスは不要である。
(C) レッスンは競争力のある価格になっている。
(D) スケジュールの変更をありがたく思う。

 意図を問われている表現❹「それは助かる」の前後を見ていくと、❷・❸で「毎月の E メール配信リストに登録することで講習ビデオを視聴できるが、登録するか」➡❹「それは助かる」➡❺「私の E メールアドレスは……」という流れになっている。つまり、毎月の E メール配信に登録して講習ビデオを見ようとしていることがわかる。この E メール配信対象として登録することを join a mailing list と言い換えた **(A)** が正解。

✎ □mailing list メーリングリスト、郵送先名簿　□unnecessary 不必要である
□competitively priced 競争力のある価格が設定された　□appreciate 〜に感謝する　□schedule change 計画変更

	1回目	2回目	3回目
59.			
60.			
61.			

 59. (D)　60. (C)　61. (A)

Questions 62 through 64 refer to the following conversation and coupon.

W: Good morning, this is Kendra DeWitt. ❶I visited your clinic for an eye test last Wednesday and ordered a pair of eyeglasses. I was wondering whether they'll be ready to pick up this week.

M: Hello, Ms. DeWitt. Thanks for calling. I'll check on that now. ❷Well, it looks like they're expected to arrive some time tomorrow morning. ❸So you can come by to get them any time after lunch tomorrow.

W: That'll be fine. ❹Could you tell me whether I can use the coupon I got when I bought a pair of contact lenses at your clinic? It's valid until November 30.

M: No problem. By the way, ❺the total price of your order before applying the coupon is $110.

問題62-64は次の会話とクーポン券に関するものです。

W: おはようございます、Kendra DeWitt です。この前の水曜日に視力検査でそちらの診療所に伺って、眼鏡を注文しました。今日の午前中に引き取ることはできるでしょうか。

M: こんにちは、DeWitt さん。お電話ありがとうございます。ただいま確認いたします。ええと、明日の朝、届く予定のようです。明日の昼休みの後でしたら、いつでも受け取りに来ていただけます。

W: わかりました。そちらの診療所でコンタクトレンズを買った際にいただいたクーポン券が使えるか教えていただけますか。11月30日が期限なのですが。

M: 問題ありません。それから、クーポン適用前のご注文の合計金額は110ドルです。

HAWK'S VISIBILITY EYE CLINIC

Discount Coupon
- -
Eyeglasses ($50 or under)	$5 off
❻ Eyeglasses (Over $50)	$10 off
Contact Lenses ($50 - $100)	$20 off
Contact Lenses (Over $100)	$30 off

- - - - - **Expires 11/30**

HAWK'S VISIBILITY 眼科クリニック

割引クーポン
- -
眼鏡 (50ドル以下)	5ドル引き
眼鏡 (50ドル超)	10 ドル引き
コンタクトレンズ (50ドル〜100ドル)	20 ドル引き
コンタクトレンズ (100ドル超)	30 ドル引き

- - - - - - 有効期限11月30日 - -

✏️ □clinic クリニック、診療所 □eye test 視力検査 □eyeglasses 眼鏡 □pick up 〜を取りに行く
□be expected to *do* 〜するはずだ □come by 立ち寄る □contact lense コンタクトレンズ □valid 有効である
□by the way ところで □apply 〜を適用する □expire 期限が切れる

62. ★☆☆☆☆

What did the woman do last Wednesday?

(A) She called an eye clinic.
(B) She purchased contact lenses.
(C) She had her eyes checked.
(D) She was given a coupon.

この前の水曜日、女性は何をしましたか。

(A) 眼科に電話をした。
(B) コンタクトレンズを購入した。
(C) 眼の検診を受けた。
(D) クーポン券をもらった。

 女性は❶で「この前の水曜日にクリニックに視力検査に行った」と述べている。以上から正解は **(C)**。

---

63. ★★☆☆☆

What does the man suggest the woman do?

(A) Pick up her order tomorrow afternoon
(B) Finalize some paperwork
(C) Contact him in November
(D) Come to his hospital today

男性は女性に何をするように勧めていますか。

(A) 明日の午後に注文品を受け取る。
(B) 事務処理を完了する。
(C) 11月に彼に連絡をする。
(D) 今日、彼の病院に来る。

 男性は❷・❸で「注文したものは明日の朝くので、明日の午後以降取りに来てほしい」と述べている。以上から正解は **(A)**。

 □finalize ～を完了させる　□contact ～に連絡する

---

64. ★★★★★

Look at the graphic. What discount will the woman probably receive?

(A) $5
(B) $10
(C) $20
(D) $30

図を見てください。女性はおそらくいくら割引を受けますか。

(A) 5ドル
(B) 10ドル
(C) 20ドル
(D) 30ドル

 まず❶から女性が眼鏡を購入しようとしていることがわかる。次に❹で女性が割引は適用されるのかと聞いたところ、男性が❺で適用されると答え、割引適用前の価格が110ドルだと話している。そこで、クーポンの内容を見ると、❻から110ドルの価格の眼鏡は10ドルの割引を受けられることがわかる。以上から正解は **(B)**。商品の種類と価格を聞き取って、割引が適用される価格帯をクーポンで参照する必要があるので、注意しよう。

	1回目	2回目	3回目
62.			
63.			
64.			

 62. (C)　63. (A)　64. (B)

Questions 65 through 67 refer to the following conversation and list.

M: Lindsay, ❶I'm scheduling job interviews for the new computer programmer for next Friday. ❷Can you send e-mails to inform all candidates?

W: ❸But did you forget we also have an important customer visiting next Friday?

M: Ah, I completely forgot.

W: You should probably schedule job interviews for a different day.

M: I see. So, could you confirm next week's schedule for the meeting room? ❹I need a period of three hours to finish the job interviews.

W: I'll check the availability calendar and reserve a time for you.

Date	Available Time
March 19 (Monday)	10:00 A.M. - 11:00 A.M.
❺March 20 (Tuesday)	2:00 P.M. - 5:00 P.M.
March 21 (Wednesday)	2:00 P.M. - 4:00 P.M.
March 22 (Thursday)	1:30 P.M. - 3:00 P.M.

📝 問題65-67は次の会話と表に関するものです。

M: Lindsay さん、今度の金曜日に新しいコンピュータープログラマーの採用面接を予定しています。全ての候補者にEメールでお知らせを送ってもらえますか。

W: でも、今度の金曜日には重要なお客様との約束もありますが、お忘れですか。

M: 本当ですね、すっかり忘れていました。

W: 採用面接は別の日にしたほうがいいですね。

M: そうですね。来週の会議室の予定を確認してください。採用面接が終わるまで3時間かかります。

W: 会議室の空き状況を確認して時間を押さえますね。

日付け	利用可能時間
3月19日 月曜日	午前10時から午前11時
3月20日 火曜日	午後2時から午後5時
3月21日 水曜日	午後2時から午後4時
3月22日 木曜日	午後1時半から午後3時

✏️ □inform ～に知らせる　□completely forget すっかり忘れる　□job interview 採用面接　□confirm ～を確認する
□period 時間　□availability (部屋の) 空き　□reserve ～を予約する　□available time 空き時間

65. ★★★☆☆

What does the man ask the woman to do?

(A) Call some applicants
(B) Arrange a customer's visit
(C) Prepare for job interviews
(D) Design a Web site

男性は女性に何をするように頼んでいますか。

(A) 応募者に電話をする。
(B) 顧客との面談の手配をする。
(C) 採用面接の準備をする。
(D) ウェブサイトをデザインする。

男性は❶でプログラマーの採用面接を予定していることを述べ、女性に❷で「候補者にEメールを送ってほしい」と話している。ここから、採用面接の準備の一部を頼んでいることがわかる。以上を表した **(C)** が正解。

□applicant 応募者　□arrange ~を手配する　□job interview 採用面接

---

66. ★★★☆☆

What problem does the woman talk about?

(A) A Web site is currently out of order.
(B) A call to an important customer was too late.
(C) A staff meeting has been delayed.
(D) There is a scheduling conflict.

女性はどんな問題について話していますか。

(A) ウェブサイトが現在利用できない。
(B) 重要な顧客への電話が遅すぎた。
(C) 職員会議が延期された。
(D) 予定がかち合っている。

男性の依頼に対して女性は❸で「今度の金曜日には重要なお客様との約束もあるが、忘れていないか」と述べている。ここから、スケジュールが重複しているという問題があることがわかる。以上から正解は **(D)**。

□out of order 故障中、利用できない　□scheduling conflict 予定の重複

---

67. ★★★★☆

Look at the graphic. What day will the woman reserve the meeting room for?

(A) Monday
(B) Tuesday
(C) Wednesday
(D) Thursday

図を見てください。女性は何曜日に会議室を予約しますか。

(A) 月曜日
(B) 火曜日
(C) 水曜日
(D) 木曜日

男性は❹で「面接を終えるのに3時間かかる」と述べている。次にリストを見ると、会議室が3時間空いているのは❺から火曜日のみであることがわかる。以上から正解は **(B)**。

	1回目	2回目	3回目
65.			
66.			
67.			

 65. (C)　66. (D)　67. (B)

267

Questions 68 through 70 refer to the following conversation and chart.

M: Tiffany, ❶I'm a little worried about our new South Storm Burger branch on Clarkson Street. ❷It's due to open this month and I don't think they are ready.

W: No? I thought the remodeling was finished on time and within the budget.

M: The renovation work is completed, but ❸I don't think the store has enough employees to deal with customer demand.

W: Really? We're in trouble then. What do you think we should do? The grand opening event is important.

M: ❹Let's check which of our branches has the highest number of part-time employees and ask the branch manager to send some employees over to the new store.

W: Great idea. I'll take a look at our employee numbers and then contact the branch manager.

📝 問題68-70は次の会話と図表に関するものです。

M: Tiffanyさん、Clarkson通りの新しいSouth Storm Burgerの店舗について少し心配なことがあります。今月開業する予定ですが、準備ができているとは思えないのです。

W: そうなのですか。改装は予定どおりに予算内で終了したと思っていました。

M: 改装は完了しましたが、店にはお客様のご要望に対処できる人数の従業員がいないと思います。

W: そうですか。それは困りましたね。どうしたらいいと思いますか。新規開店イベントは重要です。

M: アルバイトの数が最も多い店を調べて、そこの店長に新しい店にアルバイトを派遣してもらえるように頼みましょう。

W: それがいいです。従業員の数を調べて、店長に連絡します。

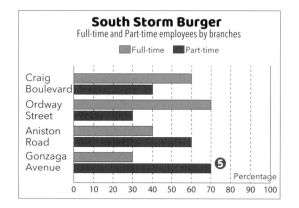

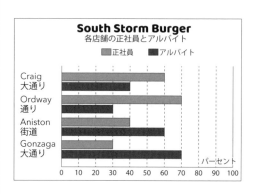

✏️ ☐be worried about ～を心配している　☐be due to *do* ～する予定である　☐remodeling 改装
☐within the budget 予算内で　☐renovation work 改装作業　☐deal with ～に対応する　☐demand 要求
☐in trouble 困った　☐grand opening 新規開店　☐part-time employee アルバイト従業員
☐full-time employee 正社員

68.

What is the topic of the conversation?	会話の話題は何ですか。
(A) The changing of a menu	(A) メニューの変更
(B) The new location of a business	(B) 会社の新しい所在地
(C) The need to hire full-time staff	(C) 常勤職員を雇用する必要性
(D) The opening of a store	**(D)** 店の開店

🔍 会話冒頭❶で男性が「新店舗について少し心配だ」と述べ、❷で「今月開業予定だが、準備ができているとは思えない」と話していることから、ある店舗の開店について話していることがわかる。以上から正解は **(D)**。

✎ □changing 変更

69.

What problem does the man talk about?	男性はどんな問題について話していますか。
(A) A location is understaffed.	**(A)** 人員不足の場所がある。
(B) A manager is unavailable.	(B) 店長は応じられない。
(C) A renovation is incomplete.	(C) 改修が完了していない。
(D) A budget has been exceeded.	(D) 予算を超えている。

🔍 男性は❸で「店には客の要望に対応できる十分な従業員がいないと思う」と話しており、人手不足であると述べている。その人手不足を understaffed と言い表した **(A)** が正解。(C) は❸の直前で既に完了していると男性が述べており、事実とは異なるため不正解。

✎ □understaffed 人員不足である　□incomplete 未完了である　□exceed ～を超える

70.

Look at the graphic. Which branch will the woman most likely contact?	図を見てください。女性はどの支店に連絡をすると考えられますか。
(A) Craig Boulevard	(A) Craig 大通り
(B) Ordway Street	(B) Ordway 通り
(C) Aniston Road	(C) Aniston 街道
(D) Gonzaga Avenue	**(D)** Gonzaga 大通り

🔍 男性は❹で「アルバイトの数が最も多い店を調べ、その店長にアルバイトの派遣を依頼しよう」と提案し、女性がそれに賛同している。次にグラフを見てみると、❺からアルバイト従業員が一番多いのは Gonzaga 大通りの店舗だとわかる。以上から、正解は **(D)**。

TEST
5

	1回目	2回目	3回目
68.			
69.			
70.			

 68. (D)　69. (A)　70. (D)

Questions 71 through 73 refer to the following advertisement.

W: ❶Are you thinking about vacationing overseas, but worried about making bad decisions with your travel plans? ❷Well, Farson Travel has the answer for you. Tell us where you wish to go, and we will find you the best transportation and hotels at affordable rates. ❸In addition to this service, if you travel with us, you could get the added advantage of reduced costs during your tours. From our wide network of business partners, we regularly receive discounts on accommodations, dining, and activities, which we'll pass on to you! ❹Farson Travel is holding a presentation on Wednesday afternoon, so if you wish to learn more about the services we offer, please visit the Kelvin Convention Center.

📝 問題71-73は次の広告に関するものです。

W: 休暇を海外で過ごしたいけれど、旅行計画で良くない判断をしてしまうのではないかと心配してはいませんか。でも、Farson Travel社にはあなたにとっての正解があります。どこへ行きたいか教えていただけましたら、お手頃な価格で最適な交通機関とホテルをお探しします。このサービスに加え、弊社を利用してご旅行になれば、ツアー中はさらに割引の特典を受けられます。弊社はさまざまなビジネスパートナーから、宿泊施設ならびにお食事やアクティビティの割引をいつも受け、それらをお客さまにご提供しています。Farson Travel社は水曜日の午後に説明会を行っていますので、弊社がご提供するサービスについてもっと詳しく知りたい方はKelvin Convention Centerにお越しください。

✏️ □vacation 休暇を過ごす　□transportation 移動手段　□affordable rate お手頃な価格　□in addition to 〜に加え
　□added 追加の　□advantage 特典　□reduced cost 割引価格　□wide network 幅広い企業・組織間の連携
　□accommodation 宿泊　□pass on to 〜に回す、譲る　□hold a presentation 説明会を行う

....

71.

What kind of business is being advertised?

(A) A travel agency
(B) A resort
(C) A hotel
(D) A restaurant

どんな事業が宣伝されていますか。

(A) 旅行代理店
(B) 行楽地
(C) ホテル
(D) レストラン

🔍 話し手はトーク冒頭❶で「旅行計画で良くない判断をしてしまうのではないかと心配していないか」と問いを投げかけ、❷で「Farson Travel社にはその正解がある」と言っていることから、個人旅行に関する対応ができる事業を行っていることがわかる。以上から正解は **(A)**。

✏️ □travel agency 旅行代理店

72. ★★★☆

What added benefit does the speaker mention?

(A) Faster Internet booking
(B) Free meals
(C) Reduced prices
(D) Exclusive access

話し手はどんな追加のメリットについて言及していますか。

(A) より速いインターネットでの予約
(B) 無料の食事
(C) 割引価格
(D) 専用の交通手段

 話し手は❸で「(交通機関とホテルを探す)サービスに加え、割引特典が受けられる」と述べている。以上から正解は**(C)**。❸の In addition to this service が「これから追加のメリットを話しますよ」というサインになっていることに着目しよう。

✎ □exclusive 専用の、独占の　□access 交通手段、接近方法

---

73. ★★★★

What are listeners invited to do on Wednesday?

(A) Tour Kelvin Convention Center
(B) Attend a presentation
(C) Collect discount vouchers
(D) Go to a dinner

聞き手は水曜日に何をすることを勧められていますか。

(A) Kelvin Convention Center を見学する。
(B) 説明会に参加する。
(C) 割引チケットを入手する。
(D) 夕食に行く。

 話し手は❹で、「Farson Travel 社は水曜日の午後に説明会を行っているので、興味のある方は Kelvin Convention Center に来てほしい」と呼びかけている。ここから、聞き手は説明会への参加を勧められていることがわかるので、**(B)** が正解。(A) は Kelvin Convention Center には行くが、施設見学までは言及がないので不正解。

✎ □collect ～を入手する、集める　□discount voucher 割引券

	1回目	2回目	3回目
71.			
72.			
73.			

🚩 **71. (A)　72. (C)　73. (B)**

Questions 74 through 76 refer to the following excerpt from a meeting.

M: ❶I called this meeting to discuss the monthly customer report. ❷Our satisfaction rate has unfortunately dropped to 85 percent. This might be due to slower response times since we have three colleagues on business trips meeting clients and Harvey is on vacation. ❸Anyway, this number is still above our average score of 80 percent, so I'm very happy with how the team is doing. And I believe we should be able to maintain these high standards in our new office in Bangkok, which is set to open in the summer. ❹Stephanie will fly out to the city next month to meet with the new branch manager, Lester Smith, who you met last month. ❺Together they'll train the new customer service team. This is a great start to the new year, and I am enthusiastic to see how our clients respond.

📝 問題74-76は次の会議の一部に関するものです。

M: この会議は月例報告について話すために開きました。我々の満足度は残念なことに85パーセントに低下しました。これは、おそらく3人の同僚が顧客との面会で出張に行っていることとHarveyさんが休暇を取っているため、応答の時間が遅くなっていることによるものでしょう。いずれにしても、この数値は当社の平均値の80パーセントを上回っていることに変わりありませんので、チームの仕事ぶりにはとても満足しています。また、夏に開業する予定の新しいバンコク営業所でもこの高水準を維持できると思います。先月、皆さんが会った新しい支部長のLester Smithさんと会うために、来月Stephanieさんがバンコクに飛びます。二人は一緒に新しい顧客サービスチームの研修を行います。これは新年に向けての素晴らしいすべり出しですし、お客様がどう反応するか楽しみです。

✏️ □call a meeting ミーティングを招集する　□satisfaction rate 満足度　□due to 〜が原因で　□business trip 出張
□on vacation 休暇中である　□above average score 平均値を上回って　□be set to do 〜する予定である
□fly out to 〜に飛行機で行く　□branch manager 支店長　□be enthusiastic to do 〜するのを楽しみにしている

---

74. ★★★★★

What is the main purpose of the talk?

(A) To introduce a new employee
(B) To describe team performance
(C) To announce a change in policy
(D) To discuss company strategy

話の主な目的は何ですか。

(A) 新入社員を紹介すること。
(B) チームの成果について説明すること。
(C) 会社の方針転換を発表すること。
(D) 会社の戦略について話し合うこと。

🔍 話し手はトーク冒頭❶で「会議を招集したのは月例報告をするためだ」と切り出し、❷で満足度について言及している。つまり、会議を招集した目的は今月のチームの成果について説明するためだとわかる。以上から正解は **(B)**。パフォーマンスについて話しているが、方針転換や戦略についてまでは言及がないので (C)・(D) はいずれも不正解。

✏️ □describe 〜を説明する　□strategy 戦略

75. ★★★☆☆

What is mentioned about the level of customer satisfaction?

(A) It is higher than the company's average.
(B) The firm has the best rate in the industry.
(C) It has been continuously increasing.
(D) It will soon be calculated differently.

顧客満足度の程度について何と言われていますか。

(A) 会社の平均値よりも高い。
(B) 会社は業界で最高の評価を得ている。
(C) 向上し続けている。
(D) 間もなく異なる方法で計算される。

 話し手は❷で「満足度は85%に下がった」と述べたものの、❸で「この数値は当社の平均値の80パーセントを上回っていることに変わりはない」と言っており、会社平均より高いということがわかる。以上から正解は **(A)**。

□firm 会社　□continuously 継続的に　□calculate 〜を計算する

76. ★★★★☆

What will happen next month?

(A) The firm will open a new office overseas.
(B) The president will be on vacation.
(C) A customer survey will be sent out.
(D) There will be training for new staff members.

来月、何がありますか。

(A) 会社が海外に新しい事務所を開設する。
(B) 社長が休暇を取る。
(C) 顧客調査書が送られる。
(D) 新人スタッフの研修がある。

話し手は❹で「来月 Stephanie さんがバンコクまで飛んで、新支部長の Lester Smith さんと会う」と触れつつ、❺で「この二人で一緒に新しい顧客サービスチームの研修を行う」と述べている。つまり、新しいスタッフへの研修が来月行われることがわかる。以上から正解は **(D)**。

□customer survey 顧客調査書

	1回目	2回目	3回目
74.			
75.			
76.			

74. (B)　75. (A)　76. (D)

273

Questions 77 through 79 refer to the following introduction.

M: ❶ You're watching our local history program on Neo Television Broadcasting Company. ❷ Today we're lucky to have a special guest, Mina Johnson, who recently wrote the book 'Beginning Boldly.' Ms. Johnson's book gives a detailed and interesting description of when our community was established. ❸ In honor of her appearance on today's show, we have arranged a special game where callers will be encouraged to answer questions about the area's past. ❹ Give the right answers, and you'll win a meal for four people at Khan's Restaurant. And now, please welcome Mina Johnson.

📖 問題77-79は次の紹介に関するものです。

M: Neo テレビ放送局がお送りする地元の歴史の番組です。今日は幸運にも特別ゲストとして最近 Beginning Boldly をお書きになった Mina Johnson さんをお迎えします。Johnson さんのご著書では、この地域社会がいつ築かれたかについて詳細で興味深い説明がなされています。今日は Johnson さんの出演を記念して、お電話いただいた方が町の歴史に関する問題に答える特別なゲームをご用意しています。正解すれば、Khan's レストランでの4人分のお食事を獲得できます。では、Mina Johnson さんをお迎えください。

✎ □be lucky to *do* 幸運にも～する　□detailed 詳細の　□description 説明　□establish ～を設立する
□in honor of ～を記念し、～を称え　□appearance 登場　□arrange ～を用意する　□caller 電話する人
□past 過去、歴史　□win ～を獲得する

---

77. ★★☆☆☆

What topic is the TV show discussing?

(A) The opening of a local restaurant
(B) Traffic conditions
(C) Saturday night entertainment
(D) The history of a community

テレビ番組のテーマは何ですか。

(A) 地元のレストランの開業
(B) 交通状況
(C) 土曜日の夜のエンターテインメント
(D) 地域社会の歴史

🔍 話し手はトーク冒頭❶で「地元の歴史番組」と述べている。これを言い換えた **(D)** が正解。

✎ □entertainment 催し、エンタメ（エンターテイメント）　□community 地域社会

78. ★★☆☆☆

Who is Mina Johnson?

(A) An author
(B) A television presenter
(C) A tour guide
(D) A chef

Mina Johnson さんとは誰ですか。

(A) 著者
(B) テレビの司会者
(C) ツアーガイド
(D) シェフ

 話し手は❷で Mina Johnson さんを紹介し、「本を書いた」と説明している。よって、本を書いた＝著者であることがわかる。以上から正解は **(A)**。

---

79. ★★★★☆

How can viewers win a prize?

(A) By accessing a homepage
(B) By participating in a quiz
(C) By attending a special meeting
(D) By making a donation

視聴者はどうしたら賞品を獲得できますか。

(A) ホームページにアクセスする。
(B) クイズに参加する。
(C) 特別な会議に出席する。
(D) 寄付をする。

 話し手は❸で「今日は Johnson さんの出演を記念して、電話クイズを用意している」と述べ、❹「正解すれば、レストランでの食事の機会を獲得できる」と述べている。つまり、視聴者は「電話クイズに参加し、正解を答える」と商品をもらえることがわかる。よって、この条件の前半部分について述べている **(B)** が正解。

✎ □quiz クイズ　□make a donation 寄付をする

	1回目	2回目	3回目
77.			
78.			
79.			

 77. (D)　78. (A)　79. (B)

Questions 80 through 82 refer to the following announcement.

M: ❶Good morning, team! ❷I think we should have some good weather today, so we'll be able to complete the construction of the foundations. Yesterday, the storm set us back a little bit, but by putting in an extra hour or two over the next week, we can get back on schedule. However, ❸remember that city ordinances do not allow us to surpass the approved noise level between 5 P.M. and 9 A.M., so we can use our heaviest equipment only from 10 A.M. to 4 P.M. ❹Let's try to get as much done as we can within that time frame. ❺Having said that, please do not rush! ❻There's a lot of dangers on the site if you don't follow the rules and procedures. We don't want anyone here getting hurt.

📝 問題80-82は次のお知らせに関するものです。

M: チームの皆さん、おはようございます。今日はいい天気になりそうなので、基礎工事を終わらせることができるでしょう。昨日は嵐のせいで少し遅れが生じましたが、来週1、2時間ほど多く取り組めば、予定に追いつくことができます。ただ気に留めておいてほしいのですが、市の条例では午後5時から午前9時までは、承認されたレベル以上の騒音を出すことが認められていませんので、最も大きな機械は午前10時から午後4時までしか使用できません。その時間枠の中でできる限り多くのことを終わらせるようにしましょう。そうは言いますが、慌ててはいけません。規則と手順に従わなければ、現場はとても危険です。ここにいらっしゃるどなたも怪我をさせたくありません。

□complete ～を完了する □construction of foundations 基礎工事 □storm 嵐 □set back ～を後退させる □get back 戻る □on schedule 計画どおりに □city ordinance 市の条例 □surpass ～を超過する □noise 騒音 □time frame 時間枠 □having said that そうは言っても □rush 慌てる、急ぐ □procedure 手順 □get hurt ケガをする

---

80. ★★☆☆☆

Where most likely are the listeners?

(A) At a government office
(B) At a construction site
(C) At an airport
(D) At a weather center

聞き手はどこにいると考えられますか。

(A) 役所
(B) 建設現場
(C) 空港
(D) 気象センター

 話し手はトーク冒頭❶で聞き手に挨拶をして、❷で「今日はいい天気になりそうなので、基礎工事を終わらせることができる」と述べている。ここから話し手と聞き手は工事現場にいることが考えられる。以上から正解は **(B)**。

 □government office 役所

81. ★★★★☆

What is mentioned about the use of some equipment?

(A) It must be operated under supervision.
(B) It requires additional training.
(C) It is only allowed at certain times.
(D) It has caused complaints about noise.

機械を使うことについて何が述べられていますか。

(A) 監督下で操作されなければならない。
(B) 追加の訓練が必要とされている。
(C) 特定の時間帯にのみ許可されている。
(D) 騒音に関する苦情を引き起こしている。

🔍 話し手は❸で「市の条例上午後5時から午前9時までは、承認レベル以上の騒音を出せないので、最も大きな機械は午前10時から午後4時までしか使用できない」と述べている。ここから、ある機械に関しては、使用できる時間帯が限定されていることがわかる。以上から、正解は一定の時間枠を at certain times と言い換えた **(C)**。

✏️ □under supervision 監督下で　□at certain times 特定の時間帯で　□cause 〜を引き起こす　□complaint 苦情

82. ★★★★☆

What does the speaker mean when he says, "please do not rush"?

(A) There is enough time for everyone to receive food.
(B) There are new speed limits in place.
(C) A deadline has been extended.
(D) Safety steps must not be skipped.

話し手が "please do not rush" と言う際、何を意味していますか。

(A) 全員が食料を受け取るのに十分な時間がある。
(B) 現場の制限速度が新しくなった。
(C) 締切期限が延長された。
(D) 安全手順をとばしてはならない。

🔍 意図を問われている表現❺「慌てないでください」の前後を見ていくと、❹「時間枠の中でできる限り多くのことを終わらせるように」➡❺「そうは言っても慌てずに」➡❻「規則と手順に従わないと現場はとても危険」という流れになっている。つまり、時間を気にして慌てると事故や怪我につながるという意図で発言したことがわかる。よって、正解は安全に関わる注意勧告を表した **(D)**。

✏️ □speed limits 制限速度　□in place 所定の場所に　□deadline 納期　□extend 〜を延長する
□safety step 安全手順　□skip 〜を飛ばす、省略する

	1回目	2回目	3回目
80.			
81.			
82.			

🚩 **80. (B)　81. (C)　82. (D)**

PART 4

TEST 5

277

Questions 83 through 85 refer to the following talk.

W: Hello everyone, and welcome to this luncheon. ❶We're honoring the recent graduates of the Everett Accountant Training Program. It takes over five years of continuous hard work for apprentices to complete this program and become nationally certified accountants. Therefore, their accomplishment deserves to be celebrated. I'm sure that many of the friends and family who've come here today are curious about what kind of training the apprentices do in the program. So before we eat, ❷I'd like to show a video about a typical day in our program. And ❸after lunch, you can join us for dancing in the ballroom.

W: 皆さま、こんにちは。昼食会にようこそ。Everett 会計士研修プログラムの今期の修了生を称えましょう。研修生がこのプログラムを修了して国家公認の会計士になるまで5年間のたゆみない取り組みが必要です。それゆえに、彼らが成し遂げたことは称賛に値します。ご来場いただいたご友人やご家族の皆さまは研修生がプログラムでどんな研修をするのかご関心をお持ちのことと思います。ですので、お食事の前に私たちのプログラムの中の典型的な一日についてのビデオをお見せします。そして昼食の後は舞踏室でのダンスにご参加いただけます。

✏️ □honor ～を称える　□continuous 継続的な　□apprentice 実習、見習い　□nationally certified 国家公認の　□accountant 会計士　□accomplishment 功績　□deserve to *do* ～するに値する　□curious about ～に興味がある　□typical 典型的な　□ballroom 舞踏室、ダンスができる大広間

83. ★★☆☆☆

What is the purpose of the event?

(A) To announce a manager's retirement
(B) To collect funds for charity
(C) To honor new graduates
(D) To attract participants to a program

イベントの目的は何ですか。

(A) 経営者の引退を発表すること。
(B) 慈善活動の資金を集めること。
(C) 新しい卒業生を称えること。
(D) 参加者の関心をプログラムに向けさせること。

🔍  話し手は❶で「Everett 会計士研修プログラムの今期の修了生を称えましょう」と述べている。以上から正解は **(C)**。

✏️ □collect funds for ～の資金集めをする　□charity 慈善活動

84.

What will the video feature?

(A) The city's landmarks
(B) A training session
(C) A new teacher
(D) The company's history

ビデオは何を取り上げていますか。

(A) 町を象徴する建物
(B) 研修会
(C) 新しい先生
(D) 会社の歴史

 話し手は❷で上映するビデオについて「プログラムに関する典型的な1日」と述べている。ここでのプログラムは研修コースのことを指すため、ビデオは研修に関する内容を取り上げていることがわかる。以上から正解は **(B)**。

✏ □landmark 象徴になる建物

85.

What will take place after the meal?

(A) A speech by the president
(B) Small group discussions
(C) Individual interviews
(D) A dance party

食事の後に何が行われますか。

(A) 学長のスピーチ
(B) 小グループでの話し合い
(C) 個別の面接
(D) ダンスパーティー

 話し手は❸で「昼食後にダンスに参加できる」と述べている。ここから、食後にダンスパーティーを行うことがわかる。以上から正解は **(D)**。

✏ □individual interview 個別面接

	1回目	2回目	3回目
83.			
84.			
85.			

🚩 **83. (C)   84. (B)   85. (D)**

Questions 86 through 88 refer to the following broadcast.

 問題86-88は次の放送に関するものです。

W: ❶And now today's entertainment news on local concerts and events. ❷Coming up next month, the rock band "Cool Sunlight" is making a stop on its tour to play here at Rattigan Arena. ❸Tickets can be bought online or at any Interpark. ❹Get yours quick. ❺The band has sold out every concert so far on this tour! ❻Ever since it released the single "The Tiger's Tale", it has been topping the charts. ❼Producers expect its new album to reach double platinum by the time it ends this tour.

W: 地元のコンサートやイベントに関する今日のエンターテインメントのニュースです。来月、ロックバンドの "Cool Sunlight" がツアーでここに来て、Rattigan Arena で公演します。チケットはインターネット、またはInterpark の各店舗で購入できます。お早めにお求めください。このバンドはツアーのこれまでの全ての公演を完売しています。シングル "The Tiger's Tale" を発売して以来、ずっとランキングで首位に立ち続けています。プロデューサーはこのツアーが終わるときまでに、新しいアルバムがダブルプラチナを達成するだろうと見込んでいます。

 □make a stop 立ち寄る □so far これまでで □release ～を発売する □top ～の首位に立つ
□reach ～に達する
□double platinum ダブルプラチナ (特定数を売り上げると platinum となり、その2倍売り上げること)
□by the time ～するまで

---

86. ★★☆☆☆

What is the topic of the broadcast?

(A) A live performance
(B) Local traffic conditions
(C) A book launch
(D) An area festival

番組のテーマは何ですか。

(A) ライブ演奏
(B) 地域の交通状況
(C) 本の出版
(D) 地域のお祭り

🔍 話し手はトーク冒頭❶で地元のコンサートやイベントに関するエンターテイメントニュースを取り上げると伝え、❷であるロックバンドが地元で公演をすると伝えている。以上から正解は **(A)**。

✎ □book launch 本の出版

87. ★★★★☆

What does the speaker mean when she says, "Get yours quick"?

(A) The concert will finish soon.
(B) Parking spaces will be limited.
(C) Seats are expected to be taken quickly.
(D) The price of an item is due to increase.

話し手が "Get yours quick" と言う際、何を意味していますか。

(A) コンサートはまもなく終了する。
(B) 駐車スペースは限られている。
(C) 座席はすぐに埋まると予想される。
(D) 商品の価格は値上がりすることになっている。

 意図を問われている表現❹「お早めにお求めを」の前後を見ていくと、❸「チケットはインターネット、もしくは店舗で購入可能」➡❹「お早めにお求めを」➡❺「このバンドの公演はこれまで全て完売している」という流れになっている。ここから、案内した購入方法で早めに手に入れないと、このバンドの公演はすぐ売り切れてしまう、つまり、すぐに座席が埋まってしまうという意図で発言していることがわかる。よって正解は **(C)**。

✎ □parking space 駐車スペース　□be expected to *do* ～する見込みだ　□due to ～が原因で

---

88. ★★★☆☆

What do the producers expect?

(A) More copies will be needed.
(B) Album sales will increase.
(C) Visitors will enjoy a redesign.
(D) A new composer will join.

プロデューサーは何を予想していますか。

(A) 多くの部数が必要になる。
(B) アルバムの売り上げが伸びる。
(C) 訪問客は新しいデザインを楽しむ。
(D) 新しい作曲家が加入する。

 話し手は❼で「プロデューサーが新アルバムがダブルプラチナを達成すると見込んでいる」と話している。ここから、このアルバムが相当売れると見込んでいることがわかる。以上から正解は **(B)**。なお、ダブルプラチナの意味がわからない場合でも、❺で発売した曲が売れているということもヒントになるので、ここから解答を導き出すこともできる。

✎ □copy 部　□redesign 新しいデザイン、再設計　□composer 作曲家

	1回目	2回目	3回目
86.			
87.			
88.			

🚩 **86. (A)　87. (C)　88. (B)**

Questions 89 through 91 refer to the following recorded message.

M: Hello, Ms. Holmes. This is Larry Foreman. ❶ I have an appointment for a physical therapy session with you tomorrow afternoon, but I'm afraid I have to cancel. I have to attend an eye examination in order to be able to renew my driver's license, and ❷ tomorrow afternoon is the only time that the optician can fit me in this week. ❸ I know this is not the first time, ❹ but would it be possible to reschedule our session for next Friday? ❺ Could you call me back sometime today and let me know? Thank you.

問題89-91は次の録音メッセージに関するものです。

M: こんにちは、Holmes 先生。Larry Foreman です。明日の午後に理学療法を予約しておりますが、申し訳ないのですが、キャンセルしなければなりません。車の免許を更新するために眼科検診を受けなければならないので、今週だと、眼科医に診てもらえるのが明日の午後しかないのです。今回が初めてではないことは自覚しておりますが、次の金曜日に時間を変更できますでしょうか。予約変更ができるか今日折り返しでお知らせいただけないでしょうか。よろしくお願いいたします。

✏️ ☐physical therapy 理学療法 　☐I'm afraid I have to *do* すまないが〜しなくてはいけない
☐eye examination 視力検査 　☐in order to *do* 〜するために 　☐renew one's driver's license 自動車免許を更新する
☐fit in 〜を予定に入れる 　☐reschedule 〜の予定を変更する

---

89. ★★★★☆

Where is the speaker calling?

(A) An eye clinic
(B) A dental office
(C) A vehicle license center
(D) A hospital

話し手はどこに電話をしていますか。

(A) 眼科医院
(B) 歯科医院
(C) 自動車免許センター
(D) 病院

🔍 話し手は❶で「明日の午後に理学療法を予約しているがキャンセルしたい」と申し出ている。ここから、理学療法を受ける医療施設に電話をかけているとわかる。以上より正解は **(D)**。❶の後に眼科が登場するが、これは予約をキャンセルしたい理由なので、(A) は不正解。

✏️ ☐eye clinic 眼科医院

90. ★★★★☆

What does the speaker imply when he says, "I know this is not the first time"?

(A) He is sorry for causing Ms. Holmes inconvenience again.
(B) He does not need to do the same training.
(C) He is unhappy at a repeated mistake.
(D) He expects Ms. Holmes to do a task easily.

話し手が "I know this is not the first time" と言う際、何を意味していますか。

(A) Holmes 先生に再度迷惑をかけることを謝っている。
(B) 同じトレーニングをする必要はない。
(C) 繰り返される失敗を好ましく思っていない。
(D) Holmes 先生は簡単に仕事をこなしてくれると予想している。

意図を問われている箇所❸「これが初めてではないことはわかっている」の前後を見ていくと、❷「今週だと、眼科で診察が可能な日が明日の午後しかない」➡❸「これが初めてではないことはわかっている」➡❼「しかしながら変更させてもらうことは可能か」という流れになっている。つまり、以前にもこのようなケースはあったので、また予約の変更をお願いすることになったことに対して申し訳なさを伝えている。以上から、謝罪の念が入っている (A) が正解。

□cause ～を引き起こす　□unhappy 不満に思う　□repeated 繰り返された　□task 任務、タスク

---

91. ★★☆☆☆

What is the listener asked to do?

(A) Confirm Mr. Foreman's bill
(B) Participate in an event
(C) Return a call
(D) Reserve a hotel room

聞き手は何をするように求められていますか。

(A) Foreman さんの請求書を確認する。
(B) イベントに参加する。
(C) 電話を折り返す。
(D) ホテルの部屋を予約する。

話し手は❺で「電話をかけ直してほしい」とお願いしている。以上から正解は (C)。

□confirm ～を確認する　□bill 請求書　□participate in ～に参加する

	1回目	2回目	3回目
89.			
90.			
91.			

🚩 **89. (D)　90. (A)　91. (C)**

Questions 92 through 94 refer to the following announcement.

M: Good morning. This is an announcement for all passengers on the City Tour Bus. On our way back to the station, you'll see the Soar Wings Tower to your right. ❶The Soar Wings Tower is the tallest clock tower in the state. It was built by the Easton family as a gift to the city over 80 years ago. ❷As we approach the end of our tour, let me remind you that you may buy souvenirs in our station's gift shop. ❸Please take a few seconds before exiting to make sure you do not leave any of your personal items on the bus.

📝 問題92-94は次のお知らせに関するものです。

M: おはようございます。市内観光バスの乗客の皆さまへお知らせいたします。駅に戻る途中で、右手に Soar Wings Tower が見えてまいります。Soar Wings Tower は州で最も高い時計台です。80年以上前に Easton 家から市への寄贈として建てられました。ツアーの終了が近づいてまいりましたので、駅にある当社のギフトショップでお土産がお求めいただけますことを再度ご案内いたします。降車の前に、身の回りの品をお忘れにならないよう少しご確認ください。

✏️ □on one's way back to 〜に戻る途中で　□gift 寄贈品　□approach 〜に近づく
□remind A that A に〜を再度案内する　□souvenir お土産　□exit 出る　□personal item 携行品、私物

---

92. ★★★★★

According to the speaker, what makes the Soar Wings Tower unique?

(A) Its unusual color
(B) Its intriguing history
(C) Its construction style
(D) Its family ownership

話し手によると、Soar Wings Tower の何が独特ですか。

(A) 珍しい色
(B) 興味深い歴史
(C) 建築様式
(D) 家族による所有

🔍 話し手は❶で、このタワーについて「州で一番の高さがあること」と「80年前にある一族から寄贈されたもの」と説明しているが、後者を歴史と言い換えて表した **(B)** が正解。(B) の intriguing は「予期しないような興味深い」という意味で interesting と同義語となる。

✏️ □unusual 珍しい　□intriguing 興味深い　□family ownership 家族所有

93. ★★★★★

What does the speaker suggest passengers do after the tour?

(A) Go to a souvenir shop
(B) Eat with the other passengers
(C) Take a photo of the Soar Wings Tower
(D) Reserve tickets for the next tour

話し手は乗客にツアーの後に何をするように勧めていますか。

(A) 土産物屋に行くこと。
(B) 他の乗客と食事すること。
(C) Soar Wings Tower の写真を撮ること。
(D) 次のツアーのチケットを予約すること。

 話し手は❷で土産物屋に行くことを念押ししている。ここから正解は **(A)** とわかる。

□souvenir お土産

---

94. ★★★★★

What does the speaker remind the listeners to do?

(A) Climb the Soar Wings Tower
(B) Keep to a schedule
(C) Gather their belongings
(D) Offer a tip to the bus driver

話し手は聞き手に何を忘れずにするよう伝えていますか。

(A) Soar Wings Tower に登ること。
(B) 予定どおりに動くこと。
(C) 持ち物をまとめること。
(D) バスの運転手にチップを渡すこと。

 話し手は❸で、バスの降車前に自分の身の回りの携行品を置き忘れないように確認してほしいと伝えている。以上から、自分の所有物を確認してまとめて身に付けるよう促していることがわかる。not leave = gather、personal items = belongings と言い換えた **(C)** が正解。(A) と (B) も場面からはあり得そうだが、トークでは触れられていないため、いずれも不正解。

□gather 〜を集める、まとめる　□belonging 所有物

	1回目	2回目	3回目
92.			
93.			
94.			

 92. (B)　93. (A)　94. (C)

Questions 95 through 97 refer to the following recorded message and ticket.

📝 問題95-97は次の録音メッセージとチケットに関するものです。

W: Hello, I'm calling for James Davenport. ❶Thank you for your inquiry about our December operas at the Hicks Opera House. You are correct that we are staging a series of well-known operas by Italian composers during that month. ❷Every Sunday, a different opera will be performed at 7:00 P.M. The series will begin on December 10th with a performance of *The Barber of Seville*. ❸The opera *Falstaff* will be performed on the 17th, and *Madame Butterfly* on the 24th. ❹The final show will be *Turandot* on the 31st. ❺If you are interested in purchasing a ticket for any of the shows, contact our box office directly at 555-1759. To find out more information about the concert hall and to view the seating plan, visit our Web site at www.hicksoh.org.

W: こんにちは、James Davenport さんにおかけしています。Hicks Opera House での12月のオペラについてお問い合わせいただきありがとうございます。お問い合わせのとおり、その月はイタリアの作曲家による一連の有名なオペラを上演いたします。毎週日曜日の午後7時に別のオペラが上演されます。このシリーズは12月10日の *The Barber of Seville* の上演から始まります。*Falstaff* というオペラは17日、*Madame Butterfly* は24日に上演されます。最終公演は31日の *Turandot* です。公演のチケットのご購入を希望の場合は、チケット窓口555-1759まで直接ご連絡ください。コンサートホールの詳しい情報と座席表をご覧になるには、ウェブサイト www.hicksoh.org にアクセスください。

The famous opera by Giacomo Puccini

❻ **Madame Butterfly**

At Hicks Opera House
Performance Starts: 7:00 P.M.
Ticket Price: $80
Seat: J15
Name: Mr. James Davenport

Giacomo Puccini による著名なオペラ

Madame Butterfly

於 Hicks Opera House
上演開始時間：午後 7 時
チケット価格：80 ドル
座席：J15
氏名：James Davenport 様

□inquiry 問い合わせ　□correct 正しい　□stage ～を上演する　□a series of 一連の、シリーズの
□well-known 有名な　□composer 作曲家　□perform ～を公演する　□be interested in ～に興味がある
□contact ～に連絡する　□view ～を見る　□seating plan 座席予定表

95. ★★★☆☆

Why is the speaker calling?

(A) To explain a performance schedule
(B) To express gratitude to a sponsor
(C) To offer information about prices
(D) To give directions to an opera house

なぜ話し手は電話をしていますか。

(A) 上演の日程について説明するため。
(B) 後援者に感謝の意を示すため。
(C) 価格についての情報を提供するため。
(D) オペラハウスへの行きかたを伝えるため。

話し手は❶で12月のオペラに関する問い合わせへの返答として電話をしており、❷・❸・❹で上演時間や演題などを伝えている。ここから、上演スケジュールについて答えていることがわかるため、正解は **(A)**。

□express gratitude 感謝する　□sponsor 後援者、スポンサー　□give direction 道順を教える

---

96. ★★★★★

Look at the graphic. When did Mr. Davenport most likely attend an opera?

(A) On December 10
(B) On December 17
(C) On December 24
(D) On December 31

図を見てください。Davenport さんはいつオペラを見に行ったと考えられますか。

(A) 12月10日
(B) 12月17日
(C) 12月24日
(D) 12月31日

チケットを見ると、Davenport さんが観たオペラの演題は❻から Madame Butterfly だとわかる。次に、この演題は❸より12月24日に上演したことがわかる。以上より正解は **(C)**。この問題は、音声が流れる前に Davenport さんが観に行ったオペラのタイトルをわかっていないと、リスニングしながら情報を保持しておく必要があるため、負担が大きくなってしまう。チケット等の文字情報がある問題には先に内容をしっかり把握しておく先読み作戦も取り入れていこう。

---

97. ★★★☆☆

According to the speaker, how can Mr. Davenport buy a ticket?

(A) By using a Web site
(B) By going to the opera house
(C) By submitting an e-mail
(D) By making a phone call

話し手によると Davenport さんはどうすればチケットを買うことができますか。

(A) ウェブサイトを利用することによって。
(B) オペラハウスに行くことによって。
(C) E メールを送ることによって。
(D) 電話をかけることによって。

話し手は❺で「チケットの購入を希望する場合は、チケット売り場に直接電話をしてほしい」と伝えている。以上より正解は **(D)**。

	1回目	2回目	3回目
95.			
96.			
97.			

 95. (A)　96. (C)　97. (D)

Questions 98 through 100 refer to the following excerpt from a meeting and chart.

M: ❶I'd like to start our meeting by reviewing the results of the factory cafeteria survey of our employees. ❷I'm happy to report that renovations to the cafeteria will start next month. Here are the results of the employees' poll on cafeteria satisfaction. These are the four areas that received an average score of six or less out of a maximum of ten. ❸First, because some employees wanted a faster Wi-Fi connection there, we've decided to install a higher quality router in the building. Additionally, we'll enlarge the room to seat more people and offer detailed nutritional information for the food we offer. ❹About the area that received the lowest satisfaction rating, that's what I want you to discuss now. Please divide yourself into small groups and share your ideas for improvement.

M: この会議は従業員に対して行った工場の食堂に関するアンケート結果を見ることから始めたいと思います。うれしいことに、食堂の改装は来月から始まることになっています。こちらが食堂の満足度に関する従業員のアンケート結果です。こちらの4つの分野は10点満点のうちの平均6点かそれ以下の点を受けました。まず、Wi-Fi 接続をもっと速くしてほしいという従業員がいたので、より高い品質のルーターを建物に設置することにしました。それだけではなく、座れる人の数が増えるように空間を広げ、出している料理の詳細な栄養に関する情報もご提供します。最も満足度が低かった分野についてですが、これが今から皆さんで話し合いたいとことです。小グループに分かれて改善案を出し合ってください。

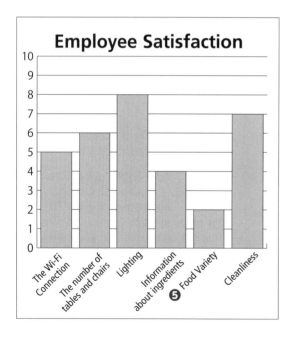

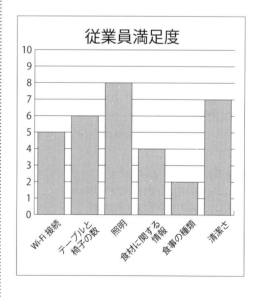

□review ～を確認する □survey 調査 □renovation 改装 □poll 投票 □install ～を設置する
□router ルーター（インターネット接続機器） □additionally 加えて □enlarge ～を拡張する □detailed 詳細の
□nutritional 栄養に関する □satisfaction rating 満足度評価 □lighting 照明 □food variety 食事の種類
□cleanliness 清潔さ

98. ★★★☆☆

What type of project is the speaker discussing?

(A) Opening a new dining area
(B) Improving employees' health
(C) Making improvements to a cafeteria
(D) Switching to a different Internet service provider

話し手はどんなプロジェクトについて話していますか。

(A) 新しい食事の場所を開設すること。
(B) 従業員の健康を改善すること。
(C) 食堂を改善すること。
(D) 別のインターネットのサービスプロバイダーに切り替えること。

 話し手は❶で「従業員に対して行った工場の食堂に関するアンケート結果を見る」と述べ、❷で「食堂の改装を来月より行う」と述べている。つまり、社員食堂の改善について述べていることがわかる。以上から正解は **(C)**。

□make improvements to ～を改善する　□switch to ～に切り替える
□Internet service provider インターネット提供会社

---

99. ★☆☆☆☆

According to the speaker, what is the problem with the current Internet connection?

(A) The security is vulnerable.
(B) The signal frequently cuts off.
(C) It has restrictions on downloads.
(D) Its speed is too slow.

話し手によると、現在のインターネット接続についてどんな問題がありますか。

(A) 安全性が脆弱である。
(B) 信号が頻繁に途切れる。
(C) ダウンロードに制限がある。
(D) 速度が遅すぎる。

 話し手は❸で「Wi-Fi接続をもっと速くしてほしいという従業員がいた」と述べていることから、インターネット回線の速度が遅いことがわかる。以上から正解は **(D)**。

□vulnerable 脆弱である　□frequently 頻繁に　□cut off 途切れる　□restriction 制限

---

100. ★★★★★

Look at the graphic. What does the speaker ask the listeners to discuss?

(A) Food variety
(B) The Wi-Fi connection
(C) Information about ingredients
(D) The number of tables and chairs

図を見てください。話し手は聞き手に何を話し合うように頼んでいますか。

(A) 食事の種類
(B) Wi-Fi 接続
(C) 食材に関する情報
(D) テーブルと椅子の数

 話し手は❹で「一番満足度が低い分野については今から話し合ってもらいたい」と議論を促している。グラフを見ると、一番評価を得ていない分野は❺の Food Variety、つまり食事の種類についてであることがわかる。以上から正解は **(A)**。

	1回目	2回目	3回目
98.			
99.			
100.			

98. (C)　99. (D)　100. (A)

GO ON TO THE NEXT TEST!

TOKIMAKURE!

PART 3&4

Test

6

32. What problem is the man reporting?

(A) He was not charged the correct amount.
(B) He got different newspapers.
(C) He can't access some online contents.
(D) He is not receiving e-mails at his home.

33. According to the woman, what does the man need to do?

(A) Open a new account
(B) Turn on the computer again
(C) Call a customer representative
(D) Provide proof of identification

34. What information does the man say he is missing?

(A) A user name
(B) An identification number
(C) A password
(D) A billing amount

35. What event does the woman want to buy tickets for?

(A) A ballet
(B) A new film
(C) A sports match
(D) A music concert

36. What problem is being discussed?

(A) There are not enough seats left.
(B) The concert has been canceled.
(C) The date has been changed.
(D) The tickets cannot be printed.

37. What does the man say about the middle front seats?

(A) They are more expensive.
(B) They are all sold out.
(C) They are under renovation.
(D) They have to be bought in advance.

38. What did the woman just do?

(A) Bought a product
(B) Changed her internet service provider
(C) Replaced the screen
(D) Upgraded some software

39. What does the man say he needs to do?

(A) Clean his desk
(B) Design a Web site
(C) Buy a computer
(D) Print a document

40. What does the woman offer to get the man?

(A) A monitor
(B) A cable
(C) A printer
(D) A computer

41. What is the woman interested in purchasing?

(A) Promotional products
(B) Flight tickets
(C) Office stationery
(D) Advertising space in a magazine

42. How can the woman receive a discount?

(A) By showing a previous receipt
(B) By placing a large order
(C) By purchasing used products
(D) By going through an agency

43. What does the man ask the woman to do?

(A) Send money in advance
(B) Design an image
(C) Contact an advertising manager
(D) Access a company Web site

GO ON TO THE NEXT PAGE ➡

T
E
S
T
6

 32-34 *P. 300*   **35-37** *P. 302*   🚩 **38-40** *P. 304*   🚩 **41-43** *P. 306*

44. What is the man preparing to do?

(A) Hire a new financial advisor
(B) Revise a pricing policy
(C) Meet a customer
(D) Make a presentation

45. Why is the man's work taking extra time to complete?

(A) Some data are not correct.
(B) Some résumés have not arrived.
(C) A computer is not working properly.
(D) A staff member is away on holiday.

46. What does the woman offer to do?

(A) Arrange a meeting
(B) Write a job description
(C) Assign someone to help with a task
(D) Talk to a department head

47. Where is the conversation taking place?

(A) At a theater
(B) At a job recruitment agency
(C) At a construction company
(D) At a real estate agency

48. What will the man do in two months?

(A) Transfer to a new city
(B) Launch his own business
(C) Request a loan
(D) Take a business trip

49. What information does the woman request from the man?

(A) His current position
(B) His next project
(C) His contact details
(D) His budget for accommodation

50. What most likely is the woman's occupation?

(A) A reporter
(B) A journalist
(C) A writer
(D) An editor

51. What does the man ask the woman to do?

(A) Look for some errors
(B) Publicize news in a periodical
(C) Schedule a conference
(D) Renew his agreement

52. What will the woman do at 1:30 P.M.?

(A) Attend a meeting
(B) Go to a branch office
(C) Interview an applicant
(D) Have lunch with some customers

53. What does the woman ask the man to do?

(A) Place a food order
(B) Arrange transportation for some employees
(C) Arrive early to help with an event
(D) Locate a place for a party

54. What does the man mean when he says, "It depends on when"?

(A) Not many workers are planning to attend.
(B) Bad weather is expected to continue over the weekend.
(C) He will be out of the office on Saturday.
(D) He is busy in the morning.

55. What does the man suggest?

(A) Visiting the venue together
(B) Rearranging the time of a meal
(C) Checking the number of customers
(D) Ordering invitations

🚩 **44-46** *P. 308*   🚩 **47-49** *P. 310*   🚩 **50-52** *P. 312*   🚩 **53-55** *P. 314*

56. Who is the man?

(A) A dance performer
(B) A festival organizer
(C) A musician
(D) A reporter

57. What problem with the festival is mentioned?

(A) Tickets are too expensive.
(B) The musical performances start too late.
(C) The location is too small.
(D) There is a shortage of parking spaces.

58. What do the women say about the festival?

(A) There are many food options.
(B) There is a wide range of musical styles.
(C) They think it is better than the last one.
(D) All the performers live nearby.

---

59. What industry do the speakers most likely work in?

(A) Advertising
(B) Education
(C) Health care
(D) Publishing

60. What does the man say will happen next quarter?

(A) A new book will be published.
(B) A new TV commercial will be aired.
(C) An awards ceremony will take place.
(D) A new class will be organized.

61. What does the man imply when he says, "Didn't Phillip draw all the illustrations"?

(A) He is seeking a graphic designer.
(B) He is worried that Phillip may not have been paid.
(C) He discovered the omission of information.
(D) He thinks the drawings are of a high quality.

Destination	Time	Platform	Status
Ashland	10:15 A.M.	4	Boarding
Sandusky	10:17 A.M.	6	Delayed
Cleveland	10:20 A.M.	8	Boarding
Akron	10:20 A.M.	3	Preparing

62. Why are the speakers taking a trip?

(A) To apologize to a customer
(B) To give a demonstration
(C) To inspect a plant
(D) To negotiate an agreement

63. What is the man worried about?

(A) Arriving late for a presentation
(B) Having trouble finding seats together
(C) Getting lost in the train station
(D) Leaving his luggage out of sight

64. Look at the graphic. Where will the speakers probably go next?

(A) Platform 4
(B) Platform 6
(C) Platform 8
(D) Platform 3

GO ON TO THE NEXT PAGE ➡

56-58 *P. 316*   59-61 *P. 318*   62-64 *P. 320*

Ms. Levine's Schedule
(April 14, Wednesday)

Speech at Presentation	10:00 A.M.
Budget committees' conference	11:00 A.M.
Review reports	3:00 P.M.
Staff meeting	5:00 P.M.

Last week's Market Share

65. Who most likely is the man?

(A) A personal assistant
(B) A furniture designer
(C) A company president
(D) A sales representative

66. What does the woman imply about Ms. Wahlberg?

(A) She is an office supply developer.
(B) She sells user-friendly software.
(C) She works with Ms. Levine.
(D) She is an important client.

67. Look at the graphic. What time will the woman meet Ms. Wahlberg?

(A) 10:00 A.M.
(B) 11:00 A.M.
(C) 3:00 P.M.
(D) 5:00 P.M.

68. Look at the graphic. Which broadcasting company do the speakers work at?

(A) Sketchers Reporting
(B) GORUN News
(C) Dazed Central
(D) Fan Cast Today

69. What is the increased market share attributed to?

(A) Adding a comedy section
(B) Focusing on regional news
(C) Covering sports matches
(D) Reporting on global issues

70. What may the woman do in the future?

(A) Review a survey result
(B) Post articles online
(C) Attend an international sports event
(D) Assist her coworkers

🚩 **65-67** *P. 322*   🚩 **68-70** *P. 324*

71. According to the speaker, what is special about the plant?

(A) It has recently been renovated.
(B) It operates all year round.
(C) It is the biggest in the state.
(D) It is the oldest in the city.

72. What will be offered to the tourists?

(A) Free clothing
(B) A tour book
(C) Audio equipment
(D) A complimentary drink

73. What are the visitors asked to do?

(A) Wear protective gloves
(B) Ask before taking photos
(C) Keep quiet
(D) Remain with the group

74. What is the speaker talking about?

(A) Expansion of an expressway
(B) Construction of new parking lots
(C) An urban improvement project
(D) Renovations to public facilities

75. According to the speaker, what does the plan involve?

(A) Placing flowers along the street
(B) Raising money from citizens
(C) Blocking a downtown area
(D) Removing some green spaces

76. What will most likely happen next?

(A) An agency will propose a plan.
(B) Materials will be chosen.
(C) Construction costs will be calculated.
(D) A group will take a vote.

77. What is being advertised?

(A) Locally-grown fruit
(B) A monthly publication
(C) Real estate opportunities
(D) A vegetarian restaurant

78. What will new customers receive for a limited time?

(A) Souvenir mugs
(B) Entry tickets to a farm
(C) Invitations to a seminar
(D) Complimentary vouchers for a restaurant

79. What are listeners asked to do on the Web site?

(A) Enter a contest
(B) Join a mailing list
(C) Use a promotional code
(D) Look at some pictures

80. What is the purpose of the message?

(A) To provide information
(B) To ask for help
(C) To make some plans public
(D) To offer a refund

81. What is the problem?

(A) Heavy rain caused traffic congestion.
(B) A company has damaged some infrastructure.
(C) Repairs will take longer than planned.
(D) Underground water pipes have burst.

82. Why does the speaker say, "Information on the Web site is updated constantly"?

(A) To reduce the number of calls
(B) To highlight improvements in technology
(C) To correct a previous statement
(D) To praise customer service agents

GO ON TO THE NEXT PAGE →

 71-73 *P. 326*   74-76 *P. 328*   77-79 *P. 330*   80-82 *P. 332*

297

83. Where is the announcement being made?

(A) In a security company
(B) In a store
(C) In a warehouse
(D) In a museum

84. What is being announced?

(A) Security staff will install new devices.
(B) A project due date is being delayed.
(C) Employees will be assigned new work hours.
(D) New inventory will be placed on display.

85. What does the speaker ask employees to do?

(A) Get the manager's approval for item returns
(B) Confirm that the cash registers are working properly
(C) Place special orders by the end of the day
(D) Make sure all cases are empty

86. What is the speaker discussing?

(A) An employee's promotion
(B) The remodeling of a shop
(C) The display of new items
(D) The relocation of a warehouse

87. What improvement does the speaker mention?

(A) Reduced prices
(B) Longer opening hours
(C) A larger parking lot
(D) More space for products

88. What does the speaker mean when she says, "It seems we were right to change contractors"?

(A) She thinks a product will sell well now.
(B) She is glad she listened to her staff's advice.
(C) Work will be finished earlier than expected.
(D) A company can offer cheaper prices than a competitor.

89. What is the main purpose of the call?

(A) To discuss a job application
(B) To sign up for a class
(C) To post a job opening
(D) To decline an invitation

90. What does the speaker plan to do next Tuesday?

(A) Conduct some interviews
(B) Make some sales calls
(C) Share the software
(D) Meet with new customers

91. What does the speaker request?

(A) Photos of consultants
(B) A list of instructors
(C) Results of job evaluations
(D) Feedback on a class

92. Who most likely is the audience?

(A) Directors
(B) New employees
(C) Recruiters
(D) Visitors

93. What should the listeners do in order to get equipment?

(A) Speak to Linda McKenna
(B) Contact the supply department
(C) Suggest it to the accounting department
(D) E-mail the security team

94. What is mentioned about the security pass?

(A) It should be kept in the supply department.
(B) It must be used to gain access to any area.
(C) It is composed of a digital code.
(D) It will be explained by Julie Kimura.

83-85 *P. 334*　　86-88 *P. 336*　　89-91 *P. 338*　　92-94 *P. 340*

Additional Services	
Print logo/name	$2.50
Color stitching	$3.50
Add pocket	$5.00
Size alterations	$8.50

95. What problem does the speaker mention?

(A) A style seems old-fashioned.
(B) A shipment is delayed.
(C) A button is missing.
(D) A name is misspelled.

96. Look at the graphic. How much will Deborah Han pay for her request?

(A) $2.50
(B) $3.50
(C) $5.00
(D) $8.50

97. What will the listener most likely do next?

(A) Ship a correct item
(B) Ask for a postal address
(C) Recalculate a bill
(D) Call a supplier

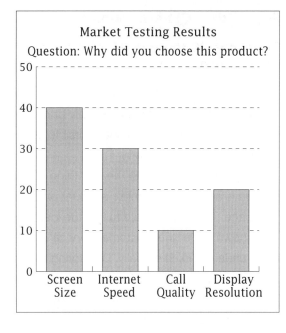

Market Testing Results
Question: Why did you choose this product?

98. What kind of product was the survey most likely about?

(A) A tablet computer
(B) A mobile phone
(C) A laptop computer
(D) An office photocopier

99. According to the speaker, what do users prefer to do?

(A) Send text messages
(B) Play games
(C) Search for information
(D) Watch videos

100. Look at the graphic. Which feature will the marketing team focus on?

(A) Screen Size
(B) Internet Speed
(C) Call Quality
(D) Display Resolution

95-97 *P. 342*

98-100 *P. 344*

PART **4**

T E S T **6**

Questions 32 through 34 refer to the following conversation.

M: Hello, I subscribed to your journal last month. ❶I have been receiving the daily print editions, but online contents are inaccessible, and I would like to know why.

W: I apologize for that. ❷The first thing you should do is activate your online account on our home page. Then you should follow the instructions shown under the 'customer service' link.

M: I understand. ❸Actually, I am trying to make an account as you mentioned. ❹The log-in screen is asking for my user name, but I don't think I have received one yet.

W: If you've not requested an ID change earlier, it is simply your e-mail address.

🗒 問題32-34は次の会話に関するものです。

M: こんにちは、先月そちらの刊行物の購読を始めました。毎日の印刷版は届いていますが、インターネットの情報にアクセスができなくて、その理由を知りたいのですが。

W: 申し訳ありません。はじめに弊社のホームページでインターネットアカウントを有効にしていただく必要があります。それから、「顧客サービス」のリンクの下に表示されている手順に従ってください。

M: わかりました。実はおっしゃったとおり、アカウントを作ろうとしているところなのです。ログイン画面でユーザー名を尋ねられますが、まだいただいていないと思うのですが。

W: 先にID変更の申請をされていないのでしたら、単純にEメールアドレスがIDになります。

✏️ □subscribe to ～を定期購読する　□journal 刊行物　□print edition 印刷版
□online content インターネット上にある情報、内容　□inaccessible 接続できない　□apologize for ～を謝る
□activate ～を有効にする　□account インターネット等のシステムを使用する個人用資格　□instruction 手順
□user name 利用者名

---

32. ★★☆☆☆

What problem is the man reporting?

(A) He was not charged the correct amount.
(B) He got different newspapers.
(C) He can't access some online contents.
(D) He is not receiving e-mails at his home.

男性はどんな問題を報告していますか。

(A) 正しい金額で請求されなかった。
(B) 違う新聞が届いた。
(C) インターネット上の情報にアクセスできない。
(D) 家でEメールを受信していない。

 会話冒頭❶で男性が「インターネットの情報に接続できない」と述べている。以上から正解は **(C)**。

 □correct 正しい　□amount 額、量　□access ～に接続する

33. ★★★☆☆

According to the woman, what does the man need to do?

(A) Open a new account
(B) Turn on the computer again
(C) Call a customer representative
(D) Provide proof of identification

女性によると男性は何をする必要がありますか。

(A) 新しいアカウントを作る。
(B) コンピューターの電源を入れなおす。
(C) 顧客窓口に電話をする。
(D) 身分証明を提出する。

男性が❶で問題を訴えたのに対し、女性は❷で「はじめに弊社のホームページでインターネットアカウントを有効にする必要がある」と述べている。以上から正解は **(A)**。❷の activate とは、作動できる状態にするという意味で、新たなアカウントを作って環境を整えることも含まれる。

□turn on ～ (の電源) をつける　□customer representative お客様相談係　□proof of identification 身分証明

---

34. ★★☆☆☆

What information does the man say he is missing?

(A) A user name
(B) An identification number
(C) A password
(D) A billing amount

男性はどんな情報が足りないと言っていますか。

(A) ユーザー名
(B) ID 番号
(C) パスワード
(D) 請求額

男性は❸で女性が言うとおりにアカウントを作成しようとしていると述べるが、❹で「ユーザー名をまだもらっていない」と女性からの指示を仰ごうとしている。ここから、男性はユーザー名が不足していることがわかる。以上から正解は **(A)**。

□billing amount 請求額

	1回目	2回目	3回目
32.			
33.			
34.			

32. (C)　33. (A)　34. (A)

Questions 35 through 37 refer to the following conversation.

W: Good morning, ❶I'd like to buy five tickets to the Boston Symphony performance this month. Could you please guarantee that all the seats are next to each other?

M: ❷I'm terribly sorry. We have only four seats left which are next to each other. Do you still want the tickets?

W: No, it has to be five. In that case, could you tell me whether there are enough tickets for the concert being held next month?

M: Yes. For the one next month, we have enough middle front seats available. ❸They each cost seven dollars more, but you will find that they are worth the price.

📝 問題35-37は次の会話に関するものです。

W: おはようございます。今月のBoston Symphonyの公演のチケットを5枚買いたいのですが。全ての席が隣り合うように押さえていただけますか。

M: 大変申し訳ありません。隣り合っている席で残っているのは4席のみになります。それでもチケットをお求めになりますか。

W: いいえ、5枚でなければならないんです。それなら、来月開催されるコンサートのチケットが十分にあるか教えていただけますか。

M: はい。来月のものですと、中央の前方に十分お席がご用意できます。1枚につき7ドル高くなりますが、それだけの価値を感じられると思います。

✏️ □symphony 交響楽団、オーケストラ □guarantee ～であることを保証する □middle front seat 中央前方席
□worth ～の価値がある

---

35. ★★★☆☆

What event does the woman want to buy tickets for?

(A) A ballet
(B) A new film
(C) A sports match
(D) A music concert

女性はどのイベントのチケットを購入したいと思っていますか。

(A) バレエ
(B) 新作映画
(C) スポーツの試合
(D) 音楽のコンサート

🔍 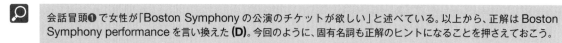 会話冒頭❶で女性が「Boston Symphonyの公演のチケットが欲しい」と述べている。以上から、正解はBoston Symphony performanceを言い換えた **(D)**。今回のように、固有名詞も正解のヒントになることを押さえておこう。

✏️ □ballet バレエ □match 試合

36. ★★★☆☆

What problem is being discussed?

(A) There are not enough seats left.
(B) The concert has been canceled.
(C) The date has been changed.
(D) The tickets cannot be printed.

どんな問題が話し合われていますか。

(A) 残っている座席が足りない。
(B) コンサートが中止になった。
(C) 日程が変更になった。
(D) チケットが印刷できない。

会話冒頭❶で女性が「公演チケットが5枚欲しい」と述べたことに対し、男性が❷で隣り合っている座席は4席しかないと返答している。ここから、座席が足りないことがわかる。以上から正解は **(A)**。

---

37. ★★★★★

What does the man say about the middle front seats?

(A) They are more expensive.
(B) They are all sold out.
(C) They are under renovation.
(D) They have to be bought in advance.

男性は中央前方の座席について何と言っていますか。

(A) より値段が高い。
(B) 完売した。
(C) 改装中である。
(D) 事前購入する必要がある。

男性は別の公演は座席が空いていると言い、❸で「中央前方の座席は価格が7ドル高い」と述べている。以上から正解は **(A)**。❸の seven dollars more の "more" をしっかり聞き取ることが重要。

□under renovation 改装中の　□in advance 事前に

	1回目	2回目	3回目
35.			
36.			
37.			

35. (D)　36. (A)　37. (A)

Questions 38 through 40 refer to the following conversation.

W: Good morning, Tony. ❶Your computer monitor was scratched, so I've just exchanged it. Everything looks to be in good order now, and the reason your computer wasn't working properly was that the inside was very dusty.

M: Thank you very much for your help. By the way, can you help me with one more thing? How can I connect the computer to a printer? ❷I need to print out a report by tomorrow, but I don't know how to do it.

W: Don't worry. ❸There's a certain cable that you need. ❹I think I have a spare in my office. ❺I'll be right back.

📝 問題38-40は次の会話に関するものです。

W: おはようございます、Tony さん。あなたのコンピューターのモニターに傷があったので、今交換したところです。今は全て正常に動いているようです。それと、コンピューターがちゃんと動いていなかった原因は内側がほこりだらけになっていたからでした。

M: 助けてくださってありがとうございます。ところで、もう一つお手伝いいただけますか。コンピューターをプリンターにつなぐにはどうしたらいいでしょうか。明日までに報告書を印刷しなければならないのですが、どうするかわからないのです。

W: ご心配なく。必要なケーブルがあるのです。オフィスに予備があったと思います。すぐに戻ります。

✎ □scratch ～に傷をつける　□in good order 正常に作動して　□work properly 正しく作動する
□dusty ほこりだらけの　□by the way ところで　□connect A to A を～に接続する　□spare 予備
□be right back すぐ戻る

---

38. ★★★☆☆

What did the woman just do?

(A) Bought a product
(B) Changed her internet service provider
(C) Replaced the screen
(D) Upgraded some software

女性は何をしたところですか。

(A) 製品を買った。
(B) インターネットサービスのプロバイダーを変更した。
(C) 画面を交換した。
(D) ソフトウェアをアップグレードした。

🔍 会話冒頭❶で女性が「コンピューターのモニターに傷があったので、今交換したところだ」と述べている。以上から、正解はモニターを screen と言い換えた **(C)**。

✎ □provider プロバイダー、供給業者　□replace ～を交換する　□upgrade ～をグレードアップする、～の等級を上げる

39. ★★★☆☆

What does the man say he needs to do?

(A) Clean his desk
(B) Design a Web site
(C) Buy a computer
(D) Print a document

男性は何をする必要があると言っていますか。

(A) デスクを掃除する。
(B) ウェブサイトをデザインする。
(C) コンピューターを買う。
(D) 書類を印刷する。

 男性は❷で「報告書を印刷する必要がある」と述べている。以上から、正解は報告書を document と言い換えた **(D)**。

---

40. ★★☆☆☆

What does the woman offer to get the man?

(A) A monitor
(B) A cable
(C) A printer
(D) A computer

女性は男性のために何を取りに行くと言っていますか。

(A) モニター
(B) ケーブル
(C) プリンター
(D) コンピューター

 女性は❸・❹・❺で「(印刷するのに必要な)ケーブルがオフィスにあるから取りに行く」と述べている。以上から正解は **(B)**。

	1回目	2回目	3回目
38.			
39.			
40.			

🚩 **38. (C) 39. (D) 40. (B)**

Questions 41 through 43 refer to the following conversation.

W: Hello, I'm calling from Jupiter Travel Agency. ❶We're interested in having leather purses made for our clients. ❷I saw them in your advertisement in the newspaper. ❸Could you give me some details on quantities and prices?

M: Yes, leather purses are 20 dollars each. ❹However, if you place an order for more than 50 leather purses, you'll get a ten percent discount off the total cost.

W: That price seems reasonable. We'd like to have our company logo printed on the leather purses. Is that hard to do?

M: No, it's very easy. ❺Just go to our Web site, upload the image of your logo, and then place your order.

📝 問題41-43は次の会話に関するものです。

W: こんにちは、Jupiter 旅行代理店と申します。お客様向けの革財布を作っていただきたいのですが。新聞で御社の広告を見ました。量と価格について詳しく教えていただけますか。

M: はい。革財布は1点20ドルです。ただ、革財布を50点以上ご注文いただきましたら、合計額から10パーセントお引きします。

W: お手頃な価格ですね。革財布に企業ロゴを印刷したいのですが。難しいですか。

M: いえ、とても簡単ですよ。弊社のウェブサイトにアクセスして、ロゴの画像をアップロードして、ご注文ください。

✏️ □interested in ～に興味がある　□leather purse 皮財布　□detail 詳細　□quantity 量
□upload ～をアップロードする (ファイルや写真をインターネット等に転送する)　□image 画像
□place an order 発注する

---

41. ★★★★★

What is the woman interested in purchasing?

(A) Promotional products
(B) Flight tickets
(C) Office stationery
(D) Advertising space in a magazine

女性は何を購入することに興味がありますか。

(A) 販促品
(B) 航空券
(C) 事務用文房具
(D) 雑誌の広告スペース

🔍 会話冒頭❶で女性が「お客様向けの財布を制作してほしい」と切り出し、❷で「新聞広告で見た」と述べ、さらに❸で価格について尋ねている。ここから、女性は広告で宣伝された製品を自分の事業の販促品として購入することに興味があるとわかる。以上から正解は **(A)**。旅行代理店が革財布を作るというところから、どんな使用目的なのかを考えることがポイント。

✏️ □promotional 販促用の　□office stationery 事務用文房具

42. ★★★☆☆

How can the woman receive a discount?

(A) By showing a previous receipt
(B) By placing a large order
(C) By purchasing used products
(D) By going through an agency

女性はどうすれば割引を受けられますか。

(A) 以前の領収書を見せることによって。
(B) 大量の注文をすることによって。
(C) 中古品を購入することによって。
(D) 代理店を介することによって。

男性は❹で「革財布を50点以上注文すれば、合計額から10パーセント引く」と述べている。ここから、大量に発注すれば割引になることがわかる。以上から正解は **(B)**。

□previous 以前の　□used 中古の　□go through ～を介する、経由する

---

43. ★★☆☆☆

What does the man ask the woman to do?

(A) Send money in advance
(B) Design an image
(C) Contact an advertising manager
(D) Access a company Web site

男性は女性に何をするように頼んでいますか。

(A) 事前に送金する。
(B) イメージをデザインする。
(C) 広告マネジャーに連絡をする。
(D) 会社のウェブサイトにアクセスする。

男性は❺で「会社のウェブサイトにアクセスする」ように案内している。以上から正解は **(D)**。

□in advance 前もって　□contact ～に連絡する　□access ～に接続する

	1回目	2回目	3回目
41.			
42.			
43.			

 41. (A)　42. (B)　43. (D)

Questions 44 through 46 refer to the following conversation.

W: Hello, Chris, ❶can we discuss the budget presentation you're giving at next week's executive conference? How's the preparation going? Has the finance department sent their expense report to you?

M: Yes, they did. However, ❷there are a few wrong calculations in the report. ❸It's taking longer than I thought to confirm the figures and make corrections.

W: I'm sorry to hear that. There are only a few more days left until the conference. ❹Do you think you need someone to help end the preparations on time? ❺I can send another employee to assist you.

M: I appreciate your cooperation. I'm sure this will go quickly if there is someone to help me.

📝 問題44-46は次の会話に関するものです。

W: こんにちは、Chris さん。来週の重役会議で発表する予算のプレゼンテーションについてお話ししてもいいですか。準備の調子はどうですか。財務部は経費報告を送ってくれましたか。

M: はい、送ってくれました。しかし、報告書には計算の間違いがありました。数字の確認と訂正に思っていたよりも時間がかかっています。

W: それは大変ですね。会議まであと数日しかありません。準備が間に合うように誰かに手伝ってもらう必要がありますか。従業員を応援に行かせますよ。

M: ご協力ありがとうございます。誰かに手伝ってもらえたら早く進むと思います。

✏️ □executive conference 重役会議　□expense 支出、経費　□wrong 間違った　□confirm ～を確認する
□figures 数値　□make a correction 修正する　□assist ～を手伝う　□appreciate ～に感謝する
□go quickly 早く進む

---

44. ★★☆☆☆

What is the man preparing to do?

(A) Hire a new financial advisor
(B) Revise a pricing policy
(C) Meet a customer
(D) Make a presentation

男性は何をする準備をしていますか。

(A) 新しい財務顧問を雇う。
(B) 価格設定の方針を改定する。
(C) 顧客に会う。
(D) プレゼンテーションをする。

🔍 会話冒頭❶で女性が「来週の会議で発表するプレゼンテーションについて話したい」と述べている。以上から正解は **(D)**。

✏️ □financial advisor 財務相談者　□revise ～を改定する　□pricing policy 価格設定方針

45. ★★★☆☆

Why is the man's work taking extra time to complete?

(A) Some data are not correct.
(B) Some résumés have not arrived.
(C) A computer is not working properly.
(D) A staff member is away on holiday.

男性の仕事はなぜ完了までに余計に時間がかかっていますか。

(A) データが正しくない。
(B) 届いていない履歴書がある。
(C) コンピューターが正常に動作していない。
(D) 従業員が休暇で不在にしている。

男性は❷・❸で「報告書には計算の間違いがあり、数字の確認と訂正に時間がかかっている」と述べている。以上から、正解は計算の間違いを Some data are not correct. と言い換えた **(A)**。

□résumé 履歴書　□work properly 正常に働く　□be away 不在である　□on holiday 休暇中で

46. ★★★★☆

What does the woman offer to do?

(A) Arrange a meeting
(B) Write a job description
(C) Assign someone to help with a task
(D) Talk to a department head

女性は何をすると申し出ていますか。

(A) 会議の手配をする。
(B) 職務内容について書く。
(C) 誰かを仕事の手伝いに充てる。
(D) 部長に相談する。

女性は❹で「会議準備が間に合うように手伝う人が必要か」と尋ね、「従業員を応援に行かせることができる」と申し出ている。ここから、女性は従業員にある業務を割り当てることが考えられる。以上から正解は **(C)**。

□job description 職務内容　□assign 〜を割り当てる　□department head 部門長

	1回目	2回目	3回目
44.			
45.			
46.			

44. (D)　45. (A)　46. (C)

Questions 47 through 49 refer to the following conversation.

M: Hi. ❶I saw a 2-bedroom house on Hardon Avenue, across from Windview Theater, that you posted on your homepage. I'm wondering how soon it would be available to move into.

W: ❷It is a beautiful home, and the owners have taken excellent care of it over the years. ❸They're moving out in October. I'd be happy to give you a tour of the house.

M: To be honest, I need something sooner than that. ❹My company is going to transfer me from Phoenix to Sedona in two months, so I'm in the process of sorting out housing.

W: I understand. ❺If you tell me the price range you are interested in, I can e-mail you a list of appropriate properties.

📝 問題47-49は次の会話に関するものです。

M: こんにちは。そちらのホームページに掲載されているWindview劇場の向かいの、Hardon大通りの寝室2間の家を見たのですが、どのぐらいで入居できるようになるか教えていただけませんか。

W: あそこは綺麗な家ですし、家主も長年にわたってしっかりと手入れをしてきています。10月には退去することになっています。喜んで中をご案内いたします。

M: 実は、それよりももっと早いのが必要なんです。2か月後にPhoenixからSedonaに転勤になるので、住む場所を探しているところなんです。

W: わかりました。ご希望の価格帯を教えていただければ、適当な物件の一覧をEメールでお送りします。

✏️ □bedroom 寝室　□post ～を掲載する　□take excellent care of ～を入念に手入れする
□over the years 長年にわたって　□move out 退去する　□I'd be happy to *do* 喜んで～する　□tour of ～の見学
□to be honest 正直に言うと　□in the process of ～の段階にある　□sort out ～を選別する　□housing 住宅
□be interested in ～に興味がある　□appropriate 適切な　□property 物件

---

47. ★★★☆☆

Where is the conversation taking place?

(A) At a theater
(B) At a job recruitment agency
(C) At a construction company
(D) At a real estate agency

会話はどこで行われていますか。

(A) 劇場
(B) 人材紹介会社
(C) 建設会社
(D) 不動産会社

🔍 会話冒頭❶で男性がある物件に言及し、「どれくらいで入居できるか」を女性に尋ねている。それに対して女性が❷で簡単な状況の説明を挟んだ後、❸で「10月に退去予定なので案内できる」と応じている。つまり、この会話は不動産賃貸に関する話であることがわかる。以上から正解は **(D)**。

✏️ □job recruitment agency 人財派遣会社　□real estate agency 不動産会社

48. ★★★☆☆

What will the man do in two months?	2か月後に男性は何をしますか。
(A) Transfer to a new city	**(A)** 新しい町に引っ越す。
(B) Launch his own business	(B) 自分の会社を立ち上げる。
(C) Request a loan	(C) 貸付金を申し込む。
(D) Take a business trip	(D) 出張する。

🔍 男性は❹で「2か月後には転勤する」と述べている。ここから、男性は引っ越しをすることがわかる。以上から正解は **(A)**。

✎ □transfer to ～に引っ越す　□launch ～を立ち上げる　□loan 貸付金　□business trip 出張

49. ★★★★☆

What information does the woman request from the man?	女性は男性にどんな情報を求めていますか。
(A) His current position	(A) 現在の役職
(B) His next project	(B) 次の計画
(C) His contact details	(C) 連絡先
(D) His budget for accommodation	**(D)** 宿泊施設のための予算

🔍 女性は❹で「希望の価格帯を教えてくれれば、適当な物件の一覧を送付する」と述べている。ここから、これから居住したい物件の価格帯を情報として求めていることがわかる。以上から、正解はこの価格帯を budget と言い換えた **(D)**。

✎ □contact detail 連絡先　□accommodation 宿泊施設

	1回目	2回目	3回目
47.			
48.			
49.			

 47. (D)　48. (A)　49. (D)

Questions 50 through 52 refer to the following conversation.

M: Hello, this is Harold Bently from human resources calling. ❶I would like to get some space in the next issue of the company newsletter. Do you think it's possible?

W: ❷Sure. We were in the middle of finding more material to fill some pages. I was about to call around to see whether anyone has any news or announcements they want in the newspaper. So, what do you have in mind?

M: Good, ❸there are a couple of events that our department would like to highlight — the annual summer picnic and the 10 km running race. ❹We would also like to publish details of the new company benefits.

W: It sounds like you need a couple of pages. Let's get together and talk about specifics and the layout. ❺I have lunch at 12 and a meeting at 1:30 P.M., so how does 4 P.M. in my office sound? I want to get everything done by 6.

📝 問題50-52は次の会話に関するものです。

M: こんにちは、人事部の Bently です。次号の社内報で少しスペースをもらえないかと思いまして。可能でしょうか。

W: いいですよ。空きページを埋めるネタを探しているところだったんです。新聞に載せたいニュースやお知らせがある人はいないか、みんなに電話をかけようと思っていたところです。それで、どんなものを考えていますか。

M: よかった。うちの課から呼びかけたいイベントが少しあります。毎年の夏のピクニックと10キロメートル競走です。それと会社の新しい福利厚生の詳細についても発表したいと思います。

W: それなら数ページ要りそうですね。直接会って詳細やレイアウトについて話しましょうか。私は12時に昼食を取って午後1時半に会議があるので、午後4時に私の事務所だとどうでしょうか。6時までには全部済ませたいです。

✏️ ☐human resources 人事部　☐issue（雑誌などの）号　☐in the middle of ～の最中である
☐fill a page ページを埋める　☐be about to *do* ～するところである
☐call around to see whether あちこちに電話して～かどうか確認する
☐What do you have in mind? どんなものを考えていますか。　☐detail 詳細　☐company benefits 福利厚生
☐specific 詳細

---

50. ★★★★☆

What most likely is the woman's occupation?

(A) A reporter
(B) A journalist
(C) A writer
(D) An editor

女性の職業は何だと考えられますか。

(A) リポーター
(B) ジャーナリスト
(C) 作家
(D) 編集者

🔍 会話冒頭❶で男性が「次号の社内報で少しスペースをもらえないかと思っている」と述べ、女性が❷でそれが可能であることを伝え、内容の確認のために問い返したのに対し、男性が❸で「課から呼びかけたいイベントについて記載したい」と述べている。ここから、女性は社内報のスペース内の記事の編集を担当していると考えられる。以上から正解は **(D)**。(B) は新聞や雑誌記事、(C) が小説等の本を書く人といった共通する要素を一部含んでいるが、書かれる内容から判断すると当てはまらないため、ここでは不正解。

51. ★★★★★

What does the man ask the woman to do?

(A) Look for some errors
(B) Publicize news in a periodical
(C) Schedule a conference
(D) Renew his agreement

男性は女性に何をするように頼んでいますか。

(A) 間違いを探す。
(B) 定期刊行誌でニュースを公表する。
(C) 会議を設定する。
(D) 契約を更新する。

 ❷で女性から社内報に載せたい内容を尋ねられた男性は、❸で「課から呼びかけたいイベントが少しある」こと、❹で「会社の新しい福利厚生の詳細について発表したい」ことを述べている。ここから、男性は女性に定期的に刊行している社内報で情報を公開する機会を求めていることがわかる。以上から正解は **(B)**。❷の newspaper が periodical と言い換えられていることを押さえておこう。

 □error 誤り　□publicize 〜を公表する　□periodical 定期刊行物　□renew 〜を更新する

---

52. ★★★★★

What will the woman do at 1:30 P.M.?

(A) Attend a meeting
(B) Go to a branch office
(C) Interview an applicant
(D) Have lunch with some customers

女性は午後1時半に何をしますか。

(A) 会議に出席する。
(B) 支社に行く。
(C) 応募者の面接をする。
(D) 顧客と昼食を取る。

 女性は❺で「午後1時半に会議がある」と述べている。以上から正解は **(A)**。

 □applicant 応募者

	1回目	2回目	3回目
50.			
51.			
52.			

 50. (D)　51. (B)　52. (A)

Questions 53 through 55 refer to the following conversation.

W: Hi, Gavin. ❶You know I'm preparing for our company's yearly picnic. ❷I was hoping that you'd be able to come early to the park on Saturday to help me get ready.

M: ❸It depends on when. ❹I have to see some clients at 11 A.M. so I won't be available until after lunch.

W: No problem. Guests will start arriving at 2:30 P.M. I wanted to start setting up around 1:30 P.M.

M: OK, then I can help you. ❺Why don't we ride over there together? That way we'll get there at the same time. I'll come by your house at 1 P.M.

📝 問題53-55は次の会話に関するものです。

W: こんにちは、Gavinさん。実は私は今会社の年次ピクニックの準備をしているんです。土曜日に準備を手伝いに早めに公園へ来てもらえたらうれしいのですが。

M: 時間によります。午前11時に顧客に会わなければならないので、昼食過ぎまでは手が空きません。

W: 問題ありません。招待客は午後2時半から到着することになっています。午後1時半ぐらいに準備を始めたいと思っていました。

M: わかりました。それならお手伝いできます。車で一緒に向かいませんか。そうすれば同じ時間に到着できます。午後1時にお宅に迎えに行きます。

✎ □get A ready A を準備する　□depend on ~による　□set up ~を設定、設営する
□ride together 車で一緒に向かう

---

53. ★★★☆☆

What does the woman ask the man to do?

(A) Place a food order
(B) Arrange transportation for some employees
(C) Arrive early to help with an event
(D) Locate a place for a party

女性は男性に何をするように頼んでいますか。

(A) 食べ物の注文をする。
(B) 従業員の交通手段を手配する。
(C) イベントの手伝いをするために早めに到着する。
(D) パーティーの場所を探す。

🔍 会話冒頭❶で女性がピクニックの準備をしていることに触れ、❷で「準備を手伝いに早めに公園へ来てほしい」と頼んでいる。以上から、picnic を event と言い換えて表現した **(C)** が正解。

✎ □place an order 注文する　□arrange ~を調整する、手配する　□transportation 交通手段　□locate ~を探す

54. ★★★★☆

What does the man mean when he says, "It depends on when"?

(A) Not many workers are planning to attend.
(B) Bad weather is expected to continue over the weekend.
(C) He will be out of the office on Saturday.
(D) He is busy in the morning.

男性が "It depends on when" という際、何を意味していますか。

(A) 参加予定の従業員はさほど多くない。
(B) 悪天候が週末にかけて続くと予想されている。
(C) 彼は土曜日に会社にいない。
(D) 彼は午前中忙しい。

 意図を問われている表現❸「それは何時かによる」の前後を見ていくと、❷「準備のために早めに来てほしい」➡❸「それは何時かによる」➡❹「11時に顧客と打合せがある」という流れになっている。つまり、午前中は他の用事があるため準備を手伝うには忙しい、という意図で発言していることがわかる。よって正解は **(D)**。

□be expected to *do* ～する見込みである　□out of office 会社にいない

---

55. ★★★★☆

What does the man suggest?

(A) Visiting the venue together
(B) Rearranging the time of a meal
(C) Checking the number of customers
(D) Ordering invitations

男性は何を勧めていますか。

(A) 会場に一緒に行くこと。
(B) 食事の時間を再調整すること。
(C) 顧客の数を確認すること。
(D) 招待状を発注すること。

 男性が❺で「車で一緒に行かないか」と提案している。ここから、会場へ一緒に行くことを勧めていることがわかる。会場を venue と言い換えて表現した **(A)** が正解。勧誘表現の Why don't we 以降を注意して聞いて正解にたどり着こう。

□venue 開催場所　□rearrange ～を再調整する

	1回目	2回目	3回目
53.			
54.			
55.			

53. (C)　54. (D)　55. (A)

Questions 56 through 58 refer to the following conversation with three speakers.

M: Hello. ❶I'm a junior reporter for the Darwin Daily Times. I'm interviewing people at the music festival. Have you seen many performances?

W1: Of course! I've been to five shows already and I'm planning to see some more. They've been very good.

M: What about you? Have you enjoyed the performances?

W2: The musical performances are excellent. However, ❷I don't like the venue. ❸I mean, there are so many people at the concert hall. ❹Also, there are long lines for everything, including the food booths.

M: The festival has always attracted people from across the country. And more tickets have been sold this year than in any other year. It could be one of the reasons for the overcrowding.

W1: ❺There are so many different kinds of music this year. ❻I hope this festival becomes an even greater success.

W2: ❼Yes, the variety of acts has been thrilling. But they need to think of changing venues for next time.

📝 問題56-58は3人の話し手による次の会話に関するものです。

M: こんにちは。Darwin Daily Times 紙のジュニアリポーターです。音楽祭で皆さんにインタビューをしています。公演はたくさん見ましたか。

W1: もちろん。もう5つのショーに行きましたし、まだもっと見るつもりです。ショーはとてもいいです。

M: あなたはどうですか。公演を楽しんでいますか。

W2: 音楽の公演は素晴らしいです。ただ、会場は気に入りません。と言うのも、コンサートホールにすごくたくさんの人がいるんです。それに食べ物の屋台なども、どこも長い列ができています。

M: この祭典はいつも国中から人がやって来ます。それに今年はこれまでのどの年にもましてチケットが売れています。それも混雑の理由の一つになっているのでしょう。

W1: 今年は本当にいろいろな種類の音楽があります。私はこのお祭りがもっと成功すればいいなと思っています。

W2: そうですね。さまざまな出し物にわくわくしています。ただ、次の会場は変更を考える必要があります。

✏️ □junior reporter ジュニアリポーター　□music festival 音楽祭　□venue 開催場所　□line 列
□attract ～を魅了する　□overcrowding 混雑　□even （比較級を強調して）ずっと　□a variety of さまざまな
□act 演出、出し物　□thrilling ワクワクする

---

56. ⭐✦✦✦✦

Who is the man?

(A) A dance performer
(B) A festival organizer
(C) A musician
(D) A reporter

男性は誰であると考えられますか。

(A) ダンサー
(B) 祭典の主催者
(C) 音楽家
(D) リポーター

🔍 会話冒頭❶で男性が「ジュニアリポーターだ」と女性に自己紹介している。以上から正解は **(D)**。

57. ★★★★☆

What problem with the festival is mentioned?

(A) Tickets are too expensive.
(B) The musical performances start too late.
(C) The location is too small.
(D) There is a shortage of parking spaces.

祭典について何が問題だと言われていますか。

(A) チケットが高すぎる。
(B) 演奏の開始が遅すぎる。
(C) 会場が小さすぎる。
(D) 駐車場に不足がある。

2人目の女性が❷で会場を好きになれないと言い、その理由として❸・❹で「コンサートホールにすごくたくさんの人がいる」ことと、「屋台もどこも行列ができている」ことを挙げている。ここから、この会場の規模が小さいと考えられる。正解はこの会場 (venue) を location と言い換えて表した **(C)**。

□a shortage of ～の不足

58. ★★★★☆

What do the women say about the festival?

(A) There are many food options.
(B) There is a wide range of musical styles.
(C) They think it is better than the last one.
(D) All the performers live nearby.

女性たちは祭典について何と言っていますか。

(A) 食事の選択肢がたくさんある。
(B) さまざまな音楽のスタイルがある。
(C) 前回よりも良いと考えている。
(D) 全ての演者は近くに住んでいる。

1人目の女性が❺・❻で「今年は本当にいろいろな種類の音楽があって、このお祭りがもっと成功してほしい」と述べたのに対し、2人目の女性も❼で賛同している。以上から、正解はこの❻・❼について部分的に述べた **(B)**。この問題は the women というところから複数の人物が同じ意見になっている箇所を聞き取って解く必要がある。ある意見が出たら、もう一方がどのような反応を示しているかを見極めて、意見の一致を確認できるように注意しよう。

□a wide range of さまざまな　□nearby 近くに

	1回目	2回目	3回目
56.			
57.			
58.			

56. (D)　57. (C)　58. (B)

Questions 59 through 61 refer to the following conversation.

W: ❶Do you have any comments about the cover design for the short story for young adults, *The Sisterhood of the Traveling Jacket*, Landon?

M: I'm very sorry, Trisha. I completely forgot about it.

W: I don't mind. ❷I know you're very busy proofreading the new novel written by Norma Smith.

M: You're right. It's been taking up all my time. But I'm finished now. ❸It will be released next quarter.

W: That's fantastic! So, do you have time to look at the cover right now?

M: Of course!

W: Thanks. I made the main illustration slightly bigger and added reviewer comments to the back cover.

M: Let me take a look. Well, the cover design is quite attractive. However, ❹the artist's name isn't written anywhere. ❺Didn't Phillip draw all the illustrations?

W: ❻Thanks for noticing. I nearly made a big mistake.

📝 問題59-61は次の会話に関するものです。

W: 若者向けの短編小説 The Sisterhood of Traveling Jacket の表紙のデザインについて意見はありますか、Landon さん。

M: 本当にすみません、Trisha さん。すっかり忘れていました。

W: 構いません。Norma Smith さんの新作小説の校正でとても忙しいのはわかっています。

M: そうなのです。時間が全てそこに割かれてしまっています。でも、今終わりました。次の四半期で発売になります。

W: それは素晴らしいです。では、今表紙を見てもらう時間はありますか。

M: もちろんです。

W: ありがとうございます。メインのイラストを少し大きくして、裏表紙に評論家のコメントを入れました。

M: 見せてください。ええと、表紙のデザインはとても魅力的です。ただ、アーティストの名前がどこにもありません。Phillip さんがイラストを全部描いたのではないですか。

W: お気づきくださりありがとうございます。大変な間違いをするところでした。

✏️ □cover design 表紙のデザイン　□short story 短編小説　□completely forget about ～についてすっかり忘れる
□proofread ～を校正する　□take up ～の時間を取る　□release ～を発売する　□next quarter 次期四半期
□have time to *do* ～する時間がある　□main 主要部の　□slightly bigger もう少し大きい
□reviewer comment 評論家の発言　□back cover 裏表紙　□attractive 魅力的な　□draw ～を描く
□nearly もう少しで

59. ★★★☆☆

What industry do the speakers most likely work in?

(A) Advertising
(B) Education
(C) Health care
(D) Publishing

話し手たちはどの業界で働いていると考えられますか。

(A) 広告
(B) 教育
(C) 健康管理
(D) 出版

 会話冒頭❶で女性は短編小説の表紙デザインについて意見を求め、❷で男性に「新作の校正で忙しいんでしょう」と状況への理解を示している。ここから、小説の表紙デザインや本の校正を手掛けている職業であることがわかる。以上から正解は **(D)**。

---

60. ★★★☆☆

What does the man say will happen next quarter?

(A) A new book will be published.
(B) A new TV commercial will be aired.
(C) An awards ceremony will take place.
(D) A new class will be organized.

男性は次の四半期に何が起こると言っていますか。

(A) 新しい本が出版される。
(B) 新しいテレビ広告が放送される。
(C) 授賞式が行われる。
(D) 新しいクラスが作られる。

 女性は❷で男性が新作の校正で忙しいことに言及し、男性は❸で「それは次の四半期に発売される」と述べている。以上から正解は **(A)**。この問題は❸の主語が it となっているため、男性が手掛けていることを会話の前半からの流れと関連づけて、内容をしっかり理解して聞く必要がある。

✎ □air ～を放送する □awards ceremony 授賞式 □take place 行う □organize ～を組織する

---

61. ★★★★★

What does the man imply when he says, "Didn't Phillip draw all the illustrations"?

(A) He is seeking a graphic designer.
(B) He is worried that Phillip may not have been paid.
(C) He discovered the omission of information.
(D) He thinks the drawings are of a high quality.

男性が"Didn't Phillip draw all the illustrations?" と言う際、何を意図していますか。

(A) グラフィックデザイナーを探している。
(B) Phillip さんへ支払いがされていないのではと心配している。
(C) 情報の抜けを見つけた。
(D) 絵の質が高いと思っている。

 意図を問われている表現❺「Phillip さんがイラストを描いたのではなかったのか」の前後を見ていくと、男性が表紙のデザインを見た際に❹「アーティストの名前がない」ことに気がつき➡❺「Phillip さんがイラストを描いたのではなかったのか」➡❻「大きな間違いをするところだった」という流れになっている。つまり、制作協力者情報が載っていないことに気づいたという意図で発言していることがわかる。この見落としを omission で表現した **(C)** が正解。

✎ □seek ～を探す、募集する □be worried about that ～ではないかと心配する □discover ～を発見する □drawing 絵 □of high quality 品質の良い

	1回目	2回目	3回目
59.			
60.			
61.			

 59. (D) 60. (A) 61. (C)

Questions 62 through 64 refer to the following conversation and sign.

W: ❶I wonder if this business trip will go well. ❷I hope the negotiations for the licensing contract with Mitchell Media Group are successful.

M: I'm sure they will be. ❸If it'll make you feel better, we can go over our strategy again on the train. ❹That is if we can get two seats next to each other. ❺These tickets don't have assigned seating, so I'm concerned that won't be possible.

W: It shouldn't be a problem. This route is never very busy during the week. Well, I think we should get going. ❻The train departs at 20 after 10, doesn't it?

M: ❼Right, and according to the departures board, our train's boarding now. We'd better hurry.

Destination	Time	Platform	Status
Ashland	10:15 A.M.	4	Boarding
Sandusky	10:17 A.M.	6	Delayed
Cleveland	❽10:20 A.M.	8	Boarding
Akron	10:20 A.M.	3	Preparing

📝 問題62-64は次の会話と標示に関するものです。

W: この出張はうまくいくでしょうか。Mitchell Media Group 社とのライセンス契約の交渉が成立するといいのですが。

M: きっとうまく行きますよ。これで気持ちが楽になるのでしたら、戦略について電車の中で再度確認できます。隣り合った2席を取れればですが。この切符は座席の指定がないので、できないのではないかと気になっています。

W: 問題ないでしょう。この路線は平日に混雑することはありませんから。では、そろそろ行ったほうがよさそうです。電車は10時20分に出発ですよね。

M: そうです。出発案内板によると、我々の電車はもう乗車が始まっているようです。急いだほうがいいでしょう。

目的地	時間	ホーム	状況
Ashland	午前10時15分	4番	乗車案内中
Sandusky	午前10時17分	6番	遅延
Cleveland	午前10時20分	8番	乗車案内中
Akron	午前10時20分	3番	準備中

✏️ □wonder if ~かどうかと思っている　□business trip 出張　□go well うまくいく　□negotiation 交渉　□licensing contract 使用許諾契約　□feel better (気分が) よくなる　□go over ~を検討する　□strategy 戦略　□assigned seating 指定座席　□be concerned 心配している　□route 路線　□depart 出発する　□according to ~によると

62. ★★★☆☆

Why are the speakers taking a trip?

(A) To apologize to a customer
(B) To give a demonstration
(C) To inspect a plant
(D) To negotiate an agreement

話し手たちはなぜ出張に行くのですか。

(A) 顧客に謝罪するため。
(B) 実演をするため。
(C) 工場を視察するため。
(D) 契約の交渉をするため。

 会話冒頭❶で女性が出張がうまくいくかどうかと不安を述べ、❷で「契約交渉がうまくいくとよい」と述べている。以上から、正解は contract を agreement と言い換えて表現した **(D)**。

 □apologize to ～に謝る　□inspect ～を視察、調査する　□plant 工場　□negotiate an agreement 契約交渉する

---

63. ★★★★☆

What is the man worried about?

(A) Arriving late for a presentation
(B) Having trouble finding seats together
(C) Getting lost in the train station
(D) Leaving his luggage out of sight

男性は何を心配していますか。

(A) プレゼンテーションに遅れること。
(B) 並びの座席を見つけるのが難しいこと。
(C) 駅で迷うこと。
(D) 目の届かない場所に荷物を置くこと。

 男性は❸・❹・❺で「出張の移動中に隣り合った席を確保できれば打ち合わせできるが、指定席ではないので、それが可能か心配だ」と述べている。ここから、並んで座る席を見つけることが困難ではないかと心配していることがわかる。以上から正解は **(B)**。

 □have trouble *doing* ～するのに苦労する　□get lost 迷う　□out of sight 目の届かないところに

---

64. ★★★★☆

Look at the graphic. Where will the speakers probably go next?

(A) Platform 4
(B) Platform 6
(C) Platform 8
(D) Platform 3

図を見てください。話し手たちはおそらく次にどこに行きますか。

(A) 4番ホーム
(B) 6番ホーム
(C) 8番ホーム
(D) 3番ホーム

 女性は❻で「私たちが乗車する電車が午前10時20分発ではないか」と男性に尋ね、それに対して❼で男性がそうだと答え、乗車案内中だから早く乗ろうと促している。表を見ると、❽から午前10時20分発の電車は8番ホームから出発することがわかる。以上から正解は **(C)**。

	1回目	2回目	3回目
62.			
63.			
64.			

 62. (D)　63. (B)　64. (C)

Questions 65 through 67 refer to the following conversation and schedule.

M: Hello, Ms. Levine. ❶I have to tell you something about your schedule tomorrow.

W: Do we need to change it?

M: Yes. ❷Ms. Wahlberg of Bella Furniture called this morning. ❸She wants to discuss our office tables. ❹Her company needs them for its upcoming furniture convention.

W: ❺Bella Furniture is one of our main customers, so we can't say no. Do I have an appointment I can reschedule?

M: There is a budget committee meeting and a staff meeting you can cancel now.

W: Well, I have to meet the directors of the budget committee. ❻I'll just skip the staff meeting. ❼Please call Ms. Wahlberg and say that I'll meet her then.

📝 問題65-67は次の会話と予定表に関するものです。

M: こんにちは、Levine さん。明日の予定についてお伝えすることがあります。

W: 変更が必要なのですか。

M: はい。今朝、Bella Furniture 社の Wahlberg さんから電話がありました。当社のオフィス用テーブルについて話がしたいとのことです。あちらは次の家具の大会のためにうちのテーブルが欲しいそうです。

W: Bella Furniture 社は、当社のお得意様ですから、断れませんね。変更できる予定はありますか。

M: 予算委員会の打ち合わせとスタッフ会議は今から取りやめられます。

W: 予算委員会の幹部には会わなければなりません。スタッフ会議は欠席します。Wahlberg さんに電話をして、その時間にお会いすると伝えてください。

Ms. Levine's Schedule (April 14, Wednesday)	
Speech at Presentation	10:00 A.M.
Budget committees' conference	11:00 A.M.
Review reports	3:00 P.M.
❽Staff meeting	5:00 P.M.

Levine さんの予定 (4月14日 水曜日)	
プレゼンテーションでのスピーチ	午前10時
予算委員会議	午前11時
報告審査	午後3時
スタッフ会議	午後5時

✎ □upcoming 来たるべき　□convention 会議　□budget committee 予算委員会　□skip ～を欠席する
□review ～を見直す、精査する

65. ★★★★★

Who most likely is the man?

(A) A personal assistant
(B) A furniture designer
(C) A company president
(D) A sales representative

男性は誰であると考えられますか。

(A) 個人付きの秘書
(B) 家具のデザイナー
(C) 社長
(D) 営業担当者

 会話冒頭❶で男性が女性に「明日の予定についてお伝えすることがある」と話しかけている。ここから、男性は女性の予定について管理・言及できる立場、つまり秘書であると考えられる。以上から正解は **(A)**。

 □sales representative 営業担当者

---

66. ★★★★☆

What does the woman imply about Ms. Wahlberg?

(A) She is an office supply developer.
(B) She sells user-friendly software.
(C) She works with Ms. Levine.
(D) She is an important client.

女性は Wahlberg さんについて何を示唆していますか。

(A) 事務用品の開発者である。
(B) 利用者目線のソフトを取り揃えている。
(C) Levine さんと一緒に働いている。
(D) 重要な顧客である。

 男性が❷・❸・❹で Bella Furniture 社の Wahlberg さんから電話があり、男性と女性の会社の家具を欲しがっていると述べ、それに対して女性が❺で「Bella Furniture 社は重要な顧客だ」と述べている。つまり、Wahlberg さんの勤務する Bella Furniture 社が重要な顧客ということは Wahlberg さん自身も重要な顧客であると言うことができる。以上から正解は **(D)**。

 □office supply 事務用品　□developer 開発者　□user-friendly 使いやすい

---

67. ★★★★☆

Look at the graphic. What time will the woman meet Ms. Wahlberg?

(A) 10:00 A.M.
(B) 11:00 A.M.
(C) 3:00 P.M.
(D) 5:00 P.M.

図を見てください。女性は何時に Wahlberg さんに会いますか。

(A) 午前10時
(B) 午前11時
(C) 午後3時
(D) 午後5時

 女性は❻・❼で「スタッフ会議を欠席にするので、その時間帯に Wahlberg さんに会う」と述べている。ここでスケジュール表を見ると、❽からスタッフ会議は午後5時から行う予定になっていることがわかる。以上から正解は **(D)**。

	1回目	2回目	3回目
65.			
66.			
67.			

 65. (A)　66. (D)　67. (D)

Questions 68 through 70 refer to the following conversation and graph.

M: Did you check our market share recently?

W: No, not recently. How are we doing?

M: ❶We jumped up to second in market share last week! We've become almost as popular as Fan Cast Today, the biggest station in the area!

W: Really? ❷I am sure it's thanks to our new section on regional current affairs that has been broadcast since last quarter.

M: Right, that was a good idea! Other news programs usually focus on sports or international events, but it seems people are really interested in hearing about what's going on right in their own neighborhoods!

W: I'm happy to hear the great news. ❸Maybe I should get out in the field and help our colleagues find more regional stories to report.

📝 問題68-70は次の会話とグラフに関するものです。

M: 最近、当社の市場占有率を確認しましたか。

W: いいえ、最近はしていません。当社はどうですか。

M: 先週の市場占有率は2位に跳ね上がりました。地域で最大の局の Fan Cast Today とほぼ同じくらいの人気です。

W: 本当ですか。前四半期から放送している地域の時事問題を扱う新番組のおかげでしょう。

M: そうですね、あれはいいアイデアでした。他のニュース番組では普通はスポーツや国際的なイベントを取り上げますが、みんな本当はまさに自分たちがいる地元で起きていることを聞きたいと思っているようです。

W: いい知らせを聞けてうれしいです。私も現場に出て、同僚が地域のニュースを探すのを手伝ったほうがいいかもしれませんね。

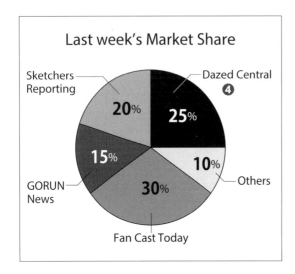

Last week's Market Share

- Sketchers Reporting 20%
- Dazed Central ❹ 25%
- Others 10%
- Fan Cast Today 30%
- GORUN News 15%

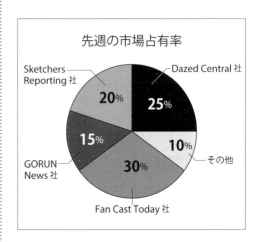

先週の市場占有率

- Sketchers Reporting 社 20%
- Dazed Central 社 25%
- その他 10%
- Fan Cast Today 社 30%
- GORUN News 社 15%

✏️ ☐market share 市場シェア、市場占有率　☐jump up 跳ね上がる　☐thanks to ～のおかげである　☐regional 地域の
☐current affairs 時事問題　☐broadcast ～を放送する　☐focus on ～に集中する、焦点を当てる
☐neighborhood 近隣　☐be happy to *do* ～してうれしい　☐maybe I should ～したほうがよいかもしれない
☐get out 外出する　☐field 現場

68. ★★★★☆

Look at the graphic. Which broadcasting company do the speakers work at?

(A) Sketchers Reporting
(B) GORUN News
(C) Dazed Central
(D) Fan Cast Today

図を見てください。話し手たちはどの放送局で働いていますか。

(A) Sketchers Reporting 社
(B) GORUN News 社
(C) Dazed Central 社
(D) Fan Cast Today 社

男性が❶で「先週市場占有率が2位になった」と述べている。ここで円グラフの市場占有率を見ると、シェア2位の会社は❹の Dazed Central 社だとわかる。以上から正解は **(C)**。

---

69. ★★★☆☆

What is the increased market share attributed to?

(A) Adding a comedy section
(B) Focusing on regional news
(C) Covering sports matches
(D) Reporting on global issues

市場占有率の増加は何に起因していますか。

(A) お笑いコーナーを追加したこと。
(B) 地域のニュースに焦点を当てたこと。
(C) スポーツの試合について報道したこと。
(D) 世界的な問題について報道したこと。

 女性は❷で「前四半期から放送している地域の時事問題を扱う新番組のおかげだ」と述べ、それに男性が即座に賛同している。ここから、地域のニュースに焦点を当てたことが要因と考えられるため、正解は **(B)**。

□comedy section お笑いコーナー　□cover 〜を報道する　□match 試合　□issue 課題

---

70. ★★★☆☆

What may the woman do in the future?

(A) Review a survey result
(B) Post articles online
(C) Attend an international sports event
(D) Assist her coworkers

女性はこれから何をすると考えられますか。

(A) 調査結果を確認する。
(B) インターネットに記事を投稿する。
(C) 国際的なスポーツイベントに参加する。
(D) 同僚を手伝う。

 女性は❸で「私も現場に出て、同僚が地域のニュースを探すのを手伝ったほうがいいかもしれない」と述べている。ここから、同僚を手伝うことが考えられる。以上から正解は **(D)**。

□review 〜を確認する　□survey result 調査結果　□post 〜を掲載する　□assist 〜を支援する

	1回目	2回目	3回目
68.			
69.			
70.			

 68. (C)　69. (B)　70. (D)

Questions 71 through 73 refer to the following announcement.

M: ❶Welcome everyone, and thank you for joining us for the tour of the Vance Apparel Plant. ❷Vance is well-known for being the first plant to open in the city, and it is still operating today in its original location. During the tour, information will be presented through a voice recording. ❸You will each be given your own set of earphones before we go into the cutting area of the factory, so please change the volume to your desired level. ❹Also, please remember to stay with the group while we are inside the plant. OK, shall we begin our tour?

問題71-73は次のお知らせに関するものです。

M: 皆さま、当社の Vance 衣料品工場のツアーにご参加いただきありがとうございます。Vance は市内に最初に開業した工場としてよく知られており、今日でも当初と同じ場所で稼働しています。ツアーの間、情報は録音音声でお伝えします。裁断区域に入る前にお一人ずつにイヤホンをお渡ししますので、お好みに合わせて音量を変えてください。また、工場内にいる間はグループと一緒にいるようにしてください。では、ツアーを始めましょうか。

□well-known 有名な　□plant 工場　□operate 操業する、稼働する　□original 当初の、もともとの
□voice recording 録音音声　□earphone イヤホン　□go into ～に入る　□cutting area 裁断区域
□desired 望ましい、適切な

---

71. ★★★☆☆

According to the speaker, what is special about the plant?

(A) It has recently been renovated.
(B) It operates all year round.
(C) It is the biggest in the state.
(D) It is the oldest in the city.

話し手によると、工場のどんな点が特別ですか。

(A) 最近改装された。
(B) 一年中稼働している。
(C) 州内で最も大きい。
(D) 市内で最も古い。

話し手はトーク冒頭❶で Vance 工場の見学に来てくれた方にお礼を言い、❷で「Vance 工場は市内で最初に開業したことで有名だ」と述べている。ここから、この工場が市内で一番古いことがわかる。以上から正解は **(D)**。「市内で最初の工場」＝「市内で一番古い」と読み換えることがポイント。

□renovate ～を改修する　□all year round 一年中　□state 州

72. ★★★☆☆

What will be offered to the tourists?

(A) Free clothing
(B) A tour book
(C) Audio equipment
(D) A complimentary drink

観光客には何が提供されますか。

(A) 無料の衣類
(B) ツアーの案内冊子
(C) 音声機器
(D) 無料の飲み物

 話し手は❸で「皆さまにはイヤホン一式が渡される」とツアー見学者に話しているので、イヤホン、つまり音声機器が提供されることがわかる。以上から正解は **(C)**。

 □audio equipment 音声機器、音響機器　□complimentary 無料の

---

73. ★★★★☆

What are the visitors asked to do?

(A) Wear protective gloves
(B) Ask before taking photos
(C) Keep quiet
(D) Remain with the group

観光客は何をするように求められていますか。

(A) 保護手袋を着ける。
(B) 撮影前に尋ねる。
(C) 静かにする。
(D) グループと一緒に居続ける。

話し手は❹で「工場内にいる間はグループと一緒にいるように」と述べている。以上から正解は **(D)**。❹の stay with が選択肢では remain with と言い換えられていることにも注目。

□protective glove 保護手袋　□keep quiet 静かにする　□remain 〜のままでいる

	1回目	2回目	3回目
71.			
72.			
73.			

71. (D)　72. (C)　73. (D)

Questions 74 through 76 refer to the following excerpt from a meeting.

M: I have a couple more things to mention before we end today's meeting. ❶ I have reviewed the project plan that the Regional Development Agency submitted. I must say I think it will do wonders! ❷ Our downtown area has never been a big attraction to visitors, and personally I've always felt that it is too gray and urban. Of course, we have Penny Park in the suburbs of the city, and a lot of people enjoy the natural environment there. ❸ However, this new idea to add flowerpots along the sidewalks will make the central area much more attractive. ❹ Before we put it to a vote, let me remind all of you that this will be an extremely beneficial and cost-effective project that could easily be completed within a month.

問題74-76は次の会議の一部に関するものです。

M: 今日の会議を終える前にいくつかお伝えすることがあります。地域開発局が提出した計画案を確認しました。すごいものになりそうです。この市の繁華街は訪れる人にとって大きな魅力にはなっていませんでしたし、いつも個人的には都会的すぎて暗いと感じていました。もちろん市の郊外には Penny 公園がありますし、多くの人がその自然環境を楽しんでいます。しかし、歩道に植木鉢を置くというこの新しいアイデアは中心地域をはるかに魅力的なものにしてくれるでしょう。投票で決める前に、改めてお伝えしておきます。これは1か月で容易に達成できる非常に有益で費用対効果の高いプロジェクトです。

✏️ ☐a couple more things もう2、3のこと　☐mention ～に言及する　☐review ～を確認する　☐project plan 計画案
☐the Regional Development Agency 地域開発局　☐do wonder 驚くべきことをする　☐attraction 魅力
☐visitor 来訪者　☐personally 自分としては　☐gray 灰色の、暗い　☐urban 都会の　☐suburb 郊外
☐natural environment 自然環境　☐flowerpot 植木鉢　☐sidewalk 歩道　☐central area 中心地域
☐attractive 魅力的な　☐put A to a vote A を投票で決める　☐extremely 非常に　☐beneficial 有益である
☐cost-effective 費用対効果のある

---

74. ★★★★☆

What is the speaker talking about?

(A) Expansion of an expressway
(B) Construction of new parking lots
(C) An urban improvement project
(D) Renovations to public facilities

話し手は何について話していますか。

(A) 高速道路の拡張
(B) 新しい駐車場の建設
(C) 都市改良計画
(D) 公共施設の改修

🔍 話し手は❶で「地域開発局が提出した計画案を確認した」と述べ、❷で「市の繁華街は今まで魅力的ではなかった」と言っていることから、都市部に関わる改良計画だと考えられる。以上から正解は **(C)**。

✏️ ☐expansion 拡張　☐expressway 高速道路　☐parking lot 駐車場　☐improvement project 改良計画
☐renovation 改修　☐public facility 公共施設

75. ★★★★☆

According to the speaker, what does the plan involve?

(A) Placing flowers along the street
(B) Raising money from citizens
(C) Blocking a downtown area
(D) Removing some green spaces

話し手によると、計画には何が含まれていますか。

(A) 道沿いに花を配置すること。
(B) 市民からお金を集めること。
(C) 繁華街地域を塞ぐこと。
(D) 緑地を取り払うこと。

 話し手は❸で「歩道に花の植木鉢を置くアイデアは中心地域を魅力的なものにしてくれる」と述べていることから、正解は (A)。❸の add が選択肢では place になっているといった細かい情報をしっかり言い換えとして判断していく必要がある。

□raise money 資金を調達する、募金する　□citizen 市民　□block ～を塞ぐ　□remove ～を取り除く

---

76. ★★★★★

What will most likely happen next?

(A) An agency will propose a plan.
(B) Materials will be chosen.
(C) Construction costs will be calculated.
(D) A group will take a vote.

次に何が起こると考えられますか。

(A) 局が計画を提出する。
(B) 原料が選ばれる。
(C) 建設費用が算出される。
(D) グループが採決を行う。

話し手はトーク後半❹で「投票で決める前に、改めて伝えておくが、これは非常に有益で費用対効果の高いプロジェクトだ」と述べて、そこまでの説明を締めくくっている。ここから、この後投票による決定がなされると考えられる。以上から正解は (D)。

□agency 局、代理店　□propose ～を提案する　□material 材料、素材　□calculate ～を計算する
□take a vote 採決する

	1回目	2回目	3回目
74.			
75.			
76.			

74. (C)　75. (A)　76. (D)

Questions 77 through 79 refer to the following advertisement.

M: ❶Now you can subscribe to Appleby Farm Magazine for only 80 dollars a year. ❷When you purchase our information-packed magazine, each month you'll receive news of the latest agricultural developments from all over the state. ❸And for a limited time only, once you subscribe to Appleby Farm Magazine, you'll receive two free coupons for the Table-Kitchen restaurant chain. You will be able to have some amazing cuisine made with fresh local produce. ❹Please go to our Web site and type in the code BF256 to take advantage of this time-limited offer.

📝 問題77-79は次の広告に関するものです。

M: 今なら『Appleby 農場誌』を年間たった80ドルで購読できます。情報たっぷりの弊社の雑誌をご購入いただけますと、毎月、州全域からの最新の農業開発ニュースをお届けします。そして『Appleby 農場誌』を購読された方には、期間限定で Table-Kitchen レストランのチェーン店で使える無料クーポン券を2枚差し上げます。地元の農産物から作られた素晴らしい料理をお召し上がりになれます。弊社のウェブサイトへ行き、コードのBF256を入力して、この期間限定特典を手に入れてください。

✎ □subscribe to ～を定期購読する □information-packed 情報の詰まった □latest 最新の
□agricultural development 農業開発 □from all over the state 州全域から □for a limited time 期間限定で
□amazing 素晴らしい □cuisine 料理 □local produce 地元の農産物 □take advantage of ～を利用する

---

77. ★★★☆☆

What is being advertised?

(A) Locally-grown fruit
(B) A monthly publication
(C) Real estate opportunities
(D) A vegetarian restaurant

何が宣伝されていますか。

(A) 地元で育てられた果物
(B) 月刊誌
(C) 不動産投資機会
(D) 菜食主義レストラン

 話し手はトーク冒頭❶で「今ならお得な価格で定期購読ができる」と切り出し、❷で（購読者は）最新の農業開発ニュースを受け取ると述べている。ここから、月刊誌の定期購読を宣伝していることがわかる。以上から正解は **(B)**。❷を聞かないと「月刊」だとわからないので、注意して聞き取ろう。

✎ □locally-grown 地元で育った □real estate 不動産 □vegetarian 菜食主義者、ベジタリアン

78. ★★★☆☆

What will new customers receive for a limited time?	新規顧客は期間限定で何をもらいますか。
(A) Souvenir mugs	(A) 記念品のマグカップ
(B) Entry tickets to a farm	(B) 農場への入場券
(C) Invitations to a seminar	(C) 講習への招待状
(D) Complimentary vouchers for a restaurant	**(D)** レストランの無料バウチャー

🔍 話し手は❸で「期間限定でレストランのチェーン店の無料クーポン券を進呈する」と述べている。以上から、正解はこれを言い換えた **(D)**。

✏️ □souvenir お土産、記念品　□mug マグカップ　□entry ticket 入場券　□complimentary 無料の

P
A
R
T
4

---

79. ★★★★☆

What are listeners asked to do on the Web site?	聞き手はウェブサイトで何をするように求められていますか。
(A) Enter a contest	
(B) Join a mailing list	(A) コンテストに出場する。
(C) Use a promotional code	(B) メーリングリストに加わる。
(D) Look at some pictures	**(C)** 販促用コードを使う。
	(D) 写真を見る。

🔍 話し手は❹で「弊社ウェブサイトからコードを入力して、特典を入手してください」と述べている。ここから、この企画の特定のコードを使用することがわかる。正解はこのコードを a promotional code と言い換えた **(C)**。

✏️ □enter a contest コンテストに出場する　□mailing list メーリングリスト、郵送先名簿
□promotional code 販売促進用コード

T
E
S
T
6

	1回目	2回目	3回目
77.			
78.			
79.			

🚩 **77. (B)　78. (D)　79. (C)**

331

Questions 80 through 82 refer to the following telephone message.

W: Thank you for calling Paragon Water Company. ❶Water service has been disrupted because of breakages in water pipes in the communities of Fort Lauderdale and Boca Raton. If you would like to report your home as being affected, please press "0". ❷The leaks in these underground pipes has currently affected fifty homes. Our crews are at the scene working to repair the damage. ❸We are experiencing a high volume of calls, so for non-emergencies please visit our Web site. ❹Information on the Web site is updated constantly. ❺Thank you for your patience.

問題80-82は次の電話のメッセージに関するものです。

W: Paragon 水道会社にお電話いただきありがとうございます。Fort Lauderdale と Boca Raton 地域の水道本管に損傷があるため、水道サービスを停止しております。お客様のお住まいが影響を受けていることを報告するには、ゼロを押してください。これらの地下パイプからの水漏れは現在50世帯に影響を与えています。弊社作業員が現在、現場で損傷の修復に取りかかっております。弊社はたくさんの電話を受けておりますため、緊急でないものは弊社のウェブサイトをご覧ください。ウェブサイトの情報は常に更新されています。お待ちいただきましてありがとうございます。

 □disrupt 〜を停止する　□breakage 損傷　□water pipe 水道配管　□affect 〜に影響を与える　□leak 漏れ
□underground pipe 地下配管　□crew 作業員　□at the scene 現場にいる　□non-emergency 緊急ではないもの
□update 〜を更新する　□constantly 常に、絶えず　□patience 忍耐、辛抱

---

80. ★★★☆☆

What is the purpose of the message?

(A) To provide information
(B) To ask for help
(C) To make some plans public
(D) To offer a refund

このメッセージの目的は何ですか。

(A) 情報を提供すること。
(B) 助けを求めること。
(C) 計画を公表すること。
(D) 払い戻しをすること。

話し手は❶で「特定の地域の水道本管に損傷があり、現在水道サービスを停止している」と公共サービスに関する情報を提供している。以上から正解は **(A)**。

 □refund 払い戻し

81. ★★★☆☆

What is the problem?	問題は何ですか。
(A) Heavy rain caused traffic congestion.	(A) 激しい雨により交通が混雑している。
(B) A company has damaged some infrastructure.	(B) 企業が基幹施設に損傷を与えた。
(C) Repairs will take longer than planned.	(C) 修理は計画よりも長くかかる。
(D) Underground water pipes have burst.	**(D)** 地下の水道管が破れた。

🔍 話し手は❷で「地下パイプからの水漏れ」と言っているので、配管が損傷したことで水漏れしていると考えられる。正解はこの損傷を burst と表現した **(D)**。

✎ □cause ～を引き起こす　□traffic congestion 交通渋滞　□infrastructure 基盤設備　□burst 破裂する

82. ★★★★☆

Why does the speaker say, "Information on the Web site is updated constantly"?	話し手はなぜ "Information on the Web site is updated constantly" と言っていますか。
(A) To reduce the number of calls	**(A)** 電話の数を減らすため。
(B) To highlight improvements in technology	(B) 技術面の向上を強調するため。
(C) To correct a previous statement	(C) 前に述べたことを訂正するため。
(D) To praise customer service agents	(D) 顧客サービスの係を称えるため。

🔍 意図を問われている表現❹「ウェブサイトの情報は常に更新している」の前後を見ていくと、❸「電話がたくさんかかっているので緊急ではない問い合わせはウェブサイトへ」➡❹「ウェブサイトで常に情報更新している」➡❺「協力の御礼」という流れになっている。つまり、電話での問い合わせが多いため、それを少しでも緩和するためにウェブサイトの閲覧の協力をお願いする意図で発言したことがわかる。よって正解は **(A)**。

✎ □reduce ～を減らす　□highlight ～を強調する　□correct ～を修正する　□previous statement 前述したこと
　□praise ～を褒める　□agent 代理人、代行者

	1回目	2回目	3回目
80.			
81.			
82.			

🚩 **80. (A)　81. (D)　82. (A)**

Questions 83 through 85 refer to the following announcement.

W: ❶Attention, staff members. As you know, our sports souvenir store's video surveillance cameras will be replaced tonight. ❷The security company will disconnect the store's current cameras and alarms while it sets up the new ones. Therefore, we have to lock up all of our merchandise tonight. ❸Before you go home, I want all sales representatives to make sure that nothing is left inside the display cases and that everything is put in the safe. The director will check the safe to make sure it's locked correctly. Thank you for your cooperation. I will see you in the morning!

問題83-85は次のアナウンスに関するものです。

W: お知らせいたします、従業員の皆さま。ご存じのとおり、スポーツ土産物店の監視カメラが今晩交換されます。新しいものを取り付けている間、警備会社は店に今あるカメラと警報機の使用を停止します。よって、今夜は全ての商品を施錠保管する必要があります。家に帰る前に、販売担当者全員に、陳列ケースの中に何も残っていないことと、全てが保管庫に入っていることを確認していただきたいと思います。部長は保管庫に施錠がされていることを確かめます。ご協力をお願いいたします。また朝にお会いしましょう。

□Attention. (聴衆に対して) お知らせします。　□souvenir お土産　□surveillance camera 監視カメラ　□replace ～を交換する　□security company 警備会社　□disconnect ～の使用を停止する　□alarm 警報器　□set up ～を設定する、設置する　□lock up ～を施錠保管する　□sales representative 営業担当者　□make sure ～を確認する　□left 残っている　□display case 陳列ケース　□safe 保管庫　□correctly 正しく　□cooperation 協力

83.

Where is the announcement being made?

(A) In a security company
(B) In a store
(C) In a warehouse
(D) In a museum

アナウンスはどこで流れていますか。

(A) 警備会社
(B) 店
(C) 倉庫
(D) 博物館

話し手はトーク冒頭❶で店舗の監視カメラを交換する旨を従業員に向けて話している。ここから、このアナウンスが店舗で行われていることがわかる。以上から正解は **(B)**。

84. ★★★☆☆

What is being announced?

(A) Security staff will install new devices.
(B) A project due date is being delayed.
(C) Employees will be assigned new work hours.
(D) New inventory will be placed on display.

何が告知されていますか。

(A) 警備スタッフが新しい機器を設置する。
(B) 期限になっているプロジェクトが遅れている。
(C) 従業員に新しい勤務時間が割り当てられる。
(D) 新しい在庫品が陳列される。

トーク冒頭❶で述べたように監視カメラの交換が行われる。以上から正解は **(A)**。❷の the security company とそれを受けた it に staff が含まれていると判断することができる。

□due date 期限日　□assign A B AにBを割り当てる　□inventory 在庫　□on display 陳列されている

---

85. ★★★☆☆

What does the speaker ask employees to do?

(A) Get the manager's approval for item returns
(B) Confirm that the cash registers are working properly
(C) Place special orders by the end of the day
(D) Make sure all cases are empty

話し手は従業員に何をするよう求めていますか。

(A) 商品の返品には店長の承認を得る。
(B) レジが正常に動作しているか確認する。
(C) 今日中に特別注文をする。
(D) 全てのケースが空であることを確認する。

話し手は❸で「帰宅前に販売陳列ケースの中に何も残っていないことを確認するように」と述べている。以上から、正解は何も残っていない (nothing is left inside) を empty と一語で言い換えた **(D)**。

□approval 承認　□item return 返品　□confirm ～を確認する　□cash register レジ
□work properly 正しく作動する

P A R T 4

TEST 6

	1回目	2回目	3回目
83.			
84.			
85.			

83. (B)　84. (A)　85. (D)

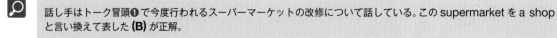

Questions 86 through 88 refer to the following excerpt from a meeting.

W: ❶This meeting is to familiarize you with the upcoming renovation of the supermarket. As you all are aware, the supermarket is beginning to look old and outdated. Well, beginning on April 12th, we will be enlarging and modernizing the building so that it appeals more to customers. In addition to a new interior design plan, our company president, Lisa Cummings, has authorized a significant expansion of the shopping area. ❷This will result in the number of aisles increasing from 11 to 17, which will allow us to carry a greater number of products. The renovation work will mostly take place between 10 P.M. and 8 A.M. in order not to cause too much disruption during business hours. What's more, ❸the work will take two weeks instead of four. ❹It seems we were right to change contractors!

📝 問題86-88は次の会議の一部に関するものです。

W: この会議はスーパーマーケットの今度の改修についてご理解いただくためにあります。皆さんもお気づきのとおり、このスーパーマーケットは古くて時代遅れに見えてきています。そこで、4月12日から、もっとお客様に関心を持ってもらえるように建物を拡張し、現代的にします。新しい内装計画に加え、当社の Lisa Cummings 社長は売り場の大幅な拡張を承認してくださいました。これにより通路の数が11本から17本に増え、さらに多くの製品を扱うことが可能になります。営業時間中にあまり混乱を生じさせないよう、改修工事は主に午後10時から午前8時の間に行われます。それだけではなく、作業にかかるのは4週間ではなく2週間です。建設請負業者の変更は正解だったようです。

✏️ ☐familiarize A with A を〜に慣れさせる　☐upcoming 来たるべき　☐renovation 改装　☐outdated 時代遅れの　☐enlarge 〜を拡大する　☐modernize 〜を現代的にする　☐appeal to 〜に訴える　☐in addition to 〜に加えて　☐interior 内装　☐authorize 〜を承認する　☐significant 大幅な　☐expansion 拡張　☐result in 〜という結果になる　☐aisle 売り場　☐carry 〜を取り扱う　☐renovation work 改修作業　☐mostly 主として　☐take place 行う　☐in order not to *do* 〜しないように　☐be right to *do* 〜するのは正しい　☐contractor 請負業者

---

86. ⭐⭐☆☆☆

What is the speaker discussing?

(A) An employee's promotion
(B) The remodeling of a shop
(C) The display of new items
(D) The relocation of a warehouse

話し手は何について話していますか。

(A) 従業員の昇進
(B) 店の改築
(C) 新しい商品の陳列
(D) 倉庫の移転

🔍 話し手はトーク冒頭❶で今度行われるスーパーマーケットの改修について話している。この supermarket を a shop と言い換えて表した **(B)** が正解。

✏️ ☐promotion 昇進　☐remodeling 改築　☐relocation 移転

87. ★★★☆☆

What improvement does the speaker mention?

(A) Reduced prices
(B) Longer opening hours
(C) A larger parking lot
(D) More space for products

話し手はどんな改良について言及していますか。

(A) 値下げ
(B) 営業時間の延長
(C) 駐車場の拡大
(D) 商品用スペースの追加

 話し手は❷で「今回の改修で通路の数が増え、さらに多くの製品を扱うことが可能になる」と述べている。ここから、商品スペースが広がることがわかる。以上から正解は **(D)**。

□reduced price 値下げ価格　□opening hours 営業時間　□parking lot 駐車場

---

88. ★★★★☆

What does the speaker mean when she says, "It seems we were right to change contractors"?

(A) She thinks a product will sell well now.
(B) She is glad she listened to her staff's advice.
(C) Work will be finished earlier than expected.
(D) A company can offer cheaper prices than a competitor.

話し手が "It seems we were right to change contractors" と言う際、何を意味していますか。

(A) 商品がよく売れると考えている。
(B) 従業員の助言を聞いて良かったと思っている。
(C) 作業は予想よりも早く完了する。
(D) 会社は競争相手よりも安い価格で提供できる。

意図を問われている表現は最後の発言❹「建設請負業者の変更は正解だったようだ」であり、この発言の前を見ていくと、❸「作業にかかるのは4週間ではなく2週間」➡❹「業者の変更は正解」という流れになっている。つまり、業者の変更により改修期間予定が早まったという意図で発言したことがわかる。よって、正解はこれを言い換えて表した **(C)**。

□sell well よく売れる　□than expected 期待していたより　□competitor 競争相手

	1回目	2回目	3回目
86.			
87.			
88.			

86. (B)　87. (D)　88. (C)

Questions 89 through 91 refer to the following recorded message.

W: Hi, Bertrand. This is Shelley calling. ❶Thank you for sending me an invitation to the training session about the new intranet messenger software. ❷Regrettably, I can't attend as I'll be interviewing some job applicants at that time next Tuesday. And I actually don't think I need the class. I tried the software on my own and I thought it had great features and was really easy to use. I love the option to record conversations and share them with colleagues. I think it'll help our consultants a lot. ❸Please give me a call after the class, though. ❹I really want to know if the rest of the consultants liked the software as much as I did.

W: こんにちは、Bertrand さん。Shelley です。新しいイントラネットメッセージソフトウェアの研修会への招待状をお送りいただきありがとうございます。あいにく、今度の火曜日のその時間に求人の応募者の面接をすることになっているため、参加することができません。それに実は私にはその研修は必要ないと思います。自分でソフトウェアを使ってみたところ、素晴らしい機能があって、とても使いやすかったです。会話を記録し、それを同僚と共有するオプションがとてもいいです。うちの相談員にとって大変役立つと思います。ただ、研修の後で電話をください。他の相談員も私と同じくらいこのソフトウェアを気に入ったか本当に知りたいです。

□invitation 招待状　□training session 研修　□intranet イントラネット (社内ネットワーク)
□regrettably 残念ながら　□attend 参加する　□interview 〜と面接する　□job applicant 仕事の応募者
□on my own 自分で　□feature 機能　□easy to use 使いやすい　□option to *do* 〜する機能
□consultant 相談者、コンサルタント　□rest of 残りの　□as much as 〜と同じくらい

89. ★★☆☆☆

What is the main purpose of the call?

(A) To discuss a job application
(B) To sign up for a class
(C) To post a job opening
(D) To decline an invitation

電話の主な目的は何ですか。

(A) 求職申込書類について話し合うこと。
(B) 研修会に申し込むこと。
(C) 求人情報を投稿すること。
(D) 誘いを断ること。

話し手はトーク冒頭❶で研修案内の御礼を述べ、その後❷で予定があり参加できないことを伝えている。以上から、ある誘いを断る目的だとわかるため、正解は **(D)**。

□job application 求職申込　□sign up for 〜に申し込む　□post 〜を掲載する　□job opening 求人
□decline 〜を断る　□invitation 招待状

90. ★★★★★

What does the speaker plan to do next Tuesday?

(A) Conduct some interviews
(B) Make some sales calls
(C) Share the software
(D) Meet with new customers

話し手は次の火曜日に何をする予定ですか。

(A) 面接をする。
(B) 営業電話をかける。
(C) ソフトウェアを共有する。
(D) 新しい顧客と会う。

 話し手は❷で「火曜日に求人面接がある」と述べている。以上から正解は **(A)**。

✏ □conduct 〜を行う □interview 面接

---

91. ★★★★★

What does the speaker request?

(A) Photos of consultants
(B) A list of instructors
(C) Results of job evaluations
(D) Feedback on a class

話し手は聞き手に何を求めていますか。

(A) 相談員の写真
(B) 講師の一覧
(C) 職務評価の結果
(D) 研修会に関する感想

 話し手は❸で研修後に電話が欲しいと述べ、❹で「自分同様に他の人もこのソフトウェアが気に入ったのか知りたい」と参加者の反応を知らせてくれるよう伝えている。よって、正解はこの参加者の反応を feedback と表現した **(D)**。

✏ □instructor 講師 □job evaluation 職務評価 □feedback 感想

	1回目	2回目	3回目
89.			
90.			
91.			

 89. (D)   90. (A)   91. (D)

Questions 92 through 94 refer to the following talk.

M: Hello, everyone. ❶Welcome to K & J Autos. As Linda McKenna mentioned, I'll be helping you get settled in over the next few days. If you need anything or have a question, just come to me. Because you already have your security badge, we're now going to go and get a laptop for each of you. ❷The supply department should already have them ready for you. ❸If you need any additional equipment like a new mouse, cables, headphones, etc., you can just e-mail the staff there with a request. James Roland, director of the supply department, will explain more when we get there. After that, I will take you on a tour of the building. ❹You'll notice that you need your security pass to get into every room in the building. When the tour concludes, we'll have lunch in the cafeteria. Lunch will be served from 1:00 to 2:00, and you can choose from a wide selection of dishes. After lunch, Julie Kimura from the personnel department will explain some basic policies.

問題92-94は次の話に関するものです。

M: こんにちは、皆さん。K&J自動車にようこそ。Linda McKennaさんが言ったように、仕事に慣れてもらえるように今後数日間私が皆さんをお手伝いします。何かが必要なときや質問がある場合は、声をかけてください。もう入館用IDバッジは渡してありますので、これから各々のコンピューターを受け取りに行きます。調達部がもう準備しているはずです。新しいマウスやケーブル、ヘッドホンなどの機材が必要な場合は、その部のスタッフにEメールで要望を送ってください。調達部に着いたらJames Roland部長から詳しい説明があります。その後、建物の見学にお連れします。建物のどの部屋に入るにも入館証が必要であることがわかると思います。見学が終わったら、食堂で昼食を取ります。昼食は1時から2時までの提供で、幅広い種類の料理から選べます。昼食後は、人事部のJulie Kimuraさんから基本方針についての説明があります。

✎ □get settled 慣れる　□security badge 入館バッジ　□laptop ノートパソコン　□supply department 調達部
□mouse (パソコン操作用の) マウス　□notice ～に気づく　□security pass 入館証　□conclude 終了する
□a wide selection of 豊富な種類の　□personnel department 人事部

92.

Who most likely is the audience?

(A) Directors
(B) New employees
(C) Recruiters
(D) Visitors

聞き手は誰であると考えられますか。

(A) 部長
(B) 新入社員
(C) 採用担当者
(D) 訪問客

🔍 話し手はトーク冒頭❶である会社に迎え入れるような発言をし、「仕事に慣れてもらえるように手伝う」と述べている。ここから、聞き手は新入社員であることが考えられる。以上から正解は **(B)**。

 □recruiter 採用担当者　□visitor 来訪者

93. ★★★☆☆

What should the listeners do in order to get equipment?

(A) Speak to Linda McKenna
(B) Contact the supply department
(C) Suggest it to the accounting department
(D) E-mail the security team

聞き手は機材を入手するために何をする必要がありますか。

(A) Linda McKenna さんに話す。
(B) 調達部に連絡する。
(C) 経理部に提案する。
(D) 保安チームに E メールを送る。

 話し手は❷・❸で「調達部がもう（機材を）準備しているが、新たな機材が必要な場合は、その部に要望を出すように」と述べている。ここから、機材を入手するためには調達部に連絡する必要があることがわかるため、正解は **(B)**。(D) の E メールは保安チームではなく調達部にするように言っているので不正解。

 □contact ～に連絡する

---

94. ★★★★☆

What is mentioned about the security pass?

(A) It should be kept in the supply department.
(B) It must be used to gain access to any area.
(C) It is composed of a digital code.
(D) It will be explained by Julie Kimura.

入館証について何と言っていますか。

(A) 調達部で保管しなければならない。
(B) どの場所に入るにも使わなければならない。
(C) デジタルコードで構成されている。
(D) Julie Kimura さんが説明する。

 話し手は❹で「建物のどの部屋に入室する際にも入館証が必要だとわかるだろう」と述べている。以上から正解は **(B)**。トーク中の get into every room in the building が選択肢では gain access to any area と言い換えられていることにも注目。

 □gain access to (場所等) に出入りする

	1回目	2回目	3回目
92.			
93.			
94.			

P A R T **4**

T E S T **6**

92. (B)　93. (B)　94. (B)

Questions 95 through 97 refer to the following recorded message and list.

W: Hello, this is Deborah Han from Angel Enterprises. I am calling about the customized blazer I ordered a week ago. I would like to request some small changes. ❶I initially chose a two-button jacket. ❷However, I think it would look a little bit out-of-date. Instead, I want to order a three-button coat. I think you said this would not result in any extra cost. Moreover, ❸I'd like my initials printed below the inside pocket. ❹I am willing to pay an additional charge for this change. Call me at 555-3926 if there are any problems. Thank you.

W: こんにちは。Angel Enterprises社のDeborah Han です。1週間前に注文した特注ブレザーの件でお電話しています。少し変更をお願いしたいです。私は最初に2つボタンのコートを選びました。ですが、少し時代遅れに見えるのではないかと思います。代わりに、3つボタンのコートを注文したいです。これは追加料金がかかることにはならないとおっしゃっていたと思います。それから、内ポケットの下に私のイニシャルをプリントしたいです。その変更での追加料金はお支払いします。問題がある場合は555-3926にお電話ください。よろしくお願いします。

Additional Services	
❺Print logo/name	$2.50
Color stitching	$3.50
Add pocket	$5.00
Size alterations	$8.50

追加サービス	
ロゴ／名前のプリント	2.50ドル
カラーステッチ	3.50ドル
ポケットの追加	5.00ドル
サイズ直し	8.50ドル

□customized 特注の　□initially 最初に　□out-of-date 時代遅れの　□instead 代わりに
□result in 結果として～になる　□extra cost 追加料金　□moreover さらに　□initial イニシャル、頭文字
□be willing to *do* ～する用意がある　□additional charge 追加料金　□stitching 縫うこと
□size alteration サイズ変更

95. ★★★☆☆

What problem does the speaker mention?	話し手はどんな問題について言及していますか。
(A) A style seems old-fashioned.	**(A)** 様式が時代遅れに見える。
(B) A shipment is delayed.	(B) 配送が遅れている。
(C) A button is missing.	(C) ボタンがなくなっている。
(D) A name is misspelled.	(D) 名前の綴りが間違っている。

話し手はトーク冒頭で特注ブレザーの件で電話したと切り出し、❶・❷で「2つボタンのコートを選んだが、少し時代遅れに見える」と述べている。以上から、正解は時代遅れ（out-of-date）を old-fashioned と言い換えた **(A)**。

□old-fashioned 時代遅れの　□misspell 綴りを間違う

---

96. ★★★☆☆

Look at the graphic. How much will Deborah Han pay for her request?	表を見てください。Deborah Han さんは要望の代金をいくら支払いますか。
(A) $2.50	**(A)** 2.50ドル
(B) $3.50	(B) 3.50ドル
(C) $5.00	(C) 5.00ドル
(D) $8.50	(D) 8.50ドル

話し手は❸で「内ポケットの下にイニシャルをプリントしたい」と述べている。ここで表の追加料金を見ると、❺より追加料金が2.50ドルだとわかる。以上から正解は **(A)**。

---

97. ★★★★★

What will the listener most likely do next?	聞き手は次に何をすると考えられますか。
(A) Ship a correct item	(A) 正しい商品を送る。
(B) Ask for a postal address	(B) 住所を尋ねる。
(C) Recalculate a bill	**(C)** 請求額を再計算する。
(D) Call a supplier	(D) 供給業者に電話する。

話し手は❸で追加料金サービスを要望し、❹で「その変更の追加料金は支払う」と述べている。ここから、聞き手は追加になった内容を含めて話し手への請求額を再計算することが考えられる。以上から正解は **(C)**。この問題は、聞き手の具体的な行動に関する言及がないため、話し手の発言から推測する必要のある難しい問題だが、追加料金を支払う＝請求額が変わるため再計算する必要があると考えて正解を導くようにしよう。

□ship 〜を送付する　□correct 正しい　□postal address 郵送先住所　□recalculate 〜を再計算する
□bill 請求額　□supplier 供給業者

	1回目	2回目	3回目
95.			
96.			
97.			

95. (A)　96. (A)　97. (C)

343

Questions 98 through 100 refer to the following excerpt from a meeting and chart.

M: Hello, everyone. I called this meeting to discuss the results of the market testing. This chart breaks down what customers thought was the most appealing feature of our new product. ❶As you can see, call quality was not very important to them. ❷A lot of the people surveyed said that they prefer using texts and messaging applications to communicate nowadays. ❸Most users consider screen size when they are purchasing a cellular phone. However, their preferences are totally personal. Some like a small one and others a large one. Therefore, it's not a feature we will focus on when we market this product. ❹Let's move down to the second most important feature. I think this makes sense, as users spend a lot of time downloading. ❺That's what I think the marketing team really needs to emphasize to appeal to potential buyers.

📝 問題98-100は次の会議の一部と図表に関するものです。

M: こんにちは、皆さん。市場テストの結果について話し合うために会議を招集しました。この図は、お客様が考える当社の新製品の最も魅力的な特徴を分類したものです。ご覧いただけるとおり、通話品質はあまり重要ではありませんでした。調査した方の多くが、最近はテキストやメッセージアプリケーションを使ってコミュニケーションするほうがいいと言っています。携帯電話を購入する際、ほとんどのユーザーが画面の大きさを気にしています。しかし、好みは完全に個人的なものです。小さいのが好きな人もいれば、大きいのがいい人もいます。ですので、この商品を市場に出す際に当社が重点的に取り上げる特徴にはなりません。2つ目の重要な特徴に移りましょう。これは、ユーザーがダウンロードに多くの時間を費やしているので、理にかなっていると思います。私が考える、マーケティングチームが潜在的な購入者に対して売り込むために本当に強調すべき点はこれです。

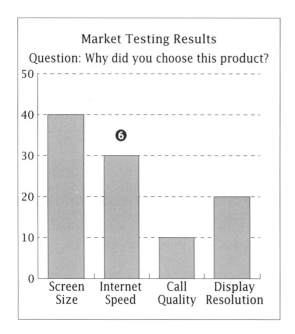

Market Testing Results
Question: Why did you choose this product?

❻

Screen Size / Internet Speed / Call Quality / Display Resolution

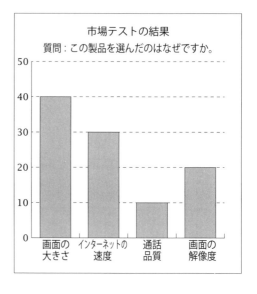

市場テストの結果
質問：この製品を選んだのはなぜですか。

画面の大きさ / インターネットの速度 / 通話品質 / 画面の解像度

□call a meeting ミーティングを招集する　□market testing 市場テスト　□break down ～を分類する
□appealing 魅力的な　□feature 特徴　□call quality 通話品質　□survey ～を調査する　□prefer ～をより好む
□text（メールやチャットなどの）テキスト　□messaging application メッセージ用アプリ　□nowadays 今日
□cellular phone 携帯電話　□preference 好み　□totally 完全に　□feature 特徴、機能　□focus on ～に集中する
□market ～を市場に出す　□move down to ～に移る　□make sense 理に適う　□emphasize ～を強調する
□potential buyer 潜在的な将来の購入者

98. ★★★☆☆

What kind of product was the survey most likely about?

(A) A tablet computer
(B) A mobile phone
(C) A laptop computer
(D) An office photocopier

どんな製品についての調査だったと考えられますか。

(A) タブレットコンピューター
(B) 携帯電話
(C) ノートパソコン
(D) オフィス用コピー機

話し手は❶で「通話品質はそんなに重要ではない」と述べており、通話機能を有する商品であることがわかる。また❸で携帯電話購入時についても言及している。以上から正解は **(B)**。

---

99. ★★★☆☆

According to the speaker, what do users prefer to do?

(A) Send text messages
(B) Play games
(C) Search for information
(D) Watch videos

話し手によると、ユーザーは何をすることを好んでいますか。

(A) テキストメッセージを送ること。
(B) ゲームをすること。
(C) 情報を検索すること。
(D) 動画を見ること。

話し手は❷で「調査した方の多くが、最近はテキストやメッセージアプリケーションを使ってコミュニケーションするほうがいいと言っている」と述べている。ここから、ユーザーはテキストメッセージの利用を好んでいることがわかる。以上から正解は **(A)**。

□text message（携帯電話等で送り合うメールやチャット等の）メッセージ　□search for 〜を探す

---

100. ★★★★☆

Look at the graphic. Which feature will the marketing team focus on?

(A) Screen Size
(B) Internet Speed
(C) Call Quality
(D) Display Resolution

図を見てください。マーケティングチームはどの特徴を取り上げますか。

(A) 画面の大きさ
(B) インターネットの速度
(C) 通話の品質
(D) 画面の解像度

話し手は❹で「2番目に重要な特徴に移りましょう」と言い、❺で「ここがマーケティングチームにとって購入者へのアピールポイントだ」と述べている。グラフを見ると、その2番目に重要な特徴は❻から Internet Speed であることがわかる。以上から正解は **(B)**。

	1回目	2回目	3回目
98.			
99.			
100.			

 98. (B)　99. (A)　100. (B)

GO ON TO THE NEXT TEST!

PART 3&4

Test

PART 3 Test 7

32. Who most likely is the man?

(A) A photographer
(B) A postal worker
(C) A receptionist
(D) A Web site designer

33. What is the woman unable to find?

(A) A certificate of receipt
(B) An account number
(C) A travel itinerary
(D) A delivery notice

34. What does the man ask the woman to bring?

(A) Some office supplies
(B) Contact information
(C) A valid credit card
(D) Photo identification

35. Where do the speakers most likely work?

(A) At a travel agency
(B) At a language school
(C) At an interior design firm
(D) At a watch manufacturer

36. According to the woman, what is the main responsibility of the position?

(A) Supervising an assembly line
(B) Advertising new products
(C) Running overseas branches
(D) Negotiating sales contracts

37. What qualifications does the man have?

(A) He has international work experience.
(B) He used to own his own shop.
(C) He is bilingual.
(D) He has a large number of customers.

38. What did the man say was wrong with the presentation?

(A) The presentation slides changed too quickly.
(B) It should have been shorter.
(C) It did not contain any special effects.
(D) The size of the text was too small to read.

39. What does the woman say about the man?

(A) He has attended the same presentation before.
(B) He has already learned some technical words.
(C) He will receive a certificate.
(D) He is a newcomer in the marketing department.

40. What does the man usually do during his presentations?

(A) Play video clips
(B) Offer his contact information
(C) Give printouts to the audience
(D) Take short breaks

41. What are the speakers expected to do?

(A) Schedule a training workshop
(B) Brainstorm a marketing campaign
(C) Improve a filing system
(D) Look over some résumés

42. What does the woman offer to do?

(A) Extend a deadline
(B) Place an advertisement online
(C) Share some work
(D) Create a project timeline

43. What does the woman ask the man to do?

(A) Submit a résumé
(B) Print out some documents
(C) Revise a journal article
(D) Fill out an application form

GO ON TO THE NEXT PAGE ➔

 32-34 *P. 356*   35-37 *P. 358*   38-40 *P. 360*   41-43 *P. 362*

44. What problem does the man talk about?

(A) A fitness center is closing.
(B) A building is under construction.
(C) He has many assignments.
(D) He has to cancel a reservation.

45. What does the woman say about the running machines?

(A) They were remodeled recently.
(B) They are not used much in the mornings.
(C) They will not be available until next month.
(D) Coaches help the members use them.

46. How can the man obtain a discount?

(A) By going to the facility on weekends only
(B) By paying in cash
(C) By presenting proof of employment
(D) By mentioning a friend's name

47. Where is the conversation taking place?

(A) At a financial institution
(B) At a tax office
(C) At a stationery shop
(D) At a job fair

48. What does the woman mean when she says, "It's usual, I'm afraid"?

(A) She is trying to reassure the men.
(B) She is confident an application will succeed.
(C) She is unsurprised by an error.
(D) She is expecting a delay in approval.

49. What will the men most likely do next?

(A) Provide a brochure
(B) Offer a mailing address
(C) Contact the woman again
(D) Check a list of requirements

50. Where is the conversation taking place?

(A) At an airport
(B) At a train station
(C) At a harbor
(D) At a bus stop

51. What does the woman tell the man about?

(A) A possible delay
(B) A passenger lounge
(C) A discounted ticket price
(D) A regulation change

52. What will the man most likely do next?

(A) Ask for a refund on a ticket
(B) Search for a seat
(C) Get his ID ready
(D) Purchase something to eat

53. In what department does the woman most likely work?

(A) Production
(B) Research and Development
(C) General Affairs
(D) Marketing

54. What does the man give the woman?

(A) Survey results
(B) A new employee's contact information
(C) A job application form
(D) A training schedule

55. What does the man suggest the woman do?

(A) Postpone a workshop
(B) Make a software program
(C) Reserve a conference room
(D) Review plans with a colleague

44-46 *P. 364*   47-49 *P. 366*   50-52 *P. 368*   53-55 *P. 370*

56. What department do the speakers work in?

(A) Personnel
(B) Sales
(C) Customer service
(D) Finance

57. What will the woman do on Thursday?

(A) Receive a performance review
(B) Have a foreign language lesson
(C) Contact her customers
(D) Change her job

58. According to the man, what did the manager say?

(A) The company will appoint a new manager.
(B) New versions of company products will be released.
(C) Some staff members will be transferred to another department.
(D) More employees will be hired.

---

59. Where is the conversation taking place?

(A) At a travel agency
(B) At a marketing firm
(C) At a security service company
(D) At a manufacturing plant

60. What does the man say about his business?

(A) It works with different media outlets.
(B) It helps reduce marketing budgets.
(C) It specializes in small, local businesses.
(D) It works with international exports.

61. What does the woman mean when she says, "I imagine so"?

(A) She expects a high price.
(B) She realizes a product will be popular.
(C) She believes the man is good at his job.
(D) She knows she will have to wait for a service.

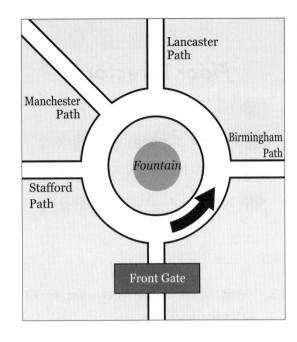

62. Why did the man call the Regional Traffic Control Center?

(A) To purchase a ticket
(B) To announce road information
(C) To renew his driver's license
(D) To mention a problem

63. What does the man imply about Birmingham Path?

(A) It is smaller than the others.
(B) Vehicles are prohibited on it.
(C) It is under renovation.
(D) A statue is blocking it.

64. Look at the graphic. Which path should the woman take?

(A) Stafford Path
(B) Birmingham Path
(C) Lancaster Path
(D) Manchester Path

GO ON TO THE NEXT PAGE ➡

 56-58 *P. 372*   59-61 *P. 374*   62-64 *P. 376*

PART **3**

T
E
S
T
7

Floor Directory

👕	Men's Clothing	7th Floor
👕	Women's Clothing	6th Floor
🏠	Household Goods	5th Floor
💎	Jewelry & Watches	4th Floor

IOWA DES MOINES AIR

Passenger Name: Ms. Dorothy Cole

From: Bellevue / **To:** Omaha

Date: Friday, April 28

Time: 1:40 P.M.

Regular Ticket Price: $80

65. What did the woman receive last week?

(A) A discount
(B) A brochure
(C) A voucher
(D) A gift

66. According to the man, what will happen in thirty minutes?

(A) The shop will close.
(B) A package will be picked up.
(C) A new shipment will arrive.
(D) A special sale will be finished.

67. Look at the graphic. Where will the man probably tell the woman to go?

(A) To the 7th floor
(B) To the 6th floor
(C) To the 5th floor
(D) To the 4th floor

68. What type of event are the speakers mainly discussing?

(A) A fundraiser
(B) A business meeting
(C) An opening ceremony
(D) A marathon

69. What problem does the woman mention?

(A) She does not know the event location.
(B) She cannot attend the event.
(C) She has lost a coupon.
(D) She has to work this weekend.

70. Look at the graphic. How much did the woman probably pay for her ticket?

(A) $75
(B) $80
(C) $85
(D) $90

🚩 **65-67** *P. 378*

🚩 **68-70** *P. 380*

71. What type of business is the speaker calling?

(A) A real estate agency
(B) A home improvement company
(C) A repair shop
(D) A cleaning service

72. What information does the speaker want?

(A) The color of a material
(B) The due date for a payment
(C) The location of a store
(D) The cost estimate of a job

73. What does the speaker say he will do at the beginning of next month?

(A) Hold a party
(B) Move to a new office
(C) Leave on holiday
(D) Make an advertisement

74. What problem does the speaker mention?

(A) The company is short of raw materials.
(B) The assembly lines are not meeting targets.
(C) Some equipment is malfunctioning.
(D) A shipment was postponed.

75. What does the speaker imply when she says, "who knows when that will be"?

(A) She is frustrated at supplier delays.
(B) She thinks the listeners may know a deadline.
(C) She has forgotten an appointment time.
(D) She is unsure when a project will be finished.

76. What will the speaker do in the afternoon next week?

(A) Prepare for a question-and-answer session
(B) Interview managerial applicants
(C) Meet with production managers
(D) Host a press conference

77. Who is the seminar most likely intended for?

(A) Event planners
(B) Book editors
(C) Advertising experts
(D) Business owners

78. What does the speaker emphasize about the event?

(A) It is economically priced.
(B) It is accessible to all.
(C) It is run by young people.
(D) It is the biggest event of its kind.

79. How can the listeners get more information?

(A) By talking to an employee
(B) By going to an office
(C) By reading a manual
(D) By using the Internet

80. Where is the announcement most likely being made?

(A) At an amusement park
(B) At a café
(C) At a stadium
(D) At a training venue

81. What is the announcement mainly about?

(A) Claiming a lost item
(B) Taking on extra duties
(C) Using the restroom
(D) Updating contact information

82. Who most likely is Ms. Parker?

(A) An event organizer
(B) A receptionist
(C) A presenter
(D) A coach

GO ON TO THE NEXT PAGE ➡

 71-73 *P. 382*   74-76 *P. 384*   77-79 *P. 386*   80-82 *P. 388*

353

83. According to the speaker, what is causing a problem?

(A) Travel costs
(B) Traffic congestion
(C) Overtime work
(D) Time differences

84. What does the speaker mean when he says, "it will be your choice"?

(A) Not all staff need to change work patterns.
(B) Staff can decide how to come to work.
(C) Attendance at a meeting is optional.
(D) Clients can use video chat for meetings.

85. What are the listeners asked to look at?

(A) An employment agreement
(B) A business message
(C) A yearly budget
(D) A work manual

86. What kind of business will the listeners most likely work in?

(A) Tourism
(B) Education
(C) Finance
(D) Real estate

87. According to the speaker, what is the most important thing?

(A) The appearance of a property
(B) The value of a service
(C) The impression a salesperson makes
(D) The online reviews of a place

88. What will happen next?

(A) A keynote speaker will give a speech.
(B) The listeners will look at photographs.
(C) The applicants will begin an exam.
(D) One of the employees will give a presentation.

89. What is the subject of the program?

(A) Public transportation
(B) An improvement project
(C) A road expansion
(D) Bus route changes

90. According to the speaker, what is important to city officials?

(A) Minimal costs
(B) An eco-friendly design
(C) Link to other transportation
(D) Accessibility for the elderly

91. According to the speaker, what will happen on Tuesday?

(A) A proposal will be announced.
(B) A renovation project will start.
(C) A new bus route will begin.
(D) A road will be closed.

92. According to the speaker, what will the listeners be asked to do next week?

(A) Install a software program
(B) Replace defective products
(C) Check a device is operating properly
(D) Learn how to use new equipment

93. What problem happened last week?

(A) Employees were not trained.
(B) Shops ran out of stock.
(C) Product demonstrations were not conducted.
(D) Some items were priced incorrectly.

94. What feature of the device does the speaker emphasize?

(A) It sends an automatic warning.
(B) It can print out price tags.
(C) It includes a manual.
(D) It is energy-efficient.

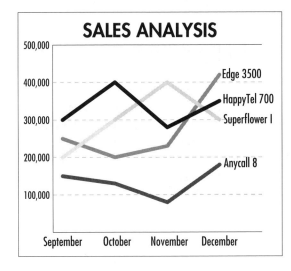

SALES ANALYSIS

Edge 3500
HappyTel 700
Superflower 1
Anycall 8

September   October   November   December

Item	Price
Force Resist Stationary Bicycle	$250
Pace Keeper Treadmill	$300
Everwear Free Weight Set	$450
Ultra Flex Lifting Machine	$600

95. Where does the speaker most likely work?

(A) At an Internet service provider
(B) At a phone accessory maker
(C) At a computer dealer
(D) At a mobile phone manufacturer

96. Look at the graphic. Which model was most recently released?

(A) Edge 3500
(B) HappyTel 700
(C) Superflower 1
(D) Anycall 8

97. What does the speaker say will happen next March?

(A) A new product will be introduced.
(B) A sales analysis will be conducted.
(C) Additional branches will be established.
(D) An old product will be discontinued.

98. What is the purpose of the call?

(A) To update personal information
(B) To announce a membership discount
(C) To check an order
(D) To place an order for equipment

99. What problem is mentioned about the Ultra Flex Lifting Machine?

(A) It has been discontinued.
(B) Production speed is low.
(C) It was recalled due to design flaws.
(D) Its price is higher than advertised.

100. Look at the graphic. How much will Mr. Goldsmith pay for a Soul Mover?

(A) $250
(B) $300
(C) $450
(D) $600

95-97   *P. 398*

98-100   *P. 400*

Questions 32 through 34 refer to the following conversation.

M: Hello, Ms. Radford. ❶We have a package for you to pick up here at the Northern Springfield Post Office. ❷You should have received a missed delivery card when we tried to deliver it yesterday.

W: ❸I'm looking at my mail now, and I can't find any notice about a missed package. I just got back from my holiday. What should I bring to pick it up?

M: OK, I understand. That shouldn't be a problem. ❹Please make sure to bring along valid photo identification when you come to pick it up.

📝 問題32-34は次の会話に関するものです。

M: こんにちは、Radfordさん。こちらのNorthern Springfield郵便局で小包をお預かりしています。昨日、配達に伺ったときの不在連絡票を受け取られていると思います。

W: 今、郵便物を確認していますが、未配達の通知は見当たりません。今、休暇先から戻ったところなのです。受け取りには何を持っていけばいいですか。

M: そうですか。わかりました。問題ございません。受け取りにいらっしゃる際には有効な写真付きの身分証明書を必ずお持ちください。

✏️ ☐package 荷物、小包　☐pick up ～を受け取る　☐missed delivery card 不在連絡票　☐mail 郵便物
☐notice 通知　☐missed package 未配達物　☐valid 有効な　☐photo identification 写真付き身分証明書

---

32. ★★★☆☆

Who most likely is the man?

(A) A photographer
(B) A postal worker
(C) A receptionist
(D) A Web site designer

男性は誰であると考えられますか。

(A) 写真家
(B) 郵便局員
(C) 受付係
(D) ウェブデザイナー

🔍 会話冒頭❶で男性が「（男性の働く）郵便局で小包をお預かりしている」と切り出し、❷で配達しようとした際に届けた不在連絡票について女性に尋ねている。ここから、男性が郵便局員であることがわかる。以上から正解は **(B)**。

✏️ ☐postal worker 郵便局員　☐receptionist 受付係

33. ★★★★★

What is the woman unable to find?

(A) A certificate of receipt
(B) An account number
(C) A travel itinerary
(D) A delivery notice

女性は何を見つけられませんか。

(A) 受領証明
(B) 口座番号
(C) 旅行の日程表
(D) 配達通知

 女性は❸で「未配達通知を見つけられない」と述べている。以上から、正解は未配達通知を delivery notice と言い換えた **(D)**。

 □certificate of receipt 受領証明　□account number 口座番号　□itinerary 旅行日程 (表)
□delivery notice 配達通知

---

34. ★★★★★

What does the man ask the woman to bring?

(A) Some office supplies
(B) Contact information
(C) A valid credit card
(D) Photo identification

男性は女性に何を持ってくるように頼んでいますか。

(A) 事務用品
(B) 連絡先の情報
(C) 有効なクレジットカード
(D) 写真付き身分証明書

 男性は❹で「写真付きの身分証明書を持ってくるように」とお願いしている。以上から正解は **(D)**。

 □office supply 事務用品　□contact information 連絡先

	1回目	2回目	3回目
32.			
33.			
34.			

 32. (B)　33. (D)　34. (D)

Questions 35 through 37 refer to the following conversation.

W: Hi, Matt. Did you hear that the company will be expanding into Europe? ❶It seems that our watches are finally getting popular there recently. Anyway, I hear a position for a new manager is opening up. Are you going to apply for it?

M: It would be a great opportunity, but I don't know if I have enough experience for the position. Do you think I have a chance?

W: ❷The job posting says that the company is going to open multiple retail units in France and the UK, and the candidate must be someone who has worked in retail outside the country and has at least five years' management experience. Is that you?

M: ❸I was assistant manager in a clothing store in London a few years back. It was difficult at first, but I really had a great time there with the employees. Maybe I should consider applying for the position.

📒 問題35-37は次の会話に関するものです。

W: こんにちは、Matt さん。会社がヨーロッパに進出することを聞きましたか。あちらでも最近ようやく当社の時計の人気が出てきたようです。それはそうとして、新しい管理職のポストがあいたそうです。応募しますか。

M: それは良い機会だと思いますが、私にその職に十分な経験があるかわかりません。私にチャンスがあると思いますか。

W: 人材公募には会社はフランスとイギリスに小売店を複数出す予定とあって、外国の小売り部門で働いたことがあり、少なくとも5年の管理職歴がなければならないとなっています。あなたがそうですか。

M: 数年前にロンドンの服屋で部長補佐をしていました。初めは大変でしたが、そこで従業員たちと素晴らしい時間を過ごしました。この仕事に応募することを考えてもいいかもしれません。

✏️ □expand into ～に進出する、拡大する　□position 職　□open up（役職などが）あく　□apply for ～に申し込む
□opportunity 機会　□job posting 社内公募　□multiple 複数の　□retail unit 小売部門　□in retail 小売部門で
□maybe A should A はおそらく～したほうがよいだろう

---

35. ★★★★☆

Where do the speakers most likely work?

(A) At a travel agency
(B) At a language school
(C) At an interior design firm
(D) At a watch manufacturer

話し手たちはどこで働いていると考えられますか。

(A) 旅行代理店
(B) 語学学校
(C) 内装業者
(D) 時計メーカー

🔍 女性は❶で「私たちの腕時計が最近人気になってきている」と述べている。ここから、話し手たちは時計に関わる仕事をしていることがわかる。以上から正解は **(D)**。

✏️ □firm 会社

36. ★★★★☆

According to the woman, what is the main responsibility of the position?

(A) Supervising an assembly line
(B) Advertising new products
(C) Running overseas branches
(D) Negotiating sales contracts

女性によると、仕事の主な責務とは何ですか。

(A) 組立ラインの監督
(B) 新製品の宣伝
(C) 海外支店の運営
(D) 売買契約の交渉

女性は❷で会社がイギリスとフランスに複数店舗を出す予定であることに触れ、それに続いて社内公募に関して「外国の小売り部門で働いたことがあり、少なくとも5年の管理職歴がなければならない」と述べている。ここから、仕事の責務は海外支店の管理に関わる業務だと考えることができる。以上から正解は **(C)**。

□responsibility 責任、責務　□supervise ～を管理する、監督する　□assembly line 組立生産ライン
□run ～を運営する　□branch 支店　□negotiate ～の交渉をする　□sales contract 販売契約

---

37. ★★★★★

What qualifications does the man have?

(A) He has international work experience.
(B) He used to own his own shop.
(C) He is bilingual.
(D) He has a large number of customers.

男性はどんな点で要件を満たしていますか。

(A) 国際的な業務経験がある。
(B) 自分の店をかつて経営していた。
(C) バイリンガルである。
(D) たくさんの顧客を抱えている。

男性は❸で「ロンドンで働いていた」と述べている。この直前❷で女性が「この職は海外経験と管理職経験がなければならない」と言っていることから、この前者に該当することがわかる。以上から正解は **(A)**。

□used to *do* かつて～していた　□bilingual バイリンガル、2か国語話す人　□a large number of 大多数の

	1回目	2回目	3回目
35.			
36.			
37.			

 35. (D)　36. (C)　37. (A)

Questions 38 through 40 refer to the following conversation.

W: I thought that presentation was wonderful. What did you think?

M: I learned a great deal. However, ❶the speaker talked too quickly and turned the slides too fast, so I missed some points.

W: Right. Most of the terms are quite familiar to me. But ❷as you recently joined the marketing division, I understand you need a little more time to learn some technical terms.

M: ❸She could have distributed handouts to all the participants. ❹That's what I usually do.

問題38-40は次の会話に関するものです。

W: プレゼンテーションは素晴らしかったと思います。どう思いましたか。

M: たくさん学べました。しかし、発表者があまりにも早口で、スライドもどんどん変えるので、いくつかの要点を聞き逃しました。

W: そうですね。ほとんどの用語は私にはなじみがあります。でも、あなたはマーケティング部に最近入ったので、専門用語を知るのにはもう少し時間が必要ですよね。

M: 参加者全員に資料を配ることもできたはずです。私はいつもそうしています。

□great deal たくさんの量　□slide（プレゼンテーション用の）スライド　□miss ～を逃す　□point 要点
□term 用語　□be familiar to ～にとってなじみのある　□technical term 専門用語　□distribute A to A を～に配る
□handout 配付資料

---

38. ★★☆☆☆

What did the man say was wrong with the presentation?

(A) The presentation slides changed too quickly.
(B) It should have been shorter.
(C) It did not contain any special effects.
(D) The size of the text was too small to read.

男性はプレゼンテーションの何が良くなかったと言っていますか。

(A) プレゼンテーションのスライド切り替えが速すぎた。
(B) もっと短い方がよかった。
(C) 特殊効果がなかった。
(D) 文字が小さすぎて読めなかった。

男性が❶でプレゼンテーションについて、「発表者があまりにも早口で、スライドもどんどん変える」と感想を述べている。この発言の後半部分に当たる **(A)** が正解。

□contain ～を含む

39. ★★★★★

What does the woman say about the man?

(A) He has attended the same presentation before.
(B) He has already learned some technical words.
(C) He will receive a certificate.
(D) He is a newcomer in the marketing department.

女性は男性について何と言っていますか。

(A) 前に同じプレゼンテーションに出席したことがある。
(B) 専門用語は既に学習している。
(C) 修了証を受け取る。
(D) マーケティング部の新顔である。

女性は❷で男性について「マーケティング部門に最近加わった」と述べている。以上から、正解は新しく部門に入った人を newcomer と言い換えた **(D)**。

□certificate 修了証書　□newcomer 新人

40. ★★★★★

What does the man usually do during his presentations?

(A) Play video clips
(B) Offer his contact information
(C) Give printouts to the audience
(D) Take short breaks

男性はプレゼンテーションの間にいつも何をしますか。

(A) 動画を再生する。
(B) 連絡先を渡す。
(C) 聴講者にプリントアウトを渡す。
(D) 短い休憩を取る。

男性は❸参加したプレゼンについて、「参加者全員に資料を配ることもできたはずだ」と述べ、❹で「私はいつもそうしている」と述べている。つまり、男性はプレゼンテーションの際には参加者に資料を配布していることがわかる。以上から、正解は handouts を printouts と言い換えた **(C)**。また、❸の distribute も give と言い換えていることに注目しておこう。

□video clip 短い動画　□contact information 連絡先　□printout 印刷物　□short break 小休止

	1回目	2回目	3回目
38.			
39.			
40.			

 38. (A)　39. (D)　40. (C)

Questions 41 through 43 refer to the following conversation.

M: ❶I am worried how I'm going to review all the résumés that were sent for the marketing positions we advertised. We've received hundreds of applications for these five openings.

W: There are too many applications. ❷I can help you look over those résumés. ❸Why don't I take some of them with me?

M: That would be helpful. I don't have hard copies of them though. The applications are all saved on my portable memory stick.

W: I see. I'd prefer to look them over on paper. ❹Would you print them out for me? I can then go over the hard copy applications thoroughly.

問題41-43は次の会話に関するものです。

M: マーケティング担当者の募集に送られてきた履歴書全てをどう確認しようか考えています。この5人の募集枠に何百人も応募がありました。

W: 応募が多すぎます。履歴書を見るのを手伝います。いくつか持っていってもいいですか。

M: 助かります。ただ、印刷したものはないのです。応募書類はすべて携帯用メモリースティックに保存しています。

W: わかりました。私は紙で見るほうがいいです。プリントアウトしてもらえますか。印刷した応募書類にじっくり目を通します。

✏️ □be worried 心配している □review ～を確認する □résumé 履歴書 □hundreds of 何百もの
□application 応募、申し込み □opening 空き □look over ～を確認する □helpful 助けになる
□save ～を保存する □portable 携帯用の □memory stick メモリースティック（パソコン等に外付けする記憶媒体）
□go over ～を確認する □hard copy（コンピューターから出力した）印刷物 □thoroughly 徹底的に、くまなく

....

41. ★★★★☆

What are the speakers expected to do?

(A) Schedule a training workshop
(B) Brainstorm a marketing campaign
(C) Improve a filing system
(D) Look over some résumés

話し手たちは何をしようとしていますか。

(A) 研修会の日時を決める。
(B) マーケティングのキャンペーンについて案を出し合う。
(C) ファイルシステムを改善する。
(D) 履歴書に目を通す。

🔍 会話冒頭❶で男性が「履歴書をどう確認しようか考えているところだ」と述べているのに対し、女性が❷で手伝うことを申し出ている。ここから、2人はこれから履歴書に目を通すことがわかる。以上から正解は **(D)**。この問題では2人が何をするかが問われているので、単に男性の❶の発言だけではなく、女性も行う意思があるところまで確認して正解を選ぶようにしよう。

✏️ □training workshop 研修 □brainstorm ～の案を出し合う

42. ★★★★★

What does the woman offer to do?	女性は何をすると申し出ていますか。
(A) Extend a deadline	(A) 締め切りを延ばす。
(B) Place an advertisement online	(B) オンラインの広告を掲載する。
(C) Share some work	**(C) 仕事を分担する。**
(D) Create a project timeline	(D) 計画のスケジュール表を作成する。

 女性は❸で「履歴書をいくつか持っていってもよいか」と男性の履歴書を見る作業を手伝うために、男性が抱えている履歴書のいくつかを引き受けようと申し出ている。以上から正解は **(C)**。Why don't I ... は相手に申し出る表現になっているので、しっかり押さえておこう。

 □extend 〜を延長する　□deadline 期限　□place an advertisement 広告を掲載する　□timeline 予定

---

43. ★★★★★

What does the woman ask the man to do?	女性は男性に何を頼んでいますか。
(A) Submit a résumé	(A) 履歴書を提出すること。
(B) Print out some documents	**(B) 書類を印刷すること。**
(C) Revise a journal article	(C) 雑誌の記事を修正すること。
(D) Fill out an application form	(D) 申請書に記入すること。

 女性は❹で「履歴書を印刷してくれないか」とお願いしている。以上から、正解は履歴書を documents と言い換えた **(B)**。

 □revise 〜を改訂する、修正する　□journal article 雑誌記事　□fill out 〜を記入する

 41. (D)　42. (C)　43. (B)

Questions 44 through 46 refer to the following conversation.

M: Hi, Ellen. I'm looking for a new fitness center for exercising. I really like the one I currently go to, but ❶I heard yesterday that it's closing down in April.

W: Why don't you join mine? The monthly fee is reasonable and the gym is equipped with some new running machines. ❷I usually go there first thing in the morning since the treadmills are almost all free then.

M: Really? I prefer going to the gym when it's less crowded, too. Can I try out the equipment before applying for membership?

W: Sure, it offers one-day trials. And now it has a promotion for new members. ❸When you sign up, mention my name, and you'll get a discount on the first month.

📝 問題44-46は次の会話に関するものです。

M: こんにちは、Ellen さん。私は運動のために新しいフィットネスセンターを探しています。今行っているところは、とても気に入っていますが、4月に閉店すると昨日聞きました。

W: 私のところに入りませんか。月額料金は手頃ですし、ジムには新型のランニングマシンが備わっています。私はいつも朝一番にそこに行っています。その時間はほとんどのトレッドミルが空いています。

M: そうなんですか。私もあまり込んでいないときにジムに行くほうが好きです。会員の申し込みをする前に設備を試すことはできますか。

W: できますよ。1日体験というのがあります。新会員対象のキャンペーンもやっています。申し込むときに、私の名前を言ってください。そうすれば初めの月は割引を受けられます。

✏️ □exercising 運動　□close down ～を閉鎖する　□monthly fee 月額料金　□reasonable（値段が）手頃である
□be equipped with ～が備わっている　□running machine ランニングマシン、トレッドミル
□first thing in the morning 午前中の最初に、朝イチで　□treadmill ランニングマシン、トレッドミル
□less crowded あまり混雑していない　□try out ～を試す　□equipment 器具、装置　□apply for ～に申し込む
□membership 会員（権）　□one-day trial 1日体験　□promotion キャンペーン、販売促進策　□sign up 申し込む
□mention ～に言及する

---

44. ★★☆☆☆

What problem does the man talk about?

(A) A fitness center is closing.
(B) A building is under construction.
(C) He has many assignments.
(D) He has to cancel a reservation.

男性はどんな問題について話していますか。

(A) フィットネスセンターが閉まる。
(B) 建物が建設中である。
(C) 仕事がたくさんある。
(D) 予約を取り消さなければならない。

 男性が❶で「（今通っている）ジムが閉鎖する」と述べている。以上から正解は **(A)**。

 □under construction 建設中の　□assignment 業務

45. ★☆☆☆☆

What does the woman say about the running machines?

(A) They were remodeled recently.
(B) They are not used much in the mornings.
(C) They will not be available until next month.
(D) Coaches help the members use them.

女性はランニングマシンについて何と言っていますか。

(A) 最近モデルチェンジされた。
(B) 朝はあまり使用されていない。
(C) 来月まで使用できない。
(D) 会員が使うのをコーチが手伝ってくれる。

 女性は❷で「いつも朝一番にジムに行っているが、その時間はほとんどのトレッドミルが空いている」と述べている。ここから、トレッドミルは朝の時間帯にあまり使われていないことがわかる。以上から正解は **(B)**。

 □remodel ～を改修する　□coach コーチ、指導員

46. ★★★★☆

How can the man obtain a discount?

(A) By going to the facility on weekends only
(B) By paying in cash
(C) By presenting proof of employment
(D) By mentioning a friend's name

男性はどうすれば割引が受けられますか。

(A) 施設に週末だけ行くことによって。
(B) 現金で支払うことによって。
(C) 雇用証明書を提示することによって。
(D) 友達の名前を言うことによって。

 女性が❸で「申し込むときに、私の名前を言えば割引を受けられる」と述べている。以上から正解は **(D)**。今回のようにカジュアルな会話をしている場合、話し手同士は友人と考えることができるため、friend という言い方ができることも押さえておこう。

 □pay in cash 現金で支払う　□proof of employment 雇用証明書

T E S T

7

	1回目	2回目	3回目
44.			
45.			
46.			

44. (A)　45. (B)　46. (D)

Questions 47 through 49 refer to the following conversation with three speakers.

M1: Hello! ❶We want to apply for a business loan for our company.

M2: ❷A friend of ours recommended this bank.

W: Good. ❸You'll need to provide tax statements, proof of earnings, a list of your debts, and a business plan.

M1: What? ❹I wasn't expecting to have to provide so many documents.

W: ❺It's usual, I'm afraid. ❻It helps us to determine which package is best for you.

M2: OK, I understand. After we are better prepared, we'll come back again.

M1: ❼Do you have a brochure or something that explains what we need?

W: ❽In fact, there's a perfect guide on our Web site. ❾The address is here on my business card, so I recommend that you check it.

問題47-49は次の3人の話し手による会話に関するものです。

M1: こんにちは。我々の会社のための企業貸付を申し込みたいのですが。

M2: 友人にこちらの銀行を勧められました。

W: はい。納税証明書、収益証明、債務一覧と企業計画をご提出いただく必要があります。

M1: えっ。そんなにたくさん書類を出さなければならないと思っていませんでした。

W: 申し訳ございませんが、これが通常になっております。お客様にとってどのパッケージが最適かを判断する際の助けになります。

M2: はい、わかりました。もっとよく準備をしてから、改めて伺います。

M1: 何が必要かを書いた冊子などがありますか。

W: 実は、当行のウェブサイトで全てご案内しております。アドレスはこの名刺に書いてありますので、そちらのご確認をお願いいたします。

□apply for ～に申し込む □business loan 企業貸付 (金) □tax statement 納税証明
□proof of earning 所得証明 □a list of ～の一覧 □debt 債務、借金 □business plan 事業計画 □usual 通常の
□I'm afraid すまないが □determine ～を決定する □package パッケージ、一連のプラン
□brochure パンフレット □explain ～を説明する □in fact 実際 □guide 案内 □business card 名刺

---

47. ★★★★☆

Where is the conversation taking place?

(A) At a financial institution
(B) At a tax office
(C) At a stationery shop
(D) At a job fair

会話はどこで行われていますか。

(A) 金融機関
(B) 税務署
(C) 文房具店
(D) 就職説明会

会話冒頭❶で1人目の男性が「企業貸付の申し込み」を希望し、2人目の男性が❷で「友人がこの銀行を紹介してくれた」と述べている。それに対して女性が❸で貸付を受けるために必要なものを述べていることから、この会話が金融機関で行われていると考えることができる。以上から正解は **(A)**。

□financial institution 金融機関 □tax office 税務署 □stationery 文房具 □job fair 就職説明会

48. ★★★★★

What does the woman mean when she says, "It's usual, I'm afraid"?

(A) She is trying to reassure the men.
(B) She is confident an application will succeed.
(C) She is unsurprised by an error.
(D) She is expecting a delay in approval.

女性が "It's usual, I'm afraid" と言う際、何を意味していますか。

(A) 男性たちを安心させようとしている。
(B) 申請がうまくいくと確信している。
(C) エラーに動じていない。
(D) 承認に遅れがあると予想している。

意図を問われている表現❺「申し訳ないが、それが通常だ」の前後を見ていくと、❹「そんなに書類を提出すると思っていなかった」➡❺「それが通常だ」➡❻「それによって、最適な提案が可能になる」という流れになっている。つまり、女性は提出書類が多いのは通常のことで、それにより男性たちにとって最適な選択ができる、と安心させる意図で発言していることがわかる。よって正解は **(A)**。

□reassure 〜を安心させる　□confident 自信がある　□application 申請、申し込み　□unsurprised 驚かない
□error 誤り　□delay 遅延　□approval 承認

....

49. ★★★★★

What will the men most likely do next?

(A) Provide a brochure
(B) Offer a mailing address
(C) Contact the woman again
(D) Check a list of requirements

男性たちは次に何をすると考えられますか。

(A) 冊子を手渡す。
(B) 郵送先住所を伝える。
(C) 女性に再度連絡をする。
(D) 要件のリストを確認する。

男性は❼で「必要なものを書いた冊子はあるか」と尋ね、それに対して女性が❽・❾で「ウェブサイトで案内しているので、そちらで確認してほしい」と返答している。ここから、この後ウェブサイトから必要な書類の一覧を確認することが考えられる。以上から正解は **(D)**。

□mailing address 郵送先住所　□requirement 要求、要件

	1回目	2回目	3回目
47.			
48.			
49.			

 47. (A)　48. (A)　49. (D)

Questions 50 through 52 refer to the following conversation.

M: Excuse me. I have a second-class ticket to Houston, but ❶I don't know where to go to catch the train. ❷Would you mind directing me to the right place?

W: The platform probably hasn't been assigned yet. It will be listed on the electronic display screens throughout the station about 30 minutes before departure. ❸However, there have been some delays today due to the heavy snow, so there's a good chance it'll leave late.

M: Okay. ❹Then I think I have some time to buy a snack. ❺Is there a concession stand nearby?

W: There sure is. You can find one at the main entrance to your right.

📝 問題50-52は次の会話に関するものです。

M: すみません。Houston 行きの二等級乗車券を持っているのですが、どこから列車に乗ったらいいのかわかりません。そこまで案内していただけないでしょうか。

W: ホームがまだ決まっていないようですね。出発の約30分前になりましたら、駅構内全ての電光掲示板に表示されます。でも、今日は大雪のため何本か遅延が発生していますので、出発が遅れる可能性が高いです。

M: わかりました。それなら、何かつまむ物を買う時間がありそうですね。近くに売店はありますか。

W: ございます。お客様の右手の正面玄関にあります。

✏️ ☐second-class ticket 2級の乗車券　☐catch a train 電車に乗る　☐direct A to A に～への道を案内する
☐right place 正しい場所　☐platform (駅などの) プラットフォーム　☐assign ～を割り当てる
☐electronic display screen 電光掲示板　☐departure 出発　☐due to ～が原因で　☐snack 軽食
☐concession stand 売店　☐nearby 近くに　☐There sure is. 確かにございます。　☐main entrance 正面玄関

---

50. ★★★☆☆

Where is the conversation taking place?

(A) At an airport
(B) At a train station
(C) At a harbor
(D) At a bus stop

会話はどこで行われていますか。

(A) 空港
(B) 駅
(C) 港
(D) バス停

🔍 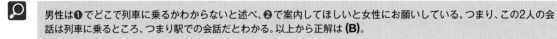 男性は❶でどこで列車に乗るかわからないと述べ、❷で案内してほしいと女性にお願いしている。つまり、この2人の会話は列車に乗るところ、つまり駅での会話だとわかる。以上から正解は **(B)**。

✏️ ☐harbor 港、波止場

51.

What does the woman tell the man about? ┊ 女性は男性に何について伝えていますか。

(A) A possible delay ┊ **(A)** 遅延の可能性
(B) A passenger lounge ┊ (B) 旅客用待合室
(C) A discounted ticket price ┊ (C) 割引チケットの価格
(D) A regulation change ┊ (D) 規定の変更

 女性は❸で大雪で本日既に遅れが出ているため、男性の乗車する列車も遅れる可能性があると伝えている。以上から正解は **(A)**。

 □regulation 規定、規制

52. ★★★★★

What will the man most likely do next? ┊ 男性は次に何をすると考えられますか。

(A) Ask for a refund on a ticket ┊ (A) チケットの払い戻しを求める。
(B) Search for a seat ┊ (B) 席を探す。
(C) Get his ID ready ┊ (C) 身分証の準備をする。
(D) Purchase something to eat ┊ **(D)** 食べる物を購入する。

 男性は❹で軽食を購入する時間がありそうだと述べ、❺で売店がないか女性に尋ねている。ここから、男性が何か食べるものを購入しようとしていると考えられる。以上から正解は **(D)**。

 □ask for ～を求める □refund 払い戻し □search for ～を探す □ID (identification) 身分証明書

	1回目	2回目	3回目
50.			
51.			
52.			

 50. (B) 51. (A) 52. (D)

🇦🇺 W 🇨🇦 M 🔊 3-7-53_55-01~02

Questions 53 through 55 refer to the following conversation.

W: ❶The director of production just told me again about the new operators' orientation next month. I'm still leading the job training, right?

M: Of course.

W: ❷And all of my training sessions with the recruits take place in the morning, don't they?

M: ❸Yes. Here's the full schedule for the orientation. You need to check it.

W: Alright.

M: Fine. There is one more thing. ❹You should coordinate your job training with Mr. Evans' afternoon safety training sessions. ❺It may be helpful to meet him briefly to get information about the material he plans on using.

W: Thanks a lot. I'll do that today.

📝 問題53-55は次の会話に関するものです。

W: こんにちは、Liam さん。生産部長から来月の新しいオペレーターのオリエンテーションについて再度連絡がありました。私が変わらず業務研修の進行をすることになっていますよね。

M: そうです。

W: それで、新人との研修は全て午前中に実施ですね。

M: そうです。これがオリエンテーション全体の予定表です。確認しておいてください。

W: 了解しました。

M: はい。それと、もう一点あります。Evans さんの午後の安全研修の内容に合わせて、あなたの業務研修を調整していただく必要があります。彼と少し打ち合わせて研修の教材について聞いておくといいのではないでしょうか。

W: ありがとうございます。今日やっておきます。

✏️ □director of production 生産部長、製造部長　□orientation 説明会、オリエンテーション　□lead ～を進行する
□job training 職務研修、業務研修　□recruit 新人　□take place 開催する　□coordinate ～を調整する
□safety training session 安全研修会　□helpful 役立つ　□briefly 簡潔に、手短に　□material 教材、素材

---

53. ★★☆☆☆

In what department does the woman most likely work?

(A) Production
(B) Research and Development
(C) General Affairs
(D) Marketing

女性はどの部署で働いていると考えられますか。

(A) 生産
(B) 研究開発
(C) 総務
(D) マーケティング

🔍 会話冒頭❶で女性が「生産部長から連絡があった」と述べている。ここから、女性は生産部門で働いていることが考えられる。以上から正解は **(A)**。

✏️ □Research and Development 研究開発　□general affair 総務

370

54. ★★★★★

What does the man give the woman?

(A) Survey results
(B) A new employee's contact information
(C) A job application form
(D) A training schedule

男性は女性に何を手渡していますか。

(A) 調査結果
(B) 新入社員の連絡先情報
(C) 求人の応募用紙
(D) 研修の予定表

 女性が❷で研修実施の時間帯について質問し、男性が❸でそれに答えて、その全体計画を渡している。以上から正解は**(D)**。オリエンテーションは通常新人に対する説明会を意味するため、今回のような文脈の場合は「研修」とほぼ同義となる。

 □survey result 調査結果　□contact information 連絡先　□job application 求人応募

---

55. ★★★★★

What does the man suggest the woman do?

(A) Postpone a workshop
(B) Make a software program
(C) Reserve a conference room
(D) Review plans with a colleague

男性は女性に何をすることを勧めていますか。

(A) 研修会を延期すること。
(B) ソフトウェアプログラムを作成すること。
(C) 会議室を予約すること。
(D) 同僚と計画を確認すること。

 男性は❹で Evans さんの研修の内容に合わせて女性の研修を調整する必要があると述べ、❺で「彼と打ち合わせて教材について聞いておいたほうがいいのでは」と促している。ここから、男性は女性が同僚と研修計画について確認することを勧めていることがわかる。以上から正解は**(D)**。

□postpone 〜を延期する　□reserve 〜を予約する、確保する　□review 〜を確認する

	1回目	2回目	3回目
53.			
54.			
55.			

 53. (A)　54. (D)　55. (D)

Questions 56 through 58 refer to the following conversation.

W: Hello, Leroy. Can I talk to you? I've lost some customers in the last month, and I'm a little concerned. ❶It doesn't look as if I'll meet my sales quota this year.

M: Don't worry. To be honest, ❷my sales are way down, too. I had several customers ready to sign an agreement, and then suddenly they decided to take more time, for reasons I still don't know. Things like that just happen when you're in sales.

W: I know, ❸but I have to talk about my performance with the general sales manager this Thursday. ❹I just hope he will be as considerate as you are.

M: You know what? ❺I met the manager in a meeting yesterday, and she actually told me that the company is launching upgrades to our products next year, which will boost our sales.

問題56-58は次の会話に関するものです。

W: こんにちは、Leroy さん。お話しできますか。先月、顧客を少々失いまして、少し心配しています。今年は販売のノルマを達成できそうもありません。

M: 心配しないでください。実を言うと、私の売り上げもかなり落ち込んでいます。契約書に顧客の署名をもらう準備まで行ったのに、理由は未だにわからないのですが、突然もっと時間をかけることになりました。営業にいると、このようなことが起こります。

W: ええ。でも、今週の木曜日に販売部長と私の業績について話さなければならないのです。あなたと同じくらい事情をわかってくれるといいのですが。

M: そうそう、昨日の会議で部長に会ったのですが、そこで部長がおっしゃった話では、うちは製品の改良版を来年発売するそうです。そうしたら、売り上げが伸びることになります。

□be concerned 心配している、懸念している □as if まるで〜のように □sales quota 販売ノルマ
□to be honest 正直に言うと □way down ずっと下がって □sign an agreement 同意書に署名する
□considerate 思いやりのある、察しのよい □You know what? そういえばですね □launch 〜を発売する
□upgrade 改良品 □boost 〜を上げる、伸ばす

---

56. ★★★☆☆

What department do the speakers work in?

(A) Personnel
(B) Sales
(C) Customer service
(D) Finance

話し手たちはどの部署で働いていますか。

(A) 人事
(B) 営業
(C) 顧客サービス
(D) 財務

🔍 まず女性が❶で「売り上げのノルマを達成できそうにない」と言うと、男性が❷で自分もそうだ、と述べている。ここから、この2人が営業の仕事をしていることがわかる。以上から正解は **(B)**。

57. ★★★★☆

What will the woman do on Thursday?

女性は木曜日に何をしますか。

(A) Receive a performance review
(B) Have a foreign language lesson
(C) Contact her customers
(D) Change her job

(A) 業績評価を受ける。
(B) 外国語のレッスンを受ける。
(C) 顧客に連絡する。
(D) 転職する。

 女性は❸で「木曜日に上司と業績について話す」と述べ、❹で「事情をわかってくれるとよい」と願望をもらしている。ここから、女性は上司と業績評価の振り返りをすると考えられる。以上から正解は **(A)**。

□performance review 業績評価　□contact 〜に連絡する　□change one's job 転職する

---

58. ★★★★☆

According to the man, what did the manager say?

男性によると、部長は何と言いましたか。

(A) The company will appoint a new manager.
(B) New versions of company products will be released.
(C) Some staff members will be transferred to another department.
(D) More employees will be hired.

(A) 会社が新しい部長を任命する。
(B) 製品の新バージョンが発売される。
(C) 数名のスタッフが別の部署に異動になる。
(D) 従業員がさらに採用される。

男性は❺で部長が話した内容に触れ、「製品の改良版を来年発売するそうだ」と話している。以上から、正解は❺の upgrades を new versions と言い換えた **(B)**。

□appoint 〜を任命する　□version 版、バージョン　□release 〜を発売する　□be transferred to 〜に異動する

PART 3

TEST 7

	1回目	2回目	3回目
56.			
57.			
58.			

56. (B)　57. (A)　58. (B)

Questions 59 through 61 refer to the following conversation.

M: ❶Welcome to our company. How can I help you?

W: ❷I believe that your agency specializes in international marketing?

M: ❸That's correct. ❹We work with some of the largest companies in the world, helping them market their products across a wide range of media outlets.

W: Does that include online marketing?

M: Yes. We help leading companies with marketing campaigns in various areas such as print, television, and online. ❺I am sure we can plan a campaign to meet your company's needs.

W: ❻I imagine so. ❼But I'm sorry, I don't have time to discuss it any further right now. In fact, I just stopped by on my way to an appointment.

M: I see. Could you give me your name and telephone number? That way I can contact you to schedule a meeting. I know that we could come up with an amazing marketing plan for you.

W: Do you have a pen I can use?

📝 問題59-61は次の会話に関するものです。

M: ご来社いただきありがとうございます。ご用件を伺います。

W: こちらの代理店では国際的なマーケティングを専門としているそうですね。

M: さようでございます。弊社は世界でも最大規模の企業様とお仕事をして、その製品のマーケティングをさまざまなメディアを活用して支援しております。

W: インターネットマーケティングもそれに含まれますか。

M: はい。大手企業のマーケティング活動を印刷媒体、テレビ、インターネットなどのさまざまな分野で支援しています。御社のご要望にかなったキャンペーンの策定をお約束します。

W: そうなんですね。ただ、すみませんが、今はこれ以上お話をする時間がありません。実は、面会に行く途中で立ち寄っただけなのです。

M: そうですか。お名前と電話番号をいただけますか。打ち合わせの日程についてご連絡差し上げますので。ご満足いただけるマーケティングプランを弊社がご提案いたします。

W: お借りできるペンがありますか。

✏️ □specialize in ～を専門とする　□market ～を市場に出す　□a wide range of 幅広い　□media outlet 報道機関　□include ～を含む　□leading company 大手企業　□various さまざまな　□such as ～といったような　□I imagine so. そうでしょうね。／そう思います。　□any further これ以上　□right now 今は　□in fact 実は　□stop by 立ち寄る　□on one's way to ～の途中で　□come up with ～を提案する　□amazing 素晴らしい

59.

Where is the conversation taking place?

(A) At a travel agency
(B) At a marketing firm
(C) At a security service company
(D) At a manufacturing plant

会話はどこで行われていますか。

(A) 旅行代理店
(B) マーケティングの会社
(C) 警備会社
(D) 製造工場

 まず会話冒頭❶で男性が女性を自分の会社に迎え入れていることがわかる。次に女性が❷で男性の事業がマーケティングに特化していることに触れている。ここから、ここがマーケティングに関わる業務をしている会社だとわかる。以上から正解は **(B)**。

 □travel agency 旅行代理店　□firm 会社　□manufacturing plant 製造工場

60.

What does the man say about his business?

(A) It works with different media outlets.
(B) It helps reduce marketing budgets.
(C) It specializes in small, local businesses.
(D) It works with international exports.

男性は事業について何と言っていますか。

(A) さまざまなメディアと共に仕事をしている。
(B) マーケティングの予算を削るのに役立つ。
(C) 小規模の地元企業に特化している。
(D) 輸出品を取り扱っている。

 男性は❹で「製品のマーケティングをさまざまなメディアを活用して支援している」と述べている。ここから、男性の事業はメディアと共に仕事をしているとわかる。以上から正解は **(A)**。

 □local business 地元企業　□export 輸出品

61.

What does the woman mean when she says, "I imagine so"?

(A) She expects a high price.
(B) She realizes a product will be popular.
(C) She believes the man is good at his job.
(D) She knows she will have to wait for a service.

女性が "I imagine so" と言う際、何を意味していますか。

(A) 高い料金になると思っている。
(B) 商品が人気になると認識している。
(C) 男性が仕事に長けていると思っている。
(D) サービスを待たなければならないとわかっている。

 意図を問われている表現❻「そうだと思う」の前後を見ていくと、❷・❸・❹のやりとりで女性が訪問前に得ていた情報と違わず、男性の会社がマーケティングに長けていることが確認できている➡❺で男性からのもう一押しとして、さまざまな手段を使って男性の会社が女性の会社の要望に適ったキャンペーンを提案できると伝え➡それに対して❻で女性は「そうだと思う」と言っている。つまり、女性はそこで男性から聞いたとおり、その会社がマーケティングに長けていることを確信したということがわかる。以上から正解は **(C)**。ちなみに今回は、❼以降で話題が転換されているので、❻の発言の文脈とはあまり関連がなくなっていることも確認しておこう。

 □realize 〜を認識する

	1回目	2回目	3回目
59.			
60.			
61.			

 59. (B)　60. (A)　61. (C)

Questions 62 through 64 refer to the following conversation and map.

W: Hello. The Regional Traffic Control Center sent us here. ❶One of your staff called to report a hazard due to a fallen tree partially blocking a sidewalk. We'll cut it up and remove it from the area today.

M: ❷I'm so glad you're here. ❸I called to report it to the Regional Traffic Control Center. One of our paths is completely blocked now. ❹To get there, drive your vehicle through the front gate and keep going straight. ❺You'll see a large fountain, and come to a circular driveway.

W: OK. And the dairy's down that way?

M: You've got to go a little further, actually. ❻The first path, Birmingham Path, is just for pedestrians. ❼So, take the second one instead. You can't miss the dairy — it's really big!

📝 問題62-64は次の会話と地図に関するものです。

W: こんにちは。地域交通管理センターから派遣されて来ました。こちらのスタッフの方からお電話で倒木が歩道を塞いでいることによる危険についての報告をいただいています。今日はそれを切り崩して、その場所から撤去します。

M: お越しいただきありがとうございます。私が地域交通管理センターに報告の電話をしました。今は通路の一つが完全に塞がっています。現場へ行くには、車で正門を抜け、そのまま真っすぐ行ってください。大きな噴水が見えたら、ロータリーに出ます。

W: わかりました。それで搾乳場はその先ですか。

M: 実はもう少し奥です。最初の小道のBirmingham通りは歩行者しか通れません。なので、二つ目の道に入ってください。搾乳場は見たらわかります。とても大きいですから。

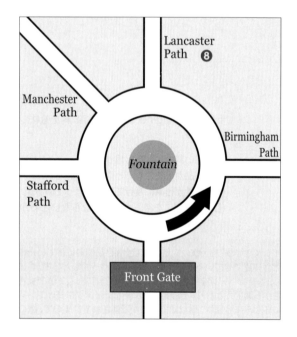

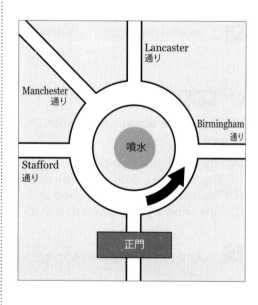

□hazard 危険、危害　□due to ～が原因で　□fallen tree 倒木　□partially 部分的に　□block ～を塞ぐ　□sidewalk 歩道　□cut up ～を切り分ける　□path 通路　□go straight 真っすぐ行く　□fountain 噴水　□circular 円形の　□driveway 車道　□dairy 酪農場、搾乳所　□down that way その道の先に　□have got to *do* ～しなくてはいけない　□go further さらに進む　□pedestrian 歩行者　□instead 代わりに　□miss ～を見逃す

62. ★★★★☆

Why did the man call the Regional Traffic Control Center?

(A) To purchase a ticket
(B) To announce road information
(C) To renew his driver's license
(D) To mention a problem

男性はなぜ地域交通管理センターに電話をしましたか。

(A) チケットを購入するため。
(B) 道路情報を発表するため。
(C) 運転免許証を更新するため。
(D) 問題について話すため。

🔍 会話冒頭❶で女性が「倒木があってかけつけた」と切り出し、男性が❷・❸で「自分がその件で電話した」と述べている。つまり、倒木という問題があったために電話したことがわかる。以上から正解は **(D)**。

✎ □road information 道路情報　□renew 〜を更新する

---

63. ★★★★☆

What does the man imply about Birmingham Path?

(A) It is smaller than the others.
(B) Vehicles are prohibited on it.
(C) It is under renovation.
(D) A statue is blocking it.

男性は Birmingham 通りについて何を示唆していますか。

(A) 他よりも小さい。
(B) 車の乗り入れは禁止されている。
(C) 改装中である。
(D) 彫像によって塞がれている。

🔍 男性は❻で「Birmingham 通りは歩行者専用」と述べている。つまり、この通りは自動車の乗り入れが禁止されていることがわかる。以上から正解は **(B)**。

✎ □prohibit 〜を禁止する　□under renovation 改装中の　□statue 像

---

64. ★★★★★

Look at the graphic. Which path should the woman take?

(A) Stafford Path
(B) Birmingham Path
(C) Lancaster Path
(D) Manchester Path

図を見てください。女性はどの小道に入るべきですか。

(A) Stafford 通り
(B) Birmingham 通り
(C) Lancaster 通り
(D) Manchester 通り

🔍 男性は女性に倒木現場までの案内として、まず❹正門を通って真っすぐ進み、❺噴水が見えたらロータリーへ行くように述べている。そして❻・❼で1つ目の通りではなく2つ目の通りに入るよう説明している。地図を見ると、正門を通ってロータリーに沿った2つ目の通りは❽から Lancaster 通りだとわかる。以上から正解は **(C)**。2つ目の通りだからといって、上から2番目の選択肢の (B) を選ばないように地図をしっかりと見て正解にたどり着くようにしよう。

	1回目	2回目	3回目
62.			
63.			
64.			

 62. (D)　63. (B)　64. (C)

Questions 65 through 67 refer to the following conversation and directory.

W: Excuse me. I want to purchase an anniversary gift for some friends of mine. ❶Is this coupon still valid? ❷I got it when I returned some merchandise a week ago.

M: Hold on. Sure, the coupon is valid until November 30.

W: Good. I've been meaning to use it for a while.

M: Is there anything in particular I can help you find? ❸We're closing early today, at 6 P.M., because of tomorrow's holiday. ❹You only have about 30 minutes.

W: ❺I'm looking for a blender. It shouldn't take me long to pick one out.

M: Great! Let me tell you where you can find them.

📝 問題65-67は次の会話と案内板に関するものです。

W: すみません。友達に送る記念品を購入したいと思っています。このクーポン券はまだ利用できますか。1週間前に商品を返品した際にいただきました。

M: お待ちください。はい、クーポンは11月30日まで有効です。

W: よかった。ずっと使いたいと思っていたのです。

M: 特に何かお探しのものはありますか。明日が祝日のため、今日は早めの午後6時に閉店します。お時間は30分しかないんです。

W: ミキサーを探しています。選ぶのに時間はかからないと思います。

M: 承知しました。売り場をご案内します。

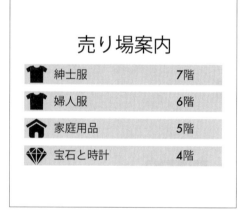

Floor Directory

👕 Men's Clothing	7th Floor
👕 Women's Clothing	6th Floor
🏠 ❻Household Goods	5th Floor
💎 Jewelry & Watches	4th Floor

売り場案内

👕 紳士服	7階
👕 婦人服	6階
🏠 家庭用品	5階
💎 宝石と時計	4階

✏️ ☐anniversary gift 記念品　☐valid 有効　☐merchandise 商品　☐hold on (電話を切らずに) 待つ
☐for a while しばらくの間　☐in particular 特に　☐blender ミキサー　☐pick out ~を選ぶ
☐floor directory 売り場案内　☐household goods 家庭用品

65. ★★★☆☆

What did the woman receive last week?

(A) A discount
(B) A brochure
(C) A voucher
(D) A gift

先週女性は何を受け取りましたか。

(A) 割引
(B) 冊子
(C) 割引券
(D) 贈り物

 会話冒頭❶で女性がクーポンの使用可否について尋ね、❷で「クーポンを1週間前に受け取った」と述べている。以上から、正解はこのクーポンを voucher と言い換えた **(C)**。

 □brochure パンフレット、冊子

66. ★★★☆☆

According to the man, what will happen in thirty minutes?

(A) The shop will close.
(B) A package will be picked up.
(C) A new shipment will arrive.
(D) A special sale will be finished.

男性によると30分後に何が起こりますか。

(A) 店が閉まる。
(B) 小包が引き取られる。
(C) 配送物が新たに届く。
(D) 特別販売が終了する。

 男性は❸・❹で「今日は店舗を早めに閉める」「時間は30分しかない」と述べている。ここから、あと30分後に店が閉まることがわかる。以上から正解は **(A)**。

 □package 荷物、小包　□pick up ～を引き取る

67. ★★★★★

Look at the graphic. Where will the man probably tell the woman to go?

(A) To the 7th floor
(B) To the 6th floor
(C) To the 5th floor
(D) To the 4th floor

図を見てください。男性はおそらく女性にどこに行くように言いますか。

(A) 7階
(B) 6階
(C) 5階
(D) 4階

 女性は❺で「ミキサーが欲しい」と述べている。そして、図の❻からミキサーは家庭用品売り場にあるものと考えられる。以上から正解は **(C)**。blender が household goods の売り場にあると気づけるかがポイント。

	1回目	2回目	3回目
65.			
66.			
67.			

 65. (C)　66. (A)　67. (C)

Questions 68 through 70 refer to the following conversation and ticket.

M: Good morning, Dorothy. ❶ I heard you got an invitation to the charity banquet in Omaha this Sunday. Are you planning to attend?

W: Of course, I don't want to miss out on such a meaningful event. It's for a really good cause.

M: ❷ I hope the charity receives a lot of donations. How are you planning to get to Omaha?

W: By airplane. ❸ The only problem is that I have to come into the office on Saturday morning to finish some work first.

M: I see. Don't forget about our corporate discount. ❹ You'll get $5 off the regular air fare.

W: Okay, thanks for reminding me. I can add that to my donation at the event.

📝 問題68-70は次の会話とチケットに関するものです。

M: おはようございます、Dorothy さん。今週の日曜日に Omaha で行われる慈善晩餐会への招待を受けたと聞きました。出席する予定ですか。

W: もちろんです。このように有意義なイベントは逃したくありません。目的がとてもいいですから。

M: 慈善活動でたくさん寄付金が集まるといいですね。Omaha まではどう行くつもりですか。

W: 飛行機です。唯一の問題点は、土曜日の朝、会社に来てまず仕事を終わらせなければならないことです。

M: そうですか。当社の企業割引を忘れないでくださいね。通常航空料金から5ドル引きになりますから。

W: わかりました。教えてくれてありがとうございます。その分、イベントの寄付金を増やせます。

IOWA DES MOINES AIR

Passenger Name: Ms. Dorothy Cole

From: Bellevue / **To:** Omaha

Date: Friday, April 28

Time: 1:40 P.M.

❺ **Regular Ticket Price:** $80

IOWA DES MOINES 航空

乗客名：Dorothy Cole 様

出発地：Bellevue ／ 到着地：Omaha

日付：4 月 28 日　金曜日

時間：午後 1 時 40 分

通常航空券価格：80 ドル

✏️ ☐ invitation 招待状　☐ charity チャリティー、慈善事業　☐ banquet 夕食会、晩餐会　☐ miss out 〜を逃す
☐ meaningful 有意義な、重要な　☐ good cause りっぱな目的　☐ donation 寄付 (金)
☐ corporate discount 企業割引　☐ air fare 航空運賃

68. ★★★★☆

What type of event are the speakers mainly discussing?

(A) A fundraiser
(B) A business meeting
(C) An opening ceremony
(D) A marathon

話し手たちは主にどんな種類のイベントについて話し合っていますか。

(A) 募金活動
(B) 商談
(C) 開会式
(D) マラソン

 会話冒頭❶で男性がチャリティーディナーについて話しており、❷で「慈善活動でたくさん寄付金が集まるといい」と述べている。ここから、話し手たちは募金活動があるイベントについて話し合っていることがわかる。以上から、正解はこのイベントを fundraiser と言い換えた **(A)**。

🖉 □fundraiser 資金集めのイベント

69. ★★★☆☆

What problem does the woman mention?

(A) She does not know the event location.
(B) She cannot attend the event.
(C) She has lost a coupon.
(D) She has to work this weekend.

女性はどんな問題について話していますか。

(A) イベントの場所がわからない。
(B) イベントに出席できない。
(C) クーポン券を失くした。
(D) 今週末働かなければならない。

 女性は❸で「問題は私は土曜日に会社に行かなくてはいけないことだ」と述べている。以上から、正解は土曜日を weekend と言い換えた **(D)**。

70. ★★★★☆

Look at the graphic. How much did the woman probably pay for her ticket?

(A) $75
(B) $80
(C) $85
(D) $90

図を見てください。女性は航空券におそらくいくら支払いましたか。

(A) 75ドル
(B) 80ドル
(C) 85ドル
(D) 90ドル

 ❹で男性は女性に「航空券は通常価格から5ドル割引される」と述べている。次にチケットを見ると、❺から通常価格は80ドルであるとわかる。この80ドルから5ドルを差し引いた75ドルが女性の支払金額だとわかる。以上から正解は **(A)**。

	1回目	2回目	3回目
68.			
69.			
70.			

 68. (A)　69. (D)　70. (A)

Questions 71 through 73 refer to the following recorded message.

M: ❶Hello, is that Clifton Flooring and Carpeting Service? My name's Malcolm Vardy. ❷I noticed your advertisement on local television. I would like to have the carpet replaced in my kitchen, living room and three of the bedrooms of my house. Please call me back to talk more in detail about the work. ❸I'd like to get a price quote from you. My telephone number is 555-9425. ❹I hope to hear back from you soon, since I'll be going on a vacation at the beginning of next month and I'd really like to have the job finished before I leave. Thank you.

🗒 問題71-73は次の録音メッセージに関するものです。

M: こんにちは、Clifton フローリング・カーペットサービスですか。Malcolm Vardy と言います。地元のテレビでそちらの広告を見ました。うちの台所と居間、それと寝室3部屋の絨毯を交換してもらいたいと考えています。作業について詳しい話をするために折り返しのお電話をください。価格の見積もりもいただきたいです。私の電話番号は555-9425です。早めにご連絡をいただけると幸いです。来月の初めは休暇に入るので、出発前に作業を終えていただきたいと思っています。よろしくお願いします。

✏ □notice 〜に気づく　□replace 〜を交換する　□call back 〜に電話をかけ直す　□in detail 詳細に
□price quote 見積もり　□go on a vacation 休暇に入る

---

71. ⭐⭐⭐☆☆

What type of business is the speaker calling?

(A) A real estate agency
(B) A home improvement company
(C) A repair shop
(D) A cleaning service

話し手はどのような業者に電話をかけていますか。

(A) 不動産業者
(B) 住宅改装会社
(C) 修理店
(D) 清掃サービス

🔍 話し手は❶で「フローリングとカーペットの会社で合っているか」と確認し、❷で絨毯を交換してほしいと述べている。ここから、電話をかけている先は住宅の改装を扱う業者だと考えられる。以上から正解は **(B)**。

✏ □real estate agency 不動産業者　□home improvement company リフォーム会社

72. ★★☆☆☆

What information does the speaker want?	話し手はどんな情報を求めていますか。
(A) The color of a material	(A) 素材の色
(B) The due date for a payment	(B) 支払いの期日
(C) The location of a store	(C) 店の場所
(D) The cost estimate of a job	**(D)** 作業の費用見積もり

 ❸で話し手が聞き手に見積もりを求めていることがわかる。以上から、price quote を cost estimate と言い換えた **(D)** が正解。

□material 素材、原料　□due date 期限日　□cost estimate 見積もり

PART **4**

73. ★★★☆☆

What does the speaker say he will do at the beginning of next month?	話し手は来月の初めに何をすると言っていますか。
(A) Hold a party	(A) パーティーを開催する。
(B) Move to a new office	(B) 新しい事業所に異動する。
(C) Leave on holiday	**(C)** 休暇で離れる。
(D) Make an advertisement	(D) 広告を出す。

話し手は❹で「来月初めから休暇に入るので出発前に作業を終わらせたい」と述べている。ここから、話し手が来月の初めに休暇でどこかに発つことがわかる。以上から正解は **(C)**。

TEST **7**

	1回目	2回目	3回目
71.			
72.			
73.			

71. (B)　72. (D)　73. (C)

Questions 74 through 76 refer to the following excerpt from a meeting.

W: ❶Hello, I've called this meeting of assembly line managers to discuss production quotas. ❷Our new mobile phone model, "Golden Berry 5", was released three months ago, and it is quite a hit in the market. ❸However, as for our existing model, "Silver Star 3", we are way behind the production schedule for a number of reasons. We had to shift around staff to work on the assembly lines for the new product. ❹It means we should set up a new production schedule and rearrange all our resources until we can meet the market demand for the new mobile phone. ❺However, who knows when that will be? ❻Therefore, I'm asking you to come up with some ideas to speed up the production of your assembly lines. ❼I will set aside an hour each afternoon next week to discuss what you have come up with. Please tell me when you are available.

W: こんにちは、生産の割り当て量について話し合うため、この組み立てライン主任の会議を招集しました。当社の新携帯電話モデル Golden Berry 5が3か月前に発売され、市場ではかなりの売れ行きです。ですが、既存モデル Silver Star 3は、さまざまな理由により、生産スケジュールに大幅な遅れが生じています。新製品の組み立てラインに取りかかるため、スタッフの配置を替えなければなりませんでした。つまり、市場での新しい携帯電話の需要を満たせるまで、生産日程を初めから組んで、全ての人手と設備を再度整理する必要があるわけです。しかし、それがいつまでになるかは誰にもわかりません。従って、皆さんには組み立てラインの生産を速めるためのアイデアを提案していただきたいと思います。皆さんが思いついたアイデアについて話し合うために、来週は午後に1時間ずつ時間を取ります。都合のつく日時を教えてください。

✏️ □call a meeting 会議を招集する　□assembly line 組立ライン　□quota 割り当て量　□release 〜を発売する　□as for 〜に関して　□existing 既存の　□way behind schedule 予定からだいぶ遅れている　□a number of 複数の　□shift 変える　□set up 〜を設定する　□rearrange 〜を再調整する、再配置する　□resource 経営資源（人員や設備）　□market demand 市場ニーズ　□come up with 〜を考案する　□speed up 〜を速める　□set aside 〜を確保する

---

74. ★★★★★

What problem does the speaker mention?

(A) The company is short of raw materials.
(B) The assembly lines are not meeting targets.
(C) Some equipment is malfunctioning.
(D) A shipment was postponed.

話し手はどんな問題について言及していますか。

(A) 会社は原材料が不足している。
(B) 組み立てラインが目標に達していない。
(C) 機材が故障している。
(D) 出荷が延期された。

🔍 まず話し手は❶で組み立てラインのマネジャーに向けて生産割り当て量について話すために招集したと伝えている。そして❷・❸で、会社の新製品は売れ行きがいいものの、既存製品の生産が遅れていることについて触れている。つまり、生産の目標に達成しない可能性を示唆しているとわかる。以上から、正解は目標が達成しないことを not meeting targets と言い換えた **(B)**。

✏️ □be short of 〜が不足している　□meet a target 目標を満たす　□malfunction 正常に動かない　□postpone 〜を延期する

75. ★★★★☆

What does the speaker imply when she says, "who knows when that will be"?

(A) She is frustrated at supplier delays.
(B) She thinks the listeners may know a deadline.
(C) She has forgotten an appointment time.
(D) She is unsure when a project will be finished.

話し手が "who knows when that will be" と言う際、何を意図していますか。

(A) 供給業者の遅れに不満を抱いている。
(B) 聞き手が締め切り日を知っているだろうと考えている。
(C) 面会時間を忘れてしまった。
(D) プロジェクトがいつ終了するかわからない。

🔍 意図を問われている表現❺「それがいつになるか誰がわかるのか」をトーク全体の流れを踏まえて見ていくと、❷新製品の売れ行きはよいが、❸既存商品の製造がさまざまな要因で遅れている➡その中で❹「市場で新しい携帯電話の需要を満たせるまで、生産日程や資源を再整理する必要がある」➡❺「それがいつになるか誰がわかるのか」➡❻「なので、皆さんに生産を速めるためのアイデアを提案してほしい」となっている。つまり、新製品の売れ行きの勢いがいつまで続くかわからない中で、既存の遅れを取り戻す改善のアイデアも現時点ではないので、プロジェクトの終わりがいつになるかわからないという意図で発言していることがわかる。よって正解は **(D)**。

✏️ □be frustrated at ～に不満を持っている　□supplier 供給業者　□deadline 納期、期限
□appointment time 面会時間　□unsure 定かではない、わからない

76. ★★★★★

What will the speaker do in the afternoon next week?

(A) Prepare for a question-and-answer session
(B) Interview managerial applicants
(C) Meet with production managers
(D) Host a press conference

話し手は来週の午後何をしますか。

(A) 質疑応答の準備をする。
(B) 管理職候補者の面接をする。
(C) 生産主任と会談する。
(D) 記者会見を主催する。

🔍 話し手は❼で「皆さんが思いついたアイデアについて話し合うために、来週は午後に1時間ずつ時間を取る」と述べている。聞き手である、この「皆さん (you)」は❶から組み立てラインの主任だとわかっている。以上から、正解は組み立てラインの主任を production managers と言い換えて表した **(C)**。冒頭の情報を理解しながら聞いて解く必要がある、難しめの問題。

✏️ □question-and-answer session 質疑応答時間　□interview ～と面接する　□managerial applicant 管理職候補者
□host ～を主催する　□press conference 記者会見

	1回目	2回目	3回目
74.			
75.			
76.			

 74. (B)　75. (D)　76. (C)

Questions 77 through 79 refer to the following advertisement.

問題77-79は次の広告に関するものです。

W: ❶When running a business, we all understand the need to beat your rivals. Alex Consulting Agency is now conducting a very useful business seminar which will help you maximize your company's profits. You can enroll in this seminar by simply calling our office. The seminar is being led by Robert Taylor, author of the biggest business bestseller of the decade. Therefore, we are sure that you will learn valuable lessons in this program. ❷In addition, our seminars are very reasonably priced. ❸To learn more about this seminar, please visit our Web site at www.alexconsulting.org.

W: 会社を経営していれば、ライバルに勝つ必要があるということは誰もが理解しています。Alex コンサルティング会社は現在、会社の利益を最大化するのに役立つ、非常に有益な企業講習を実施しています。弊社にただお電話いただくだけで、この講習にお申し込みいただけます。この講習会はこの10年で一番のビジネス書ベストセラー作家である Robert Taylor さんが担当します。ですので、このプログラムでは間違いなく貴重な学びが得られるでしょう。さらに弊社の講習会の受講料は非常にお手頃になっています。この講習に関して詳しく知るには、弊社のウェブサイト www.alexconsulting.org にアクセスしてください。

□run a business 会社・事業を経営する　□beat a rival 競合に打ち勝つ　□conduct 〜を行う
□maximize 〜を最大化する　□profit 利益　□enroll in 〜に登録する　□simply 単に　□decade 10年
□valuable 貴重な　□in addition 加えて　□reasonably priced お手頃な価格の

77.

Who is the seminar most likely intended for?

(A) Event planners
(B) Book editors
(C) Advertising experts
(D) Business owners

講習会は誰を対象にしていると考えられますか。

(A) イベントプランナー
(B) 本の編集者
(C) 広告の専門家
(D) 事業主

🔍 話し手は❶で「会社を経営していれば……」と切り出し、会社の利益を最大化する研修を紹介している。以上から、正解は会社経営者を business owners と表現した **(D)**。

78. ★★★☆☆

What does the speaker emphasize about the event?

(A) It is economically priced.
(B) It is accessible to all.
(C) It is run by young people.
(D) It is the biggest event of its kind.

話し手はイベントについて何を強調しています
か。

(A) 経済的な価格がつけられている。
(B) 誰でも出入りできる。
(C) 若者によって運営されている。
(D) その手のイベントの中で一番規模が大きい。

 話し手は❷で「研修自体はとてもお手頃な価格だ」と述べている。これを economically priced と言い換えた **(A)** が正解となる。

 □economically 経済的に　□accessible 立ち入り可能な、接続可能な

---

79. ★★☆☆☆

How can the listeners get more information?

(A) By talking to an employee
(B) By going to an office
(C) By reading a manual
(D) By using the Internet

聞き手はどうしたらさらに多くの情報を得るこ
とができますか。

(A) 従業員と話すことによって。
(B) 事業所に行くことによって。
(C) 手引きを読むことによって。
(D) インターネットを使うことによって。

 聞き手は❸で講習に関する詳細な情報はウェブサイトを見るように促している。以上から正解は **(D)**。

	1回目	2回目	3回目
77.			
78.			
79.			

 77. (D)　78. (A)　79. (D)

Questions 80 through 82 refer to the following announcement.

M: ❶Attention, participants. I hope you are enjoying this month's time management workshop. Before I introduce our next keynote speaker, I have a short announcement to make. ❷A black leather bag has been found in the restroom. ❸Please take a moment to see whether you are missing one. ❹If you are, make your way to the reception desk at the main entrance of the building. ❺Ms. Parker is the person on duty there, and she has the lost bag.

問題80-82は次の連絡に関するものです。

M: 参加者の皆さんにお知らせします。今月のタイムマネジメント講習はお楽しみいただけていることと思います。次の基調講演者を紹介する前に、1つ手短にご連絡することがあります。お手洗いで黒い革バッグが見つかりました。ご自分のものを失くされていないかご確認ください。もし失くされていましたら、建物の正面玄関の受付までお越しください。Parker さんが担当者で、落し物のバッグをお預かりしています。

□Attention. (アナウンス等で) ご注目ください。 □participant 参加者 □management workshop 管理職の研修 □keynote speaker 基調講演者 □restroom お手洗い、トイレ □take a moment to *do* 時間を取って~する □be missing ~を欠いている □reception desk 受付 □on duty 勤務中の

---

80. ★★★☆☆

Where is the announcement most likely being made?

(A) At an amusement park
(B) At a café
(C) At a stadium
(D) At a training venue

連絡はどこで行われていると考えられますか。

(A) 遊園地
(B) 喫茶店
(C) スタジアム
(D) 講習会場

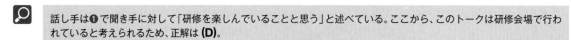

話し手は❶で聞き手に対して「研修を楽しんでいることと思う」と述べている。ここから、このトークは研修会場で行われていると考えられるため、正解は **(D)**。

□amusement park 遊園地 □training venue 講習会場

81. ★★★★☆

What is the announcement mainly about?	連絡では主に何について述べていますか。
(A) Claiming a lost item	**(A)** 遺失物を返してもらうこと。
(B) Taking on extra duties	(B) 追加業務を引き受けること。
(C) Using the restroom	(C) 休憩室を利用すること。
(D) Updating contact information	(D) 連絡先情報を更新すること。

 話し手は❷・❸で「お手洗いでバッグが見つかったので、自分のものを失くしていないか確認を」と述べている。ここから、物を失くした人に向けて、預かっているものが自分のものだと申し出るように話していることがわかる。これをclaim（自分のものだと要求する）という表現で表した **(A)** が正解。

 □claim 〜を自分のものだと要求する　□lost item 遺失物　□take on 〜を引き受ける　□extra duty 追加業務
□update 〜を更新する　□contact information 連絡先

---

82. ★★★☆☆

Who most likely is Ms. Parker?	Parker さんとは誰であると考えられますか。
(A) An event organizer	(A) 主催者
(B) A receptionist	**(B)** 受付係
(C) A presenter	(C) 司会者
(D) A coach	(D) コーチ

 話し手は❹で「紛失していたら受付まで来てほしい」と述べ、その後❺で「Parker さんが担当者だ」と述べている。ここから、Parker さんは受付にいる人と考えることができる。以上から正解は **(B)**。

 □organizer 主催者

PART 4

TEST 7

	1回目	2回目	3回目
80.			
81.			
82.			

 80. (D)　81. (A)　82. (B)

Questions 83 through 85 refer to the following excerpt from a meeting.

📝 問題83-85は次の会議の一部に関するものです。

M: Good morning, LTO Chemicals employees. As mentioned in the memo, we're planning to introduce new business hours next year. ❶It has come to the attention of management that since most of our customers are located in Asia, it is difficult to communicate with them effectively. ❷When it's morning here, it's night there, so we're going to have some employees start six hours later. ❸I realize this is a big change, but keep in mind, it will be your choice. ❹And remote working will be an option, too. Now, ❺I've written an e-mail to send to our customers to explain our new business hours. ❻I want you all to take a look at it and let me know if there is anything you think should be added.

M: おはようございます、LTO化学薬品の従業員の皆さん。社内連絡でも触れられていたとおり、来年は新しい営業時間を実施する予定です。役員が懸念してきたのは、我々の顧客の多くがアジアに拠点を置いているため効率よく連絡を取り合うことが難しいということです。こちらが朝のとき、あちらは夜です。よって当社は何名かの従業員の始業を6時間後ろにずらします。これが大きな変革であることは承知していますが、心に留めておいていただきたいのは、これは個人の選択であることです。そして、リモートワークも選択できるようになります。さて、当社の新しい営業時間を説明するためにお客様に送るEメールを作成しました。皆さんに目を通していただき、書き足したほうがよいと思われることがあれば、お知らせいただきたいと思います。

✏️ ☐as mentioned 述べたとおり　☐business hours 営業時間　☐it comes to one's attention of ～が目に留まる
☐be located in ～に拠点を置く　☐effectively 効果的に　☐realize ～を認識している、把握している
☐keep in mind 留意する　☐remote working リモートワーク（オフィスから離れた所で仕事をすること）
☐take a look at ～を見る

83.

According to the speaker, what is causing a problem?

(A) Travel costs
(B) Traffic congestion
(C) Overtime work
(D) Time differences

話し手によると、何が問題の原因となっていますか。

(A) 旅費
(B) 交通渋滞
(C) 残業
(D) 時差

🔍 まず話し手は❶で「顧客の多くがアジア拠点のため、連絡を取るのが難しい」と述べ、それに続いて❷で「こちらが朝のとき、あちらが夜なので、何人かの始業時間を遅らせる」と言っている。ここから、時差が問題の原因となっていると考えられるため、正解は **(D)**。

✏️ ☐congestion 混雑　☐overtime work 残業

84. ★★★★☆

What does the speaker mean when he says, "it will be your choice"?

(A) Not all staff need to change work patterns.
(B) Staff can decide how to come to work.
(C) Attendance at a meeting is optional.
(D) Clients can use video chat for meetings.

話し手が "it will be your choice" と言う際、何を意味していますか。

(A) 全従業員が勤務形態を変える必要はない。
(B) スタッフは仕事に来る手段を決めることができる。
(C) 会議への出席は任意である。
(D) 顧客は会議でビデオチャットを使うことができる。

 意図を問われている表現❸「あなたの選択となる」をトーク全体を踏まえて見ていくと、❶アジアの顧客と効率よく連絡を取り合うことが難しいため➡❷「何人かの始業を6時間ずらす」➡❸「これはあなたの選択となる」➡❹「リモートワークも選択の1つ」という流れになっている。❹は too と言っていることから、それがもう1つの選択であることがわかる。では1つ目の選択は何かというと、それは❷の顧客に合わせて勤務時間をずらすということになる。その変更について述べた後に❸「これはあなたの選択となる」と言っているため、勤務時間の変更が選択によるもの、つまり全従業員が合わせるものではないという意図で発言されたと考えられる。以上より、勤務開始時間の変更を change work patterns と言い換えて表現した **(A)** が正解。

□work pattern 勤務形態　□attendance 出席
□video chat ビデオチャット（お互いをディスプレイに映しながら行う会話）

---

85. ★★★★☆

What are the listeners asked to look at?

(A) An employment agreement
(B) A business message
(C) A yearly budget
(D) A work manual

聞き手は何を見るように求められていますか。

(A) 雇用契約
(B) 業務上のメッセージ
(C) 年間予算
(D) 作業の手引き

 話し手は聞き手に❺で「当社の新しい営業時間を説明するお客様用 E メールを作成した」と述べ、❻で「目を通し、書き足すべきことがあれば知らせてほしい」とお願いしている。ここから、聞き手は E メールの内容を見るように依頼されていることがわかる。以上から正解は **(B)**。

□employment agreement 雇用契約

	1回目	2回目	3回目
83.			
84.			
85.			

 83. (D)　84. (A)　85. (B)

PART 4

TEST 7

Questions 86 through 88 refer to the following talk.

W: ❶Welcome to Greenwood Property Agency. I'm pleased to see everyone here. ❷Since you have all achieved your license, I'd like to go over some important tips on selling a house. These tips are what make or break a sale. ❸First and foremost — first impressions. What does your potential buyer see when you drive up to the house? What does the outside look like? Is it inviting or is it in need of repairs? A sale is possible either way, but make sure to keep your clients informed about the properties they'll see. Many agents forget this, so to help get my point across ❹I'm going to show you some images of actual houses that are on the market. You tell me what you would tell the client before he or she sees it. Any questions so far?

問題86-88は次の話に関するものです。

W: Greenwood不動産へようこそ。皆さんを迎えることができてうれしく思います。皆さんは免許を取得したので、住宅販売の重要な秘訣を話したいと思います。この秘訣は売上を成立させるものであり、だめにするものでもあります。何よりもまず、第一印象です。家まで車でお連れするときに購入を考えている人は何を見るでしょうか。外観はどうか。魅力的か、それとも改修が必要か。どちらでも販売は可能ですが、お客様にはこれから見る物件についてしっかりと情報を伝えてください。多くの販売代理人がこの点を忘れているので、ポイントを理解してもらうために、売りに出されている実際の家の画像を見ていただきます。お客様に見せる前に何を伝えるか教えてください。ここまでで何か質問はありますか。

□property agency 不動産会社　□achieve ～を成し遂げる　□go over ～を検討する　□tip アドバイス
□break a sale 販売をダメにする　□first and foremost 何よりも最初に　□first impression 第一印象
□potential buyer 将来見込みのある購入者　□drive up to 車で～まで行く　□outside 外観　□inviting 魅力的である
□in need of ～の必要がある　□either way どちらでも　□inform ～に知らせる　□property 不動産、物件
□agent 担当者　□image 画像　□actual 実際の　□on the market 売りに出されている

---

86. ★★★★★

What kind of business will the listeners most likely work in?

(A) Tourism
(B) Education
(C) Finance
(D) Real estate

聞き手はどんな事業に従事すると考えられますか。

(A) 観光業
(B) 教育機関
(C) 金融会社
(D) 不動産業

🔍 話し手は❶で「不動産会社にようこそ」と言い、❷で免許を持つ聞き手に対して「住宅販売の秘訣を伝える」と述べている。ここから、聞き手は住宅販売に関わる事業に従事することがわかるため、正解は **(D)**。

□tourism 観光業

87. ★★★☆☆

According to the speaker, what is the most important thing?

(A) The appearance of a property
(B) The value of a service
(C) The impression a salesperson makes
(D) The online reviews of a place

話し手によると、最も重要なことは何ですか。

(A) 物件の外観
(B) サービスの価値
(C) 販売員が作る印象
(D) その場所のオンラインレビュー

 話し手は❸で「何よりも重要なのは第一印象」と話している。ここから、物件の外観が重要だと話していることがわかる。以上から正解は **(A)**。

 □appearance 外観

88. ★★★★★

What will happen next?

(A) A keynote speaker will give a speech.
(B) The listeners will look at photographs.
(C) The applicants will begin an exam.
(D) One of the employees will give a presentation.

次に何が起こりますか。

(A) 基調講演者が講演をする。
(B) 聞き手が写真を見る。
(C) 応募者が試験を始める。
(D) 従業員の一人がプレゼンテーションをする。

 話し手は❹で「これから売りに出されている物件の画像を見せる」と述べている。ここから、聞き手が画像(image)＝写真(photograph)を見ることがわかる。以上から正解は **(B)**。

 □keynote speaker 基調講演者　□applicant 候補者

PART **4**

TEST **7**

	1回目	2回目	3回目
86.			
87.			
88.			

🚩 **86. (D)　87. (A)　88. (B)**

Questions 89 through 91 refer to the following broadcast.

M: The city of Middletown would like to inform residents of exciting upcoming changes. ❶Many residents and indeed our own city hall staff have already noticed that the Western Bus Terminal is old and out-of-date. ❷That is why we asked seven architects to submit plans for renovating the terminal. ❸City hall requested that the new terminal should be more environmentally-friendly. For instance, it should allow in as much sunlight as possible to make it brighter and more energy-efficient. Moreover, all exterior lighting around the terminal must be powered by solar panels. ❹Next Tuesday, the mayor of Middletown will announce the winning design. The renovation is scheduled to begin next year.

問題89-91は次の放送に関するものです。

M: Middletown 市から住民の皆さまに今度の心躍るような改修についてお知らせいたします。多くの住民の方と実際に Middletown 市当局も既に Western バスターミナルが古くて時代遅れになったと感じています。そのため、市当局はターミナルの改修のため7人の建築家に図案の提出を依頼しました。市当局は新しいターミナルが現状より環境に配慮したものになるよう希望をしました。例えば、できるだけ多くの陽の光を取り入れて、もっと明るく、エネルギー効率が良くなることが望まれます。また、ターミナル周辺の外灯には全てソーラーパネルで電力が供給されます。今度の火曜日に Middletown 市長が選ばれたデザインを発表します。改修工事は来年開始される予定です。

✏️ □inform A of A に〜を知らせる　□upcoming 来たるべき　□indeed 実際に　□city hall 市役所　□notice 〜に気づく　□out-of-date 時代遅れの　□architect 建築家　□renovate 〜を改装する　□terminal ターミナル、終着点　□environmentally-friendly 環境に配慮した　□for instance 例えば　□allow 〜を入れる　□sunlight 太陽光　□bright 明るく　□energy-efficient エネルギー効率の良い　□moreover さらに　□exterior lighting 外灯　□power 〜の電源を供給する　□solar panel 太陽光パネル　□renovation 改修　□be scheduled to do 〜する予定である

---

89. ★★★★☆

What is the subject of the program?

(A) Public transportation
(B) An improvement project
(C) A road expansion
(D) Bus route changes

番組のテーマは何ですか。

(A) 公共交通機関
(B) 改修プロジェクト
(C) 道路の拡張
(D) バスの路線変更

🔍 話し手は❶で「Western バスターミナルが古くて時代遅れになった」と切り出し、❷で「そのため、市当局はターミナルの改修のため、建築家に図案の提出を依頼した」と述べている。ここから、改善、改修に関するテーマだとわかる。以上から正解は **(B)**。

✏️ □public transportation 公共交通機関　□road expansion 道路の拡張　□bus route バス運行路線

90. ★★★☆☆

According to the speaker, what is important to city officials?

(A) Minimal costs
(B) An eco-friendly design
(C) Link to other transportation
(D) Accessibility for the elderly

話し手によると、市当局が重要視していることとは何ですか。

(A) 最低限のコスト
(B) 環境に配慮した設計
(C) 他の交通機関への連絡
(D) お年寄りにとっての利用しやすさ

🔍 話し手は❸で「市当局は新しいターミナルが現状より環境に配慮するものになるよう要望した」と述べている。ここから、市当局は環境面の配慮を重要視していることがわかるため、正解は環境配慮を eco-friendly と言い換えた **(B)**。

✏️ □minimal 最低限の　□eco-friendly 環境に配慮した　□link to ～への連絡　□accessibility 利便性
□elderly 高齢者

91. ★★★★☆

According to the speaker, what will happen on Tuesday?

(A) A judgment will be made.
(B) A renovation project will start.
(C) A new bus route will begin.
(D) A road will be closed.

話し手によると火曜日に何がありますか。

(A) 判断がなされる。
(B) 改修プロジェクトが始まる。
(C) 新しいバス路線の運行が始まる。
(D) 道路が閉鎖される。

🔍 話し手は❹で「今度の火曜日に Middletown 市長が選ばれたデザインを発表する」と述べている。ここから、市当局が❷で募集した提案の中から採用されるものが発表されると考えられる。以上から正解は **(A)**。

✏️ □judgment 判断

	1回目	2回目	3回目
89.			
90.			
91.			

 89. (B)　90. (B)　91. (A)

Questions 92 through 94 refer to the following announcement.

W: ❶Starting next week, our shops will be equipped with new bar-code and two-dimension code scanners. By scanning the product's bar-code, the device indicates the current stock availability and the corresponding price. On the first day of use, ❷we will need sales associates like you to carefully check that the machines are displaying the correct price and stock levels. We will arrange a training session tomorrow in order for everyone to get familiar with this system before we begin to use it for sales and inventory management. ❸The new system will enable us to avoid the problem of incorrectly pricing our products, which occurred last week when we mistakenly overcharged one of our regular customers. ❹One great feature of the device is that it sends automatic alerts when we are running low on an item. ❺This feature will allow us to order new inventory automatically.

📝 問題92-94は次のお知らせに関するものです。

W: 来週から当社の店舗には新しいバーコードと二次元コードの読み取り装置が備わります。製品のバーコードを読み取ると、機械が現在の在庫の利用可能性とその価格を表示します。導入初日は機械が正しい価格と在庫量を表示しているかを販売員が慎重に確認する必要があります。販売と在庫管理で使用を開始する前に、全員がこのシステムに通じられるよう、明日は研修会を開きます。新システムにより、先週常連のお客様に誤って過大請求する原因となった、製品に誤った値付けをするという問題を回避できるようになります。この装置の優れた機能は、商品の在庫が少なくなってきたときに自動の通知を送ってくれることです。この機能により、自動的に在庫の追加注文が行われます。

✏️ □be equipped with ～が備わる □bar-code バーコード □two-dimension code 二次元コード
□scanner 読み取り装置 □device 装置 □indicate ～を表示する □stock 在庫 □availability 利用の可能性
□corresponding 対応する □sales associate 営業担当者 □carefully check ～を入念に確認する
□arrange ～を調整する □get familiar with ～になじむ □inventory management 在庫管理 □avoid ～を避ける
□incorrectly price ～に誤った値付けをする □occur 発生する □mistakenly 誤って
□overcharge ～に過大請求する □feature 特徴、機能 □automatic alert 自動警報 □run low on ～が尽きる

92. ★★★★★

According to the speaker, what will the listeners be asked to do next week?

(A) Install a software program
(B) Replace defective products
(C) Check a device is operating properly
(D) Learn how to use new equipment

話し手によると、聞き手は来週何をするように求められていますか。

(A) 新しいソフトウェアプログラムをインストールする。
(B) 不良品を交換する。
(C) 機器が正確に動作しているかを確認する。
(D) 新しい装置の使い方を学ぶ。

話し手は❶で「来週新しいバーコードと二次元コードの読み取り装置が備わる」ことについて切り出し、❷で「導入初日に機械が正しい価格と在庫量を表示しているかを販売員が慎重に確認してほしい」と依頼している。ここから、聞き手はある装置が正しく動作するか確認する必要があるとわかる。以上から、正解は装置が正しく動作することを a device is operating properly と言い換えて表した **(C)**。

□install ～をインストールする、組み込む □replace ～を交換する □defective 不良の □properly 正しく
□equipment 器具、装置

93. ★★★☆☆

What problem happened last week?

(A) Employees were not trained.
(B) Shops ran out of stock.
(C) Product demonstrations were not conducted.
(D) Some items were priced incorrectly.

話し手は先週のどんな問題について言及しましたか。

(A) 従業員が訓練されていなかった。
(B) 店が在庫切れを起こした。
(C) 製品の実演説明が実施されなかった。
(D) 値付けの不正確な商品があった。

話し手は❸で「先週常連のお客様に誤って過大請求する原因となった、製品への誤った値付けを回避できる」と述べていることから、値付けを誤ったことが問題だとわかる。以上より正解は **(D)**。

□trained 教育・訓練を受けている □run out of ～がなくなる □demonstration 実演 □conduct ～を行う

94. ★★★★★

What feature of the device does the speaker emphasize?

(A) It sends an automatic warning.
(B) It can print out price tags.
(C) It includes a manual.
(D) It is energy-efficient.

話し手は装置のどんな機能を強調していますか。

(A) 自動的に警告を出す。
(B) 値札を印刷できる。
(C) 説明書が付いている。
(D) エネルギー効率がいい。

話し手は❹・❺で「この装置の優れた機能は、商品在庫が少なくなると自動通知してくれて、この機能によって自動追加発注ができる」と述べている。その前半部分を取り上げて表した **(A)** が正解。

□warning 警告 □print out ～を印刷する □price tag 値札 □include ～を含む
□energy-efficient エネルギー効率が良い

	1回目	2回目	3回目
92.			
93.			
94.			

 92. (C) 93. (D) 94. (A)

Questions 95 through 97 refer to the following excerpt from a meeting and graph.

M: Hello, everyone. Today we have some urgent business to attend to. ❶I would like to start out by talking about the sales analysis of our mobile phones over the last four months. Now, this graph shows the performance of the four most popular products from our company. ❷As you can see, our products are selling well in the market, except for our latest model. Its sales have been declining since November. What surprised me the most from the analysis is how well our first-generation phone is doing. I believe we owe this to its affordable price. ❸You are all aware that we will launch a new model next March, right? For the rest of the meeting, I'd like you to think of ways to increase the sales of the latest product and promote it. If time permits, we will present your ideas.

📝 問題95-97は次の会議の一部とグラフに関するものです。

M: 皆さん、こんにちは。今日は注意しなければならない緊急の業務があります。まずは当社の携帯電話のここ4か月の売上分析から話を始めたいと思います。まず、グラフを見ると、当社製品の中で最も人気のある4つの売れ行きがわかります。ご覧いただけるとおり、当社の製品は市場でいい売り上げを出していますが、最新機種が例外です。その売上高は11月以降、減少傾向にあります。分析で最も驚いたことは、当社の第一世代の電話機が非常に健闘しているということです。理由はその手頃な価格でしょう。当社が今度の3月に新しいモデルを発売することは皆さんご存じですね。会議の残りの時間で最新機種の売り上げを伸ばす方法とその宣伝方法を考えていただきたいと思います。時間が許せば、アイデアの発表をします。

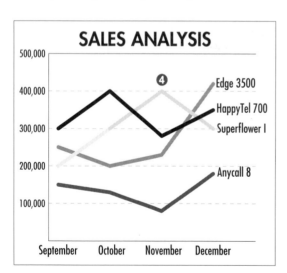

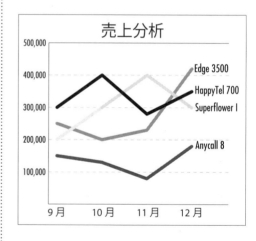

✏️ ☐attend to ～に注意を払う　☐start out by *do*ing ～することで始める　☐as you can see おわかりのとおり
☐sell well よく売れる　☐except for ～を除いて　☐decline 減少する　☐first-generation 第一世代の
☐owe A to A は～のおかげである　☐affordable 手頃な　☐aware that ～に気づいている　☐launch ～を発売する
☐latest 最新の　☐promote ～の販売を促進する　☐if time permits 時間が許せば

95.

Where does the speaker most likely work?

(A) At an Internet service provider
(B) At a phone accessory maker
(C) At a computer dealer
(D) At a mobile phone manufacturer

話し手はどこで働いていると考えられますか。

(A) インターネットのサービスプロバイダー
(B) 電話の周辺機器メーカー
(C) コンピューターの販売店
(D) 携帯電話メーカー

🔍 話し手は❶で「まずは当社の携帯電話の売上分析から話を始めたい」と話している。ここから、話し手は携帯電話メーカーで働いていることが考えられる。以上から正解は **(D)**。

96.

Look at the graphic. Which model was most recently released?

(A) Edge 3500
(B) HappyTel 700
(C) Superflower 1
(D) Anycall 8

図を見てください。最近発売されたのはどのモデルですか。

(A) Edge 3500
(B) HappyTel 700
(C) Superflower 1
(D) Anycall 8

🔍 話し手は❷で「当社の製品は市場でよく売れているが、最新機種は例外で、11月以降、売り上げが減少傾向にある」と述べている。ここでグラフを見ると、11月以降売り上げが低下しているのは❹だとわかる。以上から正解は **(C)**。

---

97. ★★★☆☆

What does the speaker say will happen next March?

(A) A new product will be introduced.
(B) A sales analysis will be conducted.
(C) Additional branches will be established.
(D) An old product will be discontinued.

話し手は今度の3月に何があると言っていますか。

(A) 新製品が発売される。
(B) 売上の分析が行われる。
(C) さらに支店が開設される。
(D) 古い製品が製造中止になる。

🔍 話し手は❸で「当社が今度の3月に新しいモデルを発売する」と述べている。以上から正解は **(A)**。

✏️ □conduct ～を行う　□additional 追加の　□branch 支店　□establish ～を開設する
□discontinue ～の製造を中止する

	1回目	2回目	3回目
95.			
96.			
97.			

 95. (D)　96. (C)　97. (A)

Questions 98 through 100 refer to the following recorded message and list.

W: Hello, Mr. Goldsmith. This is Victoria Cole from Darren Sports Supplies. ❶I'm looking over the order form you sent us for your new fitness center, and there are a few things that I want to go over very quickly. Fortunately, we have the bikes and weight sets in stock. ❷But the Ultra Flex Lifting Machine stopped being manufactured last quarter. In addition, ❸we no longer carry the Pace Keeper Treadmill, but we do carry Soul Movers, which are very similar machines. ❹We can do a special deal and sell them to you for the same price as the Pace Keeper. Please return my call at 999-3574 to discuss how you would like to proceed with the order.

📝 問題98-100は次の録音メッセージと一覧表に関するものです。

W: こんにちは、Goldsmith さん。Darren スポーツ用品店の Victoria Cole です。御社の新しいフィットネスセンター用に送付いただいた注文書を拝見しているのですが、何点かすぐに確認したいことがあります。幸い、バイクとウエイトセットは在庫があります。ですが、Ultra Flex リフティングマシンはこの前の四半期で製造中止となりました。また、当店での Pace Keeper トレッドミルの取り扱いは終了しましたが、それと同様の Soul Movers という器具を取り扱っております。特別提供として Pace Keeper と同じ価格にいたします。このご注文をどのように進めるかお話しするため、999-3574まで折り返しお電話ください。

Item	Price
Force Resist Stationary Bicycle	$250
❺ Pace Keeper Treadmill	$300
Everwear Free Weight Set	$450
Ultra Flex Lifting Machine	$600

商品	価格
Force Resist フィットネスバイク	250ドル
Pace Keeper トレッドミル	300ドル
Everwear フリーウエイトセット	450ドル
Ultra Flex リフティングマシン	600ドル

□look over ～を点検する　□go over ～を検討する、見返す　□fortunately 幸運にも　□bike バイク、自転車
□in stock 在庫のある　□manufacture ～を製造する　□in addition 加えて　□no longer もはや～ない
□carry ～を取り扱う　□treadmill トレッドミル、ランニングマシン　□similar 類似の、同様の
□special deal 特別提供　□proceed with ～を続ける

98. ★★★☆☆

What is the purpose of the call?	電話の目的は何ですか。
(A) To update personal information	(A) 個人情報を更新すること。
(B) To announce a membership discount	(B) 会員割引について知らせること。
(C) To check an order	**(C)** 注文を確認すること。
(D) To place an order for equipment	(D) 器具の注文をすること。

🔍 話し手は❶で「御社の注文書について確認したいことがある」と述べているため、これが電話の目的と考えられる。以上から正解は **(C)**。

✏️ □update ～を更新する　□personal information 個人情報　□membership discount 会員割引
□place an order 発注する　□equipment 器具、装置

---

99. ★★★☆☆

What problem is mentioned about the Ultra Flex Lifting Machine?	Ultra Flex リフティングマシンについてどんな問題が言及されていますか。
(A) It has been discontinued.	**(A)** 生産中止になっている。
(B) Production speed is low.	(B) 製造スピードが遅い。
(C) It was recalled due to design flaws.	(C) 設計上の欠陥のため、リコールとなった。
(D) Its price is higher than advertised.	(D) 宣伝されたものより高額である。

🔍 話し手は❷で「Ultra Flex リフティングマシンはこの前の四半期で製造中止となった」と話している。以上から正解は **(A)**。stopped being manufactured が has been discontinued と言い換えられていることに注目。

✏️ □discontinue ～の製造を中止する　□recall ～を回収する、リコールする　□due to ～の原因により　□flaw 欠陥

---

100. ★★★★☆

Look at the graphic. How much will Mr. Goldsmith pay for a Soul Mover?	表を見てください。Goldsmith さんは Soul Mover にいくら支払いますか。
(A) $250	(A) 250ドル
(B) $300	**(B)** 300ドル
(C) $450	(C) 450ドル
(D) $600	(D) 600ドル

🔍 ❸で「当店での Pace Keeper トレッドミルの取り扱いは終了したが、それとよく似た Soul Movers という器具がある」と述べ、加えて❹で「特別提供として Pace Keeper と同じ価格にする」と申し出ている。次に価格表を見ると、❺から Pace Keeper のトレッドミルは300ドルであることがわかる。ここから、Soul Movers の製品を購入する場合、300ドルで購入できることがわかる。以上から正解は **(B)**。

	1回目	2回目	3回目
98.			
99.			
100.			

 98. (C)　99. (A)　100. (B)

GO ON TO THE NEXT TEST!

Test

32. What was the woman expected to do yesterday?

(A) Upload a job vacancy
(B) Contact the personnel department
(C) Look over some résumés
(D) Interview job applicants

33. What caused the problem?

(A) The man made an error with dates.
(B) An e-mail was sent to the incorrect address.
(C) A voice mail message was omitted.
(D) A vacation was not allowed in advance.

34. What is indicated about the man?

(A) He will meet with the woman today.
(B) He did a task on his own.
(C) He doesn't have time for a project.
(D) He is a temporary employee.

35. Where does the man most likely work?

(A) At a clothing shop
(B) At a coffee shop
(C) At a cotton plantation
(D) At a fabric store

36. What problem does the man mention?

(A) An item can't be modified quickly.
(B) Some goods are out of stock.
(C) A delivery fee is too expensive.
(D) A promotional offer has finished.

37. When will the man call the woman?

(A) On August 11
(B) On August 13
(C) On August 16
(D) On August 20

38. What department does the woman most likely work in?

(A) In Public Relations
(B) In Marketing
(C) In Human Resources
(D) In Technical Support

39. What does the woman ask the man to do?

(A) Read the user guide
(B) Purchase a new part
(C) Restart the computer
(D) Send a report

40. What does the woman say she will do?

(A) Check an order number
(B) Pass on the problem to an expert
(C) Confirm an address
(D) Be of service on site

41. Where does the woman work?

(A) A real estate agency
(B) An investment bank
(C) An architecture practice
(D) A construction firm

42. What is the man satisfied with?

(A) A house loan has been approved.
(B) Some renovations have finally been done.
(C) A house is conveniently located.
(D) A job opening will be posted soon.

43. What is the man planning to do next week?

(A) Attend a housing exposition
(B) Inspect some work
(C) Complete some documents
(D) Look at a property

GO ON TO THE NEXT PAGE ➡

 32-34 *P. 412*   **35-37** *P. 414*   **38-40** *P. 416*   **41-43** *P. 418*

44. What does the man imply when he says, "That was only yesterday"?

(A) He corrected the woman's information.
(B) He did not attend the workshop.
(C) He will volunteer next time.
(D) He is not so busy today.

45. What is the man concerned about?

(A) Editing a difficult article
(B) Making up for lost time
(C) Handling customers' complaints
(D) Making a speech

46. What does the woman say she will do tomorrow morning?

(A) Fill out some volunteer forms
(B) Consult the man's secretary
(C) Practice some employee evaluations
(D) Mention the problem at a meeting

47. What position is the woman asking about?

(A) A sales promoter
(B) A computer programmer
(C) An account manager
(D) A web designer

48. What job qualification does the man mention?

(A) Knowledge of basic software
(B) A certification from a design school
(C) Recommendations from previous employers
(D) A portfolio of art samples

49. What does the man say will happen next week?

(A) A new office branch will be opened.
(B) An HR director will lead an orientation session.
(C) Suitable applicants will be interviewed.
(D) Computer programs will be renewed.

50. Why is the woman unavailable on Friday?

(A) She is participating in a customer meeting.
(B) She is performing at a music event.
(C) She is attending a class.
(D) She is going out of town on business.

51. What is suggested about the speakers' office building?

(A) It will undergo redecoration.
(B) It needs some electrical repairs.
(C) It will be inspected soon.
(D) It is open on weekends.

52. What is Mark required to do?

(A) Claim overtime hours
(B) Give some documents to the boss
(C) Pay an electrician
(D) Organize a desk

53. What does the man ask about?

(A) Taking a business trip
(B) Updating a work agreement
(C) Moving to another team
(D) Taking time off from work

54. Why is the woman concerned?

(A) She thinks the man lacks experience.
(B) She hopes the man can meet a customer on time.
(C) She does not want to miss a due date.
(D) She will be out of the office next month.

55. What does the woman suggest that the man do?

(A) Offer assistance to staff members
(B) Join a support program
(C) Contact her at an updated address
(D) Work overtime this month

44-46 *P. 420*   47-49 *P. 422*   50-52 *P. 424*   53-55 *P. 426*

56. Where is the conversation taking place?

(A) At a restaurant
(B) At a hotel
(C) At a real estate agency
(D) At a hospital

57. What does the woman mean, when she says, "No one told me about that"?

(A) She does not want to pay extra.
(B) She did not hear about the reschedule.
(C) She is excited about a meeting.
(D) She already made an appointment.

58. What will the woman do next?

(A) Look for other rooms
(B) Check the accommodation rates
(C) Contact her supervisor
(D) Complete a document

59. What does the woman ask about?

(A) A colleague's location
(B) A business project
(C) A sales meeting
(D) A telephone call

60. Why is the woman trying to get in touch with Briana?

(A) To educate her in sales
(B) To offer her a service
(C) To ask for some advice
(D) To introduce her to a potential customer

61. What does the man offer to do?

(A) Help out at a workshop
(B) Book an airline ticket
(C) Submit an e-mail to Briana
(D) Attend a meeting

Room No.	Room Price
9th floor (901-910)	$150
8th floor (801-815)	$135
7th floor (701-720)	$130
6th floor (601-620)	$120

62. Why is the woman calling?

(A) To change a reservation
(B) To ask for a confirmation number
(C) To get directions to the hotel
(D) To request a discount

63. Look at the graphic. What will the woman's room rate be?

(A) $150
(B) $135
(C) $130
(D) $120

64. According to the man, what will the woman receive?

(A) A list of menu options
(B) A registration form
(C) A discount code
(D) Confirmation information

GO ON TO THE NEXT PAGE ➡

🔖 56-58 *P. 428*   🔖 59-61 *P. 430*   🔖 62-64 *P. 432*

Type of binding	Price Per 500 Copies
Staple Binding	$900
Ring Binding	$1,100
Book Binding	$1,350
Hardcover Binding	$1,450

65. What does the man ask the woman to do?

(A) Reschedule a conference
(B) Prepare materials for an event
(C) Confirm some stock prices
(D) Book a seat at an event

66. What problem does the woman mention?

(A) An event is scheduled sooner than expected.
(B) A location is unavailable this week.
(C) A staff member is behind schedule with a project.
(D) A shareholders' conference has been delayed.

67. Look at the graphic. What style of binding will the woman choose?

(A) Staple Binding
(B) Ring Binding
(C) Book Binding
(D) Hardcover Binding

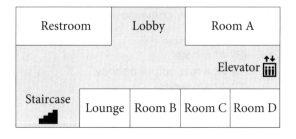

Restroom	Lobby	Room A

Elevator

Staircase	Lounge	Room B	Room C	Room D

68. What does the woman say about Mr. Manning?

(A) He has given instructions.
(B) He is awaiting a delivery.
(C) He works in a different building.
(D) He is on a business trip.

69. Look at the graphic. Where will the man most likely leave the packages?

(A) In Room A
(B) In Room B
(C) In Room C
(D) In Room D

70. What does the man ask the woman to do?

(A) Write down a mobile phone number
(B) Sign a document
(C) Make a payment
(D) Open a door

🚩 **65-67** *P. 434*

🚩 **68-70** *P. 436*

PART 4 Test 8

71. According to the speaker, what is being changed?

(A) The number of employee entrances
(B) The way of hiring new staff members
(C) The password for accessing a database
(D) The procedure for entering a building

72. What should all staff members do before the change takes place?

(A) Return their office keys
(B) Download a new program
(C) Have their photographs taken
(D) Create a new password

73. What does the speaker say was sent in an e-mail?

(A) An appointment time
(B) A list of names
(C) An identification number
(D) A set of directions

74. Where does the speaker most likely work?

(A) At a pharmacy
(B) At an accounting firm
(C) At a college
(D) At a medical facility

75. What change in the program does the speaker mention?

(A) Staff members will evaluate interns.
(B) Internship periods will be longer.
(C) The pay for interns will increase.
(D) Fewer interns will be hired.

76. What is one reason for the change?

(A) To reduce the program's budget
(B) To hire more competent staff
(C) To attract more applicants
(D) To make record keeping more efficient

77. What is the speaker planning to do?

(A) Visit a real estate agency
(B) Extend the rental period
(C) Buy her own apartment
(D) Move to a different country

78. Why does the speaker say, "but please excuse me"?

(A) She apologizes for not making a payment on time.
(B) She would like to ask several questions.
(C) She wants to apologize for giving short notice.
(D) She regrets making a change in the plan.

79. What does the speaker offer to do for the listener?

(A) Get someone to contact him
(B) Put the apartment up for sale
(C) Offer contact information
(D) Pay a penalty charge

80. What is the purpose of the announcement?

(A) To invite advertising professionals to make a speech
(B) To confirm a list of conference participants
(C) To announce an event is being held this year
(D) To ask listeners for suggestions for speech topics

81. What does the speaker ask the listeners to do?

(A) Attend the whole conference
(B) Pay fees in advance
(C) Participate in a preliminary meeting
(D) Help set up the venue

82. What is mentioned about the conference?

(A) Attendance is mandatory.
(B) It has been delayed.
(C) It is free for staff members.
(D) Seats are assigned in order of registration.

GO ON TO THE NEXT PAGE ➡

 71-73 *P. 438*   74-76 *P. 440*   77-79 *P. 442*   📎 80-82 *P. 444*

PART 4

TEST 8

409

83. What is the purpose of the broadcast?

(A) To provide local business news
(B) To report weather conditions
(C) To offer financial advice
(D) To inform people of a store opening

84. What does the announcer suggest the listeners do tomorrow?

(A) Expect extra commuting time
(B) Use public transportation
(C) Check their vehicle before a journey
(D) Change house loan providers

85. What will listeners hear soon?

(A) Political news
(B) An economic report
(C) Sports scores
(D) New music

86. Where is this announcement being heard?

(A) At a bus terminal
(B) At a subway station
(C) At a harbor
(D) At an airport

87. When can passengers start boarding?

(A) At 10:35 A.M.
(B) At 11:20 A.M.
(C) At 11:50 A.M.
(D) At 12:50 P.M.

88. What does the speaker ask passengers to do?

(A) Board according to seat number
(B) Prepare their identification for display
(C) Place large bags under the seats
(D) Go to the gate area

89. What does the speaker say about herself?

(A) She has taught a class before.
(B) She is a specialist in workshop planning.
(C) She did not attend college.
(D) She works for an international company.

90. What is the purpose of the speaker's class?

(A) To explain how to beat competitors
(B) To teach how to start up a business
(C) To give tips on reaching management level
(D) To give insight into certain business issues

91. What are the listeners invited to do next?

(A) Take notes on a presentation
(B) Introduce themselves
(C) Watch a video
(D) Raise some questions

92. What is the subject of the workshop?

(A) Advertising strategies
(B) Changing jobs
(C) Safety procedures
(D) Business presentations

93. What does the speaker recommend?

(A) Becoming aware of one's speaking speed
(B) Being very polite to clients
(C) Arriving early to a sales appointment
(D) Checking business trends online

94. What will the listeners probably do next?

(A) Work in small groups
(B) Watch videos
(C) Provide feedback on the seminar
(D) Eat together

MAP OF ORCHID HILL

[2]

[1]　　　[3]　[4]

Bridge

Tilden River

Event Schedule	
Event	Time
Opening Ceremony	12:00 P.M.
Street Activities	1:00 P.M.
Celeste Gilbert	3:00 P.M.
Closing Ceremony	4:00 P.M.

95. What is the main purpose of the call?

(A) To request a service
(B) To provide some advice
(C) To ask about a property
(D) To confirm a delivery

96. What does the speaker say she will do?

(A) Put some items outside her home
(B) Lend the listener her vehicle
(C) Give a tour of an apartment
(D) Ensure parking space is available

97. Look at the graphic. In which location is the speaker's residence located?

(A) [1]
(B) [2]
(C) [3]
(D) [4]

98. What is the theme of the event?

(A) Arts and crafts
(B) Cooking
(C) Community singing
(D) Keeping healthy

99. According to the speaker, who will be present at the event?

(A) A movie star
(B) A professional sports player
(C) A children's book writer
(D) A famous musician

100. Look at the graphic. Around what time will the prize winner be announced?

(A) 12:00 P.M.
(B) 1:00 P.M.
(C) 3:00 P.M.
(D) 4:00 P.M.

95-97　*P. 454*

98-100　*P. 456*

Questions 32 through 34 refer to the following conversation.

M: ❶Hannah, where were you yesterday? ❷You were supposed to meet me at the personnel department at 2 P.M. to help review the résumés for the temporary marketing position. I tried getting hold of you, however my calls kept getting sent to voice mail.

W: ❸Let me check the memo you sent on Tuesday. Look, it said we'd be going through the résumés today, the 26th. So, I took the afternoon off yesterday to run some private errands. Can I help you with the project today?

M: ❹Actually, I decided to do it by myself. I'm really sorry about the confusion. I've already called some of the qualified applicants and asked them to come in for interviews next week. Next time, I'll confirm any office correspondence before it goes out.

📝 問題32-34は次の会話に関するものです。

M: Hannah さん、昨日どこにいましたか。午後2時に人事部へ来て、臨時のマーケティング職の履歴書の検討を手伝ってくれるはずでした。連絡しようとしましたが、何度電話をかけても留守番電話になっていました。

W: 火曜日にいただいたメモを見させてください。ほら、これだと履歴書の検討をするのは今日、26日でした。それで、昨日は私用を済ませるために午後の休みを取りました。今日そのプロジェクトのお手伝いをしましょうか。

M: 実は一人でやることにしました。混乱してしまって、本当にすみません。条件に合う応募者にもう電話をかけ、来週の面接に来てもらうよう連絡しています。次は業務連絡を出す前に確認します。

✏️ □be supposed to *do* ～することになっている　□review ～を確認する　□résumé 履歴書
□temporary 一時的な、臨時の　□get hold of ～に連絡を取る　□voice mail 留守番電話
□go through ～を検討する、精査する　□take the afternoon off 午後休暇を取る　□run an errand お使いに行く
□private errand 私用　□confusion 混乱　□qualified applicant 条件に合う応募者　□confirm ～を確認する
□office correspondence 業務連絡　□go out 発信する

32.

What was the woman expected to do yesterday?

(A) Upload a job vacancy
(B) Contact the personnel department
(C) Look over some résumés
(D) Interview job applicants

女性は昨日何をすることになっていましたか。

(A) 求人情報を掲載する。
(B) 人事部に連絡をする。
(C) 履歴書を確認する。
(D) 求職者の面接をする。

🔍 会話冒頭❶で男性が女性に「昨日どこにいたのか」と尋ね、❷で「人事部に行って、履歴書の確認を手伝うはずだった」述べている。ここから、女性は履歴書の確認をすることになっていたことがわかる。以上から正解は **(C)**。(B) は人事部とは会うが連絡することにはなっていないので不正解。

✏️ □upload ～を掲載する　□contact ～に連絡する　□look over ～を確認する

33. ★★★☆☆

What caused the problem?

(A) The man made an error with dates.
(B) An e-mail was sent to the incorrect address.
(C) A voice mail message was omitted.
(D) A vacation was not allowed in advance.

何が問題の原因になりましたか。

(A) 男性が日付を間違えた。
(B) E メールが間違ったアドレスに送られていた。
(C) 留守番電話のメッセージが忘れられていた。
(D) 休暇が事前に承認されていなかった。

 ❶・❷で男性が女性に「昨日履歴書の確認をする予定だった」と話しかけたのに対し、女性は❸で男性のメモではその作業は今日になっている、と応じ、その後男性が謝罪している。ここから、男性が日付を誤ったことがわかる。以上から正解は **(A)**。

 □incorrect address 間違った住所　□omit ～をうっかり忘れる

34. ★★★☆☆

What is indicated about the man?

(A) He will meet with the woman today.
(B) He did a task on his own.
(C) He doesn't have time for a project.
(D) He is a temporary employee.

男性について何が示されていますか。

(A) 今日女性と打ち合わせをする。
(B) 自分一人で仕事をした。
(C) プロジェクトのための時間がない。
(D) 臨時職員である。

男性は❷・❸の女性との会話の後、❹で「履歴書の確認は自分でやることとした」と述べている。ここから、行う必要のあった業務（＝履歴書の確認）を自分で済ませたことがわかる。以上から、正解はその行うべき業務を task と言い換えた **(B)**。

□task 業務、タスク

	1回目	2回目	3回目
32.			
33.			
34.			

32. (C)　33. (A)　34. (B)

Questions 35 through 37 refer to the following conversation.

W: ❶ Thank you for recommending this suit to me. ❷ This store has so many choices that I was feeling overwhelmed. I like this one the best, though, so I'll take it. However, the jacket sleeves are a bit long. ❸ Do you offer an alteration service here? ❹ I'd like to take it home today, if possible.

M: ❺ I'm afraid it will take some time. We used to have someone working on-site, but now we send all of our suits and jackets to a tailor across town. However, I can take your measurements today.

W: All right. I was planning on wearing the suit to a important meeting on August 16th. Will it be ready by then?

M: Sure. I'll send it to the tailor first thing tomorrow, and ❻ it will be back on August 13th. ❼ I'll contact you when it's ready to be picked up.

📝 問題35-37は次の会話に関するものです。

W: このスーツを勧めてくださってありがとうございます。こちらのお店には非常にたくさんの種類があって圧倒されました。でも、これが一番気に入ったので、これにします。ただ、ジャケットの袖が少し長すぎます。こちらでは寸法直しのサービスがありますか。できれば今日持ち帰りたいのですが。

M: 申し訳ありませんが、それには時間がかかります。以前はこの場で対応する者がいたのですが、今は、当店のスーツやジャケットは全て町の反対側にある仕立屋に送っています。ただ、今日採寸することはできます。

W: わかりました。このスーツは8月16日にある重要な会議に着ていくつもりでした。それまでに仕上がりますか。

M: はい。明日の朝一番に仕立屋に送りますので、8月13日には戻ると思います。お引き取りの準備ができたら、ご連絡します。

✏️ □suit スーツ　□feel overwhelmed 圧倒される　□I'll take it. それを買うことにします。　□a bit 少し
□alteration service 寸法直しサービス　□I'm afraid すまないが　□take some time 少し時間がかかる
□used to *do* かつて~していた　□on-site 現場で、現地で　□tailor 仕立屋　□measurement 寸法
□first thing tomorrow 明日の朝一番で　□pick up ~を引き取る

35.

Where does the man most likely work?

(A) At a clothing shop
(B) At a coffee shop
(C) At a cotton plantation
(D) At a fabric store

男性はどこで働いていると考えられますか。

(A) 衣料品店
(B) コーヒーショップ
(C) 綿花農場
(D) 生地屋

🔍 会話冒頭❶で女性がスーツを薦めてくれたことのお礼を述べ、❷で「こちらのお店には非常にたくさんの種類があって圧倒された」と述べている。加えて、❸でここでサイズの直しが可能かどうかも聞いていることから、男性は衣料品に関するサービスを提供する店にいることが考えられる。以上から正解は **(A)**。

✏️ □cotton 綿花　□plantation 農場　□fabric store 生地屋

36. ★★★☆☆

What problem does the man mention?

(A) An item can't be modified quickly.
(B) Some goods are out of stock.
(C) A delivery fee is too expensive.
(D) A promotional offer has finished.

男性はどんな問題について話していますか。

(A) 商品を迅速に直すことができない。
(B) いくつかの商品は在庫がない。
(C) 配送料が高すぎる。
(D) セールは終了している。

🔍 女性が❸で、ここでスーツのサイズ直しができるか尋ね、❹で「今日家に持ち帰りたい」と述べている。それに対して、男性が❺で「時間がかかる」と述べていることから、すぐにはサイズ直しができないことがわかる。以上から正解は **(A)**。

✎ □modify ～を修正する　□out of stock 在庫切れの　□delivery fee 配送料
□promotional offer 販売促進用の売り出し、セール

37. ★★★☆☆

When will the man call the woman?

(A) On August 11
(B) On August 13
(C) On August 16
(D) On August 20

男性は女性にいつ電話をかけますか。

(A) 8月11日
(B) 8月13日
(C) 8月16日
(D) 8月20日

🔍 男性は❻で、8月13日にサイズ直しの済んだ品が戻るので、準備が整い次第女性に連絡する、と言っている。ここから、連絡が8月13日に行われることがわかる。以上から正解は **(B)**。

	1回目	2回目	3回目
35.			
36.			
37.			

🚩 **35. (A)　36. (A)　37. (B)**

Questions 38 through 40 refer to the following conversation.

M: Hello, is this the help desk? This is David Ford in office 524-B. ❶I'm calling about a problem I'm having with my desktop PC. ❷An error message suddenly pops up with a beep sound when I try to operate the word processing program.

W: Well, let me see if I can help you with that. ❸I want you to turn off the computer and then turn it on again.

M: I've tried that three times already, but it didn't solve the problem.

W: I see. Today I'm not busy, so ❹I can come to your office and take a look at it.

問題38-40は次の会話に関するものです。

M: こんにちは。そちらは問い合わせ窓口ですか。524-B 事務所の David Ford と申します。デスクトップパソコンの問題の件でお電話しています。文書作成プログラムを使おうとすると、突然エラーメッセージが出て警告音が鳴るのです。

W: では、解決できるか見てみましょう。コンピューターの電源を切って、もう一度電源を入れなおしてください。

M: それはもう3回試しました。でも問題が解決しなかったのです。

W: わかりました。今日は忙しくないので、そちらの事務所に伺って見てみます。

✏️ □pop up（画面等に）出る　□beep sound 警告音　□word processing program 文書作成プログラム
□let me see if I can ～できるかどうか見させて　□turn off ～の電源を切る　□turn on ～の電源をつける
□solve ～を解決する

---

38. ⭐⭐⭐⭐⭐

What department does the woman most likely work in?

(A) In Public Relations
(B) In Marketing
(C) In Human Resources
(D) In Technical Support

女性はどの部署で働いていると考えられますか。

(A) 広報
(B) マーケティング
(C) 人事
(D) テクニカルサポート

🔍 ❶で男性が女性に対して「パソコンに関する問題で電話した」と述べ、❷でエラーメッセージや警告音等の具体的な不具合を伝えている。ここから、女性は故障に対応するテクニカルサポート部門であることが考えられる。以上から正解は **(D)**。

39. ★★★★☆

What does the woman ask the man to do?

(A) Read the user guide
(B) Purchase a new part
(C) Restart the computer
(D) Send a report

女性は男性に何をするように頼んでいますか。

(A) ユーザーの手引きを読む。
(B) 新しい部品を購入する。
(C) コンピューターを再起動する。
(D) 報告書を送る。

 ❸で女性は男性に「一度パソコンの電源を切ってもう一度入れる」よう伝えている。以上から正解は **(C)**。❸の the computer と it は会話の流れから男性の my desktop PC であると理解しておこう。

 □user guide 利用者手引書　□restart ～を再度始める、再起動する

40. ★★★★★

What does the woman say she will do?

(A) Check an order number
(B) Pass on the problem to an expert
(C) Confirm an address
(D) Be of service on site

女性は何をすると言っていますか。

(A) 注文番号を確認する。
(B) 専門家に問題を回す。
(C) 所在地を確認する。
(D) 現場でサービスをする。

 女性は❹で「そちらの事務所に伺う」と申し出ているので、男性の現場で確認をすることがわかる。以上から、正解はその対応を現場でサービスをする (be of service on site) と言い換えた **(D)**。

 □pass on A to A を～に渡す　□be of service サービスをする、役立つ　□on site 現場で

	1回目	2回目	3回目
38.			
39.			
40.			

🚩 **38. (D)　39. (C)　40. (D)**

Questions 41 through 43 refer to the following conversation.

W: Hello, Mr. Willis. ❶This is Laura Gibson calling from Gibson Realtors. ❷A private house has just been listed that you might be interested in. ❸It's a three-bedroom house that's available right now, but best of all, it's near West Virginia Station.

M: ❹Near West Virginia Station? ❺Oh, that's good news. ❻The station is very convenient for my office. That's exactly what I was hoping for.

W: Would you like to view the house? ❼We can allow you to see it sometime next week, if you're free.

M: ❽I'm busy on Wednesday, but Thursday would be fine. Let me jot down where it is and I can meet you there.

📝 問題41-43は次の会話に関するものです。

W: こんにちは、Willis さん。Gibson 不動産の Laura Gibson です。興味を持っていただけそうな住宅がリストに追加されました。寝室が3つある、すぐに入居が可能な家で、何と言っても West Virginia 駅の近くにあります。

M: West Virginia 駅の近くですか。ああ、それは良い知らせですね。その駅は私の職場にとても便利がいいです。まさに私が希望していたものです。

W: 家をご覧になりますか。お時間があれば、来週のどこかでお見せすることができます。

M: 水曜日は忙しいですが、木曜日なら大丈夫だと思います。場所をメモさせてください。現地で落ち合えると思います。

✎ □be listed 項目に加えられる □be interested in ～に興味のある □right now 今すぐ □best of all とりわけ、何と言っても □convenient 便利である □exactly まさしく □jot down ～をさっとメモする

---

41. ★★☆☆☆

Where does the woman work?

(A) A real estate agency
(B) An investment bank
(C) An architecture practice
(D) A construction firm

女性はどこで働いていると考えられますか。

(A) 不動産事務所
(B) 投資銀行
(C) 建築設計事務所
(D) 建設会社

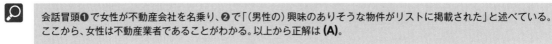

🔍 会話冒頭❶で女性が不動産会社を名乗り、❷で「（男性の）興味のありそうな物件がリストに掲載された」と述べている。ここから、女性は不動産業者であることがわかる。以上から正解は **(A)**。

✎ □real estate agency 不動産事務所 □investment bank 投資銀行 □architecture practice 建築事務所 □firm 会社

42. ★★★☆☆

What is the man satisfied with?

(A) A house loan has been approved.
(B) Some renovations have finally been done.
(C) A house is conveniently located.
(D) A job opening will be posted soon.

男性は何に満足していますか。

(A) 住宅ローンが承認された。
(B) 改修がようやく終わった。
(C) 家が便利な場所にある。
(D) 求人情報が間もなく掲載される。

女性は❷で触れた物件について❸で間取りや環境について伝える中で「West Virginia 駅に近い」と述べている。これに対して男性は❹・❺で良い知らせだ、とポジティブな反応を示し、❻で「その駅は事務所にとても便利がいい」と伝えている。ここから、紹介された物件の立地は男性にとって、とても良いことがわかる。以上から、正解はこれを言い換えた conveniently located と言い換えた **(C)**。

□be satisfied with ～に満足する　□house loan 住宅貸付金　□renovation 改修
□be conveniently located 便利な場所に位置している　□job opening 求人 (情報)　□post ～を掲載する

43. ★★★☆☆

What is the man planning to do next week?

(A) Attend a housing exposition
(B) Inspect some work
(C) Complete some documents
(D) Look at a property

男性は来週何をするつもりですか。

(A) 住宅展示会に行く。
(B) 仕事場を視察する。
(C) 書類を完成させる。
(D) 物件を見る。

女性が❼で来週男性の時間が空いていれば物件を見ることができると伝えたところ、男性は❽で木曜日なら大丈夫と応答している。ここから、男性が来週紹介された物件を見に行くことがわかる。以上から正解は **(D)**。

□housing exposition 住宅展示場　□inspect ～を視察する　□property 不動産、物件

	1回目	2回目	3回目
41.			
42.			
43.			

 41. (A)　42. (C)　43. (D)

Questions 44 through 46 refer to the following conversation.

W: Keiran, what are you doing here at the office? ❶Aren't you working at our firm's booth at the Fairfield Trade Fair this week?

M: ❷That was only yesterday. ❸Now I'm dealing with some dissatisfied customers.

W: Too bad, what happened?

M: ❹Some customers are not happy that they didn't receive their orders on time. ❺In fact, I'm really concerned since I don't know how I'm going to make up for the delays.

W: I'm sure everything will be okay. You've addressed these types of problems before. I need to get to the trade fair now, but ❻I'll bring this issue up at our staff meeting tomorrow morning to avoid it happening again.

問題44-46は次の会話に関するものです。

W: Keiran さん、会社で何をしているのですか。今週は Fairfield 展示会の当社ブースで作業するのではないのですか。

M: それは昨日だけです。今は不満をお持ちのお客様に対応しているところです。

W: 大変ですね。何があったのですか。

M: お客様の中に時間どおりに注文品が届かなかったことに不満のある方がいます。実のところ、遅れの埋め合わせをどうすればいいのかわからず、気にかかっています。

W: きっと何とかなりますよ。あなたは以前この種の問題に取り組んだことがあるじゃないですか。今私は展示会に行かなければなりませんが、この問題の再発を防げるよう明日の朝のスタッフ会議で取り上げます。

☐trade fair 産業見本市　☐deal with ~に対応する　☐dissatisfied 不満のある　☐on time 時間どおりに　☐in fact 実際　☐make up for ~を埋め合わせる　☐address ~に対応する　☐these types of これらの種類の　☐bring up ~を取り上げる　☐issue 課題　☐avoid ~を避ける

44. ★★★☆☆

What does the man imply when he says, "That was only yesterday"?

(A) He corrected the woman's information.
(B) He did not attend the workshop.
(C) He will volunteer next time.
(D) He is not so busy today.

男性が "That was only yesterday" と言う際、何を意図していますか。

(A) 女性が持つ情報を訂正している。
(B) 講習に出席しなかった。
(C) 次回志願をする。
(D) 今日はそこまで忙しくない。

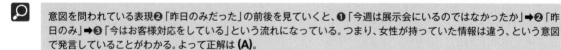

意図を問われている表現❷「昨日のみだった」の前後を見ていくと、❶「今週は展示会にいるのではなかったか」➡❷「昨日のみ」➡❸「今はお客様対応をしている」という流れになっている。つまり、女性が持っていた情報は違う、という意図で発言していることがわかる。よって正解は **(A)**。

☐correct ~を修正する　☐volunteer 志願する

45. ★★★☆☆

What is the man concerned about?

(A) Editing a difficult article
(B) Making up for lost time
(C) Handling customers' complaints
(D) Making a speech

男性は何を心配していますか。

(A) 難しい記事の編集をすること。
(B) 損失した時間の埋め合わせをすること。
(C) 顧客の苦情に対処すること。
(D) スピーチをすること。

男性は❸で不満を持ったお客様の対応をしていると話し、その後❹でお客様の不満の原因を述べ、❺でどうすればよいのか気にかかっていると話している。ここから、男性はお客様の苦情への対応について心配していることがわかる。以上から、正解は対応していること（deal with）を handle で言い換えて表した **(C)**。

□edit ～を編集する　□lost time 損失した時間　□handle ～を扱う

46. ★★★★☆

What does the woman say she will do tomorrow morning?

(A) Fill out some volunteer forms
(B) Consult the man's secretary
(C) Practice some employee evaluations
(D) Mention the problem at a meeting

女性は明日の朝何をすると言っていますか。

(A) ボランティアの用紙に記入する。
(B) 秘書に相談する。
(C) 従業員の評価を行う。
(D) 会議で問題に言及する。

男性の苦情対応に関する問題について、女性は❻で「明朝のミーティングで取り上げる」と述べている。以上から正解は **(D)**。❻の this issue が男性の抱えている案件であり、これを problem と言い換えていると理解することが重要。

□fill out ～に記入する　□consult ～に相談する　□practice an evaluation 評価を行う
□mention ～について言及する

44. (A)　45. (C)　46. (D)

421

Questions 47 through 49 refer to the following conversation.

W: Hello, this is Kelly Edith. ❶I'm calling about the advertisement I saw online for the job vacancy in your web design division. Are you still accepting applications?

M: We certainly are. There are a lot of positions you may be interested in. ❷If applicants want to be considered for the positions, they are required to have experience using several different kinds of design software.

W: Well, I know how to use all the major design software programs, so that's not a problem. I've also worked as a freelance artist. Therefore, I have a lot of experience in drawing and painting.

M: Great. ❸You sound like a qualified candidate. ❹Can you send your résumé right now? ❺The interviews are scheduled for next week.

📝 問題47-49は次の会話に関するものです。

W: こんにちは、Kelly Edith と申します。インターネットで拝見した、御社のウェブデザイン部門の求人広告のことでお電話しました。まだ応募は受け付けていますか。

M: 受け付けております。興味を持っていただけるかもしれない仕事がたくさんあります。採用の選考を受けるには、いくつかのデザインソフトウェアを使用した経験があることが条件になります。

W: なるほど。主要なデザインソフトウェアプログラムの使い方は全部知っているので、その点は問題ありません。フリーランスのアーティストとしても仕事をしていました。ですので、絵を描いた経験もたくさんあります。

M: いいですね。条件を満たしているようです。履歴書をすぐに送ってもらえますか。面接は来週を予定しています。

✏️ □job vacancy 求人　□accept an application 応募を受け付ける　□certainly 確かに
□be interested in ~に興味がある　□applicant 応募者　□be considered for ~の審議を受ける
□require ~を要求する　□major 主要な　□work as ~として働く　□freelance フリーランスの、自由契約の
□drawing and painting 絵画　□qualified candidate 条件を満たした候補者　□résumé 履歴書
□right now 今すぐ

---

47. ★★☆☆☆

What position is the woman asking about?

(A) A sales promoter
(B) A computer programmer
(C) An account manager
(D) A web designer

女性はどんな仕事について尋ねていますか。

(A) 販売促進担当
(B) コンピュータープログラマー
(C) 法人営業担当
(D) ウェブデザイナー

 会話冒頭❶で女性が「インターネットで見た、ウェブデザイン部門の求人広告のことで電話した」と言っている。ここから、ウェブデザイナーの仕事に関する問い合わせだとわかる。以上から正解は **(D)**。

 □promoter 販売促進担当者　□account 顧客、取引先

48. ★★☆☆☆

What job qualification does the man mention?

(A) Knowledge of basic software
(B) A certification from a design school
(C) Recommendations from previous employers
(D) A portfolio of art samples

男性はどんな要件について話していますか。

(A) 基本的なソフトウェアの知識
(B) デザイン学校の卒業証書
(C) 以前の雇用主からの推薦状
(D) 作品の見本

 男性は❷で「採用の選考を受けるには、いくつかのデザインソフトウェアの使用経験が条件」と言っている。ここから、ソフトウェアに関する知識が要件であることがわかる。以上から正解は **(A)**。

 □certification 修了証書 　□employer 雇用者 　□portfolio（仕事の成果となる）見本

---

49. ★★★☆☆

What does the man say will happen next week?

(A) A new office branch will be opened.
(B) An HR director will lead an orientation session.
(C) Suitable applicants will be interviewed.
(D) Computer programs will be renewed.

男性は来週何があると言っていますか。

(A) 新しい支店が開く。
(B) 人事部長がオリエンテーションを進行する。
(C) 要件を満たした応募者の面接が行われる。
(D) コンピュータープログラムが更新される。

男性は❸・❹で女性が求人の要件を満たせそうだと述べ、❺で来週面接があると伝えている。ここから、来週可能性のある求人応募者の面接が行われることがわかる。以上から正解は **(C)**。

□orientation オリエンテーション、説明会　 □suitable 適格な、ふさわしい　 □renew ～を更新する

 47. (D)　48. (A)　49. (C)

	1回目	2回目	3回目
47.			
48.			
49.			

Questions 50 through 52 refer to the following conversation with three speakers.

M1: Good morning, Sophie and Mark. ❶Are either of you free on Friday morning?

W: Sorry, but ❷I have to meet with some customers on that day.

M2: I'm not busy. What's up?

M1: ❸I need someone to be in the office from 9 A.M. to noon to let the electrician in. ❹She's going to do some work on our wiring system. I'd do it myself, but I've got that business trip to Mexico.

M2: I can be here.

W: That's really nice of you.

M1: Wow, thanks! I really appreciate that, Mark.

M2: ❺Is there anything special I have to do?

M1: Not really. You'll get a paper invoice and description of the work from the electrician. ❻Just put it on the president's desk and he'll take care of the payment.

📝 問題50-52は次の3人の話し手による会話に関するものです。

M1: おはようございます。Sophie さんに Mark さん。お二人のうちのどちらか金曜日の朝に手が空いていませんか。

W: すみませんが、その日は顧客と会わなければなりません。

M2: 私は忙しくありません。どうしましたか。

M1: 電気工の方を入れるために、午前9時から正午まで誰かに会社にいてほしいのです。配線の作業をしてもらうことになっています。私がやってもよかったのですが、メキシコへの出張が入ったのです。

M2: 私はここにいられます。

W: それは本当に助かります。

M1: ああ、ありがとうございます。Mark さん、本当にありがとうございます。

M2: 何か特別にしなければならないことはありますか。

M1: 特にありません。電気工の方から作業の請求と明細の紙を受け取ってください。それを社長の机に置いていただけたら、社長が支払いの処理をします。

✏️ □either of 〜のいずれか　□What's up? 何かありましたか。　□electrician 電気技術者　□wiring system 配線系統
□business trip 出張　□appreciate 〜に感謝する　□invoice 請求書　□description 明細
□take care of 〜を処理する　□payment 支払い

---

50. ★★★☆☆

Why is the woman unavailable on Friday?

(A) She is participating in a customer meeting.
(B) She is performing at a music event.
(C) She is attending a class.
(D) She is going out of town on business.

女性はなぜ金曜日の都合が悪いのですか。

(A) 顧客との打ち合わせに出る。
(B) 音楽イベントで演奏をする。
(C) 授業に出席する。
(D) 出張で町を出る。

🔍 会話冒頭❶で男性の1人が女性ともう1人の男性に話しかけ、「二人のうちいずれか金曜日に空いているか」と尋ねたところ、それに対して女性が「その日は顧客と会う」と述べている。ここから、女性は顧客との打ち合わせに参加することがわかる。以上から正解は **(A)**。

✏️ □participate in 〜に参加する　□go out of 〜から出る　□on business 仕事で

51. ★★★★☆

What is suggested about the speakers' office
building?

(A) It will undergo redecoration.
(B) It needs some electrical repairs.
(C) It will be inspected soon.
(D) It is open on weekends.

話し手たちの会社のビルについて何が示唆され
ていますか。

(A) 改装が施される。
(B) 電気設備の修理が必要である。
(C) もうすぐ検査がある。
(D) 平日に営業している。

 1人目の男性が❸で、午前中オフィスに電気技師を入れる必要があり、配線関係の仕事を手掛けてもらう、と述べている。ここから、会社のビルで電気関係の工事や修理作業が行われることが考えられる。以上から正解は **(B)**。会話では修理とまでは言及していないが、work から修理の可能性もあることを押さえておこう。

□undergo ～を受ける　□redecoration 改装　□electrical repair 電気設備の修理　□inspect ～を検査する

52. ★★★★★

What is Mark required to do?

(A) Claim overtime hours
(B) Give some documents to the boss
(C) Pay an electrician
(D) Organize a desk

Mark さんは何をしなければなりませんか。

(A) 残業時間を申告する。
(B) 上司に書類を渡す。
(C) 電気工に支払いをする。
(D) 机を整理する。

会話冒頭で1人目の男性が男女に Sophie と Mark と呼びかけ、❺の直前で Mark に感謝を述べていることから、Mark が2人目の男性の名前だとわかる。そして2人目の男性が❺で「何か行う必要があるか」と尋ねたところ、❻で「請求書と明細を社長の机に置くように」とお願いしている。以上から正解は **(B)**。登場人物が誰で、何をしなければいけないかを素早く把握することがポイント。

□claim ～を申告する　□overtime hours 残業時間　□organize ～を整理する

	1回目	2回目	3回目
50.			
51.			
52.			

▶ **50. (A)　51. (B)　52. (B)**

Questions 53 through 55 refer to the following conversation.

M: Can I have a word, Ms. Green? ❶I have one vacation week that must be used before the end of the month, so I wanted to get authorization to use it next week, from November 23rd to 29th.

W: Well, I know that you've been working hard and you certainly deserve a rest. But ❷what about the federal grant for our youth support program? ❸It needs to be forwarded by November 23rd. ❹I'm worried that we won't get it in on time without you here.

M: Actually, I've just finished the document this morning, and it will be ready to turn in tomorrow after the final review.

W: I see. In that case, I'm happy to approve your request. ❺In the meantime, why don't you ask your other team members if they need help catching up on anything?

📝 問題53-55は次の会話に関するものです。

M: 少しお話しできますか、Green さん。今月末までに消化しなければならない休暇が1週間分あるので、来週の11月23日から29日にそれを使うことを許可いただきたいのですが。

W: ええ。熱心に働いているので、お休みを取ってもらうのは当然です。ただ、青少年支援プログラムの連邦の助成金はどうなりますか。11月23日までに送る必要があります。あなたがここにいないと提出を間に合わせられないのではないか心配なのですが。

M: 実は、その書類は今朝仕上げましたので、最終確認の後、明日には準備が整います。

W: わかりました。それなら、喜んで申請を許可します。ところで、チームの他の従業員に間に合わせるために手助けが必要になっているものがないか聞いてもらえますか。

✏️ □Can I have a word? お話ししてもよいですか。　□authorization 許可　□deserve ～を受ける権利がある
□rest 休息　□federal 連邦の　□grant 奨学金、支援金　□youth support program 青少年支援プログラム
□forward ～を送付する　□on time 時間どおりに　□final review 最終確認　□in that case その場合
□be happy to *do* 喜んで～する　□in the meantime その間に、一方では　□catch up on ～に追いつく、間に合わせる

---

53. ★★★☆☆

What does the man ask about?

(A) Taking a business trip
(B) Updating a work agreement
(C) Moving to another team
(D) Taking time off from work

男性は何について尋ねていますか。

(A) 出張すること。
(B) 労働契約の更新をすること。
(C) 別のチームに異動すること。
(D) 仕事を休むこと。

🔍 会話冒頭❶で男性が「今月末までに消化しなければならない休暇があるので、使いたい」と許可を求めている。ここから、休暇申請について話していることがわかる。以上から正解は **(D)**。

✏️ □business trip 出張　□update ～を更新する　□work agreement 労働契約
□take time off from work 仕事を休む

54. ★★★★☆

Why is the woman concerned?

(A) She thinks the man lacks experience.
(B) She hopes the man can meet a customer on time.
(C) She does not want to miss a due date.
(D) She will be out of the office next month.

女性は何を心配していますか。

(A) 男性は経験不足であると考えている。
(B) 男性が時間どおりに顧客に会えることを願っている。
(C) 期日に遅れたくない。
(D) 来月会社を不在にする。

男性の休暇申請に対し、女性が❷・❸・❹で助成金の話を挙げ、期限に間に合うかが心配だと述べている。ここから、女性は助成金手続きの期限について話していることがわかる。以上から、正解は手続きの期限を a due date と言い換えた **(C)**。

□be concerned 心配する　□miss ～を逃す　□due date 期日　□out of the office 事務所を不在にする

55. ★★★★☆

What does the woman suggest that the man do?

(A) Offer assistance to staff members
(B) Join a support program
(C) Contact her at an updated address
(D) Work overtime this month

女性は男性に何をすることを勧めていますか。

(A) スタッフの手助けを申し出る。
(B) 支援プログラムに参加する。
(C) 更新された連絡先に連絡する。
(D) 今月残業をする。

❺で女性は男性に「チームメンバーに手助けが必要になっているものがないか尋ねてほしい」と伝えている。ここから、男性に他のスタッフに助けを申し出るように勧めていることがわかる。以上から、正解はこの助けの申し出を offer assistance と言い換えた **(A)**。

□contact ～に連絡する　□updated 更新された　□work overtime 残業する

	1回目	2回目	3回目
53.			
54.			
55.			

53. (D)　54. (C)　55. (A)

Questions 56 through 58 refer to the following conversation with three speakers.

M1: Hello. ❶Welcome to the Edith Holiday Inn and Suites.

W: Hello. ❷We'd like two rooms but have no reservation. Do you have any vacancies?

M1: Let me see what I can do for you. Fortunately, at present we have a few rooms available. How long will you be staying?

W: For three nights, please.

M2: No, Amy! ❸The convention lasts for five days. We should stay here for four nights.

W: Really? ❹No one told me about that.

M2: ❺I am terribly sorry. ❻I should have told you. ❼There was a last-minute change of dates late last night.

M1: Okay, your accommodation has been made for four nights for two rooms. ❽Please, fill out the visitors' registration form.

W: ❾I'll take care of it.

問題56-58は次の3人の話し手による会話に関するものです。

M1: こんにちは。Edith Holiday Inn and Suites へようこそ。

W: こんにちは。2部屋利用したいのですが、予約を取っていません。空きはありますか。

M1: ご用意できるか確認いたします。幸い、今いくつか空いているお部屋がございます。どのぐらいのご滞在でしょうか。

W: 3泊でお願いします。

M2: 違います、Amy さん。総会は5日間ですよ。4泊しなければなりません。

W: 本当ですか。誰からも聞いていませんが。

M2: 本当に申し訳ありません。お伝えしなければなりませんでした。昨夜の遅くに急な日程変更がありました。

M1: わかりました。ご宿泊は4泊2部屋で承りました。宿泊者登録書のご記入をお願いいたします。

W: 私がやります。

□fortunately 幸運にも □at present 現在 □night(s) ～泊 □last 続く □terribly sorry 本当に申し訳ない □last-minute change 直前の変更 □accommodation 宿泊施設 □fill out ～に記入する □registration form 登録用紙 □take care of ～を処理する

56. ★☆☆☆☆

Where is the conversation taking place?

(A) At a restaurant
(B) At a hotel
(C) At a real estate agency
(D) At a hospital

会話はどこで行われていますか。

(A) レストラン
(B) ホテル
(C) 不動産事務所
(D) 病院

会話冒頭❶で男性が宿泊施設に迎える挨拶をしており、❷で女性が部屋の利用希望を伝え、空きがあるか尋ねている。以上から正解は **(B)**。

□real estate agency 不動産事務所

57. ★★★★★

What does the woman mean, when she says, "No one told me about that"?

(A) She does not want to pay extra.
(B) She did not hear about the reschedule.
(C) She is excited about a meeting.
(D) She already made an appointment.

女性が "No one told me about that" と言う際、何を意味していますか。

(A) 追加料金を払いたくない。
(B) 日程変更について聞いていない。
(C) 会議を楽しみにしている。
(D) 既に約束を取り付けている。

 意図を問われている表現❸「誰も教えてくれなかった」の前後を見ていくと、❸「会議は5日続くので4泊すべきだ」➡❹「誰も教えてくれなかった」➡❺・❻・❼「すまない」「伝えるべきだった」「直前に変更した」という流れになっている。ここから、直前の変更を女性は知らなかったという意図で発言していることがわかる。よって正解は **(B)**。

□pay extra 追加料金を支払う　□be excited about 〜を楽しみにしている

---

58. ★★★★★

What will the woman do next?

(A) Look for other rooms
(B) Check the accommodation rates
(C) Contact her supervisor
(D) Complete a document

女性は次に何をしますか。

(A) 他の部屋を探す。
(B) 宿泊費を確認する。
(C) 上司に連絡をする。
(D) 書類を完成させる。

1人目の男性が❽で宿泊者登録書に記載するよう依頼し、❾で女性がそれに応じている。以上から、正解は登録書を a document と言い換えた **(D)**。

□accommodation rate 宿泊費　□contact 〜に連絡する　□supervisor 上司、監督者

	1回目	2回目	3回目
56.			
57.			
58.			

56. (B)　57. (B)　58. (D)

Questions 59 through 61 refer to the following conversation.

W: ❶James, have you seen Briana? ❷I've been trying to contact her, but she's not answering my calls for some reason.

M: Oh, ❸Briana's out of the office attending the monthly sales meeting in Los Angeles until next Friday. Generally, attendees are asked to turn off their mobile phones when they're listening to a speech or attending a seminar. ❹Why do you want to reach her?

W: ❺I have a meeting with Mr. Kim, who's interested in the sales service that Briana is responsible for. So ❻I wanted to introduce Briana to him. The customer is flying to Boston this Wednesday, so I don't think he'll be here when Briana comes back.

M: ❼You know, Briana and I are on the same team. ❽Why don't I go with you? I'm sure I can be of help.

📝 問題59-61は次の会話に関するものです。

W: こんにちは、James さん。Briana さんを見ましたか。連絡しようとしているのですが、なぜか電話に出ないのです。

M: Briana さんは事務所を出て、今度の金曜日までロサンゼルスで月例の営業会議に出席しています。通常は、参加者は話を聞いたり講習に参加したりしている間は、携帯電話の電源を切るように言われます。なぜ連絡を取りたいのですか。

W: Briana さんが担当する販売サービスに興味をお持ちの Kim 様と打ち合わせがあるのです。なので、Briana さんを彼に紹介したいと思いました。お客様は今週の水曜日に Boston へ発たれるので、Briana さんが戻るときには、いらっしゃらないと思います。

M: 実は、Briana さんと私は同じチームなんですよ。私が同行してもよいでしょうか。お役に立てると思います。

✏️ □contact ～に連絡する　□answer a call 電話に出る　□out of the office 事務所を出て　□generally 一般的に、通常　□attendee 出席者　□turn off ～を切る　□reach ～と連絡を取る　□be interested in ～に興味がある　□be responsible for ～を担当している　□introduce A to A を～に紹介する　□be of help 助けとなる

59. ★★★☆☆

What does the woman ask about?

(A) A colleague's location
(B) A business project
(C) A sales meeting
(D) A telephone call

女性は何について尋ねていますか。

(A) 同僚の居場所
(B) 事業計画
(C) 営業会議
(D) 電話

🔍 会話冒頭❶で女性が Briana さんの居場所を尋ね、❷で「連絡をしているが応答しない」と言っている。その後❸で男性が Briana さんは営業会議のため事務所にいないと話していることから、女性は会社の同僚である Briana さんがどこにいるかを尋ねていることがわかる。以上から正解は **(A)**。

60. ★★★★★

Why is the woman trying to get in touch with Briana?

(A) To educate her in sales
(B) To offer her a service
(C) To ask for some advice
(D) To introduce her to a potential customer

女性はなぜ Briana さんと連絡を取ろうとしていますか。

(A) 営業について指導するため。
(B) サービスを提供するため。
(C) アドバイスをお願いするため。
(D) 顧客になる可能性のある方に紹介するため。

男性が❹で Briana さんに連絡を取ろうとしている理由を尋ねると、女性は❺・❻で「（当社のサービスに興味のある）Kim さんを紹介したい」と話している。ここから、将来顧客になってくれるかもしれない人と引き合わせることが目的だとわかる。以上から正解は **(D)**。

□educate 〜を指導する、教育する　□ask for 〜を求める

---

61. ★★★☆☆

What does the man offer to do?

(A) Help out at a workshop
(B) Book an airline ticket
(C) Submit an e-mail to Briana
(D) Attend a meeting

男性は何をすることを申し出ていますか。

(A) 講習を手伝うこと。
(B) 航空券を予約すること。
(C) Briana さんに E メールを送ること。
(D) 打ち合わせに参加すること。

❻で女性が「Briana さんを顧客に紹介したいと思った」と発言したのを受けて、男性は❼で自分が Briana さんと同じチームであることを述べ、❽で Briana さんの代わりとして会議に同行することを申し出ている。以上から正解は **(D)**。

□help out 〜を手伝う　□book 〜を予約する

	1回目	2回目	3回目
59.			
60.			
61.			

 59. (A)　60. (D)　61. (D)

Questions 62 through 64 refer to the following conversation and price list.

W: Hello, this is Tiffany Stevens. ❶ I just made an online reservation at your hotel. ❷ However, when I checked the confirmation page I realized that I'd made an error with the dates. ❸ What should I do?

M: I'll be happy to make a change in your reservation, but only if we have a room available. Could you please give me your confirmation number?

W: Sure. It's TZ293. I want the reservation for the following weekend, from June 16th to June 18th. Will the price be the same?

M: Hold on, Ms. Stevens. ❹ Yes, we do have a room available for those three days at the same rate. ❺ On the 7th floor, room number 20. So, I've changed your reservation with us. ❻ You can expect an updated confirmation in your e-mail promptly.

問題62-64は次の会話と価格表に関するものです。

W: こんにちは、Tiffany Stevens と申します。そちらのホテルをインターネットで予約したところなのですが、確認ページを見たときに、日付を間違えてしまったことがわかりました。どうしたらいいでしょうか。

M: こちらで予約の変更をいたしますが、空き室があった場合でのことになります。確認番号を教えていただけますでしょうか。

W: はい。TZ293です。予約はその次の週末、6月16日から6月18日まででお願いします。価格は同じですか。

M: 少々お待ちください、Stevens 様。はい、同じ料金でその3日間利用できるお部屋があります。7階にある、20号室です。これで当ホテルでの予約を変更いたしました。新しい確認のメールがすぐに届きます。

Room No.	Room Price
9th floor (901-910)	$150
8th floor (801-815)	$135
❼ 7th floor (701-720)	$130
6th floor (601-620)	$120

部屋番号	宿泊料金
9階 (901-910)	150ドル
8階 (801-815)	135ドル
7階 (701-720)	130ドル
6階 (601-620)	120ドル

□confirmation page 確認ページ □confirmation number 確認番号 □following 次の □hold on (電話を切らずに) 待つ □updated confirmation 改訂された確認表 □promptly すぐに

62.

Why is the woman calling?

(A) To change a reservation
(B) To ask for a confirmation number
(C) To get directions to the hotel
(D) To request a discount

女性はなぜ電話をしていますか。

(A) 予約を変更するため。
(B) 確認番号について尋ねるため。
(C) ホテルへの道順を知るため。
(D) 割引を申請するため。

 会話冒頭❶・❷で女性がホテルのオンライン予約をしたが日付を間違えたと述べており、❸でどうすればよいか尋ねている。ここから、間違いをした予約を変更したいことがわかる。以上から正解は **(A)**。

 □get directions to ～への道順を知る

63.

Look at the graphic. What will the woman's room rate be?

(A) $150
(B) $135
(C) $130
(D) $120

図を見てください。女性が宿泊する部屋の料金はいくらですか。

(A) 150ドル
(B) 135ドル
(C) 130ドル
(D) 120ドル

 男性は❹で女性が変更を希望している日の部屋を確保できることを伝え、❺でそれが7階の20号室だと述べている。ここで価格表を見ると、❼で7階の部屋は130ドルであることがわかる。以上から正解は **(C)**。

64.

According to the man, what will the woman receive?

(A) A list of menu options
(B) A registration form
(C) A discount code
(D) Confirmation information

男性によると、女性は何を受け取りますか。

(A) メニューオプションの一覧
(B) 申込用紙
(C) 割引コード
(D) 確認情報

 男性は❻で「まもなく改訂された情報がEメールで送られる」と述べている。ここから、女性が確認情報を受け取るとわかる。以上から正解は **(D)**。

 □registration form 申し込み用紙

	1回目	2回目	3回目
62.			
63.			
64.			

62. (A)   63. (C)   64. (D)

Questions 65 through 67 refer to the following conversation and list.

M: Joan, ❶we need to have our company brochures printed in order to give them to new employees at next week's new employee orientation. ❷Please take care of that.

W: Let me see. ❸Isn't the orientation this Tuesday?

M: Really?

W: Yes. ❹We had to move the orientation to this week since we're scheduled to have a shareholders' meeting next week.

M: ❺In that case, please hurry to have them printed right away. Here's the pricing guide for Blissful Prints. ❻We need 500 copies. ❼Don't spend more than $1000 on printing costs.

W: Sure. I'll take a look at this and give them a call immediately.

📝 問題65-67は次の会話と表に関するものです。

M: Joan さん、来週の新入社員オリエンテーションで配布できるように会社のパンフレットを印刷してもらう必要があります。手配をお願いします。

W: ちょっとお待ちください。説明会は今週の火曜日ではないですか。

M: 本当ですか。

W: はい。来週は株主総会があるので、説明会を今週に変更しなければなりませんでした。

M: それなら、すぐに印刷してもらってください。こちらが Blissful 印刷所の料金案内です。500部必要です。印刷代に1000ドル以上かけないでください。

W: わかりました。これを見たら、すぐに電話します。

Type of binding	Price Per 500 Copies
❽Staple Binding	$900
Ring Binding	$1,100
Book Binding	$1,350
Hardcover Binding	$1,450

製本形式	500部ごとの価格
ホッチキス	900ドル
リング	1,100ドル
本	1,350ドル
ハードカバー本	1,450ドル

📝 □brochure パンフレット　□new employee orientation 新入社員説明会　□take care of ～を処理する
□Let me see. ええと。　□be scheduled to *do* ～する予定である　□shareholders' meeting 株主総会
□in that case その場合　□right away 早急に　□pricing guide 料金案内　□printing cost 印刷費用
□take a look at ～を見る　□immediately すぐに　□binding 製本、装丁　□staple ホッチキス
□hardcover ハードカバーの、堅表紙の

65. ★★★★★

What does the man ask the woman to do?

(A) Reschedule a conference
(B) Prepare materials for an event
(C) Confirm some stock prices
(D) Book a seat at an event

男性は女性に何をするように頼んでいますか。

(A) 会議の日程を変更する。
(B) イベントの資料を準備する。
(C) 株価を確認する。
(D) イベントの座席を予約する。

会話冒頭❶・❷で男性が「新入社員の説明会で使用するパンフレットを印刷する必要があるので、手配してほしい」と述べている。ここから、あるイベントの資料の準備を頼んでいることがわかる。以上から正解は **(B)**。

□reschedule 〜の日程を変更する □material 資料 □confirm 〜を確認する □stock price 株価
□book 〜を予約する

....

66. ★★★★☆

What problem does the woman mention?

(A) An event is scheduled sooner than expected.
(B) A location is unavailable this week.
(C) A staff member is behind schedule with a project.
(D) A shareholders' conference has been delayed.

女性はどんな問題について話していますか。

(A) イベントが思っていたよりも早い日時に予定されている。
(B) 今週は会場を利用できない。
(C) スタッフの作業がプロジェクトの予定より遅れている。
(D) 株主総会が遅れている。

女性はオリエンテーションについて❸で「今週の火曜日ではないのか」と尋ね、その後❹で「来週株主総会があるので今週に移動した」と1週間前倒しになったことを伝え、男性はそれを受けて❺で「それなら早急に印刷の手配を」と慌ただしくしている。ここから、オリエンテーションというイベントの開催が当初よりも早まったために準備を急がなければならなくなったことがわかる。以上から正解は **(A)**。

□sooner than expected 思ったより早く □unavailable 利用できない □behind schedule 予定より遅れている

....

67. ★★★★☆

Look at the graphic. What style of binding will the woman choose?

(A) Staple Binding
(B) Ring Binding
(C) Book Binding
(D) Hardcover Binding

図を見てください。女性はどの製本形式を選択しますか。

(A) ホッチキス
(B) リング
(C) 本
(C) ハードカバー

男性は❻・❼で印刷について「500部以上」「代金は1,000ドルを超過しない」と2つの条件を挙げている。この条件を踏まえ、価格表を見ると、後者の条件の価格帯に唯一当てはまるのが900ドルの❽だとわかる。以上から正解は **(A)**。

T
E
S
T
8

	1回目	2回目	3回目
65.			
66.			
67.			

 65. (B) 66. (A) 67. (A)

435

Questions 68 through 70 refer to the following conversation and map.

M: Good morning, ❶I've got a delivery here for Mr. Manning.

W: Yes, ❷his office is down the hall, on the right next to the elevator. ❸However, come to think of it, he's away on business, so his office won't be open. How many packages do you have?

M: Just these three.

W: I see. ❹Please put them in the stockroom. Well, now we are here in the lobby, so it's straight ahead of you, next to the employee lounge.

M: Okay. But first, ❺I need your signature on this receipt.

W: Of course, I'll do that for you.

問題68-70は次の会話と地図に関するものです。

M: おはようございます。Manning さんにお届け物です。

W: そうですか。彼のオフィスは通路の先、エレベーターのすぐ隣です。ただ、考えてみたら、彼は出張しているので、オフィスは開きません。小包はいくつありますか。

M: この3つだけです。

W: わかりました。備品室に入れておいてください。私たちは今このロビーにいますので、この真正面、従業員休憩室の隣です。

M: わかりました。ですが、まず、この受領書に署名をいただきたいです。

W: そうですね。署名いたします。

Restroom	Lobby	Room A

Elevator 🛗

Staircase	Lounge	Room B ❻	Room C	Room D

トイレ	ロビー	部屋 A

エレベータ 🛗

階段	休憩室	部屋 B	部屋 C	部屋 D

✏️ □delivery お届け物 □down the hall 廊下の先 □on the right next to ちょうど〜の隣に
□come to think of it 考えてみると □be away on business 出張で不在にする □stockroom 備品室
□straight ahead of 〜の真正面 □signature 署名 □receipt 受領書 □restroom トイレ、お手洗い
□staircase (手すりつきの) 階段

68. ★★★★★

What does the woman say about Mr. Manning?

(A) He has given instructions.
(B) He is awaiting a delivery.
(C) He works in a different building.
(D) He is on a business trip.

Manning さんについて女性は何と言っていますか。

(A) 指示を出した。
(B) 配達を待っている。
(C) 違うビルで働いている。
(D) 出張中である。

会話冒頭❶で男性が Manning さんへの荷物を持ってきたことを伝えたところ、女性は❷で彼 (Manning さん) の仕事部屋について一度言及するものの、その後❸で「よくよく考えてみると出張中だった」と彼が不在であると述べている。以上から正解は **(D)**。一瞬在室に思わせ、その後訂正している点が難しかったかもしれない。

□give instructions 指示を出す　□await 〜を待つ　□on a business trip 出張中である

---

69. ★★★★★

Look at the graphic. Where will the man most likely leave the packages?

(A) In Room A
(B) In Room B
(C) In Room C
(D) In Room D

図を見てください。男性はどこに小包を置いていくと考えられますか。

(A) 部屋 A
(B) 部屋 B
(C) 部屋 C
(D) 部屋 D

女性は❹で備品室に置くようにお願いした後に、備品室は今いる地点の真正面でラウンジの隣にある部屋だと説明している。ここで地図を見ると、❺からラウンジの隣は Room B になっている。以上から正解は **(B)**。

---

70. ★★☆☆☆

What does the man ask the woman to do?

(A) Write down a mobile phone number
(B) Sign a document
(C) Make a payment
(D) Open a door

男性は女性に何をするように頼んでいますか。

(A) 携帯電話の番号を書き留める。
(B) 書類に署名する。
(C) 支払いをする。
(D) ドアを開ける。

❺で男性は女性に「受領書にサインを」とお願いしている。以上から正解は **(B)**。

□write down 〜を書き留める

	1回目	2回目	3回目
68.			
69.			
70.			

TEST *8*

 68. (D)　69. (B)　70. (B)

Questions 71 through 73 refer to the following excerpt from a meeting.

W: ❶I called this meeting to announce a change in policy concerning the building entrance. Starting next month, you no longer have to enter a passcode on the keypad next to the main entrance. As some of you have probably seen already, we've installed a card access system. Due to this, all staff members will be given a photo identification card which you will need to swipe through the card reader to enter the building. ❷Before this change can occur, today I would like all staff members to visit the human resources department and have your pictures taken. ❸To avoid appointment conflicts, Mr. Rinebart sent you an e-mail indicating the time you should visit his office. If for any reason you can't go at the assigned time, please let him know directly.

📝 問題71-73は次の会議の一部に関するものです。

W: この会議は建物の入館に関する手続きの変更についてお知らせするためのものです。来月から正面入口横のキーパッドでパスコードを入力する必要がなくなります。既にご覧になった方もいると思いますが、当社ではカード入場システムを導入しました。そのため、スタッフ全員にビルに入る際に読み取らせる写真付き身分証をお渡しします。この変更を実施する前に、今日、スタッフは全員人事部に行って写真を撮ってもらってください。アポイントの集中を避けるために、訪問時間を示したEメールをRinebartさんが送りました。何らかの理由で指定の時間に行けない場合は、直接彼にお知らせください。

✏️ □call a meeting ミーティングを招集する　□policy 手段、方針　□concerning ～に関する　□no longer もう～ない
□passcode 暗証番号、パスコード　□keypad 入力盤、キーパッド　□next to ～の隣の
□install ～を導入する、設置する　□card access system カードによる入場システム　□due to ～が原因で
□photo identification 写真付き身分証明書　□swipe (カードなど) を機械に通す
□card reader カードリーダー、カード読み取り機　□occur 発生する、起こる　□avoid ～を避ける
□appointment conflicts 予約が重なること　□indicate ～を示す　□assigned 割り当てられた　□directly 直接

---

71. ★★★☆☆

According to the speaker, what is being changed?

(A) The number of employee entrances
(B) The way of hiring new staff members
(C) The password for accessing a database
(D) The procedure for entering a building

話し手によると、何が変更されることになりますか。

(A) 従業員入り口の数
(B) 新しいスタッフの採用方法
(C) データベースにアクセスするためのパスワード
(D) 入館時の手続き

 トーク冒頭❶で「建物の入館に関する手続きの変更について」と述べている。ここから、入館手順の変更について話していることがわかる。以上から正解は **(D)**。policy は「方針、規定」という意味のほかに「やり方、手段」という意味があり、今回のような文脈で使用された場合は procedure との言い換えとなる。

 □access ～に接続する

72. ★★☆☆☆

What should all staff members do before the change takes place?

(A) Return their office keys
(B) Download a new program
(C) Have their photographs taken
(D) Create a new password

変更が行われる前にスタッフは全員何をする必要がありますか。

(A) 事務所の鍵を返却する。
(B) 新しいプログラムをダウンロードする。
(C) 写真を撮ってもらう。
(D) 新しいパスワードを作成する。

🔍 話し手は❷で「変更前に、スタッフは全員写真を撮ってもらうように」と指示している。以上から正解は **(C)**。

✎ □office key 事務所用の鍵　□download ダウンロードする (提供元から別のコンピューター等にデータを移す)

---

73. ★★★★☆

What does the speaker say was sent in an e-mail?

(A) An appointment time
(B) A list of names
(C) An identification number
(D) A set of directions

話し手は E メールで何が送られたと言っていますか。

(A) アポイントの時間
(B) 名簿
(C) ID 番号
(D) 一連の使用方法

🔍 話し手は❸で「訪問時間を示した E メールを Rinebart さんが送った」と述べている。以上から、正解はこの訪問時間を An appointment time と言い換えた **(A)**。

✎ □a set of 一連の、一組の

P A R T 4

	1回目	2回目	3回目
71.			
72.			
73.			

T E S T *8*

🚩 **71. (D)　72. (C)　73. (A)**

Questions 74 through 76 refer to the following announcement.

M: Hi, everybody. ❶ Just a quick announcement regarding the hospital's upcoming winter internship program. ❷ Once again, we have recruited some of the top students from colleges across the state. They will be working with their assigned partners over the next three months as they learn what it takes to be a registered nurse. ❸ But this winter, I'd like to try something different. ❹ I will have all of those who supervise the interns turn in a performance report at the end of each week. ❺ I believe that the more feedback we give the interns, the more they will learn and improve. ❻ Additionally, those reports will allow us to make more informed decisions on which interns to recruit as nurses the following spring.

📝 問題74-76は次のお知らせに関するものです。

M: こんにちは、皆さん。当院の今度の冬期研修プログラムに関して少しお知らせがあります。今回も当院は州全域の大学からもっとも優秀な学生を数名採用しました。彼らは公認看護師になるのに必要なことを学びながら、今後3か月にわたり、担当のパートナーと仕事をしていきます。しかしこの冬は普段と違う試みをしたいと思います。研修生を監督する主任全員に各週の終わりに業績報告書を提出していただきます。研修生にフィードバックをする回数を増やすことで、より多くのことを学んで改善していくと思います。また、この報告書によって研修生の誰を来春から看護師として雇用するか十分な情報に基づいて判断できるようになります。

✏️ □regarding 〜に関する　□upcoming 来たるべき　□internship 実務研修　□recruit 〜を採用する
□across the state 州全域にわたる　□assigned 担当の、割り当てられた
□what it takes to *do* 〜するために必要なこと　□registered nurse 公認看護師　□those who 〜する人
□supervise 〜を監督する　□intern 実習生　□feedback 講評、感想　□additionally 加えて　□following 次の

---

74. ★★★☆☆

Where does the speaker most likely work?

(A) At a pharmacy
(B) At an accounting firm
(C) At a college
(D) At a medical facility

話し手はどこで働いていると考えられますか。

(A) 薬局
(B) 会計事務所
(C) 大学
(D) 医療施設

🔍 トーク冒頭❶で病院の研修プログラムについて触れ、❷で「今回も私たちは優秀な学生を採用した」と言っていることから、この話し手と聞き手が勤める病院で研修プログラムが行われ、その学生が採用されたと考えられる。以上から、正解は病院を a medical facility と言い換えた **(D)**。

✏️ □pharmacy 薬局　□accounting firm 会計事務所　□facility 施設

75. ★★★★☆

What change in the program does the speaker
  mention?

(A) Staff members will evaluate interns.
(B) Internship periods will be longer.
(C) The pay for interns will increase.
(D) Fewer interns will be hired.

話し手はプログラムのどんな変更について言及
していますか。

(A) 職員が研修生を評価する。
(B) 研修期間が長くなる。
(C) 研修生の賃金が増える。
(D) 研修生の採用が減る。

 話し手は聞き手に対して❹で「研修生監督者に業績報告書を提出してもらう」と伝えている。ここでの performance report は研修生の業績に関する評価報告書であり、ここから、監督者となる職員が研修生を評価することがわかる。正解は、この評価することを evaluate と表した **(A)**。

 □evaluate ～を評価する　□internship period 実務研修期間　□pay 賃金

---

76. ★★★★☆

What is one reason for the change?

(A) To reduce the program's budget
(B) To hire more competent staff
(C) To attract more applicants
(D) To make record keeping more efficient

変更の目的は何ですか。

(A) プログラムの予算を削減するため。
(B) 有能な看護師を雇うため。
(C) より多くの応募者を集めるため。
(D) より効率的な記録管理をするため。

 まず話し手は❸で「今冬は変更がある」と切り出し、❹・❺で職員が研修生を評価することと、❺で評価レポートが今後の採用につながることを述べている。ここから、評価結果で基準を満たす有能な研修者を正式に採用する際に判断しやすくするためだとわかる。以上から、正解は **(B)**。

 □competent 能力のある　□applicant 応募者　□efficient 効率的な

	1回目	2回目	3回目
74.			
75.			
76.			

74. **(D)**　75. **(A)**　76. **(B)**

Questions 77 through 79 refer to the following recorded message.

W: Hello, Mr. Miller. This is Debbie Winger from unit 9A of Samson Apartment. ❶My boss has just informed me that I will be transferred overseas, although I am not sure when exactly I will be moving. I'm thinking that it will happen before October. Therefore, I plan to move out before the renewal date of my lease in September. ❷I know that I should have notified you of this at least two months before moving out, ❸but please excuse me. ❹I, too, was only informed of my relocation this month. ❺I know someone who would like to take over the apartment from me, and I can get him to contact you. Please let me know if you'd like me to do that.

問題77-79は次の録音メッセージに関するものです。

W: こんにちは、Miller さん。Samson アパート 9A 号室の Debbie Winger です。社長から海外赴任をすることになると通達がありました。ただ正確にいつ移動することになるのかはわかりません。10月より前だと思っています。ですので、9月の賃貸契約更新前に退去する予定です。退去の2か月前までにはお伝えすべきであったことは理解していますが、どうかご容赦ください。私自身も今月、転勤のことを知らされました。私の後に契約の引き継ぎを希望している人を知っておりまして、彼から連絡させるようにできます。もしそうすることをご希望であればお知らせください。

✎ □inform ～に知らせる　□be transferred overseas 海外赴任となる　□move out 引っ越す　□lease 賃貸借契約
□notify 人 of 人に～を知らせる　□relocation 移住　□contact ～に連絡する

---

77. ★★☆☆☆

What is the speaker planning to do?

(A) Visit a real estate agency
(B) Extend the rental period
(C) Buy her own apartment
(D) Move to a different country

話し手は何をする予定ですか。

(A) 不動産屋を訪れる。
(B) 賃貸期間を延長する。
(C) マンションを購入する。
(D) 別の国に引っ越す。

🔍 話し手は❶で「海外赴任することになった」と述べている。ここから、別の国に引っ越す予定であることがわかる。以上から正解は **(D)**。

✎ □real estate agency 不動産会社　□extend ～を延長する

78. ★★★★☆

Why does the speaker say, "but please excuse me"?

(A) She apologizes for not making a payment on time.
(B) She would like to ask several questions.
(C) She wants to apologize for giving short notice.
(D) She regrets making a change in the plan.

話し手はなぜ "but please excuse me" と言っていますか。

(A) 支払いが間に合わなかったことを詫びている。
(B) いくつか質問をしたい。
(C) 急な知らせをしたことを詫びたい。
(D) 計画を変更したことを後悔している。

🔍 意図を問われている表現❸「しかし、どうか容赦してほしい」の前後を見ていくと、❷「退去の2か月前に知らせるべきだったことは知っている」➡❸「容赦してほしい」➡❹「私自身も今月知らされた」という流れになっている。つまり、異動通知がいきなりのことだったために、本来連絡すべきであったタイミングを逸して急な連絡になってしまったと伝えていることがわかる。よって、正解はこの急な連絡を short notice と表した **(C)**。

✎ □apologize for 〜を謝罪する　□short notice 急な知らせ　□regret *doing* 〜したことを後悔する

79. ★★★★★

What does the speaker offer to do for the listener?

(A) Get someone to contact him
(B) Put the apartment up for sale
(C) Offer contact information
(D) Pay a penalty charge

話し手は聞き手に何をすることを申し出ていますか。

(A) ある人から連絡をさせる。
(B) 部屋を売りに出す。
(C) 連絡先を提供する。
(D) 違約金を支払う。

🔍 ❺で話し手は聞き手に「自分の異動後に契約を引き継ぎたい人がいるので、連絡させるようにできる」と述べている。ここから、話し手の知り合いから聞き手に連絡させることを申し出ているとわかる。以上から正解は **(A)**。

✎ □put A up for sale A を売りに出す　□penalty charge 違約金

	1回目	2回目	3回目
77.			
78.			
79.			

🚩 **77. (D)　78. (C)　79. (A)**

Questions 80 through 82 refer to the following announcement.

M: ❶Last year, we couldn't hold it due to budgeting issues. ❷However, this year I'm pleased to announce that the Dynamix Conference will return. Advertising professionals from all over the country will gather and talk about the future of the industry. As always, our very own Tom Knightley will be giving a keynote speech, but we'll also have Nick Waltham from the BES Consulting Agency. ❸I strongly encourage you to attend all the sessions if you can, ❹but please be aware that seating is limited and it's first come, first served. That's why you really need to book your tickets, which will have a staff discount, soon.

問題80-82は次のお知らせに関するものです。

M: 昨年は予算の問題で開催がかないませんでした。しかし、今年は Dynamix 協議会の再開をお知らせできることを大変うれしく思います。全国から広告の専門家が集まり、業界の将来について話します。いつものように、我らが Tom Knightley さんが基調講演を行うだけでなく、BES Consulting Agency の Nick Waltham さんも参加されます。可能であれば全ての会に参加されることを強くお勧めします。ただし、座席には限りがあり、先着順となっておりますことをご承知おきください。そのような理由で、スタッフ割引があるチケットをすみやかに予約する必要があります。

☐due to ～が原因で　☐budgeting issue 予算の問題
☐be pleased to announce that 喜んで～をお知らせする　☐professional 専門家、プロ　☐all over the country 全国
☐gather 集まる　☐as always いつものように　☐one's very own ～専用の、～の　☐keynote speech 基調講演
☐strongly encourage ～を強く推奨する　☐be aware that ～に留意する　☐first come, first served 先着順で
☐book ～を予約する

---

80. ★★★☆☆

What is the purpose of the announcement?

(A) To invite advertising professionals to make a speech
(B) To confirm a list of conference participants
(C) To announce an event is being held this year
(D) To ask listeners for suggestions for speech topics

お知らせの目的は何ですか。

(A) 広告の専門家を招いてスピーチをしてもらう。
(B) 協議会参加者の名簿を確認する。
(C) 今年はイベントが開催されることを知らせる。
(D) 聞き手にスピーチの主題を提案してもらう。

会話冒頭❶・❷で「昨年は予算の問題で開催できなかったが、今年は協議会を再開する」と述べている。つまり、あるイベントを今年開催すると知らせていることがわかる。以上から正解は **(C)**。

☐confirm ～を確認する　☐participant 参加者　☐suggestion 提案

81. ★★★☆☆

What does the speaker ask the listeners to do?

(A) Attend the whole conference
(B) Pay fees in advance
(C) Participate in a preliminary meeting
(D) Help set up the venue

話し手は聞き手に何をするように求めていますか。

(A) 協議会に全て参加する。
(B) 前もって料金を支払う。
(C) 事前会議に参加する。
(D) 会場の設営を手伝う。

🔍 話し手は聞き手に対して、❸で「全ての会への参加を強く勧める」と述べている。ここから、協議会全体への参加を求めていることがわかる。以上から正解は **(A)**。

✏️ □whole 全体の　□fee 手数料　□in advance 事前に　□participate in ～に参加する
□preliminary 事前の、準備のための　□set up ～を設営する　□venue 開催地

......

82. ★★★★☆

What is mentioned about the conference?

(A) Attendance is mandatory.
(B) It has been delayed.
(C) It is free for staff members.
(D) Seats are assigned in order of registration.

協議会について何と言っていますか。

(A) 出席は必須である。
(B) 延期された。
(C) スタッフは無料である。
(D) 座席は登録順に埋まっていく。

🔍 話し手は❹で「座席には限りがあり、先着順」と述べている。以上から、正解はこの先着順 (first come, first served) を登録順 (in order of registration) と言い換えた **(D)**。

✏️ □mandatory 必須の、義務的な　□assign ～を割り当てる

	1回目	2回目	3回目
80.			
81.			
82.			

🚩 **80. (C)　81. (A)　82. (D)**

Questions 83 through 85 refer to the following broadcast.

M: ❶This is Ricky Myers with the KNCA evening forecast. Today, we all enjoyed sunny skies and warm weather. However, tomorrow will be a different story. A cold front is moving into the area overnight with temperatures reaching only 10 degrees Celsius in the morning. ❷With an 80% chance of heavy rain in the afternoon, traffic will be moving slowly, so allow extra time to make it home. And please use caution when driving in the wet. This report is sponsored by Herman Discount Supplies. ❸Stay tuned for today's baseball scores, right after this advertisement.

📝 問題83-85は次の放送に関するものです。

M: Ricky Myers が KNCA の夜の天気予報をお送りします。今日は晴天と暖かな陽気で気持ちよく過ごせました。しかし、明日はがらりと変わります。寒冷前線が夜のうちにこの地域に移動し、午前中の最高気温は摂氏10度にしかなりません。午後は80パーセントの確率で激しい雨が降るため、車の流れは遅くなるでしょう。ですので、帰宅にかかる時間は多めに見ておいてください。また雨天の運転にはお気を付けください。この予報は Herman Discount Supplies の提供でお送りしています。今日の野球のスコアはそのままのチャンネルで、コマーシャルのすぐ後です。

✏️ ☐forecast (天気) 予報　☐be a different story ～は事情が変わる　☐cold front 寒冷前線　☐overnight 夜通し
☐temperature 温度　☐reach ～に達する　☐degrees Celsius ～℃ (摂氏～度)　☐% chance of ～%の確率の
☐allow extra time to *do* 余分な時間を見て～する　☐use caution 注意する　☐sponsor ～の番組を提供する
☐stay tuned チャンネルをそのままにしておく

---

83. ★★☆☆☆

What is the purpose of the broadcast?

(A) To provide local business news
(B) To report weather conditions
(C) To offer financial advice
(D) To inform people of a store opening

放送の目的は何ですか。

(A) 地元のビジネスニュースを伝えること。
(B) 気象状況を報告すること。
(C) 金融に関する助言をすること。
(D) 店の開店を周知すること。

🔍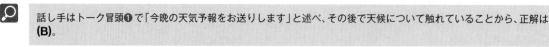

話し手はトーク冒頭❶で「今晩の天気予報をお送りします」と述べ、その後で天候について触れていることから、正解は**(B)**。

✏️ ☐weather condition 気象状況　☐financial advice 金融に関する助言

84. ★★★☆☆

What does the announcer suggest the listeners do tomorrow?

(A) Expect extra commuting time
(B) Use public transportation
(C) Check their vehicle before a journey
(D) Change house loan providers

アナウンサーは明日、聞き手に何をするように提案していますか。

(A) 通勤時間が余計にかかることを見込む。
(B) 公共交通機関を使う。
(C) 出かける前に車両を点検する。
(D) 住宅ローン会社を変える。

🔍 話し手は❷で「午後は雨で車の流れが遅くなることが予想されるので、帰宅時間は余裕を持って見ておくように」と述べている。ここから、通常以上に通勤時間がかかることを考慮するように促していることがわかる。以上から正解は **(A)**。

✎ □expect ～を見込む　□extra 余分な　□commuting time 通勤時間　□public transportation 公共交通機関
□house loan provider 住宅金融貸付会社

---

85. ★★☆☆☆

What will listeners hear soon?

(A) Political news
(B) An economic report
(C) Sports scores
(D) New music

聞き手は次に何を聞きますか。

(A) 政治報道
(B) 経済に関する報告
(C) スポーツのスコア
(D) 新曲

🔍 話し手は❸で「野球のスコアをコマーシャル後に」と述べている。以上から正解は **(C)**。厳密に言うと、天気予報の後はコマーシャルだが、選択肢にはないので、その次である (C) が正解となる。

✎ □political 政治に関する

P A R T 4

TEST 8

	1回目	2回目	3回目
83.			
84.			
85.			

🚩 **83. (B)　84. (A)　85. (C)**

Questions 86 through 88 refer to the following announcement.

M: ❶Attention, passengers for Unify Air 347 to Chicago. ❷This flight was scheduled to leave at 10:35 A.M., but has been postponed because of heavy snowstorms. ❸The new departure time is scheduled for 11:50 A.M. Boarding will commence thirty minutes earlier than the new departure time. ❹All passengers must go to the gate for their new boarding card. We ask that passengers stay inside the gate area. Passengers with premium class tickets and families with small children will board first. We apologize for the inconvenience.

M: Unify 航空347便 Chicago 行きにご搭乗の皆さまにお知らせです。当便は午前10時35分の出発を予定しておりましたが、吹雪のため延期となっております。新しい出発時刻は午前11時50分を予定しております。ご搭乗は新しい出発時刻の30分前に開始いたします。ご搭乗の皆さまは、新しい搭乗券を受け取るために搭乗口にお越しください。ご出発のお客様は搭乗エリアの中でお待ちください。プレミアムクラスチケットをお持ちのお客様と小さなお子様をお連れのご家族からご搭乗いただきます。ご不便をおかけして申し訳ありません。

□be scheduled to *do* ～する予定である □postpone ～を延期する □snowstorm 吹雪 □boarding 搭乗
□commence 開始する □premium プレミアムの、高級の
□apologize for the inconvenience 不便をかけて申し訳ない

---

86. ⭐☆☆☆☆

Where is this announcement being heard?

(A) At a bus terminal
(B) At a subway station
(C) At a harbor
(D) At an airport

アナウンスはどこで流れていますか。

(A) バスターミナル
(B) 地下鉄の駅
(C) 港
(D) 空港

話し手は❶で乗客に話しかけ、その後❷で「フライトが遅れている」と述べている。ここから、アナウンスされている場所は空港であるとわかる。以上から正解は **(D)**。

□harbor 港、波止場

87. ★★★☆☆

When can passengers start boarding?

(A) At 10:35 A.M.
(B) At 11:20 A.M.
(C) At 11:50 A.M.
(D) At 12:50 P.M.

乗客はいつ搭乗を開始しますか。

(A) 午前10時35分
(B) 午前11時20分
(C) 午前11時50分
(D) 午後12時50分

 話し手は❸で「新しい出発時刻は午前11時50分を予定しており、搭乗は出発時刻の30分前に開始」と述べている。よって、午前11時50分の30分前の午前11時20分が搭乗開始時刻だとわかる。以上から正解は **(B)**。出発時刻と搭乗時刻を勘違いしないようにしよう。

---

88. ★☆☆☆☆

What does the speaker ask passengers to do?

(A) Board according to seat number
(B) Prepare their identification for display
(C) Place large bags under the seats
(D) Go to the gate area

話し手は乗客に何をするように頼んでいますか。

(A) 座席番号の順に搭乗する。
(B) 身分証明書提示の準備をする。
(C) 大きなバッグを座席の下に置く。
(D) 搭乗エリアに行く。

 話し手は❹で「搭乗の皆さまは新しい搭乗券を受け取るために搭乗口へ」とお願いしている。ここから搭乗エリアに向かってほしい、と頼んでいることがわかる。以上から正解は **(D)**。

✎ □board 搭乗する　□according to ～に沿って　□seat number 座席番号　□identification 身分証明書

	1回目	2回目	3回目
86.			
87.			
88.			

 86. (D)　87. (B)　88. (D)

Questions 89 through 91 refer to the following talk.

📝 問題89-91は次の話に関するものです。

W: Good morning, and welcome to this annual business workshop. Before we start, I'd like to introduce myself to those I haven't met yet. I'm Jenna Dustin. I've worked as a chief executive at some major domestic companies. ❶It's my second year teaching here. This course will teach you the importance of rethinking how you do business to benefit the wider society and environment. ❷My goal is to provide the tools you need to understand social and environmental issues that arise while you are running your business. It is important to keep these issues in mind while growing your company in whatever industry you are in. ❸Now, before we start watching a video, I'd like to hear from you. ❹Please tell me your name, where you're from, and what you think social and environmental responsibility means.

W: おはようございます。年次ビジネス講習会にお越しいただきありがとうございます。始める前に、まだお会いしたことのない方々に自己紹介をしたいと思います。私の名前はJenna Dustin です。国内の大手企業数社で重役を務めました。ここで教えるのは2年目です。このコースではより広い社会と環境に貢献する仕事をどうするか考えることの重要性についてお伝えします。私が目指すのは、企業を経営する際に発生する社会及び環境の問題を理解するために必要な道具を提供することです。どの業種にいるにしても、事業を成長させるに当たって、これらの問題を気に留めておくことは重要です。さて、ビデオを視聴する前にみなさんに伺いたいと思います。お名前、ご所属、そして社会や環境に対する責任をどう考えているかお聞かせください。

✏️ □annual 年次の　□introduce oneself to ～に自己紹介する　□work as ～として働く　□domestic 国内の
□importance 重要性　□rethink ～を再考する　□benefit ～に利益をもたらす、貢献する　□society 社会
□environment 環境　□arise 発生する　□run ～を経営する　□responsibility 責任

---

89. ★★★★☆

What does the speaker say about herself?

(A) She has taught a class before.
(B) She is a specialist in workshop planning.
(C) She did not attend college.
(D) She works for an international company.

話し手について何と言っていますか。

(A) 以前講義をしたことがある。
(B) 講習会を企画する専門家である。
(C) 大学に行かなかった。
(D) 国際的な企業で働いている。

🔍 話し手は冒頭で研修参加者に挨拶し、❶で「ここで教えるのは2年目だ」と述べている。ここから、話し手が以前もここで教えた経験があることがわかる。以上から正解は **(A)**。3問付きの最初の問題にしては珍しく、キーワードが会話の中盤近くにあるという変則的な問題のため、しっかり聞き取ろう。

✏️ □specialist in ～の専門家

90. ★★★★★

What is the purpose of the speaker's class?

(A) To explain how to beat competitors
(B) To teach how to start up a business
(C) To give tips on reaching management level
(D) To give insight into certain business issues

話し手が担当するクラスの目的は何ですか。

(A) 競争相手を打ち負かす方法を説明すること。
(B) 起業する方法を教えること。
(C) 管理職になる秘訣を提供すること。
(D) ビジネスの問題に対する洞察を与えること。

話し手は❷で自分の目的について、「企業経営で発生する問題を理解するために必要な道具を提供することだ」と述べている。企業を経営する際の課題を把握する方法とは、ビジネス上の問題を見つけること、すなわち洞察力を持つことだとわかる。以上から、正解は❷の provide the tools ... to understand ... issues を give insight into ... issues と言い換えた **(D)**。

□beat 〜に打ち勝つ　□competitor 競争相手、競合他社　□start up a business 起業する　□tip 秘訣
□insight 洞察

---

91. ★★★★☆

What are the listeners invited to do next?

(A) Take notes on a presentation
(B) Introduce themselves
(C) Watch a video
(D) Raise some questions

聞き手は次に何をするように促されていますか。

(A) プレゼンテーションのメモを取る。
(B) 自己紹介をする。
(C) 動画を見る。
(D) 質問をする。

話し手は❸・❹で「名前や所属等を伺いたい」と述べていることから、聞き手である参加者に自己紹介を求めていることがわかる。以上から正解は **(B)**。(C) は動画を見る前に自己紹介してもらうと述べているため、ここでは順番の違いとして不正解。

□take note on 〜のメモを取る　□raise a question 質問をする

	1回目	2回目	3回目
89.			
90.			
91.			

 89. (A)　90. (D)　91. (B)

Questions 92 through 94 refer to the following talk.

M: Good afternoon. ❶Welcome back to this special workshop on making effective presentations to clients. I think the morning session on how to keep your speech short and interesting went well. ❷Now, another important point to consider is that some people tend to speak too fast or too slow. ❸I recommend that you practice your speech several times before you make your sales pitch. I advise you to time yourself. To start this session, ❹I'm going to play some videos showing how the speed of a presenter's speech impacts communication.

✏️ ☐welcome back to ~へ再びようこそ　☐effective 効果的な　☐go well うまくいく　☐sales pitch 営業トーク
☐impact ~に影響を与える

問題92-94は次の話に関するものです。

M: こんばんは。顧客に対して効果的なプレゼンテーションを行う特別講習会にまたお集りいただきありがとうございます。午前の、スピーチを短く、面白く保つ方法に関する講義はうまくいったと思います。では、もう一つの重要な論点はある人は話すのが早すぎたり、あるいは遅すぎたりするということです。セールストークの前に何度か話す練習をすることをお勧めします。時間を計ると良いでしょう。この講義を始めるにあたり、今から発表者の話す速度がコミュニケーションにどう影響を与えるかについて説明するビデオを流します。

---

92. ★★☆☆☆

What is the subject of the workshop?

(A) Advertising strategies
(B) Changing jobs
(C) Safety procedures
(D) Business presentations

講習会のテーマは何ですか。

(A) 広告戦略
(B) 転職
(C) 安全のための手順
(D) ビジネスプレゼンテーション

🔍 話し手は冒頭❶で「顧客へ効果的なプレゼンを行う講習会」と述べている。ここから、ビジネス上のプレゼンテーションがテーマであることがわかる。以上から正解は **(D)**。

✏️ ☐strategy 戦略　☐change jobs 転職する　☐procedure 手順

93. ★★★★☆

What does the speaker recommend?

(A) Becoming aware of one's speaking speed
(B) Being very polite to clients
(C) Arriving early to a sales appointment
(D) Checking business trends online

話し手は何を勧めていますか。

(A) 自身の話すスピードを自覚すること。
(B) 顧客に対して礼儀正しくふるまうこと。
(C) 商談の約束には早めに到着すること。
(D) ビジネスの動向をインターネットで調べること。

 話し手は❷で「重要な論点はある人は話すのが早すぎたり、あるいは遅すぎたりすることだ」と述べ、そして❸で「セールストークの前に何度か話す練習をする」ことを勧めている。ここから、話すスピードについて意識して練習することを勧めているとわかる。以上から正解は **(A)**。

□become aware of ~に気づく　□polite to ~に対して礼儀正しい　□trend 傾向、動向

---

94. ★★☆☆☆

What will the listeners probably do next?

(A) Work in small groups
(B) Watch videos
(C) Provide feedback on the seminar
(D) Eat together

聞き手はおそらく次に何をしますか。

(A) グループに分かれて作業する。
(B) 動画を見る。
(C) 講習についての感想を寄せる。
(D) 一緒に食事をする。

 話し手が❹で「今からビデオを流す」と述べているので、これから聞き手はビデオを視聴することがわかる。以上から正解は **(B)**。

□provide feedback 感想を述べる

	1回目	2回目	3回目
92.			
93.			
94.			

92. (D)　93. (A)　94. (B)

Questions 95 through 97 refer to the following telephone message and map.

W: Hello, this is Tracy Warren calling. ❶I talked to you earlier regarding the prices for your moving service. ❷I've talked things over with my husband and we'd like to use two of your moving trucks with drivers and additional helpers. As I mentioned before, our current address is 17 Ladmac Avenue, and we'll be moving to an apartment in the Orchid Hill neighborhood. Please come here at 9 A.M. on Sunday. ❸I will move my two cars beforehand, so there'll be plenty of room out front for the trucks. Getting here is easy. ❹Just come over the bridge across the Tilden River. ❺Keep going straight along that road and take the second right. ❻Go through the first crossroads, and you'll see my apartment building on your left. Let me know if you have any problems finding my place.

📝 問題95-97は次の電話のメッセージと地図に関するものです。

W: こんにちは、Tracy Warren です。引っ越し作業の費用について先ほどお話しした者です。夫と話をした結果、引っ越しトラック2台と運転手の方と、追加の手伝いの方をお願いしたいと思います。お伝えしたとおり、現在の住所は17 Ladmac 大通りで、Orchid Hill 地区のアパートに引っ越します。日曜日の午前9時にこちらに来てください。2台の車をあらかじめ動かしておくので、建物の前にトラックを停めるスペースが十分あると思います。こちらに来るのは簡単です。Tilden 川にかかる橋を渡ります。そのまま真っすぐ進んで、2つ目で右に曲がります。1つ目の交差点を通り過ぎると、左手に私のアパートが見えます。私の場所を探すのが大変なときはご連絡ください。

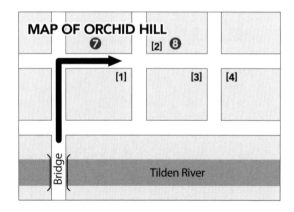

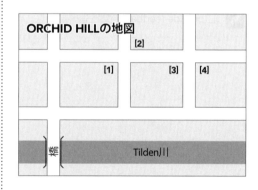

✏️ □regarding 〜について □moving truck 引っ越し用トラック □additional 追加の
□as I mentioned before 以前話したとおり □neighborhood 近隣、地区 □beforehand 事前に
□plenty of room 十分なスペース □go straight along 〜に沿って真っすぐ進む □apartment building アパート

95.

What is the main purpose of the call?

(A) To request a service
(B) To provide some advice
(C) To ask about a property
(D) To confirm a delivery

電話の主な目的は何ですか。

(A) 作業を依頼する。
(B) 助言を与える。
(C) 物件について尋ねる。
(D) 配達を確認する。

🔍 話し手は❶で「引っ越し作業の価格について」と切り出し、❷でお願いしたい引っ越しトラックの数とスタッフの人数といった具体的な作業準備の情報を伝えている。以上から正解は **(A)**。

✎ □confirm 〜を確認する

96.

What does the speaker say she will do?

(A) Put some items outside her home
(B) Lend the listener her vehicle
(C) Give a tour of an apartment
(D) Ensure parking space is available

話し手は何をすると言っていますか。

(A) 家の外に商品を置く。
(B) 聞き手に車を貸す。
(C) アパートを案内する。
(D) 駐車スペースが利用できることを保証する。

🔍 話し手は❸で「車をあらかじめ動かしておくので、トラックを停めるスペースが十分ある」と述べている。ここから、引っ越しトラックの駐停車スペースを確保していることがわかる。以上から、正解はこのスペースを parking space と言い換えた **(D)**。❸の plenty of room の room は「部屋」ではなく「余裕、スペース」を意味することを押さえておこう。

✎ □lend 〜を貸す　□give a tour 見学案内をする　□ensure 〜を保証する、確実にする

97.

Look at the graphic. In which location is the speaker's residence located?

(A) [1]
(B) [2]
(C) [3]
(D) [4]

図を見てください。話し手の住居はどこに位置していますか。

(A) [1]
(B) [2]
(C) [3]
(D) [4]

🔍 話し手は❹・❺・❻で地図上のどこに自宅があるか伝えている。まず、❹橋を渡って Tilgen 川を越え、❺2つ目の角（❼）を右に曲がり、❻そこから1つ目の交差点を過ぎた左手（❽）の [2] に話し手の自宅があることがわかる。以上から正解は **(B)**。この問題は、地図を見ながら複数の情報をたどる必要があるので、見失ってしまった場合は、しっかり復習して理解しておこう。

	1回目	2回目	3回目
95.			
96.			
97.			

 95. (A)　96. (D)　97. (B)

Questions 98 through 100 refer to the following advertisement and schedule.

M: ❶Have you purchased your tickets for this year's Oceanview Arts and Crafts Festival on August 25th? This unique community festival is held every year on Zimmer Boulevard. There are a variety of activities for both adults and kids to try, such as face painting, tie-dyeing, drawing competitions, and jewelry making. What's more, ❷the chart-topping singer-songwriter Celeste Gilbert will be giving a concert outside the Trenta Bank building. ❸Finally, after the concert one lucky ticket holder will be chosen at random to receive a five-night vacation package for two to Cooper Beach Resort in South Hamton.

M: 8月25日に開催される今年の Oceanview 工芸祭のチケットはもう購入しましたか。このユニークなコミュニティ・イベントは毎年 Zimmer 大通りで開催されています。フェイスペインティングや絞り染め、お絵描き大会、宝石作りなど、大人もお子様も挑戦できるアクティビティがたくさんあります。さらに、ヒットチャートで一番のシンガーソングライター、Celeste Gilbert さんが Trenta 銀行ビルの外でコンサートを行います。最後に、コンサートの後は当たりチケットを持っている方が発表され、South Hamton の Cooper Beach Resort への5泊休暇パッケージ旅行2名様分が贈られます。

Event Schedule	
Event	Time
Opening Ceremony	12:00 P.M.
Street Activities	1:00 P.M.
❹Celeste Gilbert	3:00 P.M.
❺Closing Ceremony	4:00 P.M.

イベント予定表	
イベント	時間
開会式	午後12時
ストリートアクティビティ	午後1時
Celeste Gilbert	午後3時
閉会式	午後4時

✏️ □arts and crafts 工芸　□unique 独特な　□a variety of さまざまな
□face painting フェイスペインティング (顔に色を塗って絵や模様を描くこと)　□tie-dyeing 絞り染め
□drawing お絵描き　□competition 大会、競争　□jewelry making 宝石作り　□what's more さらに
□chart-topping チャートのトップにいる　□singer-songwriter シンガーソングライター
□at random ランダムに、無作為に　□-night ～泊の　□vacation package 休暇用パッケージ旅行
□opening ceremony 開会式　□closing ceremony 閉会式

98.

What is the theme of the event?

(A) Arts and crafts
(B) Cooking
(C) Community singing
(D) Keeping healthy

何がテーマのイベントが開催されますか。

(A) 工芸
(B) 料理
(C) 合唱
(D) 健康維持

🔍 トーク冒頭❶で「今年の工芸祭」に言及している。以上から正解は **(A)**。

✎ □keeping healthy 健康維持

99.

According to the speaker, who will be present at the event?

(A) A movie star
(B) A professional sports player
(C) A children's book writer
(D) A famous musician

話し手によると、誰がイベントに出演しますか。

(A) 映画スター
(B) プロスポーツ選手
(C) 児童書の作家
(D) 有名な音楽家

🔍 話し手はトーク❷で「ヒットチャート1位のシンガーソングライターである Celeste Gilbert さんがコンサートを行う」と述べている。ここから、イベントに出演するのはヒットチャートで上位になるくらいの有名な歌手であることがわかる。以上から正解は **(D)**。

100.

Look at the graphic. Around what time will the prize winner be announced?

(A) 12:00 P.M.
(B) 1:00 P.M.
(C) 3:00 P.M.
(D) 4:00 P.M.

表を見てください。当せん者が発表されるのは何時ごろですか。

(A) 午後12時
(B) 午後1時
(C) 午後3時
(D) 午後4時

🔍 話し手は❸で「コンサート後に当せん者が発表される」と述べている。イベント表を見ると、❹が有名歌手の Celeste Gilbert さんのコンサートの時間帯であるため、コンサート後である❺の午後4時ごろに発表が行われることがわかる。以上から正解は **(D)**。

	1回目	2回目	3回目
98.			
99.			
100.			

🚩 **98. (A) 99. (D) 100. (D)**

PART 3 Answer

TEST 1

Part 3

No.	A	B	C	D	No.	A	B	C	D	No.	A	B	C	D	No.	A	B	C	D
32	Ⓐ	Ⓑ	Ⓒ	Ⓓ	41	Ⓐ	Ⓑ	Ⓒ	Ⓓ	51	Ⓐ	Ⓑ	Ⓒ	Ⓓ	61	Ⓐ	Ⓑ	Ⓒ	Ⓓ
33	Ⓐ	Ⓑ	Ⓒ	Ⓓ	42	Ⓐ	Ⓑ	Ⓒ	Ⓓ	52	Ⓐ	Ⓑ	Ⓒ	Ⓓ	62	Ⓐ	Ⓑ	Ⓒ	Ⓓ
34	Ⓐ	Ⓑ	Ⓒ	Ⓓ	43	Ⓐ	Ⓑ	Ⓒ	Ⓓ	53	Ⓐ	Ⓑ	Ⓒ	Ⓓ	63	Ⓐ	Ⓑ	Ⓒ	Ⓓ
35	Ⓐ	Ⓑ	Ⓒ	Ⓓ	44	Ⓐ	Ⓑ	Ⓒ	Ⓓ	54	Ⓐ	Ⓑ	Ⓒ	Ⓓ	64	Ⓐ	Ⓑ	Ⓒ	Ⓓ
36	Ⓐ	Ⓑ	Ⓒ	Ⓓ	45	Ⓐ	Ⓑ	Ⓒ	Ⓓ	55	Ⓐ	Ⓑ	Ⓒ	Ⓓ	65	Ⓐ	Ⓑ	Ⓒ	Ⓓ
37	Ⓐ	Ⓑ	Ⓒ	Ⓓ	46	Ⓐ	Ⓑ	Ⓒ	Ⓓ	56	Ⓐ	Ⓑ	Ⓒ	Ⓓ	66	Ⓐ	Ⓑ	Ⓒ	Ⓓ
38	Ⓐ	Ⓑ	Ⓒ	Ⓓ	47	Ⓐ	Ⓑ	Ⓒ	Ⓓ	57	Ⓐ	Ⓑ	Ⓒ	Ⓓ	67	Ⓐ	Ⓑ	Ⓒ	Ⓓ
39	Ⓐ	Ⓑ	Ⓒ	Ⓓ	48	Ⓐ	Ⓑ	Ⓒ	Ⓓ	58	Ⓐ	Ⓑ	Ⓒ	Ⓓ	68	Ⓐ	Ⓑ	Ⓒ	Ⓓ
40	Ⓐ	Ⓑ	Ⓒ	Ⓓ	49	Ⓐ	Ⓑ	Ⓒ	Ⓓ	59	Ⓐ	Ⓑ	Ⓒ	Ⓓ	69	Ⓐ	Ⓑ	Ⓒ	Ⓓ
					50	Ⓐ	Ⓑ	Ⓒ	Ⓓ	60	Ⓐ	Ⓑ	Ⓒ	Ⓓ	70	Ⓐ	Ⓑ	Ⓒ	Ⓓ

TEST 2

Part 3

No.	A	B	C	D	No.	A	B	C	D	No.	A	B	C	D	No.	A	B	C	D
32	Ⓐ	Ⓑ	Ⓒ	Ⓓ	41	Ⓐ	Ⓑ	Ⓒ	Ⓓ	51	Ⓐ	Ⓑ	Ⓒ	Ⓓ	61	Ⓐ	Ⓑ	Ⓒ	Ⓓ
33	Ⓐ	Ⓑ	Ⓒ	Ⓓ	42	Ⓐ	Ⓑ	Ⓒ	Ⓓ	52	Ⓐ	Ⓑ	Ⓒ	Ⓓ	62	Ⓐ	Ⓑ	Ⓒ	Ⓓ
34	Ⓐ	Ⓑ	Ⓒ	Ⓓ	43	Ⓐ	Ⓑ	Ⓒ	Ⓓ	53	Ⓐ	Ⓑ	Ⓒ	Ⓓ	63	Ⓐ	Ⓑ	Ⓒ	Ⓓ
35	Ⓐ	Ⓑ	Ⓒ	Ⓓ	44	Ⓐ	Ⓑ	Ⓒ	Ⓓ	54	Ⓐ	Ⓑ	Ⓒ	Ⓓ	64	Ⓐ	Ⓑ	Ⓒ	Ⓓ
36	Ⓐ	Ⓑ	Ⓒ	Ⓓ	45	Ⓐ	Ⓑ	Ⓒ	Ⓓ	55	Ⓐ	Ⓑ	Ⓒ	Ⓓ	65	Ⓐ	Ⓑ	Ⓒ	Ⓓ
37	Ⓐ	Ⓑ	Ⓒ	Ⓓ	46	Ⓐ	Ⓑ	Ⓒ	Ⓓ	56	Ⓐ	Ⓑ	Ⓒ	Ⓓ	66	Ⓐ	Ⓑ	Ⓒ	Ⓓ
38	Ⓐ	Ⓑ	Ⓒ	Ⓓ	47	Ⓐ	Ⓑ	Ⓒ	Ⓓ	57	Ⓐ	Ⓑ	Ⓒ	Ⓓ	67	Ⓐ	Ⓑ	Ⓒ	Ⓓ
39	Ⓐ	Ⓑ	Ⓒ	Ⓓ	48	Ⓐ	Ⓑ	Ⓒ	Ⓓ	58	Ⓐ	Ⓑ	Ⓒ	Ⓓ	68	Ⓐ	Ⓑ	Ⓒ	Ⓓ
40	Ⓐ	Ⓑ	Ⓒ	Ⓓ	49	Ⓐ	Ⓑ	Ⓒ	Ⓓ	59	Ⓐ	Ⓑ	Ⓒ	Ⓓ	69	Ⓐ	Ⓑ	Ⓒ	Ⓓ
					50	Ⓐ	Ⓑ	Ⓒ	Ⓓ	60	Ⓐ	Ⓑ	Ⓒ	Ⓓ	70	Ⓐ	Ⓑ	Ⓒ	Ⓓ

TEST 3

Part 3

No.	A	B	C	D	No.	A	B	C	D	No.	A	B	C	D	No.	A	B	C	D
32	Ⓐ	Ⓑ	Ⓒ	Ⓓ	41	Ⓐ	Ⓑ	Ⓒ	Ⓓ	51	Ⓐ	Ⓑ	Ⓒ	Ⓓ	61	Ⓐ	Ⓑ	Ⓒ	Ⓓ
33	Ⓐ	Ⓑ	Ⓒ	Ⓓ	42	Ⓐ	Ⓑ	Ⓒ	Ⓓ	52	Ⓐ	Ⓑ	Ⓒ	Ⓓ	62	Ⓐ	Ⓑ	Ⓒ	Ⓓ
34	Ⓐ	Ⓑ	Ⓒ	Ⓓ	43	Ⓐ	Ⓑ	Ⓒ	Ⓓ	53	Ⓐ	Ⓑ	Ⓒ	Ⓓ	63	Ⓐ	Ⓑ	Ⓒ	Ⓓ
35	Ⓐ	Ⓑ	Ⓒ	Ⓓ	44	Ⓐ	Ⓑ	Ⓒ	Ⓓ	54	Ⓐ	Ⓑ	Ⓒ	Ⓓ	64	Ⓐ	Ⓑ	Ⓒ	Ⓓ
36	Ⓐ	Ⓑ	Ⓒ	Ⓓ	45	Ⓐ	Ⓑ	Ⓒ	Ⓓ	55	Ⓐ	Ⓑ	Ⓒ	Ⓓ	65	Ⓐ	Ⓑ	Ⓒ	Ⓓ
37	Ⓐ	Ⓑ	Ⓒ	Ⓓ	46	Ⓐ	Ⓑ	Ⓒ	Ⓓ	56	Ⓐ	Ⓑ	Ⓒ	Ⓓ	66	Ⓐ	Ⓑ	Ⓒ	Ⓓ
38	Ⓐ	Ⓑ	Ⓒ	Ⓓ	47	Ⓐ	Ⓑ	Ⓒ	Ⓓ	57	Ⓐ	Ⓑ	Ⓒ	Ⓓ	67	Ⓐ	Ⓑ	Ⓒ	Ⓓ
39	Ⓐ	Ⓑ	Ⓒ	Ⓓ	48	Ⓐ	Ⓑ	Ⓒ	Ⓓ	58	Ⓐ	Ⓑ	Ⓒ	Ⓓ	68	Ⓐ	Ⓑ	Ⓒ	Ⓓ
40	Ⓐ	Ⓑ	Ⓒ	Ⓓ	49	Ⓐ	Ⓑ	Ⓒ	Ⓓ	59	Ⓐ	Ⓑ	Ⓒ	Ⓓ	69	Ⓐ	Ⓑ	Ⓒ	Ⓓ
					50	Ⓐ	Ⓑ	Ⓒ	Ⓓ	60	Ⓐ	Ⓑ	Ⓒ	Ⓓ	70	Ⓐ	Ⓑ	Ⓒ	Ⓓ

TEST 4

Part 3

No.	A	B	C	D	No.	A	B	C	D	No.	A	B	C	D	No.	A	B	C	D
32	Ⓐ	Ⓑ	Ⓒ	Ⓓ	41	Ⓐ	Ⓑ	Ⓒ	Ⓓ	51	Ⓐ	Ⓑ	Ⓒ	Ⓓ	61	Ⓐ	Ⓑ	Ⓒ	Ⓓ
33	Ⓐ	Ⓑ	Ⓒ	Ⓓ	42	Ⓐ	Ⓑ	Ⓒ	Ⓓ	52	Ⓐ	Ⓑ	Ⓒ	Ⓓ	62	Ⓐ	Ⓑ	Ⓒ	Ⓓ
34	Ⓐ	Ⓑ	Ⓒ	Ⓓ	43	Ⓐ	Ⓑ	Ⓒ	Ⓓ	53	Ⓐ	Ⓑ	Ⓒ	Ⓓ	63	Ⓐ	Ⓑ	Ⓒ	Ⓓ
35	Ⓐ	Ⓑ	Ⓒ	Ⓓ	44	Ⓐ	Ⓑ	Ⓒ	Ⓓ	54	Ⓐ	Ⓑ	Ⓒ	Ⓓ	64	Ⓐ	Ⓑ	Ⓒ	Ⓓ
36	Ⓐ	Ⓑ	Ⓒ	Ⓓ	45	Ⓐ	Ⓑ	Ⓒ	Ⓓ	55	Ⓐ	Ⓑ	Ⓒ	Ⓓ	65	Ⓐ	Ⓑ	Ⓒ	Ⓓ
37	Ⓐ	Ⓑ	Ⓒ	Ⓓ	46	Ⓐ	Ⓑ	Ⓒ	Ⓓ	56	Ⓐ	Ⓑ	Ⓒ	Ⓓ	66	Ⓐ	Ⓑ	Ⓒ	Ⓓ
38	Ⓐ	Ⓑ	Ⓒ	Ⓓ	47	Ⓐ	Ⓑ	Ⓒ	Ⓓ	57	Ⓐ	Ⓑ	Ⓒ	Ⓓ	67	Ⓐ	Ⓑ	Ⓒ	Ⓓ
39	Ⓐ	Ⓑ	Ⓒ	Ⓓ	48	Ⓐ	Ⓑ	Ⓒ	Ⓓ	58	Ⓐ	Ⓑ	Ⓒ	Ⓓ	68	Ⓐ	Ⓑ	Ⓒ	Ⓓ
40	Ⓐ	Ⓑ	Ⓒ	Ⓓ	49	Ⓐ	Ⓑ	Ⓒ	Ⓓ	59	Ⓐ	Ⓑ	Ⓒ	Ⓓ	69	Ⓐ	Ⓑ	Ⓒ	Ⓓ
					50	Ⓐ	Ⓑ	Ⓒ	Ⓓ	60	Ⓐ	Ⓑ	Ⓒ	Ⓓ	70	Ⓐ	Ⓑ	Ⓒ	Ⓓ

PART 3 Answer

TEST 5 — Part 3

TEST 6 — Part 3

TEST 7 — Part 3

TEST 8 — Part 3

PART 4 Answer

TEST 1

Part 4

No.	A	B	C	D	No.	A	B	C	D	No.	A	B	C	D
71			●		81				●	91				●
72			●		82				●	92			●	
73	●				83	●				93				●
74				●	84	●				94				●
75	●				85	●				95	●			
76	●				86			●		96			●	
77			●		87			●		97				●
78	●				88	●				98				●
79	●				89				●	99				●
80	●				90				●	100				●

TEST 2

Part 4

No.	A	B	C	D	No.	A	B	C	D	No.	A	B	C	D
71		●			81	●				91	●			
72				●	82	●				92				●
73			●		83			●		93			●	
74			●		84				●	94				●
75	●				85			●		95	●			
76				●	86				●	96				●
77	●				87	●				97				●
78	●				88	●				98				●
79				●	89			●		99	●			
80				●	90			●		100				●

TEST 3

Part 4

No.	A	B	C	D	No.	A	B	C	D	No.	A	B	C	D
71	●				81				●	91				●
72		●			82				●	92			●	
73	●				83			●		93				●
74	●				84				●	94	●			
75	●				85	●				95			●	
76		●			86				●	96				●
77	●				87			●		97				●
78	●				88		●			98				●
79	●				89	●				99				●
80	●				90				●	100			●	

TEST 4

Part 4

No.	A	B	C	D	No.	A	B	C	D	No.	A	B	C	D
71	●				81	●				91	●			
72	●				82		●			92				●
73				●	83				●	93			●	
74				●	84			●		94	●			
75	●				85				●	95		●		
76	●				86		●			96				●
77	●				87				●	97		●		
78	●				88				●	98			●	
79	●				89			●		99	●			
80	●				90			●		100				●

PART 4 Answer

TEST 5

Part 4

No.	ANSWER A B C D	No.	ANSWER A B C D	No.	ANSWER A B C D
71		81		91	
72		82		92	
73		83		93	
74		84		94	
75		85		95	
76		86		96	
77		87		97	
78		88		98	
79		89		99	
80		90		100	

TEST 6

Part 4

No.	ANSWER A B C D	No.	ANSWER A B C D	No.	ANSWER A B C D
71		81		91	
72		82		92	
73		83		93	
74		84		94	
75		85		95	
76		86		96	
77		87		97	
78		88		98	
79		89		99	
80		90		100	

TEST 7

Part 4

No.	ANSWER A B C D	No.	ANSWER A B C D	No.	ANSWER A B C D
71		81		91	
72		82		92	
73		83		93	
74		84		94	
75		85		95	
76		86		96	
77		87		97	
78		88		98	
79		89		99	
80		90		100	

TEST 8

Part 4

No.	ANSWER A B C D	No.	ANSWER A B C D	No.	ANSWER A B C D
71		81		91	
72		82		92	
73		83		93	
74		84		94	
75		85		95	
76		86		96	
77		87		97	
78		88		98	
79		89		99	
80		90		100	

著者紹介

大里秀介　Shusuke Osato

TOEIC L&Rテスト990点、TOEIC S&Wテスト ライティング200点満点取得の経験を持つ現役サラリーマン。2006年から英語学習を開始して、2007年スコア730点を突破、社内選考でイギリス留学を経験する。2012年からカナダに駐在勤務し、北米間の大ビジネスプロジェクトをTOEICで磨いた英語力を駆使して成功に導く。著書に『3週間で攻略 TOEIC L&Rテスト900点！』（アルク）、『TOEIC テスト新形式完全攻略模試』（学研プラス）、『TOEIC L&Rテスト壁越えトレーニングPart 7』『TOEIC L&Rテスト 壁越え模試 リーディング』（旺文社）、『極めろ！ TOEIC L&R TEST 990点 リーディング特訓』（スリーエーネットワーク）などがある。

装幀・本文デザイン	斉藤啓（ブッダプロダクションズ）
制作協力	Testing Contents Service、CPI Japan
図版制作	有限会社 ギルド
翻訳協力	河野伸治
音源制作	株式会社 巧芸創作
ナレーション	Jack Merluzzi ／ Kyle Card ／ Marcus Pittman ／ Rumiko Varnes／ Sorcha Chisholm

解きまくれ！ リスニングドリル TOEIC® L&R TEST PART 3&4

2023年3月13日　初版第1刷発行

著　者	大里秀介
発 行 者	藤嵜政子
発 行 所	株式会社　スリーエーネットワーク
	〒102-0083 東京都千代田区麹町3丁目4番 トラスティ麹町ビル2F
	電話：03-5275-2722［営業］　03-5275-2726［編集］
	https://www.3anet.co.jp/
印刷・製本	萩原印刷株式会社

Answer Sheet

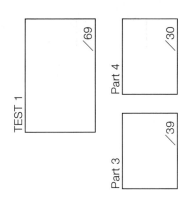

TEST 1

Part 3 /39

Part 4 /30

TEST 2

Part 3 /39

Part 4 /30

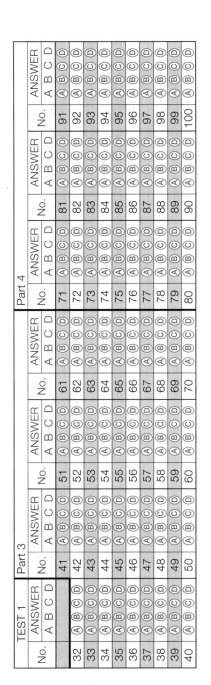

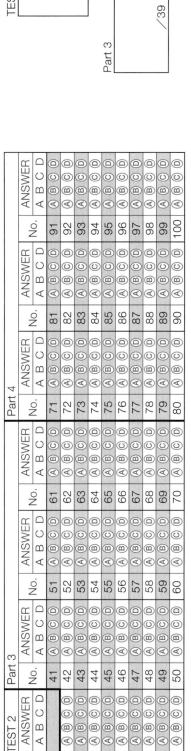

Answer Sheet

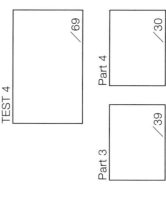

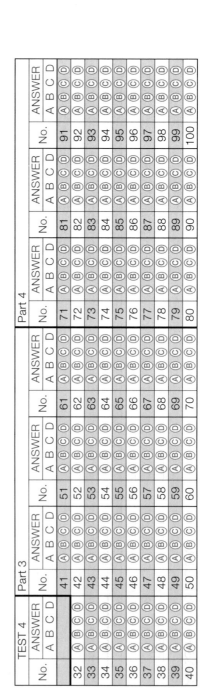

Answer Sheet

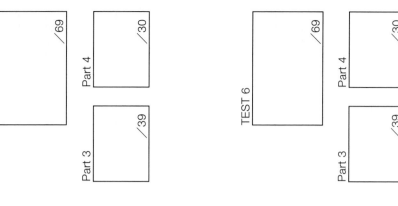

TEST 5

Part 3

No.	ANSWER A B C D	No.	ANSWER A B C D	No.	ANSWER A B C D
32	Ⓐ Ⓑ Ⓒ Ⓓ	41	Ⓐ Ⓑ Ⓒ Ⓓ	51	Ⓐ Ⓑ Ⓒ Ⓓ
33	Ⓐ Ⓑ Ⓒ Ⓓ	42	Ⓐ Ⓑ Ⓒ Ⓓ	52	Ⓐ Ⓑ Ⓒ Ⓓ
34	Ⓐ Ⓑ Ⓒ Ⓓ	43	Ⓐ Ⓑ Ⓒ Ⓓ	53	Ⓐ Ⓑ Ⓒ Ⓓ
35	Ⓐ Ⓑ Ⓒ Ⓓ	44	Ⓐ Ⓑ Ⓒ Ⓓ	54	Ⓐ Ⓑ Ⓒ Ⓓ
36	Ⓐ Ⓑ Ⓒ Ⓓ	45	Ⓐ Ⓑ Ⓒ Ⓓ	55	Ⓐ Ⓑ Ⓒ Ⓓ
37	Ⓐ Ⓑ Ⓒ Ⓓ	46	Ⓐ Ⓑ Ⓒ Ⓓ	56	Ⓐ Ⓑ Ⓒ Ⓓ
38	Ⓐ Ⓑ Ⓒ Ⓓ	47	Ⓐ Ⓑ Ⓒ Ⓓ	57	Ⓐ Ⓑ Ⓒ Ⓓ
39	Ⓐ Ⓑ Ⓒ Ⓓ	48	Ⓐ Ⓑ Ⓒ Ⓓ	58	Ⓐ Ⓑ Ⓒ Ⓓ
40	Ⓐ Ⓑ Ⓒ Ⓓ	49	Ⓐ Ⓑ Ⓒ Ⓓ	59	Ⓐ Ⓑ Ⓒ Ⓓ
		50	Ⓐ Ⓑ Ⓒ Ⓓ	60	Ⓐ Ⓑ Ⓒ Ⓓ

Part 4

No.	ANSWER A B C D	No.	ANSWER A B C D	No.	ANSWER A B C D	No.	ANSWER A B C D
61	Ⓐ Ⓑ Ⓒ Ⓓ	71	Ⓐ Ⓑ Ⓒ Ⓓ	81	Ⓐ Ⓑ Ⓒ Ⓓ	91	Ⓐ Ⓑ Ⓒ Ⓓ
62	Ⓐ Ⓑ Ⓒ Ⓓ	72	Ⓐ Ⓑ Ⓒ Ⓓ	82	Ⓐ Ⓑ Ⓒ Ⓓ	92	Ⓐ Ⓑ Ⓒ Ⓓ
63	Ⓐ Ⓑ Ⓒ Ⓓ	73	Ⓐ Ⓑ Ⓒ Ⓓ	83	Ⓐ Ⓑ Ⓒ Ⓓ	93	Ⓐ Ⓑ Ⓒ Ⓓ
64	Ⓐ Ⓑ Ⓒ Ⓓ	74	Ⓐ Ⓑ Ⓒ Ⓓ	84	Ⓐ Ⓑ Ⓒ Ⓓ	94	Ⓐ Ⓑ Ⓒ Ⓓ
65	Ⓐ Ⓑ Ⓒ Ⓓ	75	Ⓐ Ⓑ Ⓒ Ⓓ	85	Ⓐ Ⓑ Ⓒ Ⓓ	95	Ⓐ Ⓑ Ⓒ Ⓓ
66	Ⓐ Ⓑ Ⓒ Ⓓ	76	Ⓐ Ⓑ Ⓒ Ⓓ	86	Ⓐ Ⓑ Ⓒ Ⓓ	96	Ⓐ Ⓑ Ⓒ Ⓓ
67	Ⓐ Ⓑ Ⓒ Ⓓ	77	Ⓐ Ⓑ Ⓒ Ⓓ	87	Ⓐ Ⓑ Ⓒ Ⓓ	97	Ⓐ Ⓑ Ⓒ Ⓓ
68	Ⓐ Ⓑ Ⓒ Ⓓ	78	Ⓐ Ⓑ Ⓒ Ⓓ	88	Ⓐ Ⓑ Ⓒ Ⓓ	98	Ⓐ Ⓑ Ⓒ Ⓓ
69	Ⓐ Ⓑ Ⓒ Ⓓ	79	Ⓐ Ⓑ Ⓒ Ⓓ	89	Ⓐ Ⓑ Ⓒ Ⓓ	99	Ⓐ Ⓑ Ⓒ Ⓓ
70	Ⓐ Ⓑ Ⓒ Ⓓ	80	Ⓐ Ⓑ Ⓒ Ⓓ	90	Ⓐ Ⓑ Ⓒ Ⓓ	100	Ⓐ Ⓑ Ⓒ Ⓓ

TEST 6

Part 3

No.	ANSWER A B C D	No.	ANSWER A B C D	No.	ANSWER A B C D
32	Ⓐ Ⓑ Ⓒ Ⓓ	41	Ⓐ Ⓑ Ⓒ Ⓓ	51	Ⓐ Ⓑ Ⓒ Ⓓ
33	Ⓐ Ⓑ Ⓒ Ⓓ	42	Ⓐ Ⓑ Ⓒ Ⓓ	52	Ⓐ Ⓑ Ⓒ Ⓓ
34	Ⓐ Ⓑ Ⓒ Ⓓ	43	Ⓐ Ⓑ Ⓒ Ⓓ	53	Ⓐ Ⓑ Ⓒ Ⓓ
35	Ⓐ Ⓑ Ⓒ Ⓓ	44	Ⓐ Ⓑ Ⓒ Ⓓ	54	Ⓐ Ⓑ Ⓒ Ⓓ
36	Ⓐ Ⓑ Ⓒ Ⓓ	45	Ⓐ Ⓑ Ⓒ Ⓓ	55	Ⓐ Ⓑ Ⓒ Ⓓ
37	Ⓐ Ⓑ Ⓒ Ⓓ	46	Ⓐ Ⓑ Ⓒ Ⓓ	56	Ⓐ Ⓑ Ⓒ Ⓓ
38	Ⓐ Ⓑ Ⓒ Ⓓ	47	Ⓐ Ⓑ Ⓒ Ⓓ	57	Ⓐ Ⓑ Ⓒ Ⓓ
39	Ⓐ Ⓑ Ⓒ Ⓓ	48	Ⓐ Ⓑ Ⓒ Ⓓ	58	Ⓐ Ⓑ Ⓒ Ⓓ
40	Ⓐ Ⓑ Ⓒ Ⓓ	49	Ⓐ Ⓑ Ⓒ Ⓓ	59	Ⓐ Ⓑ Ⓒ Ⓓ
		50	Ⓐ Ⓑ Ⓒ Ⓓ	60	Ⓐ Ⓑ Ⓒ Ⓓ

Part 4

No.	ANSWER A B C D	No.	ANSWER A B C D	No.	ANSWER A B C D	No.	ANSWER A B C D
61	Ⓐ Ⓑ Ⓒ Ⓓ	71	Ⓐ Ⓑ Ⓒ Ⓓ	81	Ⓐ Ⓑ Ⓒ Ⓓ	91	Ⓐ Ⓑ Ⓒ Ⓓ
62	Ⓐ Ⓑ Ⓒ Ⓓ	72	Ⓐ Ⓑ Ⓒ Ⓓ	82	Ⓐ Ⓑ Ⓒ Ⓓ	92	Ⓐ Ⓑ Ⓒ Ⓓ
63	Ⓐ Ⓑ Ⓒ Ⓓ	73	Ⓐ Ⓑ Ⓒ Ⓓ	83	Ⓐ Ⓑ Ⓒ Ⓓ	93	Ⓐ Ⓑ Ⓒ Ⓓ
64	Ⓐ Ⓑ Ⓒ Ⓓ	74	Ⓐ Ⓑ Ⓒ Ⓓ	84	Ⓐ Ⓑ Ⓒ Ⓓ	94	Ⓐ Ⓑ Ⓒ Ⓓ
65	Ⓐ Ⓑ Ⓒ Ⓓ	75	Ⓐ Ⓑ Ⓒ Ⓓ	85	Ⓐ Ⓑ Ⓒ Ⓓ	95	Ⓐ Ⓑ Ⓒ Ⓓ
66	Ⓐ Ⓑ Ⓒ Ⓓ	76	Ⓐ Ⓑ Ⓒ Ⓓ	86	Ⓐ Ⓑ Ⓒ Ⓓ	96	Ⓐ Ⓑ Ⓒ Ⓓ
67	Ⓐ Ⓑ Ⓒ Ⓓ	77	Ⓐ Ⓑ Ⓒ Ⓓ	87	Ⓐ Ⓑ Ⓒ Ⓓ	97	Ⓐ Ⓑ Ⓒ Ⓓ
68	Ⓐ Ⓑ Ⓒ Ⓓ	78	Ⓐ Ⓑ Ⓒ Ⓓ	88	Ⓐ Ⓑ Ⓒ Ⓓ	98	Ⓐ Ⓑ Ⓒ Ⓓ
69	Ⓐ Ⓑ Ⓒ Ⓓ	79	Ⓐ Ⓑ Ⓒ Ⓓ	89	Ⓐ Ⓑ Ⓒ Ⓓ	99	Ⓐ Ⓑ Ⓒ Ⓓ
70	Ⓐ Ⓑ Ⓒ Ⓓ	80	Ⓐ Ⓑ Ⓒ Ⓓ	90	Ⓐ Ⓑ Ⓒ Ⓓ	100	Ⓐ Ⓑ Ⓒ Ⓓ

Answer Sheet

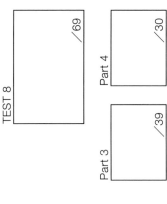

TEST 7

Part 3 /39

Part 4 /30

/69

TEST 8

Part 3 /39

Part 4 /30

/69

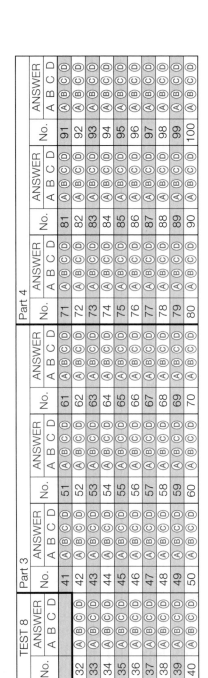

TEST 7

Part 3

No.	ANSWER	No.	ANSWER	No.	ANSWER	No.	ANSWER
	A B C D		A B C D		A B C D		A B C D
32	Ⓐ Ⓑ Ⓒ Ⓓ	41	Ⓐ Ⓑ Ⓒ Ⓓ	51	Ⓐ Ⓑ Ⓒ Ⓓ	61	Ⓐ Ⓑ Ⓒ Ⓓ
33	Ⓐ Ⓑ Ⓒ Ⓓ	42	Ⓐ Ⓑ Ⓒ Ⓓ	52	Ⓐ Ⓑ Ⓒ Ⓓ	62	Ⓐ Ⓑ Ⓒ Ⓓ
34	Ⓐ Ⓑ Ⓒ Ⓓ	43	Ⓐ Ⓑ Ⓒ Ⓓ	53	Ⓐ Ⓑ Ⓒ Ⓓ	63	Ⓐ Ⓑ Ⓒ Ⓓ
35	Ⓐ Ⓑ Ⓒ Ⓓ	44	Ⓐ Ⓑ Ⓒ Ⓓ	54	Ⓐ Ⓑ Ⓒ Ⓓ	64	Ⓐ Ⓑ Ⓒ Ⓓ
36	Ⓐ Ⓑ Ⓒ Ⓓ	45	Ⓐ Ⓑ Ⓒ Ⓓ	55	Ⓐ Ⓑ Ⓒ Ⓓ	65	Ⓐ Ⓑ Ⓒ Ⓓ
37	Ⓐ Ⓑ Ⓒ Ⓓ	46	Ⓐ Ⓑ Ⓒ Ⓓ	56	Ⓐ Ⓑ Ⓒ Ⓓ	66	Ⓐ Ⓑ Ⓒ Ⓓ
38	Ⓐ Ⓑ Ⓒ Ⓓ	47	Ⓐ Ⓑ Ⓒ Ⓓ	57	Ⓐ Ⓑ Ⓒ Ⓓ	67	Ⓐ Ⓑ Ⓒ Ⓓ
39	Ⓐ Ⓑ Ⓒ Ⓓ	48	Ⓐ Ⓑ Ⓒ Ⓓ	58	Ⓐ Ⓑ Ⓒ Ⓓ	68	Ⓐ Ⓑ Ⓒ Ⓓ
40	Ⓐ Ⓑ Ⓒ Ⓓ	49	Ⓐ Ⓑ Ⓒ Ⓓ	59	Ⓐ Ⓑ Ⓒ Ⓓ	69	Ⓐ Ⓑ Ⓒ Ⓓ
		50	Ⓐ Ⓑ Ⓒ Ⓓ	60	Ⓐ Ⓑ Ⓒ Ⓓ	70	Ⓐ Ⓑ Ⓒ Ⓓ

Part 4

No.	ANSWER	No.	ANSWER	No.	ANSWER
	A B C D		A B C D		A B C D
71	Ⓐ Ⓑ Ⓒ Ⓓ	81	Ⓐ Ⓑ Ⓒ Ⓓ	91	Ⓐ Ⓑ Ⓒ Ⓓ
72	Ⓐ Ⓑ Ⓒ Ⓓ	82	Ⓐ Ⓑ Ⓒ Ⓓ	92	Ⓐ Ⓑ Ⓒ Ⓓ
73	Ⓐ Ⓑ Ⓒ Ⓓ	83	Ⓐ Ⓑ Ⓒ Ⓓ	93	Ⓐ Ⓑ Ⓒ Ⓓ
74	Ⓐ Ⓑ Ⓒ Ⓓ	84	Ⓐ Ⓑ Ⓒ Ⓓ	94	Ⓐ Ⓑ Ⓒ Ⓓ
75	Ⓐ Ⓑ Ⓒ Ⓓ	85	Ⓐ Ⓑ Ⓒ Ⓓ	95	Ⓐ Ⓑ Ⓒ Ⓓ
76	Ⓐ Ⓑ Ⓒ Ⓓ	86	Ⓐ Ⓑ Ⓒ Ⓓ	96	Ⓐ Ⓑ Ⓒ Ⓓ
77	Ⓐ Ⓑ Ⓒ Ⓓ	87	Ⓐ Ⓑ Ⓒ Ⓓ	97	Ⓐ Ⓑ Ⓒ Ⓓ
78	Ⓐ Ⓑ Ⓒ Ⓓ	88	Ⓐ Ⓑ Ⓒ Ⓓ	98	Ⓐ Ⓑ Ⓒ Ⓓ
79	Ⓐ Ⓑ Ⓒ Ⓓ	89	Ⓐ Ⓑ Ⓒ Ⓓ	99	Ⓐ Ⓑ Ⓒ Ⓓ
80	Ⓐ Ⓑ Ⓒ Ⓓ	90	Ⓐ Ⓑ Ⓒ Ⓓ	100	Ⓐ Ⓑ Ⓒ Ⓓ

TEST 8

Part 3

No.	ANSWER	No.	ANSWER	No.	ANSWER	No.	ANSWER
	A B C D		A B C D		A B C D		A B C D
32	Ⓐ Ⓑ Ⓒ Ⓓ	41	Ⓐ Ⓑ Ⓒ Ⓓ	51	Ⓐ Ⓑ Ⓒ Ⓓ	61	Ⓐ Ⓑ Ⓒ Ⓓ
33	Ⓐ Ⓑ Ⓒ Ⓓ	42	Ⓐ Ⓑ Ⓒ Ⓓ	52	Ⓐ Ⓑ Ⓒ Ⓓ	62	Ⓐ Ⓑ Ⓒ Ⓓ
34	Ⓐ Ⓑ Ⓒ Ⓓ	43	Ⓐ Ⓑ Ⓒ Ⓓ	53	Ⓐ Ⓑ Ⓒ Ⓓ	63	Ⓐ Ⓑ Ⓒ Ⓓ
35	Ⓐ Ⓑ Ⓒ Ⓓ	44	Ⓐ Ⓑ Ⓒ Ⓓ	54	Ⓐ Ⓑ Ⓒ Ⓓ	64	Ⓐ Ⓑ Ⓒ Ⓓ
36	Ⓐ Ⓑ Ⓒ Ⓓ	45	Ⓐ Ⓑ Ⓒ Ⓓ	55	Ⓐ Ⓑ Ⓒ Ⓓ	65	Ⓐ Ⓑ Ⓒ Ⓓ
37	Ⓐ Ⓑ Ⓒ Ⓓ	46	Ⓐ Ⓑ Ⓒ Ⓓ	56	Ⓐ Ⓑ Ⓒ Ⓓ	66	Ⓐ Ⓑ Ⓒ Ⓓ
38	Ⓐ Ⓑ Ⓒ Ⓓ	47	Ⓐ Ⓑ Ⓒ Ⓓ	57	Ⓐ Ⓑ Ⓒ Ⓓ	67	Ⓐ Ⓑ Ⓒ Ⓓ
39	Ⓐ Ⓑ Ⓒ Ⓓ	48	Ⓐ Ⓑ Ⓒ Ⓓ	58	Ⓐ Ⓑ Ⓒ Ⓓ	68	Ⓐ Ⓑ Ⓒ Ⓓ
40	Ⓐ Ⓑ Ⓒ Ⓓ	49	Ⓐ Ⓑ Ⓒ Ⓓ	59	Ⓐ Ⓑ Ⓒ Ⓓ	69	Ⓐ Ⓑ Ⓒ Ⓓ
		50	Ⓐ Ⓑ Ⓒ Ⓓ	60	Ⓐ Ⓑ Ⓒ Ⓓ	70	Ⓐ Ⓑ Ⓒ Ⓓ

Part 4

No.	ANSWER	No.	ANSWER	No.	ANSWER
	A B C D		A B C D		A B C D
71	Ⓐ Ⓑ Ⓒ Ⓓ	81	Ⓐ Ⓑ Ⓒ Ⓓ	91	Ⓐ Ⓑ Ⓒ Ⓓ
72	Ⓐ Ⓑ Ⓒ Ⓓ	82	Ⓐ Ⓑ Ⓒ Ⓓ	92	Ⓐ Ⓑ Ⓒ Ⓓ
73	Ⓐ Ⓑ Ⓒ Ⓓ	83	Ⓐ Ⓑ Ⓒ Ⓓ	93	Ⓐ Ⓑ Ⓒ Ⓓ
74	Ⓐ Ⓑ Ⓒ Ⓓ	84	Ⓐ Ⓑ Ⓒ Ⓓ	94	Ⓐ Ⓑ Ⓒ Ⓓ
75	Ⓐ Ⓑ Ⓒ Ⓓ	85	Ⓐ Ⓑ Ⓒ Ⓓ	95	Ⓐ Ⓑ Ⓒ Ⓓ
76	Ⓐ Ⓑ Ⓒ Ⓓ	86	Ⓐ Ⓑ Ⓒ Ⓓ	96	Ⓐ Ⓑ Ⓒ Ⓓ
77	Ⓐ Ⓑ Ⓒ Ⓓ	87	Ⓐ Ⓑ Ⓒ Ⓓ	97	Ⓐ Ⓑ Ⓒ Ⓓ
78	Ⓐ Ⓑ Ⓒ Ⓓ	88	Ⓐ Ⓑ Ⓒ Ⓓ	98	Ⓐ Ⓑ Ⓒ Ⓓ
79	Ⓐ Ⓑ Ⓒ Ⓓ	89	Ⓐ Ⓑ Ⓒ Ⓓ	99	Ⓐ Ⓑ Ⓒ Ⓓ
80	Ⓐ Ⓑ Ⓒ Ⓓ	90	Ⓐ Ⓑ Ⓒ Ⓓ	100	Ⓐ Ⓑ Ⓒ Ⓓ

Answer Sheet

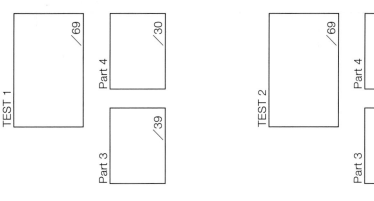

TEST 1

Part 3 /39
Part 4 /30
/69

TEST 2

Part 3 /39
Part 4 /30
/69

TEST 1

No.	ANSWER A B C D	No.	ANSWER A B C D	No.	ANSWER A B C D	No.	ANSWER A B C D	No.	ANSWER A B C D
32	Ⓐ Ⓑ Ⓒ Ⓓ	41	Ⓐ Ⓑ Ⓒ Ⓓ	51	Ⓐ Ⓑ Ⓒ Ⓓ	61	Ⓐ Ⓑ Ⓒ Ⓓ	71	Ⓐ Ⓑ Ⓒ Ⓓ
33	Ⓐ Ⓑ Ⓒ Ⓓ	42	Ⓐ Ⓑ Ⓒ Ⓓ	52	Ⓐ Ⓑ Ⓒ Ⓓ	62	Ⓐ Ⓑ Ⓒ Ⓓ	72	Ⓐ Ⓑ Ⓒ Ⓓ
34	Ⓐ Ⓑ Ⓒ Ⓓ	43	Ⓐ Ⓑ Ⓒ Ⓓ	53	Ⓐ Ⓑ Ⓒ Ⓓ	63	Ⓐ Ⓑ Ⓒ Ⓓ	73	Ⓐ Ⓑ Ⓒ Ⓓ
35	Ⓐ Ⓑ Ⓒ Ⓓ	44	Ⓐ Ⓑ Ⓒ Ⓓ	54	Ⓐ Ⓑ Ⓒ Ⓓ	64	Ⓐ Ⓑ Ⓒ Ⓓ	74	Ⓐ Ⓑ Ⓒ Ⓓ
36	Ⓐ Ⓑ Ⓒ Ⓓ	45	Ⓐ Ⓑ Ⓒ Ⓓ	55	Ⓐ Ⓑ Ⓒ Ⓓ	65	Ⓐ Ⓑ Ⓒ Ⓓ	75	Ⓐ Ⓑ Ⓒ Ⓓ
37	Ⓐ Ⓑ Ⓒ Ⓓ	46	Ⓐ Ⓑ Ⓒ Ⓓ	56	Ⓐ Ⓑ Ⓒ Ⓓ	66	Ⓐ Ⓑ Ⓒ Ⓓ	76	Ⓐ Ⓑ Ⓒ Ⓓ
38	Ⓐ Ⓑ Ⓒ Ⓓ	47	Ⓐ Ⓑ Ⓒ Ⓓ	57	Ⓐ Ⓑ Ⓒ Ⓓ	67	Ⓐ Ⓑ Ⓒ Ⓓ	77	Ⓐ Ⓑ Ⓒ Ⓓ
39	Ⓐ Ⓑ Ⓒ Ⓓ	48	Ⓐ Ⓑ Ⓒ Ⓓ	58	Ⓐ Ⓑ Ⓒ Ⓓ	68	Ⓐ Ⓑ Ⓒ Ⓓ	78	Ⓐ Ⓑ Ⓒ Ⓓ
40	Ⓐ Ⓑ Ⓒ Ⓓ	49	Ⓐ Ⓑ Ⓒ Ⓓ	59	Ⓐ Ⓑ Ⓒ Ⓓ	69	Ⓐ Ⓑ Ⓒ Ⓓ	79	Ⓐ Ⓑ Ⓒ Ⓓ
		50	Ⓐ Ⓑ Ⓒ Ⓓ	60	Ⓐ Ⓑ Ⓒ Ⓓ	70	Ⓐ Ⓑ Ⓒ Ⓓ	80	Ⓐ Ⓑ Ⓒ Ⓓ

Part 3 (No. 41–) Part 4 (No. 71–)

No.	ANSWER A B C D	No.	ANSWER A B C D
81	Ⓐ Ⓑ Ⓒ Ⓓ	91	Ⓐ Ⓑ Ⓒ Ⓓ
82	Ⓐ Ⓑ Ⓒ Ⓓ	92	Ⓐ Ⓑ Ⓒ Ⓓ
83	Ⓐ Ⓑ Ⓒ Ⓓ	93	Ⓐ Ⓑ Ⓒ Ⓓ
84	Ⓐ Ⓑ Ⓒ Ⓓ	94	Ⓐ Ⓑ Ⓒ Ⓓ
85	Ⓐ Ⓑ Ⓒ Ⓓ	95	Ⓐ Ⓑ Ⓒ Ⓓ
86	Ⓐ Ⓑ Ⓒ Ⓓ	96	Ⓐ Ⓑ Ⓒ Ⓓ
87	Ⓐ Ⓑ Ⓒ Ⓓ	97	Ⓐ Ⓑ Ⓒ Ⓓ
88	Ⓐ Ⓑ Ⓒ Ⓓ	98	Ⓐ Ⓑ Ⓒ Ⓓ
89	Ⓐ Ⓑ Ⓒ Ⓓ	99	Ⓐ Ⓑ Ⓒ Ⓓ
90	Ⓐ Ⓑ Ⓒ Ⓓ	100	Ⓐ Ⓑ Ⓒ Ⓓ

TEST 2

No.	ANSWER A B C D	No.	ANSWER A B C D	No.	ANSWER A B C D	No.	ANSWER A B C D	No.	ANSWER A B C D
32	Ⓐ Ⓑ Ⓒ Ⓓ	41	Ⓐ Ⓑ Ⓒ Ⓓ	51	Ⓐ Ⓑ Ⓒ Ⓓ	61	Ⓐ Ⓑ Ⓒ Ⓓ	71	Ⓐ Ⓑ Ⓒ Ⓓ
33	Ⓐ Ⓑ Ⓒ Ⓓ	42	Ⓐ Ⓑ Ⓒ Ⓓ	52	Ⓐ Ⓑ Ⓒ Ⓓ	62	Ⓐ Ⓑ Ⓒ Ⓓ	72	Ⓐ Ⓑ Ⓒ Ⓓ
34	Ⓐ Ⓑ Ⓒ Ⓓ	43	Ⓐ Ⓑ Ⓒ Ⓓ	53	Ⓐ Ⓑ Ⓒ Ⓓ	63	Ⓐ Ⓑ Ⓒ Ⓓ	73	Ⓐ Ⓑ Ⓒ Ⓓ
35	Ⓐ Ⓑ Ⓒ Ⓓ	44	Ⓐ Ⓑ Ⓒ Ⓓ	54	Ⓐ Ⓑ Ⓒ Ⓓ	64	Ⓐ Ⓑ Ⓒ Ⓓ	74	Ⓐ Ⓑ Ⓒ Ⓓ
36	Ⓐ Ⓑ Ⓒ Ⓓ	45	Ⓐ Ⓑ Ⓒ Ⓓ	55	Ⓐ Ⓑ Ⓒ Ⓓ	65	Ⓐ Ⓑ Ⓒ Ⓓ	75	Ⓐ Ⓑ Ⓒ Ⓓ
37	Ⓐ Ⓑ Ⓒ Ⓓ	46	Ⓐ Ⓑ Ⓒ Ⓓ	56	Ⓐ Ⓑ Ⓒ Ⓓ	66	Ⓐ Ⓑ Ⓒ Ⓓ	76	Ⓐ Ⓑ Ⓒ Ⓓ
38	Ⓐ Ⓑ Ⓒ Ⓓ	47	Ⓐ Ⓑ Ⓒ Ⓓ	57	Ⓐ Ⓑ Ⓒ Ⓓ	67	Ⓐ Ⓑ Ⓒ Ⓓ	77	Ⓐ Ⓑ Ⓒ Ⓓ
39	Ⓐ Ⓑ Ⓒ Ⓓ	48	Ⓐ Ⓑ Ⓒ Ⓓ	58	Ⓐ Ⓑ Ⓒ Ⓓ	68	Ⓐ Ⓑ Ⓒ Ⓓ	78	Ⓐ Ⓑ Ⓒ Ⓓ
40	Ⓐ Ⓑ Ⓒ Ⓓ	49	Ⓐ Ⓑ Ⓒ Ⓓ	59	Ⓐ Ⓑ Ⓒ Ⓓ	69	Ⓐ Ⓑ Ⓒ Ⓓ	79	Ⓐ Ⓑ Ⓒ Ⓓ
		50	Ⓐ Ⓑ Ⓒ Ⓓ	60	Ⓐ Ⓑ Ⓒ Ⓓ	70	Ⓐ Ⓑ Ⓒ Ⓓ	80	Ⓐ Ⓑ Ⓒ Ⓓ

Part 3 (No. 41–) Part 4 (No. 71–)

No.	ANSWER A B C D	No.	ANSWER A B C D
81	Ⓐ Ⓑ Ⓒ Ⓓ	91	Ⓐ Ⓑ Ⓒ Ⓓ
82	Ⓐ Ⓑ Ⓒ Ⓓ	92	Ⓐ Ⓑ Ⓒ Ⓓ
83	Ⓐ Ⓑ Ⓒ Ⓓ	93	Ⓐ Ⓑ Ⓒ Ⓓ
84	Ⓐ Ⓑ Ⓒ Ⓓ	94	Ⓐ Ⓑ Ⓒ Ⓓ
85	Ⓐ Ⓑ Ⓒ Ⓓ	95	Ⓐ Ⓑ Ⓒ Ⓓ
86	Ⓐ Ⓑ Ⓒ Ⓓ	96	Ⓐ Ⓑ Ⓒ Ⓓ
87	Ⓐ Ⓑ Ⓒ Ⓓ	97	Ⓐ Ⓑ Ⓒ Ⓓ
88	Ⓐ Ⓑ Ⓒ Ⓓ	98	Ⓐ Ⓑ Ⓒ Ⓓ
89	Ⓐ Ⓑ Ⓒ Ⓓ	99	Ⓐ Ⓑ Ⓒ Ⓓ
90	Ⓐ Ⓑ Ⓒ Ⓓ	100	Ⓐ Ⓑ Ⓒ Ⓓ

Answer Sheet

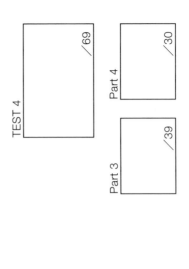

TEST 3

Part 3 /39

Part 4 /30

/69

TEST 4

Part 3 /39

Part 4 /30

/69

TEST 3

Part 3

No.	ANSWER A B C D	No.	ANSWER A B C D	No.	ANSWER A B C D
32	Ⓐ Ⓑ Ⓒ Ⓓ	41	Ⓐ Ⓑ Ⓒ Ⓓ	51	Ⓐ Ⓑ Ⓒ Ⓓ
33	Ⓐ Ⓑ Ⓒ Ⓓ	42	Ⓐ Ⓑ Ⓒ Ⓓ	52	Ⓐ Ⓑ Ⓒ Ⓓ
34	Ⓐ Ⓑ Ⓒ Ⓓ	43	Ⓐ Ⓑ Ⓒ Ⓓ	53	Ⓐ Ⓑ Ⓒ Ⓓ
35	Ⓐ Ⓑ Ⓒ Ⓓ	44	Ⓐ Ⓑ Ⓒ Ⓓ	54	Ⓐ Ⓑ Ⓒ Ⓓ
36	Ⓐ Ⓑ Ⓒ Ⓓ	45	Ⓐ Ⓑ Ⓒ Ⓓ	55	Ⓐ Ⓑ Ⓒ Ⓓ
37	Ⓐ Ⓑ Ⓒ Ⓓ	46	Ⓐ Ⓑ Ⓒ Ⓓ	56	Ⓐ Ⓑ Ⓒ Ⓓ
38	Ⓐ Ⓑ Ⓒ Ⓓ	47	Ⓐ Ⓑ Ⓒ Ⓓ	57	Ⓐ Ⓑ Ⓒ Ⓓ
39	Ⓐ Ⓑ Ⓒ Ⓓ	48	Ⓐ Ⓑ Ⓒ Ⓓ	58	Ⓐ Ⓑ Ⓒ Ⓓ
40	Ⓐ Ⓑ Ⓒ Ⓓ	49	Ⓐ Ⓑ Ⓒ Ⓓ	59	Ⓐ Ⓑ Ⓒ Ⓓ
		50	Ⓐ Ⓑ Ⓒ Ⓓ	60	Ⓐ Ⓑ Ⓒ Ⓓ

Part 4

No.	ANSWER A B C D	No.	ANSWER A B C D	No.	ANSWER A B C D
61	Ⓐ Ⓑ Ⓒ Ⓓ	71	Ⓐ Ⓑ Ⓒ Ⓓ	81	Ⓐ Ⓑ Ⓒ Ⓓ
62	Ⓐ Ⓑ Ⓒ Ⓓ	72	Ⓐ Ⓑ Ⓒ Ⓓ	82	Ⓐ Ⓑ Ⓒ Ⓓ
63	Ⓐ Ⓑ Ⓒ Ⓓ	73	Ⓐ Ⓑ Ⓒ Ⓓ	83	Ⓐ Ⓑ Ⓒ Ⓓ
64	Ⓐ Ⓑ Ⓒ Ⓓ	74	Ⓐ Ⓑ Ⓒ Ⓓ	84	Ⓐ Ⓑ Ⓒ Ⓓ
65	Ⓐ Ⓑ Ⓒ Ⓓ	75	Ⓐ Ⓑ Ⓒ Ⓓ	85	Ⓐ Ⓑ Ⓒ Ⓓ
66	Ⓐ Ⓑ Ⓒ Ⓓ	76	Ⓐ Ⓑ Ⓒ Ⓓ	86	Ⓐ Ⓑ Ⓒ Ⓓ
67	Ⓐ Ⓑ Ⓒ Ⓓ	77	Ⓐ Ⓑ Ⓒ Ⓓ	87	Ⓐ Ⓑ Ⓒ Ⓓ
68	Ⓐ Ⓑ Ⓒ Ⓓ	78	Ⓐ Ⓑ Ⓒ Ⓓ	88	Ⓐ Ⓑ Ⓒ Ⓓ
69	Ⓐ Ⓑ Ⓒ Ⓓ	79	Ⓐ Ⓑ Ⓒ Ⓓ	89	Ⓐ Ⓑ Ⓒ Ⓓ
70	Ⓐ Ⓑ Ⓒ Ⓓ	80	Ⓐ Ⓑ Ⓒ Ⓓ	90	Ⓐ Ⓑ Ⓒ Ⓓ
				91	Ⓐ Ⓑ Ⓒ Ⓓ
				92	Ⓐ Ⓑ Ⓒ Ⓓ
				93	Ⓐ Ⓑ Ⓒ Ⓓ
				94	Ⓐ Ⓑ Ⓒ Ⓓ
				95	Ⓐ Ⓑ Ⓒ Ⓓ
				96	Ⓐ Ⓑ Ⓒ Ⓓ
				97	Ⓐ Ⓑ Ⓒ Ⓓ
				98	Ⓐ Ⓑ Ⓒ Ⓓ
				99	Ⓐ Ⓑ Ⓒ Ⓓ
				100	Ⓐ Ⓑ Ⓒ Ⓓ

TEST 4

Part 3

No.	ANSWER A B C D	No.	ANSWER A B C D	No.	ANSWER A B C D
32	Ⓐ Ⓑ Ⓒ Ⓓ	41	Ⓐ Ⓑ Ⓒ Ⓓ	51	Ⓐ Ⓑ Ⓒ Ⓓ
33	Ⓐ Ⓑ Ⓒ Ⓓ	42	Ⓐ Ⓑ Ⓒ Ⓓ	52	Ⓐ Ⓑ Ⓒ Ⓓ
34	Ⓐ Ⓑ Ⓒ Ⓓ	43	Ⓐ Ⓑ Ⓒ Ⓓ	53	Ⓐ Ⓑ Ⓒ Ⓓ
35	Ⓐ Ⓑ Ⓒ Ⓓ	44	Ⓐ Ⓑ Ⓒ Ⓓ	54	Ⓐ Ⓑ Ⓒ Ⓓ
36	Ⓐ Ⓑ Ⓒ Ⓓ	45	Ⓐ Ⓑ Ⓒ Ⓓ	55	Ⓐ Ⓑ Ⓒ Ⓓ
37	Ⓐ Ⓑ Ⓒ Ⓓ	46	Ⓐ Ⓑ Ⓒ Ⓓ	56	Ⓐ Ⓑ Ⓒ Ⓓ
38	Ⓐ Ⓑ Ⓒ Ⓓ	47	Ⓐ Ⓑ Ⓒ Ⓓ	57	Ⓐ Ⓑ Ⓒ Ⓓ
39	Ⓐ Ⓑ Ⓒ Ⓓ	48	Ⓐ Ⓑ Ⓒ Ⓓ	58	Ⓐ Ⓑ Ⓒ Ⓓ
40	Ⓐ Ⓑ Ⓒ Ⓓ	49	Ⓐ Ⓑ Ⓒ Ⓓ	59	Ⓐ Ⓑ Ⓒ Ⓓ
		50	Ⓐ Ⓑ Ⓒ Ⓓ	60	Ⓐ Ⓑ Ⓒ Ⓓ

Part 4

No.	ANSWER A B C D	No.	ANSWER A B C D	No.	ANSWER A B C D
61	Ⓐ Ⓑ Ⓒ Ⓓ	71	Ⓐ Ⓑ Ⓒ Ⓓ	81	Ⓐ Ⓑ Ⓒ Ⓓ
62	Ⓐ Ⓑ Ⓒ Ⓓ	72	Ⓐ Ⓑ Ⓒ Ⓓ	82	Ⓐ Ⓑ Ⓒ Ⓓ
63	Ⓐ Ⓑ Ⓒ Ⓓ	73	Ⓐ Ⓑ Ⓒ Ⓓ	83	Ⓐ Ⓑ Ⓒ Ⓓ
64	Ⓐ Ⓑ Ⓒ Ⓓ	74	Ⓐ Ⓑ Ⓒ Ⓓ	84	Ⓐ Ⓑ Ⓒ Ⓓ
65	Ⓐ Ⓑ Ⓒ Ⓓ	75	Ⓐ Ⓑ Ⓒ Ⓓ	85	Ⓐ Ⓑ Ⓒ Ⓓ
66	Ⓐ Ⓑ Ⓒ Ⓓ	76	Ⓐ Ⓑ Ⓒ Ⓓ	86	Ⓐ Ⓑ Ⓒ Ⓓ
67	Ⓐ Ⓑ Ⓒ Ⓓ	77	Ⓐ Ⓑ Ⓒ Ⓓ	87	Ⓐ Ⓑ Ⓒ Ⓓ
68	Ⓐ Ⓑ Ⓒ Ⓓ	78	Ⓐ Ⓑ Ⓒ Ⓓ	88	Ⓐ Ⓑ Ⓒ Ⓓ
69	Ⓐ Ⓑ Ⓒ Ⓓ	79	Ⓐ Ⓑ Ⓒ Ⓓ	89	Ⓐ Ⓑ Ⓒ Ⓓ
70	Ⓐ Ⓑ Ⓒ Ⓓ	80	Ⓐ Ⓑ Ⓒ Ⓓ	90	Ⓐ Ⓑ Ⓒ Ⓓ
				91	Ⓐ Ⓑ Ⓒ Ⓓ
				92	Ⓐ Ⓑ Ⓒ Ⓓ
				93	Ⓐ Ⓑ Ⓒ Ⓓ
				94	Ⓐ Ⓑ Ⓒ Ⓓ
				95	Ⓐ Ⓑ Ⓒ Ⓓ
				96	Ⓐ Ⓑ Ⓒ Ⓓ
				97	Ⓐ Ⓑ Ⓒ Ⓓ
				98	Ⓐ Ⓑ Ⓒ Ⓓ
				99	Ⓐ Ⓑ Ⓒ Ⓓ
				100	Ⓐ Ⓑ Ⓒ Ⓓ

Answer Sheet

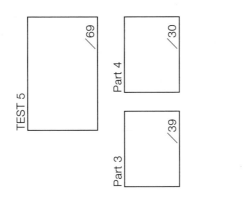

TEST 5

	Part 3														Part 4															

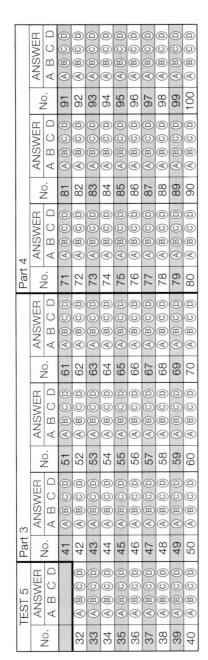

TEST 6

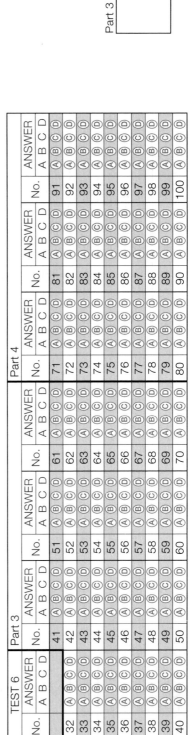

Answer Sheet

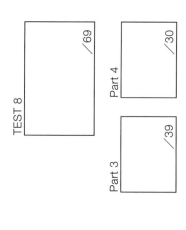

TEST 7

Part 3 — /39

Part 4 — /30

TEST 8

Part 3 — /39

Part 4 — /30

TEST 7

Part 3

No.	ANSWER
32	A B C D
33	A B C D
34	A B C D
35	A B C D
36	A B C D
37	A B C D
38	A B C D
39	A B C D
40	A B C D

No.	ANSWER
41	A B C D
42	A B C D
43	A B C D
44	A B C D
45	A B C D
46	A B C D
47	A B C D
48	A B C D
49	A B C D
50	A B C D

No.	ANSWER
51	A B C D
52	A B C D
53	A B C D
54	A B C D
55	A B C D
56	A B C D
57	A B C D
58	A B C D
59	A B C D
60	A B C D

No.	ANSWER
61	A B C D
62	A B C D
63	A B C D
64	A B C D
65	A B C D
66	A B C D
67	A B C D
68	A B C D
69	A B C D
70	A B C D

Part 4

No.	ANSWER
71	A B C D
72	A B C D
73	A B C D
74	A B C D
75	A B C D
76	A B C D
77	A B C D
78	A B C D
79	A B C D
80	A B C D

No.	ANSWER
81	A B C D
82	A B C D
83	A B C D
84	A B C D
85	A B C D
86	A B C D
87	A B C D
88	A B C D
89	A B C D
90	A B C D

No.	ANSWER
91	A B C D
92	A B C D
93	A B C D
94	A B C D
95	A B C D
96	A B C D
97	A B C D
98	A B C D
99	A B C D
100	A B C D

TEST 8

Part 3

No.	ANSWER
32	A B C D
33	A B C D
34	A B C D
35	A B C D
36	A B C D
37	A B C D
38	A B C D
39	A B C D
40	A B C D

No.	ANSWER
41	A B C D
42	A B C D
43	A B C D
44	A B C D
45	A B C D
46	A B C D
47	A B C D
48	A B C D
49	A B C D
50	A B C D

No.	ANSWER
51	A B C D
52	A B C D
53	A B C D
54	A B C D
55	A B C D
56	A B C D
57	A B C D
58	A B C D
59	A B C D
60	A B C D

No.	ANSWER
61	A B C D
62	A B C D
63	A B C D
64	A B C D
65	A B C D
66	A B C D
67	A B C D
68	A B C D
69	A B C D
70	A B C D

Part 4

No.	ANSWER
71	A B C D
72	A B C D
73	A B C D
74	A B C D
75	A B C D
76	A B C D
77	A B C D
78	A B C D
79	A B C D
80	A B C D

No.	ANSWER
81	A B C D
82	A B C D
83	A B C D
84	A B C D
85	A B C D
86	A B C D
87	A B C D
88	A B C D
89	A B C D
90	A B C D

No.	ANSWER
91	A B C D
92	A B C D
93	A B C D
94	A B C D
95	A B C D
96	A B C D
97	A B C D
98	A B C D
99	A B C D
100	A B C D

Answer Sheet

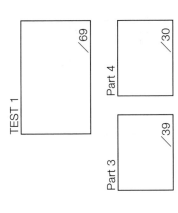

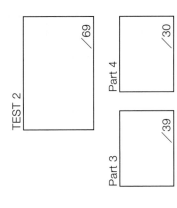

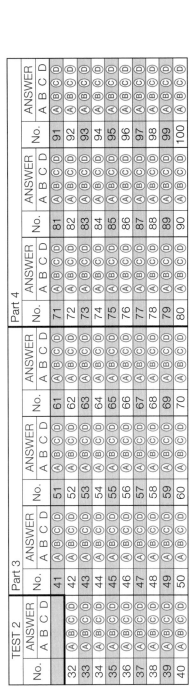

Answer Sheet

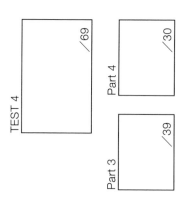

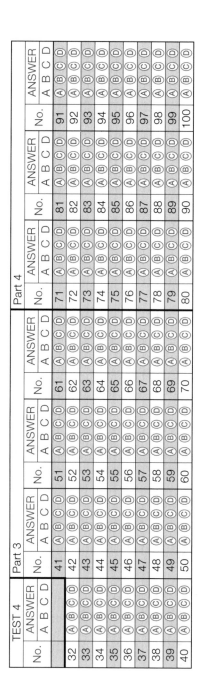

Answer Sheet

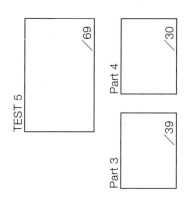

TEST 5

Part 3 /39
Part 4 /30
/69

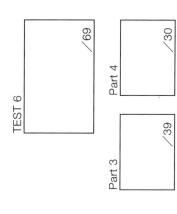

TEST 6

Part 3 /39
Part 4 /30
/69

TEST 5

Part 3

No.	ANSWER	No.	ANSWER	No.	ANSWER
	A B C D		A B C D		A B C D
32	A B C D	41	A B C D	51	A B C D
33	A B C D	42	A B C D	52	A B C D
34	A B C D	43	A B C D	53	A B C D
35	A B C D	44	A B C D	54	A B C D
36	A B C D	45	A B C D	55	A B C D
37	A B C D	46	A B C D	56	A B C D
38	A B C D	47	A B C D	57	A B C D
39	A B C D	48	A B C D	58	A B C D
40	A B C D	49	A B C D	59	A B C D
		50	A B C D	60	A B C D

Part 4

No.	ANSWER	No.	ANSWER	No.	ANSWER	No.	ANSWER
	A B C D		A B C D		A B C D		A B C D
61	A B C D	71	A B C D	81	A B C D	91	A B C D
62	A B C D	72	A B C D	82	A B C D	92	A B C D
63	A B C D	73	A B C D	83	A B C D	93	A B C D
64	A B C D	74	A B C D	84	A B C D	94	A B C D
65	A B C D	75	A B C D	85	A B C D	95	A B C D
66	A B C D	76	A B C D	86	A B C D	96	A B C D
67	A B C D	77	A B C D	87	A B C D	97	A B C D
68	A B C D	78	A B C D	88	A B C D	98	A B C D
69	A B C D	79	A B C D	89	A B C D	99	A B C D
70	A B C D	80	A B C D	90	A B C D	100	A B C D

TEST 6

Part 3

No.	ANSWER	No.	ANSWER	No.	ANSWER
	A B C D		A B C D		A B C D
32	A B C D	41	A B C D	51	A B C D
33	A B C D	42	A B C D	52	A B C D
34	A B C D	43	A B C D	53	A B C D
35	A B C D	44	A B C D	54	A B C D
36	A B C D	45	A B C D	55	A B C D
37	A B C D	46	A B C D	56	A B C D
38	A B C D	47	A B C D	57	A B C D
39	A B C D	48	A B C D	58	A B C D
40	A B C D	49	A B C D	59	A B C D
		50	A B C D	60	A B C D

Part 4

No.	ANSWER	No.	ANSWER	No.	ANSWER	No.	ANSWER
	A B C D		A B C D		A B C D		A B C D
61	A B C D	71	A B C D	81	A B C D	91	A B C D
62	A B C D	72	A B C D	82	A B C D	92	A B C D
63	A B C D	73	A B C D	83	A B C D	93	A B C D
64	A B C D	74	A B C D	84	A B C D	94	A B C D
65	A B C D	75	A B C D	85	A B C D	95	A B C D
66	A B C D	76	A B C D	86	A B C D	96	A B C D
67	A B C D	77	A B C D	87	A B C D	97	A B C D
68	A B C D	78	A B C D	88	A B C D	98	A B C D
69	A B C D	79	A B C D	89	A B C D	99	A B C D
70	A B C D	80	A B C D	90	A B C D	100	A B C D

Answer Sheet

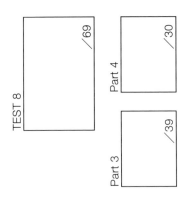

TEST 7

	/69
Part 3	/39
Part 4	/30

TEST 8

	/69
Part 3	/39
Part 4	/30

TEST 7

Part 3

No.	ANSWER	No.	ANSWER	No.	ANSWER
	A B C D		A B C D		A B C D
32	Ⓐ Ⓑ Ⓒ Ⓓ	41	Ⓐ Ⓑ Ⓒ Ⓓ	51	Ⓐ Ⓑ Ⓒ Ⓓ
33	Ⓐ Ⓑ Ⓒ Ⓓ	42	Ⓐ Ⓑ Ⓒ Ⓓ	52	Ⓐ Ⓑ Ⓒ Ⓓ
34	Ⓐ Ⓑ Ⓒ Ⓓ	43	Ⓐ Ⓑ Ⓒ Ⓓ	53	Ⓐ Ⓑ Ⓒ Ⓓ
35	Ⓐ Ⓑ Ⓒ Ⓓ	44	Ⓐ Ⓑ Ⓒ Ⓓ	54	Ⓐ Ⓑ Ⓒ Ⓓ
36	Ⓐ Ⓑ Ⓒ Ⓓ	45	Ⓐ Ⓑ Ⓒ Ⓓ	55	Ⓐ Ⓑ Ⓒ Ⓓ
37	Ⓐ Ⓑ Ⓒ Ⓓ	46	Ⓐ Ⓑ Ⓒ Ⓓ	56	Ⓐ Ⓑ Ⓒ Ⓓ
38	Ⓐ Ⓑ Ⓒ Ⓓ	47	Ⓐ Ⓑ Ⓒ Ⓓ	57	Ⓐ Ⓑ Ⓒ Ⓓ
39	Ⓐ Ⓑ Ⓒ Ⓓ	48	Ⓐ Ⓑ Ⓒ Ⓓ	58	Ⓐ Ⓑ Ⓒ Ⓓ
40	Ⓐ Ⓑ Ⓒ Ⓓ	49	Ⓐ Ⓑ Ⓒ Ⓓ	59	Ⓐ Ⓑ Ⓒ Ⓓ
		50	Ⓐ Ⓑ Ⓒ Ⓓ	60	Ⓐ Ⓑ Ⓒ Ⓓ

Part 4

No.	ANSWER	No.	ANSWER	No.	ANSWER
	A B C D		A B C D		A B C D
61	Ⓐ Ⓑ Ⓒ Ⓓ	71	Ⓐ Ⓑ Ⓒ Ⓓ	81	Ⓐ Ⓑ Ⓒ Ⓓ
62	Ⓐ Ⓑ Ⓒ Ⓓ	72	Ⓐ Ⓑ Ⓒ Ⓓ	82	Ⓐ Ⓑ Ⓒ Ⓓ
63	Ⓐ Ⓑ Ⓒ Ⓓ	73	Ⓐ Ⓑ Ⓒ Ⓓ	83	Ⓐ Ⓑ Ⓒ Ⓓ
64	Ⓐ Ⓑ Ⓒ Ⓓ	74	Ⓐ Ⓑ Ⓒ Ⓓ	84	Ⓐ Ⓑ Ⓒ Ⓓ
65	Ⓐ Ⓑ Ⓒ Ⓓ	75	Ⓐ Ⓑ Ⓒ Ⓓ	85	Ⓐ Ⓑ Ⓒ Ⓓ
66	Ⓐ Ⓑ Ⓒ Ⓓ	76	Ⓐ Ⓑ Ⓒ Ⓓ	86	Ⓐ Ⓑ Ⓒ Ⓓ
67	Ⓐ Ⓑ Ⓒ Ⓓ	77	Ⓐ Ⓑ Ⓒ Ⓓ	87	Ⓐ Ⓑ Ⓒ Ⓓ
68	Ⓐ Ⓑ Ⓒ Ⓓ	78	Ⓐ Ⓑ Ⓒ Ⓓ	88	Ⓐ Ⓑ Ⓒ Ⓓ
69	Ⓐ Ⓑ Ⓒ Ⓓ	79	Ⓐ Ⓑ Ⓒ Ⓓ	89	Ⓐ Ⓑ Ⓒ Ⓓ
70	Ⓐ Ⓑ Ⓒ Ⓓ	80	Ⓐ Ⓑ Ⓒ Ⓓ	90	Ⓐ Ⓑ Ⓒ Ⓓ
				91	Ⓐ Ⓑ Ⓒ Ⓓ
				92	Ⓐ Ⓑ Ⓒ Ⓓ
				93	Ⓐ Ⓑ Ⓒ Ⓓ
				94	Ⓐ Ⓑ Ⓒ Ⓓ
				95	Ⓐ Ⓑ Ⓒ Ⓓ
				96	Ⓐ Ⓑ Ⓒ Ⓓ
				97	Ⓐ Ⓑ Ⓒ Ⓓ
				98	Ⓐ Ⓑ Ⓒ Ⓓ
				99	Ⓐ Ⓑ Ⓒ Ⓓ
				100	Ⓐ Ⓑ Ⓒ Ⓓ

TEST 8

Part 3

No.	ANSWER	No.	ANSWER	No.	ANSWER
	A B C D		A B C D		A B C D
32	Ⓐ Ⓑ Ⓒ Ⓓ	41	Ⓐ Ⓑ Ⓒ Ⓓ	51	Ⓐ Ⓑ Ⓒ Ⓓ
33	Ⓐ Ⓑ Ⓒ Ⓓ	42	Ⓐ Ⓑ Ⓒ Ⓓ	52	Ⓐ Ⓑ Ⓒ Ⓓ
34	Ⓐ Ⓑ Ⓒ Ⓓ	43	Ⓐ Ⓑ Ⓒ Ⓓ	53	Ⓐ Ⓑ Ⓒ Ⓓ
35	Ⓐ Ⓑ Ⓒ Ⓓ	44	Ⓐ Ⓑ Ⓒ Ⓓ	54	Ⓐ Ⓑ Ⓒ Ⓓ
36	Ⓐ Ⓑ Ⓒ Ⓓ	45	Ⓐ Ⓑ Ⓒ Ⓓ	55	Ⓐ Ⓑ Ⓒ Ⓓ
37	Ⓐ Ⓑ Ⓒ Ⓓ	46	Ⓐ Ⓑ Ⓒ Ⓓ	56	Ⓐ Ⓑ Ⓒ Ⓓ
38	Ⓐ Ⓑ Ⓒ Ⓓ	47	Ⓐ Ⓑ Ⓒ Ⓓ	57	Ⓐ Ⓑ Ⓒ Ⓓ
39	Ⓐ Ⓑ Ⓒ Ⓓ	48	Ⓐ Ⓑ Ⓒ Ⓓ	58	Ⓐ Ⓑ Ⓒ Ⓓ
40	Ⓐ Ⓑ Ⓒ Ⓓ	49	Ⓐ Ⓑ Ⓒ Ⓓ	59	Ⓐ Ⓑ Ⓒ Ⓓ
		50	Ⓐ Ⓑ Ⓒ Ⓓ	60	Ⓐ Ⓑ Ⓒ Ⓓ

Part 4

No.	ANSWER	No.	ANSWER	No.	ANSWER
	A B C D		A B C D		A B C D
61	Ⓐ Ⓑ Ⓒ Ⓓ	71	Ⓐ Ⓑ Ⓒ Ⓓ	81	Ⓐ Ⓑ Ⓒ Ⓓ
62	Ⓐ Ⓑ Ⓒ Ⓓ	72	Ⓐ Ⓑ Ⓒ Ⓓ	82	Ⓐ Ⓑ Ⓒ Ⓓ
63	Ⓐ Ⓑ Ⓒ Ⓓ	73	Ⓐ Ⓑ Ⓒ Ⓓ	83	Ⓐ Ⓑ Ⓒ Ⓓ
64	Ⓐ Ⓑ Ⓒ Ⓓ	74	Ⓐ Ⓑ Ⓒ Ⓓ	84	Ⓐ Ⓑ Ⓒ Ⓓ
65	Ⓐ Ⓑ Ⓒ Ⓓ	75	Ⓐ Ⓑ Ⓒ Ⓓ	85	Ⓐ Ⓑ Ⓒ Ⓓ
66	Ⓐ Ⓑ Ⓒ Ⓓ	76	Ⓐ Ⓑ Ⓒ Ⓓ	86	Ⓐ Ⓑ Ⓒ Ⓓ
67	Ⓐ Ⓑ Ⓒ Ⓓ	77	Ⓐ Ⓑ Ⓒ Ⓓ	87	Ⓐ Ⓑ Ⓒ Ⓓ
68	Ⓐ Ⓑ Ⓒ Ⓓ	78	Ⓐ Ⓑ Ⓒ Ⓓ	88	Ⓐ Ⓑ Ⓒ Ⓓ
69	Ⓐ Ⓑ Ⓒ Ⓓ	79	Ⓐ Ⓑ Ⓒ Ⓓ	89	Ⓐ Ⓑ Ⓒ Ⓓ
70	Ⓐ Ⓑ Ⓒ Ⓓ	80	Ⓐ Ⓑ Ⓒ Ⓓ	90	Ⓐ Ⓑ Ⓒ Ⓓ
				91	Ⓐ Ⓑ Ⓒ Ⓓ
				92	Ⓐ Ⓑ Ⓒ Ⓓ
				93	Ⓐ Ⓑ Ⓒ Ⓓ
				94	Ⓐ Ⓑ Ⓒ Ⓓ
				95	Ⓐ Ⓑ Ⓒ Ⓓ
				96	Ⓐ Ⓑ Ⓒ Ⓓ
				97	Ⓐ Ⓑ Ⓒ Ⓓ
				98	Ⓐ Ⓑ Ⓒ Ⓓ
				99	Ⓐ Ⓑ Ⓒ Ⓓ
				100	Ⓐ Ⓑ Ⓒ Ⓓ